SCHOOLCRAFT COLLEGE LIBRARY
W9-BLM-610

THE MEANING OF PHILOSOPHY

HARPER & ROW, PUBLISHERS
NEW YORK, EVANSTON, AND LONDON

THE MEANING OF PHILOSOPHY

SECOND EDITION

A survey of the problems of philosophy and of the opinions of philosophers

JOSEPH GERARD BRENNAN
BARNARD COLLEGE, COLUMBIA UNIVERSITY

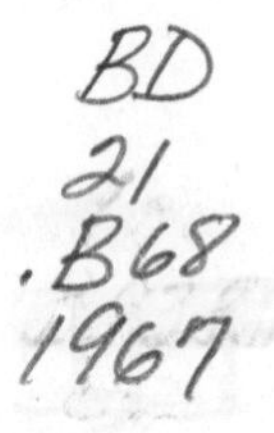

To Mary

The Meaning of Philosophy, Second Edition

For information address Harper & Row, Publishers, Incorporated, 49 East 33rd Street, New York, N.Y. 10016.

Library of Congress catalog card number: 67-11650

D-R

Contents

Part IV. Problems of Value

Preface to the Second Edition

Said Mr. Jowett, Senior, of his distinguished son Benjamin who was preparing a new edition of his commentary on the epistles of St. Paul, "I am happy to say that he appears to be carefully revising his work which certainly needed it." The first edition of *The Meaning of Philosophy* is not to be compared with the work of the Master of Balliol in any respect except that it certainly needed revision. When the first edition was published, neither Wittgenstein's nor Sartre's later work had appeared in print. To this edition I have added considerable material on the philosophy of language and the philosophy of mind, as well as new pages on Phenomenology and Existentialism. Nearly all the chapters have been extensively rewritten.

Biographical sketches of most of the principal philosophers mentioned have been placed at the end of the main text. In many of the citations of books, as well as in the suggested readings at the end of each chapter, the name of the edition I have used is followed by mention of a currently available paperbound edition ("PB"). Many of these books appear in more than one paperbound edition corresponding to the imprints of various publishers. I simply referred to the first suitable one that came to hand.

I would like to acknowledge here the benefit of many friendly conversations with my former Barnard colleagues in philosophy—Jean Potter of Bryn Mawr College, Judith Jarvis Thomson of the Massachusetts Institute of Technology, and Stanley Moore of the University of California (San Diego).

J.G.B.

November, 1966

Preface to the First Edition

Philosophy has not one, but many, meanings. As this book develops its themes from logic to the philosophy of art, some of these meanings may emerge. Here philosophy is presented by an introduction to its problems rather than to its history. Because the liveliest developments in our time have been in the fields of logic and language, these topics are given, as a place of honor, the opening chapters. Theory of knowledge comes next with new changes rung as well as old. Metaphysics is approached with respect; when all the anti-metaphysical complaints have been heard, the subject is defined in such a way that it need not be identified with nonsense. A chapter each to ethics and aesthetics, and the survey is complete.

Both student and general reader will find in these pages a cheerful assortment of philosophic names: those of contemporaries—Russell, Heidegger, Carnap, Wisdom, Sartre; those of the noble and recently deceased—Whitehead, Wittgenstein, Dewey, Croce, Santayana; and the grand old ones of the traditions—Plato, Aquinas, Kant, and the rest. In short, something for everybody.

As I wrote this modest introduction to philosophy, I thought constantly of my former teachers—J. H. Woods, A. N. Whitehead, C. I. Lewis, H. A. Wolfson, W. P. Montague. Specific aid came from my present or former colleagues. Professor John E. Smith, now of Yale, read the larger part of the book in manuscript and contributed helpful criticisms. Professor Gertrude Rich read the book in proof and made valuable suggestions. Professor Helen Huss Parkhurst read the chapter on aesthetics. Thanks are also due for various helpful things to my colleagues Professors Edgar Lorch, Henry Boorse, Gertrude Hirst, and to Professor Arthur Szathmary of Princeton. My warm thanks go to Professor William McEwen and to Hofstra College for placing numerous facilities at my disposal. Thanks, too, to Irene and Henry Acres for frequent and pleasant intervals of hospitality during the writing process.

J.G.B.

April, 1953

THE MEANING OF PHILOSOPHY

Introduction

> *For philosophy, Socrates, if pursued in moderation and at the proper age, is an elegant accomplishment, but too much philosophy is the ruin of human life.*
>
> —CALLICLES

What Is Philosophy?

Everyone knows that "philosophy" comes from Greek words meaning love of wisdom. But since "wisdom" is even harder to define than "philosophy," a definition of our subject as love of wisdom does not tell us very much. It is not easy to define philosophy in such a way as to please everybody. Some hold that "philosophy" is simply a name given to a number of quite miscellaneous inquiries which have no real common denominator. Philosophers of an older day used to define the aim of their study as "the knowledge of things generally from the point of view of their ultimate causes so far as natural reason can attain to such knowledge." The definition is now considered too ambitious. Another definition states that philosophy is that field of inquiry which studies basic assumptions or first principles —those which people take for granted in ordinary life or those assumed in systems of organized knowledge. Professional philosophers may wince when they hear businessmen talk about "the philosophy of advertising," or "the philosophy of the suburban home owner." Yet even this popular usage of the term "philosophy" shows concern with basic presuppositions or first principles. A common question, "What is your philosophy of life?" refers to some set of primary beliefs according to which a man guides his conduct. A "philosophy of history" proceeds from those fundamental assumptions upon which a particular historian's interpretation of history depends. A "philosophy of science" sets out principles more basic and comprehensive than the conclusions of the individual sciences.

Still another explanation of the task of philosophy—not inconsistent with the second offered above—states that philosophy examines those ideas or concepts which are *assumed* in all or many disciplines, but *defined* by none of them. Such concepts would include notions such as knowing, meaning, truth, certainty, cause, object, mind, existence, right, and good. Historically, not every philosopher has been interested in all these topics at once. Individual philosophers or groups of philosophers living at a certain time or place may be so interested in a particular set of concepts that they tend to define philosophy in terms of the problems which those particular concepts raise. In classical times, many philosophers concentrated on Being and "the Good." In the fourteenth century, some philosophers were preoccupied with God, others with logic. From the seventeenth to the nineteenth century, problems of knowledge claimed the attention of leading philosophers. In our own time, questions of language and meaning have come to the fore, as has a renewed interest in the problem of mind.

Now in some historical periods of culture, the philosophy of the time is marked by agreement among philosophers as to just what kind of questions philosophy should deal with. In other periods (in eras of cultural transition perhaps, such as our own), the philosophy of the day is scored by strife over what sort of things philosophers have a right to talk about. Today especially there is considerable disagreement among professional philosophers as to the meaning of their own subject. This disagreement is not just a difference of opinion about the way in which particular philosophical problems should be solved. It is a quarrel over just what the proper business of philosophy *is*. Perhaps confusion over the definition of philosophy might be reduced somewhat if we suggest that there are at least three different ways of going about philosophy, and that a philosopher's opinion of the proper business of his subject will depend upon the particular set of interests and motives that brought him to philosophy. These three fundamental approaches to philosophy we may name the *analytic*, the *metaphysical*, and the *moral*.

The Analytic Way

Many come to philosophy because they believe it important to submit to analysis and critical reflection notions which are taken for granted by most of us. Such persons are attracted by rigor and precision in thinking; they admire exactness in procedure. The analytic philosopher asks, "*How do you know?*" for he is interested in problems concerning the range, methods, and limits of human knowledge. He asks "*What do you mean?*" for he is convinced that many problems of philosophy will be solved if inquiry is made into the meaning of the terms of the argument. Today the analytic philosopher may use the highly developed techniques of modern logic to help him in his analysis of philosophical problems. He may explore the relation between the symbolic structure of logic and the rules of language. The concepts and methodologies of the special sciences interest him, and he may like to occupy himself with constructing a "philosophy of science." If he belongs to a certain school, he may say that philosophy should stick to analysis of logical, linguistic, and basic scientific notions; that it no longer has any business asking questions about God or the soul, or mind or Nature, or human existence and its place in the cosmos. Such questions he may tend to dismiss as "metaphysical."

The Metaphysical Way

"The effort after the general characterization of the world around us," says the philosopher Alfred North Whitehead, "is the romance of human thought." Many come to philosophy to find a cosmic vision, a world perspective on the universal scale; to set forth a systematic account of the nature of things in terms that go far beyond those of the special sciences both in generality and in depth. Metaphysics, or speculative philosophy as it is often called, has given Western thought some of its greatest intellectual landmarks. In ancient Greece, Plato taught that the world which our senses disclose to us is but a transient copy of an eternal realm of Forms or "Ideas" to which all individual things owe what limited measure of reality they have. In the Middle Ages, Aquinas described a hierarchy of Being, arranging all things in gradations from God down through lower levels of the spiritual world, thence to man and to corporeal Nature. In modern times, Hegel charted the history of Spirit, a force which moves toward self-realization through Nature and through Mind, generating along its dialectical course whole series of arts, cultures, religions and philosophies until at length it fulfills itself and approaches the Absolute.

Anti-metaphysical philosophers claim that the day of these grand world perspectives is over. Such visions, they say, are no more than poetry, for they do not describe the world as it is; they are but prescientific speculations, mythopoeic accounts of matters which only physical science is competent to describe. But metaphysically inclined philosophers reply that even today there is a place, and an important place, for speculative philosophy. For the physical scientist by nature of his work is restricted to those aspects of the universe and our experience of it which can be correlated with pointer readings, clocks, and rulers. The philosopher's scope is broader, so inclusive that he takes for his province *all* phases of experience—poetic, religious, moral, and social, as well as scientific. The aim of philosophy, the metaphysician claims, is to formulate categories which will help us understand the ultimate character of this all-inclusive scheme of things we call the world, and to assess with due proportion the role played within it by that tiny yet knowledgeable part of it—man.

Philosophy as Moral Teaching

There are, among others, two types of values—moral and aesthetic. Moral values have to do with good in human conduct, that is, with what a person does with his life. Aesthetic values refer to good in aesthetic experience, in a word, to beauty whether found in Nature or in art. Many come to philosophy seeking answers to the question "What is the good life for man?" Such a philosopher, whose dominant interest is *moral*, presents us with a "philosophy of life," a doctrine concerning the nature of man, desirable goals of human life, principles by which we may guide our conduct. The interest of the moral philosopher is often said to be *practical*, since moral philosophy or "ethics" is more concerned with doing or action than with knowing. From Confucius and Socrates to Nietzsche and John Dewey, moral philosophy has been more strongly marked by interest in standards and values of human action and conduct than by speculative concern with ultimate cosmological factors. Schools of philosophy in ancient Greece and Rome, such as the Stoics and Epicureans, were essentially schools of *moral* philosophy. The common saying "He took it very philosophically" derives from the Stoic ideal of the good man who lives according to reason, who is neither unduly elated by sudden blessings nor cast down by misfortune. Ancient students looked to philosophy for a rule of living. The name of our scholarly fraternity Phi Beta Kappa is formed from the initial letters of the Greek phrase *Philosophia biou kubernetes*—Philosophy (love of wisdom), the Guide of Life.

Philosophy, in the sense of traditional metaphysical and moral philosophy, has much in common with religion. It is interesting to note how many of those who teach and write philosophy have had strong religious ties at least during some period of their lives. This should not surprise us, for both philosophy (in the sense above stated) and religion are concerned with the nature and destiny of man. The difference between philosophy and religion is usually explained by saying that religion holds its conclusions on the basis of faith, whereas philosophy establishes its conclusions by natural reason alone, with no attempt to base its teachings on revelation, scriptures, religious doctrine, or tradition. In philosophy, arguments must stand on their own feet. In religious faith, there is no need for argument. If there were such need, it would no longer be religious faith. It would have become philosophy.

Integration of the Three Ways?

There is an obvious disadvantage in explaining what philosophy is by dividing the approaches to the subject into three—analytic, metaphysical, and valuational. Such a division seems to imply that any given philosophy will fall neatly into one of three compartments. Now in practice this is rarely the case. Of course it is possible to single out individual philosophers whose interests are primarily analytic, and others whose interests are chiefly moral. But many philosophers combine in their work elements from each of the three ways. This is often true in classical philosophy. Consider Plato. His reliance on philosophical analysis is obvious to anyone who reads him. Whether the topic under discussion be knowledge, virtue, beauty, justice, or piety, Plato always begins with an inquiry into the *meaning* of these concepts. This is followed by a closely reasoned analysis of the logical implications of the definitions offered. Plato's fame, however, does not rest on his talents as an analytic philosopher. The world knows him as a moralist and as a political philosopher, as well as a metaphysician on the grand scale. Not only Plato, but also most of the other great classical Western philosophers managed to combine in their thinking all three approaches to philosophy. In Aristotle, in Spinoza, in Kant, and in many others, we find a synthesis of the three ways, an integration of critical analysis, systematic world perspective, and moral doctrine.

It would seem, therefore, that the philosophy would tend toward a synthesis or integration of the three elements —analysis, metaphysics, and value. But this again is too simple. In contemporary philosophy, the tendency has for some decades run against any integration of the traditional ways of inquiry into knowledge, being, and the good. Today the word "quarrel" is inadequate to decribe differences between Anglo-American philosophy and philosophy on the continent of Europe. Geographically separated only by the English Channel, the two ways of philosophizing are so far apart that they are almost totally unaffected by one another. Under the powerful influence of the late Ludwig Wittgenstein, English and American philosophers tend to construe philosophy's task as clarification of language, a patient correction of ingrained habits of speaking plausibly but misleadingly about certain questions labelled "philosophical." In France and Germany, however, problems of knowledge, being, and existence are still discussed in a way that seems to English and American philosophers quite traditional and "first order." For his part, Sartre confesses that reading Wittgenstein only bores him.

First and Second Orders; Philosophy as Linguistic Analysis

There are two worlds—although they are not worlds in the same sense. One is the world of natural and social facts; it is the world in which we live. The other is the world of language; it is a world we have made. We use language to talk *about* the world of natural and social facts, although that is not the only use of language. We can also talk about *language*. An executive draws up a report about certain business facts. It is important that he "have his facts straight." But it is also important that he write his report in such a way that his meaning is clear. The facts the executive is writing about are affairs of the *first order*. The statements that he makes about the facts are things of the *second order*. Now, should the task of philosophy be to make statements about the world? If so, then philosophy is a science like other sciences, although much more comprehensive. That is a traditional view of the business of philosophy, a view still held by many. If, on the other hand, philosophy is essentially a second-order study, it would seem to be a subject which has for its business not new facts, but new ways of stating facts. Facts are first order.

Ways of stating facts are second order. The twentieth-century tradition of English philosophy, dominant in Anglo-American academic circles today, places the emphasis on the second order. Clarification of language rather than description of facts is taken to be philosophy's main job. That is why this contemporary philosophical tradition is widely known as the philosophy of *linguistic analysis*. G. E. Moore, one of the founders of this tradition, said "I do not think the world or the sciences would ever have suggested to me any philosophical problems. What has suggested philosophical problems to me is things which other philosophers have said about the world or the sciences."[1] Wittgenstein at Cambridge pronounced philosophy to be a battle against the bewitchment of our intelligence by means of language. In sum, according to philosophy as linguistic analysis, the task of philosophy is clarification of *meanings* rather than proclamation of *truths* about the nature of the world or of man's destiny. Its primary concern should be the analysis of our *thought* or *language*, rather than inquiry into the nature of *things*.

Conclusion: Division of the Present Survey

No position need be taken here concerning the relative value of the linguistic versus the traditional ways of philosophy. Such conclusions would be premature. It is by no means certain that the two ways of philosophizing must exclude each other. Socrates' method was an inquiry into meanings and definition. Plato's *Theaetetus*, reexamined today, reads remarkably like Wittgenstein. It is doubtful whether Aristotle really ever thought of philosophy's business as the discovery of new facts. Whichever way philosophy is approached, a good deal of the same ground is

[1] P. Schilpp, ed. *The Philosophy of G. E. Moore*, Northwestern University, 1942, p. 14.

gone over. When a classical philosopher asks, "What is the nature of Truth?" and a contemporary analyst asks, "What is the meaning of 'true'?" it is surprising how much the two discussions may have in common. We cannot ignore the contributions made to philosophy by the schools of linguistic analysis, or brush them aside as "narrow." They refreshed a subject that had gone stale in England and America. They have contributed to making the twentieth century one of the richest and subtlest in the history of philosophy. On the other hand, the philosophy of Hegel, which contains some of the wildest and most ambitious metaphysical speculations in the history of Western thought has had—through the agency of Hegel's student Marx and certain of Marx's followers—the effect of changing the shape of the world in which we live. For good or ill, we need not decide here.

Despite their very different and frequently opposing conceptions of the meaning of philosophy, nearly all philosophers, ancient and modern, are agreed on one point: that philosophy is an important enterprise and its business is serious business. Only a few of the sophists' disciples, like Callicles, believe it to be a superficial and dilettantish pursuit. It may even be that Callicles himself took philosophy quite as seriously as it deserves, and that he was maliciously misquoted by Plato. For Plato was the pupil of Socrates, and Socrates bore the sophists no love. After all, they were his bitter competitors and took money for their teaching, while Socrates' only fees were the dinners his pupils gave him.

The divisions of our survey of philosophy are rather conventional. The inquiry falls into two main parts, the first of which concentrates largely on the analytic side of philosophy, the second on the metaphysical and valuational. The analytic part of the survey is in its turn subdivided into inquiries concerning logic and language on the one hand, and on the other into epistemology or theory of knowledge in which are considered problems concerning the nature, scope, and methods of human knowledge. The second half of the survey proceeds to an examination of metaphysical topics, then enters the field of value with a brief tour of ethics, the science of the good, and concludes with aesthetics or philosophy of art.

PART I

Logic and Language

I

Logic

Contrariwise, if it was so it might be; and if it were so, it would be; but as it isn't, it ain't. That's logic.

—Tweedledee in
Through the Looking Glass

What Is Logic?

Logic is a discipline first expounded in systematic form by the ancient Greek philosopher Aristotle. Since Aristotle's time, logic has been more or less closely associated with philosophy, although it has not always been regarded as an integral part of the subject. In the last hundred years, logic has undergone extensive development; its ties to the foundations of mathematics have been carefully studied. Today logic has particular prominence as an instrument of analytic philosophy.

It is not easy to explain just what logic is. Many who teach logic and write logic books have different opinions of the proper business of the subject. Some hold that it is the purpose of logic to teach people how to "think straight." If you take a course in logic, they say, you will learn how to "reason" properly and how to avoid error. This definition is too optimistic. "Thinking" is a word which designates an area of human activity which is very broad and not clearly delimited. Everyone would agree that if people could only learn how to "think correctly" it would be a fine thing. If there were a science which provided remedies for "bad thinking," one would suppose that every man would enroll for a course. But to date no such science has been developed. Logic has been taught as an academic subject in the West for more than two thousand years, and only a comparatively small number of students have taken the trouble to study it. It is well known that logic students, as well as their less industrious fellow men, are not immune to making mistakes in many important types of thinking.

Logic the Science of Inference?

"The province of logic," says the nineteenth-century English philosopher John Stuart Mill, "must be restricted to that portion of our knowledge which consists of inferences from truths previously known." If the subject matter of logic is "restricted" to *inference*, logic is a very inclusive subject indeed, for most of what passes for human knowledge is derived by inference. Mill himself admits that it follows from his definition that the scope of logic must be wide. "By far the greatest portion of our knowledge . . . being avowedly matter of inference," he says, "nearly the whole, not only of science, but of human conduct is amenable to the authority of logic."[1] Although Mill's definition of logic as the *science of inference* is too broad to permit exactness, we may use it as the occasion of asking *what inference is*, and of stating an important distinction between two kinds of inference.

What Is Inference?

Inference, let us say, is *the process in which we pass from what we know to new knowledge.* There is an inference

[1] John Stuart Mill, *A System of Logic*, London, Longmans, 1925, p. 5.

situation whenever there is a transition from what is now known to some further knowledge. Consider these examples of simple inference situations:

1. I wake up in the morning and notice that the room is rather gloomy. I see drops of water running down the outside of my windowpane, and I hear a light drumming sound on the roof. This is what I know. I *infer* that it is raining.

2. I am introduced to a gentleman whose name is Pablo Lopez. I *infer* that he is of Spanish ancestry.

3. I put some mercuric oxide in a test tube. Holding the tube over a lighted burner, I thrust a glowing splint of wood in the open end of the tube. The splint flares up in flame. I *infer* that oxygen is being liberated from the mercuric oxide.

4. The geometry teacher points out that angle A is equal to angle B, and that angle C is equal to angle B. I *infer* that angle A is equal to angle C.

Of course, not every inference is a sound one. Despite his name, Pablo Lopez may just possibly be of Irish ancestry, and, appearances to the contrary, it may not actually be raining. In such cases, the inference leads to "apparent" knowledge only. But at this point we are not concerned with the complex question of how to distinguish sound from unsound inferences. For the moment, we shall be content to consider some more examples of inference:

	What Is Known	What Is Inferred
5.	My friend, usually ruddy and good-natured, is pale and irritable today.	Either he did not have enough sleep last night or he is not feeling well.
6.	Treason is a capital offense; to libel the king is treason.	To libel the king is a capital offense.
7.	A kettle of water is being heated on the stove.	The water will boil at 212 degrees F.

	What Is Known	What Is Inferred
8.	Two parallel lines are cut by a transversal.	The alternate interior angles are equal.
9.	My hostess yawns and glances at the clock.	She would like me to go home.
10.	The number of New Yorkers who have hair on their heads is greater than the number of hairs any one New Yorker has on his head.	There are at least two New Yorkers with the same number of hairs on their heads.
11.	After I have placed a certain mineral specimen on an exposed photographic plate, a dark area forms on the plate.	The mineral contains a radioactive element.
12.	Whatever is an element of *A* is also an element of *B*, and *X* is an element of *A*.	*X* is an element of *B*.
13.	The prisoner was in the victim's apartment at the time of the murder, and his fingerprints were found on the gun.	He is guilty of the crime.

Formal and Empirical Inference

Let us now divide these random examples of inference into two kinds. Examples 4, 6, 8, 10, and 12 are of the sort known as *formal* or *deductive* inferences. In these instances, if you take "What Is Known" as true, then it follows, on no basis other than that of the statements alone, that "What Is Inferred" is also true. If two parallel lines are cut by a transversal, then it does not merely happen to be so that the alternate interior angles are equal. Within the framework of Euclidean geometry, it is so beyond question. Similarly, if the sentences "Treason is a capital offense" and "To libel the king is treason" are taken as true without reference to anything beyond the meaning of the sentences themselves, then the sentence "To libel the king is a capital offense" is certainly true. The reason formal inferences have this peculiar "certainty" will become apparent if we compare them with inferences of the *second* type (examples 1, 2, 3, 5, 7, 9, 11, 13). Miscellaneous though they be, inferences of the second variety have this in common: they all concern the character or behavior of things and events that make up the world around us. Most of the inferences we draw every day are of this type; they are known as *empirical* or *factual* inferences.

Empirical Inference and Scientific Method

The daily run of our empirical inferences includes many that are careless and random and some that are foolish. If we see a man display fondness for children and dogs, we may infer that he is a man of good character. This is an inference about the behavior of a human being, a very variable item of the world about us, and it is obviously not a careful inference. We frequently call this kind of inference "jumping to conclusions," because the inference process is attended by little reflection upon the nature of the evidence (if any) which supports it. We make more careful inferences about the empirical world when we *reflect* upon the data we know, pausing to consider whether these data afford sufficient grounds for justifying the conclusions we have reached. A conscientious citizen in the jury box will heed the judge's instruction to "weigh the evidence carefully" before he proceeds to the conclusion that the prisoner is guilty.

A very careful type of empirical inference procedure may be found in the methods of the physical sciences. Upon the basis of certain data (*what is known*), a bacteriologist may state provisionally that a given disease is caused by a certain virus (*what is inferred*). The latter statement—conventionally called a hypothesis—is tested experimentally under numerous and varied empirical conditions. The testing is an important part of the *verification* of the statement. We should not think, however, that "scientific method" concerns a special kind of inference which is wholly empirical and which is analyzable solely in terms of categories like "hypothesis" and "verification." "Scientific method" is a name we give to a careful and reflective form of the ordinary thinking we use in everyday life. Moreover, scientific method includes complex patterns of thought which employ formal as well as empirical or factual inference.

Broad and Narrow Senses of "Logic"

Taken in a very comprehensive sense, logic is the study of inference in general. Any systematic explanation of how conclusions are drawn from various types of evidence may be called logic. More precisely, logic refers to the study of the principles of *formal* inference. Ever since the rise of the physical sciences after the Renaissance, analysts of knowledge have tried to formulate a "logic" of scientific method which would rival, in its precision, the logic of formal inference. To date, however, these attempts have not been wholly successful. Methodologies of empirical science have failed to achieve the systematic character of formal logic chiefly because empirical inference is *not* formal inference. The latter, as we shall see, by its very nature lends itself to exactness and system.

Formal or Deductive Inference

Formal inferences do not appear to be inferences about things present to sense observation. They are of the kind found in the operations of arithmetic, geometry, and other mathematical disciplines. These sciences are called *formal* sciences to distinguish them from the *empirical* sciences, which include astronomy, physics, chemistry, etc. While the empirical sciences *employ* formal science (as in the case of physics, where mathematics is an indispensable instrument), they are ultimately concerned with the behavior of Nature.

The mode of inference employed in formal science is called *deduction.* Now there are at least three senses in which the word "deduction" may be taken. The term is popularly used simply as a *synonym for "inference,"* particularly the kind of inference detectives are supposed to rely upon. Admirers of Sherlock Holmes will remember that Holmes wrote a paper about "Deduction" which his newly met acquaintance Dr. Watson criticized as "ineffable twaddle." Whereupon the sleuth proceeded to explain how he "deduced" that Watson was a medical man and former army officer invalided out of the service after wounds received in Afghanistan.[2] Throughout his career, Holmes continued to astonish his ingenuous companion by such *tours de force* of "deduction." Brilliant as Holmes' deductions were, however, they were but miscellaneous kinds of inferences about very variable components of the empirical world. There was nothing especially "deductive" about them, if the term is taken in a strict sense.

A narrower usage of the term "deduction" identifies it *that kind of inference we use in predicting an event* *nce to a general empirical law.* From this sense of

oyle, *A Study in Scarlet,* chap. 1.

"deduction" is derived the frequent definition of the term as inference which proceeds from the general to the particular. From knowledge of a general pattern of events in Nature, I may infer that some particular state exists. Knowing that mammals suckle their young, I may infer deductively that a whale will nourish its offspring in this way. Recalling the law that gases expand when heated will cause me hurriedly to punch a hole in a can of beans I am heating in a saucepan over a fire. The fact that we can refer to general empirical laws in order to predict the behavior of particular cases is of enormous importance in the investigations of the physical sciences. The term "deduction" is frequently used in this sense in contrast to *induction*—a mode of empirical inference in which examination of particular instances leads us to formulate a general law. The generalization "Infants which are frequently cuddled thrive better than those which are not" is *inductively* established on the basis of examination of particular instances of babies. If, recollecting this generalization, a mother hastens to give her baby a little extra loving, she is proceeding via *deductive* inference.

The strictest sense of "deduction" is that generally employed in logic and formal science. Strict deduction may be defined thus: *When from a given statement or statements another statement or statements necessarily follows, the first is said to imply (or "entail") the second, and inference from the first to the second is said to be deductive.*[3] From

[3] Note the distinction between "infer" and "imply." The statements "X is twice Y" and "Y is twice Z" *imply* that "X is four times Z." The relationship of *implication* exists between the first two statements and the third whether anyone "draws the conclusion" or not. But whe[illegible] someone perceives the relationship of implication, and "draws the c[illegible] clusion," then and not until then do we have *inference*. Inferenc[illegible] element of psychological activity in it that implication lacks.

the statements (1) "Danbury is due north of Stamford" and (2) "Stamford is due west of New London" we may infer deductively that (3) "Danbury is north of west of (northwest of) New London." Similarly, from the statement $2x + 5 = x + 10$, we may deduce that $x = 5$. It does not just *happen* that x equals 5. Granted the first equation, the second must follow by virtue of the formal scheme (algebra) of which these expressions are parts.

Meaning of "Formal"; Truth and Validity

We have referred to inferences of strict deductive type as *formal.* Generally speaking, a *form* is something that remains the same while that which is put into it may change. Federal Income Tax Form 1040 is the same for all who receive it from the Bureau of Internal Revenue, but the content filled in will vary with the individual taxpayer. So, in logic, inferences of strictly deductive character have nothing to do with any particular subject matter, even though the statements used in the inference process may refer to subject matter that is factual. The formal logician is concerned only with the *pattern,* with the *structure* of the relationship between the statements. Take, for instance, the example of strict deductive inference previously cited:

Danbury is due north of Stamford.
Stamford is due west of New London.
Therefore, Danbury is north of west of (northwest of) New London.

As formal logicians we are not concerned with the question of whether or not these statements are factually true. If we substitute "Buenos Aires" for "Danbury" in the first statement, the conclusion "Buenos Aires is northwest of New

London" will follow. The deductive inference will still be formally sound although the conclusion happens as a matter of empirical fact to be false. Here we meet the distinction between *truth* and *validity*. Our deduction with the modified subject matter will be *valid*, even though the conclusion is not factually *true*. As formal logicians, we are not concerned with whether there are actual things named Buenos Aires or Danbury. What we are concerned with is the *form*, the deductive *pattern* upon which the subject matter is imposed:

A certain factor (A) is related in a certain way (r_1) to a second factor (B).
Factor B is related in a certain way (r_2) to a third factor (C).
Therefore, A's relationship to C is the product of relations r_1 and r_2, that is, R.

More precisely, this may be noted:

$$\frac{\begin{array}{c} A\ r_1\ B \\ B\ r_2\ C \end{array}}{A\ R\ C}$$

The Syllogism

Consider the classical syllogism, a deductive pattern first systematized by Aristotle. A valid syllogism provides us with two statements, called *premises*, from which a third statement, the *conclusion*, necessarily follows. Let us examine the syllogism:

All marsupials carry their babies in their pockets.
All wallabies are marsupials.
Therefore, all wallabies carry their babies in their pockets.

A quick inspection of this syllogism will convince us that the premises formally (logically) imply the conclusion, if the premises are taken as true. Now consider this syllogism:

All dragons have wings.
All amoebas are dragons.
Therefore, all amoebas have wings.

Again, the conclusion follows, if the first two statements are taken as true, and the deduction is valid. It might be objected that there may be no such things as dragons, and that amoebas are not dragons but unicellular animals. But this objection is irrelevant, because the soundness of the deduction lies not in the factual truth of the statements but in the way the pattern is put together:

All *a*'s are *b*'s.
All *c*'s are *a*'s.
Therefore, all *c*'s are *b*'s.

Now consider the following syllogism:

New Englanders are Americans.
Bostonians are Americans.
Therefore, Bostonians are New Englanders.

This is clearly not a valid deduction, even though the conclusion may happen to be an empirically true statement. The fact that two subclasses happen to fall within the same class is no reason for asserting that therefore one subclass contains the other. Fish swim and so does Jane, but it does not *therefore* follow that Jane is a fish. Nor is the following syllogism valid:

Philanthropists are generous.
No beggars are philanthropists.
Therefore, no beggars are generous.

Because a class *K* has a property *P*, it does not necessarily follow that a class outside of *K* does not have the property *P*.

LOGIC AND FORMAL SCIENCE

Modern Generalized Logic

Aristotle's brilliant treatment of logic was limited to analysis of the syllogism and its constituent parts. For over two thousand years the development of formal logic moved almost wholly along lines Aristotle and the Stoics had staked out. Medieval logicians devised remarkable analytic techniques in logic and analysis of language. They did not succeed, however, in widening appreciably the borders of purely formal logic beyond the limits of the syllogism. In the seventeenth century, the German philosopher-mathematician Leibniz envisioned a universal symbolic language based on mathematical concepts. The work of Boole, Frege, and others initiated in the nineteenth century a revolutionary expansion of logic beyond the classical Aristotelian boundaries. In our own century there has been tremendous development of logic. The publication in 1910 of the monumental *Principia Mathematica* of Whitehead and Russell is the great initial landmark of this development.

It is now known that logic can be set forth as a purely formal and deductive science with a breadth and inclusiveness far beyond bounds ever dreamed of by Aristotle. This new extended logic is popularly referred to as *symbolic logic*. In some respects this is a misleading name. Modern generalized logic is not a logic *different* from the classical system founded by Aristotle in the sense that it treats of a wholly separate order of concepts. The new logic is, however, far more inclusive, and its basic concepts are far more generic than are those of classical logic.

Logic and Mathematics

Contemporary experts generally agree that formal logic, conceived in the extended modern sense, is the science of the general structure of deduction or formal inference. A widely held view of the relation between logic and mathematics derives from the "logistic" theory of Frege who taught that mathematical disciplines such as arithmetic, algebra, and geometry are *particular cases* of the amalgamation of certain general logical concepts with concepts peculiar to the special formal discipline in question (as "number" in the case of arithmetic). In other words, the various mathematical disciplines *presuppose* or assume the principles of logic and are therefore related to logic as the particular is related to the general.

Moreover, it is agreed that "logic" is not the name of any *single* formal deductive system. Rather "logic" is a name we may give to all possible sets of systems of a purely formal deductive character.

The Structure of Formal Science

Logic, then, is a formal or deductive science of very general character. The statements of logic are not derived from sense observation but "follow" from other previously established statements. Arithmetic and algebra are deductive disciplines, too, but they are not usually presented to us *as such.* Our first arithmetic teacher did not approach the subject by saying, "Now children, we shall begin the study of arithmetic with a definition of number. We will then list the primary axioms and rules of arithmetic, and proceed to deduce some interesting theorems, among them '2 + 2 = 4.' " In learning arithmetic, we plunge into the middle of it.[4] In secondary school, however, we may encounter an example of a deductive system *presented in axiomatic form.* This is plane geometry, which for most of us represents our first acquaintance with a deductive system presented *as such.* Although geometry can give us a good idea of what a logical system is like, the classical system of Euclid is less general than logic, for it supports a specifically geometrical subject matter.

A formal or deductive system is built up in the following way. Certain undefined notions are put forward, together with a set of statements which are admitted without proof. The latter are the *axioms* or *postulates* of the system. Selected *definitions* are set forth, and specific *rules* are laid down which allow us to perform certain operations upon the postulates. Using the postulates, definitions, and rules, we are able to show that certain *statements* necessarily follow. These statements are called *theorems* in the system. In the demonstration of a theorem, previously demonstrated theorems may be used as well as the basic postulates and definitions.

Analytic and Synthetic Statements

What are analytic statements, and how do they differ from *synthetic* statements? Classical logic tells us that a statement

[4] At least we used to. Nowadays schoolchildren study "modern math" which attempts to introduce arithmetic through basic concepts. In some of these courses, students examine nongeometrical axiom sets and techniques of proof. A common feature of "modern math" courses is the claim made at the outset that all mathematics, including arithmetic, derives from logic. The relevance of this claim to the teaching of mathematics is disputed by some mathematicians.

or *proposition* is composed of two *terms*, subject and predicate. In the proposition "Gold is a heavy metal" *gold* is the subject term, *heavy metal* the predicate term. Now according to classical logic, the predicate term of an analytic statement is *equivalent* to, though not necessarily identical in form with, the subject term. That is, in analytic propositions, the predicate is something like a *definition* of the subject. Consider the sentence: *Bachelors are unmarried men.* If we analyze the subject term, "bachelor," by asking what are the attributes of a bachelor, we quickly come upon the properties "man" and "unmarried." But in the sentence we are considering, these attributes are explicitly stated by the predicate term. Since, upon analysis of the subject term of the statement, we found the predicate *implicit* in it, the statement "Bachelors are unmarried men" is *analytic.* Contemporary logicians do not take the subject-predicate distinction as the logical structure of all statements. They prefer to define an analytic statement simply as one that is always true, true no matter what—a statement which cannot be falsified by a contradictory instance or exception.

Suppose someone should tell you that recently he came upon a bachelor who was married, you would not say, "What an interesting exception to the general rule—something like a white kangaroo!" Rather you would say, "You are not using the word 'bachelor' in the way I am using it." Your reply would show that you recognized the proposition "bachelors are unmarried men" to be analytic, and that such statements are not established by empirical observation but by certain rules governing the proper use of language.

Now contrast with the statement "Bachelors are unmarried men" the following sentence: *The box fell down stairs.* There is nothing in the definition of "the box" which would lead us to the knowledge that it fell down stairs. The box *happened* to take that tumble. So we classify this statement as *synthetic*, that is, one which *could* be false, although here it happens to be true. Those sentences which describe situations or "goings-on" in the empirical world are synthetic or factual statements and present a contrast to the sentences found in formal science which are analytic.

Formal Science Composed of Analytic Statements

Logical analysts today still tend to Frege's view that all statements of formal science, whether logic or mathematics, are analytic. Thus, "$2 + 2 = 4$" is an analytic statement. It does not describe an empirical situation like a bird flying or a cork popping. "Four" is *another way* of saying "two plus two," just as "unmarried man" is another way of saying "bachelor." Now if the statements of formal science are analytic, then any theorem of formal science, however complex it may be, can only make explicit what is implicit in the basic equipment of the system of which it is a part. The moves in chess, like many theorems of mathematics, can be very complicated. Yet they all derive ultimately from certain assumptions about the pieces and the rules for moving them. The statement "$2 + 2 = 4$" is often cited as an example of an obvious *truth*. But what does it mean to say that this statement is true? Strictly speaking, it means that this is a theorem of arithmetic, that is, a statement which follows from certain prior theorems, which in turn derive ultimately from certain basic notions, postulates, and rules. Now what holds for "$2 + 2 = 4$" holds as well for more complex mathematical and logical statements. They too are "true" in that they are theorems which draw their truth from the structure of the scheme which contains them.

Illustration of the Symbolic Character of Modern Logic

Just what is the difference between classical or Aristotelian logic and modern generalized or "symbolic" logic? We have spoken very generally about the two kinds, stating that logic is today considered to be the foundation of all formal science, including mathematics, and that the concepts of modern logic are far more inclusive than those of classical logic. But is it not possible to be more specific about the differences between the two logics? Unfortunately, we cannot offer such clarification without turning our book into a logic text. We can, however, show something of the "symbolic" character of modern logic by simple illustrations of types of notation used in the construction of deductive systems, such as those in *Principia Mathematica.*

Notations for Classes

The classical Aristotelian syllogism, traditionally regarded as the culmination of formal logic, is accommodated in modern logic within a more general deductive system known as the *logic of classes* or *Boolean algebra.* The reader will notice the analogy to the "set theory" now featured in so many "new math" courses. Boole showed that the letters in algebraic formulas like $a + b = b + a$ could stand for *classes* as well as for quantities. Suppose we wish to construct a deductive system involving classes. There is the class "cat," the class "fat man," the class "automobile." We need not use *words* to designate particular classes. Symbols, such as a, b, c, etc., will stand for *any* class. Here is a class, the class of "all cat" if you like:

$$a$$

Here is another class—the class of "all who are polite":

$$b$$

Now here is the class of all those things that are not cats:

$$\bar{a} \text{ (not-}a\text{)}$$

And here is the class of all those things which are not polite:

$$\bar{b} \text{ (not-}b\text{)}$$

Now consider the following two symbolic notations:

$$a \times b \qquad a + b$$

The first expression designates the *product* of classes a and b. In this class product or combined class are contained the members of both class a and class b. In terms of our subject matter, $a \times b$ represents "polite cats." The second expression designates the *sum* of the classes a and b. The class sum contains those things which are either in class a or in class b or in both. In terms of our subject matter, $a + b$ represents a class which contains all the cats and all those who are polite, a much larger group than $a \times b$ which holds only polite cats.

If we wish to represent symbolically that one class is included or contained in another class, we write:

$$a \subset b \text{ (}a\text{ is included in }b\text{)}$$

In terms of our subject matter, $a \subset b$ stands for "cats are members of the polite class."

There is a symbol used for a class that has no members. This is called the *null* class, and it is represented by the symbol:

$$0$$

The class which contains everything is called the *universal* class and is noted as:

$$1$$

For a simple illustration of some of these symbolic class notations, consider how they would work out in the case of the following four standard Aristotelian types of propositions:

1. All Italians are music lovers.

$$a\bar{b} = 0$$

The class product or combined class "Italians who are non-music lovers" is a class of no members.

2. No Spartans are cowards.

$ab = 0$

The class product "Spartans who are cowards" is a class of no members.

3. Some cassowaries are vicious.

$ab \neq 0$

The class product "vicious cassowaries" is *not* a class of no members. That is, there is at least one vicious cassowary.

4. Some choirboys are not mischievous.

$a\bar{b} \neq 0$

The class product "nonmischievous choirboys" is *not* a class of no members. That is, there is at least one nonmischievous choirboy.

A deductive system of classes can be constructed by forming postulates containing these and other class notions and developing theorems from these postulates in quasi-algebraic form.

Notation for Sentences

If we wish to construct a deductive system of propositions or *sentential calculus*, we use other basic notions, represented symbolically in the following way:

In place of a sentence with definite subject matter, like "Koalas like eucalyptus leaves," we simply use a letter symbol to stand for any sentence at all:

$$p$$

For another sentence, we use a different letter symbol. "It is cold in Greenland" may be represented by

$$q$$

Suppose we wish to represent a sentence which is to be taken as *false*. We note the sentence "It is not the case that bats are birds" as:

$\sim p$ (not-p)

If we wish to show the relation of *conjunction* or "and-ness," as in the compound sentence "America is my country and heaven is my destination," we note:

$p \cdot q$ (p and q, or p is true and q is true.)

Suppose we want to show the relation of *implication* (if . . . then) as in the sentence "if you marry me, I shall be eternally happy," we set down:

$p \supset q$ (If p is true, q is true.)

If we wish to show the relation of alternation, as in the sentence "Sue will help or Pat will help," we write:

$p \vee q$ (p is true or q is true.)

Recapitulating, our logical notions include:

p, q, r, etc.	sentence symbols (variables)
$\cdot$	"and"
$\sim$	"not"
$\supset$	"implies" or "if . . . then"
$\vee$	"or"

To illustrate, let us put into this notation three axioms singled out by classical logicians as "laws of logic."

IDENTITY: $p \supset p$
If p is true, p is true.

NONCONTRADICTION: $\sim (p \cdot \sim p)$
It is not the case that p is true and p is false.

EXCLUDED MIDDLE: $p \vee \sim p$
Either p is true or p is false.

In the *Principia Mathematica*, Whitehead and Russell begin the elementary logic of propositions with two undefined constants:

$\sim$ "not"
$\vee$ "or"

By definition we may build the "if . . . then" concept from the two notions above:

$$p \supset q \text{ means } \sim p \vee q \qquad \text{Def. 1}$$

(that is, "if p, then q" may be written "not-p or q" and vice versa.)

Now we may construct postulates or axioms out of these ideas. Here are three postulates used in the *Principia:*

I. TAUTOLOGY: $(p \vee p) \supset p$
If p is true or p is true, then p is true.

II. ADDITION: $q \supset (p \vee q)$
If q is true, then p or q is true.

III. PERMUTATION: $(p \vee q) \supset (q \vee p)$
If p or q, then q or p.

Using rules which permit substitution on variables (the p's, q's, etc. being taken as blank spaces for sentences) or by substitution of definitions ($\sim p \vee q$) being simply a *translation* of $p \supset q$ and vice versa, *theorems* of the system can now be demonstrated. Here are two examples:

THEOREM I. $q \supset (p \supset q)$

Proof

1. $q \supset (p \vee q)$ — POSTULATE II
2. $q \supset (\sim p \vee q)$ — Substituting $\sim p$ for p in step 1.
3. $q \supset (p \supset q)$ — Subst. in step 2 by Def. 1.

THEOREM II. $(p \supset \sim p) \supset \sim p$

Proof

1. $(p \vee p) \supset p$ — POSTULATE I
2. $(\sim p \vee \sim p) \supset \sim p$ — Subst. $\sim p$ for p in step 1.
3. $(p \supset \sim p) \supset \sim p$ — Subst. in step 2 by Def. 1.

There is a rule of argument that if the truth of one statement implies the falsity of a second statement, then the truth of the second implies the falsity of the first. For example, if "Jack is a bachelor" implies "Jack is not married," then "Jack is married" implies "Jack is not a bachelor." Here is the rule proved as a theorem:

THEOREM III. $(p \supset \sim q) \supset (q \supset \sim p)$

Proof

1. $(p \vee q) \supset (q \vee p)$ — POSTULATE III
2. $(\sim p \vee \sim q) \supset (q \vee \sim p)$ — Subst. $\sim p$ for p and $\sim q$ for q in step 1.
3. $(p \supset \sim q) \supset (q \supset \sim p)$ — Subst. in step 2 by Def. 1.

Logic and Ordinary Discourse

Formal logic gains in precision and exactness in almost direct proportion to its remoteness from the uses of ordinary language. Both the Aristotelian logic of propositions and syllogisms, and the modern generalized logic of the twentieth century, work with material which must be isolated from the context of ordinary discourse. Formal logic is happy with propositions like

All whales are mammals.

only when they are pulled out of the web of surrounding sentences in which we find them (when we find them at all) in ordinary speech. The following is a law of logic:

If p implies q, then not-q implies not-p.

and sometimes we do argue that way in ordinary discourse as in the case:

> If you love me, you will marry me.
> Sorry; I won't marry you.
> Then, you don't love me.

But more often than not, such strict logical arguments are rare in everyday talk. While we can abstract certain forms of argument from ordinary talk and writing, and put them into the notation of symbolic logic, many more instances of quite everyday discourse are hard to put into the standard forms of logic. Here is a bit of casual talk, well-grounded in reasoning forms of ordinary language; yet it would be the despair of a formal logician, if he were asked to throw it into one of the standard forms of class, propositional, or predicate calculus:

> I think he's going to buckle down; I heard he was in the library last night—so it's likely that he's planning to study.

We should not expect to find in a study of the logic of ordinary discourse that quality of exactness and system which belongs to formal logic. But, as P. F. Strawson says, "It is none the less true that the logic of ordinary speech provides a field of intellectual study unsurpassed in richness, complexity, and the power to absorb."[5]

FURTHER READINGS

Ambrose, A., and M. Lazerowitz, *Fundamentals of Symbolic Logic*, rev. ed., New York, Holt, Rinehart and Winston, 1962.

Aristotle, *Prior Analytics; Posterior Analytics; On Interpretation.* (The most convenient English edition of Aristotle's works is the one-volume *The Basic Works of Aristotle*, R. McKeon, ed., New York, Random House, 1941.)

Bochenski, I. M., *A History of Formal Logic*, Ivo Thomas (trans.), University of Notre Dame Press, 1961.

Brennan, J. G., *A Handbook of Logic*, 2nd ed., New York, Harper & Row, 1961.

[5] P. F. Strawson, *Introduction to Logical Theory*, London, Methuen, 1952, p. 232.

Copi, I., *Symbolic Logic*, 2nd ed., New York, Macmillan, 1965.

Hempel, C. G., "The Nature of Mathematical Truth," in H. Feigl and W. Sellars (eds.), *Readings in Philosophical Analysis*, New York, Appleton-Century-Crofts, 1949.

Jevons, W. S., *Elementary Lessons in Logic* (London, 1870), New York, Macmillan 1948.

Kneale, W., and M. Kneale, *The Development of Logic*, Oxford, Clarendon Press, 1962.

Mill, J. S., *A System of Logic* (London, 1843), New York, Longmans, 1925.

Passmore, J., *A Hundred Years of Philosophy*, London, Duckworth, 1957, chap. 6.

Quine, W. V., *Methods of Logic*, New York, Holt, Rinehart and Winston, 1950. (PB: *Elementary Logic*, Harper Torchbooks, Harper & Row, New York.)

Strawson, P. F., *Introduction to Logical Theory*, London, Methuen, 1952.

Tarski, A., *Introduction to Logic*, New York, Oxford University Press, 1941. (PB: Galaxy Books, Oxford U. P.)

Whitehead, A. N., and B. Russell, *Principia Mathematica* (1910), 2nd ed., London, Cambridge University Press, 1950, vol 1. (PB: Cambridge U. P.)

2

Language

We must speak by the card, or equivocation will undo us.

—*Hamlet*, V, i

New developments in logic in our time have been paralleled by increasing critical interest in the role played by *language* in philosophy. The word "language" here refers not to specific tongues like French or English but to language in general.

Critical awareness of the relation between philosophy and language is by no means new. The charge that philosophers' arguments are no more than *disputes about words* is of ancient origin. In the seventeenth century the philosopher Francis Bacon compiled a list of *Idols* or obstacles to the advancement of human knowledge. The "Idols of the Market-place" refers to the habit of men to use words carelessly and to mistake words for things. Says Bacon:

> ... The ill and unfit choice of words wonderfully obstructs the understanding. Nor do the definitions or explanations wherewith in some things learned men are wont to guard and defend themselves by any means set the matter right. But all words plainly force and overrule the understanding, and throw all into confusion, and lead men away into numberless empty controversies and idle fancies.[1]

[1] *Novum Organum*, xliii.

In recent years, however, critical inquiry into the relation between language and philosophy has gone far beyond warnings of a general nature concerning obscurities inherent in words and pitfalls of language which beset even the most learned men. Today, technical analysis of the structure of language, together with the development of artificial languages like modern deductive logic, have produced batteries of new techniques for the investigation of problems of language and philosophy. Since most of these devices for the analysis and construction of language are technically difficult, we shall not examine them in detail. We must be content with a few general observations and useful distinctions concerning the nature of language and its relation to philosophy.

Semantics; Syntactics; Semiotic

In the analysis of language, *semantics* refers to that discipline in which we study the relation between *words* and that which is *meant* by words. For instance, if we ask about the relation between the word "cat" or the word "blue" and the objects or properties these words stand for, this is a semantic inquiry. When we raise questions about the rules which prescribe how a language is to be used, this is a matter of *syntactics*. In grammar, *syntax* refers to the rules for putting sentences together. For example, in English and in many other particular languages it is a rule of syntax that a pronoun may be substituted for a noun. Analogously, when we treat of language *generally*, and inquire into the rules which govern the use of *any* language, ordinary or artificial, we are moving in the field of syntactics. This discipline is sometimes called the study of *logical syntax* in order to distinguish it from the study of grammatical syntax. Both semantics and syntactics are today considerd as *parts* of the general discipline of *semiotic*. The name for this study was introduced into general usage by Charles Morris. *Semiotic* is defined as the general theory of signs and languages.

Words as Linguistic Signs

Words belong to the general class of signs or symbols.[2] Not all signs are words, however. Flags, lodge pins, traffic lights, emblems of political parties, as well as tears, blushes, and sneezes may all be classed as signs, although none of them are words. What is the function of a sign? A sign *stands for something*. It leads us beyond itself to the thought of something other than itself. The hammer and sickle stands for the Communist party, the cross for Christianity, a skull and crossed bones for pirates or poison, depending on the context.

The classification of signs is a very ticklish business, but there is a rather obvious breakdown of signs into two subclasses, *natural* signs and *conventional* signs. In natural signs, the connection between sign and thing signified is a connection "of nature" rather than one which is arbitrary, conventional, and man-made. In natural signs, the sign is *part* of the thing signified. A blush and a rapidly falling barometer are natural signs. The blush is a sign of embarrassment because it is part of the total complex we call "embarrassment." The rapidly falling barometer is related to the storm as *effect* to natural *cause*.

In *conventional* signs, there is no connection "of nature" between sign and thing signified, although there may be one of *appropriateness*. The figure of a lion would have done as well as that of an elephant for the symbol of the Republican party, although the image of a pterodactyl

[2] Many philosophers, e.g., Kant, Hegel, W. M. Urban, make a distinction between "sign" and "symbol." Here, for reasons of simplicity, we take them as synonyms.

would not. A fish was once the symbol of Christianity; and a rattlesnake was proposed, though not accepted, as an emblem for the flag of the United States.

Words are *linguistic* signs. As such, they form a subclass of conventional rather than of natural signs. There is no connection "of nature" between a word and the thing signified by the word, although the peasant who said "The pig is rightly so called, for it is a very dirty animal" doubtless thought there was. If words were natural signs, the French word for "house" would be the same as the English word. It is said that primitive people commonly believe that a word *is* naturally connected with what it stands for. Hence the widespread conviction among primitives that possession of the *name* of a man or a god gives the possessor some magical control over the owner of the name. But even though we classify words as conventional rather than arbitrary signs, we should not think that all words have been chosen by some process of conscious agreement. As Bertrand Russell remarks, it is hard to imagine a scene from some bygone day in which a council of hitherto speechless elders sat down to agree to call a cow a cow and a wolf a wolf.[3] Only small classes of words—such as scientific terms like "radium" or "Parkinson's disease"—are chosen by parliamentary procedure.

Ways of Using Words

Some words form names or *terms*, like "duck-billed platypus," "hot," or "jumping." Known as *categorematic* words, names or term words can stand alone as subject or predicate of propositions (declarative sentences). *Syncategorematic* words, like prepositions, conjunctions, adverbs,

[3] Bertrand Russell, *The Analysis of Mind,* London, G. Allen, 1921, p. 190.

etc., must be used *with* other words to form names or terms.

Words are combined to form sentences. Sentences may make assertions, or they may be questions, commands, or expressions of a wish. The grammatical classification of sentences as declarative, interrogative, optative, etc., reminds us that we use language in many different ways. Some sentences are *informative*. They point out certain situations that exist, and they may describe those situations. They are generally declarative sentences, such as "It is raining," "Tibetans drink buttered tea," and "Silver is a good conductor of electricity."

A basic function of language is to produce appropriate *action* on the part of the hearer. "Look out!" and "By the left flank, march!" are action signals. There is also the *ceremonial* use of language. "How do you do" and "I'm very glad to have met you" are simple examples from everyday discourse. More complex instances of the ceremonial usage of language may be found in religious ceremonies. Language is often used to express our *feelings* or *wishes*, as in the sentences "I despise that man" and "Would to God I were a tender apple blossom!"

Descriptive and Emotive Use of Language

In the nineteen-thirties, certain philosophers of language made much of the distinction between the employment of words to inform or describe and their use to convey the state of our feelings or emotions. This distinction was frequently supported by reference to the contrast between *science* and *poetry*. Science was said to be made up of informative sentences which describe states of affairs in the actual world. Poetry is asserted to consist of statements about the poet's emotions, composed for the purpose of arousing similar emotions in us. Distinguishing between what he terms the representative and the expressive functions of language, Carnap says:

> Many linguistic utterances are analogous to laughing in that they have only an expressive function, no representative function. Examples of this are cries like "Oh, Oh" or, on a higher level, lyrical verses. The aim of a lyrical poem in which occur the words "sunshine" and "clouds" is not to inform us of certain meteorological facts, but to express certain feelings of the poet and to excite similar feelings in us. A lyrical poem has no assertional sense, no theoretical sense, it does not contain knowledge.[4]

While it is important to perceive the distinction between descriptive and emotive usage of words, and to recognize that scientists and poets use language in different ways, there is some danger in pushing the distinction too far. In the first place, the word "emotive" has acquired a subtly derogatory flavor. In a discussion of this kind, the words "emotive" and "emotions" are frequently used to make a covert value judgment in which descriptive or scientific language is implicitly accorded a high status, with "emotional" or "poetic" language relegated to inferior rank. Secondly, it is not certain that poetry (even lyric poetry) is completely defined as the expression of certain feelings on the part of the poet with the purpose of stimulating similar feelings in others. There may be implicit in such a definition the assumption that questions of poetry are nothing but questions of somebody's "feelings," and that such "feelings" are out of place in science and philosophy. Poetry is far more than mere expression of feelings. For one thing, much depends on *whose* feelings are expresed.

[4] Rudolf Carnap, *Philosophy and Logical Syntax*, London, Kegan Paul, 1935, p. 28.

For another, a poem may contain a *syntax of ideas*, a cognitive or intellectual element without which it would be nothing. It may even be the case that poets *in their way* attempt to describe "the nature of things," and that the description of "reality" is not an exclusive prerogative of empirical science.

Ambiguity, Vagueness, and Metaphor

Words that have one meaning only are traditionally called *univocal.* There are very few such words, and illustrations of them may be drawn only from a limited number of categories, such as household words ("egg beater," "teakettle") or scientific terms ("vanadium," "positron"). Most words have more than one meaning, and these are conventionally labeled *equivocal.* In many equivocal words we can clearly distinguish the separate meanings without much trouble, as in the case of "box," "bear," "note," and the like. But there is a large class of equivocal words in which various levels of meaning have become fused. In these *ambiguous* words, the multiple meanings shade over into one another and are difficult to distinguish. When such words are employed in argument, we cannot be sure, short of a definition of terms, in just what sense the words are being used. In poetry ambiguous words may add to the richness of the poetic material and may serve to invoke a host of associations. A less admirable usage of ambiguous words charged with emotion is frequently encountered in public discussion. Such "loaded" words as "aggression," "un-American" and "imperialism" are often used to prejudice the argument in favor of the speaker rather than to enlighten his audience. The role of question-begging words in everyday discourse is amusingly illustrated in Bertrand Russell's well-known conjugation:

I am firm.
You are obstinate.
He is a pig-headed fool.

It is possible to distinguish between ambiguity and *vagueness.* The word "liberal" is *ambiguous,* because we are not sure which of the various shades of meaning is intended. The word "dead," on the other hand, is *vague,* because there are borderline cases—such as that of a man whose heart has ceased to beat—to which we are not sure whether to apply the word "dead" or not. The words "knowledge" and "science" are vague. We use them appropriately, but we are not sure of the limits of their application. Does "knowledge," for example, include simple sense perception; does "science" apply to philosophy?

Scientists and philosophers have long pursued the idea of a *precise* language in which there would be neither ambiguity nor vagueness. Contemporary achievements in the construction of artificial languages such as symbolic logic or "model" linguistic systems represent a partial fulfillment of this ideal. But, precise as these symbolic languages may be, they all have the limitation of lacking *content.* While neither vague nor ambiguous, they are *vacuous.* It is Max Black's opinion that vagueness in ordinary and even in scientific language is unavoidable. But, since symbolic systems are available, he says, "the need is removed for regarding vagueness as a defect of language."[5]

The part played in language by *metaphor* is very great. A metaphor is a figure of speech which embodies a transfer of meaning by analogy or likeness, as in the expressions "a barrage of questions" or "a ship plowing the sea." Poetic language is highly metaphorical:

[5] Max Black, "Vagueness," *Language and Philosophy,* Cornell University Press, 1949, p. 27.

O the mind, mind has mountains; cliffs of fall
Frightful, sheer, no-man-fathomed.

Not only in poetry but in every type of ordinary language metaphor abounds—although this is not always obvious. The basic meaning of the word "foot" refers to the parts of our legs we walk on. By transfer of meaning, we speak of the foot of a bed and the foot of a hill. Language has grown by metaphor. The root meaning of "governor" is steersman, of "character," an engraving tool, of "spirit," breath. We speak even of scientific matters in metaphor.[6] When we explain the tides by the "pull" of the moon or the motion of iron filings by the "attraction" of the magnet, we are unconsciously using analogy words the meanings of which derive from human behavior and experience. Philosophical language, even of the soberest variety, owes much to metaphor. For example, contemporary philosophers are quite fond of the word "structure." Such expressions as "the structure of language," "the structure of personality," and "the structure of experience" are often heard today in learned discussions. A little reflection reveals the metaphorical character of the word "structure," the primary meaning of which concerns the building of houses, dams, and bridges.

Many philosophers of language warn us that indiscriminate use of metaphors and analogies leads us into error by providing us with apparent solutions or "pseudo explanations" of certain problems. Plato's explanation of the genesis of the physical universe as the production of a "Maker" or Artificer-God is sometimes given as an example of a pseudo explanation derived from uncritical use of meta-

[6] See chap. 6, "The Growth of Language," in W. S. Jevons, *Elementary Lessons in Logic* (London, 1870), New York, Macmillan, 1948.

phorical language.[7] Hans Reichenbach takes classical philosophers severely to task for their "pseudo explanations" based on naïve parallelisms. "Pernicious errors through false analogies," he says, "have been the philosopher's disease at all times."[8] It is doubtless impossible (and probably unnecessary) to purge philosophical language entirely of metaphor. But the use of metaphor and analogy is not *in itself* objectionable. These linguistic devices can be dispensed with only in artificial and symbolic language systems. The danger lies in the *uncritical* use of metaphor, in the *undiscriminating* employment of analogical expressions without realizing the limitations of analogy.

Connotation and Denotation; Definition

Two senses in which those words we call terms or names may be taken are *connotation* (or "intension") and *denotation* ("extension"). The connotation of a term refers to the attributes, essential properties, or characteristics of that which the term stands for. Denotation refers to the individuals to which the name applies. For example, the connotation of *chair* is "separate seat for one." The denotation of *chair* is this chair, that chair, and each and every other individual chair. The connotation of *bassoon* is "bass member of the double-reeded woodwind instruments." The denotation of *bassoon* is each and every bassoon. Proper names have a denotation of 1—when I say "Laura Banks" I mean one thing only. But logicians and analysts of

[7] Plato, *Timaeus*, 28 et seq. In this instance Plato warns his readers that his account of the creation of the world is no more than a "likely tale." (For convenient editions of the Dialogues of Plato, see under "Plato" in the readings listed at the end of this chapter.)

[8] Hans Reichenbach, *The Rise of Scientific Philosophy*, University of California Press, 1951, p. 11. (PB: U. of Calif. Press.)

language disagree as to whether proper names have any connotation at all.[9]

The distinction between connotation and denotation carries over into *definition.* When we define a word, we indicate in some way the appropriate *use* of the word. We try to raise thoughts in the mind of another person which he will associate with things familiar to him. Now there is more than one way of defining. We may explain what we mean by a word with a set of words whose meanings are presumed to be known. This is formal or *verbal* definition of a word and may be identified with its connotation: "A squirrel is a small animal, a rodent with a bushy tail. Squirrels live in trees, eat nuts, etc." Or we may explain what we mean by pointing to an example of that to which the word applies. This is known as *ostensive* definition, and obviously relates to the *denotation* of the term: "*That's* a squirrel." Parents of small children often rely on ostensive definition. As a rule, however, it is impractical to define ostensively since the objects to which many words refer are not of a directly observable kind or, if they are observable, are rarely at hand.

Meaning

In definition, whether verbal or ostensive, we try to make clear what we *mean* by a word. We will all concede that words with which we are familiar *mean* something, but it is not easy to explain just what *meaning* is.

Meaning is sometimes said to involve a three-part, or

[9] John Stuart Mill denies that proper names have connotation. In order that an object may properly be called "tree," it must have certain attributes—woody, plant, etc. But in order for an object to be named "Laura Banks," no such set of specifications need be met. "Laura Banks" could be the name of a race horse, a pet turtle, a private estate, as well as the name of a woman.

triadic, relationship, that is, a relation between (1) a *sign,* (2) that which the sign stands for (*referent*), and (3) the *interpreter* of the sign. A meaning situation exists whenever a sign produces in the person perceiving the sign a connection or association between the sign and that which the sign *stands for.* This will hold whether the connection or association exists (2) directly, between the sign and some physical response or action, or (b) indirectly, between the sign and referent through the medium of some concept, thought, or idea. Rapid ringing of the ship's bell produces in the sailor on a warship the immediate physical reaction of running to his battle station. The sight of the Crescent and Star may stimulate in the interpreter the thought or concept of Islam which in turn relates to that particular culture. This analysis seems also to hold for both natural and conventional signs:

	Sign		*Referent*
A. Natural	Red sky at night	means	fair weather next day.
B. Conventional			
1. Nonlinguistic	Green light	means	go.
2. Linguistic	"Sanskrit"	means	ancient language of India.

Words are linguistic signs. Their meaning involves the production in a person of some kind of connection between the word and the referent. If no such connection is produced, the word is *meaningless* to the person hearing it or reading it. If a boy, playing his first sand-lot baseball game, does not know the meaning of "Bunt!" he cannot respond to the coach's cry with appropriate action. If I *do* know the meaning of a word, I know how to use it. When a little girl points to a cat and says "cat!" her grasp of the meaning of "cat" is pretty much the same as her ability to use the word.

The Status of Referents

The question of the status or "modes of being" of the referents of words and statements raises some oddly difficult problems. Recollection of the rules of grammar may prompt us to say that nouns or names refer to things, adjectives to properties, and verbs to actions. But what manner of existence do these things, properties, and actions have? Names seem to present no difficulty, particularly names of objects. "Cat" refers to observable objects which mew, purr, scratch, etc. "Tree" refers to the familiar woody plant in my backyard and to others of its kind. The referent of a word like "atom" is not observable directly; an atom is a queer sort of object, one assumed on the basis of a long chain of inferences to have some kind of physical existence. The name "goblin" designates things which are not natural objects at all. (Where are they, then?) Some critics have poked fun at the German metaphysician Heidegger because he has written at length and very seriously about Nothing. But we should note that *meaning* and *naming* are not the same thing. Plato pointed out that "Notbeing" is not the name of anything at all. Frege showed that "the morning star" and "the evening star" name the same object—the planet Venus—although the meanings of these terms are quite different.

But language has everyday uses that go far beyond naming objects. Wittgenstein called attention to the immense variety of ways in which we employ language and the difficulty of explaining just *what* sorts of things these language utterances could possibly be signs of. Think of the differences between these uses of language: making up a story and reading it; play-acting; singing catches; guessing riddles; making a joke and telling it; solving a problem in practical arithmetic; translating from one language into another; asking, thanking, cursing, greeting, praying. Think of exclamations alone, with their completely different functions:

Water!
Away!
Ow!
Help!
Fine!
No!

"Are you inclined still," Wittgenstein asks his reader, "to call these words 'names of objects' "?[10]

J. L. Austin noticed that certain—sometimes important—statements we make could not possibly have *any* referents at all, since saying the words is identical with performing the action. He called such statements "performative utterances." When I say, "I promise to pay you back," my statement does not refer to something apart from the statement which is a promise. The phrase "I promise" *is* my promise; my word is my bond. "When I say before the altar 'I do,' " says Austin, "I am not reporting on a marriage: I am indulging in it."[11]

There is an important class of words used in ordinary discourse the status of whose referents is interesting, although difficult to analyze. These are *logical* or *syntax* words. They are syncategorematic, and include words like "if," "and," "not," and "or." Unlike *descriptive* words,

[10] *Philosophical Investigations*, New York, Macmillan, 1953, p. 27.

[11] *How to Do Things with Words*, Harvard University Press, 1962, p. 6. (PB: Galaxy, Oxford U. P., New York.)

such as "house," "unicorn," "blue," and "running," syntax words do not appear to refer to any state of affairs, actual or fictitious. They seem rather to designate logical or linguistic *attitudes*. That is, syntax words are signs of ways in which we are to "take" the words or sentences with which they are associated. For example, in the sentence "Whales are not fish," the word "not" is a sign of *rejection* of the sentence "Whales are fish." In the conjunctive sentence "Bats are mammals and they fly," the word "and" is a sign of *acceptance* of both conjuncts.

Formal and Material Modes of Speech

In the sentence "There is a cow in that field," the referent of the word "cow" is a *natural object* that moos, gives milk, etc. But in the sentence " 'Cow' is a short word," the referent of "cow" is not the object cow but the *word* "cow." These two senses of "cow" illustrate the classical distinction between the *formal* (objective; "real") and *material* modes of speech. In the syllogism:

> The emu lays large eggs.
> Emu is a three-letter word.
> At least one three-letter word lays large eggs.

the absurdity is the result of confusion between objective and material *suppositions* of the word "emu." Not all confusions between the formal and material suppositions of words and sentences are as obvious as that in the example just given. Contemporary philosophers of language tell us that it is easy to fall into the habit of talking about the syntactical properties of *sentences* while under the impression that we are talking about *things*. (We shall see a possible example of this confusion in the case of the principle of noncontradiction discussed below.) According to Carnap, a great many problems of traditional philosophy have been generated by philosophers' confounding of the objective and material modes of speech.[12] Taken broadly, this amounts to a claim that philosophers have disputed about *words* while convinced they have been disputing about *things*—a charge against philosophy about as old as philosophy itself.

Object-Language and Meta-Language; First- and Second-Order Statements

Analysts of language distinguish between *object-language* and *meta-language*.[13] This distinction helps to separate talking about objects or events and talking about the properties of a language. The referents of the sentences of a meta-language are not things or events but the properties or rules of a language. An object-language is that language to which the meta-language refers. If we wish to talk about the properties of a *special* language, we may use English as a meta-language, thus: "There are no articles in the Chinese language." Here the object-language is Chinese. If we wish to talk about the properties or rules of *language in general*, we may use the concepts and vocabulary of semantics or syntactics: "Words are linguistic signs." Shakespeare's unhappy Ophelia is speaking metalinguistically and her object-language is the language of flowers when she says: "There's rosemary, that's for remembrance; . . . and there is pansies, that's for thoughts."

A related distinction was made in our preface where we

[12] Rudolf Carnap, *The Logical Syntax of Language*, London, Kegan Paul, 1937, pp. 298–315.

[13] "Meta-language" is sometimes used as a synonym for syntactics or logical syntax of language (see above, p. 40). A distinction similar to that between object-language and meta-language is common in discussions of logic. Manipulation of syllogisms or of the various calculi in generalized logic is *logic*, while discussion of the nature of logical systems, their basic notions, postulates, rules, etc., is *meta-logic*.

noted the distinction between first- and second-order statements. There are statements about people and things—statements about the world, if you like. These are *first-order* statements. Then there are statements about statements, statements about language, about the way we use words. These are *second-order* statements. The distinction is important if we wish to understand certain basic difference between traditional philosophy and the analytic-linguistic philosophy of our time. Much of classical philosophy is cast in the form of questions derived from *first-order* statements:

1. How can the human mind be related to a body which is a material substance?
2. What is the nature of moral judgments?

Analytic-linguistic philosophy prefers to draft questions drawn from second-order statements.

1. What do we mean by "mental event" and how does our usage help us to distinguish this from "physical event"?
2. What does it mean to say "X is right," or "X is wrong"?

We shall see in the next chapter whether any of the traditional confusion surrounding the word "Truth" can be cleared away by keeping in mind this important distinction between first-order and second-order statements.

REFERENTS OF LOGICAL AXIOMS AND GENERAL NAMES

The Principle of Noncontradiction

There are at least two different points of view as to the status or mode of being of the primary laws of logic. Some philosophers hold that these laws have *ontological* status—

that is, the laws of logic have their foundation in Nature. Others (among whom may be numbered many contemporary philosophers of language) claim that the laws of logic are like the laws of any language system; they are simply *rules* which determine how we are to use language, taken generally. The difference of opinion here is a difference over the *mode of being possessed by the referents of those sentences which set forth the laws of logic.*

The problem may be illustrated by reference to the classical law of logic known as the *principle of noncontradiction.* This law was first formulated by Aristotle: "There is a principle in things about which we cannot be deceived, but must always, on the contrary, recognize the truth. It is that the same thing cannot at one and the same time be and not be."[14] That is, a door cannot be open and shut at the same time, nor can a shoe be black and white in the same place. For, says Aristotle, "the same attribute cannot at the same time belong and not belong to the same subject and in the same respect."[15] Aristotle believed that the law of noncontradiction was both a fundamental axiom of logic and of human discourse, and a first principle of Nature or *being.* That is, Aristotle was convinced that this fundamental law holds not only in the realm of logic and language but in the *natural order* as well. Indeed, according to Aristotle, it is the natural order that is the foundation and source of the principle of noncontradiction.

For more than two thousand years philosophers generally held that the principle of noncontradiction was, as Aristotle said, a fundamental law to which *things* as well as *sentences* were subject. At first sight, it does seem that natural objects "obey" this law. Dogs don't bark and "not bark" at the same time, and it is impossible for a man to be

[14] Aristotle, *Metaphysics,* W. D. Ross trans., bk. 11, 1061b34.
[15] *Ibid.*, bk. 4, 1005b18.

dead and not dead "in the same respect." Today, however, many logicians and analytic philosophers deny that the principle of noncontradiction is a fundamental law which all natural objects and events obey. Rather, they hold that the law is no more than a basic *rule of language.* It is a presupposition of human communication, a first principle of syntax, a basic rule for putting sentences together. Aristotle was right, these analysts maintain, in holding that the law of noncontradiction is a primary principle of *discourse.* But he was wrong in assuming that what is undeniably a basic rule of *language* is also a first principle of *Nature.* The reason natural objects like shoes and doors seem to "obey" the law of noncontradiction is that we cannot talk about these things without using language in which the law of noncontradiction is ingrained.

Referents of General Names; the "Problem of Universals"; Plato and Ockham

Earlier we remarked that the status or mode of being of the referent of a word like "cat" seems to offer no difficulty. Cats are observable physical objects. But we should note that the word "cat" is a *general* word or name, since it applies to *all* cats. Thus the general name "cat" stands in contrast to *singular* terms like "Purrcilla Mewriel" (a proper name) or "this cat" which apply only to one individual cat.

Now one of the most complicated problems in classical philosophy is connected with this simple classification of words as *general* and *singular.* The "problem of universals" concerns the *status or mode of being of the referents of general words.* Since the problem of universals strikingly illustrates the importance of the relation between language and philosophy, it may be useful to spend a little time on general names.

Singular names refer to specific objects, events, or instances of qualities. "Lyndon Johnson," "Boulder Dam," "that ball-playing," "this blue here" are singular terms. General names refer to *classes* or *kinds* of objects, events, or qualities. "Man," "suspension bridge," "swimming," and "yellow" are examples of general words. General names apply to each member of the class or kind. "Mouse" applies to every individual mouse, "hard" to every occurrence of that property, and "singing" to every instance of song. That general words are indispensable in human communication may be proved by the simple experiment of trying to say a few sentences without them.

Now, what kind of objects, if any, do general words refer to? Unlike singular terms, general names, *taken as such*, do not designate observable objects. Consider the sentence "The pig is a domestic animal." No one has ever observed "the pig," but only this pig, that pig, and many other individual pigs. Take the sentence "Tom is a man." We can talk to Tom and shake hands with him. Not so with man. No one has ever seen man walking down the street. What we do see are individual men.

The ancient Greek philosopher Plato drew some remarkable conclusions upon the basis of this and certain other considerations. Since general names stand for universal properties which cannot be observed *as such* by our senses, these general terms must *designate things which exist on some plane of being other than that present to sense experience.* There do exist, independently of human thought and language, certain originals or prototypes which correspond to general words. These universal objects, or Ideas, as Plato calls them, exist in a world which transcends the world of ordinary experience, a mode of being to which thought alone can penetrate. That is why these universal Forms are not observable by sense perception. Each individual thing, Plato tells us, is a *copy* (εἰκών) of one of the divine originals. Every single man—Socrates, Agathon, Callicles, etc.—derives what measure of reality he has from the *Idea of Man.* Every noble character, each honorable deed "participates" in the *Idea of Good.* Moreover, unlike mortal men and the transient goods of earth, the Universal Man and the Universal Good are imperishable and eternal. Such is Plato's theory of Ideas, which we shall meet again in our discussion of metaphysics.

Aristotle, who was Plato's pupil, thought his master's answer to the question "What sort of objects, if any, are designated by general names?" unnecessarily complicated. The referents of general words like "man" and "tree," thought Aristotle, are *classes* or *kinds* which actually exist in the natural world. These "natural kinds," however, are never experienced *as such.* Since the *universal* properties of things are copresent with *specific* features, it is impossible to observe the universal in isolation from the particular. "Man" designates an objectively existing feature of Nature which is actually present in Socrates, Agathon, etc. Nevertheless, while *humanity* exists in Nature independently of human thought or language, this property does not exist as a separate entity apart from individual men.

In the twelfth century, European universities resounded with hot debate on the question of universals. According to Abélard, the *realists* (e.g., William of Champeaux) held that there exist in Nature actual entities corresponding to general words. Man is something which exists outside the mind. It is not just a collective word for individual men. In opposition to the realists, the *nominalists* (e.g., Roscelinus) maintained that universals were nothing but *names.* "Man" is just a word, and does not designate anything in Nature, where there are only individuals, Socrates, etc.

Abélard himself taught that the referents of universals

are neither mere words (*voces*) nor things (*res*). General words are *signs*, the referents of which are concepts (*sermones*) or thoughts in the mind. These concepts in turn represent to us certain actual situations outside the mind under the mode of generality. The followers of Abélard developed the position of *conceptualism.* Conceptualists held that the referents of general names are concepts only; they are mental constructs rather than actual entities in Nature. Says conceptualist Peter Auriol: "It is clear that the notion of man and of animal is so far as it is distinguished from Socrates is a fabrication of the intellect and is nothing but a concept; for nature has not formed distinct principles of this kind as actual existences."[16]

Philosophers of the fourteenth century, keenly interested in the analysis of logic and language, tended toward the conceptualist or nominalist positions. According to William of Ockham, the referents of general words have no "ontological status"; they are logical or linguistic entities only. Nothing, says Ockham, exists in Nature outside the mind but individual things. (*Nihil est in rerum natura extra animam nisi singulare.*)[17]

A dominant tradition in modern British and American philosophy, known as *empiricism,* holds that the basis of reliable knowledge (other than formal science) lies in *sense experience,* and that true knowledge is concerned directly or indirectly with *observable things.* Now sense experience and observation present us with things which are many, separate, and individual. We should therefore rightly expect that modern empiricists take a *nominalist* position on

[16] Cited by M. H. Carré, *Nominalists and Realists,* London, Oxford University Press, 1946, pp. 106, 107.

[17] *Ibid.,* p. 112. See also S. C. Tornay, *Ockham: Studies and Selections,* La Salle, Ill., Open Court, 1938, p. 128.

the problem of universals. Philosophers of language, of the empiricist school, say that the *realist* doctrine of universals—i.e., that there are actual situations in Nature corresponding to general names—arises from a confusion of the order of *language* and the order of *things*. General words are *abstract*. All men resemble each other in certain respects. For purposes of communication, we need a word which will apply equally to all of them. Hence the general name "man." The error of the realists, say these critics, consists in the assumption (common in traditional philosophy) that to abstract words there correspond thing-like objects.

The following dialogue supports the realist position in regard to general names. The reader is invited to try his hand at linguistic analysis by evaluating the argument:

Q. Is "measles" a general word?

A. Yes, because it designates a class of events—individual cases of measles.

Q. Do individual cases of measles have any feature in common?

A. Yes. It is in terms of these common features that measles is described in medical textbooks.

Q. Now, do these characteristics which individual cases of measles have in common, and which the medical books describe, exist independently of human thought, "outside the mind," or are they subjective notions only?

A. They exist outside the mind.

Q. It follows then that realism is the correct view, and that nominalism is to be rejected. For if that which all cases of measles have in common has objective existence, then the general word "measles" designates a state of affairs in Nature.

EMPIRICIST THEORIES OF MEANING

We recall that the empiricist position in philosophy is one which may roughly be described as the doctrine that the foundation of reliable knowledge (apart from logic and mathematics) lies in *sense experience*, that true knowledge deals with things directly or indirectly *observable*. Contemporary philosophers of language inclined toward empiricism have developed a *theory of meaning* consistent with this position. It is that words and sentences (and the concepts or thoughts they express) which purport to describe facts have meaning only in so far as they are related, directly or indirectly, to observable things.

Peirce's Doctrine of Meaning

Charles Peirce, an American philosopher once neglected and now renowned, was an early advocate of such a theory of meaning. Peirce held that a term has meaning if it can be explained by other terms which *describe sensible properties*. For example, the word "hard" is meaningful because it can be replaced by the phrase "not scratchable by many other substances."[18] According to Peirce, if a term has meaning, the meaning should be capable of being set forth in such a way as to tell you *what you can do* in order to *observe* the object (referent) of that word or the object's *sensible effects*. Sentences are meaningful if they are experimentally verifiable, that is, if their truth can be tested by some kind of *publicly observable procedure*. The propositions of empirical *science* are notable examples of state-

[18] Charles Hartshorne and Paul Weiss, eds., *The Collected Papers of Charles Sanders Peirce*, Harvard University Press, 1931–1935, vol. 5, par. 403. For Peirce's theory of knowledge as inquiry, see Chapter 5, pp. 163–164 of the present text.

ments verifiable in such a way. But a large part of the propositions of traditional *philosophy*, particularly those of that part of philosophy known as *metaphysics*, are meaningless, because no public and open procedures exist for testing their truth. When the mass of meaningless propositions which constitute the bulk of traditional metaphysical philosophy is discarded, says Peirce, "what will remain of philosophy will be a series of problems capable of investigation by the observational methods of the true sciences."[19]

Logical Positivism and Logical Empiricism

One of the most popular and influential movements in analytic philosophy in our century is often identified as *logical empiricism.* Its philosophical ancestry is both British and Continental. On the British side, the line of descent may be traced back through Bertrand Russell (twentieth century) and John Stuart Mill (nineteenth century) to the Scottish philosopher David Hume (eighteenth century). The more immediate heritage of logical empiricism came from the Continent, stemming from the teachings of a group of men who met in Vienna between the two World Wars. The "Vienna Circle," as they called themselves, included Morris Schlick and Rudolf Carnap. The most remarkable of their visitors was Austrian-born Ludwig Wittgenstein, whom many believe to be the greatest philosopher of the twentieth century. The Cambridge-trained Wittgenstein was not a member of the Circle, but his early masterpiece, the *Tractatus Logico-Philosophicus* was the subject of many stimulating discussions in Vienna. Members of the Circle were particularly impressed by Wittgenstein's claim that a staggering quantity of what normally passes for meaningful statement is in fact nonsense. ("Whereof one

[19] *Ibid.*, par. 423. See Justus Buchler, *Charles Peirce's Empiricism.* London, Kegan Paul, 1939, pp. 112–120, 149.

cannot speak, thereof one must be silent.") Near the end of the *Tractatus* Wittgenstein made the startling announcement that his own book was nonsense too—but *useful* nonsense, like a ladder one climbs over, then pushes away when no longer needed.[20] Leaders of the Vienna Circle were quick to allege that most statements of traditional philosophy were nonsensical, that, apart from the sentences of logic, scientific statements were the only true statements. So the leaders of the Vienna Circle and their disciples became known as *logical positivists*—"logical" because their constructive work concerned the analysis of logic and language, "positivist" because of the kinship of their enterprise to that of the nineteenth century Frenchman Auguste Comte who believed that significant knowledge concerns only that which is open to "positive" observation. Comte held that *science* has replaced *philosophy*, just as philosophy in its day replaced theology.

Cross-fertilization took place between the Continental positivists and kindred sprits in England. A. J. Ayer's famous little book *Language, Truth and Logic* (1936) popularized the tenets of the logical positivists and became the English Testament of the movement. The general tone of the positivists of the 1930s was harsh and dogmatic, and today many of those who survive have modified the letter of their writings if not the spirit. Thus *logical empiricism* is the name often given to the philosophical tradition still influential in England and the United States which developed the methods of the positivists within a somewhat broader framework.[21]

[20] Ludwig Wittgenstein, *Tractatus Logico-Philosophicus,* New York, Harcourt, Brace & World, 1922, p. 189.

[21] A variety of the positivist-empiricist approach, with particular reference to the methods of physical science, is known as operationalism, a term introduced by P. W. Bridgman. According to Bridgman, the mean-

The Verification Theory of Meaning; A. J. Ayer

A basic tenet of logical empiricism concerns *meaning*. It was maintained that sentences intended to describe facts have meaning only if it is possible to verify them. In his *Language, Truth and Logic*, A. J. Ayer divides sentences into (1) those which convey *information* and (2) those which convey or describe *emotions*. Of the sentences which convey information he distinguishes (following Hume) two kinds: (a) statements about formal concepts and relations, such as the propositions of logic or mathematics, and statements about linguistic matters, and (b) statements about matters of fact. Now sentences which are supposed to be statements about matters of fact are significant or *meaningful* only if they are capable of being *verified*. That is, a statement which purports to describe some factual situation has *meaning* only if we are able to specify some way or ways in which the question of its truth or falsity could be settled. According to Ayer:

> The criterion which we use to test the genuineness of apparent statements of fact is the criterion of verifiability. We say that a sentence is factually significant to any given person, if, and only if, he knows how to verify the proposition which it purports to express—that is, if he knows what observations would lead him under certain conditions, to accept the proposition as being true, or reject it as being false.[22]

---

ing of a scientific concept is set forth in terms of the *operations* we use to define it. For example, the meaning of the word "foot" as a unit of length, is equivalent to the measuring *operation* we perform when we want to find out whether something is a foot long. Sentences which assert scientific hypotheses are meaningful only if the nature of those operations which could test them can be specified. See P. W. Bridgman, *The Logic of Modern Physics*, New York, Macmillan, 1927. (PB: Free Press, Macmillan.)

[22] A. J. Ayer, *Language, Truth and Logic*, rev. ed., London, Gollancz, 1948, p. 35. (PB: Dover, New York.)

The statement "There are mountains on Venus" is significant, although no means exist at present for settling the question of its truth or falsity. Since Venus is always shrouded in mist, we cannot observe its surface with our telescopes. Yet such a statement is *in principle* verifiable, since we can specify in a general way the kind of procedure which *would* settle the question, if the means for such procedure were available. In the case of Venus, the procedure would involve the construction of a space ship of sufficiently long range.[23]

Ayer then invites us to consider a typical meaningless statement. Consider the proposition "There is a God," taken as asserting the existence of an actual being who created and who sustains the world. This statement *appears* to be a factual statement—i.e., one which is either true or false—but it is actually *meaningless.* Since we cannot specify, even *in principle*, what procedures would lead us to observations relevant to the truth of falsity of the sentence "God exists," it is a nonsense statement like "The Absolute is lazy." Now what holds for the statement "There is a God" also holds for the entire class of metaphysical statements. Since these propositions make assertions about things and events which have no connection, direct or indirect, with sense observation, there is no way of determining whether they are true or false. Hence, they are meaningless.

Criticism of the Verification Theory of Meaning

The verification theory of meaning has been the subject of considerable criticism. The following are some of the ob-

[23] A similar proposition, "There are mountains on the other side of the moon," was not subjected to test until 1959 when a U.S.S.R. space vehicle photographed the far side of the moon with television cameras.

jections brought against the logical empiricist's claim that "To be meaningful, a sentence must be verifiable."

1. This doctrine lays down an arbitrary and narrow definition of "meaning" in *advance of the argument* and therefore begs the question. What gives the logical empiricist the right to decide that the meaning of a sentence is equivalent to its verifiability by experimental observation? If a man says, "God made the world," I may find this statement unclear. Yet this statement has meaning in a way that the statement "The torkin jerped boofaz" does not. To this objection, logical empiricists reply by distinguishing various *kinds* of meaning.[24] The statement "God made the world" may have *pictorial* or even *poetic* meaning, but it has no *factual* meaning.

2. Another objection concerns the vagueness of the word "verifiable." It is not at all clear just what specification must be met in order that a sentence may be considered "verified." For example, it is impossible to "verify" inductive general statements such as "Metals melt when heated" in the sense that we can examine and test every instance of metal. Defenders of the theory take account of this objection by distinguishing between (a) conclusive or complete and (b) partial or weak verification. For a factual proposition to be meaningful, say the logical empiricists, it must at least be *partly* verifiable. That is, there should exist (if only "in principle") *some* experiments involving sense observation which are relevant to deciding whether the proposition in question is true or false. Nevertheless, the problem of the meaning of "verify" and "verifiability" remains a question which is not resolved in the verification theory of meaning.

[24] Ayer, *op. cit.*, p. 15. H. Feigl, "Logical Empiricism," in H. Feigl and W. Sellars, eds., *Readings in Philosophical Analysis*, New York, Appleton-Century-Crofts, 1949, p. 7.

3. Consider once more the proposition "To be meaningful, a sentence must be verifiable." But, A. C. Ewing points out, *this statement itself is not verifiable.*[25] It is not an *analytic* statement or tautology like "7 plus 5 equals 12"; for, if it were, no one who *understood* it could fail to see that it was true. But neither is it a *factual* or synthetic statement, for the proposition is making an assertion about sentences, not about empirical facts. Further, what kind of empirical evidence could possibly support it? To answer the objection, logical empiricists frequently invoke a dictum associated with Bertrand Russell's theory of types: *No meaningful statement should ever be taken as making assertions about itself.* The proposition "To be meaningful, a sentence must be verifiable" is of a "higher logical type" than the sentences it talks about. It should not be taken as if it were talking about *itself.* To interpret the proposition thus is to confuse two different logical types or "orders" of sentences.[26]

4. Finally, the following general criticism has been urged against the verification theory of meaning, as well as against the philosophy of logical empiricism taken as a whole. The doctrine of logical empiricism is tied to a classification of sentences that is too simple and sharp-cut. The theory is based on the assumption that propositions fall into two clearly separated classes of *emotive* and *informative* statements, the latter category itself divided into two sharp-cut subclasses, *formal* (analytic) and *factual* (synthetic). Such precise compartmentalization of propositions may be

[25] A. C. Ewing, "Meaninglessness," *Mind,* 1937, p. 349.

[26] Russell's theory of types was devised to solve technical problems which arise from the existence of certain bothersome *paradoxes* or apparent contradictions in logic. A well-known example is the Antinomy of the Liar, in which Epimenides, the Cretan, says, "All Cretans are liars." A contemporary version is "The sentence you are now reading is false."

useful to us in making certain important elementary distinctions in the usage of logic and language. But these dichotomies should not be taken as ultimates. The world we experience in a very complex situation—very much mixed up with the operations of human thought. It is an error of oversimplification to isolate a single set of propositions, called "factual" (the word "fact" is vague), and to assign to these propositions the exclusive mission of "describing" the world. Those properties of Nature we describe in informative statements may shade over without a sharp break into those features of experience we speak of in emotive (poetic, pictorial) language. For purposes of formal logic, it is sometimes useful to draw a sharp distinction between formal and factual (analytic and synthetic) sentences. But the general character of the world may be such that the "formal" properties of abstract relations are not split completely apart from "factual" situations.[27] The logical empiricist's classification of statements with reference to meaning has the virtues of simplicity and clarity. But there is a danger in such clarity, the danger of reducing to a flat base the complex levels of Nature and experience.

Wittgenstein on Language

With the rise of Wittgenstein's influence—particularly as the result of his teaching after the second World War—logical empiricism was succeeded by more subtle investigations into the relation between language and philosophy. In his early work, the *Tractatus* (1922), Wittgenstein was aiming at the construction of a perfect model of a language. Such a language would have a complete logical structure

[27] See W. V. Quine, "Two Dogmas of Empiricism," in *From a Logical Point of View,* Harvard University Press, 1953. (PB: Harper Torchbooks, Harper & Row, New York.)

like that of the *Principia Mathematica*,[28] the variables in the sentence-forms (*p*'s, *q*'s, etc.) being blank spaces to be filled in with sentences about facts. This system of "logical atomism" would achieve a language which would be a kind of *picture* of the world—the world being "everything that is the case." In this ideal language, Wittgenstein believed, there must be something in common between the structure of each statement and the structure of each fact. But the element common to statement and fact could not be talked about; it could only be *shown*, since any attempt to describe the common structure would make use of it.

After he published the *Tractatus*, Wittgensten abandoned philosophy for a while, since he believed he had solved all the problems of philosophy. He returned to the subject because he came to see that his solutions were arbitrary. An account in terms of facts, using sentence forms filled in with statements about facts, is not the only way to describe the world. So Wittgenstein rejected his own earlier logical atomism. He became suspicious of ideal languages as useful modes for philosophy. Struck with the richness and sublety of the uses of ordinary language, Wittgenstein said, "It is wrong to say that in philosophy we consider an ideal language as opposed to our ordinary one. For this makes it appear as though we could improve on ordinary language. But ordinary language is all right."[29] It seemed to Wittgenstein that we should give up trying to pin-point meanings, for no words which are philosophically interesting have a fixed unitary meaning:

> . . . let us not forget that a word hasn't got a meaning given to it, as it were, by a power independent of us, so that there

[28] See pp. 33–35.

[29] Ludwig Wittgenstein, *The Blue and Brown Books,* Harper Torchbooks edition, New York, Harper & Row, 1965, p. 28.

could be a kind of scientific investigation in what the word *really* means. A word has the meaning someone has given to it.[30]

We can never achieve a satisfactory definition of language, for there is no factor common to all our uses of language —describing, joking, praying, commanding, singing, asking, and so on. Wittgenstein asks us to think of the tools in a toolbox: hammer, pliers, a saw, a screwdriver, a ruler, a gluepot, glue, nails and screws. What we do with words is as different as what we do with these objects. It is the same with *games*. Just as there is no one common element in games (hide-and-seek, chess, solitaire, hop-scotch, etc.), so there is no single core factor in *language*. Rather, all "language games" are *related*, even though we cannot identify an element possessed by all of them:

> Instead of producing something common to all that we call language, I am saying that these phenomena have no one thing in common which makes us use the same word for all—but that they are *related* to one another in many different ways. And it is because of this relationship, or these relationships, that we call them all "language."[31]

Obsession with fixed meanings and word pictures have caused philosophers to fall under the spell of language. Philosophy, says Wittgenstein, is a battle against the *bewitchment* of our intelligence by means of language. A person caught in a philosophical confusion is like a man in a room who wants to get out, but doesn't know how. He tries a window, but it is too high. He tries the chimney but it is too narrow. Yet if he would only turn around he would see that the door is open all the time.

Wittgenstein and his students agreed among themselves

[30] *Ibid.*

[31] Wittgenstein, *Philosophical Investigations*, p. 65.

that there are many ways of talking, each with its own peculiar interest and value. There are jokes. There are scientific descriptions. There is discourse about God ("God-talk"). Statements abound which cannot be "verified" by any of the standard procedures recommended by the logical empiricists, yet which seem nevertheless to have important meaning. One should treat these varieties of talking, not as nonsense, but as "language-games." The thing to do is to clarify the rules and make the games more understandable. Language is more than learning the names of objects. The meaning of the term "scissors" does not consist simply in the object it names, but in the way it is *used* in language —as, when I say "scissors" you hand me scissors, and when I say "paste" you hand me paste. Wittgenstein's maxim became a slogan, "*Don't ask for the meaning, ask for the use!*"

FURTHER READINGS

Aristotle, *Metaphysics*, bk. 4. (PB: Ann Arbor Paperbacks, Ann Arbor, Mich.)

Austin, J. L., *How To Do Things with Words*, Harvard University Press, 1962. (PB: Galaxy, Oxford U. P., New York.)

Ayer, A. J., *Language, Truth and Logic*, rev. ed., London, Gollancz, 1948. (PB: Dover, New York.)

Ayer, A. J. (ed.,) *Logical Positivism*, New York, Free Press, 1959. (PB: Free Press.)

Black, Max, *Language and Philosophy*, Cornell University Press, 1949.

Carnap, Rudolf, *Philosophy and Logical Syntax*, London, Kegan Paul, 1935.

Chappell, V. C. (ed.), *Ordinary Language*, Englewood Cliffs, N.J., Prentice- Hall, 1964.

Hayakawa, S. I., *Language in Action*, New York, Harcourt, Brace & World, 1941.

Joad, C. E. M., *A Critique of Logical Positivism*, University of Chicago Press, 1950.

Langer, Susanne K., *Philosophy in a New Key*, Harvard University Press, 1942. (PB: Mentor, New American Library, New York.)

Malcolm, N., *Ludwig Wittgenstein, A Memoir*, New York, Oxford University Press, 1958. (PB: Oxford U. P.)

Morris, Charles, *Signs, Language and Behavior*, Englewood Cliffs, N.J., 1946.

Nagel, Ernest, "Logic Without Ontology," in H. Feigl and W. Sellars (eds.), *Readings in Philosophical Analysis*, New York, Appleton-Century-Crofts, 1949.

Ogden, C. K., and I. A. Richards, *The Meaning of Meaning*, New York, Harcourt, Brace & World, 1925.

Passmore, J., *A Hundred Years of Philosophy*, London, Duckworth, 1957, chaps. 15–18.

Plato, *Republic*, Bk. 10. *Cratylus*. A convenient edition of the Platonic Dialogues is *The Dialogues of Plato*, B. Jowett (trans.), New York, Random House, 1937, in two volumes. A complete one-volume edition is *The Collected Dialogues of Plato*, E. Hamilton and H. Cairns (eds.), Random House, Pantheon Books, 1961.

Reichenbach, H., "Logic and Language," *Elements of Symbolic Logic*, New York, Macmillan, 1948.

Russell, Bertrand, *The Analysis of Mind*, London, G. Allen, 1921, chaps. 10, 11.

Russell, Bertrand, *Human Knowledge*, New York, Simon and Schuster, 1948, pt. 2. (PB: Essandess Paperbacks, Simon and Schuster.)

Urban, W. M., *Language and Reality*, London, G. Allen, 1939.

Urban, W. M., "Whitehead's Philosophy of Language," in P. A. Schlipp (ed.), *The Philosophy of Alfred North Whitehead*, Northwestern University Press, 1941.

Urmson, J. O., *Philosophical Analysis,* Oxford, Clarendon Press, 1956.

Wittgenstein, L., *Tractatus Logico-Philosophicus,* New York, Harcourt, Brace & World, 1922.

Wittgenstein, L., *Philosophical Investigations,* New York, Macmillan, 1953.

Wittgenstein, L., *The Blue and Brown Books,* New York, Harper & Row, 1958. (PB: Harper Torchbooks.)

PART II

Problems of Knowledge

3

Truth and Certainty

The necessary and sufficient conditions for knowing that something is the case are, first, that what one is said to know be true, second, that one be sure of it, and third, that one should have the right to be sure.

—A. J. AYER

Whether we can have trustworthy knowledge is an ancient question of philosophy. Plato divided human knowledge into two classes (1) *true knowledge* and (2) *belief* or *opinion*. He thought that the first kind only was reliable but that it was difficult for anyone but a mathematician or philosopher to obtain.[1] The second kind, he believed, was the equipment of the ordinary man; it was derived from sense perception, was quite unreliable, and the ultimate source of all error. The ancient Skeptics, struck by the frequency and ease with which men fall into error, challenged the possibility of obtaining *certainty* in any branch of human knowledge. With the development of modern philosophy after the Renaissance, the problem of what kinds of knowledge are "true" or "certain" became particularly acute. Since the seventeenth century the attention of a distinguished line of philosophers, from Descartes

[1] The Greek word for true knowledge ἐπιστήμη (epistemé) is the principal root of the term *epistemology*, a name given to the philosophic inquiry into knowledge.

to Bertrand Russell, has been concentrated on the question whether we can have reliable knowledge about anything. It is only in the last thirty years that the question "What do we *mean?*" has disputed the place of "How do we *know?*" as the most popular query in philosophy.

Questions about true or certain knowledge raise a number of problems which are rather difficult to disentangle. For the present we shall confine ourselves to an analysis of the meaning of truth and certainty, supplementing this with a glance at some of the problems generated by these notions and the theories of philosophers concerning them.

TRUTH

Meanings of "Truth"; "True" as Conformity to Standards

The words "truth" and "true" are used by people in a number of ways. We frequently read of the duty of the scholar or scientist to "seek truth." The shield of Harvard University bears the single word *Veritas*. Parents urge their children to "tell the truth." Everyone knows that true love is best. "To thine own self be true," counsels Polonius, and the poet Keats says, "Beauty is truth, truth beauty. . . ."

Let us distinguish *two* important senses of truth in common usage. Often we apply the word "true" (and its antonym "false") to objects. That is true gold, we say, or, those are false teeth. Historians agree that Lee was a true soldier. Zoologists state that the honey-bear or koala is not a true bear. This usage of the word "true" signifies that the objects talked about have properties that *match a standard* of some kind. Standard gold has a certain weight, chemical properties, specific gravity, lustre, etc. If the nugget I hold in my hand matches those specifications, it is "true" (or "real") gold. Lee had all the properties of the ideal soldier (courage, fighting skill, dignity, etc.) and so we call him a true soldier. But the properties of the honey bear do not conform to the standard bear described by zoologists in their classifications of mammals; the koala is, therefore, not a true bear. In each case of this usage, the adjective "true" points to a relation of matching or *conformity* between the attributes of the object we are talkng about and some kind of standard or ideal. Who *sets* that standard—whether it exists in heaven or on earth, whether it is absolute or relative, objective or subjective—we need not ask. The point is that in this usage of "true" there is an implicit reference to conformity to a standard or to some set of specifications.

Truth as a Property of Statements

An even more common usage of "true" is the way we apply it to *statements* or to beliefs which we express in statements. A man who "tells the truth" is one who makes true statements. A liar is one who frequently and knowingly makes false statements. Aristotle recognized that truth and falsity are properties of statements. "Assertion," he says, "is the saying of something concerning something . . . and is in every case either true or false."[2] In other words, when we say truth is a quality of statements, we have in mind those expressions of language which assert something to be so or not to be so. Grammar calls them declarative sentences. The assertion "The George Washington Bridge crosses the Hudson River" is true, while "Delius was an Italian composer" is false. Truth and falsity are not properties of questions or commands. Optative sentences like "If you would only love me a little!" cannot properly be called "true" or "false." Nor do we apply "true" or "false" ordinarily to *names*. If I meet a man walking along the street murmuring "horse," I cannot say that he speaks truly or

[2] Aristotle, *De Anima*, 430b27.

falsely. Of course, a child or a foreigner may point to a horse, saying "horse" and we may properly reply "true," since the expression is a shortened form of the statement "That is a horse."

Usage, then, seems to justify the claim that truth and falsity may, under some circumstances, be correctly said to be properties of statements. It follows that "truth" in this usage is a *second-order* or metalinguistic property—that is, a property of a language entity (a statement)—rather than a property of a natural object or event. Statements about objects like people and things are *first-order* statements. Statements about statements ("That claim is true") are second-order statements. Finally, we should note that "true" and "false" are sometimes said to be properties of *beliefs* or *judgments* on the ground that sentences are *expressions* of such beliefs. "Truth is a property of beliefs," says Bertrand Russell, "and derivatively of sentences which express beliefs."[3]

Theories of Truth

Just what is it that makes true sentences true? Philosophers have different theories as to just what sort of situation exists when we have true sentences or beliefs. Three well-known doctrines of what truth means are the correspondence theory, the coherence theory, and the pragmatic theory. We can give the gist of these doctrines only by oversimplification. The *correspondence* theory maintains that a sentence or belief is true if it conforms to the facts. The *coherence* theory holds that our beliefs or judgments derive their truth from their coherence or consistency with the system of human beliefs or judgments taken as a whole. The *pragmatic* theory claims that the truth of sentences or

[3] Bertrand Russell, *Human Knowledge*, New York, Simon and Schuster, 1948, p. 148. (PB: Essandess Paperbacks, Simon and Schuster.)

beliefs is identical with their success as instruments of action. Let us examine each of these theories more closely.

THE CORRESPONDENCE THEORY OF TRUTH

The classic formulation of the correspondence theory of truth is that of Aristotle. "To say of what is not that it is," says the Greek philosopher, "is false, while to say of what is that it is, or of what is not that it is not, is true."[4] Applying this formula of Aristotle, we conclude that the sentence "It is raining" is true if it is raining, and the sentence "The house next door is being painted" is true if the house next door is being painted. A true statement asserts what is the case; a false statement says what is not so.

A weaker statement of the correspondence theory is: "Truth is the correspondence of our ideas and reality." This formula has serious defects. The terms "idea" and "reality" are so ambiguous that their usage may lead to irrelevant problems. "Idea" can mean (1) a *belief* or opinion, (2) a *concept* or notion of what a thing is, or (3) a sensory *perception* or memory image. "Reality" can mean, among other things, (1) that which is most important or ultimate, (2) that which lasts or endures, (3) that which can be seen and held in the hands, (4) that which exists independently of our perception of it.

Suppose we take "idea" as perception or memory image

[4] Aristotle, *Metaphysics*, bk. 4, 1011b26. A highly sophisticated contemporary analysis of the meaning of truth is Alfred Tarski's "Semantic Theory of Truth," which is represented by its author as a modernized version of Aristotle's classic formula. See Alfred Tarski, "The Semantic Conception of Truth," in H. Feigl and W. Sellars eds., *Readings in Philosophical Analysis*, New York, Appleton-Century-Crofts, 1949, p. 52.

and "reality" as that which exists independently of our perception of it. Is our idea of "cat" a true idea? If it is, and we use the formula "Truth is the correspondence of our ideas with reality," we shall be compelled to claim that our sensory image of cat corresponds to the "real" cat as it exists independently of our perception of it. But, as we shall see in our next chapter, such an assertion could not possibly be verified.

A less ambiguous formulation of the correspondence theory is: "A sentence is true if it corresponds (or conforms) to the facts." To be sure, the word "facts" is somewhat vague, but we may take it roughly to mean things or events in the world. The word "correspond" is also troublesome. There cannot be an exact correspondence between a sentence and a situation in the world, for there are no sentences in Nature. Things do not have the structure of statements. These points aside, however, we may represent correspondence in the following way:

Sentence ————————————————→ Fact
Relationship of Correspondence

In the case of a false sentence, there is no fact to which the sentence is related, and thus no correspondence relationship. If I say, "There is a checkbook in that drawer," my sentence "corresponds" to the fact. If there is no checkbook in the drawer, there cannot be a conformity between my sentence and fact, for there is no such fact.

The correspondence theory tries to explain *what is the case* when a sentence is true. It says nothing about how we *discover* or how we *prove* that a sentence corresponds to the facts. The procedure we employ in order to find out whether a statement is true is called *verification.* In regard to a great number of everyday sentences, there is no particular difficulty in specifying what methods are used in verifying correspondence between sentence and fact. If I say, "It is raining," you may verify the correspondence between sentence and fact by stepping outside the door to observe. If I say, "There is a kangaroo in your bathroom," you will hardly require details as to what procedure to adopt in order to check the correspondence between my statement and the fact. Procedures for verification of sentences about less obvious matters may be more complicated.

Proponents of the correspondence theory urge us to keep in mind the distinction between (1) what sort of situation exists when a sentence is true and (2) how we *come to know* a sentence is true. A physician may discover that his belief "This patient has tuberculosis" is true with the aid of x-ray pictures. But this *confirmation* of the truth of the proposition did not make the proposition true. The doctor's belief "This patient has tuberculosis" was true before he examined the radiologist's photographs.

THE COHERENCE THEORY OF TRUTH

Consistency

Logic tells us that it is a mark of a true statement to be consistent with itself and with other true statements. A proposition which contradicts itself, like "This square has five sides," or "The child was dressed in a long white nightgown, but was naked," is false. A proposition which contradicts a true statement is also false. In practice, we constantly *test* the truth of statements by investigating their consistency with other propositions we know to be true. If a witness states in one part of his testimony that he was born in 1910 and in another that he was a veteran of the

First World War, we would say that these two statements are inconsistent. A man who was born in 1910 would be about eight years old at the time of the Armistice, and we have good reason to believe that no children eight years old or under were soldiers of any army engaged in that war. In Pasteur's time it was thought that putrefaction occurs whenever meat is left standing at ordinary temperatures. Exposing meat in vials, the mouths of which were covered with gauze, Pasteur was able to counter with the statement: There are *n* instances in which meat does *not* putrefy when left standing at ordinary temperatures. The logical structures of the statements are related thus:

x is *y*.
Some *x* is not *y*.

In practical inquiry, then, whether it be ordinary or scientific, testing of statements for consistency with other statements is an indispensable means of finding out whether they are true. Consistency is thus a valuable *criterion* of truth.

The Coherence Theory Stated

Suppose we grant that consistency is a test of truth and that consistency is a property of all true propositions. Could we go further and say that not only is consistency a *criterion* of truth but it is also the *meaning* of truth? That is, a proposition is true *by virtue of* its consistency with other propositions; it is the proposition's consistency with others that constitutes or "makes" its truth? Now holders of the coherence theory of truth subscribe to something similar to but not exactly like this conclusion. They say that a judgment is true in virtue of its *coherence* with the *total aggregate* of all true judgments. "Any judgment is true," says E. S. Brightman, "if it is both self-consistent and coherently connected with our system of judgments as a whole."[5]

It is very difficult to make clear just what the proponents of the coherence theory are trying to get at without some familiarity with one particular variety of a certain metaphysical doctrine we call *idealism.* This type of idealism is supported by many coherence advocates, who regard the coherence theory as an integral part of their general world perspective. Briefly, this metaphysical doctrine holds that the world is basically of the nature of mind or thought; that human knowledge is a system of interrelated judgments (appearance) constantly advancing toward a union with an absolute (reality). The metaphysical teaching of the German philosopher Hegel is a source of this doctrine. Hegel taught that the world of our experience is a necessary sequence of processes analogous to thought, and that the multiple interconnections of these processes are united with God or Absolute Spirit to form an organic whole. "In common life," says Hegel, "truth means the agreement of an object with our conception of it. . . . In the philosophical sense of the word . . . truth may be described in general abstract terms, as the agreement of a thought content with itself. . . . God alone is thorough harmony of notion and reality."[6] Reading the following passage from Brand Blanshard, a contemporary and able defender of the coherence theory of truth, we see that it is impossible to separate his coherence theory from his metaphysics:

> . . . Reality is a system, completely ordered and fully intelligible with which thought in its advance is more and more

[5] E. S. Brightman, *An Introduction to Philosophy,* New York, Holt, Rinehart and Winston, 1925, p. 61.

[6] G. Hegel, *Logic,* W. Wallace, trans., London, Oxford University Press, Humphrey Milford, 1892, pp. 51–52.

identifying itself. We may look at the growth of knowledge, individual or social, either as an attempt by our own minds to return to union with things as they are in their ordered wholeness, or the affirmation through our minds of the ordered whole itself. And if we take this view, our notion of truth is marked out for us. Truth is the approximation of thought to reality. It is thought on its way home. Its measure is the distance thought has travelled, under guidance of its inner compass, toward that intelligible system which unites its ultimate object with its ultimate end. Hence at any given time the degree of truth in our experience as a whole is the degree of system it has achieved. The degree of truth of a particular proposition is to be judged in the first instance by its coherence with experience as a whole, ultimately by its coherence with that further whole, all-comprehensive and fully articulated, in which thought can come to rest.[7]

Criticism of the Coherence Theory

Critics of the coherence theory of truth are most often those who object to the special metaphysical doctrine involved. The coherence theory, they say, cannot be defended without falling back on some variety of idealism. Moreover, this type of idealism itself ultimately relies for its definition of truth on the concept of correspondence. Suppose we grant that a certain judgment p is true because it "coheres" with the total system of true judgments q, r, s, etc. Let the accompanying diagram, then, represent the situation. If it is claimed that p, q, r, etc., being true judgments, are thoughts, and that these thoughts are true in that they are coherent parts of a "whole" which is itself of the nature of thought, then the soundness of the coherence theory of truth must depend on the doctrine that the world is essentially a process analogous to thought. Now, on the

[7] B. Blanshard, *The Nature of Thought,* New York, Macmillan, 1940, vol. 2, p. 264.

coherence assumption, truth is a matter of coherence between individual judgments and the system of our judgments taken as a whole. But by virtue of *what* is this aggregate of judgments true? The whole system of true judgments supports the truth of each judgment, taken individually. But what supports the whole system? The answer

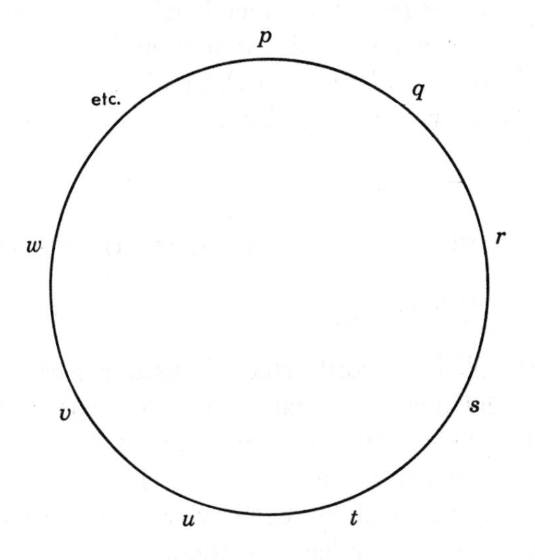

is usually given that the system of judgments approximates to or is in the process of approximating to "reality." But this means that the coherence theory is itself based on the assumption of a grand-scale ontological correspondence.

Coherence in Formal Science

There is a class of statements whose truth is, in a broad sense, constituted by their mutual consistency or coherence. These are the sentences of formal science—that is, the statements of logic and mathematics. We have already observed that a simple arithmetical statement like "$7 + 5 = 12$" is true, not because it conforms to a set of empirical facts but because it is a theorem of arithmetic which is deducible from certain prior theorems which in turn derive from the postulates, rules, and basic concepts of that system. The truth of statements of formal science is indistinguishable from their membership or "group coherence" in a system of basic notions and derivative statements. "The laws of mathematics and logic," says W. V. Quine, "are true simply by virtue of our conceptual scheme."[8]

THE PRAGMATIC THEORY OF TRUTH

Origin of "Pragmatism"

"Pragmatism" is a word which is used rather loosely to label the teachings of certain philosophers, most of them Americans, whose major writings were published during or shortly before the present century. The term "pragmatism" was introduced by C. S. Peirce in reference to a theory of *meaning* we have mentioned earlier.[9] The word "pragmatism," however, seems to have been publicly used first in 1898 by Peirce's friend William James, whose subsequent lectures and writings made pragmatism an object of popular interest. The works of F. C. S. Schiller in England and of the late John Dewey in America are also associated with pragmatism. Because of the misunderstandings and controversies that centered around the term "pragmatism," Dewey adopted the word "instrumentalism" as a label for an aspect of his own doctrine.

[8] W. V. Quine, *Methods of Logic*, New York, Holt, Rinehart and Winston, 1950, p. xiv.

[9] See Chapter 2, p. 62–63.

James' Theory of Truth

Taken generally, pragmatism is a theory of knowledge. It is that knowledge is made for action, for *doing* something about the problems that face us, for *meeting* the endless succession of obstacles and perplexities which is the condition of human existence. In his pragmatic theory of truth, James tells us that truth is an empty compliment to pay to a proposition in "cold storage." A belief *becomes* true when it is put into action. Its truth is inseparable from its successful engagement in the world of experience.

According to James, truth is an attribute of beliefs upon which we are prepared to *act*. True beliefs are those which are "successful," "expedient," "satisfactory," "useful." A true belief, if acted upon, *works*. In the long run, it is bound to produce satisfactory *results*. A false belief, put into practice, leads ultimately to failure. If a belief cannot be acted upon, or if it makes no difference one way or the other whether it is true or not, such a belief is neither true nor false; it is only meaningless and empty. Says James: "Grant an idea or belief to be true, what concrete difference will its being true make in any one's actual life? How will the truth be realized? What experiences will be different from those which would obtain if the belief were false? What, in short, is the truth's cash-value in experiential terms?"[10]

True beliefs, then, are useful beliefs. But James goes further. Truth and utility are one and the same. Comparing the statements "it is useful because it is true" and "it is true because it is useful," James says, "Both these phrases mean exactly the same thing." The truth of a belief is not only

10 William James, *Pragmatism,* New York, Longmans, 1928, p. 200. (PB: Meridian, World Publishing, Cleveland.)

discovered by testing the belief. The verification of a belief *is* its truth.

But what about fixed facts? Suppose a mouse is living behind the wall of my closet. My belief or statement to that effect is true, not because it is useful, but because it agrees with the facts. Yes, James would say, there are such things as fixed facts, and the relation between our beliefs and such facts is handled adequately enough by the correspondence theory of truth.[11] But *not all facts are fixed*, and the danger of the correspondence theory lies in its one-sided tendency to make us think that all facts *are* fixed. Yet facts *happen;* they come and they go, and the truth of our beliefs about them comes and goes too. Further, *many facts can be made by our belief in them.* Suppose a small group of citizens in a new community, now hardly more than scrub land and farms, believes that in two years there will be a fine new school here. Most of the older inhabitants are against them. People say, "There can't possibly be a school like that here; the taxpayers are all opposed to it." Yet, acting as if the belief that the community can and will support such a school were a fact, the little group goes to work to win support for the project, slowly, patiently, refusing to yield to discouragement. We know that often (although not always) it turns out that such firm beliefs *create* the facts, where there were no facts for the beliefs to correspond to. Faith can still move mountains.[12]

[11] James would point out, however, that we may analyze the truth of even such beliefs according to the pragmatic criterion. Suppose that you are disturbed nightly by a noise in your bedroom closet. You come to believe that there is a mouse living behind the closet wall. Acting on that belief, you open the wall, plant traps, poison, etc. Now suppose a mouse is caught in this way. Was not the belief "There is a mouse, etc." useful, since acting on it led you to satisfactory results? And is not the utility of such a belief all one with its truth?

[12] How faith can create facts is a leading theme of Willa Cather's novel *Death Comes for the Archbishop.*

Criticism of James' Theory of Truth

The pragmatic theory of truth, as set forth by William James, has been charged with *ambiguity*. James' enthusiastic but loose handling of words like "expedient" and "useful" in connection with truth convinced many that he was denying the "objectivity" of truth, offering in its place a subjective criterion, to the effect that the true was whatever it pleased us to think. By literal interpretations of such Jamesian remarks as "We have to live today by what truth we can get today, and be ready tomorrow to call it falsehood,"[13] critics of pragmatism support their charges of *relativism*. They denounce pragmatism as a modern version of the old Sophist doctrine that every man determines his own truth. James, of course, did not for a moment intend that his doctrine be interpreted in this way. He thought his pragmatism would help to close the gap between theory and moral practice; he believed philosophers had allowed this separation to widen to an impassible gulf.

A more specific criticism of the pragmatic theory of truth asserts that it confuses the question *what truth is* with *how we find it out*. There is no doubt that utility or workability is a valuable *test* of the truth of a sentence. In our common reliance upon observation of *results* to guide us in inquiry, we are all pragmatists, including him who said "By their fruits ye shall know them." If we are working over an automobile engine, and you say, "The dirt on the points of your spark plugs makes the engine misfire. Clean points will give you a smooth-running engine," it is obvious that pragmatic procedure is in order. I clean the points, and start the engine, which now runs smoothly. Testing the hypothesis by putting it into action solved the problem. It produced satisfying results. It *worked*.

13 James, *Pragmatism*, p. 200.

Now we employ variations of this testing procedure as a matter of course not only in problems of everyday life but also in the special sciences. The pragmatic method in inquiry, taken as a *test* of truth, is a variety of empirical verification, the general procedure we follow whenever we check the truth of a hypothesis by test and experiment.

The Instrumental Conception of Truth; Dewey

Man, says Dewey, is an organism moving within a natural and a social environment. The interaction between man and Nature, between man and society produces *experience*, which is what we philosophize about. Our dual environment raises problems; it presents difficulties and obstacles which the human organism endeavors to overcome. Now man is able to *control* to an important extent both his natural and his social environment. By controlling his environment, man can *change* it. The relation between man and Nature should not be thought of as a relation between a spectator and an aggregate of fixed and eternal facts. The correspondence theory of truth is inadequate because it covertly assumes this false, static view of man's relation to Nature and to society. Like James, Dewey points out that facts are not fixed. Man, by virtue of his intelligence, can control and modify his environment. Ideas are instruments of action, not objects of contemplation. Thus, facts can be *made*. And if facts can be made, *truth* can be made. Verification, then, is not just a way of arriving at truth. It *is* truth. "Verification and truth are two names for the same thing. We call it 'verification' when we regard it as process . . . we call it 'truth' when we take it as product."[14]

[14] John Dewey, *The Influence of Darwin on Philosophy*, New York, Holt, Rinehart and Winston, 1910, pp. 139–140. (PB: Indiana U. P.)

Critics of pragmatism readily admit, says Dewey, that the fact that a proposition *works* may lead us to know that it is true. But, they insist, that it works is not the same thing as its truth. The proposition was true all along. The artificiality of this position, says Dewey, may be illustrated by the following example: Suppose a man has just been rescued from drowning. Someone says to him that he is now a saved man. What would we think of a bystander who said, "Yes, but he was a saved man all the time. The process of rescuing, while it gives evidence of that fact, does not constitute it"? It is just as absurd, Dewey maintains, to hold that every proposition verified in experience has antecedent truth.[15] Suppose a man is lost in the woods, and he says to himself, "Acting in such and such a way will bring me safely out." He acts upon the proposition and is successful in reaching a settled area. The truth of this proposition and its success cannot be distinguished without involving oneself in triviality. There is a trap, says Dewey, in the very word "truth"; its traditional overtones of something fixed, eternal, and separated from man are so persistent that when we use the word we tend unconsciously to assume the worn-out metaphysics with which it is associated. For this reason Dewey prefers the phrase "warranted assertibility" to "truth."

Criticism of the Instrumental Theory

In certain areas of human affairs the tendency to think of truth always as something *fixed in advance* has blocked experiment, and in his criticism of this tendency most contemporary philosophers would agree that Dewey is in the right. When he says, as James did, that "the true means the verified," we can readily agree that in the case of many true

[15] *Ibid.*, p. 142.

propositions it is difficult to separate the facts they designate from their actual verification. Such statements as "Minnesota will beat Michigan this year" *become* true only at the moment of their verification. There are no present facts for the correspondence theory to point to as agreeing with the sentence. Similarly, the proposition "Democracy is the best form of government" *becomes* true as it is verified in a historical context by centuries of trial, error, adjustment, and compromise. For this reason the truth of the proposition and its verification are inextricable.

Nevertheless, Dewey's critics maintain that if we say, as Dewey does, "the true means the verified and means nothing else,"[16] there are situations where this identification simply does not hold. Some situations are *indeterminate*, and here Dewey's theory of truth as verification is applicable. An example of an indeterminate situation is that which precedes the election of a President of the United States. The truth of the proposition "Johnson is President" *becomes* true when the intrinsic doubtfulness of the situation is resolved by action of the voters. On election day, truth and verification are the same. Here truth is *made*. But other situations are *determinate*. When I open my pig bank to see if there is a dollar in it, my doing so does not constitute the truth of the proposition "There is a dollar in the pig bank." There was a dollar in it all the time. Would we be willing to say that prior to its verification the proposition "The earth is round" was neither true nor false?

The character of a philosopher's theory of truth will depend to a considerable extent upon the kinds of situations that interest him. Thus Dewey is not primarily interested in propositions about determinate situations like dollars in pig

[16] John Dewey, *Reconstruction in Philosophy*, New York, Holt, Rinehart and Winston, 1920, p. 160. (PB: Beacon Press, Boston.)

banks or the roundness of the earth. James is absorbed with situations in the moral realm—where conflict can be resolved by resolute will, where faith can bring about facts. Dewey sees the problems of philosophy in terms of problematic situations like men lost in forests, scientists searching for a working hypothesis, citizens trying to resolve a social conflict. But there are also philosophers like Bertrand Russell who are interested in propositions about determinate situations, such as the moons of Jupiter, the rate of vibration of red light, the presence of mammoths in North America. Russell was convinced that some type of correspondence theory is needed to deal with these propositions and denies that the pragmatic theory can provide an adequate explanation of the meaning of their truth.

CERTAINTY

Meanings of "Certainty"

Like "truth," "certainty" is a shifty word. Sometimes we use it to describe a *state of mind.* As such, certainty is the opposite of *doubt.* When we are certain, we assent without hesitation to a statement. When we doubt, we withhold our assent. As a state of mind, certainty is often called *subjective* or *psychological* certainty. Now subjective certainty is no guarantee of truth. When I say, "I am certain I saw Marian at Jones Beach," I may have an unshakable conviction that this proposition is true. Yet, as we know too well from experience, we may have such a strong conviction at the time, yet later be forced to admit that we were mistaken. For many centuries a large number of educated men were strongly convinced that the earth was immovable and that there were unicorns. Conviction that something is so does not mean that it is so.

Sometimes we apply certainty to *propositions.*[17] Instead of saying "I am certain that . . . ," we sometimes say "It is certain that. . . ." So we may say that the statements "I have two legs" and "$2 + 2 = 4$" are certain. Such propositions are certain, we say, because there is no reason whatever to doubt them and there is sufficient evidence of an objective character to support them. Certainty used in this sense is frequently called *objective* certainty.

In their quest for certainty, philosophers have often asked what kinds of propositions are certain. The ancient Skeptics believed there were no such propositions. Descartes, the father of modern philosophy, believed there were and recommended a remarkable method for discovering them.

Descartes's Method

The distinguished seventeenth-century French philosopher was disturbed by the fact that learned men disagreed upon every subject. Were there no propositions above dispute? he asked. If there were such, we should find them and build our knowledge upon them. Descartes believed he had a sound method for discovering propositions that were certain. He would consider all the propositions it was possible to think of and see whether it was possible to *doubt* them all. Descartes then proceeded to apply his methodic doubt to all propositions, including those drawn from ordinary experience and from the learned disciplines. He found that it was possible to doubt them all. He was able even to question the objective existence of the world of his experience, for this world *could* be a phantasm induced in him by some powerful malignant demon. But at length Des-

[17] Some would prefer to say that "certainty" pertains to *inferences* rather than to the propositions which are the conclusions of those inferences. See the discussion on inference in Chapter 1, pp. 16–20.

cartes came upon a proposition of such a nature that he could not possibly doubt it. This was the proposition *I exist.* I know that I exist, says Descartes, for I am thinking. Even if there should be an evil genius deceiving me concerning the whole world, at least there exists a René Descartes who is being deceived. He tells us: "As I observed that this truth, I THINK, HENCE I AM, was so certain and of such evidence, that no ground of doubt, however extravagant, could be alleged by the Sceptics capable of shaking it, I concluded that I might, without scruple, accept it as the first principle of the Philosophy of which I was in search."[18]

Descartes then proceeds to search for other certain propositions. The judgment "I exist" has such peculiar *clarity* and *distinctness*, he says, that it is impossible to doubt it. Are there any other judgments similarly clear and distinct? Descartes was convinced that the judgment "A perfect Being exists" had the requisite clarity and distinctness, and that the proposition expressing it was certain. Descartes claims that the truth of the proposition "God exists" is *self-evident.* Once we understand what this proposition means, we cannot possibly doubt it. Having to his own satisfaction established the certainty of "God exists," Descartes concludes that human knowledge is fundamentally reliable, provided that we use it properly. For God, being good, would not endow us with a faculty inherently deceptive.

Meaning of Self-Evidence

The reader will probably object to the soundness of the chain of inferences by means of which Descartes establishes the existence of God and the comparative reliability of

[18] R. Descartes, *Discourse on Method*, J. Veitch, trans., M. Walter Dunne, 1901, p. 171. (PB: Liberal Arts, Bobbs-Merrill, Indianapolis.)

human knowledge. One of the defects of Descartes's procedure arises from his use of clarity and distinctness or *self-evidence* to support the certainty of propositions. Now there are at least two senses in which a proposition may be said to be self-evident. A proposition is sometimes said to be self-evident in the sense that it is *indemonstrable*, that is, we cannot infer it from other propositions. In a second sense, a proposition is self-evident if it is *completely clear to me* that it is so. To those familiar with arithmetic, the proposition "$3 + 3 = 6$" is self-evident in the second sense. But not in the first, for it can be deduced from other more primitive arithmetical statements.

Now self-evidence, in the sense of "completely clear to me," may be a dangerously subjective criterion of certainty. What one man perceives clearly and distinctly another may not. The proposition "God exists" was self-evident to Descartes, but it is not at all self-evident to the majority of philosophers. "The utmost clarity in our thoughts," says Bertrand Russell, "would not enable us to demonstrate the existence of Cape Horn." The proposition "All men are created equal" was self-evident to our founding fathers, but not to the Bourbon kings.

Descartes would reply that "God exists" is a metaphysical truth, and metaphysical truths differ from mathematical truths in the following way. The axioms of geometry are in accord with sense experience and imagination. We can apply them to physical surfaces and bodies. We draw visual diagrams to help us learn geometry. It is because the laws of geometry are so compatible with the properties of things in our every-day world of experience that men readily concede these laws self-evidence. Metaphysical truths, however, do not tie in with readily observable features of the sensible world. Sense observation may be an aid in geometry, but it may get in the way of our grasping truths of metaphysics. It is only by turning the understanding away from sense experience and imagination which prejudice us against metaphysical concepts, that we can see that self-evident truths like "God exists" show themselves beyond doubt in the very act of our considering them. In a later stage of our inquiry, we shall come back to Descartes's claim of self-evidence for the proposition "God exists."

Logical Certainty

Descartes himself was a mathematician, the discoverer of analytic geometry. As a geometer, he knew he could carry on a complex series of inferences and draw it to a conclusion of unquestionable certainty. For the propositions of formal science *are* certain in the sense that they are necessarily true. It would be silly to say that "$3 + 3 = 6$" is merely *probable*. An analytic statement cannot be denied without involving the denier in a *contradiction*. But the evidence which guarantees the certainty of analytic statements is of a purely formal kind. The evidence for the certainty of "$3 + 3 = 6$" is drawn from the structure of the formal system which contains it. This proposition fits in or "coheres" with the way in which we use notions like "3," "6," "plus," and "equals" in arithmetic.

The peculiar certainty of mathematical conclusions, which philosophers have so much admired, may be classed as *logical* certainty. But we must not expect logical certainty of propositions which make assertions about matters of empirical fact. It is a characteristic of statements about people and things that their opposites may be asserted in statements which contain no internal contradiction. I have not the slightest doubt that I have a nose. Yet the proposition "I do not have a nose" does not contradict itself as does the statement "This Euclidean triangle has four sides." What detracts from the excellence of Descartes's method is his apparent conviction that something like logical certainty may be found in some propositions which have nothing to do with formal science. He tried to discover in propositions about God and the world a "clarity and distinctness" found only in mathematics and logic. "In our search for the direct road toward truth," he tells us, "we should busy ourselves with no object about which we cannot attain a certainty equal to that of the demonstrations of Arithmetic and Geometry."[19]

"Incorrigible" Propositions

Are there any propositions other than those of logic or mathematics which may be said under some circumstances to be certain? Consider those statements which refer to simple sensations, such as "I have a pain," or "I see something red." Such statements are sometimes called *incorrigible* (uncorrectable) propositions. Although it is logically possible to doubt such statements (since their opposites do not involve internal contradictions), it seems impossible to question their certainty in any other way. If we are aboard ship and you say, "I feel ill," I may doubt your statement, despire the existence of objective empirical evidence (the rough sea, your pale face, etc.) from which I may *infer* the proposition "You feel ill." But if it is *I* who feel ill, and I say, "I feel ill," *I* at least am certain of this proposition. For the evidence which supports it is immediate, sensational, internal, and—as far as I am concerned—beyond question. I do not have to *infer* the proposition. I

[19] R. Descartes, "Rules for the Direction of the Mind," in E. S. Haldane and G. R. T. Ross, trans., *The Philosophical Works of Descartes,* London, Cambridge University Press, 1931, pp. 43–44. (PB: Liberal Arts, Bobbs-Merrill, Indianapolis.)

know it directly. If Descartes's celebrated *Cogito* ("I think") is paraphrased as "I am experiencing," such a proposition may be classified as incorrigible.

Not all philosophers are in agreement about the certainty of incorrigible propositions. Some point out that, while certainty exists in such situations, the certainty is subjective and psychological only. Others say that such statements do not, properly speaking, express knowledge at all, since they are merely reports of *sensations* and do not represent any kind of inference. What is the difference between the propositions "I feel sick" and "I know I feel sick"?[20] A few analysts, extreme perhaps in their caution, may go so far as to claim that in the proposition "I feel warm" there may lurk behind the pronoun "I" the covert and unproved metaphysical assumption of a personal unity enduring through change. It would be more exact, they may say, to replace the statement "I feel warm" with the expression "There is a feeling of warmth now."[21]

Particular Factual Propositions

Apart from incorrigible propositions, are there any statements about matters of fact which may under some circumstances properly be called certain? There is a very large class of statements of this kind which we may call particular factual statements. Some of them are of this type:

[20] Wittgenstein opposed G. E. Moore's attempt to prove that a person can know that he has a sensation of warmth, of pain, etc. The concepts of knowledge and certainty, he argued, have no application to one's own sensations. I do not *know* my sensations, I *have* them.

[21] Philosophic caution may sometimes be carried to extremes. A story is told of a German professor of philosophy who was so fearful of assigning to objects attributes which the objects might not in fact possess that he habitually addressed his wife only as "Being" or "Thing"!

> There is a dictionary on the table.
> Al is playing ball.
> There is a dead mouse under the refrigerator.
> The library is open now.
> I am writing with a pen.
> The checkbook is in the drawer.

We make thousands of statements like these about simple factual matters. May such statements ever be said to be certain? They are not *logically* certain, for their opposites may be supposed true without fear of formal contradiction. Nor is the evidence which supports them of the "incorrigible" type as in the case of statements like "I feel warm." Nevertheless, it seems that such propositions may under some circumstances be called certain in the sense that (1) there is no reason to doubt them and (2) there is evidence to support them such that it would be pointless to ask for more.

The evidence which warrants the certainty of particular factual propositions like these is based on sense observation and is of a kind that can be corroborated by simple and public procedures. Suppose you approach an object which looks like a table, feels like a table, and functions as a table, and upon it you find an object which looks like a dictionary, reads like a dictionary, and functions as a dictionary. Suppose further that other members of your family behave as if they were having the same experience. Now what possible reason would there be for questioning the certainty of the proposition "There is a dictionary on the table"? What more could one ask by way of verification? What further procedures could be specified which would measurably increase the certainty of the proposition? To be sure, it *might* be, as Descartes suggests, that a malignant demon with nothing better to do is causing something which is *not* a dictionary to appear as if it *were* a dictionary. But, although this is possible, there is not the slightest reason to suppose it to be true. Besides, if the demon has gone to the trouble of making something that looks like a dictionary, can be used as a dictionary, and so on, has he not made a dictionary?

Arguments of the type above have been put forward by the English philosopher G. E. Moore in support of the certainty of such particular factual propositions. To insist, says Moore, that the proposition "I am holding a pen" is not *certain* but only *probable* is to use language in a way in which people do not employ it. The pressure exerted in this direction by Moore and his followers has forced most contemporary analysts to concede that particular empirical propositions may correctly be said to be certain, if certainty is used *in the ordinary sense*. Some philosophers, however, still have reservations about this type of proposition. Admitting ordinary certainty, they say, we may wish to use the word "certain" in special philosophic inquiry in some stricter sense.[22]

General Empirical Statements; Induction

The capacity to form general judgments is a characteristic mark of human knowledge. Without general statements there could be no science. For the essence of scientific explanation is fitting a particular observed fact into a general description or "law." Here are some samples of general statements drawn at random both from science and from ordinary discourse:

Leaves contain chlorophyll.
The subway is always crowded at five-thirty on weekdays.

[22] See A. J. Ayer, "Basic Propositions," in Max Black, ed. *Philosophical Analysis*, Cornell University Press, 1950. (PB: Prentice-Hall, Englewood Cliffs, N.J.)

The specific gravity of gold is 19.3.
Thin people tend to be nervous.
Cows get up back end first.
Human blood falls into four major groupings.
Once a thief, always a thief.
The female praying mantis, after mating, decapitates, then eats the male.
Spinach is good for you.

Suppose we note some elements common to all these general statements: (1) The statements are conclusions of *inferences.* (2) The conclusions have been drawn after *particular instances* have been examined. (3) The number of individual instances examined is *less* than the number covered by the general statement. In other words, after an examination of *some* cases, we have made a general statement concerning *all.*

The type of inference by which we establish such general statements is called *induction.* Induction may be defined as a mode of inference in which, *some* examples of an occurrence, having been observed, a conclusion is drawn concerning *all* such occurrences. Not every general statement or scientific law is established by induction. Scientists frequently derive general statements by *deduction* from other general statements. The same proposition may be derived inductively and deductively. I may base "The sun always rises" on induction, by referring to past instances of the sun's rising. Or I may deduce it by showing that this proposition follows from certain general laws of motion in their application to the earth.

The role of inductive inference in science and practical life is very important. The practical utility of inductive generalizations is that they enable us to predict *future* occurrences. If a copper alloy melts whenever I heat it to a certain temperature, I can form a general description or "law" which I can then apply to future instances of that alloy. A question for historians as well as for inductive logicians would be: how much, if anything, can we learn from the past? Our present inquiry takes this form: are there any general propositions, descriptive of natural events, that may ever be said to be *certain.* A very large number of such propositions are established inductively. Hence, the question of the certainty of general empirical statements is closely related to the question of the *soundness* of induction as a mode of inference.

THE PROBLEM OF INDUCTION

Sound and Unsound Inductions

The problem of induction may be put in this way: What gives us the right, under some conditions, to make general statements when we have only examined *some* of the instances? Formal logic tells us that the inference "Some *A* is *B;* therefore, all *A* is *B*" is *invalid.* In the course of daily life we meet many examples of inductive generalizations which we quickly recognize as dubious, such as "Tibetans are treacherous" and "Pickles and ice cream will make you sick." On the other hand, it would never occur to us to question such statements as "Fire will heat water" and "We shall all one day die." Yet both types of general statements are established by induction. Is it possible to distinguish between a sound induction and an unsound one?

Take the statement "Tibetans are treacherous." On what grounds do we question it? Apart from the ambiguity of the word "treacherous," we may challenge this induction on the following points: (1) *insufficient numbers of instances examined:* the person making the assertion has based his generalization on a small number of experiences with Tibetans; (2) *existence of contrary instances:* we ourselves know of several instances of Tibetans who are *not* treacherous; (3) *variable character of that which the generalization concerns:* human behavior is very variable, and experience tells us that general statements about human traits are frequently unreliable. (Note that here we counter with a couple of inductions of our own.)

Contrast with the weak induction "Tibetans are treacherous" the strong one "We shall all one day die." What is the nature of the evidence which supports the second statement? (1) A very large number of instances of men's deaths have been examined. (2) We know of no authenticated instance in the past of a man who has failed to die. (3) Mortality is not a variable characteristic of humans, like color of hair. (4) In addition, the statement draws independent strength from that fact that it can be *deduced* from biological laws concerning higher organisms generally.

Number of Instances Examined

We should note that *a large number of instances examined* is not *in itself* a safe criterion of the soundness of an inductive generalization. We may be tempted to say that the strength of an inductive generalization increases in proportion to the increase in the number of instances examined; that the more instances of *A* I find to be *B*, the more likely it is that any future *A* will also be *B*. Now, we *do* employ the criterion of number of instances examined to a considerable extent in ordinary life and in science. After each of a number of bad dinners at a certain restaurant, my conviction increases that any future dinner I am forced to eat there will also be bad. In medicine, in social research, in many other fields of study, the number of instances examined is frequently of great importance to the soundness of inferences drawn.

But there are large areas in both practical life and scientific investigation where the criterion of large number of instances examined does not hold. Consider the inductive statement "The density of argon is about 20." Rayleigh and Ramsay, who discovered the gas, weighed a sample or two and found the density to be 20. This figure was accepted as the measure of argon's density generally.

We need only burn our fingers once to convince ourselves of the certainty of "Fire burns painfully," but inspection of several hundred crows, each of which is black, will not persuade us that "All crows are black." In science, the strength of some general statements may be increased by testing a larger number of cases. But there are countless situations where the testing of further instances would be an obvious waste of time. What would we think of a physicist who spent his life dropping objects heavier than air, or of a business man who read dozens of copies of the same day's newspaper so he could be sure of what happened yesterday? In his treatise on induction, John Stuart Mill asks:

> Why is a single instance, in some cases, sufficient for a complete induction, while in others myriads of concurring instances, without a single exception known or presumed, go such a very little way toward establishing a universal proposition? Whoever can answer this question knows more of the philosophy of logic than the wisest of the ancients, and has solved the problem of Induction.[23]

Hume's Criticism of Induction

The rough criteria of sound induction given above—number of instances, absence of contrary instances, etc.—would not satisfy the sceptical Scottish philosopher David Hume. Hume called into question the usual reasons offered to

[23] J. S. Mill, *A System of Logic,* London, Longmans, 1925, p. 201.

"justify" induction. Admitting that he himself in practice relied upon induction, he claimed never to have heard any acceptable answer to the question as to why inductive reasons are good reasons. Hume was an empiricist; he believed that our most reliable knowledge comes from experience. According to Hume, experience brings us in contact with particular and individual occurrences only. Experience never presents us with general or universal situations.

Hume claims that when we make an inductive statement like "All men are mortal" or "Sodium ignites on contact with water" we are stating something *more* than experience warrants. What experience tells us that *in the past* men have invariably died and sodium has ignited whenever it was brought in contact with water. Experience does not tell us, however, that those men now living will die; as far as experience is concerned, we know nothing whatever about the deaths of those still living. Nor does past experience of sodium have anything to do with instances of sodium which have not yet been observed. Because something has been observed to behave in a certain way in the past is no guarantee that it will continue to behave that way. On the basis of the properties of instances observed in the past, we *assume* that the same properties will occur in the future. But this assumption is not justified by experience, since its justification would require observation of instances not yet observed. "It is impossible," says Hume, "that any arguments from experience can prove this resemblance of the past to the future; since all these arguments are founded on the supposition of that resemblance."[24]

According to Hume, then, experience gives us no warrant of certainty for inductive statements. Why then do we make them and use them so confidently to support our

[24] David Hume, *An Enquiry Concerning Human Understanding,* La Salle, Ill., Open Court, 1935, p. 37. (PB: Gateway, Regnery, Chicago.)

predictions? We make inductive generalizations, says Hume, through force of *habit*. That things have turned out in a certain way in the past accustoms us to *expect* that they will turn out that way in the future. But for this expectation there does not seem to be either a logical or a factual justification. To use Russell's example, a flock of chickens who have been fed by the farmer every day at 5 P.M. for a year will certainly *expect* to be fed today. But along comes the farmer, chops off their heads, and takes them to market. The chickens' *expectation* of being fed was lively, but that did not prevent the course of events from taking quite a different turn.

Philosophers have gone to considerable trouble to answer Hume (we shall in our next chapter see something of Kant's reply) and to find some kind of principle or "ground" upon which valid induction rests. One of these is the principle of the uniformity of Nature.

The Uniformity of Nature

"The proposition that the course of nature is uniform," says John Stuart Mill, "is the fundamental principle, or general axiom of Induction."[25] Natural events are not isolated bits of a miscellaneous jumble. They are part of a vast process of sequences of cause and effect. The principle of uniformity involves the *law of causation*. "The cause of a phenomenon," Mill tells us, is "the antecedent, or the concurrence of antecedents, on which it is invariably and *unconditionally* consequent."[26] Observation of a very few instances of fire and water convinces us that fire will heat water. For we perceive that fire and the heating of water are causally connected. They are elements in a causal se-

[25] Mill, *A System of Logic*, p. 201.
[26] *Ibid*., p. 222.

quence. Now Nature is a system of such causal sequences, a grand pattern of events which are not merely haphazardly associated but necessarily connected with one another.

The principle of the uniformity of Nature, says Mill, is the ultimate major premise of every inductive argument. It is the most general empirical proposition. Upon this principle depends not only scientific investigation, which presupposes it, but all conduct of practical affairs. Untold numbers of instances confirm this general principle, while none, of which we have reliable knowledge, runs counter to it. This most general of natural descriptions or "laws of Nature" *communicates its certainty* to the inductive statements of the several sciences. For the causal sequences investigated by these special sciences are particular exemplifications of the principle of uniformity.

It has been objected that Mill's argument is circular. For the principle "Nature is uniform" is *itself* established by induction. Mill, however, thought that his principle of uniformity was exceptional among inductive statements. He did not think that the usual challenge offered to inductive arguments could be brought against this single, all-embracing principle, unique in its comprehensive generality, verified by evidence from all possible quarters, with no known case to the contrary.

Nevertheless, many philosophers have found Mill's principle of uniformity an unsatisfactory explanation either of induction or of causality. It is objected that the principle is too vague; that it does not help us to distinguish between *sound* and *unsound* inductions, between those connections between phenomena which are *causal* and those which are merely *casual*.[27] "The doctrine of the Uniformity of Na-

[27] With his "Canons of Induction" Mill tried to formulate criteria which would help us identify genuine causal connections. See Mill, *A System of Logic*, bk. III.

ture," says Whitehead, "is to be ranked with the contrasted doctrine of magic and miracle, as an expression of a partial truth, unguarded and uncoordinated with the immensities of the Universe."[28] Despite these criticisms of the principle of uniformity, a few philosophers think that some principle analogous to the uniformity of Nature may exist, even though it has not yet successfully been formulated.[29] *Recurrence* seems to be an undeniable and basic character of Nature. Seasons recur, heartbeats recur, births and deaths recur, as do days and nights. Without recurrence—as Whitehead himself has pointed out—*prediction* of any sort would be impossible.

Inductive Statements as Probable

Many recent philosophers have felt that the quest for certainty in the case of general empirical statements should be abandoned as hopeless, and that we should be content with the conclusion that inductive statements can at best be considered *probable*. Since all instances (including future occurrences) comprehended within an inductive generalization clearly *cannot* be examined, it is obvious that we cannot be certain about them. What we *can* say is that the statements like "All men are mortal" and "Falling bodies accelerate at the rate of 32 feet per second per second" possess, by virtue of the evidence supporting them, a high degree of probability. This view of general empirical statements as probable rather than certain draws strength from the fact that historically a great number of inductive statements taken by scientists as descriptive laws have later re-

[28] Alfred North Whitehead, *Adventures of Ideas*, New York, Macmillan, 1933, p. 99. (PB: Mentor, New American Library, New York.)

[29] More specific than Mill's principle of uniformity is J. M. Keynes' *postulate of limited variety*. See J. M. Keynes, *A Treatise on Probability*, London, Macmillan, 1921.

quired correction. For example, it has been discovered that Boyle's law—which states that the volume of a gas varies inversely with the pressure—is inexact, and that it requires modification if it is applied in certain circumstances. Newton's laws, once considered absolute, have had to be modified to account for certain properties of space subsequently observed.

The trouble with invoking *probability* as a solution of the problem as to why inductive reasons are good reasons is this: If past observed instances cannot, as Hume claimed, confer certainty on inductive inferences, why should they communicate probability? If past occurrences cannot influence future occurrences, how can we say there is a probability of the latter—unless we mean by "probability" our subjective sense of expectation which Hume grants at the outset? Further, there is more than one sense of the term "probable." One is the precise sense of mathematical or a priori probability. Using a calculation based on this I can predict that the probability of a penny thrown three times in succession, turning up heads each time, is one-eighth. But I must assume here that I am tossing an *ideal* penny, that is, a coin which is equally likely to turn up heads or tails. Another sense of "probability" is *relative frequency*. Automobile insurance companies construct tables of accident frequencies, modify these by taking into account new trends, and set their premium rates accordingly. Useful as this probability concept is, it makes only statistical (not individual) predictions, and assumes that what has happened in the past will (roughly) continue to happen in the future. The probable, says Aristotle, is what usually happens. Finally, there is the sense of "probable" that means *likely*. When I say "I'll probably come to dinner," I mean I'll try to get there—you should not be surprised to see me turn up, but it is by no means out of the question that I shall miss it. In view of these varying senses of "probability," then, it does not seem to help very much to say that inductive generalizations are never certain, but that under some circumstances, they may have a high degree of probability.

The Problem of Induction; Conclusion

A certain number of instances of *A* have been found to be *B*. Therefore, all future instances of *A* will be *B*.

As it stands above, schematically represented and taken abstractly, the principle of induction has no justification. There is nothing about induction *as such* which guarantees its soundness. This we know by the enormous number of unsound inductions which follow the pattern above. We cannot formulate induction as a formal logical principle which, when applied, will provide reliable security in inference. Induction is concerned with *empirical* inference; therefore we can never expect it to have *formal* or *deductive* certainty. We draw inductions concerning a huge variety of matters, ranging from the freezing point of mercury to the dispositions of red-headed girls. We cannot discuss the soundness of induction in the abstract *without reference to the nature of the particular evidence which supports the given induction.*

Does Hume's question have an answer? Can we give any explanation as to why inductive reasons are sometimes good reasons, even when all we have observed are particular facts which are not in themselves general laws? Some critics say that the way Hume's challenge is formulated makes it impossible to answer it. For Hume presupposes that the instances examined constitute all the evidence for the general inductive conclusion. If the function of particular instances is to provide the sole support of the general conclusion, this support is fated to be partial because of the particular and instantial nature of the evidence. But it may be that the particular favorable instances (those men that have died; those mammals with four-chambered hearts) do more than make partial support for a generalization never experienced as such. The obvious uselessness of trying to increase the number of instances examined to support certain classes of general statements ("A body tends to fall toward the center of the earth," and "Fish have backbones") convinced Aristotle long ago that the function of induction in such cases is not to *prove* anything by the number of favorable instances observed, but rather *to call our attention* to the existence of certain general patterns in Nature.[30] The role of induction is to nudge us into awareness of the existence of these general natural features, statements about which form the premises of the sciences. Aristotle did not believe there was any need to prove by extended nose counting (simple enumeration of instances) that which he thought any reasonable man could see for himself after he had observed a few cases.

Some recent philosophers of science (H. Reichenbach, for one) have tried to avoid Hume's difficulty by denying that inductive conclusions are general statements at all. Such conclusions, they say, may have the *form* of propositions, but they are really *hypotheses* or suppositions. Consider an example of a conclusion drawn about the relation between iodine injections and thyroid response. To formulate a conclusion "All injections of *n* units of radioactive iodine are followed by such and such thyroid reactions" would be to invite Hume's objection. To put the conclusion in the form of a flat universal proposition does not really represent what we are doing. Our conclusion would

[30] Aristotle, *Posterior Analytics*, 99b15 et seq.

be rendered more accurately by putting it into hypothetical form: "*If* you inject *n* units of radioactive iodine, *then* the thyroid will react in such and such ways." This hypothesis would hold, then, not as a universal statement of fact, but as an instrument of inquiry; we apply it to problematic situations to see whether or not by successive observations and experiments we can obtain *confirmation* of the hypothesis. Once more we should remind ourselves that inductive hypotheses which may take the form of generalizations are of little use in isolation. They are parts of a closely knit web of strands of inquiry (other hypotheses, conclusions, laws) which lend each other mutual support and confirmation.

As to the question whether any general empirical propositions may correctly be described as *certain*, the answer will depend upon the meaning assigned to the word "certain." If "certain" is to be used in the sense of *ordinary* or *practical* certainty, then the answer will be yes. Whatever our theoretical doubts, we *behave* as if unexamined instances of fire will burn us and kisses of our loved ones will comfort us. But if by "certain" is meant *logical* certainty, the certainty which attends the inferences of formal science when correctly drawn, the answer will be no. Nor can general empirical statements properly be called certain if by "certainty" is meant *incorrigibility*. We cannot claim that any inductive statement is beyond the possibility of correction or revision, or that the behavior of future unobserved instances can in any case of induction be unconditionally guaranteed in advance.

FURTHER READINGS

Truth

Aquinas, Thomas, *Truth* (*De Veritate*), R. W. Mulligan, S. J. (trans.), Chicago, Regnery, 1952, vol. 1, qu. 1.

Blanshard, Brand, *The Nature of Thought*, New York, Macmillan, 1940.

Dewey, John, *The Philosophy of John Dewey*, Joseph Ratner (ed.), New York, Holt, Rinehart and Winston, 1928, chap. 7.

Dewey, John, "Propositions, Warranted Assertibility, and Truth," *The Journal of Philosophy*, March 27, 1941.

James, William, *The Meaning of Truth*, New York, Longmans, 1909.

James, William, *Pragmatism*, New York, Longmans, 1928, chap. 6. (PB: Meridian, World Publishing, Cleveland.)

Joachim, H. H., *The Nature of Truth*, Oxford, Clarendon Press, 1906.

Pap, Arthur, *Elements of Analytic Philosophy*, New York, Macmillan, 1949, chap. 14.

Russell, Bertrand, *An Inquiry into Meaning and Truth*, New York, Norton, 1940.

Tarski, Alfred, "The Semantic Conception of Truth," in H. Feigl and W. Sellars (eds.), *Readings in Philosophical Analysis*, New York, Appleton-Century-Crofts, 1949.

Thayer, H. S., "Pragmatism" in *A Critical History of Western Philosophy*, D. J. O'Connor (ed.), New York, Free Press, 1964.

Whitehead, Alfred North, *Adventures of Ideas*, New York, Macmillan, 1933, chap. 16.

Certainty and Induction

Black, Max, "The Justification of Induction," in *Language and Philosophy*, Cornell University Press, 1949.

Cohen, Morris, and Ernest Nagel, *An Introduction to Logic and Scientific Method*, New York, Harcourt, Brace, & World, 1934, chap. 14.

Descartes, René, *Discourse on Method*, J. Veitch (trans.), M. Walter Dunne, 1901. (PB: Liberal Arts, Bobbs-Merrill, Indianapolis.)

Dewey, John, *The Quest for Certainty*, New York, Minton, 1929. (PB: Capricorn, Putnam, New York.)

Goodman, Nelson, "The New Riddle of Induction," in *Fact, Fiction, and Forecast*, Harvard University Press, 1955.

Hume, David, *An Enquiry Concerning Human Understanding*, La Salle, Ill., Open Court, 1935, sec. 3. (PB: Gateway, Regnery, Chicago.)

Keynes, John Maynard, *A Treatise on Probability*, London, Macmillan, 1921.

Mill, John Stuart, *A System of Logic*, London, Longmans, 1925, bk. III.

Pap, Arthur, *Elements of Analytic Philosophy*, New York, Macmillan, 1949, chap. 8.

Reichenbach, Hans, "The Logical Character of the Principle of Induction" and "The Logical Foundations of Probability," in H. Feigl and W. Sellars (eds.), *Readings in Philosophical Analysis*, New York, Appleton-Century-Crofts, 1949.

Russell, Bertrand, *Human Knowledge*, New York, Simon and Schuster, 1948, pt. 6. (PB: Essandess Paperbacks, Simon and Schuster.)

Russell, Bertrand, "On Induction," *The Problems of Philosophy*, New York, Holt, Rinehart and Winston, 1912, chap. VI. (PB: Galaxy, Oxford U. P., New York.)

4

Our Knowledge of the World Outside Us

Wherein, he resembled my Right Reverend friend, Bishop Berkeley—truly, one of your lords spiritual—who, metaphysically speaking, holding all objects to be mere optical delusions, was, notwithstanding, extremely matter-of-fact in all matters touching matter itself. Besides being pervious to the points of pins, and possessing a palate capable of appreciating plum-puddings.

—*Mardi*, HERMAN MELVILLE

In the preceding chapter it was suggested that many types of propositions may under some circumstances be correctly described as *certain* in the ordinary sense of the word. That is, I firmly hold them to be true on the ground of objective and reliable evidence. Among these propositions we included the type based on simple perceptual judgments like "There is a black cat on that chair." Since the evidence supporting such propositions is our sense observation which can be corroborated by similar observations by others, it seemed that there is no reason to doubt them.

But suppose the following questions are raised: What

evidence do we have that there exists a cat and a chair *independently* of me and other percipients? What evidence is there that these objects (assuming that they do exist "out there") actually possess in their own right the properties they appear to have? If no such evidence exists, or if the evidence is questionable, it would seem that the certainty of the proposition "There is a black cat on that chair" is, after all, a rather dubious matter. In the external world we distinguish innumerable objects such as cats, trees, tables, houses, and rivers. Common sense tells us that these things exist independently of us and that they themselves possess the properties they seem to have. But suppose it were argued that there is no guarantee whatever that the character of the external world as it is given to us through sense perception is reliably reported.

Now human knowledge goes far beyond particular sense observations. To know is to generalize. We cannot describe the external world solely in terms of individual *percepts*, of colored shapes that feel hard or soft and move this way and that. We must use general notions, ideas, *concepts* to tie our scattered percepts together, to *interpret* our sense observation, and thus bring order, system, and explanation into knowledge. No man has ever *perceived* an atom, yet the concept of "atom" holds up the world of modern physics and enables us to control mighty forces of Nature.

But if the reliability of sense perception can be questioned, so can the reliability of conceptual knowledge. Our perceptions, at least, are affairs of present sense experience. But concepts go *beyond* sense experience. They deal with what is not immediately present to sense observation. They are abstract. They are general. That an event is the *cause* of another is not seen but inferred. No one perceives "heat" or "electricity" or "gravity" as such. "Evolution" and the "subconscious" are not matters given directly in sense experience. General notions such as these are indispensable to science. But is there any assurance that there actually exists in the external world such situations as they purport to describe?

In modern times philosophers have raised many questions concerning the reliability of perception and the validity of concepts. These problems are conventionally called *epistemological*, that is, problems concerned with the trustworthiness of human knowledge. We shall first examine the problem of perception and then consider some questions relating to conceptual knowledge.

THE PROBLEM OF PERCEPTION

Sense Percepts and Objects

Sensations are the simplest elements of human knowledge. They are the reports given to us by the senses of sight, hearing, taste, touch, etc. The name "percept" is often given to a group of associated sensations (red sphere; hard block). But we need not drive too sharp a distinction between "sensations" and "perceptions." Let us say that on the basis of sense perception, we assume the independent existence of objects, such as trees and cats. Now common sense tells us that there is a basic distinction between the perceiver of an object (myself) and the object perceived (the black cat). The question is: what is the nature of the relationship between the perceiver and the perceived object? We shall see that there is more than one way of analyzing this relationship.

Common-Sense Realism or Objectivism

The doctrine of perception which makes the most immediate appeal to common sense may be expressed in the following three propositions: (1) We perceive physical objects *directly*. (2) These objects exist independently of ourselves and occupy a definite position in space. (3) The character of these objects is such as we perceive them to be. In sum, when I see a black cat, I perceive directly and without intermediary a physical body in space which exists independently of me and which in its own right possesses the properties it appears to possess. This theory we may call *common-sense realism* or *objectivism.* Its account of perception may be represented by the accompanying diagram.

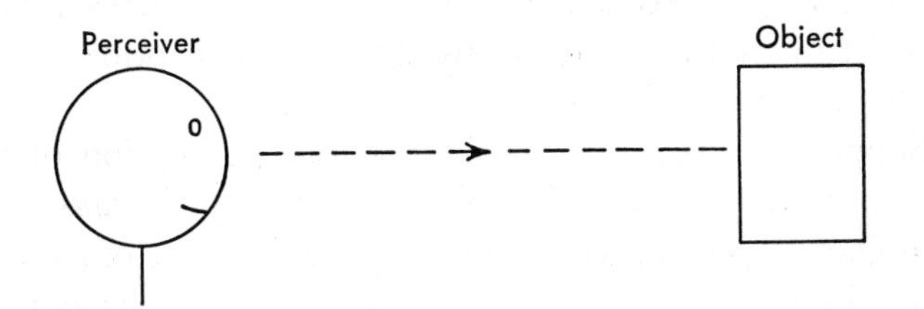

While the common-sense realist holds that we perceive physical objects, he would not claim that everything we perceive is a physical object. In dreams and illusions we have perceptions to which no physical objects correspond. The pile of money I dreamed of last night was dream money only. The dagger Macbeth saw before him was not "real." The oar which appears bent in water is objective enough, but its "bent-ness" is not. The common-sense realist admits the *subjective* character of dreams and illusions. But this admission does not affect his basic claim that we can and do directly perceive physical bodies which have objective and independent existence.

The Dualistic or Representational Theory of Perception

Common-sense realism tells us that we perceive objects directly. The penny I see and the penny itself are one and the same thing. But is there not some kind of distinction between the penny and our perception of it? Our perception of the penny can and does *vary*, whereas the penny (we assume) does not. If you and I are sitting before a table upon which a penny rests, you perceive the penny as *elliptical* in shape. From my angle of vision, the penny is of a slightly different elliptical shape. Only when we stand up and in turn look directly down upon the penny does it appear *circular*. Now despite the many elliptical penny shapes we experience, we believe that the penny, that is, the object itself, is circular. We find ourselves, therefore, compelled to admit that the penny and our perception of the penny are *two* different things.

Suppose, however, we insist that our perception of the penny—though it is distinct from the penny—is *caused* by an objective penny. Suppose we say further that our penny is *like* its cause, the objective penny. By now our analysis of perception is no longer quite that of common-sense realism. The latter view holds to the *directness* of the relationship between perceiver and object perceived. Our present position, however, suggests that the relationship is *indirect;* that the perception of an object is in some way *intermediate* between the object perceived and the perceiver. We now hold that our perception of an object is *something distinct* from the external object, that it is *causally produced* by the object, and that it is *similar* to the object. Such an analysis of perception is called a *dualistic* theory (or "epistemological dualism") since it claims that our perception of an object and the object itself are *two* distinct entities rather than one and the same thing. It may also be referred to as a *representational* theory of perception in contrast to the *presentational* account given by the common-sense realist. Diagrammatically, we may represent the dualist analysis of perception as it appears on the following page.

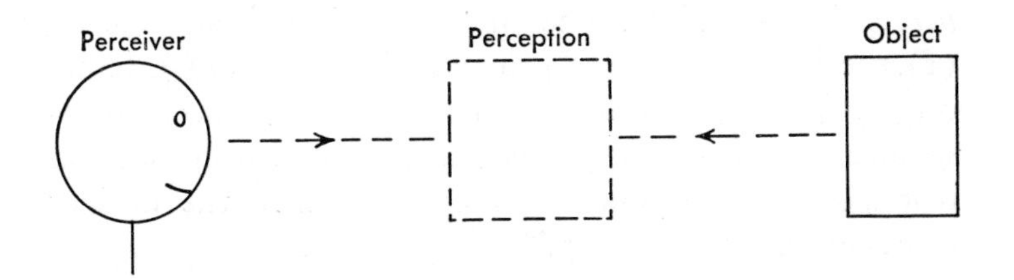

Locke's Analysis of Perception

A classic example of the dualistic analysis of perception is that offered by the seventeenth-century English philosopher John Locke. In his book *An Essay Concerning Human Understanding* Locke tried to determine the scope and limits of human knowledge. He took as his point of departure the proposition that all knowledge comes from *experience.* The mind is like a sheet of white paper or a blank tablet (*tabula rasa*) on which experience makes its marks. Experience furnishes us with *sensations* and the mind *reflects* upon these. Sensations and the internal operations of the mind consequent upon sensations Locke calls *ideas.* Ideas are what we know, and all that we *can* know directly. "We can have knowledge no further than we have ideas . . . ," says Locke. "Since the mind, in all its thoughts and reasonings, hath no other immediate object but its own ideas, which it alone does or can contemplate, it is evident that our knowledge is only conversant about them."[1]

Locke believed that the *causes* of our sensations are external to us. We do not know the nature of these external causes immediately, but we infer this from our ideas, which are representations of the external causes. The *dualistic* nature of Locke's analysis of perception is evident. In the act of perception, we do not know *things;* we know *our*

[1] J. Locke, *An Essay Concerning Human Understanding,* A. C. Fraser, ed., London, Oxford University Press, 1894, vol. 2, p. 190 and p. 167. (PB: Meridian, World Publishing, Cleveland.)

perceptions of things. The "understanding" is affected by (1) the ideas, which are produced in us by (2) external causes. Between (1) and (2) there is a likeness or correspondence. The reality of our ideas, says Locke, lies "in that steady correspondence they have with the distinct constitutions of real beings."[2]

Locke's Primary and Secondary Qualities

The correspondence between our ideas and the external objects which cause them is partial only. Following the assumptions of Newtonian physics, Locke divides the qualities of physical objects into *primary* and *secondary* qualities. The primary qualities include extension, figure, rest, motion—those properties which Aristotle had named "common sensibles" since they could be perceived by more than one sense. The secondary qualities ("proper sensibles") are those properties of an object which can be perceived by one sense only—its color, sound, taste, smell, etc. Now, like his scientific contemporaries, Locke states that *only the primary qualities have objective existence;* that is, only those properties like mass and "taking-up-space-ness" exist "out there" independently of the perceiver. The secondary qualities like taste and color have subjective existence only. They are wholly effects produced *in us* by the contact of external objects with our senses. Sugar is not objectively sweet; sweetness is the effect of the sugar upon our sense of taste. The blue is not actually in the flower; it is the effect of the flower upon our visual sense that produces the sensation of blue in us. Locke's doctrine of the subjectivity of secondary qualities, together with his earlier claim that the mind knows not things but ideas, raised difficulties which led to the formation of a new analysis of perception—that known as *subjectivism.*

[2] Locke, *Essay,* p. 498.

Subjectivism

Locke's analysis of perception tells us (1) that what we know are our sensations or "ideas," (2) that these sensations are produced in us by physical objects external to us, (3) that there is at least a partial correspondence between our perceptions and these external causes. But it is just at this point that a difficulty rises. What assurance have we that there is any correspondence at all between our "ideas" and their external causes? What justifies our belief in this likeness between perceptions and the things which produce them in us, if what we know are perceptions only? There is simply no way of showing that any correspondence whatever exists between our "ideas" and the physical objects which are supposed to cause them. Indeed, there is no way

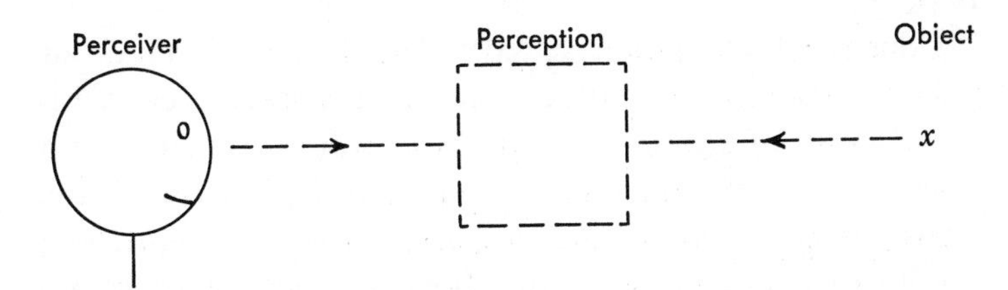

of demonstrating that there *are* any physical objects existing independently of us. Consider the accompanying diagram. In order to show that there is a conformity between our perception P and the assumed object *x*, we would have to take a stand at some point *outside* our perceptions in order to compare P and *x* to see if there were a similarity between them or to see if there were any object at all. But this is impossible, for no one can stand outside his perceptions. This argument favors a *subjectivist* analysis of perception, since it tends to the conclusion that the character of perceived objects is determined by the character of the perceiving subject.

Berkeley on Things and Ideas

The difficulties implicit in Locke's dualistic analysis of perception were made clear by an eighteenth-century Anglo-Irishman, George Berkeley, who in his later years became Bishop of Cloyne and a Platonist as well. What the youthful Berkeley did was to draw from Locke's analysis certain *subjectivist* conclusions which the older philosopher sought to avoid. Berkeley heartily seconded Locke's announcement that what we know are ideas, and that these ideas are of two kinds—sensations, and reflections of the mind upon these sensations. Now, if what we know consists of ideas and ideas only, if an idea cannot be compared with a "thing," but only with another idea, what evidence is there of the existence of physical objects? None whatever, said Berkeley.

Consider for a moment, says Berkeley, an instance of what we take to be a physical object—a cherry. A cherry is a *collection of sensations*—red color, soft to touch, round shape, tart taste, etc. Can we point to a property of the cherry which is not a sense property? If there is *something more* to the cherry over and above a collection of sensations, we should be able to tell what it is. An underlying substance or substratum perhaps? But there is no contact between us and this *assumed* substratum; there is not one whit of evidence for the existence of anything besides the sensed qualities of the cherry. In Berkeley's words:

> I see this *cherry*, I feel it, I taste it: and I am sure *nothing* cannot be seen, or felt, or tasted: it is therefore *real.* Take away the sensations of softness, moisture, redness, tartness, and you take away the cherry. Since it is not a being distinct from sensations; a *cherry*, I say, is nothing but a congeries of sensible impressions, or ideas perceived by various senses; which ideas are united into one thing (or have one name given to them)

by the mind; because they are observed to attend each other. . . . Hence, when I see, and feel, and taste, in sundry certain manners, I am sure the *cherry* exists, or is real; its reality being in my opinion nothing abstracted from those sensations. But if by the word *cherry* you mean an unknown nature distinct from all those sensible qualities, and by its existence something distinct from its being perceived; then indeed I own, neither you, nor I, nor anyone else can be sure it exists.[3]

To Berkeley, then, the cherry is a collection of sense qualities and nothing more. The dualist analysis of perception asserts a distinction between a complex of sensations or "ideas" and an external object. Berkeley denies this distinction. The complex of sensations *is* the object. The dualist claims that this complex of sensations is *caused* in us by something outside us. Berkeley replies that he admits that our sensations are caused by a source other than ourselves. He maintains, however, that the nature of this source is *not* physical. We cannot demonstrate the existence of the "material substances" which common opinion wrongly supposes to exist. For we cannot compare our sensations with their alleged physical causes.

Berkeley reinforces his argument by collapsing the distinction between primary and secondary qualities. He agrees with Locke that secondary qualities have subjective status only and do not exist independently of perception. "The red and blue which we see," he says, "are not real colours, but certain unknown motions and figures which no man ever did or can see."[4] To prove the subjectivity of secondary qualities Berkeley uses the argument (as old as the Greek Sophists and Skeptics) of the relativity of sense

[3] G. Berkeley, "Three Dialogues," in *A New Theory of Vision and Other Writings*, New York, Dutton, 1934, p. 287. (PB: Liberal Arts, Bobbs-Merrill, Indianapolis.)

[4] Berkeley, "Three Dialogues," p. 218.

perception. What is sweet to one man may be sour to another. Lukewarm water can be made to seem hot to one hand and cold to another. But the same substance cannot be sweet and not-sweet or hot and not-hot.

The primary qualities, "extension, figure, solidity, gravity, motion, and rest," are just as relative to perception as the secondary qualities. Take extension, for example. A tower, looked at from nearby, appears large and square-cornered. Seen from afar, however, it seems small and round. Moreover, we infer the very existence of the primary qualities from the secondary or sense qualities. How do we know that an object takes up space except by our *seeing* a colored patch, *touching* something hard, etc.? Now if both primary and secondary qualities are relative to perception—if neither has absolute or independent existence in itself—then *all* the qualities of so-called physical objects are relative to the perceiving mind. No idea can exist without the mind, says Berkeley. Things are collections of ideas. Therefore, things do not and cannot exist apart from minds. *Esse est percipi.* For a thing to be, it must be perceived.

When asked by Boswell how he would refute Bishop Berkeley, the illustrious Dr. Johnson fetched a nearby stone a mighty kick and roared, "I refute him *thus!*" Like many who read Berkeley, Dr. Johnson thought that the philosopher was denying that objects in the external world are "real." But if we have followed Berkeley's argument carefully, we can see that it was not his intention to deny the reality of objects. Tables and chairs and stones are real. They are *not* "optical delusions." They are exactly what they appear to be. Berkeley's theory of perception is not subjectivist in the sense that it means the visible world is but the vaporous stuff of my imagination. To Berkeley, the objectivity of the world lies in the fact that a common process of images flows through all minds in rational and orderly sequence. That these images are fundamentally located in minds rather than caused in us by external material bodies does not—in Berkeley's view—destroy their objectivity. What he is denying is that the world is a mass of matter, that tables and chairs are material substances throwing off "appearances" at us. Experience gives us tables and chairs and stones as collections of sensations, as perceptions and nothing more. These objects have no existence apart from perceiving minds, although my mind or yours may not happen to be perceiving them at the moment. If some critics object that what *they* mean by "real" is existence independent of anyone's mind, Berkeley would reply that reality in *that* sense is an indemonstrable as well as a wholly unnecessary assumption.

Berkeley: Other Minds and God's; Solipsism

Reality, then, says Berkeley, is a system of minds. There are minds other than my own—other perceivers in whose collective consciousness the external world exists. Above all, there is a supreme Mind or Spirit which is the cause, distinct from myself, of the mighty complex of ideas which is the visible world. This Mind is God, who produces in us that system of perceptions which, taken as an ordered whole, we call Nature. "There is an *omnipresent eternal Mind*," says Berkeley, "which knows and comprehends all things and exhibits them to our view in such a manner, and according to such rules as he himself hath ordained, and by us termed the *laws of nature*."[5] Thus we can see that Berkeley's analysis of perception has led him at length to the metaphysical doctrine of *idealism*, the view that the fundamental character of reality is that of mind or thought. God produces sensations in us without *need* of matter or a

[5] Berkley, "Three Dialogues," p. 266.

physical world. Our perceptions derive their order and coherence from the nature and operations of the Divine Mind.

Berkeley's critics complain that the philosopher supports his mentalistic theory of bodies only by anchoring the theory on God. That God, they say, is a *deus ex machina*, a device arbitrarily brought in to save his doctrine. But in fairness to Berkeley we must point out that in making God the ultimate cause of the totality of perceptions in minds (that is to say, Nature, the external world), he is doing no more than the majority of classical philosophers who held that God was the first or ultimate cause of the world. In claiming that God (the supreme Mind) keeps the world in being by his eternal knowledge of it, Berkeley simply offers his own individual variety of the traditional metaphysical doctrine that God is a *sustaining* cause, the continuous creator of the world.

A more ticklish question concerns Berkeley's reason for accepting so readily the existence of *other minds.* How does he know that minds other than his own exist, when he can know of their existence only by perceiving the behavior of human *bodies* whose physical nature Berkeley denies? If Berkeley's analysis of bodies into complexes of sensations (*his* sensations) is correct, what warrant has he for assuming that there are any perceiving minds besides his own? I do not observe another person's mind, but *infer* this via analogy by observing his body. But the body of another is just as much a congeries of my sensations as a cherry or a tower. If all I know are perceptions, and these perceptions are *my* perceptions, what evidence have I for the existence of other perceivers. Indeed, how do I know that there exists anything but *myself?* Thus, by pushing Berkeley's analysis of perception to its logical conclusion, it would seem that I find myself in what Ralph Barton Perry called the *egocentric predicament.* I cannot get beyond my own "ideas." I am walled in by my perceptions. Hence I find myself in the strange position of *solipsism,* the belief that only I and my thoughts exist. So a common line of objection to Berkeley's theory of perception goes like this: A theory which leads to a false conclusion must itself be false. But Berkeley's theory of perception leads to solipsism, and solipsism is false. Therefore. . . .

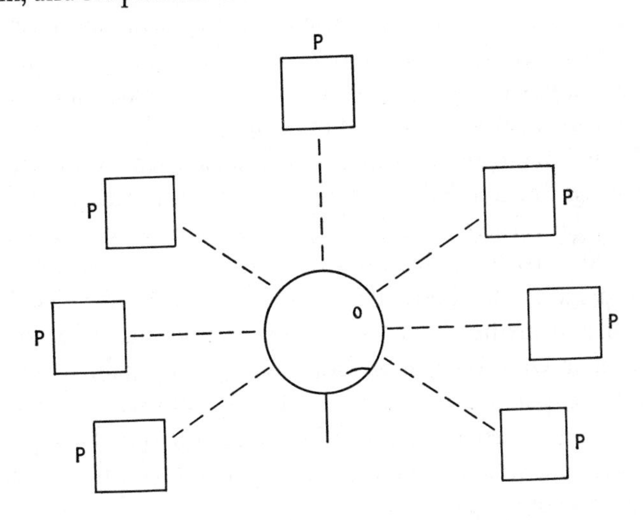

Can Solipsism Be Refuted?

Solipsism is the belief that I alone exist. No major philosopher has ever accepted solipsism.[6] On the contrary, philosophers have done everything they could to avoid it. But it is sometimes said that solipsism cannot be refuted. Since the world and everything in it is known to me through

6 Bertrand Russell states that he once received a letter from the eminent logician, the late Mrs. Christine Ladd Franklin, saying that she was a solipsist and was surprised nobody else was. "Coming from a logician," Russell remarks, "this surprise surprised me." *Human Knowledge,* p. 180.

sense perception, I cannot get outside my percepts to verify the existence of something other than these perceptions. The universe is my perception of it; the world is my Idea. There is no way of *disproving* that my perceptions alone exist. On the basis of these considerations, it is often said that solipsism is logically irrefutable. But because a certain position is "logically irrefutable," it does not on that account follow that it is true. Schopenhauer recommends that we treat this argument of "theoretical egoism" as an army would handle a frontier fortress. "The fortress cannot indeed be taken, but the garrison can never sally forth from it, and therefore we pass it by without danger, and are not afraid to have it in our rear."[7] Further, we can ask what is meant by the word "refutable." Even those who claim that solipsism cannot be refuted usually admit that it is psychologically impossible to hold this position and that the attitude of a sane person who pretends to hold it may be dismissed as trivial and artificial, as "classroom scepticism." Moreover, even if it were true, solipsism could not be held by more than one person. It would be fatally awkward for two solipsists to meet each other in the street. But if solipsism cannot be a serious conviction, why not take this fact as a refutation of solipsism?[8]

There may be such a state of affairs as *moral solipsism.* All of us know at least one person who acts as if he were the only person in the world—the man who acts as if everything and everyone should function as an extension of *him.* In many cases, we would have to admit that this person is ourselves, that it requires a considerable act of the will on our part to transcend our own ego. The problem of breaking through the self to others is one of the root

[7] A. Schopenhauer, *The World as Will and Idea,* vol. 1, bk. 1, p. 19.

[8] See A. P. Ushenko, *Power and Events,* Princeton University Press, 1946, p. 87.

puzzles of the philosophy we call Existentialism. Much of the British philosophy of our century has tended to center around the problem of *epistemological* solipsism (Russell, Ayer) while Continental philosophy has been fascinated by the problem of *moral* solipsism (Sartre).

Russell's Analysis of Perception; a Causal Theory

Bertrand Russell once said that a physiologist examining the brain of a patient is actually seeing his own brain.[9] When he made this startling remark, Russell was thinking of the scientific analysis of perception. From a physiological point of view, sense perception is a highly complex and indirect affair. When we see a cat or any other physical object, certain light waves coming from an external source act upon the eye in such a way that nerve currents produce a stimulus within the brain. The effect of this brain stimulus is "seeing a cat." If what science tells us is true, our eyes and ears function as intermediate transmission stations in the chain of events which constitutes sensory perception. Our visual and auditory apparatuses act as delicate selectors of certain light and sound waves. They transform these impulses, which are sent along nerve paths to certain areas of the brain. In the brain the impulses are further transformed into sensory experiences which fall into patterns instantaneously interpreted by us as "cat" or "table." Indeed, it is theoretically possible, by means of application of electrical stimulus to the proper brain area, to produce the sight of a cat when there is no cat in the ordinary sense.[10]

[9] Bertrand Russell, *An Outline of Philosophy*, London, G. Allen, 1927, p. 146. (PB: Meridian, World Publishing, Cleveland.)

[10] One of the practical consequences of current researches by neuroanatomists may be the possibility of artifically stimulating the brain in blind persons to produce significant flashes so that by means of these "letters" they may be able to read.

Now if scientific analysis of perception is reliable, thinks Russell, we must admit that seeing a cat or a star is in a very important respect an event in the brain. "What occurs when I see a star," he says, "occurs as the result of light-waves impinging on the retina and causing a process in the optic nerve and brain; therefore the occurrence called 'seeing a star' must be in the brain."[11] But if we concede this, then we must also concede that the external world as a whole is a series of brain events. And if the external world is no more than this we seem to be moving rapidly toward solipsism. How does Russell avoid the solipsist's predicament?

Russell's answer takes the form of a dualistic theory of perception. Percepts have independently existing external causes. Between the two exists a relationship of correspondence, although this correspondence is limited. If science is true, our percepts do not greatly resemble their ultimate sources. To common observation, the sun is a rather small yellow disk. To the astrophysicist, the sun is a body many times larger than the earth, the scene of enormous electrical activity. But there *is* a correlation between our perceptual world and the world of external objects. This correlation Russell explains in terms of the *continuity of causal lines* between the two.

Source $\longrightarrow a \longrightarrow b \longrightarrow c \longrightarrow d \longrightarrow$ Percept

Each one of the terms in this series, which represents the chain of events leading to a perception, is independent and may be qualitatively quite different from any other. For example, the nerve impulse traveling along a nerve path toward the brain is an event independent of the percept of

[11] Bertrand Russell, *Our Knowledge of the External World*, rev. ed., London, G. Allen, 1949, p. 129.

the sun, and it does not resemble its source, which is the sun itself. But in the percept of the sun may be correlated with the sun in that the percept is causally connected with the sun through the chain of intermediate events.

We may say further, Russell tells us, that there is a *similarity* between the "ordinary" world of experience and the system of events which causes these experiences, if we understand by "similarity" a correspondence of *structure.* Considers (*A*) the score of Beethoven's C *Minor Symphony* as it rests on the stand before the conductor, and (*B*) the sounds we hear when we listen to a radio broadcast of a recording of the conductor's interpretation of the symphony.[12] Now *A* and *B* have a structural similarity despite the many intermediate stages which occur between the score and our hearing of the music. While some of these stages are qualitatively different from and independent of one another—the musicians' translation of notes into sounds, the transcription of sounds into impressions on tape, the change of sound waves into radio waves—they all center about a structure which is constant. Analogously, the perceptual world and the system of external causes which produces these perceptions in us have a common structure. The principle of constancy of structure, says Russell,

> . . . implies that in circumstances which occur frequently, but not invariably, the structure of a percept is the same as that of each of a series of occurrences, leading backward in time to an original occurrence. . . . This original occurrence is what we are said to "perceive" when it is held that different people can "perceive" the same object. . . . The sameness of structure between our sensational experiences and their physical

[12] In his music score analogy, Russell adapts an illustration used by Wittgenstein (*Tractatus,* 4.014) to explain the "picture" relation between language and the world. See Chapter 2, p. 70.

causes explains how it comes about that naive realism, though false, gives rise to so little confusion in practice.[13]

Phenomenalism

Phenomenalism is a theory of perception that has much in common with Berkeley's analysis of objects perceived. It is definitely not a causal theory of perception, for it denies a dualism between perceptual experiences and their supposed independent causes. The object as perceived by me and the object which "causes" the perception are one and the same. As perceived, a table is a combination of percepts or *sense data*—rectangular brown surface, hard and smooth, etc. Now consider the "real" table which a dualist or causal theory tends to represent as existing independently of us and "causing" the appearance of the table in us. To a phenomenalist, there is no distinction between the two; the "real" and the perceived table are one and the same thing. Appearance is reality. Describing the phenomenalist position, W. P. Montague (himself not a phenomenalist) says:

> There are no things in themselves, but only things in relation to our experience. There is no "reality" hidden behind the veil of sensory appearance; the appearances of things are their reality. And for the sceptic to bewail the fact that we can know nothing but appearance is as silly as it would be to bewail the fact that we have nothing to wear but clothes and nothing to eat but food.[14]

The phenomenalist analysis of perception is usually associated with certain types of empiricism or positivism, that is, with doctrines which claim that sense experience is the

[13] Bertrand Russell, *Human Knowledge*, New York, Simon and Schuster, 1948, pp. 473–474. (PB: Essandess Paperbacks, Simon and Schuster.)

[14] W. P. Montague, *The Ways of Knowing*, London, G. Allen, 1925, p. 185.

most reliable form of knowledge. Hume defined physical objects as collections of sense data and no more. Ernst Mach imported phenomenalism into nineteenth-century philosophy of science, stating that "Bodies do not produce sensations, but complexes of sensation make up bodies."[15]

The phenomenalist's analysis of perception resembles Berkeley's in that both hold that what is experienced (sense data) is real, and that there is nothing "behind" sense data—no Lockian "substance" or substratum distinct from the sense qualities and "causing" them. But phenomenalism denies Berkeley's doctrine of *esse est percipi*—that for an object to exist it must be perceived. Admitting Berkeley's contention that we cannot prove that anything exists unperceived, the phenomenalist states that the independent existence of objects can easily be verified if only "independent existence" is taken in the proper sense. To say of a physical object that it exists is to say that it is possible to perceive it. Consider the sentence "There is a telephone in that cabinet." If this sentence is taken (and the phenomenalist thinks it should be so taken) as the equivalent in meaning of the sentence, "If you were to open that cabinet, you would see a telephone," then there is no problem at all about verifying the independent existence of the telephone. To the phenomenalist, Berkeley is right in his analysis of perceived objects as collections of sense data—right too in seeing the uselessness of constructing unnecessary "material causes" to project these sense data. But he is wrong in pushing his phenomenalistic analysis over into an exaggerated *mentalistic* interpretation of the sensible world. A phenomenalist analysis need not lead one to the conclusion that this is a world of minds or spirits. It is enough that analysis of physical objects *in sense-data language* is more useful,

[15] E. Mach, *Analysis of Sensations*, La Salle, Ill., Open Court, 1915, p. 29. (PB: Dover, New York.)

tends to make fewer mistakes, than does a dualistic, representational, or "causal" theory of perception. Anything we know about physical objects may be expressed in statements referring to sense data.

One of the difficulties encountered by phenomenalism is the situation the phenomenalist meets when he tries to reconcile his doctrine of "appearances are reality" with scientific descriptions of objects. To the normal observer, a table is a brown, hard, solid, static object. To the physicist, however, the table is a dynamic society of atoms, continually gaining and losing electrons. If appearances *are* reality, how does the phenomenalist dispose of the scientific description of the table, which is certainly not a description in terms of ordinary appearances or sense data?

One answer to this difficulty is given by the nineteenth-century philosophers Ernst Mach and Hans Vaihinger, to the effect that scientific descriptions like the atomic theory are *fictions* which do not correspond to anything real. Scientific statements about unobservable entities like atoms are to be taken only "as if" they were true. Such descriptions are instruments for finding our way about more easily in the world. They are not descriptions of what is real. Such fictions, says Vaihinger, are "practically useful and necessary though theoretically false deviations from reality."[16] Variations of this "fictionalism" are present in certain more recent positivistic philosophies of science.

Some contemporary phenomenalists, however, reject the fictionalist account of scientific descriptions because it appears to reduce scientific propositions about the external world to false statements. While atomic events cannot be observed in the same way we observe rocks and trees, yet these micro-events are observable *theoretically*. An electron

[16] See H. Vaihinger, *The Philosophy of "As-If,"* C. K. Ogden, trans., New York, Harcourt, Brace & World, 1924, pp. 15, 16.

may be very much smaller than the wave length of light needed to make it visible to a human observer. Yet we may suppose the existence of a hypothetical superhuman observer who could directly see an electron with the help of light of wave lengths smaller than the electron. In other words, while micro-events are unobservable in the ordinary sense, they are observable *in principle.*[17]

Critics of phenomenalism believe that this reply does not dispose of the original difficulty. If what we observe and what is real are one and the same thing, are the atoms which we do *not* observe real or not? The introduction of a superhuman observer, say the anti-phenomenalists, is a strained attempt to "save the appearances." It amounts to no more than saying that all real things, whether ordinary objects or micro-events, are observable; but the latter are observable only in a very peculiar or Pickwickian sense.

Another objection to phenomenalism is that in its effort to avoid an "iron-curtain" theory of perception, it falls into what R. Chisholm calls *the sense-datum fallacy.*[18] The phenomenalist believes that if there *is* a difference between a material object and its appearances, we can never get *behind* the appearances to the object itself. Therefore he says, "All we can observe is sense data." But this is false, if by "observe sense data" we mean that *we perceive sense impressions*—much as Locke's claim that the immediate objects of our knowledge are "ideas" or sensations. But sense impressions are not the *objects* of our perceptions; they do not stand between us and the object in such a way that we are fated never to know the object. A man's eyeglasses, stand between him and the object he is looking at. Yet it

17 See A. Pap, *Elements of Analytic Philosophy,* New York, Macmillan, 1949, p. 138.

18 "Phenomenalism" in *Perceiving: a Philosophical Study,* Cornell University Press, 1957, Appendix.

would be absurd to hold that what the man is looking at is the lenses of his glasses. He does not look *at* the lenses but *through* them.

CONCEPTUAL KNOWLEDGE OF THE EXTERNAL WORLD

Percepts and Concepts

Sense reports may be the simplest elements of human knowledge; but we cannot give an adequate account of our knowledge of the external world solely in terms of sense perceptions. A world consisting of sense data alone would be confused and meaningless, a world like that present to a tiny infant, echoing with the sound of "a thousand twangling instruments" and shot through with random shapes and lights. In a world composed only of percepts, all knowledge would be immediate and none inferred.

Now human knowledge is largely *inferred* knowledge. This is not to say that animals cannot infer, and that they are restricted to sense data. Animals *build up* knowledge out of sense data as humans do. But human knowledge is distinguished by its power to *explain* and *to interpret* immediate happenings. It has the capacity to perform inferences of a complexity and generality that far outrun those within the powers of the cleverest nonhuman animal.

We may call that all-important area of human knowledge which goes beyond what is immediately given in sense experience *conceptual* knowledge. Sensations are immediate and particular, like a flash of light or the sound of a bell. Percepts, or complexes of sensations are particular, like my perception of you walking toward me. But *concepts* are not particular; they are general and abstract, like the notion of "mammal" or "electron." Whether it concerns the realm of everyday experience or that revealed to us by science, our knowledge of the external world is saturated with concepts. No description of the world is possible without their constant employment.

There is no wide and observable gulf between percepts and concepts. What some call concepts others call percepts. Indeed, it is very difficult to say just where the percepts leave off and the concepts begin. For example, we would naturally be inclined to say that our knowledge of *physical objects*, like tables and trees, is perceptual rather than conceptual. But the notion of a physical object existing independently of me and preserving its identity from moment to moment is to some extent a learned, built up, or inferred notion. Anyone who doubts this should watch the behavior of a very young baby who drops his rattle out of sight. When this happens, the infant behaves as if the rattle had dropped out of existence as well. Small babies are Berkeleyans; to them, *esse est percipi.*

There are *gradations* in concepts, or *constructs*, as they are sometimes called, according to the degree of abstractness they represent. The notion of an independently existing physical object may be regarded as a concept of the lowest grade, a very elementary construct. Above this may be ranked other types of concepts of progressively higher degrees of abstractness. A sample selection from the hierarchy of concepts may be given as follows:

1. The concept of an independently existing physical object.
2. The concept of "minds" or selves other than our own.
3. Concepts of general classes such as "plant" or "metal."
4. Concepts of general properties such as "red" or "heat."
5. Concepts of "laws" of physical nature such as "Gases expand when heated."
6. The concept of "cause."
7. Concepts of a highly abstract nature employed in scientific descriptions of the external world such as that of "gravity" or "relativity."
8. Purely mathematical or logical concepts.

If we concede that only particulars are immediately given in experience, then all of our knowledge employing notions like those above must be considered to be in lesser or greater degree *conceptual* knowledge. Now the question is: If these concepts are not given to us directly by sense experience, what validity do they have? How can we be sure that there are situations in the external world which correspond to these concepts? Two famous answers to this question are those given respectively by David Hume and Immanuel Kant. Hume says that most of these concepts have no demonstrable validity simply because they are *not* given in experience. Kant says these concepts *have* validity, but that their nature is essentially mental. They are the products of the *mind* operating upon material of unknowable character.

The Skepticism of David Hume

From premises laid down by Locke and Berkeley, Hume proceeded to draw some remarkably skeptical conclusions. Like his predecessors, Hume took the primary data of human knowledge to be perceptions and reflections about perceptions. To the question "What do we know?" Hume answers that we know (1) sense impressions and (2) ideas or "faint images" of these impressions (by the latter we "remember" the impressions). According to Hume, human knowledge is built up by *association* of these impressions according to certain patterns: (a) similarity, (b) contiguity, and (c) invariable sequence. All we are given in experience is impressions, perceptions, sense data.

Now Hume claims that these impressions are always given to us as *separate* and *distinct* from one another. "All our distinct perceptions," he says, "are distinct existences, and the mind never perceives any real connection among distinct existences."[19] Through *habit* we associate these impressions with one another, as, for instance, our association of the visual impression we name "dog" with the auditory impression we call "bark." But as far as *experience* goes, these impressions are all given as distinct and separate elements.

Consider a physical object—for example, a box. Locke admitted that all we know directly of the box is a complex of sense data—"red," "hard," "square," etc. On the basis of these distinct impressions, Locke concluded (though not without hesitation) that underlying the impressions was a *thing*, a substance, something enduring through time; something that was the *same*, although its qualities might change. But, Hume points out, if all we know of the box amounts to a collection of separate, sense qualities we have no right to infer the existence of a supposed enduring substratum which is the "same" from one moment to the next. Hume agreed with Berkeley that since all we know of physical objects is that they are collections of sensible properties, there is no proof that physical objects are anything more than "ideas" in our minds.

But Hume disagreed with Berkeley on the latter's assumption without proof that there were "minds" other than his own. Experience gives us no warrant for the assumption of any such thing as a mind or self. Just as experience tells me that this box is a collection of sense data and nothing more, so experience tells me that my "mind" or "self" is just a bundle of perceptions and no more. Says Hume: "What we call a *mind* is nothing but a heap or collection of different perceptions united together by certain relations, and supposed, tho falsely, to be endowed with a perfect simplicity and identity."[20]

[19] D. Hume, *A Treatise on Human Nature*, Oxford, Clarendon Press, 1896, p. 636. (PB: Meridian, World Publishing, Cleveland.)

[20] Hume, *Treatise*, p. 207.

Now if we grant, says Hume, that all we know are sense impressions, or ideas built up out of them, and if we grant further that experience gives us no hint of any necessary connection between them, then we must concede that we have no ground (other than that of habit or custom) to justify belief in the existence of enduring *physical objects* which preserve their identity from one moment to the next; we have no basis on which to infer the existence of enduring *selves* or *minds* which underlie the string of sensory impressions or memories of these.

Hume's Analysis of Causality

Having shown to his own satisfaction how infirm are the foundations of our belief in the existence of physical objects and enduring selves, Hume next turns to demolish two other presuppositions of science and practical life—induction and causality. We have already encountered Hume's arguments on induction. Experience presents us with *particulars*, that is, with separate and detached instances of sensory impressions. With no warrant other than habit, we slip in a *connection* between these instances. Upon a set of given particulars we superimpose a *general* principle which experience has failed to provide. Experience gives us separate occurrences of "This *A* is *B*," "This *A* is *B*," etc. After a while, we conclude that "All *A* is *B*" and use this generalization to predict that future *A*'s will be *B*'s. But, Hume tells us, however much habit may incline us to such general conclusions, we must admit that they are not given to us in our observation of natural bodies.

Hume's analysis of *causality* is similar to his approach to induction. Does experience provide us with any instance of *A* causing *B?* If by "cause" is meant some *universal and necessary relation* between *A* and *B*, a relation which is more than *A together with B*, the answer is "No." "Causality" is a term for a *general* relation, while experience gives us particulars only. A proper definition of cause, says Hume, amounts to no more than this: "An object precedent and contiguous to another, and so united with it that the idea of the one determines the mind to form the idea of the other, and the impression of the one to form a more lively idea of the other."[21]

Experience may furnish us with numerous separate instances of *A attended by B*. Experience may even go so far as to offer us *invariable sequences* in each of which *A* is followed by *B*. But each experience of *B* followed *A* is always something separate and distinct from the next. Sense observation tells us "*A* then *B*," "*A* then *B*," and so on. No more. Now through *habit*, says Hume, we insert between *A* and *B* a fictitious necessary connection—which we call a "Causal relation"—and conclude that "*A* causes *B*." But we do not find this necessary connection in experience.

Hume asks us to consider an example. Whenever I go into my garden, he says, I notice that a certain stone is warm to touch. At the same time, I also observe that the sun is shining. I further note that sometimes the stone is cold. At these times, the sun is not shining. I then infer that *the sun warms the stone*. But sense observation does not disclose this causal connection. What I do observe is (*A*) the sun, and (*B*) the warm stone, and again (*A*) the sun, and (*B*) the warm stone, and again and again. Since human inclination tends to supply the necessary connection which experience does *not* supply, I say, "The sun *causes* the stone to get warm," or more briefly, "The sun warms the stone." My conclusion is reinforced by repeated observations that when the sun is not shining, the stone is not warm. But we should note that our conclusion does *more*

[21] Hume, *Treatise*, p. 172.

than sum up what we have actually observed. We have experienced particular instances of associated facts. But "cause" means some kind of general relation between these facts, some kind of universal and necessary (unceasing) connection. "Causality" is the name of a concept and has the usual general and abstract quality of concepts. But the ground of the concept, says Hume, is not to be found in sense experience, since the *extent* of the concept is far wider than the extent of the experienced facts. The true ground of the concept lies simply in the "lively expectation," born of habit, that events we have in the past found to be *associated*—that is, presented together—will continue to be associated in the future. Thus, remembering in the past that pouring water on the fire is immediately followed by the fire going out, I expect the same result this time.

Thus, by pushing the Locke-Berkeley analysis of knowledge to extreme conclusions, Hume has reached a position of skepticism concerning our ability to show that the general character of concepts is grounded in correspondingly general patterns in Nature. Percepts are given in experience, but concepts are not. There are no good reasons to justify our belief in the existence of those universal and necessary connections which men suppose to exist in Nature and to which they appeal to justify inductive and causal inference.

We should note that Hume's skepticism, and the solipsism to which this skepticism appears to lead, is cheerfully admitted by its author to have no relation to practical life. Hume tells us that he does not for a moment doubt that there are independently existing physical objects like the backgammon board before him. Nor does he doubt that he, David Hume, is something more than a bundle of sensations. Nor does he doubt general statements like "Fire burns" or causal inferences like "Water quenches thirst."

What I do doubt, says Hume, is the *possibility of any rational justification* of these beliefs. I told them on no basis other than instinct, inclination, habit, or custom.

Kant's Problem

Hume's skepticism struck the great German philosopher Immanuel Kant as a challenge to the very foundations of philosophy and science. It was the warning voice of David Hume, Kant tells us, "which many years ago first interrupted my dogmatic slumber, and gave my investigations in the field of speculative philosophy a quite new direction."[22] Both philosophy and science, Kant perceived, presuppose the validity of universal or general judgments such as those of inductive generalization and causal inference. If Hume is right, and there is no foundation in *experience* for these indispensable general judgments, what basis can there possibly be for them? If there is no rational justification of our belief in necessary connections between things in Nature, then the foundations of both philosophy and science rest on thin air. Should the situation actually be as Hume represents it, thought Kant, the only defensible philosophic attitude is skepticism.

If skepticism is to be avoided, says Kant, we must show how those universal and necessary connections, which Hume claims experience does not provide, are rationally justifiable. Or, in Kant's formidable terminology, we must show how a priori synthetic judgments are possible.[23]

[22] I. Kant, *Prolegomena to Any Future Metaphysics*, P. Carus, ed., La Salle, Ill., Open Court, 1902, p. 6. (PB: Open Court.)

[23] Inductive and causal judgments are *synthetic* and unlike *analytic* judgments, because the definition of their subjects does not disclose their predicates. They are a priori since their general or universal character is never given in experience; that is, we do not directly observe that *all* phosphorus is inflammable. Contrasting with a priori judgments are a posteriori judgments which *are* supported by direct experience. "This box is red" is an example of an a posteriori judgment.

Hume pointed out that in inductive inference sense experience gives us separate and unconnected particulars, "This *A* is *B*," "This *A* is *B*," etc. In causal inference sense experience offers us again only separate particulars, "*X* then *Y*," "*X* then *Y*," etc. Whence comes the universal and necessary character of the judgments "All *A* is *B*" and "*X* causes *Y*" which we so swiftly form from these particular and disconnected items of experience?

Kant's Categories

Kant's answer is this: The universal and necessary quality of causal, inductive, and other judgments of a general nature is determined *by the structure of mind itself*. The mind is not like an inert block of wax passively receiving and recording the impressions of sense, as Locke and the other British sensationalists held. The mind is a creative, dynamic, *active* process. It is equipped with certain innate forms which order and interpret sense experience.

The data which sense experience presents to us are first oriented in *space* and *time*. Now space and time have no objective existence independently of us. They are forms of the mind which impress themselves on all human experience. After the data of experience are coordinated in space and time, that part of the mind Kant calls the "understanding" takes over. The "understanding" possesses twelve innate forms or *categories*. It is from the categories that our experience derives its quality of universality and necessary connectedness. Those general and necessary judgments which Hume declared impossible to justify are the products of the operation of the categories of the mind upon the stuff of experience. In a causal inference, for example, experience provides us with the data "*X* then *Y*," "*X* then *Y*," etc. These data are then interpreted by the category of *causality*, and the judgment "*X* causes *Y*" results. Different types of general judgments are produced by the operation of other appropriate categories upon the data of experience. The role of Kant's categories may very roughly be illustrated by the accompanying diagram.

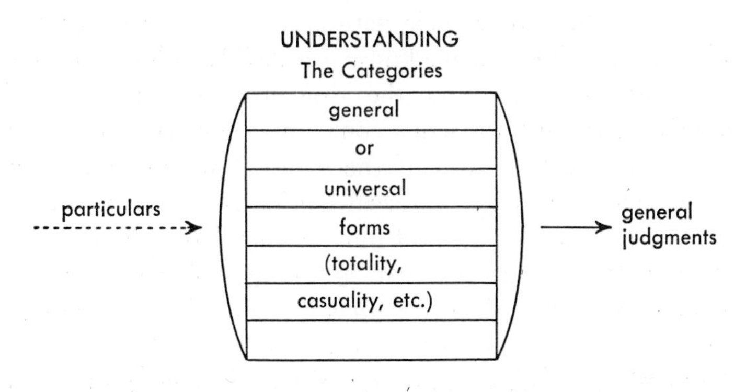

"*Percepts Without Concepts Are Blind*"

Knowledge in which universal and necessary judgments are present is *conceptual.* Both percepts and concepts are elements of human knowledge, the former distinguished by their *particular* and immediate character, the latter by *general* nature. Percepts are provided by experience. Concepts, according to Kant, are formed by the internal structure of the mind itself. Both percepts and concepts are necessary ingredients in any act of knowledge which does not lead to deception. "Concepts without percepts are empty," says Kant. "Percepts without concepts are blind."[24]

Any concept formed without a basis in sense experience will be little better than a fiction, and percepts, without concepts to order and interpret them, cannot advance knowledge one step beyond themselves. For percepts lack the quickening, moving, creative element of conceptual knowledge which distinguishes human thought from the simple immediacy of sensation.

[24] See I. Kant, *Critique of Pure Reason,* Norman Kemp Smith, trans., New York, Humanities Press, 1950, p. 93. (PB: St. Martin's, New York.)

Phenomena and Things-in-Themselves

According to Kant, percepts derive from an objective source external to us. But, since percepts are organized by concepts which owe their nature to the structure of the mind, everything that we know is indelibly colored by our knowing faculty. Now the dramatic consequences of Kant's theory of knowledge come into view. We can never know the "real" nature of the external world or of any object within it, if by "external world" is meant the world as it exists independently of human knowledge. *Things-in-themselves,* as Kant calls them, are unknowable and forever hidden from us. What we *do* know are the appearances (*phenomena*) produced by the operation of the forms of the mind upon this unknowable X-world. The mind transforms things-in-themselves in such a way as to make them intelligible. Our world is one of appearances only; behind those appearances the understanding can never penetrate. In Kant's words:

> . . . Things which we see are not by themselves what we see. . . . They cannot, as phenomena, exist by themselves, but in us only. It remains completely unknown to us what the objects may be by themselves and apart from the receptivity of our senses. We know nothing but our manner of perceiving them, that manner being peculiar to us and not necessarily shared in by every being, though, no doubt by every human being.[25]

Kant's "Copernican Revolution"; Conclusion

Perhaps Kant's meaning can be made clearer by a familiar simile. A man born with undetachable blue spectacles of whose presence he was unaware would see the world blue and think it *was* blue. But we know that the blueness

[25] I. Kant, *Critique of Pure Reason,* rev. ed., Max Müller, trans., New York, Macmillan, 1922, p. 34.

comes, not from the world, but from the glasses. Now, if Kant's theory is correct, we are all born with minds like *ordering glasses.* Through these mental lenses there filters the flux of the external world in such a way that we see this world as an ordered, connected, rational whole. "Common sense" attributes this order, connectedness, and rationality *to the world.* But Hume's analysis of experience shows that experience does not warrant any such assumption. The only alternative, Kant believes, is to place the origin of the world order in the human mind itself. By finding the source of time, space, and the natural order as a whole within *mind* rather than in the external world, Kant believed that he had accomplished a "Copernican revolution" in philosophy.[26]

Is the phenomenal world, the world of science and common sense, *real?* It is certainly not illusion, says Kant. While we cannot say that the external world we know is *absolutely* real, we may say it is relatively or *phenomenally* real. The objects of perception, the vistas of Nature, the laws of science are the products of an interaction between ordering minds and the *ground* of experience. The existence of this ground or base (the world-in-itself) is beyond doubt, although we cannot know what it is like apart from human knowledge. The laws of Nature are not mere figments of a mind. Causality, physical uniformities, the law-like interaction of things and events, have a phenomenal objectivity; they are "in" the phenomenal world, not just "in" men.

Kant has offered a theory of knowledge to explain and to justify belief in the existence of orderly, scientific knowledge of the external world. He has claimed for con-

[26] In Kant's view, it may be more than just the *human mind* that orders our experience. He seems sometimes to hold that in the nature of things, over and above the individual human consciousness, is some sort of rational order with a logical structure in its own right. (We shall see in Chapter 7 how Hegel develops this notion.)

cepts, such as those of general laws and causal relations, the rational justification which Hume declared impossible. But this justification has been achieved only at the cost of a surrender of all claims to knowledge of the properties of the world as it is independent of human perception. In place of such claims, Kant offers a *critical* epistemology which holds that human knowledge has certain inherent *limitations*, that what we know is a world which reflects the structure of the human mind, a world fashioned and shaped by the categories of the understanding out of a raw material whose existence is indubitable but whose nature we can never know. Historically, this Kantian theory of knowledge led to significant developments in the metaphysics of *idealism*, the philosophic doctrine that the world of our experience is essentially of the nature of *thought*.

The Role of Concepts in Scientific Knowledge

An Alternative to Hume and Kant

Does conceptual knowledge give us reliable descriptions of the nature of the external world? Hume's analysis of knowledge appears to have shown that conceptual knowledge does not come to us directly from sense experience. Must we then accept as the only alternative Kant's theory that conceptual knowledge is valid but phenomenal only, that the external world we know is no more than *appearance*, an ordered image created by the human mind?

Let us consider some conditions of a third alternative. Such a theory would hold that concepts, while to an important degree the products of the human mind, are nevertheless *correlated with the structure of the external world*. That is, concepts are, to a degree, *constructed* by us; but they are not fictions, nor are they wholly products of innate forms of the mind.[27] Concepts are not given to us *as such* by experience, yet

[27] An analysis of conceptual knowledge in science in terms of "constructs," which are neither fictions nor products of Kantian categories,

descriptions of the nature of the external world taken as existing independently of human thought.

Concepts of Wave and Particle in Modern Physics

Consider two concepts used today in describing the nature of the atom. Scientists speak of the atom as a group of *particles.* Yet in dealing with certain problems it is often necessary to describe the basic processes of physical nature in terms of *waves* or stresses within an electrodynamic *field.* The ancient concept of the atom was that of a particle, although of an indivisible particle. The notion of the atom as a tiny indivisible bit of matter was held in modern physics until the late nineteenth century, when the behavior of radioactive elements, such as uranium and radium, forced the beginning of a radical revision of the concept of the atom. Now we see the atom no longer as an indivisible particle but as a group or society of particles—protons, electrons, neutrons, etc., held together by powerful forces. Yet even in this highly modified contemporary view of the atom, the notion of ultimate micro-events as *particles* still remains.

In classical physics, *light* was successfully described in terms of *waves* rather than particles. True, Newton had suggested that light was made up of corpuscles, but it was generally held that there was little evidence for this theory. But in our own century, certain fundamental problems arose which required a reinterpretation of light in terms of corpuscles, and the name "photon" was given to the basic particle of light energy. To this day, the behavior of light seems to require description in terms of *both* wave and particle. These two concepts, however, do not seem compatible or consistent with one another, for the concept of "particle" entails that of "mass," while the notion of "wave" is related to mass only in a much more shadowy way. An analogous problem exists in regard to the nature of the electron. Evidence exists which supports the concept of the electron as a particle; evidence also exists which suggests that the electron is a wave.

At the heart of quantum mechanics, a theory basic to

twentieth century physics, is the possibility of one and the same sub-atomic event appearing either as a wave or as a particle. To resolve the contradiction, Bohr and Heisenberg offered the solution of *complementarity* which says that we cannot simultaneously measure a micro-event's position (a particle property) and its momentum (a wave property). Thus wave and particle both exist, but each only at the moment the physicist is measuring. Certain scientists, particularly in the Soviet Union, have challenged the complementarity way of resolving the wave-particle dualism.[28]

Now the lesson of the wave-particle dualism in modern physics may be this: "Wave" and "particle" are *concepts*, and concepts are not literal descriptions or mental photographs of the external world. They are human constructs which *interpret* the nature of the world even though they do not *create* it out of whole cloth. The conflict between the wave and particle concepts seems to indicate a certain limitation inherent in these valuable notions, a lack which up to the present time it has been impossible to remedy. But reflection on the history of science encourages us to believe that sooner or later a *new* concept will appear in modern physics which will reconcile and unify the wave and particle concepts, and which will at the same time achieve even greater success in explaining the nature of events in the external world.

Einstein on Concepts

According to Einstein, the nature of the external world is not immediately given in experience. What are given are *data*, the data of consciousness. There is only one way to pass from the data of consciousness to knowledge of the external world,

[28] Many Soviet theorists charged that the complementarity solution of the wave-particle dualism confused the objective reality of material micro-events with our knowledge about them, thus leading to a Kantianism or idealism inconsistent with the Soviet philosophy of dialectical materialism. (See ahead, "Dialectical Materialism," pp. 269–275.) A very interesting analysis of the controversy in the U.S.S.R. over quantum mechanics is Loren R. Graham's "Quantum Mechanics and Dialectical Materialism," *Slavic Review*, Sept. 1966.

and that is the way of *intellectual construction.* The most elementary concept of everyday experience is that of independently existing objects, such as the table in the room. The table, however, is not given to us as an independently existing object, but rather as a complex of sensations to which we attribute the name and concept "table." In Einstein's words: "In my opinion, it is of the greatest importance to be conscious of the fact that such a concept ['table'], like all other concepts, is of a speculative-constructive kind. Otherwise one cannot do justice to those concepts which in physics claim to describe reality, and one is in danger of being misled by the illusion that the 'real' of our daily experience 'exists really' and that certain concepts of physics are 'mere ideas' separated from the 'real' by an unbridgeable gulf."[29]

"Speculative-constructive" though they may be, such concepts as those of independently existing physical objects are not mere fancies, Einstein maintains. These concepts "stand in a relation of correspondence with our sensations." Now in physics, the correspondence or correlation between concepts and sensations becomes more and more indirect. But because the concepts of physics are highly abstract and only indirectly correlated with ordinary experience, it does not follow that they are fictions. Euclidean geometry contains the concept of a straight line. This concept may be correlated with physics if for a straight line we substitute a rigid rod. But a rigid rod is conceptual also, for we do not find perfectly rigid rods in everyday experience. Yet the notion of a rigid rod may be correlated with the metal rods of everyday experience if we coördinate this concept with others such as that of heat expansion. Scientific concepts are tied to experience in so far as they help us to establish correct and verifiable relations between our experiences.

Although convinced that our knowledge of the physical world is highly conceptual, Einstein believes that we should not feel ourselves confined to a choice of two alternatives between which contemporary physicists seem to him to waver:

[29] "Reply" in H. L. Samuel, *Essay in Physics,* New York, Harcourt, Brace & World, 1952, p. 158.

(1) that there is a physical reality, but its laws do not permit of any other than statistical expressions; (2) that there is nothing at all which "really" corresponds to the description of a physical situation—only "probabilities" exist. In opposition to this attitude, which seems to him undesirably skeptical, Einstein maintains a remarkably optimistic and "realist" position. "We believe," he says, "in the possibility of a theory which is able to give a complete description of reality, the laws of which establish relations between the things themselves and not merely between their probabilities."[30]

FURTHER READINGS

Adrian, E. D., *The Physical Background of Perception*, New York, Oxford University Press, 1947.

Ayer, A. J., *The Foundations of Empirical Knowledge*, New York, St Martin's, 1958. (PB: St Martins.)

Berkeley, George, "Three Dialogues Between Hylas and Philonous," *A New Theory of Vision and Other Writings*, New York, Dutton, 1934. (PB: Liberal Arts, Bobbs-Merrill, Indianapolis.)

Berkeley, George, *A Treatise Concerning the Principles of Human Knowledge*, La Salle, Ill., Open Court, 1903. (PB: Liberal Arts, Bobbs-Merrill, Indianapolis.)

Chisholm, Roderick M., *Perceiving: A Philosophical Study*, Cornell University Press, 1957. (PB: Meridian, World Publishing, Cleveland.)

De Broglie, L., *Matter and Light*, New York, Norton, 1939.

Eddington, A. S., *The Nature of the Physical World*, New York, Macmillan, 1929. (PB: Ann Arbor Paperbacks, Ann Arbor, Mich.)

Einstein, A., and L. Infeld, *The Evolution of Physics*, New York, Simon and Schuster, 1938. (PB: Essandess Paperbacks, Simon and Schuster.)

Hanson, N. R., *The Concept of the Positron*, London, Cambridge University Press, 1963.

[30] Samuel, *Essay in Physics*, p. 161.

Hume, David, *An Enquiry Concerning Human Understanding*, La Salle, Ill., Open Court, 1935. (PB: Gateway, Regnery, Chicago.)

Hume, David, *A Treatise on Human Nature*, Oxford, Clarendon, 1896. (PB: Meridian, World Publishing, Cleveland.)

Kant, Immanuel, *Critique of Pure Reason*, rev. ed., Max Müller (trans.), New York, Macmillan, 1922. (PB: St Martins, New York.)

Kant, Immanuel, *Prolegomena to Any Future Metaphysics*, P. Carus ed., La Salle, Ill., Open Court, 1902. (PB: Open Court.)

Lewis, C. I., *Mind and the World Order*, New York, Scribner, 1929. (PB: Dover, New York.)

Locke, John, *An Essay Concerning Human Understanding*, A. C. Fraser (ed.), London, Oxford University Press, 1894. (PB: Meridian, World Publishing, Cleveland.)

Mach, Ernst, *Analysis of Sensations*, La Salle, Ill., Open Court, 1915. (PB: Dover, New York.)

Margenau, Henry, *The Nature of Physical Reality*, New York, McGraw-Hill, 1950. (PB: McGraw-Hill.)

Merleau-Ponty, M., *The Phenomenology of Perception*, Colin Smith (trans.), New York, Humanities Press, 1962.

Meyerson, Emile, *Identity and Reality*, K. Loewenberg (trans.), New York, Macmillan, 1930. (PB: Dover, New York.)

Moore, G. E., "Proof of an External World" (British Academy Annual Philosophic Lecture, 1939), British Academy, *Proceedings*, 1939, vol. 25, pp. 273–300.

Price, H. H., *Perception* (1933), rev. ed., London, Methuen, 1961.

Russell, Bertrand, *Human Knowledge*, Simon and Schuster, 1948, pt. 3. (PB: Essandess, Simon and Schuster.)

Russell, Bertrand, *Our Knowledge of the External World* (rev. ed.), London, G. Allen, 1949. (PB: Mentor New American Library, New York.)

Vaihinger, H., *The Philosophy of "As-If,"* C. K. Ogden (trans.), Harcourt, Brace & World, 1924.

5

Methods of Knowledge

We can never arrive at the real nature of things from the outside. However much we investigate, we can never reach anything but images and names. We are like a man who goes round a castle seeking in vain for an entrance and sometimes sketching the facades.

—SCHOPENHAUER

In a dialogue called the *Theaetetus*, Plato has Socrates ask the young mathematician for whom the dialogue is named, "What is knowledge?" Theaetetus replies in effect, "Well, Socrates, there is the knowledge of the geometricians; the knowledge of the cobblers; the knowledge of the carpenters. . . ." But Socrates interrupts him, saying that he is not interested in having the various kinds of knowledge enumerated. He wants to find out what knowledge *is*. One of the answers suggested by Theaetetus is that "*Knowledge is true belief*." The definition is good as far as it goes. But—as Socrates points out in the *Theaetetus*—I may arrive at a belief which happens to be true, but my *reasons* for arriving at it may not be sound. For example, a jury may be convinced by the clever but invalid arguments of a lawyer that the defendant is not guilty. Now it may actually be the case that the defendant is in fact innocent. Yet the jury can hardly be said to have knowledge, if they arrived at this conclusion for the wrong reasons.[1] That is why Bertrand Russell defines knowledge as a *subclass* of true beliefs; I may be said to know something if I hold a true belief *and* have sound reasons to justify that belief.

Knowing How and Knowing That

There is another limitation of the definition of knowledge as true belief: it is onesided. "True belief" fits *knowing that* something is so. I believe that there are pandas in China, that Trotsky wrote an autobiography, that vinegar contains acetic acid. These are true beliefs, and—assuming that I hold them on the basis of good reasons—the word "knowledge" may properly be applied to them. But what about *knowing how?* You know how to tie a bowline knot, how to feed a small baby, how to operate a drill press, how to play Chopin's *Nocturne in E flat* on the piano. Surely you have knowledge of these things. But we would hardly say you have "true beliefs" about them—no more than Plato would say that the art of cobblers and cooks consists primarily of true beliefs. *Knowing that* things are so can usually be put rather easily into the form of statements, and hence is sometimes called "propositional knowledge." *Knowing how* fits less easily into propositional form, since it is more directly related to *action* than simply knowing that something is so. Of course, people write books with titles like "How to Play Chess" and "How to Navigate Small Boats," and these books are full of statements as well as illustrations. Nonetheless, it remains true that in philosophizing about knowledge, we tend to emphasize "knowing that" at the expense of "knowing how." People in academic life, like professors and dons, often talk as if propositional knowledge were the only kind of knowledge—or, at least,

[1] Plato, *Theaetetus,* 201. (References to the dialogues of Plato are usually made by the so-called Stephens numbers; these are marginal numbers which are the same for all modern editions of Plato. A similar method is used in citations from Aristotle's works.)

the most important kind. Gilbert Ryle warns against this tendency:

> Theorists have been so preoccupied with the task of investigating the nature, the source and the credentials of the theories that we adopt that they have for the most part ignored the question what it is for someone to know how to perform tasks. In ordinary life, on the contrary, as well as in the special business of teaching, we are much more concerned with people's competences than with their cognitive repertoires, with the operations than with the truths they learn. Indeed even when we are concerned with their intellectual excellences and deficiencies, we are interested less in the stocks of truths that they acquire and retain than in their capacities to find out truths for themselves and their ability to organize and exploit them, when discovered.[2]

Sources of True Beliefs

With these reservations let us accept the incomplete definition of knowledge as "true belief," and ask: from what general sources do we derive our beliefs, and are these sources reliable? We have already raised these questions in a *particular* form in connection with the problem of our knowledge of the external world. There we have said that our knowledge of physical Nature derives from sense observations (percepts) and from intellectual interpretations of them (concepts). Now we wish to put the question in a more *general* way. We all carry about with us a very large number of beliefs about many different things, and these beliefs we hold to be true. Now what are the various ways by which we derive our beliefs? What is the comparative reliability of these methods of obtaining belief? These questions are quite common in modern philosophy, and the

[2] Gilbert Ryle, *The Concept of Mind*, London, Hutchinson, 1949. (PB: Barnes & Noble, New York, p. 28.)

term *methodology* or *theory of inquiry* is used to name that part of philosophy which considers them.

In 1877 C. S. Peirce published an article called "The Fixation of Belief." *Belief*, said Peirce, is the opposite of *doubt*, and the two attitudes of mind may be contrasted as follows:

> Doubt is an uneasy and dissatisfied state from which we struggle to free ourselves and pass into the state of belief; while the latter is a calm and satisfactory state which we do not wish to avoid, or to change to a belief in anything else. On the contrary, we cling tenaciously, not merely to believing, but to believing just what we do believe.[3]

The irritation of doubt, Peirce said, causes a struggle to obtain belief. This struggle is *inquiry*. The object of inquiry is to find out, on the basis of what we already know, something else which we do not know. Now there are four ways of removing doubt and fixing our beliefs firmly. One is the method of *tenacity*, in which we hold fast to our beliefs simply because we want to continue believing them. Another is the a priori method, in which we support our beliefs by appealing to their alleged *reasonableness*. A third way is the method of *authority*, in which propositions are held to be true on the word of a powerful social agency such as church or state. (For the mass of mankind, says Peirce, there is perhaps no better method than this.) A fourth way of fixating belief is *scientific method*. This method begins with the study of observable occurrences. Hypotheses are formed to explain these occurrences. The conclusions derived from these hypotheses are then subjected to experimental verification. Of the four methods of fixating belief, Peirce held scientific method by far the most

[3] C. S. Peirce, "The Fixation of Belief," in Morris Cohen, ed., *Chance, Love, and Logic*, Harcourt, Brace & World, 1923, p. 15. (PB: J. H. Randall, Jr., J. Buchler, and E. Shirk, *Readings in Philosophy*, Barnes and Noble, New York.)

reliable, since it involves test by sensory observation and is open to public inspection.

Since Peirce's time American philosophers have shown much interest in classifying the various means of obtaining knowledge and in estimating their comparative value as methods of inquiry. The following division of the sources of knowledge may be considered typical:[4]

Authority
Intuition
Reason
Experience

AUTHORITY

A moment's reflection on the number of our beliefs that we have acquired through authority should convince us that this number is very great. One of the major problems of *historical knowledge* is the question of evaluating the credentials of authorities and the authenticity of the documents they use to support their claims—since comparatively few living people are direct witnesses of historical events. Nearly all of what we know through "book learning" comes to us on the testimony of others. The proportion of our beliefs that we have taken on the say-so of parents, teachers, friends, neighbors, government officials, clergymen, physicians, newspaper writers, and radio or television speakers is impressively large. That we are thus able by means of authority to increase our knowledge so greatly without going to the trouble of investigating the situation personally is a very wonderful thing. Indeed, the capacity to accumulate and to pass along large bodies of

[4] See, for example, W. P. Montague, *The Ways of Knowing*, London, G. Allen, 1925, pt. I.

knowledge to others is a human talent which gives man an immense advantage over the other animals.

Of course, there are dangers implicit in the way of knowledge of authority. Man is a credulous animal and tends to believe what he is told. Historically, philosophers (like Bacon and Descartes) have taken great pains to point out that authority is at least as important a source of error as it is of knowledge. But there are certain precautions which can be employed to reduce the perils implicit in the way of knowledge of authority. Some of these safeguards will become apparent as we examine the following distinctions.

In the first place, authority is not, strictly speaking, a "true" way of knowledge at all; it is a way of knowing in a derivative sense only. That is, authority always reduces to some other way of knowing which is not authority. For example, I may believe the statement "Copper is a better conductor of heat than iron" because I have read it in my physics textbook. But this proposition is originally derived *from somebody's experience.* Back of the propositions "Lhasa is the largest city in Tibet" and "Caesar crossed the Rubicon" stands somebody's presence in Lhasa and somebody's sight of Caesar. These propositions have been communicated to us by the testimony of others. But the persons who first believed in their truth did not derive their beliefs from someone's say-so but from personal experience.

In the second place, we must distinguish between authority as a means by which we *come to know* a proposition to be true and authority as the reason *why* a proposition is true. A reliable authority communicates truth; it does not make it. Any agency which claims that its authority *constitutes* the truth of the propositions it utters should be regarded with the most profound distrust. Suppose a child, told by its father that "Spinach is good for you," asks why, and is informed, "Because I say so. That's why." In making his authority constitute the goodness of spinach, the father allows his temper to cloud his good sense. It is authority conceived in this second way—that of constituting rather than communicating truth—that is today widely repudiated under the label of "authoritarianism." Rulers of twentieth-century totalitarian states have not hesitated to manufacture their own truth. The techniques employed in this efficient method of preserving power over ignorant men have been wittily satirized by George Orwell in his novel *1984* and by Ignazio Silone in *Bread and Wine*.

"An authority is only as good as his argument" is a prudent saying. It tells us that the reliability of an authority is inseparable from the *possibility of that authority's being checked by some other way of knowing*. Yet it would be foolish not to accept a proposition stated by a competent authority unless we had *personally* checked it. The technical and specialized character of much of modern knowledge requires our reliance on the opinions of experts within their respective fields of competence. The fact that the statements made by the authority in question are open to independent investigation is usually a sufficient warrant of reliability. If a reputable physicist who has been investigating the properties of the metal niobium tells us that it has a very low lattice heat capacity, we would not think of subjecting ourselves to rigorous training in laboratory technique simply in order to verify his statement. The possibility that we *could* do so, if we so desired, is assurance enough.

If, however, my history book tells me that Napoleon was defeated at Waterloo, and I am disposed to doubt the truth of that statement, it is not even theoretically possible for me to check it by personal observation. What I can do is to check it against the statements of other authorities trained in the field of history. If I find that all competent historians agree that Napoleon was defeated at Waterloo, I am faced with the following alternatives: (1) The statement "Napoleon was defeated at Waterloo" is true, or (2) expert historians, who have made independent investigation of the documents concerned, have one and all been made victims of an incredible deception or they themselves have engaged in an inexplicable conspiracy to deceive the students of the present day. Now I can ask: Of these alternatives, which is the more *reasonable?* That is, which alternative is more nearly consistent with a large number of propositions which we have independent grounds to believe to be true? Thus we have introduced as a check on authority a method of inquiry independent of authority, a method to which the classical name *reason* may be applied.

When authorities *disagree*, the question of determining which is in the right may be very complicated. Suppose two experts of roughly equal competence have examined a painting and have subjected it to exhaustive tests. Expert X says that it is a genuine Titian. Expert Y says that it is not. A third expert brought in to settle the dispute is unable to decide. In situations like this, evidence may exist which can be interpreted to support both contentions. But the total evidence may not be complete enough to be conclusive. Sometimes in such unsettled cases the only thing one can do is to suspend judgment in the hope that some further evidence can be turned up.

INTUITION

A Feeling in the Bones?

"Intuition" is often taken to mean a direct, immediate, and certain way of knowledge which dispenses with both the element of logical inference present in *reason* and the element of sensory observation associated with *experience*. When the writer of this book was a small boy, he secretly decided one Sunday to go to a baseball game instead of attending Sunday School. Now he had never before absented himself from Sunday School for a reason of this kind. On the day in question, he left the house at the usual time and walked part of the way through the usual streets. After enjoying as much of the ball game as coincided with the Sunday School period, he returned home to find his mother waiting for him at the door with lightnings playing about her head. Long after the storm had blown over, the mother confided that, as she was working in the kitchen that afternoon, a sudden conviction came to her that her boy was not in Sunday School. "It was a feeling that came over me all at once," she said, "I didn't know why, but I just *knew* you weren't there." From that day onward, the writer has entertained a wholesome respect for the way of knowledge called intuition.

Intuition and Mysticism

"Intuition" has been applied to many different kinds of knowledge situations. A common meaning (as in the incident related above) refers to a person's sudden feeling of certain knowledge for which there is no *apparent* evidence other than the power of the conviction itself. A related meaning concerns knowledge which has come to many remarkable characters in history by way of visions, interior illuminations, *aperçus*, inner voices, and the like. Such intuitions commonly have the effect of suddenly resolving metaphysical, moral, or religious conflicts within the person concerned. In many cases they effect a complete reorientation of life and action. Ancient Indian sages taught that a holy man, who subjected himself to long periods of self-discipline, would suddenly know the reality that lay behind the veil of Maya which is this world. In a famous passage of the *Symposium*, Plato says that a philosopher, after laboriously mounting upward by way of the disciplines of earthly love and mathematics, may achieve a vision of eternal beauty. Socrates and Joan of Arc differed widely in beliefs and culture, but both listened to inner voices at critical moments of their lives. St. Paul had a shattering vision on the road to Damascus and went forth to spread Christianity throughout the Roman world.

Such intuitions are characteristic of the way of knowledge of *mysticism*. The mystic is a saintly person who, after long exercise in prayer and ascetic self-denial, suddenly experiences a moment of luminous certitude; he "sees" beyond the world's illusion that one Divine Reality with which he feels himself united. Mystics of the religions of the West—St. Theresa, Ruysbroeck, Meister Eckhart, and others—all speak of an exhausting spiritual struggle (St. John of the Cross calls its most depressing moment "The Dark Night of the Soul") which is brought to an end by climactic experience of incandescence in which the mystic no longer "knows" but "sees."

Other Meanings of "Intuition"

"Intuition" is frequently used to refer to the direct and immediate way in which we apprehend an artistic object. Philosophers of art often refer to a certain instantaneous insight into "form" as essential to the creation or appreciation of a work of art. The sudden clarity with which important hypotheses sometimes present themselves to great scientists is commonly labeled "intuition." The history of science, from Archimedes to Darwin, furnishes dramatic examples of revolutionary scientific ideas which have come to their authors "all at once." "Every one of these great discoveries," says Schopenhauer, "is an immediate intuition, and as such the work on an instant, an *aperçu*, a flash of insight. They are not the result of a process of abstract reasoning." Kekule *saw* the benzine ring in his fireplace.

Propositions of which we can have immediate certainty without proof ("self-evident" propositions) are often said to be intuitively known. However, as we have seen, there may be disagreement as to just what kinds of propositions may properly be described as self-evident. Some philosophers restrict the class of propositions intuitively known to statements about simple perceptions, such as "This is blue." Others hold that the axioms of logic are intuitively known. Descartes used "intuition" as a synonym for his "clear and distinct" basic knowledge. "Each individual," he says, "can mentally have intuition of the fact that he exists, and that he thinks; that the triangle is bounded by three lines only, the sphere by a single superficies, and so on."[5] Some moral philosophers hold that the fundamental principles of ethics are intuitively known. Since basic moral axioms can be neither rationally demonstrated nor experimentally confirmed, they say, the truth of such ethical principles is "self-evident" and can be grasped only by direct and immediate knowledge.

Limitations of Intuition

Suppose intuition is taken to mean a way of knowledge which is immediate, direct, and certain. It is the opinion of many analysts that, while such knowledge may exist, it does not come to us by way of a mysterious faculty set apart

[5] R. Descartes, "Rules for the Direction of the Mind," in E. S. Haldane and G. R. T. Ross, trans., *The Philosophical Works of Descartes*, London, Cambridge University Press, 1931, p. 7. (PB: Liberal Arts, Bobbs-Merrill, Indianapolis.)

from other channels of knowledge. Psychologists tend to agree that the larger number of instances of "intuition" can be explained in terms of reflection upon sense experience. The mother of the truant boy, they would say, probably observed a certain unusual tenseness or caution in his behavior that day. Subsequent reflection on these observations, below the level of her conscious attention, produced a build-up of latent responses which finally "broke through" in the form of a sudden conviction of her son's absence from Sunday School.

While psychologists generally agree that the solution of problems frequently comes to us "in a flash," they usually deny that such insight affords sufficient evidence of the existence of a special intuitive faculty.[6] The sudden illumination which discloses to a Newton or a Lavoisier the hypothesis for which he has been searching can be taken simply as the product of a long period of mental incubation in which concepts built up from sensory observation and logical inference have been mentally matched against one another in an imaginative process of trial and error. Psychologists interested in the phenomena of religious experience, yet skeptical of revelations and visions, have analyzed the illumination of religious mysticism in terms of complex

[6] In recent years certain psychologists have investigated the possibility of the existence of a quasi-intuitive way of knowledge known as "extrasensory perception." During the thirties and forties the American psychologist. J. B. Rhine conducted a long series of experiments at Duke University designed to discover whether or not certain persons have the power to "know" if something is so without observing the situation. In these experiments, the subject tried to identify concealed cards upon which special designs were printed. According to Rhine, the results of these experiments indicate that some people actually do possess a special way of knowing by means of which unobserved states of affairs are directly disclosed to them in consciousness. A considerable number of psychologists and other scientists disagree with Rhine on the value of these experiments.

forms of latent sensory and emotional build-ups. An example of such an analysis may be found in J. H. Leuba's *The Psychology of Religious Mysticism*, in which the author claims that any information obtained by mystics in their moments of illumination has "really" come to them through their senses. This is an attitude common among students of mysticism who do not themselves move within a context of religious belief.

Perhaps the most important limitation of intuition as a way of knowledge is its *lack of public character*. Critics of intuitionism point out that what is disclosed in intuition is not publicly verifiable; it is an essentially private affair. We are quite properly suspicious of those people who say they "see" things which others do not see, and who claim that they have interior illuminations in which important truths are revealed to them alone. Indeed, the claim of private revelation is all too often the first mark of a psychotic state. Mental hospitals are full of persons who claim such particular visions. Now most contemporary methodologists are inclined to believe that truth is not a private but a social affair. If a proposition is true, they say, what it designates should in some way or other be open to public inspection. An important reason why the methodology of the sciences is so productive is that scientific statements are amenable to public test and confirmation.

At this juncture, however, a distinction should be made. Suppose, for the sake of argument, that on occasion it is possible for one to arrive at the knowledge of important propositions via the direct and private route of intuition. Now if the truth of these propositions, disclosed in intuition, can be confirmed by some way of knowing which *does* have a public character, then the objection to intuition on the ground of its essentially private character will lose something of its force.

Intuition and Intellect; Bergson's Theory of Knowledge

The modern French philosopher Henri Bergson offers an interesting theory of knowledge in which *intuition* and *intellect* are suggested as the two basic ways of knowing; yet neither intuition nor intellect, in this two-part division, are segregated from experience, which enters into both. Of the two ways of knowing, Bergson says:

> The first implies that we move round the object; the second that we enter into it. The first depends on the point of view at which we are placed and on the symbols by which we express ourselves. The second neither depends on a point of view nor relies on any symbol. The first kind of knowledge may be said to stop at the *relative;* the second, in those cases where it is possible, to attain the *absolute.*[7]

The first kind of knowledge is the indirect, conceptual, rational, abstract way of intellect. The second is the direct, immediate, concrete, life-penetrating way of *intuition.* The way of intellect is best observed in *science,* whose function is to understand and to control material objects. The way of intuition may be found in artistic creation, human love, and in the experiences of the saint and the mystic. By means of the conceptual, symbolic way of intellect we *know about* the object—that is, we move all around it and see it from every side. By means of the direct, immediate way of intutition we *know* the object—that is, we enter into it and become at one with it. The task of philosophy, says Bergson, is to integrate *both* these fundamental ways of knowing.

[7] H. Bergson, *Introduction to Metaphysics,* rev. ed., T. E. Hulme, trans., New York, Putnam, 1936, p. 1. (PB: Liberal Arts, Bobbs-Merrill, Indianapolis.)

William James—who admired Bergson—distinguishes between (1) knowledge by acquaintance, and (2) knowledge "about." A similar distinction is made by Bertrand Russell between (1) knowledge by acquaintance and (2) knowledge by description. I know New York City by acquaintance, but I only know *about* Katmandu. I know Schubert's *D Minor Quartet* by acquaintance, but I only know *about* atoms. We may add an example of a mother and a pediatrician. Both mother and pediatrician *know* the baby. But their knowledge is different. That of the mother is direct, immediate, inseparable from, although not identical with, her love for the baby. The pediatrician's knowledge is scientific, conceptual, external. To Bergson, the first is intuitive, the second intellectual knowledge. We note that neither is separated from experience. Similarly, in the realm of art, we know best those works for which we have the most sympathy. Is it not true that the most valuable literary criticism is of those books and writers the critic loves? Perhaps that is why the poet Rilke says, "Works of art are of an infinite loneliness and with nothing to be so little reached as 'criticism'; it is through love that we may truly reach them."[8]

Bergson's view of intellect is pragmatic and instrumental. Intellect, he tells us, has a *functional* character. It is an instrument which man has acquired and developed in the course of evolution, a natural tool by means of which the human organism is able to cope with its environment. Intellectual knowledge enables us to handle, to manipulate, and to control the material world. Because the function of intel-

[8] In medieval philosophy, the meaning of the term "connatural knowledge" is something like the intuition or the "knowledge from within" that Bergson talks of. Thomas Aquinas says that while it is possible to acquire considerable knowledge *about* virtue by studying moral philosophy (e.g., Aristotle's *Ethics*), only a *good* man has *connatural* knowledge of virtue.

lect is to handle *matter*, the intellect cannot help but see the world as if it were made up entirely of *material bodies*. Thus, when faced with an object it seeks to understand, intellect by its very nature tends to conceive of it in terms of an assemblage of material particles. Intellect *analyzes* the object which confronts it, splits that object up into parts, examining them from every side, making mechanical models of it, ever striving to establish the relation of the parts of the model to each other as well as the relation of the model as a whole to other objects. This is the way of knowledge of science, which is intellectual knowledge *par excellence*–indirect, analytic, conceptual, rational, abstract.

But intellect, says Bergson, is not all there is to human consciousness; it is a contraction, a focusing, a special use of that consciousness. Surrounding intellect, as a vague but luminous fringe, is *intuition*. In man, this way of knowledge is a higher development of what appears in the animal world as *instinct*. Intuition is not analytic; it does not break up the object which confronts it into a collection of movable parts. It does not seek to understand its object, as does intellect, by indirect reference to concepts and ideas. In intuition, we grasp the object as a whole. We no longer move around it; we are at one with it.

Now if the object of intellect is matter, what then is the object of intuition? Bergson answers: *Life*. When science (which is to say the intellectual or rational way of knowledge) is faced with the phenomenon of life and seeks to understand the nature of the organic, it breaks up the unified living thing into parts, into atoms, into material bits, and seeks to "explain" life in terms of physical particles combined in some complex way. But, Bergson is convinced, life will never thus be understood. For intellect, striving to grasp the nature of life, handles it as if it were *not* living. It turns life into a collection of tiny material blocks and, in so doing, presents us with a conception of life which is one-sided and misleading, if not actually false. Intuition, on the other hand, is at home with life. Directly, immediately, without need of conceptual reference, we know life as it flows and wells up within ourselves. We know, without intellectual demonstration, that our *mode of being* is fundamentally different from the mode of being exhibited by physical objects:

> Intelligence, by means of science, which is its work, will deliver up to us more and more completely the secret of physical operations; of life it brings us, and moreover only claims to bring us, a translation in terms of inertia. It goes all round life, taking from outside the greatest number of views of it, drawing it into itself instead of entering into it. But it is to the very inwardness of life that *intuition* leads us—by intuition I mean instinct that has become disinterested, self-conscious, capable of reflecting upon its object and of enlarging it indefinitely.[9]

Bergson tells us that if we extend beyond ourselves this intuition of life—given to us in our awareness of the inward flow of our own consciousness—we can at significant moments touch the pulse of life as it surges in the world behind the crust of matter. For, Bergson believes, something analogous to organic life, but far more fundamental, strives to unite itself with everything that is. This *élan vital*, conceived as a primordial cosmic impulse, is the ultimate source of organic life. In such a way does Bergson's concept of intuition lead him to a particular *metaphysical* theory, that is, to a general doctrine of the nature of things. It should not surprise us to learn that in his later

[9] H. Bergson, *Creative Evolution*, A. Mitchell, trans., New York, Holt, Rinehart and Winston, 1911, p. 176. (There is a Modern Library edition.)

years Bergson became absorbed with the problem of *mysticism* and approached, if he did not actually undergo, religious conversion.

REASON

The Rational Animal

Long ago, Aristotle said that the definition of "man" is "*rational animal.*" According to the Greek philosopher, the function of definition is to set forth the essence, the nature, the "what-ness" of that which is defined. We do this by first giving the *genus* or *kind* to which the thing we are defining belongs. In the case of man, the genus is "animal," for he shares with animals capacities which are characteristic of them. The second element in definition is *difference*, the characteristic which marks off what is being defined from all other members of its genus. In man, said Aristotle, the "difference" is *reason.* Like animality, rationality is part of man's essence or nature, but it is that element which man does *not* share with other members of his genus. Reason is that property which sets man *apart* from other animals. Man's rational capacity, said Aristotle, is the source of all properly human activities—our ability to talk, to laugh, to engage in scientific inquiry, etc.

Philosophers, of our century, as a rule, do not accept the implication in Aristotle's definition that "reason" is a unified inborn faculty with which man is "by nature" endowed. Such a conception of reason, thinks John Dewey, draws attention away from the fact that "reason" is a set of learned habits, achieved with difficulty through long runs of trial and error in experience. Dewey prefers the word "intelligence" to "reason." Nevertheless, most philosophers have agreed with the *spirit* of Aristotle's definition. Human knowledge can certainly be distinguished from animal knowledge by virtue of its *results*. At the very least, it is a legitimate linguistic convenience to include under one name —whether this be "reason" or "intelligence"—those capacities by means of which men produce mathematical theorems, Diesel locomotives, systems of both cost accounting and philosophy.

The classical word "reason" has many senses, all of them more or less closely related, which are determined by the particular context of subject matter in which the word is used. Two or three of these related meanings of "reason" are rather important to an understanding of frequently heard discussions in which the word "reason" occurs, and we shall try to distinguish between them.

Reason and Impulse

One of the many shades of meaning which have gathered about "reason" is that taken on by the word when it is used in opposition to "impulse." Impulse plays a tremendous part in human life. The *power* of the instinctive, dynamic, infrarational side of human nature has been a matter of serious concern to Western thinkers from Plato to Freud. The way of impulse is to act without reflection, to "shoot first and ask questions afterward." Impulse is powerful and, if undirected, blind. Poets and moralists alike have mourned the havoc wrought in human affairs by uncontrolled sexual love and the compulsion to strike down one's fellow man. Human beings have the capacity to achieve, at the cost of pain and frequent defeat, control of impulse and the ability to channel it in productive directions. To that specifically human capacity to foresee the results of impulse, and to govern and direct compulsive drives accordingly, we give the name of "reason" or "intelligence."

Some moralists have been content to stress the *negative*

role of reason in relation to impulse. Like the Stoics and Spinoza, they have focused one-sidedly on the power of reason to control or even to eliminate the emotions. Other analysts of human nature—aware of the thin and ineffective quality of thought without the driving force of passion—have insisted that the function of reason is not to conquer impulse but to guide it. The function of reason, *positively* conceived, is to direct impulse and vital energy toward the achievement of fruitful ends. Impulse urges us to act—to act at once without thought of consequences. The part of reason is to make us look before we leap; to foresee the consequences of the act to which impulse drives us; to reflect upon these consequences; and to adjust our plan of action accordingly. Such a conception of reason in relation to impulse is presented by John Dewey in his analysis of "intelligence."

> Impulse is primary and intelligence is secondary and in some sense derivative. There should be no blinking of this fact. But recognition of it as fact exalts intelligence. For thought is not the slave of impulse to do its bidding. Impulse does not know what it is after; it cannot give orders, not even if it wants to. ... What intelligence has to do in the service of impulse is to act not as its obedient servant but as it clarifier and liberator. ... Rationality ... is not a force to evoke against impulse and habit. It is the attainment of a working harmony among diverse desires. "Reason" as a noun signifies the happy cooperation of a multitude of dispositions, such as sympathy, curiosity, exploration, experimentation, frankness, pursuit—to follow things through—circumspection, to look about at the context. ... The clew of impulse is, as we say, to start something. It is in a hurry. It rushes us off our feet. It leaves no time for examination, memory and foresight. But the clew of reason is, as the phrase also goes, to stop and think.[10]

[10] J. Dewey, *The Philosophy of John Dewey*, J. Ratner, ed., New York, Holt, Rinehart and Winston, 1928, pp. 292–293.

Reason and Sense Perception

A somewhat different sense of "reason" is used when we contrast reason with sense perception. Here "reason" refers to our capacity for *conceptual knowledge*, the power of the human mind to go beyond the particular and separate items of sense experience to form abstract concepts or "laws" of a general nature. To describe and to interpret the world it is necessary to go beyond what is immediately given in sense perception, to fix upon general patterns of experience rather than on particular and isolated bits of it. Since Plato, who believed that "the mind, by a power of her own, contemplates the universal in all things," it has been traditional to associate reason with conceptual knowledge.

A very broad division of types of philosophic thinking is suggested by the contrast between reason and sense experience. Those philosophers who stress the importance of sense observation in reliable knowledge are called *empiricists*. Those who emphasize the power of reason or conceptual knowledge are labeled *rationalists*. Historically, no philosophers have said of sense perception and conceptual knowledge that one was utterly valueless and the other completely trustworthy. But there have been major differences of emphasis on the relative importance of these two ways of knowing.

Philosophic Rationalism

Generally speaking, philosophic rationalism can be identified with confidence in the capacity of human reason or conceptual knowledge to attain to truth. With this confidence is associated a tendency to relegate sense experience, as a way of knowledge, to a role of secondary importance.

It is only natural to be impressed by the power of the

human mind to carry on complex processes of inference without the need of constant stopping and turning to the observable world to verify conclusions established at each link of the chain of thought. The mathematical disciplines most clearly reveal the successful working of this human talent. Philosopher-mathematician that he was, Plato exulted over the ability of the human mind to reach knowledge without apparent aid of sense observation. Knowledge is not sense perception, he says; it is not even reasoning about sense perceptions. The objects to which reason leads us are not observable at all. They are the universal patterns of being to which mind alone can penetrate. Those who place their trust in sense perception Plato calls "the earth-born," and scornfully refers to them as "the people who believe in nothing but what they can hold in their hands."

Perhaps the most radical philosophical rationalist of all time was Plato's predecessor Parmenides, who convinced himself and his disciples by apparently logical reasoning that neither multiplicity nor motion exists. There is only one thing that is, says Parmenides, and that is Being. Since Nothing is not, it does not exist. Now space is nothing. In order for there to be *many* things, there must be space between them. But space does not exist, since it is Nothing; therefore there is only *one* Being. Similarly, in order for there to be motion, there must be space to move in. But there is no space; therefore, motion is impossible. The one eternal Being does not move or change in any way. If the senses tell us there are many different things, and that there is motion, so much the worse for the senses.

Parmenides' pupil Zeno used antinomies or puzzles to prove his master's doctrine of the impossibility of motion. Zeno's best known puzzle is that of Achilles and the tortoise. Supposedly the faster runner, Achilles gives the tortoise a handicap such that the tortoise starts off at *A*, Achilles starting some distance behind him. Now to overtake the tortoise Achilles has to pass through *A*. But the supposition is that the tortoise is moving too; hence he has moved ahead to *B*. To catch up with the tortoise, Achilles has to pass through *B*. But by that time the tortoise has moved ahead to *C*, and so on. Thus Achilles can never catch the tortoise. The assumption that motion is real, that one runner can move faster than another, has led to a contradictory conclusion. Therefore the proposition, "Motion is real," is false.[11]

Philosophers of the seventeenth century were struck by the power of mathematics, which was brilliantly developed in their age. Continental rationalists like Descartes, Leibniz, and Spinoza were convinced that the human mind possessed certain innate capacities or a priori truths upon which complex inferences could be built up without important aid from sense perception. Kant was a rationalist in that he believed our knowledge of the external world is primarily conceptual; the material which these concepts set in order is not directly known. Thinkers as different as Thomas Aquinas and Hegel are frequently described as rationalists because of the way they relied on the powers of conceptual inference in their construction of grand-scale philosophical systems.

Another Meaning of Rationalism; Reason and Faith

A large number of educated persons of the seventeenth and eighteenth centuries shared with Descartes and Leibniz the general confidence of the period in the competence of human reason to reach true knowldge. Not everyone, however, (particularly in England) agreed with the Continental rationalists in believing that sense observation plays

[11] For further information on Parmenides and Zeno, see J. Burnett, *Early Greek Philosophy*, London, A & C Black, 1920, chaps. 4, 8. (PB: Meridian, World Publishing, Cleveland.)

a minor role in reliable knowledge. Many showed their confidence in human reason by crying down, not sense experience, but another type of knowledge—hitherto considered as basic. This was knowledge derived from *religion*—from faith and the authority of sacred revelation.

In medieval culture it was generally held that there were two primary ways of knowledge, which we may distinguish as *faith* and *reason.* To the philosopher of the Middle Ages the information contained in Scriptures (which he considered as divinely revealed knowledge) together with the teaching of his religion constituted a broad path of knowledge which reached farther and higher than reason. But the medieval philosopher did not think that religious faith supported by the authority of Scriptures and tradition was the only way of knowing or even the only important way. He believed that reliable knowledge could also be attained through the exercise of the natural power of human reason unaided by revelation. Men like Aquinas and Maimonides set themselves the task of organizing systems of human knowledge in which the findings of faith and reason would be integrated within a synthesis which did justice to both. Religious faith was never considered by medieval thinkers to be an *obstacle* to human thought; they took it as a *stimulus* to intellectual activity. "*Credo ut intellegam,*" said Anselm. "I believe in order that I may understand."

Modern times, beginning with the Renaissance, saw the gradual breakup of the medieval synthesis. Little by little, educated men pushed the presuppositions of faith further and further into the background. By the eighteenth century, the rise of confidence in the power of human reason was paralleled by a decline of trust in religious beliefs. Faith became associated with clericalism, superstition, fanaticism, and "enthusiasm." All necessary knowledge of God and his relation to the world could be obtained by natural reason.

No need of revelation, Scriptures, or a teaching church. In this climate of eighteenth-century rationalism there developed the "rational" or "natural" religion known as *deism.*

Nineteenth-century scholars turned to the scriptural writings themselves, and, treating them as they would any other set of historical documents, subjected them to critical analysis. They challenged the authenticity of some parts of the Scriptures, called into question the authorship of others, pointed out interpolated and corrupt passages, and so forth. In this way the term "rationalism" became associated with the so-called "higher criticism" of the Bible.

Thus we can distinguish two basic meanings of the difficult word "rationalism," each of which has an element in common with the other. *Philosophic rationalism* entails (1) confidence in the power of human reason to reach true knowledge (2) without important aid from sense perception. What we may call *secularist* or *naturalistic* rationalism implies (1) confidence in the power of human reason to attain to true knowledge (2) without the aid of faith, revelation, or a teaching church. In the definition of philosophic rationalism, "reason" is taken as synonymous with conceptual knowledge in contrast to sense perception. In secularist rationalism, reason is interpreted in a broader sense which does not necessarily exclude the element of sense observation and experiment.

EXPERIENCE

Some Meanings of "Experience"

"We learn by experience," we say. "Experience is a great teacher." But what is experience? The word is even more difficult to define than "reason." Its varied usages form concentric rings of meaning that blur into one another in such a way that it is impossible to separate them clearly.

The narrowest meaning of "experience" is *sensation.* In this sense, the perception of a colored shape, a flash of light, or a feeling of warmth is said to be an experience. A less restricted meaning is *observation.* We know via experience that it is raining, that the stove is hot, that the subway is crowded, etc. Another meaning refers to an event or happening in which we are involved and which makes a *strong impression* on us. Thus a man who has just been robbed may say, "I had a terrible experience last night."

If we translate Descartes's famous "*Je pense, donc je suis*" as "I am experiencing, therefore I am," we are using "experience" as a synonym for *consciousness.* A person whose capacity to do a job has been built up by *past practice* in the skills required is referred to as "experienced." A still broader usage of "experience" suggests *knowledge by acquaintance* in contrast to *knowledge about.* I know from experience that my father was a gentle and kind man while my children know this only by my testimony. When I ask, "In your experience, did you ever encounter a case like this?" I refer to a series of past events in which you were concerned and your response to these. This last usage gives us a clue to a working definition of "experience" in a fairly comprehensive sense. *Experience is what happens to us and what we do about it.*

Philosophical Empiricism

An empiricist is usually defined as one who believes that experience is the most reliable method of knowledge. Such a person is the legendary man from Missouri who said, "Show me." Philosophical empiricism is associated with confidence in the reliability of experience as a way of knowing together with a tendency to distrust conceptual knowledge. The philosophical empiricist is critical of the rationalist's claim that the mind has powers of its own to disclose the nature of things. He also tends to suspect the reliability of intuition and many forms of authority as ways of knowing. There is one shortcoming of our simple definition of an empiricist. The term "experience" has such broad extension that there is hardly a philosopher in history who has not at one time appealed to "experience" to justify his theories.

Credit for the most eloquent and influential defense of *experience* as the most important source of human knowledge goes to John Locke. In his *Essay Concerning Human Understanding* Locke rejects the teaching of the rationalist Descartes that the human mind is by nature endowed with certain innate ideas:

> Let us suppose the mind to be, as we say, white paper, void of all characters, without any ideas. How comes it to be furnished? Whence comes it by that vast store which the busy and boundless fancy of man has painted on it with an almost endless variety? Whence has it all the *materials* of reason and knowledge? To this I answer in one word: EXPERIENCE. All our knowledge is founded in experience, and from experience it ultimately derives itself.[12]

Locke never tells us just what he means by "experience," but he tends much of the time to take it in the narrow sense of *sensations*. British empiricists who succeeded Locke applied his doctrine "All knowledge from experience" strictly as "All knowledge from sense data." A rigorous application of this sensationalistic interpretation of "experience" led to Hume's doctrine of objects and minds as clusters of sensations. Thus empiricism turned into skepticism. The greatest twentieth-century representative of British empiricism is

[12] J. Locke, *An Essay Concerning Human Understanding*, A. C. Fraser, ed., London, Oxford University Press, 1894, vol. 1, pp. 121–123. (P.B.: Open Court, La Salle, Ill.)

Bertrand Russell. Russell himself inclines toward an analysis of "experience" in terms of sensations or "brain states." But he admits that a theory of knowledge based on "experience" alone is inadequate. Our knowledge of the general principles which guide human behavior, he says, "cannot be based on experience, though all their verifiable consequences are such as experience will confirm."

The recent doctrine known as *logical empiricism* is descended in part from the British empiricist tradition. This fact may throw some light on the tendency of many of its adherents toward a sensationalistic analysis of experience. We have seen earlier that logical empiricists hold (with Hume) that informative statements must be either formal or factual if they are to be significant. It follows that for the logical empiricist there are two basic methods of reliable knowledge: (1) logical and linguistic analysis and (2) inferences from observed "facts." Propositions which are analytic are true in virtue of the rules of logic and language. "Factual" propositions are meaningful only if verifiable; their truth can be determined only by a testing process in which some element of sensory observation is present. In our discusion of "Language," we have noted some opinions concerning the limitations of this form of empiricism.[13]

A good part of twentieth-century American philosophy may be described as "empiricist," if we interpret the word in a broad sense to refer to a general underlying assumption that the most reliable knowledge is that which is subject to confirmation by scientific experiment or social practice. American philosophy was given its empiricist orientation by the philosophers of the pragmatist tradition, Peirce, James, and Dewey. The current popularity of "phi-

[13] Chapter 2, pp. 67–69.

losophy of science" and "philosophy of language" and the influence of logical empiricism have introduced more specialized and technical strains of empiricism into philosophic tendencies in the United States.

A Broader Concept of Experience; Dewey's Empiricism

John Dewey's interpretation of "experience" is probably the broadest of any philosophy this side of rationalism. He forcefully rejects the notion that experience is *sensation,* and that what we know are *sense data.* He has no patience with those self-styled empiricists who tell us that when we look at a chair we "really" experience only a colored patch. A man experiences the chair most fully, says Dewey, not when looking at it, but when he is intending to sit down in it. And he can intend to sit down in the chair precisely because his experience of the chair is *not* limited to a colored shape. Far from experiencing only a colored patch which is *less* than a chair, that man experiences a good deal *more* than a chair. He "lays hold of a wide spatial context, such as the room where the chair is, and a spread of its history, including the chair's period, price paid for it, consequences, public as well as personal which follow from its use as household furniture, and so on."[14] In Dewey's opinion, the contemporary "colored-patch" empiricist is not talking about experience or knowledge at all:

> Sensations are not parts of *any* knowledge, good or bad, superior or inferior, imperfect or complete. They are rather provocations, incitements, challenges to an act of inquiry which is to *terminate* in knowledge. . . . When the isolated and simple existences of Locke and Hume are seen not to be truly

[14] J. Dewey, *Experience and Nature,* La Salle, Ill., Open Court, 1925, p. 5. (PB: Dover, New York.)

empirical but to answer certain demands of their theory of mind, the necessity ceases for the elaborate Kantian and post-Kantian machinery of *a priori* concepts and categories to synthesize the alleged stuff of experience. The true "stuff" of experience is recognized to be adaptive courses of action, habit, active functions, connections of doing and undergoing; sensori-motor co-ordinations. Experience carries principles of connection and organization within itself.[15]

What then is experience? Of all the varied definitions of the term we have outlined in a previous section, the one closest to Dewey's conception is "Experience is what happens to us and what we do about it." But Dewey would insist that the primary stress be put on the *doing* rather than the *undergoing*. As we have said earlier, Dewey sees man as an organism acting upon the being acted upon by the dual environment of Nature and society. The human organism does not stand passive and inert, like Locke's blank tablet, waiting for something to impress itself upon it from outside. Man *acts* upon his environment, changing its character, and the environment, so modified, reacts upon him. Experience is the *product* of this interaction between the human organism and its natural and social environment. Experience is the outcome of transactions between man, Nature, and society. This Dewey takes to be the business of human knowledge, whether common-sense, scientific, or philosophical. To him, knowledge is not just propositional knowledge, not just *knowing that*. The essential relation of

[15] J. Dewey, *Reconstruction in Philosophy*, New York, Holt, Rinehart and Winston, 1920, pp. 89–91. (PB: Beacon Press, Boston.) Compare Merleau-Ponty in *The Phenomenology of Perception:* "Pure sensation, defined as the action of *stimuli* on our body is the 'last effect' of knowledge, particularly of scientific knowledge, and it is an illusion that causes us to put it at the beginning and to believe that it precedes knowledge."

knowledge to action requires stress on *knowing how* as essential to its meaning.

Like Bergson, Dewey holds a *genetic* theory of knowledge—although, unlike the French philosopher, he does not separate intuition from intellect. To Dewey, intelligence has arisen in the course of evolution as a means of successful adaptation of the human organism to its environment. Ideas, says Dewey, are tools of practical action, not objects of contemplation. It is not the business of human thought to uncover a "reality" which has always been "there." The primary function of intelligence is to grapple with the succession of problems, obstacles, difficulties, and doubtful situations which man's natural and social environment press constantly upon him.

Dewey's Analysis of Thinking

With Peirce, Dewey holds that knowledge begins with a doubtful situation and moves toward a settled one. Knowledge does not spring up out of nothing. A problem, an obstacle, a sense of trouble and unease must exist to stimulate productive thought. Dewey distinguishes five stages in the process of reflective thinking which practical everyday thought and scientific investigation have in common.[16] We may illustrate these phases by a rather simplified and mechanical example (not Dewey's):

Suppose a man wants to listen to his bedside radio and finds that it will not operate. Here is the typical start of a thinking process—the situation is uncertain; action is blocked. (1) The first phase, *suggestion:* Action blocked leads to hasty notions as to how action may quickly be resumed. The man twists the dials of his radio at random, then taps the instrument with his hand. (2) The second

[16] See J. Dewey, *How We Think,* rev. ed., Boston, Heath, 1933, chap. 7.

phase, *intellectualization:* A problem clearly formulated is a problem half-solved. The man observes that at least some tubes are lighted up. Current is flowing through his receiver, but he has no sound. This is the central difficulty. (3) The third phase, *hypothesis:* Ideas now occur as to possible causes of the failure. Could a single tube be out? Or maybe there is a break in the circuit within the receiver itself. Or it could possibly be line cord or plug trouble. (4) The fourth phase, *reasoning:* Here the hypotheses are tested mentally by comparing them with what we already know. The man considers the suggestion that one tube has blown, but rejects it on the ground that in an ordinary radio like this all tubes are wired in series; if one tube goes, all go. If any tubes are lighted, this is evidence current is getting to the set. This fact eliminates line cord or plug trouble as well as the possibility of a defective off-on switch. Finally he considers the likelihood of a circuit break in the receiver itself. This could be caused by a crack in the printed circuitry—especially if someone had dropped the set or set it down too hard. (5) The fifth phase, *testing the hypothesis:* A hypothesis which has survived the test of consistency with what we already know is ready for test in action. The man examines the fine etched wires in the printed circuitry. What appears to be a small crack is faintly visible on one wire. He taps on the area, pushes up and down on the circuit board. Now he hears a crackle followed by the sound of an announcer's voice. A little solder does the rest, and the man settles back to listen to his favorite station. The troubled situation is over; equilibrium has been restored.

Dewey would not insist that our analysis of problem solving must exhibit precisely these five stages. He would ask us simply to note that the thinking process is stimulated by blocked action; that thinking is under way as we form hypotheses (suppositions) to deal with the unsatisfactory situation; that this is followed by our eliminating of certain hypotheses, and the selection and testing of others. The successful hypothesis is evidently the one which, when acted upon, resolves the unsatisfactory situation by removing the block and allowing action to resume.[17]

Is All Knowledge Problem Solving?

Dewey has been reproved for reducing all knowledge to problem solving, for representing every worthwhile situation of human thought in terms of fixing an automobile engine. He has also been criticized on the ground that his analysis of knowledge leaves no room for theoretical research which does not have practical application in mind. It is true that Dewey's view of man in the universe struggling with the problems imposed on him by his environment

[17] The reader may be interested in the way a television repairman might deal with the problem of a set brought to his attention by a customer who claims that the set is "not working." What is the complaint? No picture, says the customer. Does that mean there is no brightness or illumination of the screen ("raster") or that there is no image? The customer replies that he gets brightness but no image. The TV man then knows that certain circuits (high voltage and sweep) are working, for if they were not, there would be no illumination. So the trouble must lie in the "video" aspect of the set. Now the TV man listens for sound. There is none. But if there is no video and no sound, this means it is likely that the trouble lies in the tuner, that is, in the tubes in front of the set. (80 to 85 percent of all TV troubles stems from the tubes.) Now the TV man has the problem of deciding which of the tubes in front of the set to replace. Suppose he sees small black and white dots on the illuminated but imageless screen. This means that the video amplifier is working. So he must replace tubes in the RF amplifier or in the mixer oscillator. Which? He listens attentively to the set and hears a faint warbling sound: this generally means that the mixer oscillator is working. Then one of the IF amplifier tubes (there are only two or three) must be out. The TV man replaces each tube in turn, and on the second try, he gets both sound and image. The set is once more working and the customer is satisfied.

orients his theory of knowledge toward practical action. But Dewey would insist that practical action need not be problem solving in the narrow sense of the word. It may mean the resolution of doubtful situations on purely theoretical levels. "Ideas may be of intellectual use to a penetrating mind," says Dewey, "even when they do not find any immediate reference to actuality, provided they stay in the mind for use when new facts come to light."[18] It is not to speculative knowledge that Dewey objects, but to knowledge which is *merely* speculative. Ideas, concepts, theories, and speculations are utterly necessary to productive knowledge. But unless they make some difference one way or another, they are just ideas and no more. Ideas which are not used as *instruments*, as operational plans to guide future action, are no better than daydreams. Dewey would be the first to admit that the ideas which contribute to great poetry and art are very valuable. But he does not (at least in his earlier writings) consider them the material of knowledge. We shall see in our survey of moral philosophy how Dewey takes ethical judgments as instruments of problem solving.

Rationalism and Empiricism as Methods of Science; Conclusion

In the sciences we can observe a happy union of the two great methods of knowledge we have labeled rationalism and empiricism. The truth of a proposition may be determined by testing it. But there are two general methods of testing propositions. We may show that the proposition may be deduced by logical inference from other propositions already established. Or we may try it out in an experiment in which some element of sense perception is

[18] Dewey, *How We Think*, p. 106.

involved. The first is the way of deduction or *rationalism*, the second the way of observation and experiment or *empiricism*. In the realm of logic and mathematics only does the method of rationalism operate successfully *solo*. To be sure, it is prominent and successful also in those physical sciences in which mathematics plays an essential role. But even theoretical physics—which carries on so much of its work by mathematical reasoning—requires an occasional crucial check by experiment. *All* the natural sciences are more or less rationalistic. There is no science which confines itself to sense observations without reasoning about them. But the propositions of the empirical sciences (in contrast to those of logic and mathematics) must somewhere along the line be subject to confirmation by experiment. And experiments are procedures in which *some* kind of sense observation is concerned.

From propositions contained in his revolutionary theory of relativity Einstein deduced by a complex process of inference that light rays are bent as they pass near the sun. Some years later, astronomers at Greenwich took photographs of an eclipse of the sun which showed the bending of the light waves. The astronomical photographs which correlated Einstein's theory with sense observations showed, as Whitehead expresses it, that a great adventure in thought had come safe to shore.[19]

In the form of observation and experiment, the empiricist element plays an indispensable role in the methodology of the physical sciences. But observation and experiment of themselves do not produce great scientific theories. These are the products of the creative, speculative, *rational* aspects of human thought stimulated by the problems and uncertainties of the world of sense.

[19] Alfred North Whitehead, *Science and the Modern World*, New York, Macmillan, 1925, p. 15. (PB: Mentor, New American Library, New York.)

FURTHER READINGS

Bergson, Henri, *Creative Evolution*, A. Mitchell (trans.), New York, Holt, Rinehart and Winston, 1911, chap. 2. (There is a Modern Library edition.)

Cohen, Morris, *Reason and Nature*, New York, Harcourt, Brace & World, 1931. (PB: Free Press, Macmillan, New York.)

Cohen, Morris, and Ernest Nagel, *An Introduction to Logic and Scientific Method*, Harcourt, Brace & World, 1934, chaps. 10, 11, 20.

The Columbia Associates, *An Introduction to Reflective Thinking*, Boston, Houghton Mifflin, 1923.

Descartes, René, "Discourse on Method," in E. S. Haldane and G. R. T. Ross (trans.), *The Philosophical Works of Descartes*, London, Cambridge University Press, 1931. (PB: Liberal Arts, Bobbs-Merrill, Indianapolis.)

Dewey, John, "Changed Conceptions of Reason and Experience," in *Reconstruction in Philosophy*, New York, Holt, Rinehart and Winston, 1920. (PB: Beacon Press, Boston; Mentor, New American Library, New York.)

Dewey, John, "The Instrumental Theory of Knowledge," in J. Ratner (ed.), *The Philosophy of John Dewey*, New York, Holt, Rinehart and Winston, 1928.

Dewey, John, *How We Think*, rev. ed., Boston, Heath, 1933.

Feigl, Herbert, "Logical Empiricism," in H. Feigl and W. Sellars (eds.), *Readings in Philosophical Analysis*, New York, Appleton-Century-Crofts, 1949.

James, William, *Pragmatism*, London, Longmans, 1928, chaps. 1 and 2. (PB: Meridian, World Publishing, Cleveland.)

Leuba, J. H., *The Psychology of Religious Mysticism*, New York, Harcourt, Brace & World, 1925.

Maritain, J., "On Knowledge through Connaturality," in *The Range of Reason*, New York, Scribner, 1952. (PB: Scribner.)

Montague, Wm. Pepperell, *The Ways of Knowing*, London, G. Allen, 1925, pt. 1.

Peirce, Charles Sanders, "The Fixation of Belief," in Morris Cohen (ed.), *Chance, Love, and Logic*, New York, Harcourt, Brace & World, 1923. (PB: Randall, J. H., Jr., J. Buchler, and E. Shirk, *Readings in Philosophy*, *Barnes & Noble*, New York.)

Plato, Socrates' Speech in "The Symposium," *The Dialogues of Plato*, B. Jowett (trans.), New York, Random House, 1937, vol. 1. (PB: Liberal Arts, Bobbs-Merrill, Indianapolis.)

Plato, "Theaetetus," *The Dialogues of Plato*, B. Jowett (trans.), Random House, 1937, vol. 2. (PB: Liberal Arts, Bobbs-Merrill, Indianapolis.)

Reichenbach, Hans, "The Empiricist Approach," in *The Rise of Scientific Philosophy*, University of California Press, 1951. (PB: U. of Calif. Press.)

Russell, Bertrand, "Knowledge by Acquaintance and Knowledge by Description," in *Mysticism and Logic*, London, Longmans, 1918. (PB: Anchor, Doubleday, Garden City, N.Y.)

Russell, Bertrand, *Scientific Method in Philosophy*, La Salle, Ill., Open Court, 1914.

Walsh, W. H., *Reason and Experience*, London, Oxford University Press, 1947.

PART III

Metaphysics or Speculative Philosophy

6

What Is Metaphysics?

Metaphysicians are musicians without musical talent.
R. CARNAP

Metaphysics or speculative philosophy has been described as that part of philosophy which raises basic questions about the nature of the world and man's place in it. The description is too broad, since philosophy itself might be defined that way. Hardly less wide is the definition of metaphysics as the study of *being* and *existence*, that is, of certain general conditions of things, over and above those studied by the special sciences. At times in the history of philosophy, metaphysics has been declared suspect, or denounced outright as the study of vain and idle questions. Kant thought that metaphysics was a dialectical and deceptive study, and his *Critique of Pure Reason* culminated in a criticism of metaphysics and its pretensions. In the 1930s and 1940s, British and American philosophy was strongly influenced by *positivism* (the doctrine that truth is best expressed in statements of science) and hence tended to reject metaphysics as a legitimate study. The 1950s and 1960s saw fairer weather for metaphysics, although recent theorists in England have tended to take metaphysical problems as second- rather than as first-order questions—

preferring to ask "What kind of statements are metaphysical statements?" rather than "What is metaphysics?"[1] Some Oxford philosophers go further than this modest concern with metaphysical *language.* Reminding us that there are categories and concepts which, in their most fundamental character, do not change at all, P. F. Strawson identifies what he calls "descriptive" metaphysics as *the study of the most general features of our conceptual structure.*[2] Despite the influence of nineteenth-century positivism, which was hostile to metaphysics, the subject never fell out of favor on the continent of Europe, and the popularity of Phenomenology and Existentialism in our own time has contributed to the relatively high prestige metaphysics enjoys in academic circles of France and Germany today.

Since the term "metaphysics" can be understood in more than one sense, it is possible that, defined one way, metaphysics will seem to us a fruitless enterprise, while, defined in another, it may appear to be a legitimate study. Accordingly, we shall set out two or three different opinions as to what the object of metaphysical inquiry is, and then go on to look at a few problems of classical and modern metaphysics.

[1] For the distinction between first- and second-order statements, see pp. 8–9.

[2] P. F. Strawson, *Individuals: an Essay in Descriptive Metaphysics,* London, Methuen, 1959. (PB: Anchor, Doubleday, Garden City, N.Y.) Strawson contrasts "descriptive" metaphysics with what he calls "revisionary" metaphysics. The latter attempts to construct a world-picture basically different and "better" than the world as it comes to us in experience. An example (not Strawson's) of a revisionary metaphysics would be that of Parmenides, who tells us that the world, which seems to change and to have many things in it, is really changeless and one. (See Chapter 5, p. 181.)

METAPHYSICS AND SCIENCE

Metaphysics as Prescientific Speculation

The ancient Greeks made little distinction between philosophy and what we would call physical science. In fact, the study of the nature of the physical world was considered the business of the philosopher until quite recent times. As a synonym for "physics" the term "natural philosophy" has not been extinct very long. The very first philosophers in the West, the Ionian Greek cosmologists of the sixth century B.C., were absorbed by the question "What kind of stuff is the world made of?" Thales, the first philosopher of whom we have any record, said that all things ultimately derived from water. Anaximenes stated that the elemental principle of things was a primordial vapor. Heraclitus held that fire was the cause of all things. Democritus' theory that the simplest units of world stuff were tiny, indivisible, material particles or *atoms* is the most remarkable product of the same ancient line of inquiry. Such prescientific speculations as to the ultimate principle of things are frequently called "metaphysical."

Today we believe that the constitution of matter and the structure of the physical universe are no longer questions for philosophy to answer, but rather for the empirical sciences, physics, astronomy, and the rest. These sciences are special disciplines which do not rely wholly upon speculation and logical reasoning but employ experimental means of confirming the hypotheses they put forward. These methods include the use of sensitive instruments of measurement which the Greeks did not have. To be sure, most scientists today will quickly decline to answer the question which the prescientific Ionian cosmologists had in mind: What is the ultimate origin or "first cause" of the universe? They usually explain their reluctance by stating that such a question is "metaphysical"; that it cannot be answered by science, since there are no methods by which it can be settled.[3]

Metaphysics as the Synthesis of Conclusions of Sciences

One modern view of the task of metaphysics is this: While metaphysics should not occupy itself with questions which the special sciences have experimental means of treating, yet it is possible to construct a metaphysical doctrine on the basis of the findings of these sciences. According to this opinion, the business of metaphysics is to fashion a synthesis of the general conclusions of the special sciences and in this way to arrive at a world perspective more comprehensive than any one of the particular sciences can offer. The aim of metaphysical philosophy, says the Danish philosopher Höffding, "is to attain points of view from which the fundamental phenomena and the principles of the special sciences can be seen in their relative importance and connection." Comte arranged the sciences according to the order of their abstractness, beginning with mathematics and ending with sociology. Referring with approval to this classification, the American philosopher W. P. Montague says:

[3] Some contemporary scientists have committed themselves on the question of the origin of the physical universe. In his *The Nature of the Universe*, New York, Harper & Row, 1951 (PB: Signet, New American Library, New York), Fred Hoyle says that the universe had no beginning; while George Gamow, in his *The Creation of the Universe*, New York, Viking, 1952 (PB: Compass, Viking), maintains that it had a definite beginning. The first is sometimes referred to informally as the "continuous creation" theory, the second as the "Big Bang" theory.

We now have the six fundamental branches of science: Mathematics, Physics, Chemistry, Biology, Psychology, and Sociology, each of them (except, of course, the first) logically dependent on its predecessor. And all of them are to be represented as the successive spokes of a wheel... but so far there is nothing to bind the spokes together. It is this binding or unifying function which *metaphysics* aspires to perform.... Accepting humbly and gratefully from the sciences their verified discoveries of this and this and that and that, we must still ask, *what is it all about?*[4]

Even the anti-metaphysical Carnap, whose view of philosophy is very different from Montague's, has no quarrel with "those theories–sometimes called metaphysical–whose object is to arrange the most general propositions of the various regions of scientific knowledge in a well ordered system."[5]

Some metaphysicians object to this conception of the task of their subject as one of integrating the broad conclusions of the special sciences. Among their number are those who believe that speculative philosophy should be constructed from material drawn from every major phase of human experience–poetic, moral, and religious, as well as scientific. To these philosophers the "scientific synthesis" view of metaphysics is too narrow and positivistic–for it seems to take for granted that scientific propositions are the most important if not the only true propositions. This conception of metaphysics, says Bergson, is altogether too modest; it reduces metaphysics to the role of a "registration court, charged at most with wording more precisely the sentences that are brought to it, pronounced and irrevo-

[4] W. P. Montague, *The Ways of Things*, Englewood Cliffs, N.J., Prentice-Hall, 1940, pp. 10–11.

[5] R. Carnap, *Philosophy and Logical Syntax*, London, Kegan Paul, 1935, p. 15.

cable."[6] Such a view leaves to the metaphysician only the passive role of awaiting delivery of various sets of propositions which he must assume in advance to be true as well as adequate representations of the character of things. Scientific descriptions, though true, may be somewhat abstract and one-sided. Metaphysicians, restricted to the task of integrating the general statements of science, may be content to offer a world picture which is no more than a pastiche of scientific conclusions. Such an outlook will be limited in its perspective; it will fail to do justice to many basic aspects of human experience.

METAPHYSICS AS THE STUDY OF BEING

Aristotle's "First Philosophy"

We do not know just how the word "metaphysics" came into use. One account says that a Greek editor, collating the writings of Aristotle, inserted the published lectures in which the philosopher deals with what he calls "first philosophy" or "theology" *after* (μετά) the treatise titled *Physics*. In any event, this particular work of Aristotle is now known as the *Metaphysics*.

According to Aristotle, "first philosophy" investigates *being*. The special sciences treat of particular *parts* of being; zoology, for example, deals with animal and political science with constitutions. But "first philosophy" deals with being *qua* being, that is, with being in general, without primary reference to some particular variety of being: "There is a science which investigates Being as Being and the attributes which belong to this in virtue of its own

[6] H. Bergson, *Creative Evolution,* A. Mitchell, trans., New York, Holt, Rinehart and Winston, 1911, p. 195. (There is a Modern Library edition.)

nature. Now this is not the same as any of the so-called special sciences; for none of these treats universally of Being as Being. They cut off a part of Being and investigate the attribute of this part."[7]

Metaphysics as Ontology

Taken in Aristotle's sense of an inquiry into being, metaphysics is frequently called *ontology* (literally, the study of being). Since there is no category more comprehensive than being, ontology is the most generic and abstract of all intellectual inquiries. Some analytic philosophers, such as Carnap, hold that ontology consists wholly of pseudo problems; that metaphysicians who ask questions about being and its kinds are under the impression that they are discussing actual objects, while in fact they are merely talking about special grammatical forms–particularly in the German language where variations of the verb "to be" have a particularly deep and mysterious sound. Others, like Tarski, maintain that ontology is not objectionable, if we understand by it "a general theory of objects . . . a discipline which is to be developed in a purely empirical way, and which differs from other empirical sciences only by its generality."[8] Without further ado about the various senses in which "ontology" may be taken, we shall proceed to mention a few well-known classic and contemporary distinctions between various *modes of being.*

Modes of Being; Permanence and Change

Aristotle divides being into two basic kinds: (1) *immutable* or changeless being and (2) *mutable* or changing being.

[7] Aristotle, *Metaphysics,* W. D. Ross, trans., bk. 4, 1003a21.

[8] A. Tarski, "The Semantic Conception of Truth," in H. Feigl and W. Sellars, eds., *Readings in Analytic Philosophy,* Appleton-Century-Crofts, 1949, p. 72.

The study of the second kind, mutable being—which, according to Aristotle, is the only kind we see in the world about us—belongs to the subject of physics or (as we would say) philosophy of Nature.[9] The study whose subject matter is the first kind of being, immutable being, is theology; for there is only one being "eternal and immovable" and this is God.

The belief that there is a mode of being which is *changeless* is characteristic of a dominant tradition in Greek metaphysics. Aristotle derived his dual classification of being from Plato, his teacher, who held that "true being" was something not subject to change and decay. According to Plato, our world exhibits only *becoming;* in the world of sense everything is coming into being and going out of being, but nothing really *is.* Only that which is changeless is real, thought Plato; reality is permanent and immutable. The world of sense experience in which everything is subject to generation and corruption is only a *reflection* of reality. Of the two primary modes of being, permanence and change, permanence is primary, more important, "realer," while change is derivative, secondary, less real.

The conviction that permanence is the primary mode of being has an interesting relationship to the classical doctrine of *substance.* One of Aristotle's classifications of being divides being into the two modes of "substance" and "accident." A substance or "thing" manifests a relatively *independent* "way" of being. Examples of substances are objects like books or men. Substances (things) are the basic existences, what we must start with if we want to think about *what is.* In contrast to substance, an *accident* or quality has no independent being, but exists *in* a substance. Blue and soft do not have the relatively self-contained being of trees and men. Qualities must "inhere" in sub-

[9] Aristotle, *Metaphysics,* Bk. 6, 1026a10.

stances such as coats or fruit. Now substances, in some fundamental way, remain the same, although their qualities may change; that is, substances retain their identity through change. A man may display the property of running or talking. But these modifications of the man pass away and are replaced by different ones. Yet the man remains, his identity is preserved through change. Substances, then, represent the relatively permanent side of Nature. The substantial aspect of things enables us to identify them on separate occasions. Thus the old and bald Socrates is in some important way the *same* Socrates as he was when he was young and had curly hair.

The Greek notion that permanence is the "realer" or "better" mode of being and that change is derivative and less real is not at all characteristic of more recent systems of metaphysics. In the world-perspectives of men like Hegel, Bergson, and Whitehead, change, process, passage is taken as primary, while the permanent and stable side of things is considered derivative, secondary, less fundamental. Along with the *general* concept of the importance of permanence, metaphysicans of our epoch have also tended to abandon the *particular* notion of substance. To them, the concept of substance is inseparable from a view of the universe in terms of basic units which are fixed, static, and enduring. The discovery of modern science that basic physical entities are electrical agitations, dynamic processes rather than static pellets of enduring matter, reinforces the conviction of the "process philosopher" that ultimate units are *happenings* rather than substances; not things but *events* are really real.

Several reasons have been offered to account for the shift from the priority of permanence to that of change in the transition from classical to nineteenth- and twentieth-century metaphysics. Some say that a reason is the decline of the great religions and their visions of eternity. Others point out that science and technology entered men's lives, that steam and factories changed the world around them. The French Revolution showed men that they can *make history*, that they can *change* the social order. The modern ideal of *progress* is another important factor in this shift of emphasis from permanence to change—although whether it is cause or effect is hard to say. The concept of biological *evolution*, which shook the intellectual fabric of Europe and the United States, stimulating scientists and philosophers to interpret the cosmos and its processes in terms of growth and development, is an additional influence.

Being and Time

Despite Aristotle's emphasis on the positive or "good" side of change shown in biological development, Greek philosophers generally tended to think of change as *katagenesis*, as falling away from being, as decay and corruption. Greek poets lamented the transiency of the world: love, life itself, the fair, the wise, the valorous, all go down to the grave. Epicurus' disciples bewailed the fate of this vast world condemned to death and ruin. What is time? To the Greeks, time was basically a *measure of motion*, a particular kind of change shown by the movement of the sidereal universe. Hence time is a category subordinate to space. Now since time measures the motion of the heavenly bodies which move in circular orbits, endlessly repeating their patterns, the Greeks thought that a law of *eternal recurrence* ruled the universe. Since there was a limited stock of matter in the cosmos, and endless time in which to recombine it, the Stoic philosophers believed that each historical epoch would one day repeat itself. To Plato and Plotinus, time was semireal, something that came into being only with the creation of the world. In the realm of true being, *eternity*, not time, prevails. Despite a new sense of the reality of history lacking in their Greek predecessors, medieval philosophers too tended to follow the ancients in distinguishing the world of time from God's world where there is no time but eternity.[10] In contrast, twentieth-century metaphysicians like Bergson and Whitehead advanced the notion, handed on from the preceding century, that time is an inseparable dimension of the nature of things; there is nothing "outside" time. They taught that reality is a continuous creativity, an endless advance into real novelty, as well as "perpetual perishing." Earlier, Hegel's historically oriented philosophy had nourished the belief among Continental thinkers that man is *essentially a temporal being*, that human nature cannot be understood outside of time and history. From this source ran a stream that led to the current of thought we call Existentialism.

Essence and Existence

When Aristotle remarked " 'What man is' and 'That man exists' are two different questions,"[11] he introduced a distinction between essence and existence, and sent it off to a distinguished metaphysical career which has lasted to the present day. "Essence" refers to *what a thing is*, to its nature, its definition or its description, if you like. "Existence" refers to *whether it is*. Existences are actualities. Essences are not actual, although we may describe them in detail. Shakespeare's Miranda is an essence. She is a possible, not an actual being. But we can answer the question "Who is Miranda?" by replying that she is the daughter of Prince Prospero, that she lives with her father on a remote and magic island, that she meets a young man cast up by the sea, and so on. Miranda is an essence, for she can be

10 "What is time?" writes St. Augustine, "If no one asks me, I know. If I try to explain it to someone asking me, I don't know." *Confessions*, 11, XIV. (PB: Penguin, Baltimore, Md.)

11 Aristotle, *Posterior Analytics*, 11, 7, 92b, 10–11.

described; she is not an existence, for she lacks actuality. The reader of this book, on the other hand, is both an essence and an existence. He can not only define himself by answering the question "Who are you?" he is, as well, an actual being. New York City combines essence and existence; it is both possible and actual. But the land of Hy Brasil where the Celtic heroes rest, is an essence only. Colors are said by some philosophers to be "pure" essences; blue is a universal quality which has an elusively simple way of actualizing itself in eyes, sapphires, oceans, cornflowers, skies, and Greek flags. In classical metaphysics, the distinction between essence and existence raised questions which concern the so-called ontological argument for the existence of God. Existentialist philosophers apply the principle "actuality is prior to possibility" to man, and state as an axiom that in human nature, existence precedes essence. We shall discuss some of these questions in due course.

The Realm of Essence; Santayana

When the existence of something comes to an end, we can no longer say that the thing exists. But we can still talk of its "what-ness" or character. The lost continent of Atlantis may once have been an existing thing; now it is an essence only. As George Santayana says:

> After things lose their existence, as before they attain it, although it is true of them that they have existed or will exist, they have no internal being except their essences, quite as if they had never broached Existence at all: yet the identity of each essence with itself and difference from every other essence suffices to distinguish and define them all in eternity, where they form the Realm of Essence.[12]

[12] G. Santayana, *The Realm of Essence*, New York, Scribner, 1927, p. 24.

In Santayana's philosophy there are two worlds. Over against the world of natural facts and events, there is an immense realm of possibilities or essences. Through sense observation and practical action we know the world of natural fact; but we reach the realm of essences through the clear intuitive insight of the imagination. The realm of essences is a world of ideal eternal objects, incredibly rich in variety, infinite in number. God and the devil are essences, as well as sky blue and B flat. The human mind has laid hold of a small part only of this inexhaustible store of timeless forms. The domain of essences is full of things no one has yet imagined, "tortures undreamed of in hell and delights unthought of in heaven." From this nonactual region come the things that matter most—all the values that enrich our lives and make our natural existence bearable. The metaphysical speculations of Plato, the theology of the Catholic church, the great visions of the poets, moralists, and saints—all are products of fertile contact between the creative imagination of man and the limitless world of essences.

The natural world has only one advantage (if it can be called an advantage) over the realm of essence—that of actual existence. Essences have "aesthetic immediacy and logical definition," says Santayana, but they have no natural being. Men have cherished the illusion that essences particularly precious to them have somewhere, somehow a footing in the world of natural fact. Frequently such men try to force their belief on others. But the wisely doubting spirit knows that essences do not exist, yet loves them all the more:

Thus a mind enlightened by scepticism and cured of noisy dogma, a mind discounting all reports, and free from all tormenting anxiety about its own fortunes or existence, finds in the wilderness of essence a very sweet and marvellous solitude. The ultimate reaches of doubt and renunciation open out for it, by an easy transition, into fields of endless variety and peace, as if through the gorges of death it had passed into a paradise where all things are crystallised into the image of themselves, and have lost their urgency and their venom.[13]

"Our" Kind of Being; Bergson; Descartes; Pascal

Many philosophers have been struck by the peculiar and immediate "feel" of our personal existence, as it is given to us directly in consciousness. Bergson, as we have seen, believed that there were two kinds of knowledge: the inward, direct knowledge he calls "intuition"; and the external, indirect, and conceptual knowledge he terms "intellect." Each of these ways of knowing deals with one of two basic modes of being. By intuition, "our" kind of being, *life*, is disclosed to us directly in the immediate data of consciousness. By intellect or conceptual knowledge, we reach and control *matter*, the kind of being physical objects represent. We have seen also that, long before Bergson, the great Descartes was so impressed by the immediacy of his knowledge of his own existence that he drew from it a primary principle upon which to base all human knowledge. Descartes's contemporary, Pascal, pondered not only on the immediacy with which we know our individual existence but also on the *unique quality* of this existence. That he, Blaise Pascal, should exist at this time, in this place, with this utterly personal and inimitable *individuality* seemed to him a subject worthy of much meditation. In Pascal's words:

When I consider the short duration of my life, swallowed up in the eternity before and after, the little space which I fill, and even can see, engulfed in the infinite immensity of spaces

[13] G. Santayana, *Scepticism and Animal Faith,* New York, Scribner, 1923, p. 76. (PB: Dover, New York.)

of which I am ignorant, and which know me not, I am frightened, and am astonished at being here rather than there; for there is no reason why here rather than there, why now rather than then. Who has put me here? By whose order and direction have this place and time been allotted to me? ... The eternal silence of these infinite spaces frightens me.[14]

To philosophize about our kind of being, about human reality, or, as Sartre would say, "to start with the subjective," is a characteristic mark of two related types of ontological method prominent in twentieth-century Continental European thought—Phenomenology and Existentialism. The distinction between essence and existence is important in Existentialism; a postulate of Sartre's *Being and Nothingness* is that existence is the first fact of human reality, while essence, character, or nature, is a subsequent construct.

PHENOMENOLOGY AND EXISTENTIALISM

Phenomenology; Husserl

The kind of philosophizing known as *Phenomenology* is most closely associated with the name of the German theorist Edmund Husserl who died just before the second World War. Husserl's general problem is one basic to any theory of knowledge: how to reconcile reality with our thoughts about reality. We recall the distinction Kant made between the object we know (*phenomenon;* appearance) and the unknowable thing-in-itself, the object as it is apart from our knowing minds. In effect, Husserl recommends that we abandon any concern we may have for things-in-themselves. Instead he asks us to give our whole attention to phenomena, that is, to things as they are ex-

[14] B. Pascal, *Pensées,* 205, 206, Everyman's Library, W. F. Trotter, trans., New York, Dutton, 1948, p. 61. (PB: Dutton.)

perienced by us. Now these objects and events are not "mere" appearances; they are the authentic data of experience. The phenomenological method requires us to take experience at its face value, to accept the credentials which things carry with them as they come. We should not approach things as if they were sets of appearances with their reality lying *behind* them. Patient, careful analysis of things and events that come to us "showing themselves" is the way of phenomenology. "It tries to give a direct description of our experience as it is," says Merleau-Ponty, "without taking account of its psychological origin and the causal explanations which the scientist, the historian or the sociologist may be able to provide."[15]

Perhaps an illustration (not Husserl's) may make the point of the distinction clearer. Take the case of jealousy. In ordinary life, when we encounter a striking instance of jealousy, our "scientific" reaction is usually to rush to explain the feeling in terms of its supposed *causes*. We say that the jealous person is immature, or that his conduct betrays a hidden form of infantile behavior, that his mother was overattentive to him, and so on. But to explain jealousy in this way, in terms of its supposed causes, is to turn away from jealousy to something other than jealousy, to something supposed to lie "behind" jealousy, although causally connected with it. So the usual popular psychological account treats jealousy as "mere" appearance, as a symptom, as surface behavior: the causes of the feeling are distinct from jealousy. Now a quite different account of jealousy may be given in a literary work. In his novel *A la recherche du temps perdu*, Marcel Proust constructs a description of jealousy in exquisite and painful detail. As presented by the novelist, the jealousy of Swann in the case of Odette, of the narrator in the case of Albertine, is jealousy as it comes, as

[15] Maurice Merleau-Ponty, *Phenomenology of Perception*, Colin Smith, trans. New York, Humanities Press, 1962, p. vii.

it is experienced, as it presents itself. In Proust's book, jealousy, minutely observed, offers no credentials other than itself. We do not have to wonder what lies behind it. No *causal* explanation is offered. None need be. So we can say that Proust's novel offers a phenomenology of jealousy just as, at an earlier date, Balzac's *Eugénie Grandet* set forth a phenomenology of avarice.

But the illustration above should not lead us to suppose that Husserl's phenomenology is a literary affair. From beginning to end, Husserl is deeply concerned with the philosophical problem of the relation of *knowing* to *being*. From his predecessor Franz Brentano, who died in 1916, Husserl derived the proposition that objects are always affected by our *intentions toward them*—they are always "objects-for-us." There is no such thing as an isolated object; the nature of every object is to an important extent the effect of our attitude toward it. Yet, for all his emphasis on the importance of intentionality in our experience of objects, Husserl insists that the things and qualities we encounter in experience are real natures, authentic *essences*. To reduce colors, for example, to "secondary qualities," or to conclude that they are "really" light vibrations is exactly the opposite of the phenomenological method. Yellow as it is experienced by us is a pure essence, a real kind. It is not mere appearance.

Neither Husserl nor his teacher Brentano ever got over their admiration for the Cartesian method. To start with the *Cogito* ("I think"), to begin philosophy with analysis of the kind of being we know best—our own immediate experience—is completely in accord with the method of phenomenology's founders. But, says Husserl, it is necessary to *correct* Descartes; "I think; therefore I am," is excessively subjective. The Cartesian *Cogito* tends to isolate the "I" from the rest of being, to make us think we have simply rescued a little tag-end of the world from doubt.[16] But the true "I" *transcends* such isolation. We may start, as did Descartes, with the immediate data of experience, but we must realize that consciousness its always consciousness of *something*. Consciousness that is *only* consciousness would be a vacuum. Experience is not just empty thought, but thought with *content*. That content is the world as we experience it. The certitude of the true *Cogito* is an *objective* certitude.

Husserl's phenomenology, followed as it was by Heidegger's metaphysics, made an enormous impression on the young students of philosophy in the French universities. They were pleased that Descartes was now revealed as the father of the phenomenological method. For it was Cartesian method to base philosophical inquiry on that kind of bring with which we are in direct contact—the Self. The renowned Bergson, whose philosophy had been overlaid by a once-fashionable "evolutionism" turned out to have had a phenomenological method of his own. His first book had for its subject "the immediate data of consciousness." His *Creative Evolution* began with the words:

> The existence of which we are most assured and which we know best is unquestionably our own, for of every other object we have notions which may be considered external and superficial, whereas, of ourselves, our perception is internal and profound.[17]

Bergson's analysis of material bodies was from the beginning marked by the concept of intentionality. The character of material bodies, said the author of *Matter and*

[16] *Cartesian Meditations.* (PB: Martinus Nijhoff, The Hague, 1964, p. 24.)

[17] Bergson, *Creative Evolution, op. cit.*, p. 1.

Memory, is determined by our possible action upon them. While the most famous product of phenomenological influence in France was Sartre's *Being and Nothingness* (1943) —subtitled "An Essay in Phenomenological Ontology"— a number of striking phenomenological studies followed it in France, of which the best known is *Phenomenology of Perception* by Sartre's one-time pupil and associate, Maurice Merleau-Ponty.

Heidegger's Ontology

Although his big unfinished book *Being and Time* ("*Sein und Zeit*") is dedicated to Husserl, Martin Heidegger criticizes the phenomenology of his predecessor as oversubjective, too Cartesian in its concentration on the consciousness of the "I." Heidegger prefers to begin with an objective ontological division of being and its kinds. Yet the type of being that concerns him most is what he calls *Dasein*, which is sometimes translated "human reality." *Dasein* ("being there," "being-in-the-world") is the kind of being exhibited by human life as it is disclosed to us, with all its uniqueness and authenticity, in consciousness. "We are ourselves the entities to be analysed," says Heidegger, "The Being of any such entity is *in each case mine*."[18] There are other kinds of being—that of ordinary objects (*Vorhanden*, as well as that of the things we can use as tools (*Zuhanden*). But it is in the analysis of *Dasein* that Heidegger puts forth his greatest effort. The reality that we know so directly and immediately, "our kind of being," is attended by a deep-rooted feeling of "care" (*Sorge*), manifesting itself in a profound sense of insecurity, an all-pervasive apprehension we may call "anxiety" or "dread" (*Angst*). We are aware

[18] M. Heidegger, *Being and Time*, J. Macquarrie and E. Robinson, trans., New York, Harper & Row, 1962, p. 67.

that our foothold in being is fundamentally shaky. We do not *have* to be; we *happen* to be. Man is *thrown* into existence, and this sense of contingency or "thrown-ness" (*Geworfenheit*) contributes to our profound metaphysical uneasiness. Dread is to be distinguished from fear. The object of fear is always *something*—a storm, an enemy, the loss of a job, and so on. But the object of dread is *Nothing*. To Heidegger (as to Plato long ago), Nothing is not a metaphysical zero. Nothing is related to being. It is "other-than-being." On those rare occasions when we apprehend Nothing, what oppresses us is the feeling that everything has slipped away and ourselves with it.[19]

Heidegger is one of few modern philosophers who has constructed a *metaphysics of death*. Death is something peculiarly and intimately related to *Dasein*, to human reality, to that reality which is temporal, which can never be abstracted from time. In Heidegger's words, "Death is Dasein's ownmost possibility," a possibility which is *veiled*. To act in the light of the importance of this possibility is to act authentically. Most of us do not do this; we do not really believe we will die. "Death certainly comes," we say, "but not right away." But in saying this, we *evade* death. We admit that death is empirically certain, but not for *Dasein*, not for our human reality. "They" die, but "I" don't. Death is something that happens to "the others." But to act as if this "ownmost non-relational possibility of Dasein" is *ours*, really ours, is to act with authentic *freedom towards death*.[20] Such is Heidegger's philosophy of death, a twentieth-century variation of Socrates' teaching that the life of a philosopher should be a continuous dying.

[19] M. Heidegger, "What is Metaphysics?" R. F. Hull and Alan Crick, trans., in *Existence and Being,* Chicago, Regnery, 1949, p. 366. (PB: Gateway, Regnery.)

[20] Heidegger, *Being and Time,* p. 311.

Existentialism

Jean-Paul Sartre took up some of Heidegger's ways of dividing being and incorporated them into his own philosophy. Sartre popularized the doctrine known as Existentialism which attracted world-wide attention after the close of World War II. It is not easy to explain just what Existentialism is, for men who are labelled "existentialists" frequently differ in basic beliefs. Sartre, for example, is an atheist, while Karl Jaspers and Gabriel Marcel are Christian believers.

The term itself has acquired several concentric circles of meaning. Sometimes "Existentialism" is used to refer broadly to that type of philosophy in which the starting point is the personal experience of the philosopher himself. Brilliant and hard-to-classify men like St. Augustine, Pascal, Nietzsche, and Kierkegaard develop their thought autobiographically in their writings; their deepest insights are often drawn from their own personal histories. More particularly, "Existentialism" designates a certain quality common to the writings of such men as those named above, an interest in the *philosophy of man*, rather than in scientific philosophy, an interest which often goes together with a certain hostility to systematic metaphysics. It is the predicament of man, the human situation, that such thinkers take as central, and "man" in this usage is neither Aristotle's rational animal nor John Dewey's intelligent agent. The starting point is, as the Spanish philosopher Unamuno puts it, "the man of flesh and bone," *this* man in all his individual and unique *existence* which is inseparable from his passion and suffering. Nietzsche and Kierkegaard are frequently cited as forbears of existential philosophy, although the first was a bitter anti-Christian, the second a Protestant theologian. Søren Kierkegaard was an eccentric Danish preacher who wrote polemics against the systematic philosophy of Hegel as well as against the complacency of bourgeois Christianity. Nietzsche too, a pastor's son, railed against pastors and professors as well; in his brilliant and aphoristic style, he wrote of the reality of suffering and the nobility of overcoming, of transcending it. "Nothing great," said Nietzsche, "comes into being except in *despite* of something." Heidegger (who is as formidably systematic as any German metaphysician) took from Kierkegaard his concept of *dread*, from Nietzsche his doctrine of the *absence of God*.[21]

Sartre's Existentialism

Our being-in-the-world is the starting point of Sartre's existentialism. Like Heidegger, he teaches that philosophy must begin from human reality, the kind of being we know better than any other, because it is our own. Sartre distinguishes between human reality (*l'être pour soi*) and the kind of being that things or objects have (*l'être en soi*). Human reality is incomplete, filled with a consciousness of a lack at its base. We yearn for the wholeness, for the foursquare completeness that physical objects, even nonhuman animals, have. Yet the contradiction that arises between my knowing myself as a center of human reality, and my inevitable tendency to treat humans as objects only, lies at the heart of the relation between ourselves and others.[22]

[21] See pp. 334–336.

[22] In her book *The Second Sex*, Sartre's disciple Simone de Beauvoir comments at length on the human male's inevitable inclination to regard woman only as body, as an object, as a sexual thing—and the resulting anguish in the feminine soul. But Merleau-Ponty says, "In sexuality, what we try to possess is not just a body, but a body brought to life by consciousness." Merleau-Ponty has developed Sartre's insight into the peculiar relation of a human being to his body. I am never at one with my body. I am always projecting myself forward from it toward the future, toward that which is not. Outward from my body stands an *intentional arc*. Failure to take this intentional arc into account limits the value of

From what source comes this lack we find in our own being? From the *nothingness* that is part of us, Sartre answers. Man is the "nothing-making animal." An earthquake, a flood, any natural disaster simply redistributes matter; only man can actually destroy. Yet the nothingness at the heart of our reality is all one with our freedom. In things, in objects, says Sartre, *essence* precedes *existence.* The nature, the what-ness, the character of a table I am designing is prior to its actual manufacture. We can have a pretty good idea of that table before it comes into existence. But, apart from being a vertebrate that talks and walks erect, man's nature does not exist before he begins to act, to *make himself* out of the choices that spring from his freedom. Man alone is able to erase the moment just past, to *cancel out* and to start making himself again. Alone among living things, he has the power to modify Being, to throw the past out of court, to create himself. Human freedom precedes essence in man, for out of our freedom, we become what we are. All our lives long, we are painting a self-portrait. This picture—our essence, our character—will not be finished until we lay down the brush at the moment of death. Even before the firing squad, as he dies for an idea, a man can define himself. Here Sartre supports Hegel's slogan, "*Wesen ist was gewesen ist,*"—essence is what has been.[23]

For a human to *be,* then, is to *act.* A man is the sum of his actions. In Sartre's book, there is no place for mute inglorious Miltons. A man is what he has done. And what

---

the usual mechanistic or conditioned-reflex psychological explanation of human behavior. The reader may wish to ask himself how much the distinction between the "*in itself*" and "*for itself*" of Sartre and Merleau-Ponty reflects the old distinction between *body* and *soul.*

[23] The simplest account of the priority of existence over essence in man appears in Sartre's lecture, "Existentialism is a Humanism" (1946). But the argument appears earlier in the first chapter of *Being and Nothingness.*

he has done, he has chosen to do. A man is not simply the product of his environment—his family, his church, his government, his poverty, his neuroses—although in their name he may deny his freedom and thus stand in "bad faith." Freedom is hard to bear; knowing that I am responsible for my acts is the source of anguish. There is no set of reasons inclining us to act one way, outweighting a set of reasons for another course. When I deliberate, I have already chosen; the chips are down. I alone act. The choice to engage myself is mine. I may try to escape the burden of freedom's anguish by denying my freedom, by appealing to this or that kind of determinism. But whatever course I choose, whatever side of the barricades I find myself on, even if I decide not to act at all, it is *my* choice. In the world of *Being and Nothingness*, there are no innocent victims.

The greater part of *Being and Nothingness* was worked out before the Second World War, although the book was not published until 1943. A remarkable development of Sartre's thought can be seen in his post-war writings, particularly in his *Critique of Dialectical Reason* (1960) together with its prefatory essay "Search for a Method." The premise of Sartre's *Critique* is that Marxism is the philosophy of our time, the only philosophy that takes man in his totality. We cannot go beyond Marxism because we have not gone beyond the circumstances that have brought it about. Marxism does not mean the Marxism of Stalin or Khrushchev or of the French Communist Party. Sartre defends what he calls "Marx's own Marxism," by which he understands a theory of history and of Nature in which facts are never taken as isolated appearances. When facts come into being together, it is always within a higher unity of a whole. As Hegel pointed out, man is part of a historical process which has its reasons and its laws; these reasons and laws can be known and used by men. Under "Capitalism" men have become alienated from the fruits of their labor. The products of men's sweat—a factory combine or an immense business corporation, say—stands to them as something threatening and hostile. Under Capitalism, it is impossible to understand a man by abstracting him from his social and economic situation. The truth of a man is the nature of his work and his wages.

Now the obvious question is: how can one be an Existentialist and a Marxist at the same time? For the one claims a radical freedom of the individual person; the other implies a historical determinism in which the individual man seems to be no more than a product of social forces. Engels taught that if Napoleon had not existed, another would have filled his place, and the replacement would have made no historical difference. Sartre denies that Marxism need entail the denial of human freedom. He finds Engels' statement on Napoleon arbitrary; it gives up the reality of an individual human life and career far too easily. Sartre prefers to cite another passage taken from a letter of Engels to Marx, "*Men themselves make their history, but in a given environment which conditions them.*" Sartre reconciles Marxist theory with his own earlier views by saying that Existentialism

> . . . intends, without being unfaithful to Marxist principles, to find mediations which allow the individual concrete—the particular life, the real and dated conflict, the person—to emerge from the background of the *general* contradictions of productive forces and relations of production.[24]

[24] J-P. Sartre, *Search for a Method*, Hazel Barnes, trans., New York, Knopf, 1963, p. 57. Sartre points out that "abstract" Marxism has much to learn from American sociology and from psychoanalysis; in their different ways these disciplines have shown how human behavior, while moving within economic class-structure, is not always simply determined by it.

In Sartre's post-war writings we find the teaching that future Marxism will develop to a point where its abstract and theoretical character will be filled out by a specifically human dimension, that is, the Marxist theory will take up into itself the existentialist truth of the reality of the individual concrete life and act. From that day existentialism will fade out as a separate doctrine, for it will have been absorbed in the totalizing "philosophy of our time," the only one which takes man in "the materiality of his condition."

Further discussion of the possibility of reconciling Sartrean Existentialism with Marxism would not be profitable, until we are familiar with some elements of the philosophy of Hegel and of dialectical materialism. We will try to accomplish this in the next chapter.

CRITICAL CONCEPTIONS OF METAPHYSICS

Since the eighteenth century there have been a number of conceptions of metaphysics which agree on this: that *metaphysics is concerned with things which cannot be shown to have actual existence.* While these critical conceptions of metaphysics are generally in accord concerning the indemonstrability of the actual existence of those entities talked about by metaphysicians, they differ as to the value or importance of metaphysics as an intellectual discipline.

Kant's Metaphysical Agnosticism

According to Kant, metaphysics is a study peculiar to that department of the knowing mind he calls reason. *Intuition* or sensibility furnishes us with the concepts of mathematics. *Understanding* is divided into categories which supply the general concepts necessary for physical science. *Reason* provides the concepts of metaphysics. Now the "ideas" of mathematics and physical science order or pull together some kind of material which comes to us in *experience*, even though we can never know the nature of that material as it exists independently of our minds. But, says Kant, the "ideas" of metaphysics have *no* foundation in experience.

What are these metaphysical "ideas" for which experience fails to provide any basis? There are three of them: (1) the *psychological idea* deals with the question of the permanence of the "self" and the immortality of the soul; (2) the *cosmological idea* treats of the question whether the world is eternal or had a beginning in time and whether *freedom* exists anywhere in the series of causes and effects which constitutes the world; (3) the *theological idea* concerns the existence of God, the first cause or "ground" of the world. In sum, the three primary metaphysical "ideas" are God, freedom, and immortality.

Kant uses the word "idea" in a special sense in this connection. "By idea," he says, "I understand the necessary concept of reason to which the senses can supply no corresponding object."[25] In other words, sensory experience gives us no ground to support convictions such as the existence of God, freedom, and the immortality of the soul. Metaphysics can never tell us more than this: it is *possible* that objects exist which correspond to these concepts. It may be that there is an enduring self and a God upon whom the world depends. But human reason can never show that these things have actual existence. Metaphysics, says Kant, is a study for which we have a natural inclination; but it is deceptive and *dialectical* in its nature. For

[25] I. Kant, *Critique of Pure Reason*, rev. ed., Max Müller, trans., New York, Macmillan, 1922, p. 266.

reason will provide us with arguments of equal force for *either side* of the disputed issues. For example, the weight of the arguments supporting free will are exactly balanced by the weight of the arguments which prove that all our acts are determined.

But Kant has a word of comfort for metaphysicians. Even though reason cannot establish the actual existence of metaphysical objects, such as God, neither can reason demonstrate that they do *not* exist. Therefore, metaphysics can at least teach us not to adopt uncritical dogmatic views such as atheism and materialism. If nothing else, the ideas of reason are valuable as *ideals*. Moreover, the concern of metaphysics for subjects like God, freedom, and immortality can prepare us for sympathetic consideration of these topics in *moral philosophy*. There we learn that, while we cannot *prove* the existence of God, freedom, and immortality through our knowing minds, nevertheless as moral agents we must *postulate* their existence.

Metaphysics as the Study of Nonnatural Objects; G. E. Moore

The British philosopher G. E. Moore takes the position that metaphysics deals with things which are *possible* rather than things which are *actual*. Moore calls anything which has actual existence a "natural object." Now metaphysical statements, he believes, are never about natural objects. Such propositions are always statements about something *supersensible*. That is, they concern things which are not objects of perception and which cannot be inferred from things which *are* objects of perception. According to Moore, inquiry into the realm of things which have not actual but only possible existence is by no means an illegitimate enterprise. Metaphysics has the edifying effect of teaching us that not all objects of knowledge are natural objects. In other words, metaphysics can inform us that there are many interesting forms of *being* which do not have actual *existence*. According to Moore, the trouble with most metaphysicians to date is that they do not realize that they are talking about objects which have no actual existence. When, like Plato, they refer to a supersensible reality—a world of eternal Forms, for example—they mistakenly suppose that this nonobservable realm has actual existence. In Moore's words:

> I admit that "metaphysics" should investigate what reasons there may be for belief in such a supersensible reality; since I hold that its peculiar province is the truth about all objects which are not natural objects. And I think that the most prominent characteristic of metaphysics in history has been its profession to *prove* the truth about non-natural existents. I define "metaphysical," therefore, by a reference to supersensible *reality;* although I think that the only non-natural objects about which it has succeeded in obtaining truth, are objects which do not exist at all.[26]

To put what Moore is saying in another way: Metaphysics would be thoroughly admirable enterprise if only metaphysicians would realize that they are talking about those objects which Santayana calls "essences"—things which are quite wonderful in their way, but which have no status in the world of natural fact.

The Empiricist Critique of Metaphysics

The conceptions of metaphysics examined in the preceding sections are *critical* in that they set limits to the subject. Yet they are essentially friendly criticisms, since they concede to metaphysics a legitimate, if restricted, status. There are, however, many contemporary philosophers whose attitude

[26] G. E. Moore, *Principia Ethica* (1902) London, Cambridge University Press, 1951, p. 112. (PB: Cambridge U. P.)

toward metaphysics is not only critical but skeptical. The most that metaphysics can offer, they say, is poetry; the rest is nonsense.

Most of these anti-metaphysical philosophers belong to that tradition of extreme empiricism which derives from Continental positivism and from Hume. Comte, the father of positivism, considered metaphysics as a prescientific stage of the development of human knowledge.[27] With science available. Comte believed, philosophers should abandon metaphysical speculation and devote their energies to constructing a unified encyclopedia of the sciences. Hume, as we have seen, believed that there were only two kinds of significant statements: those which treat of formal relations such as we find in mathematics and those which refer to observable facts. Metaphysics consists of statements which fall into neither one of these categories. Therefore, the study should be abandoned as a vain pursuit. In Hume's words:

> If we take in our hand any volume; of divinity, or school metaphysics, for instance; let us ask, *Does it contain any abstract reasoning concerning quantity or number?* No. *Does it contain any experimental reasoning concerning matter of fact and existence?* Commit it to the flames. For it can contain nothing but sophistry and illusion.[28]

Contemporary anti-metaphysical empiricists and "philosophers of language" attack metaphysics, as we have noted before, on the ground that metaphysical propositions are

[27] Comte distinguished three stages in the development of the intellectual life of man: (1) the *theological* stage, during which men explained everything by gods and spirits, (2) the *metaphysical* stage, in which men accounted for things by invoking essences and hidden causes, (3) the *positive* stage, under which men would not go beyond the observable facts in constructing explanations.

[28] D. Hume, *An Enquiry Concerning Human Understanding,* La Salle, Ill., Open Court, 1935, sec. 12, pt. 3.

unverifiable by procedures involving sense experience. From such propositions we are not able to deduce any statement asserting any experience whatever which may be expected for the future. Metaphysical propositions, says Carnap, assert nothing at all.[29] Carnap's supporter A. J. Ayer opens his assault on metaphysics with Hume's gambit:

> We may . . . define a metaphysical sentence as a sentence which purports to express a genuine proposition, but does in fact express neither a tautology nor an empirical hypothesis. And as tautologies and empirical hypotheses form the entire class of significant propositions, we are justified in concluding that all metaphysical assertions are nonsensical.[30]

Consider, says Ayer, a statement chosen at random from the pages of a metaphysical book *Appearance and Reality* by F. H. Bradley: "The Absolute enters into, but is itself incapable of, evolution and progress."[31] No means whatever can be specified which would determine whether this statement is true or false. It is therefore not a genuine proposition but a pseudo proposition. The quantity of metaphysical statements about such topics as "being" or "transcendental reality" arises from defective linguistic analysis. Because philosophers have found that they can talk about all sorts of names which do not designate actual existents, they have supposed that there must be a special mode of being, differing from actual existence, which is inhabited by these nonexistents.[32] What remains in metaphysics,

[29] Carnap, *Philosophy and Logical Syntax*, p. 17.

[30] A. J. Ayer, *Language, Truth and Logic*, rev. ed., London, Gollancz, 1948, p. 41. (PB: Dover, New York.)

[31] F. H. Bradley, *Appearance and Reality*, rev. ed., New York, Oxford University Press, 1946, p. 442.

[32] Ayer found Heidegger guilty of a naive linguistic fallacy: since "Nothing" is a word, Heidegger believes it must be the *name* of something. Thus, if you say, "Nobody is in the room," I conclude that the room cannot be empty because Nobody is in there. Heidegger, however,

Ayer concludes, over and above statements about some transcendent reality or other entities generated in linguistic confusion, are a number of passages which manifest genuine mystical feeling and which may have some moral or aesthetic value.

Can Metaphysics Be Defended?

F. H. Bradley, the author of the now notorious proposition about the Absolute and evolution quoted above, once jocosely defined metaphysics as "the finding of bad reasons for what one believes on instinct." In a more serious vein, Bradley remarks that a man who is ready to prove that metaphysics is impossible is a brother metaphysician with a rival theory of his own. With reference to Bradley's second statement, his critics point out that this type of *tu quoque* argument ("You yourself do it!") can easily be overworked. For example, it is not a very powerful argument against atheism to claim that a man who says "There is no God" is himself making a theological statement. Nevertheless, there is some strength in Bradley's implicit charge of dogmatism against the anti-metaphysical empiricists. It is probably never wise to include in one's philosophic doctrine a rule that people are forever barred by that rule from pursuing certain lines of inquiry, however unprofitable they may appear to be. For such an attitude tends to suggest that the critic is thoroughly familiar with what lies beyond the boundary he has marked "Closed."

But now to the point. The question of the legitimacy of metaphysics depends in large part on how one interprets the term "metaphysics." It is doubtless true that philosophic minds of certain types are inclined to construct systems of explanation which have little to do in any impor-

---

has denied that his "Nothing" names an object, and has urged his positivist critics to read his analysis of this concept more carefully.

tant way with human experience. In so far as critiques of metaphysics serve to recognize this inclination and to expose the absurdities to which it frequently leads, such critiques are valuable *correctives.* But the usual empiricist criticism assumes that metaphysics *must* by its very nature lack contact with experience. Metaphysics is identified as a subject which *by definition* deals with that which lies beyond experience. The subject is alleged to be the study of a "transcendent reality" or some other inaccessible domain. "I will call *metaphysical,*" says Carnap, "all those propositions which claim to represent knowledge about something which is over and beyond all experience."[33] It would be pretty difficult to find any philosopher today who would defend a subject defined in those terms.

There is no compulsion to believe that metaphysics can be defined only as an inquiry into things which are beyond experience. A metaphysician is not necessarily committed to belief in the existence of some mysterious realm which has no contact at all with the world of sense. "Metaphysics" may be understood in some other way—for example, as *an attempt to provide some unified and systematic explanation of the numerous and widely different kinds of experience we have.* To those (like Carnap) who believe that science can provide such explanation, and that this explanation is adequate, metaphysics will have the task of arranging the broad conclusions of the special sciences in systematic form. To those (like Whitehead), on the other hand, who do *not* believe that scientific statements can adequately describe all phases of human experience, metaphysics will have the work of integrating scientific conclusions with accounts of those phases of human experience for which scientific explanations are deemed insufficient. In either case, metaphysics would appear to be quite unobjec-

[33] Carnap, *Philosophy and Logical Syntax,* p. 15.

tionable, and its study a legitimate and important intellectual pursuit.

METAPHYSICS AND EXPERIENCE; WHITEHEAD

Whitehead's Conception of Metaphysics

Metaphysics or speculative philosophy is defined by Whitehead as the endeavor to frame a system of general ideas in terms of which every element of our experience can be interpreted.[34] In contrast to conceptions of metaphysics as a subject which inquires into things no one can experience, Whitehead's definition emphasizes that speculative philosophy can have meaning only in so far as it is based on and continuous with experience. "Experience," in Whitehead's view, is not just one especially selected set of experiences like science. The data of science are important and must be taken up into any system of speculative philosophy which pretends to be adequate. But science takes a special and abstract view of things. There are important facts, Whitehead believes, which elude scientific method. An example of an experience which cannot adequately be described in scientific concepts would be that arising from a poet's contact with Nature, the sort of experience Wordsworth had when he wrote:

> Ye Presences of Nature in the sky
> And on the earth! Ye visions of the hills!
> And Souls of lonely places! . . .

[34] Whitehead's exact wording is: "Speculative Philosophy is the endeavor to frame a coherent, logical, necessary system of general ideas in terms of which every element of our experience can be interpreted." *Process and Reality*, New York, Macmillan, 1929, p. 4. (PB: Torchbooks, Harper & Row, New York.)

Speculative philosophy, Whitehead believes, must be constructed on the basis of *all* phases of experience; this includes poetic, moral, social, and religious experiences, as well as scientific. The task of metaphysics is the endeavor to bring together under a general system of explanation the abstractions of science and the concrete experiences for which scientific explanations are inadequate.

The Character of Whitehead's Metaphysics

It is possible to agree with Whitehead's conception of *what metaphysics is* without accepting his own highly individual metaphysical doctrine. Nevertheless, it is only natural that this philosopher's definition of metaphysics should tie in with his particular view of the universe. Basic to Whitehead's world view is his teaching of the *interconnectedness of things*. For purposes of a particular interest—such as scientific experiment or religious meditation—we may fix our attention on certain aspects of experience as if they were separate from the total context of experience. But within that total context all things are interrelated.

The word "things" may be misleading. In Whitehead's lexicon there are no things; there are *events*. The basic units of experience are not *substances*—fixed, permanent, static entities which can be separated and isolated from changing qualities. Change is at the very heart of "things." "One all-pervasive fact," says Whitehead, "inherent in the very character of what is real is the transition of things, the passage one to another."[35] We are involved in a great *process* which includes myriads of interrelated events. Within this shifting flux we can point to unities or patterns, such as a mountain, the American nation, or a rose. These unities or patterns have varying degrees of stability and

[35] A. N. Whitehead, *Science and the Modern World*, New York, Macmillan, 1925, p. 135. (PB: Mentor, New American Library, New York.)

definiteness. But even the most permanent of these unities are ever shifting and blurring their lines with those of other unities with which they are fused. The most stable of patterns fade and finally disappear as fresh forces of creative novelty emerge in the world process. For practical purposes, we speak of the world as if it were made up of "facts." But facts are not ultimate. Process is ultimate.

The universe, then, consists not of passive enduring matter but of centers of activity. Now these active unities which constitute the world are *interrelated.* They are entwined with one another as organisms merge with their environments. And, just as organism and environment reciprocally influence one another, so it is with all the events we discern in the world process: each contributes to the other's character and qualities. "There is no possibility of a detached, self-contained local existence," says Whitehead. "The environment enters into the nature of each thing."[36]

To Whitehead, Nature is a seamless web. Throughout the world process run feelings of mutual awareness. Each individual activity takes account of all the activities with which it is connected. We participate in natural processes, and these, in some way, take account of us and of each other. There are no gaps, no sharp-cut divisions, no "bifurcations" in the nature of things. Feeling and consciousness, life and mind, are no monopolies of man. They are qualities of the world process with which we are integrated. *Value* —the quality we sense in aesthetic, moral, social, or religious experience—is not a purely subjective reaction confined to the human sphere. Value is an ingredient in the cosmos, an element of the total metaphysical situation, not just of that part of it man occupies. Nature, of which all these factors are components, cannot be described in terms of one isolated set of categories—moral, poetic, or scien-

[36] A. N. Whitehead, *Modes of Thought,* New York, Macmillan, 1938, p. 188. (PB: Capricorn, Putnam, New York.)

tific. Description of Nature in terms of sense perception approaches adequacy least of all:

> Sense-perception, for all its practical importance, is very superficial in its disclosure of the nature of things. . . . My quarrel with modern epistemology concerns its exclusive stress upon sense-perception for the provision of data respecting Nature. Sense-perception does not provide the data in terms of which we interpret it.[37]

These are the words of a philosopher in the great rationalist tradition.

Through the many-sidedness of human experience, Whitehead tells us, we become aware of the multiple aspects of the great cosmic adventure in which we are involved. The mathematician, the poet, the religious teacher, the physicist, the social reformer, the political leader—each has experiences which yield partial insights into the character of the world process. The task of speculative philosophy is to show this character in its totality. The metaphysician's view must be synoptic.

Whitehead's emphasis on the primacy of process, of the interconnectedness of things, of the interpenetration of events, shows the influence of certain *idealist* metaphysicians (Bradley, for example) who studied the German philosopher Hegel. A brief examination of the idealist tradition forms the first part of our next inquiry.

FURTHER READINGS

Aquinas, Thomas, *Concerning Being and Essence*, C. G. Leckie (trans.), New York, Appleton-Century-Crofts, 1937. (PB: Appleton-Century-Crofts.)

Aristotle, *Metaphysics*, bks. 3–9. (PB: Ann Arbor Paperbacks, Ann Arbor, Mich.)

[37] Whitehead, *Modes of Thought*, p. 182.

Ayer, A. J., *Language, Truth and Logic*, rev. ed., London, Gollancz, 1948. (PB: Dover, New York.)

Bergson, Henri, *An Introduction to Metaphysics*, T. E. Hulme (trans.), New York, Putnam, 1912. (PB: Liberal Arts, Bobbs-Merrill, Indianapolis.)

Carnap, R., *Philosophy and Logical Syntax*, London, Kegan Paul, 1935.

Collingwood, R. G., *Metaphysics*, Oxford, Clarendon Press, 1940.

Kant, Immanuel, "Transcendental Dialectic," *Critique of Pure Reason*, Norman Kemp Smith (trans.). (PB: St Martin's, New York, 1966.)

Kant, Immanuel, *Prolegomena to Any Future Metaphysics*. (PB: Liberal Arts, Bobbs-Merrill, Indianapolis.)

Plato, *Sophist*.

Santayana, G., *The Realm of Essence*, New York, Scribner, 1927.

Strawson, P. F., *Individuals: an Essay in Descriptive Metaphysics*, London, Methuen, 1959. (PB: Anchor, Doubleday, Garden City, N.Y.)

Taylor, Richard, *Metaphysics*. (PB: Prentice-Hall, Englewood Cliffs, N.J., 1963.)

Whitehead, A. N., "Nature and Life," *Modes of Thought*, New York, Macmillan, 1938. (PB: Capricorn, Putnam, New York.)

Whitehead, A. N., *Process and Reality*, New York, Macmillan, 1929. (PB: Harper Torchbooks, Harper & Row, New York.)

Whitehead, A. N., *Science and the Modern World*, New York, Macmillan, 1925. (PB: Mentor, New American Library, New York.)

In Connection with Existentialism and Phenomenology

Barrett, William, *What is Existentialism*, New York, Grove Press, 1964.

Beauvoir, Simone de, *The Ethics of Ambiguity*. (PB: Citadel, New York, 1964.)

Heidegger, Martin, *Being and Time*, J. Macquarrie and E. Robinson (trans.), New York, Harper & Row, 1962.

Heidegger, Martin, "What Is Metaphysics?" *Existence and Being*, Chicago, Regnery, 1949. (PB: Gateway, Regnery.)

Husserl, Edmund, *Cartesian Meditations* (1929), The Hague, Martinus Nijhoff, 1960. (PB: Martinus Nijhoff, 1964.)

Husserl, Edmund, *Ideas: General Introduction to Pure Phenomenology* (1913), W. R. Boyce Gibson (trans.), New York, Macmillan, 1952. (PB: Collier, Crowell-Collier, New York.)

Kierkegaard, Søren, *A Kierkegaard Anthology*, Robert Bretall (ed.), Princeton University Press, 1946.

Kierkegaard, Søren, *Either/Or*, Princeton University Press, 1944. (PB: Anchor, Doubleday, Garden City, N.Y., 2 vols.)

MacIntyre, A., "Existentialism," in D. J. O'Connor (ed.), *A Critical History of Western Philosophy*, New York, Free Press, 1964.

Merleau-Ponty, M., *Phenomenology of Perception*, Colin Smith (trans.), New York, Humanities Press, 1962.

Pascal, Blaise, *Pensées*, W. F. Trotter (trans.), Everyman's Library, Dutton, 1948. (PB: Anchor, Doubleday, Garden City, N.Y.)

Sartre, Jean-Paul, "Existentialism Is a Humanism," in W. Kaufmann (ed.), *Existentialism from Dostoyevsky to Sartre* (PB: Meridian, World Publishing, Cleveland, 1946).

Sartre, Jean-Paul, *Being and Nothingness*, Hazel Barnes (trans.), Philosophical Library, 1956. (PB: Citadel, New York.)

Sartre, Jean-Paul, *Search for a Method*, Hazel Barnes (trans.), New York, Knopf, 1963.

"Search for a Method" is a sizable essay Sartre has placed before his *Critique of Dialectical Reason* (*Critique de la raison dialectique*), a large work not yet available in English translation.

Unamuno, Miguel de, *The Tragic Sense of Life*, London, Macmillan, 1926. (PB: Dover, New York.)

7

Mind, Matter, and Nature

Almost all philosophers have confused ideas of things. They speak of material things in spiritual terms, and of spiritual things in material terms.

—PASCAL

There seem to be two very different kinds or states of "being" in the world. On the one hand, there are physical objects and events. On the other, there are our thoughts and feelings. We often refer to this distinction as that between *mind* and *matter*. The distinction is complicated by the fact that we who have these thoughts and feelings are also physical objects. However noble a man's thoughts, when you trip him with a stick, he falls downstairs just like any other physical object. Assuming that both types of being, mental and physical, have some kind of status in the world, the question may be raised: Which kind of being is primary and basic, and which is secondary or derivative? Perhaps this question cannot be answered well because of the way it is put. It may be that we make a mistake when we separate mental events and physical events into two radically different types, and then insist that somehow they coexist in human beings.

Metaphysicians often say that the subject of their study is the nature of reality. What is reality? It is that to which we refer when we are pushed to ultimate explanations of the character of things. In terms of which kind of being, mental or physical, is reality most adequately described? To this question the philosophical *idealist* will reply: the basic character of reality is analogous to mind, thought, consciousness. Physical being cannot be understood without reference to the activity of a knowing mind. The order of physical things and events is secondary to and dependent upon the order of mind and knowledge. On the other hand, the philosophical *materialist* will say that the basic character of reality should be interpreted in physical terms. All things and events, including life, consciousness, and mind, are best explained as particular states of matter or energy. The philosophical *naturalist* will answer that both the idealist and the materialist focus one-sidedly on each of two genuine aspects of what is essentially *one* real situation, that is, Nature. To the naturalist, Nature is the basic reality, and the natural is the ultimate category. From Nature arise both mind and matter, and to Nature both must be referred as their ultimate source. Nature is all that there is; *no supernatural order exists.* Our present task is to gain some further understanding of these three world perspectives, which we may label respectively idealism, materialism, and naturalism.

IDEALISM

The Meaning of "Idealism"

In ordinary conversation we use the word "idealist" to refer to a person who envisions and strives to reach goals so high that their complete achievement is unlikely. Thus, we say that Woodrow Wilson was an idealist or that the supporters of the United Nations are idealistic men and women. *Philosophical* idealism must be taken in a different sense. Very generally, the philosophical idealist takes the position that what is real, what is fundamental in the nature of things, resembles or has some important affinity to human thought, mind, consciousness, or spirit. "Outside of spirit," says idealist F. H. Bradley, "there is not and there cannot be, any reality, and the more that anything is spiritual, so much the more it is veritably real."[1]

We may distinguish three main types of idealism: (1) ancient Greek idealism, particularly that of Plato, (2) the "empirical" idealism developed by Berkeley in the eighteenth century, (3) modern German idealism and its related forms. German idealism comprehends the doctrines of a whole line of philosophers including Leibniz, Kant, Fichte, Schelling, Hegel, and Schopenhauer. What is called "absolute idealism" is related to the Hegelian type and includes among its proponents the late nineteenth-century English philosophers Bernard Bosanquet and F. H. Bradley, the Italian Benedetto Croce, and the American Josiah Royce, who was a colleague of William James at Harvard. The metaphysics of the "transcendentalist" movement in America, of which Emerson is the best-known representative, derives in part from German idealism.

Platonic Idealism

Plato's "Ideas" are not psychological states; they are not simply ideas "in somebody's head." They are neither the subjective sensations of Berkeley nor the innate categories of Kant. Platonic Ideas are timeless and heavenly models. The multitude of things in the world are but imperfect copies of these unities. Thoughts in our minds are dim reflections of them. Plato, following a line of thought suggested by his master Socrates, arrived at this position in the following way.

[1] F. H. Bradley, *Appearance and Reality*, rev. ed., New York, Oxford University Press, 1946, p. 489.

Experience conveys to us this truth, says Plato, that there is nothing that can be observed by the senses which endures. All objects perceived by the senses are perpetually changing, becoming, perishing; they never really *are*. Now, in contrast to the shifting quality of the multiple and ephemeral objects which make up the world of sense, there is the quality of general notions or concepts like "man," "triangle," or "justice" which are constantly employed in human discourse. To these general notions sense experience gives us no corresponding objects. For no one of us ever did see triangle; we see only this triangle. Nor did we ever observe good; we see only this good man. Now any particular triangle is subject to erasure; any individual good man changes with age and finally dies. But the concepts of triangle, man, good, justice, and the rest survive the passing away of any one of their particular embodiments. Long after the death of Socrates, we continue to speak of "good" and "man" in connection with other individuals.

How can we explain the existence in our minds of these universal concepts whose originals are never disclosed by sense experience, yet which outlast the objects we perceive by our senses? These notions, says Plato, are the products of reason or intelligence. To these notions correspond real objects. Unlike the objects of sense perception which are multiple and subject to change and decay, the objects with which reason puts us in touch are single and changeless. But where are these changeless unities? Plato tells us that they inhabit another world, a world that is stable and eternal in contrast to the shifting world of sense: "But of the heaven which is above the heavens, what earthly poet ever did or will sing worthily? It is such as I will describe. . . . There abides the very being with which true knowledge is concerned; the colourless, formless, intangible essence, visible only to the mind, the pilot of the soul."[2]

[2] Plato, *Phaedrus*, 247. (PB: Liberal Arts, Bobbs-Merrill, Indianapolis.)

The hierarchy of eternal Ideas is the original source of what poor measure of reality our world possesses. Whatever imperfect suggestion of order and unity we may find in the world of sense must be traced back to these deathless models, the archetypes of all order and unity. Not only are the Ideas (or "Forms") the cause of all *being;* they are the cause of all *knowledge* as well. For the universal concepts or general notions we have in our minds are but reflections within us of the light from this realm of real being. Sense percepts report only the unstable, flickering character of the physical world. Sense observation discloses to us only the *many* and the ever-changing; mind discloses *unities* that abide. True explanation of things can be only the product of the comparison of a thing with its eternal paradigm or Idea. "There are two patterns eternally set before us," says Plato, "the one blessed and divine, the other godless and wretched."[3] Or again, "There are two ruling powers, and one of them is set over the intellectual world, the other over the visible."[4] In sum, the world disclosed by sense perception is appearance or semireal only, in contrast to "true being," the supremely rational order of things upon which the world depends and to which mind alone can penetrate.

Platonic scholars disagree on what mode of being Plato believed his Ideas to have, as well as their degree of separation from things we observe by our senses. Aristotle understood his master's Forms as "separate things," dwelling in a divine world quite apart from this one. Some modern commentators believe that the Forms are more on the order of scientific laws or unchanging logical concepts to which we must refer observed things in order properly to understand them. One reason for the difficulty of grasping just what

[3] Plato, *Theaetetus,* 176.
[4] Plato, *Republic,* 509.

Plato means by the Ideas is that in his various dialogues their role seems to differ according to the subject matter of the particular discussion—temperance, justice, the State, love, being and existence, God, and so on. But in all cases, Plato's Forms seem to be universals, timeless models to which things must be referred if we wish to have a rational explanation of them.

Berkeley's Idealism

Unlike that of Plato, whose theory of knowledge is strongly *rationalistic*, Berkeley's idealism arises out of an *empiricist* analysis of knowledge he shares with Locke and Hume. This consists, as we have seen, in taking sense date as the material of knowledge. The line of argument Berkeley uses to establish the proposition that the real world is a mental world is familiar to us. What we know are our sensations and ideas compounded from these. These sensations are popularly (and wrongly) believed to be caused by material things to which they correspond. Berkeley says that there is no way of demonstrating that physical objects exist independently of us with the properties they appear to have, for every object of which we can have knowledge is a "sensed" or "experienced" object. Since we cannot know objects apart from our experience of them, the properties of objects, and indeed their very existence, depend upon a perceiving mind or experiencing consciousness.

On the basis of these arguments Berkeley concludes that the external world is the sum total of a series of effects produced in our consciousness by a cause which is not a physical thing at all. This ultimate cause of our ideas is God, a Supreme Mind or Spirit who presides over a society of finite minds or spirits. Berkeley's God is the benevolent counterpart of Descartes's malignant demon; a good genius rather than an evil one, and real rather than possible. What we call "Nature" is the result of God's stimulating in our several minds a coherent and rational system of sensations or ideas. By his constant production of ideas in human consciousness, God sustains the existence of the world. His is a continuous creation. In Berkeley's words:

> Some truths there are so near and obvious to the mind that a man need only open his eyes to them. Such I take this important one to be, to wit, that all the choir of heaven and furniture of the earth, in a word all those bodies which compose the mighty frame of the world, have not any subsistence without a mind, that their *being* is to be perceived or known; that consequently so long as they are not actually perceived by me, or do not exist in my mind or that of any other created spirit, they must either have no existence at all, or else subsist in the mind of some Eternal Spirit. . . .[5]

Hegel's Idealism

Kant's theory of knowledge implies idealism. According to Kant what we know is appearance only. Things as they exist independently of ourselves (things-in-themselves) are unknowable to us. The world of appearance, however, is not a deceptive phantasm. It is an orderly and rational world. And it is orderly and rational because its structure is the product of the knowing *mind*. Now is the rational character of our world entirely the effect of the *human* mind ordering and arranging the data of experience by means of its innate categories? Or does the nature of things possess of itself a rational or intelligible character which transcends the human mind? Kant never made his answer to these questions wholly clear. But Kant's great successor, G. W. F. Hegel, leaves us in no doubt. Hegel denies that

[5] G. Berkeley, *Principles of Human Knowledge,* La Salle, Ill., Open Court, 1903, p. 32. (PB: Liberal Arts, Bobbs-Merrill, Indianapolis.)

the rational structure of the world is simply the creation of the human mind. In Hegel's view, the human mind is but one particular aspect of a cosmic process, a world-embracing system which has a logical and rational structure in its own right. That is why Hegel's brand of idealism is sometimes called "Objective Idealism." Hegel does not deny the reality of material Nature, although to him this reality is limited compared to *Spirit* which is Hegel's "really real."

According to Hegel, there is at work in the heart of things something we may call "self-consciousness." Now self-consciousness is a property of human thought. Not only do we know; we know that we know. Self-consciousness, however, transcends or goes beyond the thought of the individual human. The universe is an all-encompassing organic whole which is in a constant state of development toward greater consciousness of itself. This cosmic process is something like a mighty system of logical thought which contains both mind and Nature. The world is a series of progressive stages of development toward a state of supreme self-consciousness, free of limitation, which Hegel calls Absolute Spirit. If we view things and events—history, art, religion, science, Nature itself—against the background of their widest set of relations, we see that they are stages of development thrown off, as it were, by Spirit as it moves through the world via progressively higher levels of growth toward complete self-realization. Now the meaning of this rational, spiritual First Principal cannot be grasped until we have studied its development from the partial and limited forms in which it reveals itself to its final all-embracing unity. The task of philosophy is to chart the development of Spirit. In order to accomplish this, we must understand the laws through which the stages of Spirit's growth are disclosed.

Hegel's "Phenomenology"

Hegel's *The Phenomenology of the Spirit* is a wildly difficult book, but many notable men (including Karl Marx, and Walt Whitman) have succumbed to its peculiar fascination. Like much of Hegel's work, the material of the *Phenomenology* is ordered by a triadic or three-stage rule. Any one stage of knowledge or of being is bound to be one-sided and limited. If a proposition is pushed to its logical extreme, this one-sidedness will be revealed together with the need to pass over to a position which is "other" than the first—often its opposite or *negation.* But this second stage may well reveal a similar one-sidedness or limitation, forcing us to move to a higher and more "self-conscious" level of inquiry, where the stages we have worked through are cancelled, yet "taken up" onto a higher level. In this triadic way the development continues progressively through higher levels, moving ever through greater clarification of concepts and more clearly exposed realities. Both knowing *subject* and known *object* are involved in a continuous process of mutual reflection as they move ever closer to their ideal actuality or "*Concept.*" The nature of this process is "*dialectical,*" a term we may apply basically to any advance through opposites. To Hegel, dialectic is *the* method of philosophy.

From the *Phenomenology* let us take a sample of Hegel's dialectical analysis. I am aware of myself as a conscious self among other conscious selves. My immediate reaction to my awareness of "the others" is double—my own pride suffers a blow, my egotism is diminished; at the same time, I want to wipe out these rival conscious selves. In primitive societies the second reaction is actualized in a modified or sublimated form. My egotism is satisfied if I can be master over a slave. My rival is now permanently fixed in inferior status. But the relation between master and slave develops in a dialectical way to the disadvantage of the former. Forced to live by his own work, the slave develops a certain self-reliance or independence, while the freedom of the master, who finds himself dependent on the slave, is relatively diminished. In the relation between Marcus Aurelius, the philosopher-emperor, and Epictetus, the philosopher-slave, Hegel sees a classical example of the master-slave duality raised to a high level of self-consciousness. Aurelius was a Stoic, and to the Stoic, all men, masters and slaves, were brothers.

But the Stoic ideal of human brotherhood, rational and noble as it was, remained essentially *abstract.* This deficiency in Stoic philosophy is reflected in the claims of a rival school, whose attitude toward the Stoic criterion of the rational is *negative.* In turn, the Sceptic philosophy reveals its limitation or one-sidedness. For the Sceptic, who holds that nothing is certain, cannot put this belief in practice in the conduct of his everyday life. His theoretical doctrine is implicitly negated by his concrete acts. The doubleness implicit in classical moral philosophy becomes sharper in the Christianity which succeeded it. From the "unhappy consciousness" of the Christian springs his vision of himself alienated, estranged from God; the divine has become remote from man. Later, modern man will try to reduce or to bridge his dualism between suffering creature and remote creator.

Hegel believed that, more than any preceding religion, Christianity revealed the nature of Spirit. We can see that Christian doctrine lends itself to dialectical interpretation. In primeval blessedness, man was at one with God. With the Fall, he became estranged from God. But with the Redemption this estrangement is overcome. God, as God, stands apart from the world, an essence tending to abstractness. In the begetting of the Son, who becomes man and world saviour, the abstract is made concrete. The third person of the Trinity, the Holy Spirit, remains with the world after its redeemer has ascended to the Father whence he came. Theologically minded Hegelians stressed the dialectical character of Jesus' moral teaching—"He that saveth his life shall lose it, and he that loseth his life shall save it." The way to self-realization is through self-renunciation. Yet Hegel believed that philosophy stands higher than religion. Religion discloses the progressive development of Spirit in terms of images and pictures. But philosophy deals with the career of Spirit in categories whose nature is Spirit's own—*rational.*

Hegel's Logic

Hegel's *Logic* is a more systematic book than the *Phenomenology*—here the dialectic is more sharply defined, the triads presented in almost Scholastic fashion. This logic is not a formal science composed of tautologies, but a "real" logic which has *content.* Since human thought and Nature are but interrelated parts of a rational cosmic process, the laws of thought are inseparable from the laws of reality. The rational is the actual. Hence logic *includes* metaphysics. Hegel invites us to consider the ontological concept of *Being.* Analysis of Being discloses that this concept is so empty and abstract that it passes over into its opposite, *Nothing.* In the dialectical process, *Being* and its opposite *Nothing* are "taken up" into the higher concept of *Becoming,* which includes them both and yet transcends them: "Being, as Being, is nothing fixed or ultimate: it yields to dialectic and sinks into its opposite Nothing.... Nothing, if it be thus immediate and equal to itself, is also conversely the same as being is. The Truth of Being and of Nothing is accordingly the unity of the two: and this unit is BECOMING."[6] Thus the process of thought is carried

[6] *The Logic of Hegel,* rev. ed., William Wallace trans., Oxford, Clarendon Press, 1892, pp. 161, 163.

to successively higher stages in which that final rational synthesis Hegel calls "Idea" becomes progressively more manifest. The highest unity of thought, within which all opposition is finally reconciled and integrated, is the Absolute Idea.

The Absolute Idea which is the goal of the dialectical process of thought is but one stage in the ultimate dialectic of the real. In that final process of the whole, we see *Idea* and *Nature* united in *Spirit*. Here the "objective" character of Hegel's idealism manifests itself on grand dimensions. The *subjective* side of things–mind, thought, Idea–forms but one pole of reality. The opposite side is the sphere of the *objective* which is Nature. But subject (Idea) and object (Nature) do not exhaust the actual, for these two realms are taken up within one final all-containing unity. This ultimate reconciliation of opposites is the work of Absolute Spirit, the history of whose progress toward self-realization is the ground of all histories, political as well as cultural. Thus philosophy, which begins with a particular striving toward self-awareness by an individual mind at length discovers itself on the universal scale in the self-knowledge of Absolute Spirit. Each stage of historical development, whether of science, art, religion, politics, or philosophy, reveals itself as a phase of the process of self-realization by Absolute Spirit. Each moment in cultural history–oriental art, Greek ethics, the modern state–is a concrete manifestation, thrown off, as it were, by Spirit as it strives to greater and clearer self-knowledge.

Philosophy itself is more than a collection of "opinions of the philosophers." Opinion, says Hegel,

> ... does not comprehend the difference of philosophical systems in terms of the progressive development of the truth, but sees only the contradiction in this difference. The bud disappears as the blossom bursts forth, and one could say that the

former is refuted by the latter. In the same way, the fruit declares the blossom to be a false existence of the plant, and the fruit supplants the blossom as the truth of the plant.[7]

The history of philosophy is more than a mere chronicle of particular doctrines, each contradicting the other. Philosophy is one, and each philosopher's teaching is a contribution—partial and one-sided though it may be—to the science of truth. The latest philosophy conserves all the work of the earlier. Nothing is lost. The history of philosophy is the concrete result of the strivings of the Spirit through twenty-five hundred years of Western thought.

Hegel's metaphysics is regarded by many critics as an outrageous farrago of nonsense. Nonsense or no, the German philosopher's doctrine made a deep impression on a modern century's thought. Although many creative minds who have used Hegel have failed to stick to the letter of his text, they have harnessed his intellectual dynamic to their own teachings in order to organize and promulgate their views. We shall see that Hegel's dialectical method was adapted by Marx and Engels in such a way as to provide a theoretical base for Communism. Sartre's major books presuppose a grounding in Hegelian philosophy. The study of Hegel was the source of *absolute idealism*, a movement that dominated academic philosophy in Europe and the United States for more than half a century.

Absolute Idealism

Certain idealist followers of Hegel described the world as a process akin to a system of thought, this thought system being a partial aspect of a comprehensive principle or absolute which is the ground of everything. What is called

[7] *Phenomenology*, in Walter Kaufmann, trans., *Hegel*, New York, Doubleday, 1965, Preface, p. 370.

absolute idealism—the doctrine associated with men like F. H. Bradley, Benedetto Croce, and Josiah Royce—may be regarded as a development of this thesis.[8] Absolute idealism may not describe the real as a system of *thought*, but rather (more broadly) as a system of *experience*. The absolute idealist holds that there is no reality apart from some experience, and that reality is a vast unified system of experiences internally coherent and mutually independent. Whose experiences? Who or what is *having* the experiences? Human experience is partial and limited; one would not expect human experience to be identical with the ultimate foundations of reality. True, says the absolute idealist, but human experience is always developing; our knowledge is constantly growing. As human experience progressively widens, it approximates more and more closely to a total system of interrelated experiences in which no single experience can be completely understood apart from the perspective of the whole. As human knowledge increases, it moves nearer and nearer to identifying itself with an all-embracing system of experiences which contains, and indeed makes possible, any particular experience. This all-containing system of experiences is reality, the absolute. Since human knowledge represents only an approximation of this final system of experiences, we do not know reality, but appearances only. But human experience is constantly widening out. It is at the same time becoming the subject of increasingly more systematic interpretation, with one realm of experience after another seen to be interdependent within the whole. Therefore, appearances may become progressively less unreal. Says F. H. Bradley:

[8] For a survey of the various channels of American Idealism, see J. H. Randall, Jr., "Josiah Royce and American Idealism," *The Journal of Philosophy*, Feb. 3, 1966.

> Reality is one . . . it is essentially experience. There is nothing in the Whole beside appearance, and every fragment of appearance qualifies the Whole; while on the other hand, so taken together, appearances, as such, cease. Nothing in the universe can be lost, nothing fails to contribute to the single Reality. . . . And hence, because nothing in the end can be *merely* itself, in the end no appearance, as such, can be real. But appearances fail of reality in varying degrees; and to assert that one on the whole is worth no more than another, is fundamentally vicious.[9]

Perhaps we can see now a little more clearly why a coherence theory of truth is essential to absolute idealism. A judgment is made on the basis of experience. Its truth depends on whether that experience ties in with other experiences. If my judgments, based on my present experience, cohere with other judgments based on a wider set of experiences, my judgments acquire a higher degree of truth. But this wider set of experiences is itself tied in with still wider sets of experience. These in turn derive what reality they possess from the all-embracing system of experiences which is reality itself. Therefore, the truth of any judgment derived from experience is ultimately constituted by its coherence with that complete system of judgments which would be formed if human knowledge could identify itself with the widest possible set of experiences, which is reality or the absolute.

MATERIALISM

Meaning of "Materialism"

We often hear popular moralists, who deplore the present state of the world, blame the world's shortcomings on "materialism." In this context of meaning, the word has a de-

[9] Bradley, *Appearance and Reality*, p. 453.

rogatory flavor; a materialist is one who attaches undue importance to money, property, power, and the like. In philosophy, the word is used quite differently. Philosophical materialism is that metaphysical view which holds that physical matter or energy determines the basic character of things and events. The kind of being physical objects or events have is fundamental; what we call mental or conscious experience derives from matter or energy and can best be explained in terms of these categories. An alternate word for this general philosophical view is *physicalism*. Let us oversimplify and put the basic tenets of materialism in the form of three propositions:

1. All things and events, including life, consciousness, and mind, are effects, on different levels of complexity, of the behavior of physical matter or energy.
2. Whatever happens can be explained in terms of the operation of a uniform system of physical laws to which all things and events, conscious or not, conform.
3. No God or any other supernatural being is required, to explain the existence and nature of the world.

The Monistic Character of Materialism

Both materialism and idealism are *monistic* systems of explanation. Any monism accounts for the world in terms of *one* fundamental category. The idealist's one all-inclusive principle is *mind* or thought; the materialist's is *matter* or physical energy. In this context, we may take the opposite of monism to be *dualism*. A dualistic position explains things in terms of two basic categories. The traditional account of the nature of man in terms of body and soul is dualistic. So is the traditional distinction between God and the world. Perhaps the most extreme form of dualism in Western philosophy is found in the metaphysics of Descartes, who held that there are two kinds of substances, material things and spiritual things, which are utterly *unlike.*

Now the first proposition of materialism denies any dualism between matter and life or matter and mind. Physical matter or energy, says the materialist, is the *one* fundamental reality; everything which seems to be different from matter or energy may be explained in terms of matter or energy. The second proposition implies that there is but *one* system of laws governing the totality of things and events. These are the patterns of behavior of matter and energy which the investigations of physical science have partly disclosed. The materialist denies any dualism which would set a particular kind of events apart from the uniform control of physical laws—those human actions, for example, which many suppose to be "free." The third proposition of materialism asserts that there is but *one* all-inclusive cosmological category—physical nature. This proposition denies the dualism implied by belief in the existence of any world transcending the physical universe—such as the Platonic ideas or the realm of supernature assumed in traditional theology or religion. Materialism denies the existence of God as a being distinct from the world.

Mechanism

The second proposition of materialism maintains that all things without exception are governed by a uniform system of physical laws. Implicit in this assertion is a doctrine known as *mechanism,* which together with its corollary *determinism* has been defended by most "classical" materialists. Mechanism asserts the primacy of a familiar type of causal sequence called *mechanical causality* in contrast to "free" or "purposive" causality. When one billiard ball knocks another into a certain position, we do not assume that the rolling ball "chooses" to act that way. Rather we assume that the ball "must" act that way if it is impelled by a certain force in a certain direction. Further, we would say that if, before the event occurred, we had all the relevant data—the weight of the ball, the point on its surface where it was hit, the force and direction of the stroke, etc.—we could by prior calculation *predict* the behavior of the ball.

The investigations of the first three hundred years of modern science proceeded on the assumption that some kind of uniform mechanical causality operated throughout Nature. The enormous success of these investigations naturally enough led scientists and philosophers to affirm that any event is predictable in principle.[10] The astronomer Laplace maintained that an intellect which knew the situations of all the bodies in Nature and the forces operating upon them could then calculate with certainty, not only all the past states of the universe, but every future state as well. A similar confidence radiates from Thomas Huxley:

> If the fundamental proposition of evolution is true, that the entire world, living and not living, is the result of the mutual interaction, according to definite laws, of the forces possessed by the molecules of which the primitive nebulosity of the universe was composed, it is no less certain that the existing world lay, potentially, in the cosmic vapor, and that a sufficient intellect could, from a knowledge of the properties of the molecules of that vapor, have predicted, say the state of the Fauna of Great Britain in 1869, with as much certainty as one can say

[10] The reader doubtless knows that contemporary physicists are not quite so sure of the universal predictability of physical events as were their nineteenth-century predecessors. Heisenberg's principle of indeterminacy was formed on the basis of experiments which indicate that certain aspects of the behavior of subatomic particles, taken individually, are not predictable. The more exactly the position of a subatomic particle is known, the less exactly is its momentum known, and vice versa. But it is doubtful whether the uncertainty principle has any bearing on the problem of freedom of human choice.

what will happen to the vapor of the breath in a cold winter's day.[11]

What does the materialist do with his concept of mechanical causality? He extends it in such a way that he sees it governing *all* things and events, including those we do not ordinarily think of in terms of mechanism. Human behavior can hardly be subject to the same laws that hold for the motion of billiard balls. Now the materialist will concede a far greater *complexity* in the human situation. Human beings are not simple objects like billiard balls. But, he will maintain, if we knew (and through science we are gradually coming to know) as much about the physical structure of the human organism as we do about simpler physical objects and events, we would realize that the difference between them is one of *degree* of complexity of structure rather than a radical distinction of *kind*. If we had sufficient data and could control the variables, we would see that whatever a human organism does can be explained in terms of the antecedent physical states of that organism together with those of its environment—just as the motion of an electrical particle may be adequately accounted for by a consideration of all the relevant physical circumstances.

Freedom and Determinism

If a uniform system of mechanical causality holds throughout Nature, then should not purposive or "teleological" causality be abandoned as a category of adequate explanation? The fact that a sunflower orients itself toward the sun is not to be accounted for on the ground that the sunflower *intends* to do so or because it unconsciously fulfills a

[11] T. Huxley, cited by H. Bergson in *Creative Evolution*, A. Mitchell, trans., New York, Holt, Rinehart and Winston, 1911, p. 38.

purpose thereby. The behavior of the sunflower is *determined* by the physical factors present in the situation. The interpretation of physical, chemical, and biological events in terms of nonpurposive causality is basic to scientific method. Struck by the wonderful success of that method, the materialist would like to extend nonpurposive explanation to include everything, including human behavior of the type usually considered purposeful. Some materialists admit the existence of purposive cause in Nature but insist on the primacy of nonpurposive causality. Does it follow that human freedom is an illusion? No, but by "freedom" is meant exemption of any part of human behavior from basic or derivative physical laws, human actions are not "free."

According to John Watson, famous American behaviorist psychologist, human behavior is simply the result of conditioned reflexes. Pavlov's dog drooled at the sight of a steak accompanied by the sound of a bell; at length, the bell's ring alone produced the salivary response. Watson claimed that human behavior can be explained wholly in terms of conditioned reflexes, allowing, of course, for the greater complexity of many human behavior situations. Could society only make up its mind what it wants, Watson said, psychologists with data and technical equipment sufficient to permit application of the necessary conditioning could turn out any kind of human being desired:

> Give me a dozen healthy infants, well-formed, and my own specified world to bring them up in and I'll guarantee to take any one at random and train him to become any type of specialist I might select—doctor, lawyer, artist, merchant-chief, and, yes, even beggar-man and thief, regardless of his talents, penchants, tendencies, abilities, vocations, and race of his ancestors.[12]

[12] J. B. Watson, *Behaviorism*, rev. ed., New York, Norton, 1930, p. 104. (PB: Phoenix, U. of Chicago Press.)

Today Watson's behaviorism is considered oversimple; but behaviorism remains at the conceptual center of much, if not most, American experimental psychology. B. F. Skinner's brilliant work on learning problems testifies to the continuing importance of behaviorism as a method, if not as a metaphysics. Skinner's book *Science and Human Behavior* considers problems incident to a behaviorist-conditioned society of the future. It does not follow from the above that every behaviorist is a materialist, although materialists often employ behaviorist explanations in defence of their doctrine. There is, however, such a high positive correlation between materialism and determinism that we may say that determinism is a *corollary* of materialism.[13]

The question of freedom versus determinism is a tricky one. Whether we are materialists or not, all of us are able to distinguish between an act done under compulsion, and one performed where no such compulsion is present. To give money to a poor man is one thing; to give money to a robber with a gun is another. There is an important difference between a confession made out of a genuine desire to admit a wrong and one wrung from a man by torture. A long line of philosophers from Aristotle to Sartre agrees that for an act to be free a possibility of *choice* must exist. Suppose I fall off a subway platform as the result of a push by another man. The event, lacking all intention on my part, is *something that happens to me* rather than an act of mine. The materialist admits the distinction, but says that it is not relevant to his claim that all acts are (1) the effects of causes, and (2) there are no causes which are not explainable in material or physical terms. When something happens, we look for a cause. A door bangs. Was it the wind,

[13] Not all determinists are materialists. A *theological* determinist would hold that every act is the necessary result of an omnipotent God's will.

or did someone slam it? A child is sick. Did he eat too much, or is he "coming down" with chickenpox? We never think, "*X* happened, but nothing caused it," although we may admit that we do not know the causes of *X*.[14] Now why should we exempt human behavior or any part of it from the rule of causality? Large areas of human behavior can be predicted successfully. Business, services, and industry are geared to this rule. A prudent beach-store manager will increase his order for hamburgers and frankfurters in expectation of a hot summer weekend crowd. Young husbands will buy more insurance. Old ones will be in the market for smaller living quarters. True, the foregoing examples are statistical in nature. They do not show that an individual person's behavior is predictable, and it is well known that some persons have the trait of being "unpredictable." The determinist would reply that this amounts to no more than saying that we do not know the antecedent conditions of such people's unexpected behavior. If we did have such knowledge, we could have predicted the effect. It does not follow that because we were unable to predict an act, that act was not determined.

But if all human behavior is determined, and none is free, we might ask the determinist why we should praise or blame? Why reward people for some deeds, and put them in jail for others? The determinist might reply that praise and blame are by no means incompatible with determinism. Praise and blame, rewards and punishments, are means of *changing people's behavior* in some desired way. To introduce children into approved modes of behavior, parents laud or scold them. Medals are pinned on soldiers to rein-

[14] Children often say tearfully, "He hit me *for no reason*." This does not mean there was no *cause* for the assault (which might have been the essential meanness of the assailant), but only that no rational explanation of why they were struck can be offered.

force in them and others the tendency toward a desired manner of conduct in battle. Putting criminals in jail is quite compatible with the truth of determinism; we may simply wish to preserve ourselves from their destructive behavior.

Determinism is difficult to refute, although we seem instinctively to react to the determinist's claim as if it were false when applied to ourselves. A well-known psychologist once admitted with humorous resignation, "For practical purposes, I act as if I had free-will but that the behavior of everybody else is determined." The claim that for every event that happens, there are antecedent causal conditions which bring it about that this event happens and not some other, seems to admit of no exception. Yet commonest experience testifies that we sometimes do deliberate, that we sometimes do think over whether we will do this or that. In a direct and simple way, we are aware that it is sometimes *up to us* whether we do this or that. My immediate consciousness tells me that I can, under certain circumstances, control my actions—whether I shall go out for a walk or stay at home and practice my guitar. Some philosophers have tried to dissolve the difficulty by distinguishing between two forms of determination, the second being compatible with the claim of human freedom. Determination need not be a compulsion upon the organism from the outside. Human beings are organisms capable of a certain measure of *self*-determination. I am an *agent*, and my acts have their source and ground in me. As an intelligent agent, I am able to foresee the results of different courses of action I contemplate. I am able to weigh the benefits of these results against one another and to make a choice accordingly. But it is *I* who make the choice; this is what is meant by self-determination.

Determinism is also subject to the following objection,

one which tries to force the determinist to admit that his claim can only be a tautology, that is, true only by definition. Consider the proposition, "All acts are determined and none are free." Now does the determinist claim that his thesis is true only because he defines it that way? No, for anybody could win any argument by making his conclusion true by definition. Then the determinist's claim "All acts are determined," must be a description of fact, rather than a tautology. But if the determinist's claim is a description of fact, we could conceive of a human act that would falsify it—as, for example, I could conceive of a mammal with a two-chambered heart, even though I believe "All mammals have four-chambered hearts" to be true. But according to the determinist, there is no exception to the determinist rule that there are antecedent causal conditions which bring it about that this event happens and not some other. The determinist would find it very difficult, if not impossible, to think up an example of a human act which *was* an exception, which *would* falsify the determinist rule. But a proposition which admits of no conceivable exception cannot be a factual or descriptive proposition. Hence the determinist's claim can only be true by definition; it is a taulology and tautologies (though always true) tell us nothing about how things are with the world or with human behavior.[15]

Mind, Life, and Value

Materialism holds that life, consciousness, and mind are adequately explained in terms of the activity of matter or

[15] This refutation of determinism is open to the objection that the argument must assume a radical separation between definitions and descriptive statements, a dualism of a kind which has been challenged by Quine and others. See p. 69.

energy. "I wish to argue for the view," says J. J. C. Smart, "that conscious experiences are simply *brain processes*."[16] The materialist claims that—while we do not as yet understand fully the nature of mental activity—there is no reason why mind cannot satisfactorily be explained in physical terms. We know that the brain is in a constant state of electrical activity. We know that mind depends on brain. A minute fragment of bone driven from the inner table of the skull into the brain can transform a statesman or philosopher into a driveling idiot. It has been known since the days of the Greeks that human functions, including mental ones, can be correlated with specific parts or areas of the brain. But the brain is a pound or two of matter. It can be held and weighed on a small scale. Is it a confusion of language to refer to the *mind* as "that seven inches of inner space between the root of the nose and the occiput"? How can the richness and interiority of our mental life be equated with the behavior of a smallish mass of matter? How can we say that the creativity of mind is "simply" brain states? Nineteenth-century materialists taught that mind is an *epiphenomenon*, a by-product of the processes of the physical organism, like the electrical glow that may sometimes be seen hovering over a machine at work. Later, behaviorist psychologists said that mind can be described adequately in terms of observable behavior. Mental life is a fiction, said Watson, for thinking is but subvocal talking; that is, thinking is essentially motor contractions. Contemporary materialists are confident that recently developed calculating machines will dispel much of the mystery associated with human thought. These marvelous devices, they say, are like human brains; an important difference between the two is that the computers have a compara-

[16] J. J. C. Smart, *Philosophy and Scientific Realism*, New York, Humanities Press, 1963, p. 88.

tively small number of electrical circuits, while the brain has millions.

The materialist reminds us that we inhabit a little planet which revolves about a rather unimportant star which is a member of a galaxy of stupendous dimensions, this galaxy itself only one of thirty million or so composing the physical universe. *Life* has arisen on our small planet as the result of a chance collocation of atoms. Temperature and other conditions happened to be suitable for life's development. The evolution of life is accounted for by the adaptation of living forms to the less highly organized physical environment. The complex character that life forms have assumed in the course of evolutionary history is no more to be put down to purposes inherent within these living forms than the shape of the human nose is to be explained on the ground that such a shape is most suitable for the wearing of spectacles. The universe itself has no inherent purposive direction. The man who said that there is "one far-off divine event toward which all creation moves" was no scientist, but a poet influenced by theology.

The materialist does not deny that human beings have values and ideals. These, however, he generally views as subjective in nature and related to external material factors as effect to cause. Ethical values develop from the desire of the organism to preserve its life and well-being. Aesthetic values arise from the need on the part of the organism to release emotional tensions brought about by physiological or environmental conditions. Religious values have their origin in the fears and insecurities of a highly sensitive animal organism, frightened by physical phenomena and overborne by the immensity of the universe.

There are a number of difficulties raised by the materialist concept of mind. Some of these may be seen indirectly in our discussion of mental events at the end of this chapter. But here are a few common objections put down by way of sample.

1. The materialist argues that mind's dependence on brain shows that mental events are essentially physical in nature. Bergson holds that this line of argument confuses "dependence on" with "nature of." The coat hanging on the coat-hook is dependent on the hook, and when the hook breaks, the coat falls to the ground. But it does not follow that the coat *is* the coat hook. So damage to the brain may destroy mind. But it does not prove that mental events are identical with brain states.[17]

2. It is dangerous to argue to the physical nature of mind by way of analogy to machines, computing or other. We often compare organic functions to machines. We may say, for example, that the human body is like a locomotive, taking in fuel, expending energy in the form of work, discharging waste, etc. Or that the human arm is like a crane, or the eye like a camera. But such analogies cut two ways. While a man may be compared to a locomotive, the locomotive in turn may be thought of as a crude man, with limited functions (muscular) powerfully exaggerated. Or we may say that a crane is a simple arm, or that the camera is a crude eye. Similarly, specialists in *cybernetics* may find it useful to compare human thinking with the behavior of calculating machines, but a computer may just as easily be thought of as a simplified brain. In any case, to compare a human organism to a machine is not to prove that the human organism *is* a machine, for the analogy turned around could then be used to "prove" that machines are human organisms.

3. A scientific explanation of something is important and useful. Yet such an explanation need not exhaust the meaning of that thing. According to modern science,

[17] H. Bergson, *Matter and Memory*, London, G. Allen, 1911, p. 80. (PB: Anchor, Doubleday, Garden City, N.Y.)

lightning is a movement of electric charges from one ionized layer of cloud to another such layer or to the earth. Yet it is misleading to conclude that "This is what lightning *really* is." An explanation of something in terms of its *causes* need not be identical with what that thing "really is." A child may know nothing of ionized layers. Yet the lightning he sees during a thunderstorm is part of what lightning "really is."

4. Materialism commits the fallacy of *reductionism*. The reductive or "nothing-but" fallacy is explaining *A* by saying "*A* is nothing but *B*." We are in danger of falling into reductionism whever we try to account for something by saying it is not what it is, but something else. Extreme examples of the reductive fallacy are contained in assertions like "Romantic love is nothing but glands" or "Religion is nothing but magic." In his anxiety to prove that "All is matter in motion," the materialist reduces genuinely *different* levels of experience to *one* only. To say that life is simply highly organized matter is to say that life is nothing but matter. But this explanation ignores real differences between living and nonliving things. Instead of explaining life, the materialist explains it away. To say mind is nothing but electrical activity is to refuse to treat mind as an important type of experience. The materialist tendency to fit all things into the categories of physics and chemistry:

> ... is equivalent to the denial that certain kinds of facts are "really" facts. To say that the phenomenon of a living organism is "nothing but" an arrangement of chemical compounds is to disregard relationships of which experience gives clear testimony. To say that values are no more than names given to purely physical situations is to dismiss one portion of experience *in favor* of another.[18]

[18] J. H. Randall, Jr. and J. Buchler, *Philosophy: An Introduction*, New York, Barnes & Noble, 1942, p. 231.

Historical Background of Materialism

The doctrine that the ultimate cause of the world is physical stuff is found in the earliest Western philosophy. The Greek atomists (Leucippus, Democritus, and Epicurus) held that this physical material occurs in the form of tiny indivisible particles called *atoms* which move through space or *void* according to a principle of *necessity* inherent in things. All objects are combinations of atoms. The human mind is composed of particularly light and delicate particles. There are gods, but they too are physical beings composed of atoms. They have no control over the laws of Nature, nor do they interfere in human affairs. In his great philosophical poem *On the Nature of Things*, the Roman poet Lucretius sets this metaphysical doctrine in Latin verse. No need to fear death, Lucretius tells us, for death is but the dissolution of the society of atoms of which we are composed. There is no afterlife in which we shall be judged and punished for our misdeeds.

Materialism disappeared during the religious Middle Ages for obvious reasons. The rise of materialism in modern times is directly related to the development of the physical sciences. The conception of a world composed of physical bodies operating upon one another in regular predictable patterns went hand in hand with enormous advances in the understanding and control of natural processes. Newton's wonderful picture of a cosmic mechanism was quickly detached by his materialist admirers from his belief in God. Earlier, Thomas Hobbes had already explained everything in terms of bodies in motion. His French contemporary, Descartes, was no materialist; but the Cartesian dictum that all living substances other than man were machines inevitably led to the question "Why not man also?" The eighteenth-century French materialist

La Mettrie wrote a book titled *Man a Machine*. La Mettrie belonged to a group of free-thinking, anti-clerical writers of the French Enlightenment—men such as Diderot, d'Holbach, and d'Alembert—who helped popularize a rather naive mechanical materialism.

The history of materialism shows that materialists have adjusted their doctrines in different ways in order to meet objections to the *determinism* implied in their doctrine. Epicurus held that the atoms falling through space have a slight tendency to swerve, an *exiguum clinamen*, a minute deviation from a perfectly straight trajectory. In this way, an incalculable element is introduced into Nature, and in the human soul there is present a "nameless element" which accounts for freedom of choice. French materialists of the eighteenth century met the difficulty head on. They admitted that their doctrine precluded moral responsibility, claimed that crime was nothing but a disease, and recommended hospitals for the wicked. They conceded, however, that legal punishment was a necessary though regrettable social expedient; but they urged that correction should be as mild as possible. In our own century, the physicist Schrödinger wrote a fascinating little book, *What Is Life?*, offering an analysis of living organisms in terms of an enlightened but relentless materialism. Organic life is at its base nothing but the protein molecule, and this molecule is a complex arrangement of atoms in the pattern of an aperiodic crystal. But when he comes to account for his own unshakeable conviction that it is he, Erwin Schrödlinger, who controls the aggregate of molecules that is himself, he confesses that the only plausible answer to the problem seems to be that of the ancient Indian philosophers—"I am God."

The triumph of Darwin's evolutionary theory in the nineteenth century was followed by a wave of popular materialist essays couched in the idiom of biology rather than physics. Huxley in England and Haeckel in Germany contributed to the growing popularity of the belief that living forms, including man, were but chance products of molecular combinations in a vast process of cosmic evolution. The disciples of Hegel in Germany included not only a religious and theologically inclined group—the "right-wing" Hegelians—but also a left wing, sympathetic to materialism and absorbed by problems of social and political reform. The disputations of these men provided an intellectual setting from which Karl Marx and Friedrich Engels developed the most powerful form of modern materialism. This is *dialectical materialism*, for years the official metaphysics of the Soviet Union and, as such, well deserving our separate attention below.

Apart from the dialectical variety, materialism is rather rare today. Few academic philosophers in Britain or the United States would now describe themselves as materialists, although a number would describe their doctrine as *naturalism*, which some critics take to be a modified form of materialism. Materialism is a general world view, and world views are somewhat out of fashion in academic philosophy today. Materialism is rather more common among intelligent amateurs. Indeed, this has almost always been so. Apart from the old Greek atomists and certain of their predecessors, the history of philosophy includes very few philosophers of the first rank who can be classified as materialists. But this fact should not necessarily be taken as discrediting materialism. It may be that philosophy is at fault. Lenin, a brilliant philosophical amateur, has said that philosophy, throughout nearly its whole history, has yielded to a dominant *idealist* tendency. The reader of this book is invited to judge.

Dialectical Materialism

This theory combines the fundamental materialist thesis that matter alone is real with the following propositions of Hegelian origin: (1) all things are interconnected; (2) all things are in the process of development; (3) this development proceeds according to dialectical laws. This theoretical framework supports an explanation of human social and economic development in terms of the material needs of men, and of the social classes which have control of the production of necessities which satisfy those needs.

As we should expect, dialectical materialism asserts the primacy of matter. Says Engels:

> The material, sensuously perceptible world to which we ourselves belong is the only reality.... Our consciousness and thinking are the product of a material, bodily organ, the brain. Matter is not a product of mind, but mind itself is merely the highest product of matter.[19]

And Lenin says:

> Matter is that which, acting upon our sense-organs, produces sensation; matter is the objective reality given to us in sensation.... Matter, nature, being, the physical–is primary, and spirit, consciousness, sensation, the psychical–is secondary. ... The world picture is a picture of how matter moves and of how "*matter thinks.*"[20]

To the dialectical materialist the world of matter does not consist in a simple mechanical assemblage of physical

[19] F. Engels, *Ludwig Feuerbach,* New York, International Publishers, n.d., pp. 39, 43.

[20] V. I. Lenin, *Materialism and Empirio-Criticism,* in *Selected Works,* New York, International Publishers, 1943, vol. 11, pp. 207–208, 402.

bodies isolated from and independent of each other. This, they say, is eighteenth-century "mechanical" materialism which must be corrected. The material world is "a connected and integral whole, in which things, phenomena, are organically connected with, dependent on, and determined by, each other."[21] Not only is every part of this material system interrelated with every other part; the entire system is constantly undergoing change and development. The older mechanical materialism, says Marx, fails to account for change. It treats of change simply as the relocation of static bits of matter in new positions—which is no change at all. Dialectical materialism holds that change is at the heart of Nature. Matter is not static, but dynamic. It is constantly in development, which continually manifests itself in the formation of new forces and phenomena and in the breakdown of the old.

How does matter change? The answer given by Marx and Engels is that matter develops *dialectically*. Hegel was wrong in claiming primacy for Idea and Spirit. His idealism must be rejected. But Hegel was right in his belief that the world process moves dialectically, that is, by means of opposites inherent in the development of things. "In its proper meaning," says Lenin, "dialectics is the study of the contradiction within the very essence of things." The history of every object and event can be understood only in terms of the development within that object or event of its own opposite or contradiction, and the emergence of that opposite upon the dissolution of that which gave it birth.

To describe the dialectical development of the material world Marx and Engels adapted three Hegelian principles: (1) the law of transformation of quantity into quality; (2)

[21] J. V. Stalin, *Dialectical and Historical Materialism*, New York, International Publishers, 1940, p. 7.

the law of unity of opposites; (3) the law of the negation of the negation.

1. The law of transformation of quantity into quality is invoked to do justice to the genuine qualitative difference of things and to avoid the oversimplification of the older materialism in which qualitative differences are conceived merely as rearrangements of quantities of matter. Dialectical materialists say that in the development of matter new qualities arise at certain critical points or "nodes." The qualitative transformation is not gradual, for when the nodal point is reached, there is a comparatively quick change or "leap" into the new state. This may be illustrated by changing states of natural substances, as in the case of the freezing of a liquid. When the temperature of water is lowered, there comes a critical point at which the liquid changes quickly into a qualitatively new state—ice. Dialectical materialists see this law at work in the realm of social action as well as in physics. Industrial capitalism, a qualitatively new social order, sprang comparatively quickly into being, although the conditions favorable to its development had been in existence for a long time. So also with the Soviet Socialist order.

2. The law of the unity of opposites states the familiar dialectical principal of the essentially contradictory character of things. The unity of all objects and events covers an internal polarity of opposites. This doctrine was taught in early Greek philosophy by Heraclitus, who held that the apparent stability of things was the result of tension between opposite forces, as in the case of a bow or lyre string. Hegel maintained in his *Logic* that opposites, like positive and negative, never represent an absolute difference but are in some way identified. What is negative to the debtor is positive to the creditor. A way to the East is also a way to the West. We cannot have the north pole of a magnet without a south pole. Applying this law to social theory, Marx asserted that at the basis of social conflict or "class struggle" was a contradiction between the methods of production available to a particular society and the social re-

lationships characteristic of that society. Under capitalism, the proletariat or working class seeks to expand and to change the system of social relations to an extent comparable to the massive changes in the means of production brought about under capitalism. The proletariat, however, is opposed by the "bourgeoisie," who control the means of production; they strive to prevent or to limit the social changes demanded by the working class. When the conflict between the two opposing forces reaches its nodal or "breaking" point, there will occur, in accordance with the first of the three dialectical laws, a sudden and violent leap, via revolution, from bourgeois capitalism to a new social order, *scientific socialism.*

3. The law of the negation of the negation may be clarified if we consider any state of affairs to be developing its opposite or negation within itself in Hegelian fashion. This negation in time breaks away to stand over against and in opposition to the state which gave it birth. But this second state (the first negation) generates its own opposite, which then stands forth as the negation of the first negation. According to Marx, capitalism cannot exist without its own negations. But these negations will ultimately negate capitalism. An example of the internal contradictions of capitalism is its tendency to overproduction, which brings about unemployment. This in turn prevents the workers from buying the goods produced. Thus arise economic crises or depressions in which the very existence of capitalist economy trembles in the balance. With the final collapse of capitalism will emerge the world socialism envisioned by Marx. This new social order is thus the negation of the negation. Here is Marx's illustration of this law: "The capitalist mode of appropriation, the result of the capitalist mode of production, produces capitalist private property. This is the first negation of individual private property, as founded on the labor of the proprietor. But capitalist production begets, with the inexorability of a law of Nature, its own negation. It is the negation of the negation."[22]

[22] Karl Marx, *Capital,* New York, International Publishers, n.d., vol. 1, p. 789.

Comment on Dialectical Materialism

It is difficult to appraise dialectical materialism impartially. The doctrine depends heavily on key concepts drawn from Marx's social philosophy, such as the "materialist conception of history." The adequacy of these concepts has been widely challenged by historians and economists. Charges of "scholasticism" and "academicism" have been raised by some critics who point to the fact that Marx had no systematic metaphysics, that dialectical materialism as a system owes its existence to the more pedantic Engels. (The three famous "Laws of material dialectics" appear for the first time in Engel's uncompleted *Dialectics of Nature.*) The soundness of dialectical materialism is in part contingent on the worth of its Hegelian conceptual framework. Much of it reflects the *Logic*, the more abstract and systematic side of Hegel, rather than his more "existential" *Phenomenology*. Marx himself was fascinated by the *Phenomenology*, deriving from it his early concept of "Alienation."[23]

The writings of older dialectical materialists are so full of violent attacks on other positions that it is not easy to disengage exposition and support of the theory from the mass of polemic in which it is embedded. Lenin's chief philosophical book, *Materialism and Empirio-Criticism* is essentially a defense of a realist or objectivist theory of

[23] Marx uses the terms "alienation" (Entaüsserung) and "estrangement" (Entfremdung) interchangeably in his early *Economic and Philosophical Manuscripts* (1844). Hegel distinguishes between the two—"alienation" involving "estrangement" only if what is relinquished or transferred ("alienated") confronts the alienator as a hostile power. Marx extends the concept of alienation to modern society as a whole. Work, wealth, and the state—although created by man—turn to confront him as alien and hostile powers. The instruments of production, the factory, the mill, the business house, are not within his control and stand over against him, alien, threatening, strange.

knowledge against certain positivist and phenomenalist theories. But its diatribes against dozens of now-forgotten theorists distract our attention from the central thesis. The polemic trend in dialectical materialism reached the high fever point in the Stalin era. Here is an extract from an outline of a (then) projected Soviet history of philosophy:

> The tasks of this chapter are to subject to partisan Bolshevik criticism the reactionary, bourgeois ideology of the imperialist period; to show its connection with the general crisis of capitalism and with the corruption of all contemporary bourgeois culture; to pull to pieces with particular severity the reactionary philosophical and sociological doctrines used nowadays by the enemies of Marxism; to show that V. I. Lenin and J. V. Stalin tirelessly attacked the rotten anti-Marxist idealistic doctrines and reactionary social ideas of the imperialistic bourgeoisie and mercilessly exposed every kind of tendency toward idealism and priestcraft; and to emphasize that the contemporary bourgeois ideology is an arsenal of reactionary and odious ideas for the right-wing socialists—the lackeys of the imperialistic bourgeoisie.[24]

Since the death of Stalin, the abusive tone of Soviet philosophy has moderated somewhat. In 1963 Soviet philosophers visited the annual meeting of the American Philosophical Association and took part in a symposium sponsored by the Society for the Philosophical Study of Dialectical Materialism, an American organization. Since that time a number of philosophers from the U.S.S.R. have been invited to joint meetings with their Western colleagues.

Supporters believe that dialectical materialism represents an important landmark in the development of materialism. It brings into materialism the causal role of social factors which the older materialism neglected. Its Hegelian "rational kernel" enables it to correct many of the inade-

[24] *A Soviet History of Philosophy*, William Edgerton, trans., Washington, D.C., Public Affairs Press, 1950.

quacies of "mechanical" materialism. It recognizes the limitations of any materialism founded on a conception of the world as an essentially static system of isolated bodies moving about one another. The Marxian metaphysics replaces this "mechanical" materialism with a world perspective in which change and development are treated as internal and basic, rather than as external and accidental relocations of permanent particles in space.

Nevertheless, critics maintain that the dialectical materialist's claim that "matter moves dialectically" is itself open to serious question. While striking instances of "dialectic" can be pointed out in Nature (for example, the polar character of electricity), there are many natural objects and events which do not seem to behave in a particularly dialectical manner. Such phenomena can be accounted for dialectically only by forcing the facts to fit the theory. It is also objected that dialectical materialism lacks power to *predict* and hence is of no use to science. But its defenders argue that the concept of Evolution has little or no predictive power, yet it has served a useful purpose as an ordering concept in the biological sciences as well as stimulating philosophical thinking.

NATURALISM

We recall that one of the basic propositions of materialism is: no God or any other supernatural being is required to explain the existence and nature of the world. That is, if a philosopher is a materialist, he is almost certainly an atheist. True, ancient materialists like Epicurus and Lucretius said there were gods. But these gods were natural, although superior, beings who dwelt in a realm above the world in blessed tranquility and took no thought of the affairs of men. Indeed, some scholars hold that neither Epicurus nor Lucretius really believed in the gods at all, but included these beings in their cosmologies in order not to offend against patriotism and good taste. Materialism, then, claims that God does not exist, except as a construct of the human mind. But materialism does not have a monopoly on this negative belief concerning God. A philosopher may hold that the materialist is wrong in claiming that all is matter or energy, wrong in his mechanistic determinism, but right in his claim that there is no God. What then would be an appropriate name for the view of the philosopher in question? In recent years, the name "*naturalism*" has been suggested as appropriate. Naturalism may be defined very generally as the belief that things and events have natural rather than supernatural causes; that the cosmos has a natural rather than a supernatural origin; that man has a natural rather than a supernatural end.[25] Naturalism is a "this-worldly" rather than an "other-worldly" view of things. That is why, for example, we speak of the "naturalism" of Chinese classical philosophy. Confucius was averse to any form of supernatural explanation and found all problems of interest to him in Nature and in human relations. For the same reason, we describe Aristotle's general approach to problems as "naturalistic," even though this philosopher believed in a God who was distinct from the world. For, despite his theology, Aristotle tends to explain things pretty generally without reference to another world. In this respect, we contrast Aristotle

[25] In literary criticism the word "naturalism" refers to a factual and realist treatment of subject-matter such as we would find in the works of Zola and Dreiser. The American novelist James T. Farrell claims philosophical naturalism as well. The author of *Studs Lonigan* says "I have been called a naturalist and I have never denied it. However my own conception of naturalism is not that which is usually attributed to me. By naturalism I mean that whatever happens in this world must ultimately be explainable in terms of events of this world. I assume or believe that all events are explainable in terms of natural origins rather than of extranatural or supernatural origins." *New York Times Book Review*, Sun., Nov. 21, 1957.

with the "other-worldly" Plato, who held that the ultimate explanation of things must be sought in the divine world of Ideas. Aristotle criticized his master's doctrine of the ideal world on the ground that it is superfluous to erect another world in order to explain this one. Such criticism is typical of the naturalist attitude.

Taken less broadly "naturalism" refers to a general approach to philosophy—not specific philosophical teachings—that developed in the United States after the ascendancy of the pragmatists. Toward the close of the last century the philosophy taught in American colleges and universities was generally some form of idealism. The reaction against idealist metaphysics, led by Peirce, James, Dewey, and their followers, helped develop interests less concerned with systematic metaphysics and comprehensive world views than with inquiry into scientific method and an empirical approach to moral and social problems. Nevertheless, the new American empiricism required a metaphysical stand on the question of Nature versus Supernature. The empiricists, generally, declared themselves on the side of Nature. This is pretty much the position of the majority of American philosophers in secular schools today, although they tend to be less concerned about it than teachers of an older generation. Santayana helped to popularize the term "naturalism," although he himself was interested neither in empiricism nor scientific method. Santayana found his own this-worldly outlook compatible with the ideals of reason and harmony of classical Greece.

Naturalism and Religion

Naturalism denies the existence of God, if God is conceived as an *actual* being distinct from the transcending Nature. Does it follow that every naturalist is an atheist? Or can belief in naturalism and conviction of the importance of religious values be reconciled? Historically, materialistic naturalism has been identified with militant atheism, aggressive secularism, and anti-religious and anti-clerical movements. But, in American naturalism, there has been considerable effort on the part of *some* philosophers to grant religious experience a genuine status, to recognize religious values, and to integrate religion within a naturalistic world outlook. Contemporary naturalists may be divided into "right-wing" and "left-wing" groups, or, to borrow William James' terminology, into those who are "tender-minded" and those who are "tough-minded." "Tough-minded" naturalists are closer in spirit to the older materialists. They are indifferent to the problem of religious values, or actively opposed to attempts to bring religion in any sense into a naturalistic world outlook. "Tender-minded" naturalists are sympathetic to religion. While they generally reject the forms of orthodox or traditional religions, they believe that religious values are important and can be incorporated within a naturalistic philosophy.

Santayana's attitude toward religion has had considerable effect upon American naturalism. This philosopher, as we know, holds that, in addition to the world of natural fact, there is a world of essences which can be reached through man's creative imagination. These essences are *not* natural facts, but, taken as *ideals*, they can give meaning to life; they can and do lend color, richness, and value to experience. Among these ideals are those of poetry and religion: "Religion and poetry are identical in essence and differ merely in the way in which they are attached to practical affairs. Poetry is called religion when it intervenes in life, and religion, when it merely supervenes upon life, is seen to be nothing but poetry."[26] To Santayana, God is an ideal,

[26] G. Santayana, cited by J. Dewey in *A Common Faith*, Yale University Press, 1934, p. 17. (PB: Yale U. P.)

not a fact. Theology deals with essences rather than existences. Yet ideals and essences communicate with life by providing centers about which our lives can be organized and made significant. Without them life could hardly be human. But, Santayana reminds us, while everything natural has an ideal fulfillment, every ideal has a natural basis. Taken as descriptions of natural fact, the traditional religions can only lead to disillusion. Taken as symbolic interpretations of life, they can help us to accommodate ourselves to destiny in a tranquil spirit.

John Dewey is a naturalist whom it would be misleading to classify as "right-wing" or "tender-minded." Yet he admires Santayana's conception of religion as concerning ideal values. Santayana distinguishes two elements in religion—a moral consciousness and a poetic or mythological conception of things. It is religion's connection with the moral life that interests Dewey. He is concerned with religion's relation to the ideals by which men set their goals and with the effect that these ideals have on practical action. To Dewey, the religious life consists of commitment to ideals and continuing efforts to realize them. Since ideals have the power to guide action, religious values occupy a high place among those norms which govern human conduct. God is a name for our ideals conceived as a unity:

> Suppose ... that the word "God" means the ideal ends that at a given time and place one acknowledges as having authority over his volition and emotion, the values to which one is supremely devoted, as far as these ends, through imagination, take on unity. If we make this supposition, the issue will stand out clearly in contrast with the doctrine of religions that "God" designates some kind of Being having prior and therefore non-ideal existence.[27]

[27] Dewey, *A Common Faith*, p. 42.

The general direction taken by Santayana and Dewey is followed by those contemporary naturalists who are anxious to find a place for religious values within a naturalistic scheme. Their approach is humanistic, since religious values are seen as grounded, not in any supernatural source, but in human nature itself. "Right-wing" naturalists hold that there is a place for religion in a naturalist philosophy, since religion is a fact of human experience. What the naturalist usually means by "religion," however, is not some historical form of religion, not an "organized" religion. Santayana is an exception here, for he believes that the naturalist can enjoy a traditional religion. One cannot speak in language in general, he says, but only in a particular language. But most American naturalists shy away from "orthodox" religions, preferring to take religion as Dewey's "common faith," a devotion to those unified patterns of ideals by which one guides one's life. Says S. P. Lamprecht: "The religious life is . . . a life in which multiple interests and diverse values are brought into effective and organic unity through central allegiance to some integrating ideal. . . . Religion ought to be the ornament of a rich life, not the driving passion of a fixed commitment."[28] It is obvious that such a concept of religion is very different from religion in the sense in which it has been traditionally conceived.

However sympathetic he may be toward religion, the "right-wing" naturalist gently, occasionally almost reluctantly, declines to concede the existence of God as an actual being distinct from the universe. The naturalist position in regard to this question is generally that, while the notion of a transcendent God is not inherently self-contradictory, there is no empirical evidence to warrant belief in the

[28] S. P. Lamprecht, "Naturalism and Religion," in Y. Krikorian, ed., *Naturalism and the Human Spirit*, Columbia University Press, 1944, pp. 20, 38.

actuality of such a being. In the following chapter we shall examine some elements of traditional philosophical theology, as well as certain modern concepts of God as a "real" being. The reader may then consider whether these theological claims have a place only within an older religious culture from which our secular age has long since drifted away, or whether they have some weight in their own right.

In sum, naturalism excludes theism, the philosophical doctrine that God exists as an *actual* being. It denies a dualism between God and the world; it denies the existence of a supernatural order as over against the natural order. But *some* forms of naturalism are compatible with the teaching that God is an *ideal* and that this ideal may influence human lives for the good.

SOUL AND MIND

Old philosophers liked to compare man to a "little world" or *microcosm* within a "great world" or *macrocosm* which is the universe. On the macroscopic level, the naturalist philosopher rejects any dualism between Nature and Supernature, God and the world. On the scale of the microcosm—that is, the human being—the naturalist rejects any body-mind or body-soul dualism in which mind or soul is conceived as a spiritual or divine principle separable from the body. He rejects the view that the soul is radically "other" than the body. At the same time, he insists on the crucial importance of mind and the human capacity of intelligence, and denies the classical materialist's thesis that mind is nothing but matter behaving in a complicated way.

Two Concepts of Mind; Plato and Aristotle

In Western thought there developed two great concepts of mind which we may call the Platonic and the Aristotelian views—after the philosophers who started them on their way through history. To Plato the mind is a faculty of the *soul*, and the soul is our real self, an incorruptible spiritual entity radically different from and opposed to the body. The body is composed of matter, the principle of heaviness, sluggishness, and inertia; it weighs down the soul and prevents its clear vision through its highest power—mind. But the soul is not fated to die with the body. By nature, soul is immortal. Says Socrates in the *Phaedo:*

> The body is a source of endless trouble to us by reason of the mere requirement of food; and is liable also to diseases which overtake us and impede us in the search after true being: it fills us full of loves, and lusts, and fears, and fancies of all kinds, and endless foolery, and in fact, as men say, takes away from us the power of thinking at all. . . . In this present life, I think that we make the nearest approach to knowledge when we have the least possible intercourse or communion with the body and are not surfeited with the bodily nature, but keep ourselves pure until the hour when God himself is pleased to release us.[29]

Aristotle has a different notion of soul. Like Plato, he believes that mind is a faculty of the soul. But to Aristotle the soul is not a spiritual principle imprisoned in a body as a bird in a cage. The soul, he says, is *the form of the body*. That is, the soul is the principle of organization of any living thing. A man's soul is his *life*, and mind or "reason" is the highest activity of that life. Thus conceived, body and soul are as inseparable as the structure of anything is inseparable from the material of which it is composed. "That is why," says Aristotle, "we can wholly dismiss as unnecessary the question whether the body and soul are one: it is as

[29] Plato, *Phaedo*, B. Jowett, trans., 66, 67.

meaningless as to ask whether the wax and shape given to it by the stamp are one. . . ."[30] Traditional Christian religion, deeming belief in a separable and immortal soul as basic, inclines somewhat to the Platonic concept of the soul. The early Fathers of the church had no *philosophical* doctrine of their own with which to explain the *religious* teaching of the nature and destiny of the human soul. So they used Platonic concepts and metaphors in teaching about the soul. But theologians pointed out that, while to Plato the soul was immortal by its very nature (*de jure*), the Christian teaching is that the soul's immortality is a gift, the result of the sustaining power of God's grace (*de facto*). Moreover, a spiritual soul totally at odds with a material body does not fit well with the religious doctrines of the Incarnation and Resurrection. Christ did not come to save souls, said Tertullian, he came to save *men*. Thomas Aquinas denied that the soul was in the body "like a sailor in a ship" and tried to reconcile the Aristotelian concept of the soul as the form of the body with the notion of the separable soul of Christian faith. But despite this *totus homo* ("whole man") view of theologians, the language of popular Christian teaching about the soul has remained to this day deeply colored by Platonism.

Mind and Body; Descartes' Problem

Descartes is well named "the father of modern philosophy," for he raised a number of questions which affected the subsequent course of philosophy down to the present day. One of the important problems he treated was that of the relation between *mind* and *body*. According to Des-

[30] Aristotle, *De Anima*, 512b6. The neat opposition of the Platonic and Aristotelian concepts of the soul is marred by the fact that Aristotle hesitates over the question whether the "active intellect" might not, after all, be immortal; while in his *Republic*, Plato reorients his concept of

cartes, there are two kinds of substances or things in the universe—*mental* things (minds) and *physical* things (bodies). These two kinds of being are radically different. But what about humans, who seem to be both mind and body? I am a conscious, thinking being, said Descartes. Immediate experience tells me that I am a mind, that it is my nature to think. It is as a thinking substance that I cannot doubt my existence. But I perceive that I have a body which is a physical thing. How can these two fundamentally different kinds of being—a thinking substance and an extended, physical substance—coexist to form the unity which is myself? How do these totally different entities cooperate? That mind and body *do* interact seems plain enough. When my mind apprehends bad news, my face turns pale. When my body is injured, my power to think may be impaired or lost. But how is this possible? How can one kind of being affect the other which seems completely different?

Descartes thought that mind and body affected each other through the medium of what he called "animal spirits." In addition, he believed that the pineal gland in the brain served as a locus of exchange of influence between mental and physical events. This solution was regarded as unsatisfactory even in Descartes' time. But the French philosopher's answer to the mind-body problem is less important than the fact that he raised the question. Certain of his successors stressed the role of the *mental* side of human nature, and played down the physical. This line of thought led to modern *idealism*. Other philosophers after Descartes focused on the importance of *material* things, and endeavored to explain life, consciousness, and mind as subclasses of physical events. This tradition led to modern *materialism*.

---

soul in a rather more "naturalistic" direction. Nevertheless, the contrast between the two classic interpretations of soul remains.

How Are Mind and Body Related?

The simplest answer to this question is given by *materialism.* A human being is, fundamentally, a body, a material thing. Now he is not a *simple* material body like a penny or a stone. Rather, he is a combination of material parts in a highly complex pattern. All the parts of a human being are in constant activity. The activity of the brain includes all those events we call *mental*—thinking, sensing, feeling, wishing, etc. In sum, a human being is a highly complicated active organization of matter. Part of that activity is the circulation of the blood. This can be pretty well observed and measured. Another part of that activity is mental activity. This cannot as yet be as well observed and measured, because of the greater complexity of the brain's composition and behavior compared with that of the blood and its circulation. Much of the brain's activity appears to be electrical in nature. Some of this electrical activity can be measured by machines like the electroencephalograph. It is true that we cannot now tell, by observing brain activity, what a person is thinking. But because we cannot now do so, this does not mean that mental events are totally "other" than physical events. In fact, we can often tell about mental events by watching physical events. I can tell if a small child is in pain by watching his behavior. Thinking may simply be a kind of talking, as the behaviorist Watson held, a kind of talking which we cannot as yet hear and record.

A *dualist* theory of the mind-body relation holds that mental events and physical events are different in kind, not just in degree. My mind and my body are two quite different affairs, and one is not to be explained in terms of the other. Descartes's dualism was extreme, for he held that mental and bodily happenings were utterly different, and that they coexisted only in man. Nonhuman animals, he thought, were complex mechanisms; the cry of an injured dog, "the crash of broken machinery." But any dualism, Cartesian or modified, which holds to an essential difference between mind and body leads to the same difficulty that bothered Descartes: how, if mind and body are different in kind, do they interact? They certainly *seem* to interact. But, if mental events and physical events belong to two different orders, how can one have causal power over the other? What goes on in my mind, I assume, is private and internal; and I hold the same goes for your mind. But my body is publicly observable and has a pushing effect on people in the subway; and so, I assume, is yours.

So the dualist theory seems to square with common sense, for in ordinary life we draw a fairly sharp distinction between mind and body. Now the materialist theory does not seem to square with this common-sense distinction. If the materialist is right, you and your body are identical. Your mind is a complicated part of your body's behavior. Yet it seems queer to say that "I enjoyed the concert" and "My body enjoyed the concert" mean the same thing. If the materialist is right, thought is no more than an activity of the brain. But it is odd to try to imagine, even in principle, a machine which could peer so closely into my brain that it could *see* what I was thinking about—my mother's favorite chair, let us say. In his turn, the dualist is stuck with the seemingly insoluble difficulty of having to explain clearly and coherently how mind and body interact. The great Leibniz was so puzzled by this problem that he finally declared that mental and bodily events do *not* interact; they only seem to because God in his goodness and power sees that the two orders of events—those of my mind and those of my body—*parallel* each other in such a way that they appear to interact although in reality they do not affect each other at all.

Ryle's Concept of Mind

An influential book on the mind-body problem appeared in England in 1949—Gilbert Ryle's *The Concept of Mind.* Ryle denies a dualism between mental and physical events, yet declines to accept the materialist's claim that mental events are just a special kind of physical events. The trouble started, he says, by the traditional dualist assumption that there are two totally different kinds of existence—mental and physical. It is supposed that every man is made in two parts, so to speak, (1) a *body* that is material, located in space, and publicly observable, (2) a *mind* that is immaterial, that cannot be located in space, that cannot be publically observed since it is utterly private to each person. This false dualism, Ryle thinks, has been arrived at by assuming that every *physical* self must be attended or backed by a second, *mental* self. Around me are observable persons walking about, talking, reading books, scolding children, repairing engines. Now each one of these observable persons carries about with him a corresponding second self, but invisible, nonpublic, known only to himself. In short, a mental self. Such is the traditional dualism assumption.

But in assuming the existence of a second mental self that must stand behind or within each physical self, we commit what Ryle calls a *category mistake.* Suppose I were to be taken to visit a university. I am shown the buildings, meet some professors, see the students in the lecture rooms, inspect the offices and residence halls. Now suppose I were to say, "Yes, I've seen the students, the teachers, the buildings, and all that, but when are you going to show me the *university?*" Why is my question silly? Because it makes out that I think a university is a thing similar to but separate from a group of students, faculty, buildings, and so on. The truth is that a university does not belong to the same type or order of things as buildings, teachers, or students. Nor is it something over and in addition to them. So too the following belief involves a category mistake: that corresponding to my physical self there is a related, but private and invisible *mind* which I alone can know. This essentially dualist view assumes that every visible human body must be doubled by an associated invisible mind.[31] Ryle holds that this mind-body dualism, now traditional and ingrained in "common-sense," comes down to us from Descartes who held that each person is a mental self standing behind a complex physical apparatus called the body. Ryle labels this Cartesian dualism and its descendants "the dogma of the ghost in the machine." Santayana, an earlier critic of this mind-body dualism, called it "the clumsy conjunction of an automaton with a ghost."

Ryle rejects any dualism between mind and body that would make the first private and unobservable and the second a mindless material object. Human beings are unities. There is no impassable gulf between the behavior of the bodies and the thoughts and intentions of their minds. Novelists like Jane Austen do not hesitate for a moment to assume that their characters' observable actions show quite well what is going on "in their mind." Parents, teachers, and children, draw a large part of their practical conclusions by watching people's behavior. Depending on how you act, I assume that you are tired, interested, hopeful, or in love. And if I am a perspicacious observer, chances are I shall be in the right of it more often than not. So much for the myth of essentially private, impenetrable mental worlds—yours or mine. Human beings are unities; they come in one piece. For certain purposes, we distinguish between (a) what goes on when a person falls on the ice, is raised in a ski-lift, or runs 100 yards in ten seconds flat, and (b) what goes on when a person is thinking of last summer, wanting the class to end, or mentally testing a new theorem or dress design. But the fact that we do so distinguish

[31] Opposing higher education for women at Harvard, President Eliot may have fallen into a category mistake when he argued that women's minds could not be like men's minds, since their bodies were so different.

between the two sorts of events does not mean that humans are packaged in two watertight compartments, the first bodily, material, and publically observable; the second interior, mental, and forever private. Once we appreciate the fact of the essential unity of human beings and the artificiality of the physical-public mental-private distinction, says Ryle, we shall appreciate as well the origin and refutation of the materialist-dualist dispute. The materialist is wrong because he holds that there *are* no really mental events; everything is physical. The dualist is wrong, because he tries to repair the essential shakiness of the house of materialism by doubling it with a *shadow of that house*. Because a house has an inside and an outside is no reason for claiming either that (a) the inside of the house is really a complicated form of the outside, or that (b) the outside and the inside are totally different kinds of being whose intimate connection with one another will remain forever mysterious.[32] Of the two solutions to the mind-body problem, Ryle sympathizes more with dualism than with materialism, although he believes both theories are false. Human beings *are* mysterious. But the mystery will never be solved by reducing humans to mechanisms, then attempting to activate the mechanisms by inserting shadow-mechanisms within them to make them work.

The influence of Ryle's philosophical behaviorism on recent Anglo-American philosophy has been considerable. His work stimulated a new area of interest in contemporary philosophy, a field that has come to be known as Philosophical Psychology or *Philosophy of Mind.* The fact that Wittgenstein's later philosophical studies raised questions concerning the relation between our thoughts, feelings, and intentions, on the one hand—and our actions, on the other—has added to the interest in this area of philosophical inquiry.

32 The comparison of the inside and outside of the house is not Ryle's example, and may be misleading. After all, we *can* enter houses to look at the inside directly, and the exterior of *some* houses provides no information as to their probable interior character.

FURTHER READINGS

Idealism

Berkeley, G., *Principles of Human Knowledge*, La Salle, Ill., Open Court, 1903. (PB: Liberal Arts, Bobbs-Merrill, Indianapolis.)

Blanshard, Brand, *The Nature of Thought*, New York, Macmillan, 1941.

Bradley, F. H., *Appearance and Reality*, rev. ed., Oxford, Clarendon Press, 1946.

Ewing, A. C., *Idealism: A Critical Survey*, New York, Humanities Press, 1950.

Hegel, G. W. F., *Logic*, in *The Logic of Hegel*, rev. ed., William Wallace (trans.), Oxford, Clarendon Press, 1892.

Hegel, G. W. F., *The Phenomenology of the Spirit*. Translated as *The Phenomenology of Mind* by J. B. Baillie, rev. ed., New York, Macmillan, 1931.

Kaufmann, Walter (ed. and trans.), *Hegel*, New York, Doubleday, 1965.

Plato, *Phaedo*. (PB: Liberal Arts, Bobbs-Merrill, Indianapolis.)

Plato, *Phaedrus*. (PB: Liberal Arts, Bobbs-Merrill, Indianapolis.)

Royce, J., *The Spirit of Modern Philosophy*, Boston, Houghton Mifflin, 1892.

Materialism

Elliot, Hugh, *Modern Science and Materialism*, New York, Longmans, 1919.

La Mettrie, J. de, *Man a Machine* (1748), La Salle, Ill., Open Court, 1927. (PB: Open Court.)

Schrödinger, E., *What is Life?* New York, Macmillan, 1945.

Sellars, R. W., M. Farber, and V. J. McGill (eds.), *Philosophy for the Future: The Quest of Modern Materialism*, New York, Macmillan, 1949.

Smart, J. J. C., *Philosophy and Scientific Realism*, New York, Humanities Press, 1963.

Smith, H., "Kamango," in A. Woolcott (ed.), *The Woolcott Reader*, New York, Viking, 1935. (PB: Compass, Viking.)

Dialectical Materialism

Engels, Friedrich, *Dialectics of Nature*, New York, International Publishers, 1940.

Lenin, V. I. *Materialism and Empirio-Criticism*, in *Selected Works*, New York, International Publishers, 1943, vol. 11.

Marx, Karl. *Karl Marx: Early Writings*, T. B. Bottomore (ed.), New York, McGraw-Hill, 1964. (PB: McGraw-Hill.)

Stalin, J. V. *Dialectical and Historical Materialism*, New York, International Publishers, 1940.

Wetter, G., *Dialectical Materialism*, New York, Praeger, 1958. (PB: Praeger.)

Naturalism

Dewey, John, *A Common Faith*, Yale University Press, 1934. (PB: Yale U. P.)

Dewey, John, *Experience and Nature*, New York, Norton, 1929. (PB: Dover, New York.)

Krikorian, Y. (ed.), *Naturalism and The Human Spirit*, Columbia University Press, 1944.

Nagel, Ernest, "Naturalism Reconsidered," *Proceedings and Addresses*, American Philosophical Association, Oct., 1955, vol. 28. Reprinted in M. Mandelbaum *et al.* (eds.) *Philosophical Problems*, New York, Macmillan, 1957, pp. 751 ff.; and Y. H. Krikorian and A. Edel (eds.), *Contemporary Philosophical Problems*, New York, Macmillan, 1959, pp. 337 ff.

Randall, J. H., Jr., and J. Buchler, "The Broader Conception of Nature," *Philosophy: An Introduction*, New York, Barnes & Noble, 1942. (PB: Barnes & Noble.)

Santayana, G., *The Life of Reason*, Vol. 4: *Reason in Religion*, New York, Scribner, 1905–1906. (PB: Collier, Crowell-Collier, New York.)

Santayana, G. *The Realm of Matter*, New York, Scribner, 1930.

Freedom and Determinism

James, William, "The Dilemma of Determinism," *The Will to Believe and Other Essays*, London, Longmans, 1908.

Lehrer, Keither (ed.), *Freedom and Determinism*. (PB: Random House, New York, 1966.)

Mill, J. S. "Of Liberty and Necessity," *A System of Logic* (1843), London, Longmans, 1925, chap. 2, bk. VI.

Morganbesser, S., and J. Walsh (eds.), *Free Will*. (PB: Prentice-Hall, Englewood Cliffs, N.J., 1962.)

Skinner, B. F. *Science and Human Behavior*, New York, Macmillan, 1953. (PB: Free Press, Macmillan.)

Taylor, R., *Metaphysics*. (PB: Prentice-Hall, Englewood Cliffs, N.J., 1963, chap. 4.)

Watson, J. B., *Behaviorism*, rev. ed., New York, Norton, 1930. (PB: Phoenix, U. of Chicago Press.)

Philosophy of Mind

Chappell, V. C. (ed.), *The Philosophy of Mind*. (PB: Prentice-Hall, Englewood Cliffs, N.J., 1962.)

Descartes, Rene, *Meditations*. (PB: Liberal Arts, Bobbs-Merrill, Indianapolis.)

Ryle, Gilbert, *The Concept of Mind*, London, Hutchinson, 1949. (PB: Barnes & Noble, New York.)

Taylor, Richard, *Metaphysics*. (PB: Prentice-Hall, Englewood Cliffs, N.J., 1963, chaps. 1–4.)

8

Theism

The world is charged with the grandeur of God.
It will flame out, like shining from shook foil.
—G. M. Hopkins

"THEISM" refers to that metaphysical position which asserts the existence of God as an actual being. We have seen that some naturalist philosophers use the word "God" to mean a concept which binds human values or goals into a unity. But this position is not usually considered a form of theism, since God is treated by the naturalist as an ideal rather than as a "real" being. A very large part of the traditional philosophy of the West is theistic. Those metaphysical systems which developed within the religious traditions of Judaism, Christianity, and Islam unanimously took as their point of departure the existence of a God who had created the world and who was distinct from it. Although early Greek philosophy and the atomist school that developed from it represented a frank naturalism, the dominant metaphysical tradition—that of Plato and Aristotle—was theistic. In modern times, despite the rise of naturalism, many systems of theistic metaphysics have been formulated. Modern theistic doctrines have been marked by increasing degrees of individualism and a lessening reliance on the presuppositions of the religious traditions.

Theology has been defined as that division of metaphysics which treats of the existence and nature of God and his relation to the world. We should take note of the traditional distinction between "natural" theology and "revealed" or "sacred" theology. In the religious culture of the Middle Ages it was generally assumed that there were two main sources of reliable knowledge, revelation and human reason. Medieval theologians held that, while the richest source of theological knowledge was to be found in revelation, it was perfectly possible to acquire knowledge about God "by the light of natural reason." Later, philosophers came to refer to any inquiry into the existence and nature of God without the aid of Scriptures, faith, tradition, a teaching church, etc., as "natural theology," "natural religion," "theodicy," or (as in the case of Kant) simply "theology." Our present inquiry is concerned, not with "revealed," but with "natural" theology.

CLASSICAL ARGUMENTS FOR THE EXISTENCE OF GOD

In the course of Western philosophy, a number of arguments for the existence of God have been developed. Let us say at the outset that these arguments can be taken or construed in at least four ways:

1. *As strict demonstrations.* That is, granting of the premises of these arguments necessarily leads to the conclusions.
2. *As offering good reasons.* Less strict than the first, this way of understanding the arguments is to construe them as giving good reasons why we should believe that God exists, but not as formal proofs of that existence.

3. *As disproofs of the irrationality of belief in God.* That is to say, the arguments have some value, but only to the point of indicating that the existence of God is not contrary to reason.
4. *As bad arguments.* That is, the arguments for the existence of God are essentially fallacious.

We should also note that in the past these arguments usually appeared within a context of religious faith. Traditional theologians did not believe that God's existence could be proved "from scratch." They were aware of the difficulty of proving the existence of something without first knowing in some way what kind of being it is that they were looking for. Sensitive to this type of problem, theologians have usually been reluctant to allow the arguments for the existence of God to be isolated entirely from the presuppositions of faith. Yet philosophers who did not believe themselves bound by such presuppositions—Aristotle, and Spinoza, for example—have gone on record as claiming that these arguments are sound *apart* from religious context.

Let us consider the three best-known classical arguments for the existence of God together with some of their variations. They are usually labelled (1) the cosmological argument; (2) the ontological argument; (3) the teleological argument.

The Cosmological Argument

This argument has at least three forms. The proof from *motion* as set forth by Aristotle and reproduced in various ways in traditional philosophy runs this way: The world is composed of things which move or change. Of these, none has the power to move itself. All things are moved by others. But these other things also lack the capacity of self-movement and are themselves moved by others, which in turn are moved by still other agents. Now, unless we are to conclude that the world is an *infinite* series of moving things, none of which has the power of self-motion, we must conclude that it is ultimately moved by a mover which is itself unmoved. "It is evident," says Aristotle, "that the first mover must be something that is one and eternal."[1] This unmoved mover is God.

Of course, many things "move themselves." Animals, for instance, have the power of locomotion. In the context of the argument, however, the word "move" may be taken in a broad meaning akin to "cause." If we substitute "cause" for "move," we may obtain that variation of the cosmological argument which is known as the proof from *causality*. This argument goes as follows: Experience tells us that nothing which exists has brought itself into existence. That is, everything that exists has a cause or causes. But the causes of things are themselves caused, and those causes in turn are the effects of still other causes. It is evident, then, that the world is composed of things none of which has the power to cause itself; hence the world cannot be its own cause. Therefore it is concluded that the world is caused by some cause other than itself, a cause which is uncaused. This uncaused cause is God.

A third variety of the cosmological argument is the argument from *necessity and contingency*. It is found in the writings of Thomas Aquinas in this form:

> If everything is possible not to be, then at one time there could have been nothing in existence. Now if this were true, even now there would be nothing in existence, because that which does not exist only begins to exist by something already existing. Therefore, if at one time nothing was in existence,

[1] Aristotle, *Physics*, 259a15.

it would have been impossible for anything to have begun to exist; and thus even now nothing would be in existence—which is absurd. Therefore, not all beings are merely possible, but there must exist something the existence of which is necessary. . . . This all men speak of as God.[2]

In other words, a thing may be said to have *necessary* existence, if it *has* to exist. It has *contingent* or possible being only, if it *happens* to exist. Now experience tells us that nothing in the world *need* exist. That a table does not have to exist can be demonstrated by chopping it up. That a man need not be is attested by the fact of his death. The world as a whole, then, is a contingent rather than a necessary being, since it is composed of contingent beings. But if the world is contingent, there is no reason why there should be a world in the first place. The alternative is to assume the existence of a being who *has* to exist, who is a *necessary* being, who is the "reason" for the existence of the world. This is God.

Comment on the Cosmological Argument

The reader may care to sharpen his skill in analysis by subjecting the cosmological argument (as well as those proofs we have yet to examine) to his own criticism. Here are a few well-known objections to the cosmological argument set down without further development:

1. The Aristotelian proof from motion rests upon an erroneous physical cosmology in which the earth was thought to receive motion transmitted by relatively im-

[2] Thomas Aquinas, *Summa Theologica*, pt. 1, q. 2, art. 3; Fathers of the English Dominican Province, trans., London, Burns and Oates, 1924, p. 26. Aquinas avoids saying that what is reached by these arguments *is* God. Rather, he says, it is what men *call* God. Only when speaking of God's essence or nature—in connection with the unity or oneness of God—does he say "And this is God" (pt. 1, q. 9, art. 3).

mutable heavenly bodies which in turn were moved by the Unmoved Mover. Further, Aristotle's argument assumes that an infinite series of movers is impossible. But there is nothing about an infinite series, as such, which is self-contradictory. It is possible to construct such a series in arithmetic.

2. The argument from causality does not answer the child's question "Who made God?" Those who defend this argument deny self-causing power to Nature but attribute it without hesitation to God. But, when we make God, rather than Nature, the exception to causality as ordinarily experienced, we evade rather than solve the difficulty of accounting for the world. What we have done is simply to ser the difficulty back one stage, by postulating a cause outside of Nature which is unlike other causes.

Further, the argument assumes that causality, which we experience only in Nature, holds good outside of Nature. That is, we have experience of causal laws holding among finite or contingent things. But we have no basis for the belief that causal laws hold between Nature as a whole and some being supposedly apart from and above Nature.

3. It may be admitted that nothing in Nature contains its own reason for being, and that therefore things and events are indeed contingent. But to infer from the contingency of things and events, taken individually, that Nature as a whole is contingent, and thus dependent upon another being, is to commit the fallacy of composition. This fallacy consists in arguing from the properties of the parts, taken separately, to a property of the whole, taken together. Because sodium and chlorine are poisonous, it does not follow that table salt, which is composed of these elements, is equally poisonous. Although any part of Nature, taken singly, may be contingent or dependent for its existence on something else, it does not follow that Nature, taken as a

whole, is also contingent. In other words, there is no reason why Nature cannot be considered to be the ultimate ground of all existence, even though its parts depend for their existence on other parts.

The Ontological Argument

This argument, which has many interesting and subtle variations, is associated with the name of St. Anselm, a theologian of the eleventh century. It was popular with the Continental rationalists of the seventeenth century and may be found in the writings of Descartes, Spinoza, and Leibniz. The Anselmian form of the argument may be freely paraphrased thus: Let us conceive of a perfect being (*ens realissimus*). Now such a being will contain all the attributes of perfection. Existence is one of these attributes, for, of two supposed "perfect beings," one of which exists and one of which does not exist, the former will possess something that the latter lacks, and hence alone will be the "perfect being." Now to say that the perfect being includes the attribute of existence is simply another way of saying that he (God) exists. From the very conception of God, therefore, his existence may be inferred.

But, it will be objected, by means of such an argument it would be possible to prove the existence of all manner of fictitious beings. This difficulty was actually offered to Anselm himself by a monk named Gaunilon, who observed that, although he could think very hard of a perfect island, this perfect island was not on that account brought into existence. Defenders of the ontological argument, however, deny the validity of the comparison between the conception of God and that of an island or any other created thing. We may conceive of an island perfect in its own kind, that is, having all the perfections of an island. But an absolutely perfect island—one containing all the attributes of perfection—would no longer be an island, but God. Now God is a *necessary* being. That is, his essence (what he is) and his existence (that he is) are one and the same. Therefore God *must* exist. In created things, on the other hand, essence and existence are *not* the same. A particular flower has essence, for it may be described; it has existence, for there it is. But that the flower's essence and existence are two different things is proved by the flower's dying. After the flower's existence ceases, its character may be described in a poem. But its character did not suffice to hold the flower in existence. So with all created things. In God, however, essence and existence are identical. If they were not, if God did not *have* to exist, he would be just like a created thing and subject to passing out of existence like the flower. But such a God would not be a God at all. Now if in God essence and existence are one and the same, merely to define him—indeed, merely to *conceive* of him (as a perfect being, for example)—is to show that he exists. Or, as Descartes puts it, the existence of God follows from the idea of God just as the property of 180 degrees follows from the idea of triangle.

Comment on the Ontological Argument

The ontological argument has been rejected by a variety of philosophers, including Thomas Aquinas and Kant. Aquinas interprets the argument as asserting that the existence of God is *self-evident.* But, he says:

> No one can mentally admit the opposite of what is self-evident; as the Philosopher [i.e., Aristotle] states concerning the first principles of demonstration. But the opposite of the proposition "God is" can be mentally admitted: *The fool said in his heart, There is no God* (Ps. lii 1). Therefore, that God exists is not self-evident.[3]

[3] Aquinas, *Summa Theologica,* pt. 1, q. 2, art. 1.

To put Aquinas in modern terminology, he is saying that the proposition "God exists" is not a tautology or an analytic statement like "A triangle has three sides," which is true *by definition.* "God exists" is to him a synthetic or factual statement whose truth cannot be established merely by examining its syntactical structure.

Kant sees in the ontological argument the confusion of a *logical* kind of existence with a *real* kind. Actual existence is not an attribute in the sense that "blue" and "perfect" are attributes. When we assert that the concept of God includes the attribute of existence, such existence can never be anything more than *possible* being. What happens in the ontological proof is that at the outset we covertly assert the actual existence of God. We can no more prove the actual existence of anything from its possibility than we can increase our bank balance by adding merely possible dollars to it.

Critics of the ontological argument agree that it commits the fallacy of begging the question—that is, of assuming as true what is to be proved. What should be established is that God exists; but this is taken for granted, under the counter, as it were, in the premises of the argument. All that the ontological argument asserts amounts to no more than this: if there *were* a perfect being, then he *would* actually exist; if there *were* a necessary being, then in him essence and existence *would* be identical and he would necessarily exist. What the argument fails to do is to "catch" the perfect or necessary being by showing that there actually *is* such a being.

The Teleological Argument

This argument is sometimes known as the proof from design. It has two closely related forms. One points to the apparently purposive character of natural objects, citing such examples as the marvelous coordination of the parts of the human or animal eye or the wonderful instances of adaptation which abound in the world of plants and animals. Such purpose in Nature, it is argued, cannot be the result of mere chance, but must be the work of an intelligent author of Nature, who is God. A more general form of the argument appeals to the uniformity and order of physical Nature, taken as a whole. This argument interprets the order of Nature as evidence of intelligent design, and proceeds from this to infer the existence of God as the designer.

The notion that the ultimate cause of the order of physical Nature is something akin to mind or intelligence is as old as Anaxagoras, and is considerably developed in the philosophies of Plato and Aristotle. Cicero uses the argument from design in his *De Natura Deorum.* Medieval theologians employed the teleological proof in their writings, although they tended to give more prominence to the cosmological argument. The rise of the physical sciences in modern times produced among educated men a heightened admiration for the complex harmony of Nature. This in turn increased the popularity of the teleological proof. The argument from design was a particular favorite of the eighteenth-century *deists*—men who preferred a minimal "natural religion," based on reason and experience, to one founded on revelation or a teaching church. The deists liked to think of the universe as a wonderful machine (its laws so brilliantly revealed by the incomparable Newton) which God had created and then left to run according to its own laws without interference on his part.

The proof from design was popular with eighteenth-century English churchmen. William Paley, Archdeacon of Carlisle, argued in his *Natural Theology* for "the necessity, in each particular case, of an intelligent designing mind for the contriving and determining of the forms which organized bodies bear." Paley used the famous "watch" illustration, which he borrowed from the Dutch philosopher Nieuwentyt. If we should find a watch on an uninhabited island, argues Paley, we would naturally infer that this clever mechanism was the work of an intelligent craftsman rather than the product of chance. Now the universe is a mechanism incomparably more wonderful than a watch. Do we not therefore have the right to conclude that the universe is the product of a mind of surpassing intelligence, and that this mind is God?

The teleological argument appeared with renewed vigor after the triumph of the theory of biological evolution in the nineteenth century. To be sure, the "tough-minded" Darwinians took the data of evolution as proof that organic life is the chance product of nonpurposive adaptation to the material environment. But others interpreted the impressive history of the development of living forms as evidence of a cosmic direction and purpose which could only be attributed to God or something like a God. Bergson's *Creative Evolution* is full of examples of the marvels of adaptation to be found in organic Nature, from which he infers the existence of a cosmic purposive force. Twenty years ago the biologist Lecomte du Noüy used probability calculus to demonstrate that the probability of a single protein molecule's having organized itself by chance is incredibly small—2.02×10^{-321}, to be exact.[4] In his popular book *Human Destiny*, du Noüy stated that any man with respect for the methods of science can only infer that there is an anti-chance factor at work in the universe. This is God.

Comment on the Teleological Argument

Critics of the teleological proof point out that the form of the argument which appeals to the *purposive character of*

[4] L. du Noüy, *Human Destiny*, New York, Longmans, 1947. (PB: Mentor, New American Library, New York.)

natural objects developed within a period in history which lacked the concepts and techniques of empirical science. The behavior of natural objects was interpreted, in those days, almost exclusively according to an Aristotelian principle of internal and purposive causality with little attention to the role of external physical causality. For example, the falling of a stone was explained in terms of a tendency within the stone itself to fall, rather than as the result of an influence external to the stone. This type of thinking produced an exaggerated teleology, of which Voltaire makes fun in his *Candide*. In that book Dr. Pangloss, professor of metaphysico-theologo-cosmolonigology, addresses his ingenuous pupil thus:

> 'Tis demonstrated . . . that things cannot be otherwise; for, since everything is made for an end, everything is necessarily for the best end. Observe that noses were made to wear spectacles; and so we have spectacles. Legs were visibly instituted to be breeched, and we have breeches. Stones were formed to be quarried and to build castles; and My Lord has a very noble castle; the greatest Baron in the province should have the best house; and as pigs were made to be eaten, we eat pork all the year round; consequently, those who have asserted that all is well talk nonsense; they ought to have said that all is for the best.[5]

The more general form of the teleological argument—that based on the evidence of a world order—was vigorously attacked by David Hume. It is true, says Hume, that from the existence of a house we may infer the existence of a builder. We may do this because we have *experience* of houses *and* of architects who design them and builders who construct them. But, Hume points out, although the order

[5] Voltaire, *Candide*, New York, Modern Library, 1930, p. 4. (PB: Anchor, Doubleday, Garden City, N.Y.)

of Nature is given to us in experience, the existence of a cosmic designer is not. Therefore the argument rests on a bad analogy. Further, says Hume, even if we grant the existence of an intelligence which is responsible for the world order, it does not follow that this intelligence is God. At best, the argument from design indicates the existence of a finite being of whom nothing more can be said than that it is the cause of the order of Nature. We cannot conclude that this being is a God, who is infinite, omnipotent, all-good, etc. The very most the argument can support, says Hume, is the inference that "The cause or causes of order in the universe probably bear some remote analogy to human intelligence."[6]

Du Noüy's use of probability calculus to demonstrate the existence of an anti-chance factor in the cosmos is open to the following objection. When we say the probability of a penny's turning up heads on any given throw is ½, we are making an assumption concerning the behavior of pennies, namely, that it is equally likely that they will turn up one of two ways on any given throw. Assumptions of this kind do no harm in the case of simple objects like pennies and dice, but may be very misleading when applied without care to more complex situations. We have no assurance that formulas of mathematical probability, the theory of which is still under development, may safely be applied to such complicated and inclusive areas as organic life or the cosmos taken as a whole.

Postscript to the Arguments

The traditional arguments for the existence of God have had a bad press. The majority of critics believe these argu-

[6] D. Hume, *Dialogues Concerning Natural Religion*, E. D. Aiken, ed., New York, Hafner, 1948, p. 94. (PB: Liberal Arts, Bobbs-Merrill, Indianapolis.)

ments have never recovered from the assaults of Kant and Hume. Empiricists claim that the proofs have no possible verification. Existentialist theologians question whether God can be said to "exist" at all, since he is the *ground* of existence. Even Thomists concede that the five ways of Aquinas have been wrongly abstracted from their context for apologetic purposes. Poets dislike the arguments. André Gide writes in *Nourritures Terrestres:*

> There is, of course, the proof by two and two make four. —But, Nathaniel, we aren't all good at arithmetic.
>
> There is the proof of the First Cause.—But there is always another that came before it.

The famous British Broadcasting Corporation debate between Bertrand Russell and F. C. Copleston, S.J., was a public example of the failure of these arguments to help agnostic and theist find a common basis of discussion.[7]

But in the last few years a number of philosophers and theologians have reexamined the old arguments with interest. Austin Farrer subjects them to careful scrutiny in his *Finite and Infinite.* E. L. Mascall restates and supports the proofs formulated by Aquinas. Independent defense of the arguments may be found in the metaphysical writings of the American philosopher Richard Taylor. The argument from causality, Taylor claims, may be usefully widened by an appeal to the "Principle of Sufficient Reason"—*Nothing occurs without a sufficient reason for its occurence.*" There seems to be no basis for belief that the universe as a whole is exempt from this law, Taylor claims. But if this is the case, that is, if the universe is not exempt from the principle of sufficient reason, then the theist is justified in claiming that

[7] This debate has been reprinted in a number of anthologies, including John Hick, ed., *The Existence of God,* New York, Macmillan, 1964.

a sufficient reason for the universe must exist, and he may call this God. He concludes:

> No more is claimed for these arguments, however, than that they are good arguments, and that they seem to yield the conclusions derived from them. If they are defective, the defects are not gross or obvious. The reader may suit himself whether they yield those conclusions, and if so, what their human significance might be.[8]

RELATION OF GOD TO THE WORLD

Causality of God; Creation

In traditional theism, the world is considered to be related to God as effect to cause.[9] Does this mean that all forms of classical theism take God to be the creator of the world? Not if we mean by "creator" a being who makes the world from nothing (*ex nihilo*). In the theology of the Greek philosophers, for example, we find no notion of a God who creates from nothing. The Greeks had two different conceptions of the manner in which God and the world are related, neither of them involving "strict" creation. One of these we may call *transformation*, the other *emanation*.

In most Greek theologies matter is eternal. What God does is to give *form* to this matter. In his *Timaeus*, Plato explains the creation of the world by means of a poetic myth. God, gazing upon the eternal Forms, takes in hand

[8] Richard Taylor, *Metaphysics*, Prentice-Hall, 1963, p. 56.

[9] It is commonly said by theologians that the causality of God cannot be *identical* with the finite cause-effect relations we encounter in experience. At most, the divine causality is more or less *analogous* to finite causality. To this, sceptics often object that since we have no experience of divine causality as we do with ordinary runs of cause and effect in nature and society, it is questionable whether the alleged relation between God and the world can properly be called "causal" at all.

the formless flux of matter and molds it according to the timeless patterns he sees before him. God fashions the world as a sculptor who, with his eyes on a fair model, gives form to the imperfect clay that is the only material available to him. Aristotle's account is hardly less poetic. God, the Unmoved Mover, is absorbed in self-contemplation and has no knowledge of anything beyond himself. The effect of his presence, however, is such as to induce form within the eternal matter. Like a magnet unaware of the iron, or like a man whose life is changed by a beautiful woman who does not even know he notices her, God has from all eternity drawn matter toward him, this matter acquiring form as it moves toward "the object of its appetition." Because of God's ever-present influence, matter has always had some degree of form. Hence the world is eternal. To Aristotle, God is the object of the world's desire.

Later Greek philosophers, called Neoplatonists, explained the creativity of God in terms of emanation rather than transformation. According to Plotinus, God—"the One"—is Being itself. In the plenitude of his being (and in his wish to share it), God "spills over" being like wine from a brimming cup. Or, to change the metaphor, God *radiates* being, as the sun pours forth light and heat. These radiations or *emanations* assume the form of a hierarchy of stages of being, ranging from higher to lower. The world is one of the lower stages of this graduated system of emanations. Matter—which the Greeks regarded as the principle of imperfection—arises at that stage of the emanation process which is farthest from God. The imperfection of matter (communicated to the world, which is partly matter) is not to be explained by any original limitations within God. Rather, matter is the poor stuff it is, because it is the last in the series of emanations, and is therefore, metaphysically speaking, at the greatest distance from the creative source.

The notion that God creates the world *from nothing* (*ex nihilo*) is Judaic rather than Greek and arises from considerations of the story of creation as given in Genesis. This Biblical document gives a curious double account of creation, one aspect of which can be interpreted as a type of transformism. Historically, there was considerable debate among both Jewish and Christian theologians as to whether the world was formed by God's creative energy operating on a primordial chaos or material substratum, or whether God simply created the world from nothing. In general, traditional theologians tended to agree that revelation indicated that the world was created from nothing, but that this could not be proved from "natural reason." We shall see that the manner in which God is conceived to have created the world has some bearing upon the question of the attributes of God and upon what is called the problem of evil.

The Attributes of God

In the traditional theology of the West, God was represented as having a number of attributes or qualities. Jewish and Christian philosophers went to great lengths to avoid the charge of what today we call *anthropomorphism*—the attributing to God of human qualities. God, they agreed, is to a large extent beyond human knowledge. Therefore, strictly speaking, we can say nothing about his nature which will adequately represent that nature. Yet in seeking to avoid the Scylla of anthropomorphism theologians feared to fall into the Charybdis of *agnosticism*, the position that God is unknowable and that nothing at all can be said about him. Various attempts to avoid this dilemma were devised. The Jewish philosopher Maimonides recommended the *vis negativa.* While we cannot attribute positive qualities to God, we can indirectly describe his nature by making negative statements. We cannot say, for example, that God is wise, but we can say that he is not unwise. This is not intended as mere word-play; Maimonides means that if there is any perfection in human wisdom, we may be sure that God does not lack it. Thomas Aquinas suggested the doctrine of *analogy*. We cannot apply to God attributes like "wisdom" or "goodness" *in the same sense* in which these words are applied to things of the created order. Such attributes can only be predicated of God *analogically* in a way which admits the need for correction.

Traditional theologians agreed that God had in *some* sense attributes such as infinity (that is, God is without limitations), goodness, omnipotence, omniscience, etc. While certain of the early fathers had difficulty in conceiving of God as something immaterial, it was generally held that God was a spiritual rather than a corporeal being. It was also agreed that God *thought* or was a mind; that in the work of the creation of the world he proceeded in a fashion not wholly different from that of a rational creature who carries a plan or design into effect and knows what he is doing.

The Problem of Evil

The traditional doctrines of the creativity and attributes of God produced many difficulties. One of the best known of these is the so-called problem of evil. The problem may be stated in this way: While there is in the world evidence of much that is orderly, good, and rational, there is even more compelling evidence of all-pervasive evil. There are physical evils, such as famine, earthquakes, and other natural catastrophes. There is pain, sickness, and death. There are moral evils—injustice, sin, the wickedness of men. There is war, which is a pandemonium of evils, both physical and moral. Now, if God *cannot* prevent evil in the world, it would seem that he is not all-powerful, and if he *will not* prevent evil, it would seem that he is not all-good. Consider these two alternatives: (1) God is not all-powerful; (2) God is not all-good. The Greek philosophers tended to favor the first alternative. To them, *matter* is the principle of limitation and disorder, hence indirectly the source of all evil. God did not create matter. It coexists with God from all eternity. God is not an absolute lord over matter. Plato explicitly admits that God is *limited* by something outside himself which he calls "necessity." Indeed it is only by "persuasion" that his God can elicit a partial order within the material flux from which the world is formed. On the other hand, *Manicheism*, a religion which at one time nearly defeated Christianity in the West, was more receptive to the alternative of divine ill will. The Manicheans taught a *theistic dualism* in which two Gods, one of Light or Good, the other of Darkness or Evil, eternally coexisted. The order and harmony of the world was attributed to the God of Light, the disorder to the God of Darkness.[10]

Neither of these alternatives, however, was acceptable to traditional Christian theology, which attributed *both* in-

[10] The doctrine preached by the prophet Mani had its origin in ancient Persia, which seems to have been the home of theistic dualism. A notable example is the Persian fire cult we call Zoroastrianism, which taught the coexistence of a God of Light (Ormuzd or Ahura Mazda) and a God of Darkness (Ahriman). For ten centuries Manicheism was widespread throughout Europe. Incorporating the cosmological doctrines of Platonism plus the speculations of the Gnostics, the Manicheans held spirit responsible for good and matter for evil. Their radical dualism between body and soul led the Manicheans to strange theories and practices that proved intolerable to the medieval Church. In a move inspired more by greed than religious zeal, the northern French knights exterminated the Manicheans (they were also known as Albigensians or Cathars) in southern France. Troubadour poetry died with them.

finite goodness and power to God. God is absolutely without limitation and he is all-good. Hence, other solutions to the problem of evil were formulated, none of which is completely satisfactory. One of the classic solutions, first developed by St. Augustine, suggests that evil is not something positive, but rather a privation or lack of an order which "ought to be there." Thus blindness is an absence or derangement of the physiological order which would normally permit sight. In the moral realm, sin is the lack of a spiritual order proper to the soul. Now if evil is a privation or lack rather than a positive created thing, then God cannot be said to have created it.

The obvious objection to this attempt to answer the problem of evil is that an all-powerful God could *prevent* the occurrence of this lack of privation. But theologians would perhaps invite our attention to a more general way of taking evil as the result of privation—that is, evil may be the necessary result of *limitation* inherent in creatureliness. God himself is complete and infinite Being. Now created things, in virtue of the very fact that they *are* created, cannot possess complete being. They are not necessary beings, but contingent only. Because of this, created things have a tendency to slip away from being toward nonbeing. This *finitude* of things implies limitation and imperfection. To demand of God the removal of finitude from creatures is to ask that he make them God. "People complain," says Lactantius, "that man is subjected to sicknesses and untimely death. They are angry that they have not been born gods."[11] Now no reasonable man would complain of his lack of unlimited perfection. But it is from this finitude of things, from the contingency and dependence of the created order, that evil arises. "It may well be," says Austin Farrer, "that the chaotic interrelation of forms in space and

[11] Lactantius, *The Workmanship of God*, chap. 4.

time is the simple condition of finitude or of our level of finitude, that it does not and cannot positively express the mind of God, nor be overruled by His direction for the benefit of the higher finite beings, such as we flatter ourselves to be."[12]

Interesting as these metaphysical considerations of evil may be, we should note that Augustine and other Christian theologians based their *primary* explanation of the presence of evil in the world upon certain historical events described wholly within the bounds of Scripture. According to this account, man brought his troubles on himself. There was a certain primal fault committed by man, a fault so serious as to turn God away away from him. As a result of this estrangement between man and his creator, there was a fall from man's once blessed estate. [13] The consequence of this fall was a shattering of man's nature and the appearance of suffering and death. Why did God permit man to commit this primal fault? Why does he allow his creatures, over whom he has domination, to choose evil instead of good? Theologians may reply that, since God created man in his image, he created him a *free* being and not merely a good-doing automaton. Since man is free, the choice between good and evil is open to him.

Certain philosophers have not been content to allow the problem of evil to rest within the context of religious faith but have striven to work out a solution consistent with the Christian view in terms of a "natural theology." Leibniz, for example, maintains in his *Theodicy* a position which has been called *cosmological optimism.* According to Leibniz,

[12] Farrer Austin, *Finite and Infinite,* Westminster, Glasgow, Dacre Press, 1943, p. 299.

[13] The doctrine of a primordial fault and a fall occurs in religions and philosophies of various cultures. The notion is present in Indian metaphysics. It is elaborated in mythopoeic language in Plato's *Phaedrus.*

God has created the world according to the best possible plan. But the best plan, says Leibniz, "is not always that which seeks to avoid evil, since it may happen that *the evil is accompanied by a greater good.*"[14] Since experience tells us that evil frequently brings about good (an illness, for example, may give a man time to reflect on a misspent career and thus lead him to a nobler life), it may be concluded that all evil serves some higher good of which we may not have knowledge. Leibniz' reasoning on this problem has rarely been found convincing. His doctrine that "this is the best of all possible worlds" is mercilessly satirized by Voltaire.[15]

GOD AS THE WHOLE

Spinoza's Concept of God

As Western thought gradually broke away from the framework of traditional religion within which it had operated for sixteen hundred years, the character of metaphysical systems became increasingly independent and individualistic. Some philosophers, like Descartes, tried to tie their new systems to traditional theology. Others, like the seventeenth-century Dutch-Jewish philosopher Spinoza, sharply criticized the traditional concept of God and put forward their own. Spinoza's theology is particularly interesting because it breaks down the traditional distinction between God and Nature. God and Nature are one and the same, he

[14] G. W. F. Leibniz, *Theodicy*. See *Leibnitz: Selections*, P. P. Wiener, ed., New York, Scribner, 1951, p. 510. (PB: Scribner.)

[15] See the excerpt from *Candide* on p. 304. A more recent French criticism of the claim that evil serves a higher good occurs in Albert Camus' novel *The Plague;* Father Paneloux preaches to the stricken city that the pestilence is God's will, but is confounded by the suffering and death of a child.

says, but Nature is *more* than the physical universe. This is puzzling, and Spinoza has been called everything from "God-intoxicated man" to a "forerunner of contemporary Naturalism." Some years ago, when Albert Einstein was questioned by newspaper reporters as to his belief in God, he replied, "My God is the God of Spinoza." This left the reporters little wiser than before.

According to Spinoza, God, while not identical with the physical universe, is inseparable from it. To God, Spinoza gives the impersonal name of *Substance*. The traditional definition of substance is "any independently existing thing." A coat is a substance; its properties, like red or soft, were known as "accidents" or "modes." Applying this definition with rigorous exactness, Spinoza states that there can be but one *absolutely* independent thing. This is God, upon whom everything else depends. All other beings, says Spinoza, including the physical universe and everything in it, are *modes* or aspects of this infinite Substance. These modes follow from the nature of Substance by the same inexorable necessity by which the properties of a geometrical figure follow from the figure itself as given. The world, there, *proceeds* from God by *necessity*. The world is a necessary consequence of the nature of God and it is part of that nature.

An analogy may be drawn between the Spinozistic relation between God and the world, and that which exists between the premises and the conclusion of any syllogism:

Men are rational.
Greeks are men.
———————————
Therefore, Greeks are rational.

The premises of this syllogism imply or "contain" the conclusion, which is, of course, *part* of the total syllogism. The conclusion itself "follows" from the premises necessarily. In an analogous fashion God or Substance "contains" the world which is a *part* of God and *follows necessarily* from the nature of God. Now if the physical universe is a necessary consequence of God's nature, it would seem that God must implicitly contain *matter*. This Spinoza readily concedes. The infinite Substance contains not only the infinite attribute of *thought* or mind (which traditional theologians had always ascribed to God) but also the infinite attribute of matter, or *extension*, as Spinoza puts it.

The consequences of Spinoza's concept of God show certain radical differences between this God and the God of traditional theology. First, orthodox theologians held that God was spirit only. Spinoza maintains that God is matter as well as mind. Second, the traditional God produced the world by a free creative act according to a certain plan or design in his mind. Spinoza denies that God creates in this quasi-human and arbitrary manner. The world has existed from all eternity as a mode or aspect of infinite Substance, and it is a necessary consequence of that Substance's nature. Third, the traditional doctrine of the relation of God to the world emphasized the *transcendence* of God. That is, God is a causal power who is apart from and beyond the world which is his effect. Now Spinoza *denies the separation* between God and the world. To him, God is an *immanent* rather than a transcendent cause—an indwelling or inseparable cause with which the effect (the world) is continuous. But God does not dwell within the physical universe as a part lies within a whole. Rather the reverse. The world, which is the part, dwells within God, who is the Whole. Now, while the terms "God" and "Nature" are interchangeable, God is not identical with *physical* Nature; rather does he include or contain the physical universe. That is why Spinoza approves the saying of St. Paul, "In Him we live and move and have our being."

Spinoza then proceeds to the following conclusion: Since all that exists in the universe is a necessary consequence of God's nature, there is no freedom in the world. Every event in the universe, from the fall of a stone to the act of a man, is inexorably determined by the necessity of God's nature. Only that man can be called "free" who *understands* that God alone is a free cause, and that all else follows from God by necessity.

God as Immanent and Transcendent Cause

The concept of God as the immanent or inseparable cause of the world is not peculiar to Spinoza, although his particular metaphysical system is unique. In the religious traditions of the West we may distinguish two different lines of emphasis on the relation of God to the world. One line is that of those theologians who have endeavored to interpret the meaning of God in highly rational or "scientific" terms. The result is "the God of the philosophers," the Infinite Cause of the cosmos, the creator and foundation of the total hierarchy of being. In this context the stress is nearly always on the *transcendence* of God, his distinctness or separation from the world, rather than on his *immanence* or indwellingness. But the God of the Western religious traditions is not only the impersonal First Cause of the world. He is also a God of Love who cares for man. According to Christian doctrine, the love of God for his creatures is so great that he *came into the world* as Jesus, the Son of God, the second person of the Trinity; and *remains with* the world in the form of the Paraclete, the Holy Spirit, the third person of the Trinity.

Devout Christian writers, absorbed with the God of Love, rather than with the infinite First Cause, invariably emphasized God's *closeness* to the world. The mystics—of whom the Christian tradition includes Theresa of Avila, John of the Cross, Ruysbroeck, Eckhart, and Jacob Boehme

—particularly stressed the immanence of God, the unity of all things within the Divine. But orthodox theologians were fearful of pushing the concept of God's immanence to extremes. Although a large measure of truth was conceded to the mystics, the balance of orthodoxy tipped toward transcendence. Excessive emphasis on God's immanence was regarded with suspicion. Later, this was to be called "pantheism."

Pantheism

"Pantheism" is a word which seems to have been used first by John Toland in 1705 and means literally "All is God." The illustrious Dr. Johnson defined a pantheist as "one who confused God and Nature" and referred to the followers of Spinoza as pantheists. Spinoza is, of course, a pantheist by definition, if we take "pantheism" to mean (1) God is inseparable from Nature or (2) God is the infinite Whole, and everything which exists is a part or "mode" of that Whole. We frequently hear the word "pantheism" applied to certain poetry in which the poets sing of the unity of all things within the Divine. Goethe, who admired Spinoza, tells us in his poem "One in All" that the best way to find oneself is to lose oneself in the Infinite. We have it didactically from Pope that:

> All are but parts of one stupendous whole,
> Whose body Nature is, and God the soul.[16]

Or in Emerson, under the spell of Indian mysticism:

> They reckon ill who leave me out;
> When me they fly, I am the wings;
> I am the doubter and the doubt,
> And I the hymn the Brahmin sings.[17]

[16] A. Pope, *Essay on Man.*
[17] R. W. Emerson, "Brahma."

The indwellingness of Deity in Nature is a theme of Edna Millay's *Renascence:*

> God, I can push the grass apart
> And lay my finger on thy heart![18]

Of all poets, Wordsworth is most absorbed with the immanence of the Divine in Nature:

> . . . And I have felt
> A presence that disturbs me with the joy
> Of elevated thought; a sense sublime
> Of something far more deeply interfused,
> Whose dwelling is the light of setting suns,
> And the round ocean and the living air,
> And the blue sky, and in the mind of man:
> A motion and a spirit, that impels
> All thinking things, all objects of all thought
> And rolls through all things.[19]

God as All-Soul or All-Mind

The same generic concept of God, which in some settings we label "pantheism," occurs again in the doctrine of the All-Soul or All-Mind—an idea of God both ancient and modern. The philosophers of ancient India held that the individual soul (atman) is but a particularization of the infinite all-encompassing soul which is God (brahma). In the West, the Stoics regarded individual minds as parts of an all-containing Universal Reason. Certain commentators on Aristotle, such as Alexander of Aphrodisias, interpreted the master's puzzling doctrine of the immortality of the "active intellect" to mean that individual minds are related to the Divine as sparks to a flame. It was the preference of

[18] E. Millay, *Renascence*, New York, Harper & Row, 1917.

[19] W. Wordsworth, "Lines Composed a Few Miles Above Tintern Abbey."

medieval Arabian philosophers for this interpretation of Aristotle that caused Christian philosophers to condemn Moslem theology for what today we would call "pantheism." The All-Mind occurs in Yankee dress in New England transcendentalism; Emerson's "oversoul" owes much to atman and brahma. Another version of the All-Soul was offered by the late Dean Inge:

> The entire cosmic process is the life-frame of the universal Soul, the Divine Logos. With this life we are vitally connected, however brief and unimportant the span and the task of an individual career may seem to us. If my particular life-meaning passes out of activity, it will be because the larger life, to which I belong, no longer needs that form of expression.[20]

Is the Absolute God?

Not unrelated to the concept of God as All-Mind is the Absolute of the idealist philosophers. It is not easy to say just what the Absolute is, since various absolute idealists speak of it in somewhat different ways. They agree, however, that the Absolute is the ground of all being; that upon the Absolute all things depend. Hence the Absolute fulfills the primary role of the God of traditional theology. The Absolute is the Whole, of which everything is a finite fragment. It is the one reality, and all else is appearance. The Absolute is something like an all-pervasive thought which reveals itself through Nature and through all things—these being but *aspects* of the Absolute. Hegel tells us that the Absolute is "not just the Supreme Being," transcending the world and distinct from it: "Common fancy puts the Absolute far away in a world beyond. The Absolute is rather directly before us, so present that so long as we think, we

[20] W. R. Inge, *Outspoken Essays* (First Series), London, Longmans, 1924, p. 273.

must, though without express consciousness of it, always carry it with us and always use it."[21]

According to Josiah Royce, the Absolute is that "larger Self" which includes all individual selves. He tells us that the Absolute is at the very least a person and more definitely conscious than we are. All the problems of the world are solved within the Absolute; the darkest mysteries are known to it. Nor can we escape the Absolute, for:

> Flee where we will, . . . the net of the larger Self ensnares us. We are lost and imprisoned in the thickets of its tangled labyrinth. The moments are not at all in themselves, for as moments they have no meaning; they exist only in relation to the beyond. The larger Self alone is, and they are by reason of it, organic parts of it. They perish, but it remains; they have truth or error only in its overshadowing presence. . . . There is, then, at last, but one Self, organically, reflectively, consciously inclusive of all the selves, and so of truth.[22]

F. H. Bradley sees the Absolute not as a larger Self or Person, but as "superpersonal." The Absolute is the foundation of all reality, it *is* reality, but it is not the God of the traditional religions. "God," says Bradley, "is not God, till he has become all in all, and . . . a God which is all in all is not the God of religion. God is but an aspect, and that must mean but an appearance of the Absolute."[23]

In any metaphysical system in which God or the Absolute is taken as the Whole—everything else being an aspect or part of that Whole—the problem of evil is there to be

[21] G. W. F. Hegel, *Logic*, rev. ed., William Wallace, trans., Oxford, Clarendon, 1892, p. 50.

[22] J. Royce, *The Spirit of Modern Philosophy*, Boston, Mifflin, 1892, p. 379.

[23] F. H. Bradley, *Appearance and Reality*, rev. ed., Oxford, Clarendon Press, 1946, p. 433.

reckoned with just as an orthodox theology. For if God or the Absolute contains all, it must contain evil as well as good. Some absolute idealists endeavor to meet this difficulty by saying that evil is conflict and disharmony on the scale of the *part*, but within the *whole* all conflict is resolved. In the Absolute, evil disappears. As in Meredith's poem:

> Stop a moment: I seize an idea from the pit.
> They tell us that discord, though discord alone,
> Can be harmony when the notes properly fit:
> Am I judging all things from a single false tone?[24]

According to Bradley, we may say that the Absolute *has* evil, since it contains a province of which evil is a partial element. But we cannot say that the Absolute *is* evil on the basis of the character of one of its "fragmentary and dependent details." It was possibly argument of this sort William James had in mind when he said "Damn the Absolute!"

GOD AS FINITE

Concepts of God fall into two kinds: (1) God as *infinite;* he is the ultimate metaphysical factor, the foundation of everything, the cause of all being. God, as infinite, is not limited by anything outside himself. (2) God as *finite*—at least in respect to some of his attributes. He is one of the ultimate cosmic factors, but he is not the only one. God is limited by something other than himself. Greek philosophers, like Plato, hesitated to make God responsible for *everything*. Would that not make God responsible for the

[24] George Meredith, "Martin's Puzzle."

presence of imperfection and disorder in the world? God is the author of good things only, says Plato; the Father and Shepherd of the *Timaeus* is infinite in respect to his goodness, but not in respect to his power. He can persuade order and reason out of Necessity, but he cannot compel. So Plato made matter a cosmological factor coeternal with God. Thus conceived, God is in some ways finite; he is limited by something other than himself, something beyond his complete control. The God of traditional Judaeo-Christian theology, on the other hand, is infinite, for he is unlimited by anything outside himself. He is the Supreme Being, the single, ultimate, metaphysical fact upon which everything else depends. As Aquinas puts it, God is Being itself (*Ens*).

Modern concepts of God may be classified in the same way. Spinoza's God is infinite, the one self-caused Substance of which everything else is but a mode. The Absolute of the idealists is very much like Spinoza's God in this respect. The Absolute, too, is unlimited by anything other than itself. It is the sole reality, containing within itself the whole complex system of appearances which is our world. The Absolute is the ultimate ground of all being.

But despite Spinoza and the Absolute idealists, modern theism shows an emphatic trend in favor of a *finite* deity. This limited God plays an important role in the cosmos, but he is circumscribed, even thwarted, by other metaphysical elements. Alexander's Deity has not yet emerged from the womb of the cosmos. Whitehead's God can persuade but cannot compel. Bergson's vital force is struggling through matter. James' wider self is partially dependent for his very existence upon our belief in him. In this section of our brief theological survey we shall examine these restricted deities in further detail.

Evolutionary and Emergent Deity

One effect of the concept of evolution upon the generation of philosophers preceding our own by one or two was to stimulate the production of natural theologies of an evolutionary type. These philosophers saw the state of present living forms to be but a stage in a vast biological process of transformation and development. The physical universe itself they accepted as a mere moment in the stupendous scheme of cosmic evolution. But what, they asked, is the force behind all this? It is God. But it is God conceived as a power not so much outside the cosmic process as within it, at its heart. God is part of the evolutionary process. Deity itself evolves. It may be that God is at this moment "hatching out" from the mighty universe, emerging gradually as from a cosmic womb, to transcend the process of which he is the immanent cause. Says W. P. Montague:

> We are confronted with a God, or something very like a God that exists . . . as an ascending force, a nisus, a thrust toward concentration, organization, and life. This power appears to labor slowly and under difficulties. We can liken it to a yeast that, through the aeons, pervades the chaos of matter and slowly leavens it with spirit.[25]

In his *Creative Evolution*, Bergson conceives of God as a vital force, the *élan vital*, the primal source of creative energy. Like Plotinus' One, this pure and undifferentiated Life finds itself thwarted and blocked by *matter*, which has come into being as an indirect and unwanted by-product of itself. The *élan vital* is like a fountain surging upward or a rocket shooting toward the sky. Matter is like the drops which fall back against the upswelling thrust of the foun-

[25] W. P. Montague, *Belief Unbound*, Yale University Press, 1930, p. 74.

tain or the dead ashes that drop earthward from the rocket. Its free creative play hindered by matter, the *élan* plunges into the inert stuff that resists it, and the marvelous multiplicity of living forms arises. The story of evolution is the history of the attempts the life force has made—and is still making—to overcome the matter into which it has entered, to regain its original undifferentiated one-ness, to win through to its primordial freedom.

Another form of evolutionary theism is the doctrine of *emergent evolution*, associated with C. Lloyd Morgan and S. Alexander. According to the emergent evolutionists, cosmic evolution is not just a mechanistic regrouping of atoms but an organic process in which we may discern the emergence of qualitatively different levels of being:

> Within the all-embracing stuff of Space-Time, the universe exhibits an emergence in Time of successive levels of finite existences, each with its characteristic empirical quality. The highest of these empirical qualities known to us is mind or consciousness. Deity is the next higher empirical quality to the highest we know. . . .[26]

That is, within *Space-Time*, the primordial matrix of things, the cosmic womb from which all successive orders of being emerge, there is at work a creative *nisus* or upward thrust which pushes to the surface, as it were, a succession of qualitatively different emergents. *Matter* represents but one stage in the emergent process—the comparatively primitive level of physical, inorganic being. From matter there arises a new and relatively independent level of being—*life*. From life emerges *consciousness*, a still more highly organized state of things. From within consciousness *mind* separates out to form the next higher autonomous

[26] S. Alexander, *Space, Time, and Deity*, London, Macmillan, 1934, vol. 2, p. 345.

realm of being. *Value*, to Lloyd Morgan, is an emergent level higher still. Finally, there is *deity*, the creative nisus itself, which has been slowly driving upward and outward these various strata of being. Deity has not yet emerged but is in the process of emerging from the cosmos. As yet we can but faintly sense its "numinous" presence. In the diagram given, deity forms the apex of the cosmic pyramid, and it is represented by dotted rather than solid lines to show that it has not yet emerged:[27]

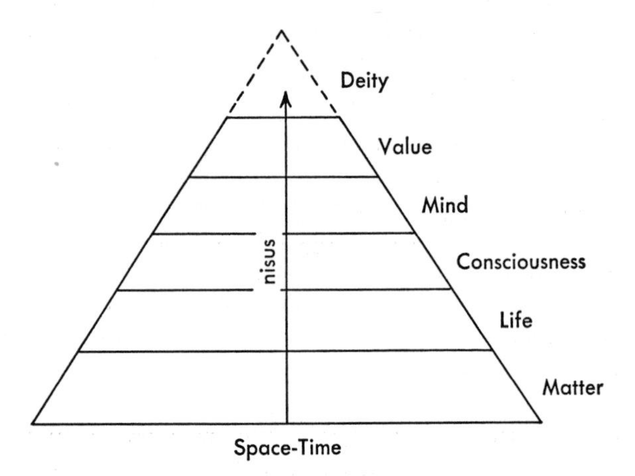

To Alexander the infinite God of traditional theism is not actual but ideal. God, thus conceived, has not yet *become* actual. The actual God is the universe viewed as *tending toward* deity. The universe is God's *body* and includes all the gradations of being which have emerged up to this time. The quality of deity, straining to the cosmic surface, is the *mind* of God. Deity is both created and creating, immanent and transcendent. "God," say Alexander, "is

[27] See C. Lloyd Morgan, *Emergent Evolution*, New York, Holt, Rinehart and Winston, 1927, pp. 9–14.

immanent in respect of his body, but transcendent in respect of his deity."

The evolutionary theism of Teilhard de Chardin is also an emergent theory. The Jesuit anthropologist's book *The Phenomenon of Man* is a highly individual work, bristling with neologisms and a technical vocabulary which fails to mask a religious vision, deeply held. The divine impulse immanent in the universe is there in Teilhard's work as we find it in Alexander, Lloyd Morgan, Bergson, even Whitehead. Evolution is growing complexification—matter, life, consciousness, mind. Human society is the scene of future evolution. Teilhard's *Noosphere* corresponds to Alexander's emergent level of "mind," while his *Omega point* is Deity toward which the universe moves as it throws off successively higher evolutionary levels of development. God, the Omega point, is a soul of souls developing at the summit of the world, the last state of emergence. "After all," asks Teilhard, "is there any other way in which our thought can generalise the Principle of Emergence?"

Whitehead's God

We know that to Whitehead the world is a process in which we may discern a vast interrelated scheme of actual events—a table, a rainbow, the life of a man, the explosion of a star—no one of which can be adequately understood apart from its relation to other events. Now these actual happenings which constitute the world are only *part* of what Whitehead calls "the total metaphysical situation." Over and above the *actual* lies the vast domain of the *possible*, a realm which comprises all the things that *could be*. But the two spheres are not cut off from each other. Since any event is, so to speak, an *actualized possibility*, the realm of the possible must have an area of contact with the actual.

The possible enters into the actual; it has *ingress* into the spatiotemporal world.

Now a puzzling question arises. How does the world come to have the particular character it possesses? How is it that, out of the boundless stock of possibilities, *this* particular set has been actualized? Why *this* world rather than another? To answer this question, Whitehead finds it necessary to introduce a metaphysical factor which is responsible for this particular crimp in the nature of things. He postulates an agent which causes to emerge from the timeless domain of possibilities that particular, concrete system of patterns which is the actual cosmos. This agent is God, whom Whitehead calls "the Principle of Concretion." God's function is to impose a *limit* upon the limitless system of possibilities. God determines an actual course of events which, "metaphysically speaking, might have been otherwise."

Why is it that God makes concrete or actual *this* set of possibilities which is our world? If, metaphysically speaking, it might have been otherwise, what *reason* can be offered for God's having selected *this* world to actualize rather than another? Whitehead's answer is that no reason can be assigned. That is why we must say that God's existence is the ultimate *irrationality*. "No reason can be given for the nature of God," says Whitehead, "because that nature is the ground of rationality."[28]

But God, thus conceived, appears as remote from the human heart as Aristotle's Prime Mover—to which Whitehead's Principle of Concretion bears some resemblance. Thus, Whitehead is faced with the old problem of the two Gods. One is the cosmic force, the impersonal, metaphysical Deity of the philosophers. The other is the God of

[28] A. N. Whitehead, *Science and the Modern World*, New York, Macmillan, 1931, p. 257.

Love, who is close to us, embracing all things in his tender care. In the history of theism, says Whitehead, these two Gods have never satisfactorily been reconciled. He himself attempts a reconciliation by suggesting that the nature of God is *dipolar*, that is, it has a double aspect. One aspect of God is his *antecedent* nature, the other is his *consequent* nature.

In his antecedent nature God is the Principle of Concretion, the cosmic factor which elicits actuality from possibility. But God, taken as the Principle of Concretion, is more *conceptual* than he is *actual*. This is a supreme metaphysical paradox. For, although God is the Principle of Actuality, he is himself deficient in actuality. Conceived as the metaphysical agent which presses the actual out of the possible, God is not quite a "real" being. In this respect, Whitehead's God is like Alexander's Deity, who, as creative nisus, is responsible for the emergence of all the various levels of being in the cosmos, yet is himself not yet actual.

But Whitehead's God has also a consequent or derivative nature. This is God as he is here and now related to and affected by the world he has brought into existence. In this aspect of God's nature we find the God who is the object of religious worship. This is the God who dwells in the world and in whom the world dwells. This is the God who is near to us, whom we love, and who loves us:

> The image under which this operative growth of God's nature is best conceived, is that of a tender care that nothing be lost.... He does not create the world, he saves it; or, more accurately, he is the poet of the world, with tender patience leading it by his vision of truth, beauty, and goodness.[29]

[29] A. N. Whitehead, *Process and Reality*, New York, Macmillan, 1928, pp. 525, 526.

What about evil? If God is conceived, as in traditional theism, as a supreme and all-powerful creator, or as the Absolute, the infinite ground of all being, then such a God must be held responsible for the evil as well as the good. "He is then," says Whitehead, "the supreme author of the play, and to Him must therefore be ascribed its shortcoming as well as its success."[30] But God, as conceived by Whitehead, is not the foundation of the total metaphysical situation. He is but *one* of the cosmological factors, his function being to lure the possible over into the actual. In his consequent nature, God is a power which bends the world by persuasion toward the good. With Plato, Whitehead says, "God is the author of good things only."

The ultimate source of evil lies not in God but in the nature of things. The basic character of the cosmos is process, change, passage. In the actual world there is nothing which can escape this transiency; there is nothing which abides forever. God cannot prevent the passingness of things. "The ultimate evil in the temporal world," says Whitehead, "lies in the fact that the past fades, that time is a 'perpetual perishing.' "[31] There is another reason for the presence of evil in the world. Whenever any given possibility is actualized, the realization of certain other possibilities is thereby excluded. One of life's tragedies is that we must choose between beautiful things. Acceptance of one desired object all too often entails the rejection of others. To try to hold on to two incompatible goods is to risk catastrophe. We cannot eat our cake and have it. Or, as Whitehead puts it, "The nature of evil is that the characters of things are mutually obstructive."

[30] Whitehead, *Science and the Modern World*, p. 258.
[31] Whitehead, *Process and Reality*, p. 517.

A Modern Fideist Approach; William James

All this philosophizing about God is quite repugnant to William James, who has himself had considerable influence on modern religious thinking. To James, natural theology is an abomination of desolations. For just about all such rationalistic speculations can show for their trouble is some kind of metaphysical deity whose dubious existence is of little interest to anybody besides theistically inclined metaphysicians. James' approach to the problem of God is quite different. It is *fideistic* rather than rationalistic. That is, for James, God is not primarily an object of knowledge. He is an object of faith: "There is one element of our active nature which the Christian religion has emphatically recognized, but which philosophers as a rule have with great insincerity tried to huddle out of sight in their pretensions to found systems of absolute certainty. I mean the element of faith."[32]

To many critics, James' emphasis on the primacy of faith suggests a modern return to what the fathers of the church considered the only direct way to God: *Credo ut intellegam!* First, we must *believe*, and then understanding will be added. But James attributes a power to faith which the old fathers would never have dared to claim for it—the power *to bring God into existence*, or at least to sustain and increase his being. "I firmly disbelieve," says James, "that our human experience is the highest form of experience extant in the universe."[33] In religious experience, he tells us, we are conscious of a continuity between ourselves and

[32] William James, *The Will to Believe*, London, Longmans, 1912, p. 90. (PB: Dover, New York.)

[33] William James, *Pragmatism*, New York, Longmans, 1928, p. 299. (PB: Meridian, World Publishing, Cleveland.)

"a wider self through which saving experiences come."[34] Between this wider self and our individual selves there exists a relation of mutual dependence: "I do not see why the very existence of an invisible world may not in part depend on the personal response which any one of us may make to the religious appeal. God himself, in short, may draw vital strength and increase of his very being from our fidelity."[35]

Pragmatism teaches that there is no complete separation between beliefs and facts. Within the moral and religious realm, James seeks evidence to support his pragmatism. In a famous illustration, he tells us how a belief can create a fact. A man, fleeing for his life, finds himself on the brink of a chasm. It is just possible to jump it. A successful leap will take the man to safety. A miss means death. Now if the man believes with every fiber of his being that he can jump the chasm, the chances are he will be successful. If he entertains doubts and hesitations, he will fail. So it is with judgments of the moral and religious order. We have no final assurance of God's existence. If we had such assurances, faith in God would not be a primary element of religion. Religious faith is positive commitment in regard to a situation the outcome of which is not assured.

On pragmatic principles, says James, if the hypothesis of God *works* satisfactorily, in the widest sense of the word, it is true. Does it make a difference, he asks, whether God exists or not? James believes that it does. If the materialist is right, he says, then the things that matter most are at the mercy of the things that matter least. If, however, there is a

[34] William James, *Varieties of Religious Experience*, London, Longmans, 1908, p. 515. (PB: Collier, Crowell-Collier, New York.)

[35] James, *The Will to Believe*, p. 61. An unkind critic once compared James' notion that our belief in God contributes to his existence to that of Peter Pan who tells us that our belief in fairies keeps them alive.

being which is the deepest power in the universe, a power conceived under the form of mental personality and which works for good, then life becomes immeasurably richer and more meaningful; an incomparable vista of values opens out before us. Is not the second alternative worth believing in? Should we shrink from it because we *may* be in error? To James (as to Pascal) belief in God represents the choice of a live option, a momentous choice well worth a gambler's risk.

God and Linguistic Analysis

In his essay "Gods," the English philosopher John Wisdom tells a now-famous story about two people who return to their long-neglected garden and find flowers growing among the weeds. One says to the other, "There must be a gardener who comes and tends this garden." The other says no, the flowers just happened to grow without tending. But the first man says, "Look at the way those flowers are arranged. There's a purpose and feeling for beauty here." The other shakes his head; a gardener would have done something about those weeds. The two people make inquiries, but they can find no one who has seen a gardener come. They return to the garden and look at it more closely. Both see the same garden. Both examine the same evidence. But each interprets it differently. "I still believe a gardener comes," says the first man. But his companion says, "There is no gardener." He thinks the first man credulous. But *he* in turn thinks the other blind.

Wisdom was the pupil of Wittgenstein, and in the master's "second age," theological propositions were no longer dismissed as meaningless. In fact, Wittgenstein came to admit the existence of a wide range of propositions from jokes to "God-talk" that could not be verified empirically but were not on that account devoid of meaning. Like many other kinds of discourse, God-talk is a "language game." The important thing is not to sweep it off the table, but to clarify the rules. In the propositions of psychoanalysis Wisdom found examples of statements that could not be verified empirically but were nonetheless useful and meaningful. We may consider that theological statements belong to the same type as those of psychoanalysis—not verifiable in the ordinary observational way, but significant and valuable just the same. By this, Wisdom did not intend to suggest that the propositions of theology are *reducible* to statements of psychoanalysis; that would mean subscribing to Freud's cheerful positivism in theological and religious matters—God is merely a Father image, a lingering authority-ghost of childhood. Wisdom's point of view is, rather. that psychoanalytical and theological propositions are special kinds of statements, significant in their own special way, not subject to verification by the usual empirical tests we employ as criteria in scientific investigation or in everyday conduct. Thus when a mother says to her child, "God is invisible," we should understand this to mean, not that God is standing right here in this room undetectable by our eyes, but simply, "Looking around for him won't do any good."

The Death of God

In recent years there have been many lively debates on the proposition, "God is dead." For the most part, these discussions have been carried on in theological or religious contexts, and in the popular press. Neither the topic itself, nor the loose and uncritical language in which it has so often been discussed have appealed to the interest of philosophers, in this country at least. Still, philosophy must bear some responsibility for the topic, since it was the philosopher Friederich Nietzsche who introduced the concept of the death of God into the stream of late nineteenth-century thought. The theme of the death of God is put forward in two of Nietzsche's books, *Joyful Wisdom* (1881) and *Thus Spake Zarathustra* (1883). These books are written in a dithyrambic, prophetic style, and it is not easy to state in just what way Nietzsche wished his parables to be understood. It may be useful to quote in full here, despite its length, the most self-contained passage from *Joyful Wisdom.* The passage is headed "*The Madman.*":

> Have you ever heard of the madman who on a bright morning lighted a lantern and ran to the market-place calling out unceasingly: "I seek God! I seek God!"—As there were many people standing about who did not believe in God, he caused a great deal of amusement. Why! is he lost? said one. Has he strayed away like a child? said another. Or does he keep himself hidden? Is he afraid of us? Has he taken a sea-voyage? Has he emigrated?—the people cried out laughingly, all in a hubbub. The insane man jumped into their midst and transfixed them with his glances. "Where is God gone?" he called out. "I mean to tell you! *We have killed him*, you and I! We are all his murderers! But how have we done it? How were we able to drink up the sea? Who gave us the sponge to wipe away the whole horizon? What did we do when we loosened this earth from its sun? Whither does it now move? Whither do we move? Away from all suns? Do we not dash on unceasingly? Backwards, sideways, forwards, in all directions? Is there still an above and below? Do we not stray, as through infinite nothingness? Does not empty space breathe upon us? Has it not become colder? Does not night come on continually darker and darker? Shall we not have to light lanterns in the morning? Do we not hear the noise of the grave-diggers who are burying God? Do we not smell the divine putrefaction?—for even Gods putrefy! God is dead! God remains dead! And we have killed him! How shall we console ourselves, the most

murderous of all murderers? The holiest and the mightiest that the world has hitherto possessed, has bled to death under our knife,—who will wipe the blood from us? With what water could we cleanse ourselves? What lustrums, what sacred games shall we have to devise? Is not the magnitude of this deed too great for us? Shall we not ourselves have to become Gods, merely to seem worthy of it? There never was a greater event,—and on account of it, all who are born after us belong to a higher history than any history hitherto!"—Here the madman was silent and looked again at his hearers; they also were silent and looked at him in surprise. At last he threw his lantern on the ground, so that it broke in pieces and was extinguished. "I come too early," he then said, "I am not yet at the right time." This prodigious event is still on its way, and is travelling —it has not yet reached men's ears. Lightning and thunder need time, the light of the stars need time, deeds need time, even after they are done, to be seen and heard. This deed is as yet further from them than the furthest star,— *and yet they have done it!*—It is further stated that the madman made his way into different churches on the same day, and there intoned his *Requiem aeternam deo*. When led out and called to account, he always gave the reply: "What are these churches now, if they are not the tombs and monuments of God?"[36]

Like Kierkegaard's notion of the abyss between man and God, Dostoyevsky's presentation of the irrationality that lies in the depths of human consciousness, and Kafka's parables of the absurdity of existence—Nietzsche's concept of the death of God has touched a responsive chord in the hearts of the generations of and after the second World War. Atheism was nothing new—the encyclopedists and philosophes of the eighteenth century had made it respectable, and the militant humanists of the nineteenth century had replaced their lost faith

[36] Nietzsche, *The Joyful Wisdom*, T. Common (trans.), p. 125. (See bibliographical note at end of section.)

in man's supernatural destiny by enthusiastic belief in the Idea of Man. Announcements of the death of God seem to be linked not only to a general decline of belief in traditional religion, but also, and rather more particularly, to the loss of faith in the humanist ideal—the essential goodness, rationality, and self-perfectability of Man. The appalling things done to men by men in our educated and humanistically enlightened twentieth century cracked faith—not so much faith in the goodness of God, which had gone by the board anyway, but faith in the trustworthiness of human nature. "Hitler came too close to winning," Sartre remarks, "I am not going to trust humanity to the men of two hundred years in the future."

Why Dostoyevsky's writings seem pertinent is that so many of his characters (in *The Brothers Karamazov*, for instance) seem to realize that if God does not exist, then some embarrassing questions have to be faced. Dostoyevsky put little faith in humanism; "man will prevail!" meant nothing to him. In sum, loss of faith in the humanist ideal makes men *aware* of the absence of God and what a difference that absence makes. Without faith in God *or* Man, the human situation appears utterly lonely and irrational. The acclaim given Albert Camus' writings in the years immediately following the second World War stemmed in large part from public sympathy with the French novelist's awareness of the problems of men in a post-Christian and post-Humanist context as well as with his endeavor, both poetic and polemic, to redefine humanism.

More specific stimulus to the "death of God" current of thought came from European theology in the twentieth century. A sense that Christianity had become estranged from a world whose social problems were so pressing that half that world declared itself for Marxism awakened certain theologians to the need to pointing out that the mission of Christ was not to protect the rights of the middle classes. In the preceding century, Kierkegaard angrily distinguished Christianity, witness of Christ, from Christendom, the world of the church-going bourgeoisie, propertied and complacent. "If a man feels the need and the desire to hear about Christ's suffering and death," said Kierkegaard, "the state has no right to push itself in and say 'Good, that will cost you ten dollars, and we'll fix it up for you.' " Post-war twentieth-century theology went beyond Kierkegaard in emphasizing the gulf between finite man and infinite God. Paul Tillich declared that one could not even say of God that he exists, since God is the "ground" of existence. Karl Barth urged on a secularized Europe a return to eschatological, Biblical theology. Fresh impetus in the direction of "God is dead" came from Rudolf Bultmann who urged Christianity to rid itself of the dead weight of old stories and pictures from ages past and to "demythologize" itself. The claim that man, for the first time in the history of the world, now lives in an agnostic culture has drawn words of confirmation from many European theologians. Dietrich Bonhoeffer, a Lutheran minister who died under the Nazis, wrote from his prison, "We are proceeding to a time of no religion at all." He added that we must learn to live without God.

The "radical theology" which has stimulated so much recent discussion in this country on the "death of God" motif has taken that theme for its slogan. The group promoting "radical theology," made up of younger men from U.S. seminaries and campuses, has no formidable intellectual originality of its own, but draws heavily on the sources mentioned above, and has succeeded in bringing these sources to public attention. A brief reading list from these and older sources related to the topic of the death of God follows. Suggestions for more general reading in philosophical theology may be found in the Further Readings at the chapter's end.

FURTHER READINGS

Alexander, S., "Deity," *Space, Time, and Deity*, London, Macmillan, 1934, vol. 2, bk. 4.

Aquinas, Thomas, "The Existence of God," *Summa Theologica*, pt. 1, q. 2. This may be found in Anton Pegis (ed.), *The Basic Writings of Thomas Aquinas*, New York, Random House, 1945, vol. 1, pp. 18 ff.

Aristotle, *Metaphysics*, in *The Basic Works of Aristotle*, New York, Random House, 1941, bk. 12.

Bergson, Henri, *Creative Evolution*, A. Mitchell (trans.), New York, Holt, Rinehart and Winston, 1911. (There is a Modern Library edition.)

Du Noüy, Lecomte, *Human Destiny*, London, Longmans, 1947; New York, New American Library, 1949. (PB: Mentor, New American Library.)

Farrer, Austin, *Finite and Infinite*, Westminster, Glasgow, Dacre Press, 1943.

Flew, A., and A. Macintyre (eds.), *New Essays in Philosophical Theology*, London, Macmillan, 1955. (PB: Free Press, Macmillan, New York.)

Hartshorne, Charles, and Wm. L. Reese (eds.), *Philosophers Speak of God*, University of Chicago Press, 1953. (PB: Phoenix, U. of Chicago Press.)

Hick, John (ed.), *The Existence of God*, New York, Macmillan, 1964.

Hume, David, *Dialogues Concerning Natural Religion*, E. D. Aiken (ed.), New York, Hafner, 1948. (PB: Liberal Arts, Bobbs-Merrill, Indianapolis.)

James, William, *Varieties of Religious Experience*, London, Longmans, 1908. (PB: Collier, Crowell-Collier, New York.)

James, William, *The Will to Believe and Other Essays*, London, Longmans, 1912. (PB: Dover, New York.)

Kant, Immanuel, "The Ideal of Pure Reason," *Critique of Pure Reason* rev. ed., F. Max Müller (trans.), New York, Macmillan, 1922, pp. 459–516. (PB: St Martin's, New York.)

Leibniz, G. W. F., *Theodicy* (abridgment), in P. P. Weiner (ed.), *Leibniz: Selections*, New York, Scribner, 1951, pp. 510 ff. (PB: Scribner.)

Lloyd Morgan, C., *Emergent Evolution*, New York, Holt, Rinehart and Winston, 1927.

Mascall, E. L., *Existence and Analogy*, New York, Longmans, 1949.

Mascall, E. L., *He Who Is*, New York, Longmans, 1943.

Montague, W. P., *Belief Unbound*, Yale University Press, 1930.

Plato, *Timaeus*.

Spinoza, Baruch (Benedict), *Ethics* (Everymans Library), New York, Dutton, 1938. (PB: Hafner Library of World Classics, Hafner, New York.)

Taylor, Richard, *Metaphysics*. (PB: Prentice-Hall, Englewood Cliffs, N.J., 1963, chap. 7.)

Teilhard de Chardin, *The Phenomenon of Man*, New York, Harper & Row, 1956. (PB: Harper Torchbooks, Harper & Row.)

Whitehead, A. N., *Process and Reality*, New York, Macmillan, 1929, chap. 3, sec. 1. (PB: Harper Torchbooks, Harper & Row, New York.)

Whitehead, A. N., *Science and the Modern World*, New York, Macmillan, 1925, chap. 11. (PB: Mentor, New American Library, New York.)

Wisdom, John, "Gods," in A. G. N. Flew (ed.), *Essays on Logic and Language*, Oxford, Blackwell, 1951. (PB: Anchor, Doubleday, Garden City, N.Y.)

READINGS IN RADICAL THEOLOGY

Altizer, T. J. J., and W. Hamilton, *Radical Theology and the Death of God*. (PB: Liberal Arts, Bobbs-Merrill, Indianapolis, 1966.)

Bonhoeffer, Dietrich, *Letters and Papers from Prison*, New York, Macmillan, 1962. (PB: Macmillan.)

Bultmann, Rudolf, "New Testament and Mythology," in *Kerygma and Myth*. (PB: Harper Torchbooks, Harper & Row, New York, 1961.)

Harper, Ralph, *The Seventh Solitude*, Baltimore, Johns Hopkins, 1965.

Kierkegaard, Søren, *The Last Years: Journals 1853–1855*, R. G. Smith (trans.), New York, Harper & Row, 1965.
Nietzsche, Friedrich, *The Joyful Wisdom*, T. Common (trans.), in Oscar Levy (ed.), *The Complete Works of Friedrich Nietzsche*, London, T. N. Foulis, 1910, vol. 10. Reprinted, New York, Russell & Russell, 1964. (PB: Ungar, New York.)
Nietzsche, Friedrich, *Thus Spake Zarathustra* (vol. 11 of *The Complete Works*) (PB: Gateway, Regnery, Chicago.)
Tillich, Paul, *The Courage to Be*, Yale University Press, 1952. (PB: Yale U. P.)
Vahanian, Gabriel, *The Death of God*, New York, Braziller, 1961. (PB: Braziller.)

PART IV

Problems of Value

9

Ethics

It is by the Rules of Propriety that the character is established....

—Confucius

Ethics or moral philosophy is sometimes defined as the study of those principles by which we determine what actions are *right* and what ends are *good*. This definition is useful up to a point, but it is too broad. There are many kinds of rightness and goodness which are not *moral* rightness and goodness, and it is the moral right and good that philosophers have singled out as the object of ethical inquiry. Both "ethics" and "morals" derive from words meaning *custom*, but it would be too easy on that account to conclude that questions of morals are nothing but questions of customs. We often use "ethics" in the narrow sense of rules for professional conduct. Thus we say that a physician who tries to take a patient away from a colleague is violating the ethics of the medical profession, although he is not breaking a local or state law. More broadly, ethics is said to be concerned with the rules for human conduct with a view to inquiring what may be the nature of those principles upon which the rules are based. Ethics is often called a "normative," as opposed to a "positive," science, since it deals with questions relating to human conduct as it *ought* to be rather than as it *is*. But such attempts to identify ethics leave too wide an opening. There are many types of "oughts" and kinds of rules for human conduct—such as those for playing games or opening cans—that need have nothing to do with the problems of human conduct we specify as *moral.*

Many classical and modern philosophers have taken the basic question of ethics to be, "*What is the nature of the good life?*" They analyze the claims of a life defined in terms of reason, or of pleasure, or social usefulness, then attempt to settle the question in terms of what they believe to be the superior claims. A less wide-open approach to ethics is made by those philosophers who choose as their leading question, "*What is the nature of ethical judgments?*" They try to identify the first principles from which we derive moral judgments like "It is right to keep promises," or "It is wrong to steal." Recent philosophers in the Anglo-American tradition adopt second-order or linguistic tactics in dealing with ethics. Preferring not to enter into substantive questions concerning the foundation of moral good, they take the proper business of ethics to be inquiry into the meanings of ethical terms and statements. For them, the problem of moral philosophy is not, "What is the nature of the right and the good?" but rather, "*What do terms like 'right' and 'good' in their moral sense mean?*"

The Language of Ethics: the Meaning of "Good"

Classical moral philosophers did not altogether lack a sense of the importance of "second-order" inquiry into moral philosophy. Indeed, since the time of Socrates, ethical theorists have worked very hard to define their terms. There is an old distinction in moral philosophy among three kinds of good or (to use "second-order" idiom) among three senses of the word "good": (1) the good as useful (*bonum utile*); (2) the good as pleasing (*bonum delectabile*); (3) the specifically moral good (*bonum honestum*). This three-part division corresponds to a distinction of three senses of "good" we make in ordinary discourse. Usually, "a good watch" means one that keeps time, and "a good pen" is one that writes clearly and easily. That is, a good watch and a good pen fulfill the purpose for which they were made; their good lies in their utility. But we also apply the term "good" to what pleases or delights us. A child tasting an ice-cream cone will say, "This is good," and lovers exchanging kisses have been known to say the same thing despite the moral disapprobation of their elders. The meaning of "good" in the *moral* sense may be shown by such statements as "That act of kindness was a good deed," or "Adlai Stevenson was a good man." Although we are able to distinguish the moral sense of "good" from others, it is not easy to say just what it is that makes the moral good specifically moral and a good. Moreover, we often use the word "good" in contexts that show a blurring or a telescoping of these three senses of the term. When we speak of a good husband, for example, we do not seem to intend the word "good" in any one of these three senses *alone*. A good husband is likely to be a useful being; he pleases, or at least tries to; and he is, as well, worthy of moral approbation.

Are there any factors common to all senses of the word "good"? First, there is always an element of praise or approval. When we say something is good, says R. M. Hare, we always commend it. Second, there is an element of conformity to a standard, a matching-up with a set of attributes or specifications. A good watch will keep time, not need frequent repairs, have a pleasant appearance, and so on. A good husband will be loving and attentive to his wife and children, be a faithful provider, and so forth. A man I call "good" will have qualities that square with some set of standards or attributes I have in mind. In this way, the word "good" resembles that sense of the word "true" which we saw was almost synonymous with "real." The statements, "He is a true [real] soldier," and "He is a good soldier," mean about the same thing. Hare calls these two elements entailed in our usage of "good" the *evaluative* and the *descriptive* aspects of the term. That is, when I say "*X* is good," I am doing two things: (1) I am commending or approving of *X*, and (2) claiming that *X* squares up to a certain standard, a set of qualities or attributes.[1] In some usages of "good" the evaluative factor is weak and the descriptive element is strong, as when I say "That's a good road map." Sometimes the commendatory factor has the upper hand over the descriptive, as in the case of telling a child that he is a good boy.

But the question remains: how can we distinguish the *moral* good from the good as useful and pleasing? A long line of ethical theorists have answered this question by claiming that the moral good applies to *people*, not to *things*. A good watch keeps accurate time; a good plane transports us quickly and safely to a distant point. But we do not on that account praise watches and planes as morally good beings. They are instrumental goods only, not ends in themselves. Of course, the good of an ice-cream cone is not a means to an end—the child enjoys the ice cream for itself. But ice-cream cones too are things, not people. Questions of moral good seem to have to do with relations between human beings *as* human beings. Only people, not things, says Kant, can be truly moral agents. Only the

[1] R. M. Hare, *The Language of Morals*, New York, Oxford University Press, 1952, chap. 7. (PB: Galaxy, Oxford U. P.) But is there always a factor of conformity to a standard in our use of the word "good"? Suppose a child is given some food he has neither seen nor tasted before. He takes a bite and says "This is good." What is the descriptive element in the child's use of "good" here?

actions of persons can be judged morally right or wrong; the moral "ought" applies to human beings alone.

"Right" and "Ought"

Corresponding to the same distinction in the case of "good," there is a difference between the specifically moral and the morally indifferent sense of the term "right." The difference between the two senses is sometimes blurred, but frequently clear. Suppose you are trying to open a can or to put together a model car. When I say "You are not doing that right," or "That's the wrong way to go about it," I am not claiming that your actions are *morally* wrong. There are ways to secure certain desired ends. *If* you want to open the can neatly and quickly, there are one or more ways to do it, and the way you are doing it is not one of those ways. Similar considerations hold in the case of right roads and right answers to arithmetic problems. Tentatively, we may hazard that the *morally* right act is an act *toward* a human being *as* a human being which conforms to a certain principle or rule. Suppose you return some money you have found that the owner will never miss. I say that your action is "right." First, it is a true act—that is, one done with intention, freely, without compulsion. It is an act in which genuine *choice* exists. It is an act which concerns a human as a human. It conforms to a rule, this rule having a general or universal character. The rule may have been formulated by yourself, or implanted in you by others. It may be only dimly present in your consciousness, or it may be clearly written down in a book in the words "Always give back to others what belongs to them," or "Thou shalt not steal." In sum, your action is one that I commend as "right" in the specifically moral sense of the term.

A similar distinction applies to "*ought*"—a word of great

interest to moral philosophers. There are ethical "oughts" and nonethical "oughts." If you are driving me someplace in your car, and I say "You ought to turn here," I do not state this as a *moral* obligation. As in the case of the morally neutral "right," I mean: "If you want to get to the farm by the most direct route, or if you want to avoid five miles of road construction, you will turn here." The usage of the specifically moral "ought" will correspond roughly to the usage of the moral "right" sketched above. The philosopher Kant, as we shall see, held that the moral "ought" is always one with no strings attached, no reasons of self-benefit. No *reason* apart from moral duty can be given for the ethical "ought." One ought to be honest, not because it pays or because it lets one sleep at night, but because it is the right thing to do. That is, it is one's duty.

David Hume remarked that statements expressing moral judgments tend to contain the words "ought" or "ought not" in contrast to statements about matters of fact which say "is" or "is not." Hume concluded that moral statements belong to a type quite different from factual or descriptive statements. One cannot validly derive a moral conclusion from factual premises; one cannot get an "ought" out of an "is." Factual judgments are descriptive, we would say, while moral judgments are prescriptive. Kant's way of pointing up the difference between ethical judgments and others was to say that the former are commands or *imperatives*. All imperatives are expressed by the word *ought*, Kant said, and then drew his distinction between ethical and nonethical "oughts." Contemporary moral philosophers approve of Kant's identification of ethical judgments as a subclass of imperatives or commands. Because of their outward form, they say, ethical statements may be easily mistaken for assertions about what actually is the case. But the logic of statements like "You took the money" and

"You ought not to have taken the money" are completely different. The first is a description of fact; the second is a disguised command. The former asserts what is the case; the latter prescribes *acting* or withholding from action. "You ought to give some of your time to help others," may be paraphrased, "Give some of your time to help others."

MORALS, POLITICS, RELIGION

Ethics and Politics

The Greeks commonly regarded ethics as a subclass of *politics*. Ethics treats of the good of the individual person only, while politics attends to the good of the corporate entity of which the individual person is a member. Plato believed that the crucial question "What is justice?" could not be answered satisfactorily if the problem was restricted to the conduct of men taken individually. In his famous political treatise *The Republic*, Plato expands the framework of the problem of justice so that it includes the state, which Plato regarded as the individual person "in capital letters."

Something of the Greek distinction between ethics and politics remains today in the common practice of dividing ethics into *individual* and *social* ethics. But our conception of the relation between the individual person and the state is somewhat different from that of the Greek theorists. For they thought that the state was prior in importance to the individual person. Modern thought on the relative priority of person and state is less clear. Moreover, for certain historical reasons—one of which is the split between political and moral theory dating from the Renaissance, and not yet completely closed—it is more difficult for us than it was for the Greeks to bring politics and ethics into sharp focus within the same frame. Nearly everyone today, however, would agree that a closer union between personal morals and the conduct of politics would be a very good thing.

Religious and Autonomous Ethics

If we have been brought up within a religious tradition, we naturally think of the distinction between right and wrong as having ultimately a religious foundation. Western theologians have generally maintained that all particular good proceeds from God, who is the source of the right and identical with the good. It is true that we live in a secular age. But the continuity between the ideas of our time and the ages of faith (which take up about sixteen hundred years of Western culture) is still not wholly broken. This situation frequently produces in us a *dual* attitude toward moral principles. Sometimes we grant them authority in their own right; sometimes we appeal to their religious origin. This dual attitude is illustrated by the remarks of former President Truman in an address made to a group of law-enforcement officers. "We must teach that we should do right because it is right," he said. Yet he coupled this assertion with the further statement that the fundamental basis of "right" as embodied in the nation's law "was given to Moses on the Mount," that it "comes from the teaching we get from Exodus and St. Matthew, from Isaiah and St. Paul."[2]

Consider for a moment the notion of "human dignity." This belief that there is in each human person a fundamental worth or value which may not rightly be ignored is probably one of the basic presuppositions of Western society. In what does this dignity consist? What is its foundation? To those who still live within one of the religious

[2] Reported in *The New York Times*, February 16, 1950.

traditions of the West, the answer to this moral question is not difficult. The foundation of human dignity, they say, lies in the fact that God created a man in his image, that all men regardless of condition are equally dear to God. Or, in the words of Mr. Truman on another occasion, "We believe that men are equal because of that relation between God and man, we believe that each man in himself has dignity and individual worth."[3] This answer to the problem of the foundation of human dignity is a simple version of that offered by traditional theologians.

Now many philosophers take exception to this traditional position on "human dignity" because (being naturalists) they object to making the validity of ethical concepts depend on a supernaturalist metaphysics. John Dewey, for example, finds that "the assertion that the rights and freedom which constitute democracy have no validity or significance save as they are referred to some center and authority outside nature" reflects an "intrinsically skeptical, cynical and pessimistic view of human nature." "The fact of the case," says Dewey, "is that naturalism finds the values in question, the worth and dignity of men and women, residing in human nature itself."[4]

As far as the purposes of our ethical survey are concerned, no issue need be raised in terms of naturalism or supernaturalism. Whether their backgrounds be religious or not, most moral philosophers have agreed that an ethical doctrine can be constructed at least without immediate reference to a religious framework. Kant, for example, was a pious Lutheran, yet he produced an ethical system which he put forward as independent of particular religious tradi-

[3] Reported in *The New York Times,* May 15, 1950.

[4] John Dewey, "Anti-Naturalism in Extremis," in Y. Krikorian, ed., *Naturalism and the Human Spirit,* Columbia University Press, 1944, pp. 8, 9.

tions, holding it to be a practical basis of moral doctrine to which all reasonable men could agree. Outright disbelief in the metaphysical assumptions of the Judaeo-Christian tradition has not prevented modern philosophers from writing valuable books on ethics. Indeed, long before there was a Judaeo-Christian tradition in the West, the pagan Aristotle had written a naturalistic ethical treatise marked by such shrewdness and common sense that the theologians of later times incorporated his views in their own writings on ethical questions. To an important extent it was the study of Aristotle's ethical writings which convinced these theologians that the science of ethics possessed a relatively but nonetheless real autonomy. All men by the light of "natural reason," they conceded, could know the principles of ethics, the science which pertains to man's natural, if not his supernatural, end.

We shall now examine a few classic and modern types of ethical theory together with the views of the philosophers who support them. If the reader has never troubled to formulate his own moral first principles, this survey may stimulate him to the attempt.

REASON AND SELF-REALIZATION; ARISTOTLE AND DEWEY

An ethics of *reason* (ethical rationalism) holds that moral acts must be defined in terms of intelligent choice. An ethics of *self-realization* maintains that the good life for man consists in the harmonious development of all his capacities. An examination of the ethics of Aristotle and John Dewey will show us how an ancient and a modern moral doctrine incorporate these elements, together with strong emphasis on the inseparability of the good life from *social* relations.

Aristotle and the Good

According to Aristotle, the good is that at which all things aim. The good for man is what we desire for itself, that for the sake of which everything else is done. Happiness is this good.[5] Now happiness is not a passive state, but activity in accordance with virtue. We are not *endowed* with virtues. We acquire them by learning, habit, and practice. Virtues are of two kinds: intellectual and moral. The highest intellectual virtue is *wisdom*. The moral virtues are many, and may be defined in terms of a mean between an excess and a defect. Courage, for instance, stands between rashness and cowardice, and generosity between prodigality and meanness. Aristotle says:

> Virtue must have the quality of aiming at the intermediate. ... Hence it is no easy task to be good. For in everything it is no easy task to find the middle, e.g. to find the middle of a circle is not for everyone but for him who knows; so, too, any one can get angry—that is easy—or give or spend money; but to do this to the right person, to the right extent, at the right time, with the right motive, and in the right way, *that* is not for every one, nor is it easy; wherefore goodness is both rare and laudable and noble.[6]

To Aristotle, ethics belongs to *practical* philosophy. Its basic concern is not knowing but doing. The conclusions of ethical or practical syllogisms should lead us to *act*. Now a necessary ingredient of the moral act is the element of *choice*. Actions in which choice is present form a subclass

[5] The late President Kennedy liked to quote Aristotle's definition of happiness: "The good of man is in the active exercise of his soul's faculties in conformity with excellence or virtue, or, if there be several human excellences or virtues, in conformity with the best and most perfect of them." (*Nichomachean Ethics*, 1098a17.)

[6] Aristotle, *Nichomachean Ethics*, W. D. Ross, trans., 1106b14, 1109a24. (PB: Penguin, Baltimore, Md.)

of voluntary actions. Choice, however, is distinct from other voluntary actions in that it reflects the element of reason or intelligence in man's nature. Moral acts are *free* and *reasonable* acts.

According to Aristotle, the complete development of anything is its highest good. Development requires the transformation of potentialities into actualities. Development means capacities realized. The end or goal of a sapling is to be as much of a tree as possible. In man's case, his end is to be as much of a man as possible. Now man is a rational animal. Those capacities which he shares with other animals (for instance, eating and reproducing) should be realized, since he *is* animal. But he is a *rational* animal. It follows that those capacities which man does not share with other animals—those powers which set him apart *as a man*—should be fulfilled in such a way that they will have priority and control over the development of man's animal capacities.

A good man, then, will act according to that aspect of his nature which marks him off from the other animals. The moral life will be of a specifically human character. Life conceived only in terms of eating, bodily comfort, fighting, and sexual pleasure is a life open to irrational animals. Such a life is not characteristically *human*, and therefore it is not good *for a man*. Aristotle does not mean that eating, sexual activity, and the rest are *bad*. They are good, provided that they operate under the control of activities which are specifically human. Thus the good life may be defined in terms of the development of all our capacities under the control of reason or intelligence. The highest of the rational capacities, Aristotle thought, is that of contemplation, a theoretical and disinterested knowledge of things which only a few men can achieve. But all this is only a partial definition of the good life, since it omits the *social* or, as Aristotle would say, the *political* element. Human capacities cannot be realized in isolation. They can come to fruition only within the larger frame of relations between man and his political community. A man who attempts to live apart from the social environment which is natural to him is not living as a human: "Man is by nature a political animal. . . . The individual, when isolated, is not self-sufficing; and therefore he is like a part in relation to the whole. He who is unable to live in society or who has no need because he is sufficient for himself, must be either a beast or a god."[7]

Moderation and Reason

Aristotle's definition of moral virtue in terms of a *mean* brings his teaching within the group of ethical creeds which hold up *moderation* as an ideal of conduct. This includes the Stoic tradition from which we derive the tags *Nihil nimis* ("Nothing too much") and *In medio virtus stat* ("Virtue stands in the middle"). Classical Chinese philosophy also taught a doctrine of the mean. Confucius' "superior man" always took hold of extremes of doctrine, determined the mean, and employed it in the government of the people. Some critics say that moderation is a characteristic ideal of *naturalistic* ethical doctrines in contrast to the ideal of complete commitment and self-abandonment found in the ethics of *religious* teaching. It is as difficult to imagine Aristotle and Confucius exhorting their disciples to sell all they had and give the money to the poor as it is to imagine Jesus defining virtue as a mean between an excess and a defect. But virtue, to Aristotle, is no mere bourgeois compromise. The metaphor he uses to describe the good man is not fence-sitting but striking the center of the target. To hit the gold is is not easy. That is why Aristotle says, "It is hard to be good."

[7] Aristotle, *Politics*, B. Jowett, trans., bk. 1, 1253a1, 27.

Emphasis on the role of *reason* in moral acts enables us to classify Aristotle's doctrine as an example of *ethical rationalism.* The common denominator of the various forms of ethical rationalism is the belief that a truly moral act is a reasonable act. There are comparatively few moral philosophers who are not in some sense ethical rationalists—although Hume said pretty flatly, "The rules of morality . . . are not conclusions of our reason." The Greeks, who did not make the sharp distinction between "intellect" and "will" later emphasized by the Christian tradition, tended to think of ethical goodness as a *species of wisdom.* Socrates has traditionally been credited with teaching that knowledge is virtue. The Stoics, who believed that everything in Nature proceeded according to the metaphysical principle of universal reason, quite naturally regarded rationality as a criterion of moral acts. Scholastic philosophers said that "right reason" tells us what is good. Spinoza considered reason, not only as the means by which we can control natural forces, but also as the instrument of analysis by which the passions which hold us in bondage can be mastered. Even Kant, who held that right acts proceed from the *will* rather than from *knowledge,* believed that in ethical matters reason had the function of guiding the will according to rational principles. The truly good will, says Kant, is a rational will. John Dewey, as we shall see, holds that reason plays the dominant role in moral acts, if "reason" be interpreted as "intelligent insight into complete and remote consequences of desire." In practical life, we are all ethical rationalists to a degree. It is a presupposition of society that reason guides us in matters of right and wrong. In law, the actions of a defendant in certain circumstances are considered in the light of what a "reasonable man" would do in similar circumstances.

Moral Ideas as Practical Instruments; Dewey

Like Aristotle, Dewey believes that intelligence plays a dominant role in moral acts and that the good life consists in self-realization within a system of social relations. It is in Dewey's *instrumental* conception of the nature of moral acts that we see a distinctively modern emphasis. According to Dewey, there is no fixed eternal good to which all men by nature aspire. There are *goods*—natural goods such as health, wealth, friendship, and aesthetic appreciation; moral goods, such as justice, temperance, and benevolence. But even these goods are too generic to be sought *as such.* For practical purposes, the good always lies in a particular situation. "Every moral situation," says Dewey, "is a unique situation having its own irreplaceable good."[8]

Moral acts are not directed toward the achievement of goals or ends which are established and permanent. Goals or ends are *instruments* we use in intelligent solutions of problems raised by our natural and social environment. "Why have men become so attached," asks Dewey, "to fixed, eternal ends? Why is it not universally recognized that an end is a device of intelligence in guiding action, instrumental to freeing and harmonizing troubled and divided tendencies?"[9] Scientific method is concerned with the control of our natural environment. Methods in morals help us meet those problems which arise from our relations to other men. Yet the two methodologies are not cut off from each other. Rather, they interpenetrate. Science has enormous moral potentialities; for it has the power to better the human condition. Moral problems can yield to

[8] John Dewey, *Reconstruction in Philosophy,* Holt, Rinehart and Winston, 1920, p. 163. (PB: Beacon Press, Boston.)

[9] John Dewey, *Human Nature and Conduct,* New York, Modern Library, 1930, p. 231.

the application of scientific method; for a moral problem is a situation of blocked action calling for reflection, hypothesis, intelligent choice, and confirmation in experience. Like other ends, moral ends are instruments by which we remove obstacles to practical action. That is, they are ends which are at the same time means.

Man's proper business is practical activity, says Dewey. Aristotle was wrong in fixing on contemplation as the fulfillment of the highest capacity of man, even though he limited it to a knowledgeable few. Esteem of the contemplative life arises from a false "spectator" theory of the relation of man to Nature. Since contemplation affects nothing, it is worth nothing. "While saints are engaged in introspection," says Dewey, "burly sinners run the world."[10] Practical activity involves the attainment of ends which are relevant to the solution of problems which our ever-developing natural and social environment poses to us. An ethical act derives its moral content, not from an eternal moral law externally imposed from above, but rather from its relevance to the practical situation at hand.

Moral Conduct as Intelligent Choice

Like Aristotle, Dewey holds that a moral act must contain the factor of *choice*. "Only deliberate action," says Dewey, "conduct into which reflective choice enters, is distinctively moral, for only then does there enter the question of better or worse."[11] Like Aristotle too, Dewey emphasizes the critical role of reason in the moral act. But the "reason" which guides moral conduct is not a divine endowment as the Greek philosopher sometimes seems to suggest. Rather, "reason" is a set of habits which enables us to discriminate among possible alternatives of action. Reason in morality is

[10] Dewey, *Reconstruction in Philosophy*, p. 154.
[11] Dewey, *Human Nature and Conduct*, p. 279.

intelligent choice in a practical situation. It is the ability to foresee imaginatively the consequences of a proposed act; it is the capacity to compare and to evaluate those alternative consequences in the light of the goals we wish to achieve; it is competence in assessing the claims of others who may be affected by those consequences. "Moral insight, and therefore moral theory," says Dewey, "consist simply in the every-day workings of the same ordinary intelligence that measures dry-goods, drives nails, sells wheat, and invents the telephone."[12]

Suppose a man, after many years at a particular job, becomes dissatisfied and wishes to change his vocation. This moral situation, like all others, begins with an unsettled, troubled state of affairs in which the routine of daily living is disturbed by doubts and uncertainty. Sound moral decision resolves doubts, restores equilibrium, and clears the way for action. The man who is considering changing his job can make a sound moral decision only by intelligent reflection. This will involve formulating his desires within his own mind more clearly; consideration of the alternative consequences of this or that choice; attention to the claims of others, such as members of his family who may be committed by his decision. No all-binding moral law will help here. This moral situation, like most, simply cannot be abstracted from particular circumstances. Successful solution will be just as specific, and will depend upon the quality of intelligent insight the man can bring to bear on the probable net results of each of the alternatives between which he must choose and their relevance to the ends he desires to attain.

We might derive from Dewey's view a simple answer to

[12] John Dewey, "Moral Theory and Practice" in *The Philosophy of John Dewey*, J. Ratner, ed., New York, Holt, Rinehart and Winston, 1928, p. 310.

the question: what is the basic nature of moral judgments? Just as scientific judgments are intelligent judgments dealing with problems raised by our *natural* environment, so moral judgments are intelligent judgments dealing with problems raised by our *social* environment, the problems, that is, which spring from relations between ourselves and other people. It would then follow as a corollary that a morally defective judgment is an unintelligent judgment, and that acting on it amounts to careless or stupid handling of a matter involving our relations with other persons. "Stupidity pushed to a certain point *is*, you know, immorality," says Mrs. Assingham in Henry James' novel *The Golden Bowl*. "Just so, what is morality but high intelligence?"

Self-Realization within Democracy

In Dewey's ethical doctrine we find an emphasis on the social nature of moral acts which is kindred to Aristotle's. The American philosopher admires the Greek's "profound insight into the relation of man to society, and the dependence of the individual upon the social body." But Dewey sees moral acts deriving their meaning with reference to a *modern* social structure, which in complexity far transcends the democracy of the small city-state within which Greek life was so tightly contracted. Modern democracy, Dewey believes, is the widest and most inclusive category of social adaptation. It is by no means "prior to the individual," as the Greeks thought their state was. Democracy has emerged "as a kind of net consequence of a vast multitude of responsive adjustments to a vast number of situations, no two of which were alike, but which tended to converge to a common outcome." Men are best able to realize their individual capacities within a democratic society, for:

. . . All social institutions have a meaning, a purpose. That purpose is to set free and develop the capacities of human individuals without respect to race, sex, class or economic status. And this is all one with saying that the test of their value is the extent to which they educate every individual into the full stature of his possibility. Democracy has many meanings, but if it has a moral meaning, it is found in resolving that the supreme test of all political institutions and industrial arrangements shall be the contribution they make to the all-around growth of every member of society.[13]

The significant word here is "growth." The metaphor is biological. Aristotle defined the good of anything as its highest development. The goal of an organism is maturity. So, in the case of man, Dewey sees his good, not in fixed results to be attained, but in continuing improvement and progress. Creative development of individual capacities within a democratic society is the highest good. "Growth itself," says Dewey, "is the only moral 'end.' "[14]

THE GOOD AS PLEASURE AND UTILITY

Hedonism

There is a classic theory concerning the nature of the good which asserts that all good (including moral good) is identical with pleasure; that the greatest good for man is defined negatively as the avoidance of pain, positively as the attainment of maximum pleasure. This theory is known as *Hedonism* (from the Greek ἡδονή—pleasure) and was held by certain ancient ethical schools such as the Cyrenaics and the Epicureans. Tradition has assigned the slogan "Let us eat, drink, and me merry, for tomorrow we die"

[13] Dewey, *Reconstruction in Philosophy*, p. 147.
[14] *Ibid.*, p. 141.

to the Epicureans, but there is no evidence that Epicurus himself or any of the philosophers of his school identified the good with an earthly paradise of sensual delights. Rather, Epicurus esteemed the pleasures of the mind as superior to those of the body and held that "the painless state" (ataraxia) in which the gods dwelt was most nearly approached by the untroubled contemplation of the sage discussing philosophy with friends in his garden. An American hedonism of the earthly paradise sort was offered as his personal credo by George Jean Nathan:

> As it is given to few men to die happy, the best that man can hope and strive and pray for is momentary happiness during life, repeated as frequently as the cards allow. Pleasure, whatever its species, is the drink in the desert. It is the beautiful transient reward of travail and pain. There is no other reward except for those still sufficiently aboriginal to believe in a hereafter.
>
> The ambrosia of the gods, the lovely angels, eternal blue skies and peace, the music of golden harps, are too far off and dubious so far as my own metaphysics goes. I prefer to trust to the more realistic and visible Grand Montrachet, pretty girls, Mediterranean coast and symphony orchestras of the here and now.[15]

What is pleasure? It is hard to tell just what it is. The antonym of "pleasure" is "pain," but, unlike pain, pleasure is hard to localize. We do not hesitate to say "my foot hurts," or "I have a pain in my shoulder." But do we as often speak of having pleasure in a particular part of ourselves? Sometimes we talk of pleasure as if it were simply a feeling that occurs at this or that time ("He blushed with

[15] *The New York Times*, April 9, 1958. The prudent will be relieved to know that the renowned theatre critic modified his credo in later life and died a convert to religious orthodoxy.

pleasure at the compliment"). Again, we speak of it as enjoyment, not in such a way as to suggest that pleasure comes and goes in the course of what we are doing ("I had a very pleasant talk with Bill after the meeting"). Often we mention pleasure as if it were some kind of end or goal ("Those who prefer Grand Montrachet and pretty girls are pleasure seekers"). The philosophers have had many things to say about pleasure, not always as if they had quite the same understanding of the concept. Plato speaks of pleasure as a replenishment, a making up for a deficiency. Sometimes he dismisses it as no more than the scratch of an itch; yet he admits the existence of certain pleasures that are pure and unmixed, like the smell of a rose. Aristotle would have pleasure as the concommitant of unimpeded activity; as, we would say, one enjoys a walk, not for the sake of its destination, but for "the pleasure of walking." Augustine holds that pleasure is a passion or emotion and links it to the *will* and its satisfaction. Aquinas says that pleasure is the *arrest* of desire for a loved object, "the enjoyment of the possession of an object when desire does not fail."[16] A number of philosophers distinguish pleasure from *happiness* by pointing to the relative transiency or brevity of pleasure. Yet others, like John Stuart Mill, *define* happiness in terms of pleasure.

Utilitarianism; Kinds of Pleasure

"Utilitarianism" was the name given by John Stuart Mill to a doctrine first expounded by Jeremy Bentham, in whose teachings Mill was rigorously indoctrinated by his father, James Mill. According to the younger Mill, utilitarianism:

[16] So Aquinas is rendered by Elizabeth Anscombe to whose analysis of pleasure I am here indebted. J.G.B.

> The creed which accepts as the foundation of morals utility, or the greatest happiness principle, holds that actions are right in proportion as they tend to promote happiness, wrong as they tend to produce the reverse of happiness. By happiness is intended pleasure and the absence of pain: by unhappiness, pain and the privation of pleasure.[17]

The first part of this statement has nothing directly to do with hedonism. It is the second part, in which happiness is identified with pleasure, that interests us here. Bentham took pleasure as something *quantitative*, something which is open to measurement. *More* pleasure is simply the heightening of pleasure and this increase is at least theoretically capable of being calculated. Now Mill modifies this Benthamist hedonism in an important respect. While he identifies happiness with pleasure, he distinguishes between *kinds* of pleasure. There are *qualitative* differences in pleasures. Some pleasures are "lower" or "grosser," others are "higher" or "nobler," the former generally being bodily pleasures, the latter intellectual. "It is quite compatible with the principle of utility," Mill thought, "to recognize the fact that some kinds of pleasure are more desirable and more valuable than others."[18] He quickly saw that to maintain hedonism in a purely quantitative form would lead to awkward conclusions. For, if pleasure were merely quantitative, if all pleasures were qualitatively alike, then there would be no reason to suppose that the human ideal of happiness would be on a different level from that of a pig. Mill rejects Bentham's undifferentiated hedonism because he is convinced that "It is better to be a human being

[17] John Stuart Mill, *Utilitarianism.* (PB: Liberal Arts, Bobbs-Merrill, Indianapolis, 1949, p. 7.)

[18] *Ibid.*, p. 8.

dissatisfied than a pig satisfied; better to be Socrates dissatisfied than a fool satisfied."[19]

Now, if we are to distinguish between "higher" and "lower" pleasures, the former to be pursued rather than the latter, the question arises: How are we to know which pleasure is higher and which lower? A loyal empiricist and suspicious of anything savoring of "mysticism," Mill sternly rejects any attempt to settle this question by an appeal to *intuition*, by which Mill understood a form of direct knowledge independent of empirical reference or public confirmation. He prefers to point to those who have had experience of *both* "higher" and "lower" pleasures, with the claim that by far the greater number of these men have shown by their actions that the "higher" pleasures are to be desired. "Of two pleasures," says Mill, "if there be one to which all or almost all who have experience of both give a decided preference, irrespective of any feeling of moral obligation to prefer it, that is the more desirable pleasure."[20]

Altruism in Utilitarianism

There is another way in which Mill is forced to modify Bentham's hedonism, and this stems partly from the importance Mill attaches to man's *social* character. Like Aristotle, Mill believed that man is a social animal and cannot live the good life apart from society. "The social state," says Mill, "is at once so natural, so necessary and so habitual to man, that, except in some unusual circumstances or by an effort of voluntary abstraction, he never conceives himself otherwise than as a member of a body."[21] Now Bentham be-

[19] *Ibid.*, p. 10.
[20] *Ibid.*, p. 9.
[21] *Ibid.*, p. 33.

lieved that men who constitute society are motivated by their own selfish interests. Mill, however, amends this egoism to the point of admitting that men frequently desire to bring about happiness *for others*, and that this is a good thing. For, in order to bring about the greatest amount of *total* happiness, there will be times when we must sacrifice our particular pleasure for that of others. A nurse who stays to die at her post in order that her patients may live is a case in point.

Because of his inclusion within utilitarianism of the element of sacrifice of personal happiness for the good of others, Mill's doctrine has been labeled *altruistic hedonism.* Mill derives his altruism, however, from frankly naturalistic premises. In animals, he says, we find not only the drive of *self-preservation* or self-defense but also the instinct of *sympathy*. In the animal kingdom this sympathy rarely reaches beyond the immediate offspring, but in man it may be extended to include all men. As he develops this argument, Mill turns it back in the direction of egoism. Due to his superior intelligence, Mill says, man can discern that his own personal welfare is bound up with that of the community, so that when he sees that community imperiled in any way he feels his own security threatened.

Is Pleasure the Good?

Some critics of Mill's utilitarianism have claimed that his insistence on identifying his theory of happiness and human good with the pleasure principle weakens his doctrine. He could have had his utilitarianism, they say, without mixing it up with hedonism. Mill's teaching is a social-utility ethics which he tries to derive from a definition of happiness in terms of pleasure, an axiom as unnecessary to his system as it is mistaken. Why many moral philosophers believe that the pleasure theory of ethics is mistaken may further be clarified if we consider the following objections, two applying to hedonism in general, the other two referring more particularly to Mill's version of it:

1. In one of its most common usages, pleasure refers to a relatively brief response, a relatively short period of exalted good feeling. If the hedonists claim that pleasure is the good and *the only good* (for, of course, one need not be a hedonist to hold that pleasure *is* good), then one need only to point to common experience to show that the lives of many good men are determined by goals other than pleasure in the usual sense. If, on the other hand, by "pleasure" is meant something more than a brief span of heightened good feeling—for example, the satisfaction which accompanies intellectual endeavor or activity in behalf of social welfare—then the word "pleasure" is inflated to cover too extensive an area of experience. The word "happiness" would fit as well, and perhaps better; for "happiness" is commonly used to designate a satisfaction which endures.

Mill himself admits this distinction between pleasure and happiness but claims that the happy life is the one with the fewest pains and the most pleasures. It is questionable, however, if the good men Mill admired defined their goals in terms of a life of maximum pleasure. Pleasure and, for that matter, happiness itself seem to be by-products, arising from activities which are not aimed at pleasure or happiness *as such*. The sick man does not want happiness as such; he wants to be well. The scholar does not want to be happy; he wants to finish his book. It is not happiness the lover desires, but his beloved.

2. When we admit, as Mill does, that there are *kinds* of pleasure, some "lower" and some "higher," do we not at the same time admit the presence of a factor *by virtue of which* these pleasures are "lower" and "higher"? But this factor by means of which we distinguish between the *quali-*

ties of pleasures can hardly *itself* be a pleasure principle, unless "higher" pleasure means merely an increase in the *quantity* of pleasure—which Mill denies.

3. To assert, as Mill does, that there are some pleasures which are more *desirable* than others is subject to the preceding difficulty. In addition, Mill's use of the word *desirable* ("ought to be desired") as a synonym for *desired* produces confusion. He states that (a) happiness (pleasure) is the only thing *desirable*, and supports this assertion by the claim that (b) happiness (pleasure) *is in fact desired.* But "desirable" and "desired" do not mean the same thing. The first, with its compressed "ought," refers to a criterion or standard by which actions are to be judged, and thus has a *normative* reference. "Desired," however, points simply to what in fact is, and thus has only a *positive* reference.

4. To claim pleasure as *the* good is to deny the independence and autonomy of ethical judgments. For when I assert that moral good is but a *species* of pleasure, I give ethical values a secondary and derivative rank: what is primary and basic is pleasure; the moral good, being a kind of pleasure, is a second-line phenomenon only. The hedonist's alleged reduction of the moral to questions of pleasure is an example of what G. E. Moore calls *the naturalistic fallacy*.

Is Social Utility the Good?

Let us forget about the hedonist element in utilitarianism and compress what remains into the following proposition: *The morally good is the same thing as the socially useful.* Such a definition of the good seems quite reasonable. Killing a man except in self-defense is morally wrong because such an action is not only harmful to the victim; it also imperils the welfare of the social group. Giving food and clothing to the poor is morally right because such charity not only makes the poor people happier; it also improves the condition of society as a whole. What is the end of human life but usefulness to others? Do we not send our children to good schools so that they will grow up to become useful citizens in a democratic society? Christian doctrine itself seems to make morality equivalent to helping others. Does not Jesus' teaching that we should feed the hungry and clothe the naked constitute (as Mill declares) "the ideal perfection of utilitarian morality"?

Can such a warm-hearted and altruistic definition of the good be criticized? Some critics object to the term "socially useful" on the grounds of vagueness. It is just as difficult to define what is "socially useful," they say, as it is to define what is "morally good." From a social-utility point of view, we might all agree that murder, being socially harmful, is properly considered morally bad, while ameliorating the condition of the poor, being socially useful, is morally good. But suppose the case under consideration were that of a man who proposes to enter a monastery, there to spend the rest of his life in prayer and contemplation. To reach agreement on the moral rightness of his act and the moral desirability of his goal would require a searching inquiry into the *meaning* of social utility.

Other critics hold that a definition of the good in terms of social utility can never be any more than secondary. For, they say, whenever we assert that the good is the same thing as the useful, we are forced to make an exception of that for the attainment of which the good *is* useful. That is, a thing can be said to be useful only if it helps to bring about a state of affairs other than itself. Thus, a hammer is useful in that it helps us drive nails through wood. Now what is that for which the socially useful *is* useful? If the aim of good schools is to produce useful citizens, what are the citizens to be useful *for?*

Mill, of course, would reply to this last objection that there is only one state of affairs which is *good in itself*, this being the maximum amount of general happiness; all other goods are to be defined in terms of their utility in bringing this about. John Dewey, on the other hand, would reply that both the objection and Mill's answer are wrongly conceived. For they both assume that any definition of moral good must be in terms of a single good-in-itself to which all other goods are instrumental and subordinate. Dewey, as we have seen, holds that there is no single good-in-itself, whether this be taken as maximum happiness, the welfare of the social group, or something else. To Dewey there is no good, there are only goods. There is no end, there are only ends. And ends are always *ends-in-view*. The only thing which qualifies for the title of *the* moral end is creative growth of the individual within a society—and this concept precludes fixed ends.

Some critics find an excessive emphasis on *altruism* in social-utility doctrines of the good. The "morally good," they say, cannot be quite the same thing as the "socially useful," because there are morally good acts which do not involve our relation to others. Not only does one owe moral obligation to others, says W. P. Montague; one owes it to oneself. "To say that Robinson Crusoe had no moral duties because he had no neighbors is to forget that one's nearest neighbor is one's own future self."[22] As for utilitarians and social-good theorists who support their doctrine by reference to the Christian ethic, is it possible that they assume the presence of an exaggerated altruism in the teachings of Jesus which may not be there at all? Says C. G. Jung:

[22] W. P. Montague, *Ways of Things*, Englewood Cliffs, N.J., Prentice-Hall, 1940, p. 149.

The acceptance of oneself is the essence of the moral problem and the epitome of a whole outlook upon life. That I feed the hungry, that I forgive an insult, that I love my enemy in the name of Christ—all these are undoubtedly great virtues. What I do unto the least of my brethren, that I do unto Christ. But what if I should discover that the least amongst them all, the poorest of all the beggars, the most impudent of all offenders, the very enemy himself—that these are within me, and that I myself stand in need of my own kindness—that I myself am the enemy who must be loved—what then?[23]

MOTIVES AND INTUITION

Consequences, Intent, and Motive

What makes an act morally right or wrong? Is it the consequences, the results of that act, or is it the motive or the intention of the doer? First, we should distinguish between *intent* and *motive*. Consider the case of a man who has killed another with his car. The consequences of the deed are clear enough and bad enough—the victim is dead. Now consider the question of intent. Did the driver *intend* to kill the man? In most such cases, the answer is no. Although there may have been an element of carelessness present on the driver's part, the killing of the man was an *accident*, that is, it was not the intention of the driver to kill the man. Suppose, however, that in this instance the driver *did* intend to kill the victim, and that he hit him with his car to make the death *look like* an accident: Now there is, morally speaking, a great difference between the two situations, although the principal result—a man dead—is the same. Legally, the second killing is a murder and the law would exact far more severe punishment if the killer's intentions were found by a jury to have been murderous.

[23] C. G. Jung, *Modern Man in Search of a Soul*, New York, Harcourt, Brace & World, 1933. (PB: Harvest, Harcourt, Brace & World.)

Suppose it is known that the driver did in fact intentionally kill the victim. We might now ask what was his *motive* for so doing? We know that the killing was intentional, but still we wonder why he did it. Was he jealous? Impelled by desire to revenge an old wrong? Trying to rid himself of a blackmailer? In sum, *intent* has to do with an agent's wanting to achieve a certain end, but *motive* has to do with his reasons for wanting that end.

Most of us would admit that intent is an important factor in judging the morality of an act, yet we would hesitate to pronounce a deed morally right or wrong solely on the basis of the intention of the doer. The cry of a child, "I didn't *mean* it," checks the upraised hand over the broken vase. Yet to say of a man, "Poor fellow, he *means* well," is decidedly not a tribute of moral esteem. There is a saying that virtue is its own reward, but there is another to the effect that the road to Hell is paved with good intentions. Sometimes a deed entails such evil consequences that we may be tempted to refuse to consider the question of intent or to say that it is unimportant. Consider the following example. A certain nation X tries to put down an insurgency hostile to X, its cause, and its allies. In the fighting that ensues, many noncombatants are killed or injured by X's bombing attacks. Critics of nation X say that X's action in *Y* is *immoral*, and as evidence of immorality point to the large number of innocent civilians killed by X's bombers. But defenders of X reply that this evidence does not support the charge of immorality. X's military commanders do not *intend* to kill or injure innocent noncombatants; they try to avoid it if they can. What X intends to do is to destroy military objectives and to interdict certain areas to the insurgents. Objectors reply that the killing of so many innocent civilians is a *result* so bad in itself, as well as being inextricable from achieving military objectives in this case, that the question of *X*'s *intent* fades to the point of irrelevancy. Defenders of *X* in turn reply that. . . . But the reader may want to carry on the argument from this point by himself.[24]

There can be little doubt that we judge the ethical quality of an action by *motive*. Giving money to those in want, let us concede, is an action worthy of moral approval. Yet suppose a teacher gives some money to a beggar on the streets, his motive being a desire to impress with his generosity some students who are standing about. The results of the act, so far as the beggar is concerned, are identical with the gift of the same amount of money by another man who offers it simply because he considers it his duty to help the poor. The dollar from the first man buys as much food as the dollar from the second. Yet if the students knew what had moved their teacher to perform his charitable act, they would probably not think so highly of him. Similarly, if we discovered that the primary motive of nation *X*'s counter-insurgency military action was to protect its economic markets rather than to promote social justice, we should think considerably less of the moral worth of *X*'s cause.

Ethical theories are sometimes classified according to whether their primary stress is on motives or consequences. But there is no important moral theory which states that the moral content of an act lies entirely within the motive of the agent, nor is there any major ethical doctrine which

[24] An old-fashioned way of putting the distinction is to say that a deed may be *materially* but not *formally* bad. A surgeon who amputates a patient's leg has produced a situation which is materially evil—through his intervention the patient has lost his leg. But while the material object of the surgeon's intent was the amputation of the patient's leg, his formal object was to save the patient's life. In less pedantic language: the surgeon chooses to effect a lesser evil in order to prevent a greater. The reader may judge whether any analogy exists between this example and the war situation outlined above.

would judge morality wholly in terms of consequences. It is often said that Utilitarianism and instrumental theories of the good, such as those of Mill and Dewey, tend to stress consequences, while ethical theories like that of Kant emphasize the role of motive in the moral act. Mill recognized the fundamental importance of *intention* in moral situations. "The morality of the action," he says, "depends entirely upon the intention that is, upon what the agent wills to do." But the question of *motive* he declared a quite different matter. "The motive," says Mill, "has nothing to do with the morality of the action, though much with the worth of the agent."[25] Certainly the question of the purity of the agent's motive is important to Kant. According to the German philosopher, true moral acts are never done for the sake of personal advantage. Ethical deeds are *disinterested*, that is, no element of self-benefit can be present in them. Kant found his analysis of ethical judgments quite consistent with the Biblical injunction, "Purefy thy heart!" To Kant, moral acts are performed, not for profit, but from *duty*. "Honesty is the best policy," would be for him a *prudential* rather than an ethical maxim. Kant admits that some things we do with an eye to profit will happen to be in accord with duty. Such actions are not morally bad. In fact, certain deeds, like that of a rich man giving a great sum to charity from a motive of vainglory, may even be *praiseworthy*. But praiseworthiness does not coincide at all crucial points with morality. Let us look at Kant's moral theory in further detail.

Kant's Voluntarism

Voluntarism in ethical theory refers to an emphasis on the primary role played by *will* in the moral situation. According to Kant, there are two principal faculties of man: (1)

[25] Mill, *Utilitarianism*, chap. 2.

the *knowing* faculty and (2) the *willing* faculty. Knowledge makes *science* possible. But it is the *will* which is the foundation of morals, as well as the sole source of that which alone is good in itself. "Nothing can possibly be conceived in the world," says Kant, "or even out of it, which can be called good without qualification, except a *good will*."[26]

Now reason and will are not wholly cut off from each other, says Kant, for reason can and does guide the will according to its own rational principles. Yet man, as *willing*, man as a *moral* being, can penetrate to depths which are closed to *knowing* man, whose understanding is confined to appearances which derive their systematic order from the categories of the mind. To illustrate: Kant says that through reason we can never come to know the existence of God. To man, as a *knowing* being, God remains only a *possible* entity. Nevertheless, although we can never demonstrate that God is, our *will* directly acquaints us with the necessity of postulating his existence. We cannot *prove* God by pointing to the starry heavens above, but the moral law within our breast *convinces* us of him. Similarly, reason can tell us only of the possibility of immortality, but the will compels us to assert its actuality. For the *summum bonum* (the union of virtue and happiness) toward which the will strives cannot be reached in this life. Yet a good will is *worthy* of this highest good.

Kant's Intuitionism; Conscience; the Imperatives

By "intuitionism" in ethical theory we mean any view which holds that the basic principles of morality are directly recognized by us without any need of proof or con-

[26] I. Kant, *Fundamental Principles of the Metaphysic of Morals*, T. K. Abbott, trans. (PB: Liberal Arts, Bobbs-Merrill, Indianapolis, 1949, p. 11.)

firmation from external sources. According to Kant, we can know for ourselves what is right and wrong, and this direct and immediate knowledge comes from an inner moral awareness. This internal apprehension of moral law men commonly name *conscience.* Now conscience, Kant tells us, acquaints us with the moral law in the form of a command or *imperative.* The imperative of conscience is known as the *categorical* imperative to distinguish it from a *hypothetical* imperative. Both categorical and hypothetical imperatives, when expressed, contain the word "ought"; but the categorical imperative is *unconditional*, while the hypothetical imperative refers to results which benefit the doer in some way. "It pays to tell the truth" and "You ought to be honest, because honesty is the best policy" are examples of hypothetical imperatives. But the categorical imperative simply commands, "Thou oughtst!" If we ask "Why?" we receive no reply beyond "Thou oughtst, because thou oughtst."

The categorical imperative, Kant tells us, may be formulated in a number of alternate ways. One is: "Act only on that maxim whereby thou canst at the same time will that it should become a universal law."[27] To test the morality of a proposed act the agent should ask himself, "Can I honestly will that which I am about to do should be generally done? Or am I making an exception in favor of myself?" We can see that this formulation of the categorical imperative is related to the "golden rule": "Do unto others as you would have others do unto you."[28] Another formulation of the categorical imperative is stated by Kant as: "So act as to treat humanity, whether in thine own

[27] *Ibid.*, p. 38.

[28] The golden rule is found in the Sermon on the Mount thus: "Therefore all things whatsoever ye would that men should do to you, do ye even so to them" (Matthew 7:12). The golden rule occurs in negative phrasing (but with positive import) in the Confucian teaching of reciprocity.

person or in that of any other, in every case as an end, never as a means only."[29]

Importance of Kant's Theory

In so far as it emphasizes the relevance of motive to moral judgment, Kant's ethical doctrine provides a check to the potential one-sidedness of utilitarian or pragmatic ethics. The German moralist's insistence on the independence of ethical judgment, on the autonomy of morals, alerts us to the need for careful thinking before we construe ethical judgments simply as particular kinds of psychological or social beliefs. In the sense that Kant claims a unique quality to inhere in moral judgment, his moral theory may be classified as a kind of *ethical absolutism.* It was pointed out earlier (pp. 350–351) that Kant's teaching that fundamental ethical judgments are *imperatives* anticipates the analysis of many contemporary ethical theorists who hold that ethical claims are not true descriptive statements, but commands disguised in propositional form. Important too is Kant's attention to the element of *universalization* in moral judgments. When I say "You shouldn't break a promise," I am not limiting myself to the specifics of your case, but I bring to bear on that case a universal rule—"No one should break promises" or "It is wrong to break promises." Despite the power of Kant's ethical analysis, many critics are not satisfied with certain implications of his moral theory. Should the reader wish to take some questions along to his future reading of Kant, here are a few adapted from various critiques of Kant's theory:

1. Kant's voluntarism seems to create an exaggerated dualism between the theoretical or "scientific" realm and the sphere of the moral or practical. Is such a radical dualism between man as *knowing* and man as *willing* defensible?
2. Is Kant's claim that a good will is the only conceivable

[29] Kant, *Fundamental Principles,* p. 47.

good-in-itself consistent with his claim that the good will is *worthy of happiness?* (Would not happiness then be the good-in-itself?)

3. Kant seems to assume that a moral sense is something *innate*, a faculty with which man is endowed, rather than a capacity he acquires. Can this assumption be defended?

4. From what source do the imperatives of conscience derive their authority?

5. Will any of the various formulations of the categorical imperative tell us what to do in any specific situation? If not, what function do they have?

The Good as Indefinable; G. E. Moore

A highly individual form of ethical intuitionism, very different from Kant's, is held by the English analytic philosopher G. E. Moore. Moore maintains that all ethical propositions are based on the notion of "good." Now we can know what "good" is only by direct acquaintance (intuition). For "good" is qualitatively unique. There is nothing else like it. It is *sui generis.* "Good" is something simple (that is, it has no parts) and therefore cannot be defined. We cannot set forth the *meaning* of "good" in propositions which do not include the notion of good:

> "Good," then, if we mean by it that quality which we assert to belong to a thing, when we say that the thing is good, is incapable of any definition, in the most important sense of that word. The most important sense of "definition" is that in which a definition states what are the parts which invariably compose a certain whole; and in this sense "good" has no definition because it is simple and has no parts. It is one of those innumerable objects of thought which are themselves incapable of defintion, because they are the ultimate terms by reference to which whatever *is* capable of definition must be defined.[30]

[30] G. E. Moore, *Principia Ethica* (1902), London, Cambridge University Press, 1951, pp. 9, 10. (PB: Cambridge U. P.)

"Good," says Moore, is unanalyzable in much the same way as the perceived quality "yellow" is unanalyzable. To be sure, yellow may be defined in terms of light vibrations. But it is not light vibrations we perceive when we experience yellow. What we do enjoy when we have the experience of yellow is just the unique, indefinable quality "yellow" and that is all there is to it. In the same way, "good," as experienced, is not explainable in terms of anything but itself.

But what about those ethical theorists who *have* explained "good" in terms of something else? Hedonists say the good is pleasure; utilitarians say it is the greatest happiness of the greatest number, etc. They are wrong, says Moore. Whoever defines "good" in terms of something other than good, such as pleasure or utility, is guilty of the *naturalistic fallacy*. Moore does not object to the proposition "Pleasure is good," or "Social utility is good." It is statements such as "Pleasure is the *only* good" and "Social utility is what we *mean* by good" that he refuses to accept. For the same reason, Moore rejects any attempt to define "good" by appeal to the descriptive sentences of the special sciences. The claim, for example, that "good" can be explained in terms of certain psychological states would be dismissed by Moore as another instance of the naturalistic fallacy.

Moore's claim that "good" is indefinable has reminded some of G. K. Chesterton's attitude to the quality "mean." According to Chesterton, you cannot explain what it is that constitutes meanness in a man. A mean man is just plain *mean*, and that's all. More seriously, some critics of Moore's position think he has failed to make an important distinction between two kinds of definition corresponding to the two kinds of knowledge—knowledge by acquaintance and knowledge by description.[31] Yellow is yellow, as Moore

[31] See p. 174.

says, and to state that yellow is light vibrations of such and such a kind does not do justice to the *unique perceptual quality* of yellow. Yet we may *understand* what yellow is, we may know *about* yellow, by defining it in terms of its wave length. Moore may well be right in claiming that, when we know "good," the peculiar quality of this direct experience is unanalyzable in terms of predicates other than "good." But could it not be the case that we can *know about* good by means of predicates which do not refer to its unanalyzable quality? If so, it would seem that an attempt to define "good" in terms of predicates other than good is—in principle, at least—not fallacious. It does not follow, of course, that defining "good" in predicates other than good is necessarily acceptable when such definition involves *reductionism*—as, for example, the statements "Good is nothing but pleasure" and "Conscience is nothing but internalized authority."

ETHICAL STATEMENTS AS EXPRESSIONS OF FEELING

Approval and Disapproval

Are ethical propositions reducible to statements concerning someone's feelings? This question has received considerable attention from recent moral philosophers. Some years ago, Bertrand Russell put forward the suggestion that ethical propositions are essentially implicit expressions of approval or disapproval. That is, when a person says "*x* is good," or "*y* is morally right," he is expressing approval of *x* and *y* and implicitly exhorting others to feel the same way. Similarly, when a person says "*x* is bad," or "*y* is morally wrong," he is expressing disapproval of *x* and *y* together with his desire to persuade others to disapprove as well.

The view that ethical propositions are basically expressions of approval or disapproval has been considered seriously by a number of contemporary philosophers who have subjected various types of ethical statements to linguistic analysis. For example, C. L. Stevenson offers the following schema as a "working model" suitable for the preliminary stages of analysis of ethical meaning:

1. "This is wrong" means *I disapprove of this; do so as well.*
2. "He ought to do this" means *I disapprove of his leaving this undone; do so as well.*
3. "This is good" means *I approve of this; do so as well.*[32]

Ayer's Four Types of Ethical Propositions

About thirty years ago, A. J. Ayer made his controversial claim that a large number of moral judgments are no more than *disguised* expressions of approval or disapproval. The statement "It was wrong to steal that money" is equivalent to the exclamation "You stole!" uttered in a tone of disapprobation. In *Language, Truth and Logic,* Ayer distinguished four types of ethical propositions: (1) propositions which express the *meanings* of ethical terms; (2) propositions which express the phenomena of moral experience; (3) exhortations to moral virtue; and (4) actual ethical judgments, such as "It is wrong to steal." Now only propositions of the first type—that is, those in which the meanings of ethical terms are analyzed—properly belong to ethical philosophy. That is, the legitimate boundaries of ethics are those of a *second-order study*. The second type of proposition, which describes the phenomena of moral experience and their causes, is not the proper business of philosophy, but should be relegated to psychology or sociology. Propositions of the third type—exhortations to

[32] C. L. Stevenson, *Ethics and Language,* Yale University Press, 1944, p. 21. (PB: Yale U. P.)

moral virtue—are not propositions at all, but ejaculations designed to make the reader or hearer act in a certain way. Propositions of the fourth type—actual ethical judgments such as "It is wrong to steal" are not genuine propositions either. They are not *analytic* statements, that is to say true be definition, nor are they *synthetic* statements, descriptions of fact. They are pseudo-propositions: "In saying that a certain type of action is right or wrong, I am not making any factual statement, nor even a statement about my own mind. I am merely expressing certain moral sentiments. And the man who is ostensibly contradicting me is merely expressing his moral sentiments. So that there is plainly no sense in asking which of us is in the right. For neither of us is asserting a genuine proposition."[33] It would seem then, according to Ayer's view here, that there can be no argument about ethical judgments of the sort "Murder is wrong" and "Giving to charity is right" since each party to a dispute about them is doing no more than *expressing his feelings*—the kind of feelings we call "moral sentiments." Ethical utterances, such as "It is right to defend the weak," have the *grammatical form* of descriptive statements or propositions, but these utterances function so very differently from factual or descriptive statements that we may conclude they have an entirely different *logical form*. It is a fact that Raskolnikov killed the old woman. It is not a fact, in anything like the same sense of "fact," that it was right or wrong for him to do so. In short, ethical statements are not statements about facts but about our *attitudes* toward facts.

Nothing but Feelings?

Many moral philosophers strongly disagree with the opinion that ethical statements are no more than the expressions

[33] A. J. Ayer, *Language, Truth and Logic*, rev. ed., London, Gollancz, 1948, pp. 107, 108. (PB: Dover, New York.)

of someone's feelings or attitudes. If we concede, say the objectors, that ethical judgments are at base expressions of attitudes, surely there are some attitudes that are right and some that are wrong, or at least some attitudes that are better than others. These critics invite reflection on the two sets of attitudes represented respectively by a Nazi SS officer in charge of an extermination squad and a protesting clergyman who holds "It is wrong to gas these Jews (or Poles or Gypsies)." Is not one of these attitudes right and the other wrong, even though the SS officer may *believe* his attitude is the right one? Further the statement that "strictly ethical" judgments are not propositions at all seems true *only by definition* if the premise upon which it depends is the claim that there are only two kinds of genuine propositions analytical or tautologies, and synthetic or factual-descriptive. But it is by no means self-evident, say the objectors, that these are the only two types of "genuine" propositions.[34] It is true that ethical statements of the type "X is right" and "*Y* is wrong" are not empirical statements of the kind "Ten thousand Jews were gassed." But it does not follow that statements of the former class reflect nothing but subjective feelings of approval or disapproval. Russell himself has doubts on the matter. He stoutly maintains that the good must be defined in terms of desire, and that a person who judges "X is good" is wishing others to feel certain desires. But, he asks:

> What are "good" desires? Are they anything more than desires that you share? Certainly there *seems* to be something more. Suppose, for example, that some one were to advocate the introduction of bull-fighting in this country. In opposing the proposal, I should *feel*, not only that I was expressing my desires, but that my desires in the matter are *right*, whatever that may mean. As a matter of argument, I can, I think, show

[34] See discussion of the analytic-synthetic distinction on p. 69.

that I am not guilty of any logical inconsistency in holding to the above interpretation of ethics, and at the same time expressing strong ethical preferences. But in feeling, I am not satisfied. I can only say that, while my own opinions as to ethics do not satisfy me, other people's satisfy me still less.[35]

Ayer himself, while defending his claim that ethical judgments are basically emotive, would not maintain that each of two attitudes toward the proposed courses of action illustrated above are equally preferable, since "equally preferable" involves a contradiction. "The moral problem," says Ayer, "is: What am I to do? What attitude am I to take? And moral judgments are directives in this sense."[36]

ETHICAL RELATIVISM; POWER MORALITY

The Relativity of Morals

We have seen that some philosophers conclude, upon the basis of linguistic analysis, that the difference between ethical statements of the type "*X* is wrong" and "*X* is right" is simply a question of different *attitudes*. An apparently similar conclusion is reached by another type of argument, which asserts that the validity of all statements about moral matters is relative to the individual person or to the particular group to which the person belongs. The view that moral right and wrong are relative to the individual or to the group is a very old one. It appears to have been held by certain Sophists in ancient Greece and was vigorously attacked by Socrates, who believed that moral

[35] Bertrand Russell, "Reply to Criticism," in P. A. Schilpp, ed., *The Philosophy of Bertrand Russell*, Northwestern University Press, 1944, p. 724.

[36] A. J. Ayer, "On the Analysis of Moral Judgments," *Horizon*, XX, no. 117 (September, 1949).

principles were objective, transcending personal opinions or particular interests. Quite common today–though rare among moral philosophers–is the opinion that moral principles are entirely relative to the culture or folk pattern in which they are found. This point of view–which we may call *cultural relativism*–derives from a popular interpretation of evidence drawn from anthropology and related studies. In the nineteenth century, brilliant works such as Frazer's *The Golden Bough* and Westermarck's *The Origin and Development of Moral Ideas* marshaled quantities of data to show how closely the notions of right and wrong were bound up with the customs and beliefs of individual cultures. In our own century, continued study of primitive cultures has thrown much light on the origin and growth of morals and their relation to custom and taboo. From such evidence, cultural relativists argue that moral principles have no objective status. Since moral codes are dependent on the particular culture within which they develop, no one set of moral principles is "better" than any other. Therefore, it is idle to dispute about ethical matters. "It's all relative!"

Unfortunately we cannot here give this type of argument the attention that its popularity warrants. We can only suggest in passing the following criticisms that have been offered against it. First, suppose we grant that morals originated in custom. It does not therefore follow that one set of moral teachings is as good as another, any more than it follows that one custom is as good as another.[37] Second, morality may have *begun* in custom and local practice. But

[37] It was the custom of the ancient Carthaginians to burn children alive to propitiate the god Moloch. One can say flatly that the custom was bad and whatever moral principle might be derived from it wrong, for these reasons: the practice did no good–Moloch paid no heed to the sacrifice, for there was no such supernatural being; the practice did much bad–innocent children suffered and died. The reader may wish to add analogous examples from our own more enlightened century.

this is not the same as to say that morality is *identical* with custom and local practice. Because religion may have begun with shamans, it does not follow that religion is *nothing but* shammanism. Third, the doctrines of many moral teachers have been conspicuous by their *difference* from the accepted moral teaching of their day, a difference which sometimes resulted in the violent deaths of the moralists in question at the hands of the official representatives of the culture in which they lived. Jesus and Socrates are cases in point.

Perhaps we do not wish to subscribe to a doctrine of absolute ethical objectivism which asserts the existence, antecedent to experience, of a fixed eternal moral law, externally imposed from above and binding upon all men. But we are not therefore compelled to hold as the only alternative the radical form of ethical relativism which states that moral doctrines are entirely subjective and relative, and binding upon no man. The position that one manner of moral behavior is as good as another is no more tenable than the position that one opinion is as good as another. Such assertions are perhaps logically irrefutable, but only because when we retreat to them we implicitly reject the effectiveness of intelligent discourse and deny the human power to judge, discriminate, and evaluate.

Moral conduct requires both handed-down principles and individual decisions in applying them. A society that relies too heavily on handed-down principles may find itself handicapped by moral rigidity. In his *Two Sources of Religion and Morality*, Bergson describes such a society as conceiving of moral behavior solely in terms of compliance to the eternal rule of law. On the other hand, a people that pays little or no attention to moral principles, focussing exclusively on the worth of individual decision or the promptings of the individual heart, may lack moral stability. Reflection on the age-old vacillation between reliance on tried-and-true principles and the instinctive seeking of new and individual decisions may clarify for us the role of those who revolt. The rebels will shout from the housetops, says R. M. Hare, that some or all of the old moral principles are worthless:

> . . . some of these rebels will advocate new principles of their own; some will have nothing to offer. Though they increase the confusion, these rebels perform the useful function of making people decide between their rival principles; and if they not only advocate new principles, but sincerely try to live by them, they are conducting a moral experiment which may be of the utmost value to man (in which case they go down in history as great moral teachers), or may, on the other hand, prove disastrous both to them and to their disciples. . . . Morality regains its vigour when ordinary people have learnt afresh to decide for themselves what principles to live by, and more especially what principles to teach their children.[38]

Might Makes Right; Natural and Conventional Morality

The teaching that the root of ethical principles lies in custom and folkway is a *genetic* theory of morals, that is, a theory which claims that the true character of moral judgments may be found in their origin and development. A genetic account of morals has also been offered to support the doctrine that *right* is a function of superior *power.* Moralists who hold this position frequently distinguish between two kinds of morality (1) *natural* morality, in which what is right is identical with what the strong are able to do, end (2) *conventional* morality, in which a moral system opposed to the first is constructed by the weak in order to protect themselves. Various formulations of

[38] Hare, *The Language of Morals*, p. 73.

power morality have appeared at different stages of the history of Western culture. We find it in Machiavelli's arguments supporting the power of Renaissance princes; in some nineteenth-centure Darwinists who drew it as an ethical corollary from the biological principle of the survival of the fittest; and in the sociopolitical theories of the prophets of Fascism. The classic exposition of the morality of the strong is put into the mouth of Callicles by Plato in the *Gorgias:*

> For the truth is, Socrates, that you who pretend to be engaged in the pursuit of truth, are appealing now to the popular and vulgar notions of right, which are not natural, but only conventional. Convention and nature are generally at variance with one another . . . the makers of laws are the majority who are weak; and they make laws and distribute praises and censures with a view to themselves and to their own interests; and they terrify the stronger sort of men, and those who are able to get the better of them, in order that they may not get the better of them; and they say, that dishonesty is shameful and unjust; meaning, by the word injustice, the desire of a man to have more than his neighbors; for knowing their own inferiority, I suspect that they are too glad of equality. And therefore the endeavor to have more than the many, is conventionally said to be shameful and unjust, and is called injustice, whereas nature herself intimates that it is just for the better to have more than the worse, the more powerful than the weaker.[39]

Aristocratic and Slave Morality; Nietzsche

Friedrich Nietzsche accounts for the development of morality in something of the fashion of Callicles. In his *Genealogy of Morals*, the nineteenth-century German philosopher asserts the existence of a primitive aristocratic era in

[39] Plato, *Gorgias*, B. Jowett, trans., 482–483. (PB: Liberal Arts, Bobbs-Merrill, Indianapolis.)

which morality was identical with the will of the noble. Conceived thus, natural morality is aristocratic, inseparable from the will of the superior few which is imposed on the inferior many. The modern moral tradition of Europe, says Nietzsche, arose from Christianity, which was originally a conspiracy of slaves determined to thwart the aristocratic will of their overlords. Just as sheep, subject to the predations of wolves, might formally agree that "Eating sheep is bad," so the Christians devised a moral system in which weakness and humility were converted into virtues, the exercise of strength and power into *sin*, their own incompetence into immortality:

> These weaklings!—they also, forsooth, wish to be strong some time; there is no doubt about it, some time *their* kingdom also must come—"the kingdom of God" is their name for it, as has been mentioned—they are so meek in everything! Yet in order to experience *that* kingdom it is necessary to live long, to live beyond death, yes *eternal* life. . . .[40]

Using their slave morality cunningly as an instrument of social control, says Nietzsche, the Christians were able to overthrow the domination of their noble masters and to introduce to the Western world a morality of inferiority and weakness which has since effectively held in check the aristocratic aspirations of the strong. He looked forward to the day when this traditional morality with what he understood to be its emphasis on the *feminine* virtues (compassion, gentleness, not hurting others) would be taken up into a higher union with the transfigured *male* virtues of courage, hardness, and strength. From this "Transvaluation of All Values" would emerge a new type of human, the Super-

[40] F. Nietzsche, *Genealogy of Morals,* in O. Levy, ed., *The Complete Works of Friedrich Nietzsche,* H. B. Samuels, trans., New York, Macmillan, 1924, pp. 50, 51. (Also in Modern Library "Giant" edition.)

man (*Übermensch*) in whom power and virtue would again be one.

Summaries of Nietzsche's moral theory, such as the above, are frequently followed by observations to the effect that such a detestable doctrine is self-evidently false, together with pious allusions to Nietzsche's death in a madhouse. This is indeed the less attractive aspect of Nietzsche, his "misunderstood" side, the side which is said to have appealed to Hitler and the Nazi theorists.[41] Nietzsche himself, however, seems *not* to have thought of the Superman in the terms in which this questionable concept has so often been interpreted—a "blonde Teuton beast" who would lead a new "master race" to world domination. Nietzsche made a distinction between two principles of human nature and culture; (1) the *Dionysian* principle, which designates the dynamic and infra-rational side of man—impulse, feeling, instinct, power; and (2) the *Apollonian* principle which refers to reason and order, to man's rational and

[41] Compare Adolf Hitler: "The whole work of Nature is a mighty struggle between strength and weakness—an eternal victory of the strong over the weak. There would be nothing but decay in the whole of Nature if this were not so. States which offend against this elementary law fall into decay." or "Always before God and the world, the stronger has the right to carry through what he wills. History proves: He who has not the strength—him the 'right in itself' profits not a whit." Cited by Alan Bullock in *Hitler: A Study in Tyranny*, London, Odhams Press, pp. 362–363. (PB: Harper Torchbooks, Harper & Row, New York.)

Although Hitler had himself photographed beside a bust of Nietzsche and made Mussolini a birthday present of the philosopher's collected works, it is doubtful if he took more than a perfunctory interest in Nietzsche's writings. Hitler had an intense, if amateurish, interest in painting and music (Wagner was his favorite composer, with Bruckner a poor second), but showed little inclination to works of imaginative literature or of philosophy. We must leave to scholarly specialists the question as to whether or not Hitler tapped a certain source of ideas and feelings to which Nietzsche had access, a reservoir of culture and ideology we call "German romanticism," with its cult of frenzied genius and sympathy with death.

ethical aspect. The historical effect of the Judaeo-Christian moral tradition, Nietzsche thought, was to split the two apart with the result that we tend to accord to reason and morality a shallow independence, a fictitious mastery over the instinctive and dynamic side of human nature. What Nietzsche seems to have had in mind when he spoke of the Superman is an ideal *integration* of the dynamic and instinctive elements of human nature with its rational and ethical components. Thus conceived, the Superman is nearer to Goethe than he is to a glorified storm trooper.

Conclusion

Some critics of Nietzsche hold that the trouble with his moral doctrine lies in its assumption that instinct, impulse, the "will to power," and the dynamic, infra-rational side of human nature generally, need to be defended against the encroachments of intellect and morality. They concede to Nietzsche that exaggerated confidence in the power of reason may lead to shallow optimism; complacency in regard to the effectiveness of enlightened moral doctrine may engender a superficial and one-sided view of human nature. But, they ask, has the instinctive and "natural" side of man ever seriously been threatened by the pretensions of his rational and ethical side? Certainly, we must admit the importance of impulse and subrational drives, agree that they are powerful and rooted deep in man. We should welcome their study so as to understand their nature and effects. But was there ever a time when impulse and "will to power" required *protection* against reason and morals? Do not the actual practices of men and nations plainly show that power morality stands in no danger of losing its popularity?

The world events of the present century and of the present day have demonstrated (indeed, there was never any need to demonstrate it) that the rational and ethical equipment of men is as yet a thin and fragile instrument, still far outweighed by powerful drives, irrational and amoral, which sleep lightly under the most enlightened humanistic surface and are easily aroused from their slumber. The humane tradition of the West—among whose ingredients are the rationalism of the Greeks, the ethics of the Judaeo-Christian tradition, and the science of the modern world—has been built up slowly and painfully over twenty-five hundred years of time, never at any moment proof against the wildest excesses of human passion and cruelty, against the drive to be master at all costs. From this tradition we have derived a rational and ethical deposit, which is not yet so strong that the need of guarding it is past.

FURTHER READINGS

Aristotle, *Nicomachean Ethics.* (PB: Penguin, Baltimore, Md.)

Ayer, A. J., *Language, Truth and Logic*, rev. ed., London, Gollancz, 1948, chap. 6 (PB: Dover, New York.)

Dewey, John, *Human Nature and Conduct,* New York, Modern Library, 1930.

Dewey, John, "Moral Reconstruction," *Reconstruction in Philosophy* (1920). (PB: Mentor, New American Library, New York, 1950; also Beacon Press, Boston.)

Hare, R. M., *The Language of Morals,* New York, Oxford University Press, 1952. (PB: Galaxy, Oxford U. P.)

Hume, David, *An Enquiry into the Principles of Morals,* Oxford, Clarendon Press, 1894. (PB: Liberal Arts, Bobbs-Merrill, Indianapolis.)

Kant, Immanuel, *Critique of Practical Reason and Other Writings in Moral Philosophy*, L. W. Beck (trans.), University of Chicago Press, 1949. (PB: Liberal Arts, Bobbs-Merrill, Indianapolis.)

Kant, Immanuel, *Fundamental Principles of the Metaphysic of Morals*, T. K. Abbott (trans.). (PB: Liberal Arts, Bobbs-Merrill, Indianapolis, 1949.)

Mill, John Stuart, *Utilitarianism.* (PB: Liberal Arts, Bobbs-Merrill, Indianapolis, 1949.)

Moore, G. E. *Principia Ethica* (1902), London, Cambridge University Press, 1951. (PB: Cambridge U. P.)

Nietzsche, Friederich, *The Birth of Tragedy*, *Thus Spake Zarathustra*, and *The Genealogy of Morals*, in *The Works of Nietzsche*, New York, Modern Library, 1931.

Nowell-Smith, P. H., *Ethics.* (PB: Penguin, Baltimore, Md.)

Plato, *Gorgias*, *Protagoras.* (PB: Liberal Arts, Bobbs-Merrill, Indianapolis.)

Stevenson, C. L. *Ethics and Language*, Yale University Press, 1944. (PB: Yale U. P.)

10

Aesthetics

It is from Music that the finish is received.
—Confucius

Ethics and aesthetics, it is commonly said, are both concerned with "value" or "the good" the difference between them being that ethics has for its object of study "moral good," while aesthetics deals with "the beautiful." Less broadly taken, aesthetics is identified with "the philosophy of art," that is, the study of the general principles of artistic creation and appreciation. Thus defined, aesthetics is contrasted with *criticism*, whose task is to analyze and appraise particular works of art. As a separate division of philosophy, aesthetics has had a relatively brief history. The word "aesthetics" seems to have been publicly used for the first time in 1735 by the German philosopher A. G. Baumgarten, who afterward published a book titled *Aesthetica.* One of the first influential formal treatments of aesthetics, conceived as a special discipline, was offered by Kant (who studied Baumgarten) in his *Critique of Judgment.* But philosophers did not wait until the eighteenth century to discuss the nature of the beautiful, the function of art, and the role of the artist. Ancients like Plato, Aristotle, and Plotinus had much to say on these topics. Even the medievals, who tended to concentrate on those two plain sisters, the True and the Good, had kind words to spare for the Cinderella of philosophy, the Beautiful—although they sometimes suspected her, metaphysically speaking, of waywardness.

Aesthetic Terms

There are certain words we use which indicate to those listening to us that we are referring to aesthetic properties. A list of such words would include "beautiful," "pretty," "dainty," "graceful," "charming," "brilliant," "powerful," "handsome," etc. Of particular works of art, we speak of their balance, tension, warmth, remoteness, rhythm, symbolism, control, tranquility, fervor, and so on. We use these words, not as empty noises, but to refer to qualities of things. Yet it is not easy to explain what these qualities are. They are not color properties like those designated by words such as "yellow" or "violet," nor are they moral properties like "right" and "honest" as applied to a man or his actions. Suppose, for the sake of argument, we were able to lay down specifications for the correct use of "*beautiful*" in this way: "beautiful" applies to an object if and only if the object has all three properties *A*, *B*, *C*. Such a statement of specifications for beauty would set out the necessary and sufficient conditions which an object must meet in order properly to be called "beautiful." If such a set of specifications could be laid down, then any object having qualities that match the specifications could properly be called "beautiful." On the other hand, we could not justifiably call "beautiful" any object which lacked these properties. Under these conditions we would know *in advance* just what things to call "beautiful," just as we now know in advance what objects may correctly be called "goat," "hot," and "red." But no philosophers of art today claim to be able to set down in advance specifications for the correct use of "beautiful" or any other aesthetic term. The reason for this difficulty is not because there is dispute about these matters, or that aesthetic qualities are "relative" or "subjective." There are disputes about color properties too, but this does not mean that "red" and "green" fail to refer to objective qualities. We pay hard cash in fines for passing red traffic lights.

We should note that aesthetic terms have a way of coming into and going out of fashion, a fate they share with certain moral terms. (Who today would praise a man for "righteousness"?) Only a few generations ago, the word "*sublime*" referred to a type of aesthetic experience associated with watching a tremendous storm or the starry heavens above. Today we rarely classify experiences as sublime. Even "*beautiful*" is used less comprehensively now than in the day of Keat's Grecian urn which told us that all we need to know is that beauty is truth and truth beauty. It may be that the idea of the beautiful belongs to an era rapidly becoming more remote. The classical ideal of repose, order, and harmony was exalted by the ancient Greeks possibly because they themselves were an excitable people. It was revived by the Renaissance, and romanticized in eighteenth- and nineteenth-century Europe. Even if we concede that "beautiful" is still good currency as an aesthetic term, there are many objects of aesthetic interest and value it seems inappropriate to call beautiful. Joyce's *Ulysses*, Berg's *Wozzeck*, and Picasso's *Guernica* are cases in point. Sophocles' *Oedipus* could be added.

Natural Beauty

Let us grant that beauty is an important aesthetic property, though by no means the only one. Now if the subject of aesthetic study is taken to be *beauty*, then the province of aesthetics is wider than "the philosophy of art." For there are many other things, beside artistic objects, to which people apply the adjective "beautiful." The beauty of sunsets, tigers, flowers, and women falls within the realm of *natural* beauty. We moderns seem to find more beauty in Nature than did our classical forebears. What could be more beautiful than sunlight on snow-capped mountain peaks? Yet, as late as the seventeenth century, persons of considerable sensitivity wrote of "the high and hideous Alps." Indeed, says Havelock Ellis, for most travelers before Rousseau's time "The Alps still remained what they had been for Livy and for Amianus, a scene of unmitigated horror which no one could approach for the sake of pleasure."[1]

The natural beauty which the Romans admired was of a tidy and cultivated kind, like that of Horace's garden. Even Plato, archpoet that he was, describes natural scenes in terms of what we would call the pleasant rather than the beautiful. Socrates, sitting down by the bank of the Ilissus with Phaedrus says:

> By Herè, a fair resting-place, full of summer sounds and scents. Here is this lofty and spreading plane-tree, and the agnus castus high and clustering, in the fullest blossom and the greatest fragrance; and the stream which flows beneath the plane-tree is deliciously cold to the feet. . . . How delightful is the breeze:—so very sweet; and there is a sound in the air shrill and summerlike which makes answer to the chorus of the cicadas. But the greatest charm of all is the grass, like a pillow gently sloping to the head. My dear Phaedrus, you have been an admirable guide.[2]

It is the comfort of it all—the cold water on his feet, the grass pillowing his head—that seems to make the greatest impression on Socrates. He goes on to observe to his

[1] Havelock Ellis, *From Rousseau to Proust*, Boston, Houghton Mifflin, 1935, p. 78.

[2] Plato, *Phaedrus*, B. Jowett (trans.), 220.

pupil that he rarely goes out to the country. "I am a lover of knowledge," says Socrates, "and the men who dwell in the city are my teachers, and not the trees or the country." How different from Wordsworth:

> One impulse from a vernal wood
> Will teach you more of man
> Of moral evil and of good
> Than all the sages can.

The Arts and the Artist

Besides natural beauty, there is beauty (or other aesthetic qualities) in art. But what is art? There are the useful arts, and the fine arts, and some which appear to be both. In premodern times the notions of "art" and "craft" were not as widely separated as they are today. Some say that all art originated in the desire of the craftsman to make his handiwork not only useful but pleasing. The plain bowl was adequate for food, but the prehistoric potter added some bright colors in a pleasing design. Visitors to Sardinia or Sicily are charmed by these colorful paintings with which the peasants, in accord with tradition, decorate their simple carts. A fine Persian or Chinese rug is a pleasure both to walk on and to look at. The Greeks built their temples and the medievals their cathedrals for communal worship. In modern America, the finest products of engineering and construction often combine beauty with utility. New York City's RCA tower soars into the sky with a grace far surpassing that of its taller rival, the Empire State Building; and the Whitestone Bridge arches over the East River as if it had no weight at all. It is a pity, say philosophers Santayana and Dewey, that in the contemporary world we have come to think of art as something divorced from experience, something to be gawked at on Sunday afternoons in a special building with the sepulchral name of "*museum*."

Since Flaubert, we apply the word "artist" to poet, composer, and novelist, as well as to painter and sculptor. But in ancient and medieval times, the word for "artist" was even more comprehensive in meaning; it stood for any technician or craftsman. To the Greeks, a man who made pots and one who made statues were both *artificers*. Originally, the word "poet" meant *maker*. To the medievals, an artist was not a man who "expressed himself." He *made* things.

The Fine Arts

The "fine" arts include the spatial and visual arts of architecture, sculpture, painting, and drawing; and the temporal and auditory art of music.[3] The "literary" arts include poetry, drama, and (a late-comer) the novel. The history of art tells us how in the past many of these forms have combined with and served one another. The Greek drama required the accompaniment of music and the dance. The medieval cathedral needed sculptured figures for the exterior, paintings for the altar, and the music of plain chant for the Mass. Drama and poetry were one in the plays of Shakespeare, Racine, and Goethe. In modern times, however, the arts have split apart from one another, each form tending to go its separate and autonomous way. True, music, drama, and even the dance are combined (uneasily, some think) in the modern opera. The old Russian ballet was an admirable synthesis of the dancing of Fokine and Nijinsky, the music of Stravinsky and Ravel, and the scene

[3] It was not until the eighteenth century that the fine arts were officially separated from the mechanical or useful arts by the French Encyclopedists. *Les beaux arts* included painting, sculpture, poetry, music, and the dance. Oratory and architecture were considered to have both pleasure and utility as their end.

painting of Bakst. And today there is something of a revival of the poetic drama—notably the work of T. S. Eliot and Dylan Thomas. But, generally speaking, at present the individual art forms are cultivated on separate levels.

The conventional classification of the arts gives no indication of historical development. Some art forms have declined, others have risen from lowly state. Our poets no longer write epics, leaving this to the novelists. Indeed, the audience for poetry of any kind today seems to have dwindled. The great ages of sculpture seem to be past. But music, once a humble auxiliary among the arts, is now loved for its own sake. It has been said that music is the art most characteristic of modern Western culture. Schopenhauer pronounced it "the art of arts," and Pater claimed that all art aspires to the condition of music. Some pessimists (and they may be right) tell us that the day of great artistic creation is over for the West, that all that remains for art today is repetition or parody.

There seems to be no reason why "fine" art should be restricted to the conventional categories. In the eighteenth century, hydraulics and landscape gardening were taken quite seriously as art forms, and in our own century, Ernest Hemingway's *Death in the Afternoon* convinced many that bull fighting has its own aesthetic. The motion picture has enormous resources which have from time to time been employed to produce an artistic masterpiece.

Types of Aesthetic Theory

Here is a man looking at a Chinese vase or listening to a Schubert quartet. He says, "That's beautiful." Now, we ask, how do philosophers of art deal with the problem of the beautiful—or whatever they wish to call the quality of aesthetic excellence? Do they talk about those generic properties which both the vase and the music possess? Or do they talk about the effect produced in the man? In other words, do philosophers of art assume that beauty is something *in the object,* and proceed to analyze those qualities by virtue of which an object is a work of art? Or are they more interested in discussing what happens *in the man* as he sits there enjoying the beautiful thing? Philosophers of art are usually quick to reply that beauty is a cooperative affair; that it cannot be discussed in terms of either subject or object alone. Both, they say, must be taken into account in any discussion of aesthetics, for in the aesthetic experience there is an attunement or rapport between subject and object—something like a sympathetic vibration between two strings. "Art," says DeWitt Parker, "is sympathetic representation; the effort not only to reveal an object to us, but to unite us with it."[4] Analysis of the role of *perception* in visual art alone indicates both that the perceived object possesses a complex set of properties in its own right (shape, color, even "feeling"), while on his side the perceiver brings to bear an equally complex set of relevant attitudes.

Nevertheless, it is possible to distinguish (very roughly) between those theories which approach the problem of art and aesthetic excellence from the side of the *object* and those that come to it from the side of the *subject.* This contrast is sometimes recognized by dividing aesthetic doctrines into theories of *form* and theories of *expression.* In theories of form the approach is "objective." The philosopher tries to tell us what it is that makes an object beautiful or otherwise aesthetically valuable. For example, he may say that the object possesses certain properties, such as unity, wholeness, balance, symmetry, and so on. In theories of expression the perspective is more "subjective." The philosopher is not so much interested in talking about the

[4] D. H. Parker, *The Principles of Aesthetics,* rev. ed., New York, Appleton-Century-Crofts, 1946, p. 82.

formal properties of the beautiful object as he is in discussing the nature of *the aesthetic experience.* He wants to tell us what occurs *in us* when we are enjoying a beautiful thing. A similar (and overlapping) contrast between types of aesthetic theory may be observed if we compare *metaphysical* theories of art—particularly those of the classic Platonic type, which suggest that art reveals the universal in the particular—with *psychological* theories, which stress the appreciator's state of mind.

Related to theories of the psychological type are *genetic* accounts of art. In this case the philosopher endeavors to explain how art came about in the first place. He explains art through its origins. Art begins in decoration of useful objects; or it begins in play; or in imitation. Or the genetic theorist may suggest that art has biological roots and call our attention to the role of bright and pleasing colors in sexual selection in the animal kingdom, or to the habits of certain birds who collect pretty stones.

METAPHYSICAL THEORIES: ART AND THE UNIVERSAL

Art as Imitation and Vision; Plato

In Plato's writings we find the first statements of a number of subsequent theories of art and the beautiful. His doctrine of art as *imitation* stirred questions that even today rise to trouble the critics. On the psychological side, he suggests in one dialogue that art is *pleasure;* in another he gives a striking description of the *emotional state* of one who beholds a beautiful object. He even foreshadows the romantic notion of the pathological nature of art; the poet is a madman, although it is a divine kind of madness that afflicts him. Most characteristically, he tells us that in the experience of beauty we have a *vision of a universal form.* This side of the Platonic aesthetic comes to us through a long line of philosophers of art down to Schopenhauer and Croce.

When he is thinking of art as "imitation" (*mimesis*), Plato tends to take a dim view of the artist. His objections are based on both metaphysical and political grounds. The actor imitates men's actions; he empties himself of his own identity to take on the identity of others. The painter makes an image of a bed, the real maker of which is the carpenter. But according to the Platonic theory of Ideas, all objects—including beds—are themselves copies of the eternal Forms which alone are truly real. The carpenter makes this particular bed according to the Idea of bed. The painter imitates what the carpenter has made. Thus the painter is one who makes a copy of a copy; his work is appearance twice over, and thus his art is twice removed from reality.[5] Since he is thus occupied with shadows of shadows, it is hard for the imitative artist to be a solid citizen. By nature the poet tends to *mis*represent; hence politically he is unreliable. Accordingly, in his capacity of political philosopher, Plato reluctantly excludes poets from his Ideal Republic.

In his capacity of poet-philosopher, however, Plato has more favorable words for the artist. Once more the reason is metaphysical. The eternal Forms, which are the sole reality, are invisible. Accessible to reason alone, they cannot be disclosed by the senses. There is one exception, though. One only of the immmutable essence is revealed to us, at least partially, by the senses. This is the Form of beauty:

[5] Plato, *Republic*, 596–597. Today we can defend a mimetic theory of art without taking "imitation" in the narrow sense of literal copying. The poet Guillaume Apollinaire says, "When a man wanted to imitate walking he created the wheel, which does not resemble a leg."

And the essence of beauty, as I have explained, was revealed to us along with the other essences, but in this world it is beauty that we apprehend the most clearly shining through the clearest of our senses. For sight is the sharpest of all our bodily senses. Wisdom cannot be seen; for if wisdom could have afforded any such lively and visible image of herself, we should have been mad with love of her, or any other of the essences that are lovely. But, as it is, beauty alone has this privilege, so that it is the most manifest and lovable of all things.[6]

The lover, says Plato, is inflamed by the beauty of his beloved. He too, like the poet, is visited by a sort of divine madness. And it is well that this should be so. For mortal beauty, if we but follow where it points, can lead us as it were up a ladder which we mount step by step with the indispensable aid of intellectual discipline. At each stage of our ascent we come nearer and nearer to the kingdom of the real, until at last the soul, shot through with a kind of incandescence, no longer knows but *sees* in an all but blinding moment of illumination—the Form of beauty itself.

What is suggestive in Plato's parables of beauty is not only the idea that beautiful objects disclose a universal form but also the notion of the *intuitive* character of aesthetic experience. Since Plato, many philosophers of art have called our attention to the immediacy and directness with which we know the beautiful. Beauty, they tell us, is not reached by syllogisms or demonstrated by theorems; it is something directly apprehended. In Bergson's language, we do not move around the object of art; we do not know it discursively by means of its external relations; we enter into it and find ourselves at one with it. Croce denies to art the character of conceptual knowledge, and makes intuition the key to his entire theory of aesthetic.

[6] Plato, *Phaedrus,* E. F. Carritt, trans., 250.

Universal and Radiant Form; Aristotle and Aquinas

In Aristotle we find something of each of what have come to be standard ways of art philosophizing. There is the genetic point of view. Art begins in imitation. It is natural in man to imitate others, and it is also natural for him to delight in representative works which successfully imitate things. From the psychological side, there is the effect of art upon the emotions which Aristotle calls *catharsis* or purgation—and of this we shall have a little more to say further on. Finally, from the "objective" side, art embodies the universal. According to Aristotle, the function of the poet is to describe, not the particular—the kind of thing that has happened. The poet's task is to describe the universal—the kind of thing that might happen. "Hence poetry," says Aristotle, "is something more philosophic and of graver import than history, since its statements are of the nature rather of universals, whereas those of history are singulars."

In Aquinas too we find the teaching that in the beautiful object the universal is made manifest in the particular—at least this is how many of his commentators interpret him. According to St. Thomas, there are three formal properties which beautiful things possess: (1) *integritas* or unity (of the whole), (2) *consonantia*, the harmony, balance, or order (of the parts); (3) *claritas*—clarity, brightness, or radiance.[7] Now the first two properties of the beautiful are classic in aesthetic tradition. The unity and simplicity of the admired object (*unus et simplex*) had been noted by Aristotle. Plotinus had specified the harmony and propor-

[7] Aquinas, *Summa Theologica*, pt. 1, q. 39, art. 8. Aquinas' remarks on beauty occur in the context of a discussion of the Trinity, not of a work of art. To St. Thomas "art" is any kind of skilled work.

tion of the parts. But *claritas* or "radiance"—what is this? Readers of James Joyce will recall that in his novel *Portrait of the Artist as a Young Man* the hero Stephen Dedalus ponders this very question. Is the Thomistic *claritas* the universal form made manifest in the sensible object? Or does *claritas* refer to the instantaneous apprehension of the form or character of the object itself?

> The radiance of which he [Aquinas] speaks is the scholastic *quidditas*, the *whatness* of a thing. This supreme quality is felt by the artist when the esthetic image is first conceived in his imagination. The mind in that mysterious instant Shelley likened beautifully to a fading coal. The instant wherein that supreme quality of beauty, the clear radiance of the esthetic image, is apprehended luminously by the mind which has been arrested by its wholeness and fascinated by its harmony is the luminous silent stasis of esthetic pleasure. . . .[8]

E. F. Carritt interprets the Thomistic *claritas* in this way: Aquinas believes that if we knew ultimate reality (God), we would know it, not by conceptual knowledge, but directly and intuitively. Now when we encounter what is beautiful, we are able to grasp its nature in an act of immediate apprehension. This intuitive knowledge of a sensible thing is a small-scale analogue of the apprehension of ultimate reality. In fact, the ultimate reality may be said to appear in or through those sensible objects which are beautiful:

> The reason why it thus appears in or through *some* individual sensible objects, is that there is a real difference in these objects, not a difference in man's attitude to them. They are objects where the matter and form or essential character are mutually adequate, so that there is completeness and due proportion of parts, and distinctness like the clarity of colour.

[8] James Joyce, *Portrait of the Artist as a Young Man,* New York, Modern Library, 1928, p. 250.

Objects which the form thus shines through or illuminates are peculiarly suited to our faculties of perception and are beautiful.[9]

In this way, the universal is made manifest in the particular.

The Platonic Forms and the Wheel of Ixion; Schopenhauer

According to the nineteenth-century German philosopher Arthur Schopenhauer, we know the world under two aspects—idea and will. Viewed as idea, the world is what Kant said it was—*appearance*, ordered by the mental forms of space, time, and causality. That is to say, from the standpoint of knowledge, the world is but a coherent dream, orderly illusion. But there is also the world as it is *in itself*. This is *will*. Reality is one eternally striving will, blind and amoral, immanent in all individual things. The omnipresence of the indwelling will is revealed to us directly in our own restlessness, passion, and never satisfied desire. The will, which is the sole reality, is one. But seen from our point of view, that is, under the forms of space, time, and causality (idea), the will becomes multiple; it divides into its members or creatures, in each of which it is present like the Godhead in the several hosts of the Eucharist. The infinite Will thus *objectifies* itself in its numberless finite parts. The multiplicity of natural objects is no more than the will itself seen from the secondary and derivative level of human knowledge.

On the one hand, then, we have the cosmic will—one, eternal, ever striving. And on the other, there is the multiplicity of finite things into which the will seems to divide. But between the two realms stand the *Platonic Ideas*. These are the universal types of things, the models which Nature seems to strive in vain to copy. These Forms have a kind of

[9] E. F. Carritt, ed., *Philosophies of Beauty from Socrates to Robert Bridges*, Oxford, Clarendon Press, 1931, p. 50.

demi-existence outside human knowledge and hence are unaffected by time and multiplicity. We may compare the world will to a roaring waterfall—blind and irresistible in its senseless power. The multiple individuals in the world of space and time are the countless fragmentary drops into which the raging torrent shivers in its plunge. Now the rainbow, hovering beautiful and motionless above the boiling torrent, is the realm of the universal Forms, the archetypes of all things. Existing independently of the categories of the mind, the Platonic Forms inhabit, so to speak, a lovely half-world somewhere between the cosmic will, taken as one and undivided, and the crawling multiplicity of the individuals in which the will objectifies itself.

It is these universal Forms—located outside the struggle and compulsion of things, detached from the blind striving of the will—which are the objects of the artist's vision. The artist is a genius, a special man, not like "the common mortal, that manufacture of Nature which she turns out by the thousand every day." He alone among his fellows can contemplate the timeless Form behind the particular object. He alone can understand what Nature, in all its multiplicity and dividedness, is trying unsuccessfully to express:

> The true genius . . . recognizes the Idea in the particular thing, and thus, as it were, *understands the half-uttered speech of nature,* and articulates clearly what she only stammered forth. He expresses in the hard marble that beauty of form which in a thousand attempts she failed to produce, he presents it to nature, saying, as it were, to her, "That is what you wanted to say!" And whoever is able to judge replies, "Yes, that is it."[10]

[10] A. Schopenhauer, *The World as Will and Idea,* R. B. Haldane and J. Kemp, trans., London, Routledge, 1948, vol. 1, p. 287. (PB: Dolphin, Doubleday, Garden City, N.Y.)

From this metaphysical account of art in terms of contemplation of Platonic Form, Schopenhauer proceeds to draw a psychological and moral conclusion concerning the function of art. *Art is escape*. Escape from what? Escape from the relentless striving of the will within us; escape from the never-to-be-satisfied longing produced in us by the infinite demands of the will. For we are creatures of the will, tormented by the thirst of a thousand desires. Of these, the most powerful is the sexual, in which the blind and irrational character of the will most nakedly reveals itself. For sex is but the means the will employs to perpetuate itself in other creatures in order to go on striving endlessly. We know from bitter experience that to satisfy one desire is to cause ten others to spring up in its place; to indulge desire is to throw an alms to a beggar—it keeps him alive today so that he may starve tomorrow. We are slaves of *wanting*, bound as prisoners to an endlessly turning wheel as was Ixion of old. But in art we find a real—if temporary—release from the anguish of life. Art is like sweet balm on wounds. For it has the power to detach us from desire, and therefore from suffering. When we behold the beautiful, we slip loose from the will for a blessed moment of respite; we gaze upon the universal in things in pure, objective, will-less contemplation:

Then all at once the peace which we were always seeking, but which always fled from us on the former path of the desires, comes to us of its own accord, and it is well with us. It is the painless state which Epicurus prized as the highest good and as the state of the gods; for we are for the moment set free from the miserable striving of the will; we keep the Sabbath of the penal servitude of willing; the wheel of Ixion stands still.[11]

[11] *Ibid.*, p. 254.

PSYCHOLOGICAL THEORIES: THE NATURE OF AESTHETIC EXPERIENCE

Art as the Expression of Emotion

Here is a tale about the origin of art. A primitive man once encountered a strange animal, a buffalo. The huge beast came very close to the man and frightened him. The man hurried back to the shelter of his cave. Safe there, but still aroused, the man seized some soft colored stone and on the wall of the cave traced the outline of the fearsome thing. His drawing finished, he felt calmer. Fellow cave dwellers crowded around the picture, grunting and nodding appreciatively. Art was born.

This little story presents an entirely imaginary account of the genesis of art.[12] Nevertheless it is consistent with a popular conception of art as basically *the expression of emotions.* This is a doctrine consistently taught to school children. Rarely does the sixth grade make its first formal trip to the museum without instruction in some simplified emotive theory of art. Here, for example, is a report of a visit by students and a teacher of art appreciation from a New York City junior high school to the Museum of Modern Art:

[12] There is wide agreement among contemporary experts on primitive art that such cave paintings had a primarily *magical* significance. "The best proof," says Arnold Hauser, "that this art was concerned with a magical and not an esthetic effect, at least in its conscious purpose, lies in the fact that the animals in these pictures were often represented as pierced by spears and arrows or were actually shot at with such weapons after the completion of the work." *The Social History of Art,* New York, Knopf, 1951, vol. 1, p. 28. (PB: Vintage, 2 vols., Random House, New York.)

"The artist is making you feel something. An emotion." On to a mandolin-shaped figure in bright colors. What did the color do to them? One girl said it made her feel dizzy. Andrea said it made her feel a little nauseous. "Good! Good!" cried Mrs. Milgram. On the way to the next painting she said she liked the children to have strong reactions. She liked them to feel free to say what they felt, even if it made them want to vomit.... She recalled a young girl who studied a canvas and began to twitch....[13]

Reader's of Proust's novel *Remembrance of Things Past* will recall Madame Verdurin's claim that the playing of Vinteuil's Sonata moves her so profoundly that she invariably suffers a bad headache. "No, no, no, not my sonata," she screams, "I don't want to be made to cry until I get a cold . . . and neuralgia all down my face. . . ."[14]

Not all emotive theories of art are at once so simple and so drastic as to equate aesthetic response with our somatic reactions. But many distinguished critics and philosophers of art have claimed that in some fundamental way art is concerned with expression or communication of emotions. "Created form moves us so profoundly because it expresses the emotion of its creator," says Clive Bell, ".... No one ever doubted that a Sung pot or a Romanesque church was as much an expression of emotion as any picture that was ever painted."[15] Tolstoy says that the artist hands on to others the feelings he has lived through, and that these others are infected by these feelings and experience them: "To evoke in oneself a feeling one has once experienced

13 "The Day They Discovered Art," *The New York World-Telegram and Sun*, Feb. 7, 1966, p. 17.

14 *Swanns Way*, New York, Modern Library, 1928, p. 294.

15 Clive Bell, *Art*, London, Chatto & Windus, 1914, pp. 49, 58. (PB: Capricorn, Putnam, New York.)

and having evoked it in oneself then by means of movements, lines, colours, sounds, or forms expressed in words, so to transmit that feeling that others experience the same feeling—this is the activity of art."[16]

But even those of us inclined to favor an emotive theory of art are aware that aesthetic response is not expression of just any emotion. A kick in the shins or the sight of a street accident will excite our feelings, but they are not on that account aesthetic reactions. Most philosophers of art who have held emotive theories say that in the aesthetic experience our feelings are aroused, but they are *put into some kind of special condition.* Aristotle declares that when we view a tragic drama the feelings of pity end fear are stimulated, but in such a manner that these feelings undergo a *catharsis* or purgation.[17] Nearer our own day, the English critic I. A. Richards says that the feelings awakened in aesthetic experience are put into a state of harmony or equilibrium he names *synaesthesia.* The ordinary man suppresses nine-tenths of his impulses, Richards claims, because he is incapable of managing them without confusion; the most valuable effects of poetry, on the other hand, must be described in terms of the resolution and balancing of the impulses.[18]

[16] L. Tolstoy, *What Is Art?* A. Maude, trans., London, Oxford University Press, 1931, p. 123. (PB: Liberal Arts, Bobbs-Merrill, Indianapolis.)

[17] Aristotle, *Poetics,* 1449b28. In *Portrait of the Artist as a Young Man,* James Joyce's Stephen Dedalus labels the state of the feelings in aesthetic response *stasis* or "arrest." The feelings aroused by nongenuine aesthetic situations are "kinetic." Kinetic feelings, like desire or loathing, push us toward or pull us away from the perceived object, while in the aesthetic state we are "raised above desire and loathing. Stephen's "stasis" bears some resemblance to Kant's "disinterest" and Schopenhauer's "will-less state" as well as to Clive Bell's "arrest" of our anticipations and memories when we view a painting properly.

[18] I. A. Richards, C. K. Ogden, and J. Wood, *The Foundations of Aesthetics,* New York, Lear Publishers, 1929, p. 14.

Richards was influenced in his aesthetic theory by the positivism of the nineteen-thirties which inclined toward an emotive theory of aesthetics. A number of positivists, as we know, made a sharp distinction between "factual statements" and "pseudo-statements." The scientific man makes statements, they said; but the poet composes his feelings. Poetic expressions are not statements of fact, although they may have the appearance of such statements. Taken as sentences which purport to say something about the world, emotive utterances are but pseudo-statements. Poetic expressions have no claim to *truth*—for truth and falsity, properly so called, are properties of scientific or factual statements, and of no other kind. Truth in the strict sense is "ultimately a matter of verification as this is understood in the laboratory." To emotive utterances, including those which constitute poetry, "truth" is applicable only in the Pickwickian sense of "acceptability by some attitude." Rudolf Carnap's "oh-oh" theory of aesthetics claims that:

> Many linguistic utterances are analogous to laughing in that they have only an expressive function, no representative function. Examples of this are cries like "Oh, oh" or, on a higher level, lyrical verses. The aim of the lyrical poem in which the words "sunshine" and "clouds" appear is not to inform us of certain meteorological facts but to express certain feelings of the poet and to excite similar feelings in us. A lyrical poem has no assertional sense, no theoretical sense, it does not contain knowledge.[19]

In her study of aesthetics, *Feeling and Form,* Susanne Langer rejects any attempt to understand art simply as an affair of expressed emotion. If art is no more than expression of feelings, then there is no distinction between good and bad art. If self-expression is the end or goal of art, then

[19] Rudolf Carnap, *Philosophy and Logical Syntax,* London, Kegan Paul, 1937, p. 61.

only the artist himself can judge the value of his products. If his sole purpose is to produce emotional excitement, the artist should study his audience and let his psychological findings guide his work, as advertising agents do. "The psychological approach dictated by the general empiricist trend in philosophy," says Mrs. Langer, "has not brought us within range of any genuine problems of art." That feelings play an important role in aesthetic experience Mrs. Langer is far from denying. What she objects to in crude emotive theories of art is their failure to do justice to the *cognitive* ingredient in aesthetic experience. Form in art is inseparable from feeling; art, like science, aims primarily at being understood. But what then does art express?

> What art expresses is not actual feeling, but ideas of feeling, just as language does not express actual things and events, but ideas about them. . . . Not feelings, but knowledge about feelings. . . . Art is the creation of form symbolic of human feeling.[20]

While commending her emphasis on the cognitive side of art, critics of Mrs. Langer's view claim that she herself has failed to escape from difficulties inherent in any emotive theory of art. For to say that art expresses, not emotions, but *ideas about them*, is to retain an emotive theory—although an indirect one. If art is "form symbolic of human feeling," then the conclusion seems inescapable that in art what is symbolized are the emotions. But this conclusion is quite compatible with nearly every emotive theory of art.

So vague and all-inclusive are the concepts "emotion" and "feeling" that it is often hard to tell what is meant by an aesthetic theory which bases itself upon them. From the time of Plato on philosophers and nonphilosophers alike

[20] Susanne K. Langer, *Feeling and Form*, New York, Scribner, 1953, pp. 38–39.

have perpetuated the existence of a model man with his reason or *cognition* (symbolically located in the head) elevated above feeling or *emotion* (located in the breast or gut).

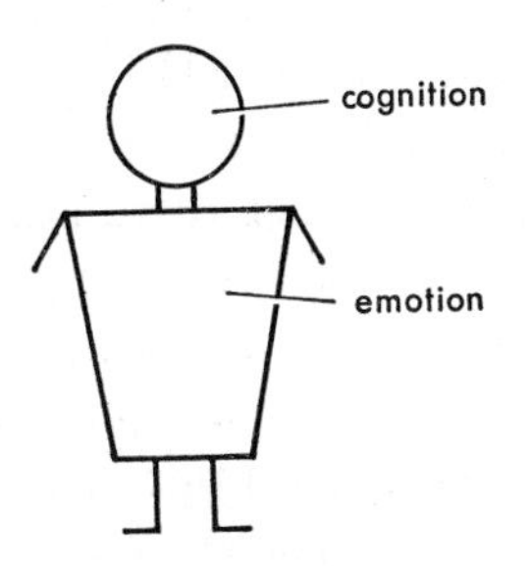

But this radical separation of cognition and emotion is misleading, for it fails to take account of the way our intelligence and feelings are unified. Cognition has emotional content and feelings have their cognitive aspect. Consider the experience of fear—fear of a tiger, perhaps. Now the somatic side of fear has a static, even a paralyzing effect. But the cognitive aspect of fear is one with conscious awareness which results not in paralysis but in practical action. That is, fear leads us to take account of the tiger in such a way that a meeting with him is successfully avoided. What is basic in our encounter with a tiger or a work of art is our *perception* of it, and perception is a cognitive affair. Our perception may be pervaded by tension or excitement. Before the tiger or the painting our *attention* is, in different ways, intense. But that makes the perception no less cognitive.

Art and Expression; Croce

At the turn of the century, one of the most renowned philosophers of art, the Italian Benedetto Croce, defined art as expression. Expression of the emotions? No, just expression. But expression of *what?* Of intuitions. In fact, art *is* intuition. Intuition and expression are correlative. To intuit is to express, and nothing else.

Croce's theory of art is quite difficult to understand, although there is widespread agreement that it is very important. One reason for its difficulty is that Croce was a philosophical idealist, holding that everything which exists is mental or spiritual and that there are no such things as physical facts. A work of art has no formal properties; what we find in it is our own spirit smiling at us. Art is intuition, and intuition is imaginative, nonconceptual knowledge which comes from our feelings. "Intuitions are truly such because they represent feeling, and only thence can they arise."[21] Now no one has intuitions without expressing them. To have a genuine intuition of a geometrical figure is inseparable from our ability to draw it. So, in art, to *have* an intuition is to *express* it.

But how does an artistic or aesthetic intuition differ from any other kind of intuition—such as that of a triangle? Croce replies that there is no important difference between the two types of intuition. *All* intuitions are beautiful. This explains why sensitive people can find beauty in everything, even in an old shoe. "One artist is thrown into transports by a smiling landscape, another by a rag shop, another by the pretty face of a young girl, another by the squalid countenance of an old rascal."[22] If there *is* any difference between the ordinary run of intuitions and those of art, it is quantitative only—not qualitative. That is, the intuitions of art are wider and more complex than those we generally experience. The intuition of a popular love song

[21] B. Croce, *A Breviary of Aesthetics*, E. F. Carritt, trans., in Carritt, *Philosophies of Beauty*, p. 241.

[22] B. Croce, *Aesthetics*, D. Ainslie, trans., London, Macmillan, 1929, p. 99.

is truly beautiful, but it is beautiful in a limited way compared to the complex intuition of a love song by Leopardi.

In art, intuition (or, if you prefer, imagination) expresses itself in images, and these take from in words, colors, lines, tones. They are neither good nor bad, real nor unreal, useful nor useless. They are beautiful. "Art is vision or intuition. The artist produces an image or a dream; and those who appreciate his art turn their eyes in the direction he has indicated, look through the loophole which he has opened, and reproduce in themselves that image."[23]

Art as Pleasure

Beauty, says Santayana, is pleasure. It is pleasure *objectified* —pleasure regarded as the quality of a thing. Some may object that Santayana stresses the subjectivity of beauty at the expense of its formal qualities. But at least he reminds us that all art is, in some sense, an entertainment and a delight. In the aesthetic experience the emotions are aroused, but the excitement is pleasurable, not painful. Art frequently deals with the painful and the ugly, but in some way—hard to explain—representation of these things produces satisfaction. Is it because, as Aristotle says, successful imitation always pleases even when the subject is ugly? Or is it that in art we never take the painful situation literally, but only "as if" painful? Perhaps Schopenhauer is right when he says that in contemplating a representation of the tragic side of things we find austere satisfaction in the compelling way in which the artist lays hold of the universal by means of the particular. ("Yes, that is it.") Says Santayana:

> We are more thankful for the presentation of the unlovely truth in a lovely form than for the like presentation of an abstract beauty: what is lost in the purity of the pleasure is

[23] B. Croce, *A Breviary of Aesthetics*, cited in Carritt, *Philosophies of Beauty*, p. 233.

gained in the stimulation of our attention, and in the relief of viewing with aesthetic detachment the same things that in practical life hold tyrannous dominion over our souls. . . .[24]

The beautiful, says Aquinas, is that which, when beheld, pleases. (*Pulchra enim dicuntur quae visa placent.*) Of course, not everything which pleases is beautiful. But, say the critics, if a work of art does not please, it fails. This does not mean that a work of art must please everybody. Beautiful things can be difficult, and may not yield us pleasure easily.[25] Art is not simply an affair of warm-hearted good feeling; Schönberg's *Pierrot Lunaire* does not wear its beauty on its sleeve. The peculiar quality of aesthetic pleasure has been a problem of interest to generations of philosophers of art. Plato speaks of "unmixed" pleasures, such as the smell of a rose, and says that the pleasures of art are "pure" pleasures, since they are not followed by pain. Kant tells us that the pleasure we take in the beautiful is *disinterested* pleasure. There is no suggestion of utility or profit in the satisfaction we derive from the beautiful. The object of art is not regarded as a means or instrument; it pleases us as an end in itself. Thus the aesthetic state is pleasure "without interest" (*interesseloses Wohlgefallen*).

Art as Play

Kant's conception of aesthetic experience as enjoyment of an object, not for profit or utility, but for its own sweet sake is related to his suggestion that art is *play*. Work is activity for an end. Play is an activity agreeable in itself. Hence art is more closely related to play than to work.

24 G. Santayana, *The Sense of Beauty*, New York, Scribner, 1896, pp. 207, 208. (PB: Dover, New York.)

25 "*Schuppanzigh*," said Beethoven to his violinist who complained that his part in one of the last quartets was impossible for him to play, "*Do you think I write my quartets for you and your puling fiddle?*"

The poet Friedrich Schiller picked up this notion from Kant and in his *Aesthetic Letters* developed it into a theory of the genesis of art. Art begins in the play impulse, and play is a kind of overflow or discharge of superfluous energy. Man works when motivated by need; he plays when his superabundant vitality overflows and takes form in pleasurable activity which is its own end. The highest form of human play is art. Taking his cue from Schiller, Herbert Spencer finds the origin of aesthetic activity in animal play, which he also interprets as the expression of superfluous energy. In his *Principles of Psychology* he tells us that in animals of higher types the energy not wholly drawn off by the satisfaction of physical needs is expended in play which awakens all kinds of agreeable feelings. In aesthetic experience the faculties of the organism are exercised in such a way that a maximum of activity is combined with a minimum of strain.

To Karl Groos, art is the highest form of the universal game of *make-believe*. The frolicking puppy pretends to attack his master. The little girl treats her doll "as if" it were her child. Adult sport—wrestling, tennis, etc.—provides make-believe fights, conventionalized struggles for supremacy, which are far more pleasurable than the "real thing." The artist, too, desires supremacy; he does not create for pleasure alone. Out of his own "make-believe" he achieves a spiritual ascendancy over his fellow men. "Spiritual supremacy," says Groos, "is the aim of the highest art, and there is no real genius without the desire for it."[26]

Art as Wish Fulfillment; Freud

Groos' notion of the artist's achieving supremacy through make-believe is not unlike the theory of Sigmund Freud,

[26] K. Groos, *The Play of Animals*, New York, Appleton, 1898, p. 295.

the father of psychoanalysis. Freud's teaching on the subject of the artist is the very opposite of classical *disinterest* theory. According to Freud, art is the projection in fantasy of the heart's desire. The artist (an introverted, almost neurotic type) is motivated—like all men—by deep-rooted, instinctive drives. He wants power, fame, honor, riches, women. But he lacks the means to gratify these longings. So he projects his desires into fantasy. This might lead a person of lesser capacities to preoccupation with unreality and ultimately to neurosis. But not to the artist. He finds his way back to reality because the products of his fantasy bring to him by an indirect route the very things he really wants. The artist is able to create fantasies to which the ordinary man turns with delight—for the ordinary man is not satisfied by his own poor daydreams. Out of his ability to project his fantasies in such a way that other men find pleasure and consolation in them the artist reaps his reward in their gratitude and love. Thus he wins "through his phantasy—what before he could only win in phantasy: honor, power, and the love of women."[27]

Empathy

In Freud's theory as cited above, the idea of the projection of the self in art is a rather simple one.[28] The artist has certain basic longings; these are projected in fantasy, which is then objectified in the art work. But among aesthetic theories we find another which involves a concept of self-projection more difficult to grasp. This is the empathy or

[27] S. Freud, *A General Introduction to Psychoanalysis* (1920), Garden City (New York, Doubleday), 1952, pp. 327, 328. (PB: Washington Square Press, New York.)

[28] That is to say, Freud's writing about the artist in *A General Introduction to Psychoanalysis.* Freud has more complex things to say about art and the artist in other books, for example, in his *Leonardo Da Vinci.* (PB: Vintage, Random House, New York.)

Einfühling ("in-feeling") theory identified with the aesthetic doctrine of Theodor Lipps and his disciple Vernon Lee.

In aesthetic experience there are present in us what the psychologists call "sympathetic motor responses." The conventional illustrations of this are drawn from architecture. The Doric column seems to press down firmly on its foundations; we "read into it" our own unconscious muscular tensions. Faced with a splendid skyscraper, the human organism exhibits sympathetic muscular behavior, as if it were straining for flight. Now if the empathy theory of aesthetic enjoyment amounted to nothing beyond calling our attention to the sympathetic postural or muscular attitudes provoked by or projected into art, we should have little difficulty understanding it. But the empathy theory means more than the projection of kinesthetic tension into objects. True, says Lipps, so complete is the unity in aesthetic experience of self and object that we may fall into sympathetic muscular attitudes. But these are only external, behavioristic signs of the "in-feeling." What really brings about the unity of subject and object in art is that we project into the object all kinds of activities and feelings, ranging from simple physical attitudes to the most developed processes of the human spirit. In the enjoyment of the sight of a human figure in motion:

> I am now with my feeling of activity entirely and wholly in the moving figure. Even spatially, if we can speak of the spatial extent of the ego, I am in its place. I am transported into it. I am, so far as my consciousness is concerned, entirely and wholly identical with it. Thus feeling myself active in the observed human figure, I feel also in it free, facile, proud. This is esthetic imitation and this imitation is at the same time esthetic empathy.[29]

[29] T. Lipps, cited in M. M. Rader, ed., *A Modern Book of Esthetics*, Holt, Rinehart and Winston, 1935, p. 298.

Lipp's empathy theory suggests that in the aesthetic experience the "ego" is projected into the object admired. Vernon Lee disassociates herself from this "metaphysical" interpretation of empathy and rests content with defining it as the "complex mental process by which we invest objects with the stored up and averaged and essential modes of our activity."[30]

ART AND LIFE

Form and Content

The fine arts use a sensuous medium—stone, wood, metal, glass, in the case of architecture and sculpture; color and line in painting and drawing; tones and rhythm in music. The literary arts have no comparable sensuous media at their disposal; they must use words, which are comparatively conceptual. So it is hard for aesthetic philosophy to set out principles which illumine both "fine" and "literary" arts. Can we distinguish between *form* and *content* in a work of art? A poem seems to be about something—Satan, a blacksmith, or a woman's hair. A musical composition is built up out of themes. A painting presents this rather than that material to our eyes—a goddess, a room in Ajaccio, a yellow square inside a grey one. But in every art the content is disposed in a certain way. The material is shaped, ordered, controlled.

> . . . fettle for the great grey drayhorse his bright and battering sandal!

is about the same as far as content is concerned as

> . . . hammer for the big grey work horse his red-hot iron horseshoe.

[30] V. Lee, *The Beautiful,* London, Cambridge University Press, 1913, p. 66.

But there is a difference of art, and not just because "sandal" is a fancier way of saying "horseshoe." Philosophers of art have often declared that in the best art work there is a perfect union or balance between the elements of content and form. Form, they say, is far more than something superadded to the content of an art work—like icing on the cake or vanilla flavoring. Imagery and metaphor are not tacked on to the subject matter of a poem in order to make it read nicely. Form is integral to art, not an embellishment of it. When content gets the upper hand at the expense of form, the value of a work of art is compromised. A painting is spoiled when the meaning has more weight than the line.

Representation and Life

Questions about the relation of content and form in a work of art raise all kinds of difficult problems. Take the case of *representation* in painting. Some paintings represent actual objects such as trees or sitters for portraits. Here it seems quite easy to say what the "subject matter" of the painting is. But other important kinds of painting—those popularly known as "abstract," for example—present material which does not resemble actual objects. Some critics hold that the representative element in painting is irrelevant. They are worried lest in looking at a painting of a child we bring with us from life our own favorable attitudes toward children and allow these to weight our valuation of the picture. Everybody loves Picasso's picture of the little girl with the soup bowl. How much of our response to it is prepared in advance? Best known for his doctrine that "*significant form*" is the one quality common to all works of visual art, critic Clive Bell lays down this rule:

> The representative element in a work of art may or may not be harmful; always it is irrelevant. For, to appreciate a work

of art we need to bring with us nothing about life, no knowledge of its ideas and affairs, no familiarity with its emotions. Art transports us from the world of man's activity to a world of aesthetic exaltation. For a moment we are shut off from human interests; our anticipations and memories are arrested; we are lifted above the stream of life.[31]

It is commonplace to claim that the way a painter handles the "solids" or the "volumes" of a picture is more to the point than whether his subject is people or apples. But subject matter has a way of refusing to let itself be brushed out of the picture entirely. Is a painting by Uccello a picture of solids or of horses? Did Cimabue's contemporaries value his Madonna primarily as a colored surface? To charges that he was painting erotic nudes Matisse replied "It is not a woman, it is a picture." But is a Renoir painting more concerned with a woman's volumes than with her femininity?

Belief that the attitudes and convictions we bring with us from life are just as irrelevant to art as is the representative element in a painting is only one expression of an influential modern tradition that art and life are in some basic way incompatible. This tradition has philosophical precedent in Kant who taught that aesthetic pleasure is *disinterested;* that is, aesthetic enjoyment has nothing to do with gratification of our personal interests. Schopenhauer went further: the true aesthetic state, he claimed, is one of will-less contemplation in which all desire, all reaching out for our particular good, is put out of action. In mid-nineteenth-century France, Gautier exalted *l'art pour l'art,* a slogan popularized as "Art for art's sake." Later the Symbolists insisted that the duty of a poet to his art required that he turn his back on life. "As for living," said Villiers de l'Isle Adam, "We can let our servants do that for us." André

[31] Bell, *Art,* p. 25.

Malraux, our contemporary, declares that men do not make art out of life; art is the rival of life—"All art is a revolt against man's fate."[32]

Art and Morality

"Morality" in its broad meaning refers to right relations between men; in a narrower meaning, it touches on sex. Art is related to morality in both senses. Time and again throughout the ages, moralists have charged that art encourages idleness and stimulates sexual passion. In every era, guardians of public morals have covered up statues, turned paintings to the wall, banned poetry, burned books, halted operas, censored plays—all on the ground that the works in question offended moral decency. Renowned philosophers of art have themselves had anxieties on this score. Plato was convinced that music and poetry could soften the sinews of the soul, leading the young to lives of idleness and dreams. Tolstoy feared art's dangerous proclivity for stirring the flesh; he denounced paintings of naked women and novels about adultery; he wrote *The Kreutzer Sonata* to show how music could inflame the passions.

We tend today to pass over the outraged cries of moralists and Philistines with a smile and a shake of the head. Yet, in a way, they are right. If art has the power to awaken all our faculties, we cannot expect the sexual side of our nature to remain unkindled. As Santayana says, "The whole sentimental side of our aesthetic sensibility—without which it would be perceptive and mathematical rather than aesthetic—is due to our sexual organization remotely stirred. . . ."[33] When Kant said that the pleasure of aesthetic experience is *disinterested*, Schopenhauer interpreted this to

[32] André Malraux, *The Voices of Silence*, Garden City, N.Y., Doubleday, 1953, p. 639.
[33] Santayana, *The Sense of Beauty*, p. 59.

mean that in art the faculties are detached from all willing, most particularly from sexual desire. With his doctrine of art as escape from the will, Schopenhauer took the aesthetic state to be a pure will-less contemplation in which sensuality is put out of action. Nietzsche denies this. Art does not calm the will; rather it excites it, even when refining it. For all its capacity to soar in the realm of spirit, art is rooted in sense, even in the sensual. The inspiration found by painters and sculptors of all ages in the nude female body shows that in art something very different from Kantian "disinterest" is involved. (Nietzsche cites the example of Pygmalion.)

Using the word "morality" in a broader sense: it is almost a classic thesis in aesthetics that art and morality occupy different spheres. The realm of the moral is the practical, says Croce; morality is an affair of the will. But aesthetic activity is essentially contemplative and, as such, has nothing to do with practical activity:

> Art, in fact, as was long ago observed, is not produced by an act of the will; the good will which makes a good man does not make an artist. And since it is not produced by an act of will, art is exempt from moral distinctions, not by any privilege of immunity, but because moral distinctions simply do not apply. An artist may imaginatively represent an act worthy of moral praise or blame; but his representation, being imagination, is worthy of neither. Not only can no penal code condemn an imaginative representation to death or to prison, but no reasonable man can make it the object of a moral judgement. To judge immoral Dante's Francesca, or moral Shakespeare's Cordelia, whose functions are purely artistic and who are like notes of music from the soul of Dante or Shakespeare, would be no better than to judge a triangle wicked, or a square moral.[34]

[34] Croce, *Breviary of Aesthetics*, cited in Carritt, *Philosophies of Beauty*, p. 236.

But, adds Croce, if art is outside the sphere of morality, the artist is not. "As a man he comes under its laws and never escapes the duties of a man."[35]

Art for Art's Sake

Radical emphasis on the separation of art and morality marks the views of certain critics and literary men of the latter half of the last century. Théophile Gautier, author of the scandalous *Mlle de Maupin*, brandished the slogan "*L'art pour l'art*" to confound the Philistine bourgeoisie. Walter Pater inspired a generation of budding artists to "burn with a hard gem-like flame," to get into the brief interval of life "as many pulsations as possible":

> Only be sure it is passion—that it does yield you this fruit of a quickened, multiplied consciousness. Of this wisdom, the poetic passion, the desire of beauty, the love of art for art's sake, has most. For art comes to you proposing to give nothing but the highest quality to your moments as they pass, and simply for those moments' sake.[36]

Oscar Wilde made epigrams: "All art is quite useless.... There is no such thing as a moral or immoral book. Books are well written or badly written. That is all.... No artist has ethical sympathies. An ethical sympathy in an artist is an unpardonable mannerism of style."[37] The attitude of Gautier, Pater, and Wilde, as well as any view of art as radically isolated from morality or "life," is sometimes labelled "*aestheticism.*"

Critics of the "art for art's sake" doctrine admit that the

[35] *Ibid.*, p. 237.

[36] W. Pater, *The Renaissance*, rev. ed., London, Macmillan, 1925, pp. 238, 239. (PB: Mentor, New American Library, New York.)

[37] O. Wilde, *The Picture of Dorian Gray*, Preface. (PB: Dolphin, Doubleday, Garden City, New York.)

artist should not be expected to concern himself in his work with moral and ethical matters. But they find implicit in *l'art pour l'art* an erroneous belief that aesthetic values are somehow set apart from human values, taken generally. But art is an intensely human affair and, as such, cannot be compartmented away from human good. "Beauty, being a good," says Santayana, "is a moral good; and the practice and enjoyment of art . . . fall within the sphere of morals—at least if by morals we understand moral economy and not moral superstition."[38] But the classic criticism of the "art for art's sake" doctrine remains Nietzsche's:

> If art is deprived of the purpose of teaching morality and of improving mankind, it does not by any means follow that art is absolutely pointless, purposeless, senseless, in short *l'art pour l'art*—a snake which bites its own tail . . . what does all art do? does it not praise? does it not glorify? does it not select? does it not bring things into prominence? In all this it strengthens or weakens certain valuations. . . . Is his [the artist's] most fundamental instinct concerned with art? Is it not rather concerned with the purpose of art, with life? with a certain desirable kind of life? Art is the great stimulus to life; how can it be regarded as purposeless, as pointless, as *l'art pour l'art?*[39]

Conclusion

People often talk as if art were a special form of communication akin to ordinary language. We sometimes refer to music as "the language of the emotions." A man looking at

[38] G. Santayana, "A Brief History of My Opinions," in Irwin Edman, ed., *The Philosophy of Santayana*, New York, Modern Library, 1936, p. 20.

[39] F. Nietzsche, *Twilight of the Idols*, in Oscar Levy, ed., *The Complete Works of Frederick Nietzsche*, New York, Macmillan, 1924, vol. 16, pp. 79, 80. (PB: *The Portable Nietzsche*, W. Kauffman, ed., Viking, New York.)

a piece of sculpture may declare, "It doesn't speak to me." A schoolteacher may ask his pupils, "What is Hawthorne trying to say in *The Scarlet Letter?*" or (indicating a painting) "What is the artist trying to tell you about life?" This way of talking may show that the speaker takes the end or aim of a poem or a painting to be the communication of a "message," that a work of art is a kind of vehicle to convey "ideas." He may believe that an artist puts "ideas" in paint or sets them to music. Such notions of art puzzle artists themselves, even literary men whose art uses the written word, and is in this way more directly related to the order of concepts than are the nonverbal arts. "Idea?" asked Goethe when queried about what concepts he chose in writing this or that play, "Not that I know of. They come and ask me what ideas I have tried to embody in my *Faust;* as if I myself knew or could say."[40] A work of art is not a servant of ideas, said Andre Gide; rather, "the role of ideas should always be to serve beauty."[41]

While philosophers of art are divided on the difficult question as to whether or in what sense art is or is not a language, they are (with the exception of Tolstoy) pretty generally at one in rejecting any notion that the primary function of art is to convey moral messages. Such a view, they say, denies the autonomy of art; it makes of art works mere vehicles to convey ideas, and, as such, relegates art to second-rank status. But if we reject the "message" view of art as untutored and juvenile, it by no means follows that artists never back moral or social values in their works. They often do. The notion that the artist does not—or if he does, *should* not—allow his personal support or condemnation of values to become visible, is a corollary of the classical *disinterest* theory of aesthetic experience which

[40] *Conversations with Eckermann,* New York, Dutton, Everyman's Library, 1930, p. 205. (PB: Ungar, New York.)

[41] Preface to *King Candaulus.*

found its philosophical justification in Kant and Schopenhauer. The novelists Flaubert and Joyce thought that the artist should be as impersonal as Aristotle's God, a God who takes no sides, who steps back from the world which is his handiwork, paring his fingernails. Still, this is only one tradition. It happens to be one which formed the tastes of the writer of this book. But there is another tradition, one of art as *interested*, whose claim must be heard. Just before the outbreak of World War II, Antonin Artaud composed a fiery manifesto proclaiming a new aesthetic for the theatre. "To our disinterested and inert idea of art," Artaud wrote, "an authentic culture opposes a violently egotistical and magical, that is, *interested* idea."[42] The father of the "Theatre of Cruelty" declares that the aim of art is to *break through language* in order to touch life. But when we pronounce the word "life," he says:

> ... it must be understood we are not referring to life as we know it from its surface of fact, but to that fragile fluctuating center which *forms* never reach. And if there is still one hellish, truly accursed thing in our time, it is our artistic dallying with forms, instead of being like victims burnt at the stake, signalling through the flames.

FURTHER READINGS

Aristotle, *Poetics*. (PB: "On the Art of Poetry," Liberal Arts, Bobbs-Merrill, Indianapolis.)

Bell, Clive, *Art*, London, Chatto & Windus, 1914. (PB: Capricorn, Putnum, New York.)

[42] *The Theatre and its Double* (1938), M. C. Richards, trans., Grove Press, 1958, p. 83. (PB: Evergreen, Grove Press, New York.)

Carritt, E. F. (ed), *Philosophies of Beauty, from Socrates to Robert Bridges*, Oxford, Clarendon Press, 1931.

Croce, Benedetto, *Aesthetics*, D. Ainslie (trans.), London, Macmillan, 1929. (PB: Noonday, Farrar, Straus & Giroux, New York.)

Dewey, John, *Art as Experience*, New York, Macmillan, 1934. (PB: Capricorn, Putnam, New York.)

Ducasse, C. J., *Art, the Critics and You*, O. Piest, New York, 1944. (PB: The Liberal Arts, Bobbs-Merrill, Indianapolis.)

Edman, Irwin, *Arts and the Man*, New York, Norton, 1939. (PB: Norton.)

Gilbert, K. E., and H. Kuhn, *A History of Esthetics*, New York, Macmillan, 1939.

Gombrich, E. H., *Art and Illusion*, Pantheon Books, Inc., 1960.

Hauser, Arnold, *The Social History of Art*, New York, Knopf, 1951, 2 vols. (PB: Vintage, Random House, New York, 2 vols.)

Kant, Immanuel, *Critique of Judgment*, J. H. Bernard (trans.), London, Macmillan, 1892. (PB: Hafner Library of World Classics, Hafner, New York.)

Langer, Susanne K., *Feeling and Form*, New York, Scribner, 1953.

Lee, Vernon, *The Beautiful*, London, Cambridge University Press, 1913

Malraux, André, *The Voices of Silence*, Garden City, N.Y., Doubleday, 1953.

Margolis, J. (ed.), *Philosophy Looks at the Arts*. (PB: Scribner, New York, 1962.)

Panofsky, Erwin, *Meaning in the Visual Arts*, Garden City, N.Y., Doubleday, 1957. (PB: Anchor, Doubleday.)

Parker, DeWitt, H., *The Principles of Aesthetics*, New York, Appleton-Century-Crofts, 1946.

Parkhurst, Helen Huss, *Beauty: An Interpretation of Art and the Imaginative Life*, Harcourt, Brace & World, 1930.

Plato, *Phaedrus*. (PB: Liberal Arts, Bobbs-Merrill, Indianapolis.)

Plato, *Republic*, F. M. Cornford (trans.). (PB: Galaxy, Oxford U.P., New York, pp. 400–402, 597–607.)

Plato, *Symposium*, Socrates Speech, 199–212. (PB: Liberal Arts, Bobbs-Merrill, Indianapolis.)

Rader, M. M. (ed.), *A Modern Book on Esthetics*, 3rd ed., Holt, Rinehart, and Winston, 1960.

Richards, I. A., C. K. Ogden, and J. Wood, *The Foundations of Aesthetics*, New York, Lear Publishers, 1929.

Santayana, G., *Reason in Art*, Scribner, 1934. (PB: Collier, Crowell-Collier, New York.)

Santayana, G., *The Sense of Beauty*, New York, Scribner, 1896. (PB: Dover, New York.)

Schopenhauer, A., *The World as Will and Idea*, R. B. Haldane and J. Kemp (trans.), London, Routledge and Kegan Paul, 1948, vol. 1, bk. 3. (PB: Dolphin, Doubleday, Garden City, N.Y.)

Tolstoy, Leo, *What Is Art?* A. Maude (trans.), London, Oxford University Press, 1931. (PB: Liberal Arts, Bobbs-Merrill, Indianapolis.)

Vivas, E., and M. Krieger (eds.), *The Problems of Aesthetics*, New York, Holt, Rinehart and Winston, 1953.

Biographical Sketches

SOCRATES

469–399 B.C.

Socrates is said to have been the son of a stonecutter and a midwife. He lived all his life in Athens, where he taught young men, including Plato and Xenophon. In his old age he was tried and condemned by an Athenian court on the dubious charge of "teaching strange things about the gods" and corrupting the youth. He was executed in prison. According to Plato, Socrates delivered a final discourse to his favorite students before he drank the cup of poison (hemlock or aconite) handed to him by the weeping jailer.

The origin of the Athenian government's hostility to Socrates is obscure, but it seems likely that the Democrats, who were in power, were worried about the continued presence of Socrates in Athens after the overthrow of the terror-ridden junta of Oligarchs in 403 B.C. Socrates had a number of pupils, including Plato, whose relatives either had taken part in or sympathized with the short-lived rule of the hated Thirty. Socrates himself may have been suspected of anti-Democratic leanings. It is unlikely that the Athenian rulers desired Socrates' death; rather, they appeared to hope that he would slip out of the city to exile. But he stubbornly remained.

Socrates left no writings. The discourses presented to us by Plato in his so-called "Socratic" dialogues (*Apology: Crito*) and by Xenophon in his *Memorabilia* are considered to be highly imaginative reconstructions of Socrates' teaching. All parties agree that Socrates' chief object of interest was moral values and that his question-and-answer method of teaching was aimed at achieving satisfactory *definitions* of the concept under discussion, whether this was justice, piety, temperance, or some other moral excellence.

Tradition makes Socrates the hen-pecked husband of Xanthippe, but such stories about the philosopher's marital infelicities appear to be inventions of later commentators. There is some ancient gossip to the effect that Socrates had a second wife called Myrto. Whatever the actual circumstances of his life may have been, Socrates was a man who made an unforgettable impression on those who knew him. "Of all the men of his time whom I have known," says his pupil Plato, "he was the wisest and justest and best."

PLATO

427–347 B.C.

Plato was the son of an aristocratic Athenian family, and lived most of his life in his native city. As a young man, he was a devoted pupil of Socrates; and the execution of his master inspired in him a life-long horror of bad government. Some years after the death of Socrates, Plato, who had withdrawn from Athens at the time of the execution, returned to found the Academy, a school for higher learning which lasted nine centuries. It was abolished in 529 A.D. by the Edict of Justinian. The higher curriculum of the Academy consisted of the intensive study of mathematics and philosophy. Aristotle was the most distinguished graduate of the Academy.

Plato is said to have made two excursions to Sicily to teach at the court of Dionysius II, the young ruler of Syracuse. The philosopher's experiences were disillusioning, however, and at one time during the political turmoil Plato seems to have been in danger of his life. On his return to Athens, Plato continued to teach at the Academy until his death at the age of eighty.

The Platonic philosophy is written in the form of *dialogues*, all of which have come down to us. The early dialogues are dominated by the spirit of Socrates. In the great middle dialogues, like the *Republic*, *Phaedrus*, and *Phaedo*, two momentous concepts are elaborated—the theory of Ideas or Forms, perhaps the most famous of all metaphysical theories, and the doctrine of Soul, which had an immense effect on philosophy, religion, and literature.

Plato never married, and such love as he knew seems to have been directed to members of his own sex. The well-known notion of "Platonic Love" probably derives from the dialogue *Symposium* in which Socrates, as guest speaker as well as life of the party, tells of Love which has its beginning in sexual attraction, but mounts from the visible beauty of the flesh to the higher and invisible beauty of Mind. In its highest manifestation, Eros is a mighty force which plays between heaven and earth, linking the divine and the mortal.

So great was the admiration for Plato among Renaissance humanists that there was talk of having him canonized as a Saint. All subsequent philosophy, said Alfred North Whitehead, "is a footnote to Plato."

ARISTOTLE

384—322 B.C.

Aristotle was the son of a Macedonian physician. As a young man he came to Athens to study under Plato. Tradition says that he remained a member of the Academy for 20 years, and would have succeeded to its headship, had he not been of Macedonian origin. After some travelling, he was summoned in 342 to the court of Philip of Macedon, there to serve as tutor to the king's son Alexander, later known as "the Great." Later he returned to Athens to found his own school, the Lyceum. Shortly before his death, there was an outbreak of anti-Macedonian feeling in Athens; and Aristotle, recalling the fate of Socrates, left the city determined, so the story goes, "not to let Athens sin against philosophy twice." He died on the island of Euboea.

Plato's most famous student had broad scientific as well as philosophical interests, and his tremendous technical competence is even today hard to believe. His treatises on physics, astronomy, embryology, zoology, political theory, ethics, poetic criticism, metaphysics, and logic constitute the first text books in these subjects. The writings of Aristotle that have come down to us seem to be notes made for or taken from his lectures to advanced students. This may account for their rather dry and succinct character. The philosopher's earlier writings, which are lost, are said to have had greater literary charm.

Aristotle taught that philosophy and science must begin by considering *things* ("substances"). All things are composed of matter (what they are made of) and *form* (the organization of the matter which makes the thing the kind of thing it is). In all things, too, we may distinguish *potentiality* (what a thing is capable of becoming) from *actuality* (the achieving of its capacities). To *define* a thing we should place it as species into its larger class or natural kind (genus), then seek the differentiating property that marks off the species from the other members of the genus. Aristotle's methods of division gave to the biological sciences their first techniques of classification.

According to tradition, Aristotle was married, but had, besides a wife, a charming mistress named Herpyllis to whom he bequeathed a house and his second-best furniture. His treatise on moral philosophy, the *Nichomachean Ethics*, was named for his son Nichomachus. Aristotle's authority stood so high in the medieval universities that he was referred to simply as "The Philosopher."

PLOTINUS

205—270

Plotinus was ashamed that he had a body. At least so his pupil Porphyry says, even though in his writings Plotinus praises the body, remarking that we should no more criticize it than the house of a host who entertains us overnight. Porphyry is the source of the meagre biographical information available about the last and greatest of the neo-Platonic philosophers. Indeed, it is to Plotinus' alleged embarrassment in his fleshly envelope that Porphyry credits the philosopher's reluctance to give out any information concerning his birthplace, race, or family.

Plotinus came to Alexandria to study philosophy in 232 and became the pupil of the enigmatical Ammonius Saccas, a kind of ancient Wittgenstein whose disciples were forbidden to disclose their master's teaching. Whatever its content, the teaching of Ammonius seems to have determined the course of Plotinus' philosophical enterprise. After sitting at Ammonius' feet for 11 years, Plotinus decided that he should learn Persian and Indian wisdom, and set off with the Emperor Gordian's journey to the East. But Gordian was murdered in Mesopotamia in 244; the royal expedition broke up, and Plotinus made his way with difficulty to Antioch. There is no evidence to show that Plotinus ever learned enough Eastern philosophy or religion to be influenced by it.

At the age of 40 Plotinus turned up in Rome where he became a teacher of philosophy. Soon he found himself a favorite of the Emperor Gallienus and almost persuaded that monarch to found a Platonic republic in southern Italy with a constitution modelled after Plato's *Laws*. This ideal city-state was to have been called "Platonopolis." Plotinus died, after a long illness, of a disease akin to leprosy. He bore his affliction with the fortitude worthy of his calling.

The treatises of this great contemplative—he wrote that all action is a weakening of contemplation—are called the *Enneads*. Plotinus' writing, all of which seems to have been done during the last 16 years of his life, shows the character of doctrine rather than inquiry. His teaching had a lasting impact on Christian theology, particularly on the Cappadocian Fathers Basil and Gregory of Nyssa in the East, and on Augustine in the West.

AUGUSTINE

353–430 A.D.

Augustine was born at Tagaste in the Roman province of Numidia, not far from the site of ancient Carthage, near the modern border of Algeria and Tunisia. Imaginative paintings of this Christian saint often represent him as dark skinned, a complexion consistent with his African birth. Augustine's father was a Roman official and a pagan. His mother, Monica, was a Christian, and it is to her persistent anxiety over his spiritual welfare that her son credits his conversion to the Church. Augustine dedicated his fiery and passionate youth to study and to the pursuit of pleasure. Ambitious for his success, his parents sent him to good teachers to study rhetoric. Augustine learned to love philosophy from the *Hortensius*, a lost work of Cicero that may have been based on an early treatise of Aristotle on immortality. In his search for truth, Augustine joined the Manichaeans whose explanation of evil in terms of a Principle of Darkness opposing a Principle of Light held him for a while. Then he turned to Scepticism, and later to the teachings of the Neoplatonists. Plato seemed to him the wisest philosopher of antiquity.

Leaving Africa for Italy, Augustine was appointed professor of rhetoric in Milan. There he met Ambrose, archbishop of Milan, through whose efforts, joined by those of his mother, Augustine became converted to Christianity. A distinguished career in the Church opened out before him, and in 395 he was made Bishop of Hippo (the modern Bône in Algeria). Augustine's numerous writings include his *Confessions*, *The City of God*, and *On the Trinity*.

Despite his training in the classical philosophy of antiquity, Augustine is essentially a theologian and religious teacher rather than a philosopher. To him the most important truth comes through Revelation rather than from the natural light of reason. His method is to work from Biblical texts rather than from philosophical arguments. Nevertheless, Augustine's penetrating comments on knowledge, certainty, time, history, freedom, and the predicament of man, often have a peculiarly modern flavor.

Augustine's great importance to the West stems from the crucial point in history at which he stood, a point where the classical culture of the ancient world began to flow into the new barbarian world of Europe, soon to be converted to Christianity. He died in his episcopal residence of Hippo as the Vandals were hammering at the city gates with their swords.

MOSES MAIMONIDES

1135–1204

The greatest of Jewish philosophers was born in Cordova, Spain. The ruling Moors loved art and learning, lived in peace with their Jewish subjects, and permitted them a generous measure of religious and cultural independence. Maimonides' father was a member of the rabbinical college in Cordova, besides carrying on a family business in precious stones. Young Moses was a brilliant scholar, writing his first commentaries on the Talmud while still in his teens. But this scholarly tranquility was destroyed by the ascendancy of the fanatical Almohades, a rigorist sect of North African Moslems who seized Cordova in 1148. The Koran or the sword were the hard alternatives presented to the Iberian Jews. Maimonides' family fled from Cordova to Fez, for reasons not clear, since the Almohades controlled Morocco as well. It was in North Africa that Maimonides wrote his *Letter Concerning Apostasy*, counselling his suffering brethren to remain faithful to the religion of their fathers, even though they might be forced (and would not do wrong) to utter the Moslem formula with the sword at their throats. Years later a similar epistle, the *Letter to the South*, brought consolation to the suffering Jews in Yemen and spread Maimonides' fame to Jewish communities throughout the Mediterranean world.

Maimonides left Morocco for Palestine in 1165, remaining in the Holy Land for a short time before moving on to a permanent home in Egypt, first in Alexandria and then to the old Arabic capital of Fostat. In 1168 he finished his Commentary on the *Mishnah*, a compilation of Jewish ritual and law that formed the basis on which both the Jerusalem and Babylonian Talmuds were written. The second of his three great works is the *Mishneh Torah*, an immense legal commentary representing ten years of toil. The third and best known is *The Guide to the Perplexed* ("Moreh Nebukim"), a book which made its author famous in the non-Jewish intellectual community of Europe. Albertus Magnus, and through him Thomas Aquinas, studied the *Guide* in which Maimonides delicately balances the claims of faith and reason.

The last part of Maimonides' life was spent as a physician in the court of Saladin the Great. It is said that Saladin's conqueror, Richard the Lionhearted, offered the learned Jew a post in the English court, but that the offer was respectfully declined. The final years of Maimonides' life were disturbed by controversies and criticism of his teaching. Many pious Jews thought that Rabbi Moses relied too much on the natural light of reason, that he compromised the Scriptures by questioning their literal interpretation. Worn out by his labors, Maimonides died in his seventieth year. Moslems joined Jews in lamenting his death, and in the synagogues the faithful mourned, "The glory is departed from Israel, for the Ark of God is taken."

THOMAS AQUINAS

1225—1274

Thomas of Aquin was born in Rocca Secca in the kingdom of Naples of a noble Norman-Lombard family. His father was Landulph, Count of Aquino; his mother, Countess of Teano. The boy was sent to study at the Benedictine abbey at Monte Cassino, where he startled his teachers by asking repeatedly, "*What* is God?" In 1236 he went to the University of Naples where he was trained in logic and the natural sciences by Peter the Irishman. In 1240 (or it may have been 1243) he made the startling decision to join the order of St. Dominic. The idea of her noble son living the life of a mendicant friar was too much for his proud mother, and she took part in an arrangement whereby Thomas' brothers kidnapped him and confined him in a fortress for two years, hoping to change his mind. They even went so far as to secrete a lady of easy virtue in the fortress in the hope of distracting Thomas from his vocation; but the stout lad seized a burning brand from the fire and chased the temptress to a shrieking exit. Thomas' kind-hearted sister smuggled in to him copies of the Bible, Aristotle's *Metaphysics*, and the *Sentences* of Peter Lombard.

At last his mother relented, and Thomas was allowed to join his order which sent him to Cologne to study with Albertus Magnus. Albert took him to Paris where Thomas obtained his bachelor's degree in theology. He returned to Cologne where he was ordained priest in 1250, after which he returned to teach at the University of Paris. A doubtful tradition says that he and his colleague Bonaventure took their doctor's degrees in theology on the same day in 1257.

Thomas quickly became famous as a teacher at Paris, but did not confine his activities to that city. He travelled the length of France and Italy, preaching and compiling notes for his monumental *Summa Theologica.* The archbishopric of Naples was offered him, but he humbly declined it. He was swamped with offers from abbeys and universities. The Pope appointed him to his advisory council. Louis XIV of France invited him to dine and was amused by the scholar's absent-mindedness at table. Thomas' excessive weight may have contributed to an early breakdown in health. He died at Fossanova on his way to the second Council of Lyons. Certain theses based on his work concerning the soul (following Aristotle, he considered the soul related to body as form to matter) were condemned in Paris, and later at Oxford, after his death; but the proscription was short lived. Thomas was canonized by John XXII without the usual inquiry into miracles. His writings, the Pope said, were miracles enough.

RENÉ DESCARTES

1596–1650

A Frenchman has said that the true biography of Descartes is the history of his thought. Although he passed years of his life in court, foreign travel, and military service, the external events of the great French philosopher's career are interesting only so far as they throw light on the development of his inward reflections. Descartes was born at La Haye in Touraine, the third child of "*un gentilhomme de robe,*" councilor to the parliament of Rennes. At 10, the boy was sent off to the famous Jesuit school of La Flèche where he studied for 8 years. From childhood. Descartes was constitutionally averse to getting up in the morning, and the good fathers allowed him to study in bed until noon.

Although mathematics was his favorite study "because of the certainty of its proofs and the evidence of its reasonings,"

Descartes took his degree at the University of Poitiers in law. Bored with study, he joined the army of Prince Maurice of Nassau and followed the wars in Europe. In a small German town he had a dream in which the marvellous interconnections of the sciences were revealed to him. This moment of luminous certitude was followed by years of meditation on science and philosophy with a view to working out a reliable method of reaching true conclusions. That line of research was epitomized in his *Discourse on Method* which made a sensation in the small world of scientists and men of learning when it was published at Leyden in 1637.

Descartes moved to Holland in 1629 and lived there for the greater part of the rest of his life. He composed treatises on mathematics, physics, and philosophy. He devised the geometry we call "analytic" or "coordinate." A work on cosmology, in which he supported the Copernican theory, remained unpublished because of possible offense to church authorities. Descartes's principle philosophical work, the *Meditations*, was published in Amsterdam in 1642. He was now the intellectual leader of a generation that included Fermat, Galileo, Torricelli, Huyghens, and Harvey.

In 1647 Descartes made one of his infrequent visits to France and took occasion to call on young Pascal in Paris. Two years later he reluctantly left Amsterdam for Stockholm to take up an appointment to give instruction to Queen Christina of Sweden. The Queen, being less indulgent than his old teachers, required Descartes's presence at five each morning. Returning from the palace one cold morning, the philosopher caught a chill, contracted pneumonia, and died five months after his arrival in Sweden.

JOHN LOCKE

1632–1704

John Locke was born in Somerset, England, son of a family of the Puritan trading class. His grandfather was a prosperous clothier, his father an attorney and small landowner. Locke was sent to school in Westminster where he received a scholarship at Christ Church, at that time Oxford's most important college. He took his B.A. in 1656 and his M.A. two years later. Locke is sometimes said to have been a passionless man, but in these years at least he was brisk upon the ladies, many of whose identities he concealed in his letters by coding their initials. Locke was secretive by nature and cloaked many of his activities in shorthand or cipher. He never married.

The year 1660 saw the restoration of the Stuart monarchy. Locke stayed on at Oxford as tutor and occupied himself with the study of medicine. This enabled him to remain at Christ Church without taking holy orders. In 1667 he accepted the invitation of Lord Ashley Cooper, later Earl of Shaftesbury, to live with him as his secretary and personal physician. Shaftesbury, spokesman of the commercial imperialism of the time, fell under royal disfavor for plotting a "Protestant Revolt" and fled to Holland where he died. Later Locke was expelled from Oxford by the King's express command and a warrant for his arrest issued. But Locke had already moved to Holland where he resided from 1682 until the "Glorious Revolution" of 1688 when King William landed an army from Dutch ships and accepted the English throne.

Locke returned to England in 1689. That same year three of his books were in the press, the *Essay Concerning Human Understanding*, *Two Treatises of Government*, and *A Letter Concerning Toleration.* A year later his popular pedagogic treatise, *Some Thoughts on Education,* appeared, a book Rousseau had before him when he wrote *Emile.* Locke was now a famous man. His liberal and tolerant political views entered into the dominant ideology of the time. The chemist Boyle was his friend, and he corresponded with Sir Isaac Newton. In 1695 he was appointed a Commissioner of Trade. In this capacity he pronounced unemployment and pauperism to be caused not by scarcity but by lack of discipline and corruption of manners. His attitude toward child labor was the same that horrified Dickens a century and a half later.

Locke was personally a devout man, believing in the truths of the New Testament which he considered amenable to the tests of reason. He was a latitudinarian Anglican, favoring tolerance of dissenting sects with the exception of Jews (infidels) and Catholics (agents of a foreign power). His enlightened views on natural rights, necessity of consent of people to their government, and their right of revolt in circumstances of flagrant injustice, are said to have had considerable influence on the political thinking of the founding fathers of the United States.

BENEDICT SPINOZA

1632–1677

Baruch Spinoza, or Benedict as he later called himself, was born in Amsterdam of Iberian Jews of the kind known in Spain as "Maranos"—that is, Jews who had become nominally Catholic to escape persecution. Little is known about Spinoza's parents or his childhood. He studied at the Amsterdam synagogue under the distinguished rabbi Manasseh ben Israel and became familiar with the writings of Maimonides and Crescas. The Gentile scholar and revolutionary Franciscus van den Enden helped him with his Latin so that he might devour the works of Descartes, the *beau idéal* of scientifically-inclined young men of the day. A story has it that the bachelor Spinoza fell in love with van den Enden's daughter Clara, but that a rival won her instead with a gift of pearls.

Young Spinoza's unorthodox views became a subject of grave concern to his congregation and he was pressed to abjure them. Unyielding to persuasion backed by a monetary offer, Spinoza left the synagogue. He was excommunicated from the Jewish community with formal ritual curses, a harsh measure to be understood in the light of the Amsterdam Jews' anxiety not to offend their Protestant hosts by spectacles of impiety. Spinoza took to a solitary scholar's life, grinding telescope lenses when he was not reading or writing. It is doubtful whether he made a living by his lens grinding; he probably derived financial support from certain well-placed admirers.

One of the remarkable things about Spinoza was his ability to attract so much attention and esteem from the learned world, although he published comparatively little during his lifetime. A commentary on Descartes was the only book printed with his name on it while Spinoza was alive. His magnum opus, the *Ethics*, was not published until after his death, and his *Tractatus Theologico-Politicus* appeared anonymously. The philosopher circulated much of his work privately. In any case, he was admired by important contemporaries. He knew Huyghens and corresponded voluminously with Oldenburg, secretary of the Royal Society in London. Leibniz visited him at his last dwelling place in the Hague. The Elector of the Palatinate offered him a chair of philosophy at the University of Heidelberg, but Spinoza declined the honor.

Spinoza died at the age of 44 of tuberculosis. It is likely that glass dust from his lens grinding hastened the end. For many years his name brought a shudder to the orthodox, but the European enlightenment rehabilitated him. Goethe and Coleridge were among his ardent partisans. Some years after World War II, a petition was presented to the board of rabbis in Amsterdam with the object of removing the ban of excommunication from Spinoza's name. But the rabbis of postwar Amsterdam confessed themselves unable to take action, since in order to remove such a ban it would have been necessary for them to demonstrate that they were wiser than the rabbis of the community that condemned Spinoza. Such a demonstration, they regretfully concluded, was beyond their power.

GOTTFRIED WILHELM LEIBNIZ

1646–1716

Like Descartes, Leibniz lived as a courtier rather than as a professor, and for this reason wrote no magnum opus in philosophy. Instead, there flowed from his pen a series of theses, papers, monographs, letters, and treatises, many of which obscure the brilliant insights of his genius. Leibniz was born in Leipzig where his father was a professor of moral philosophy. The boy entered the University of Leipzig at 15 and 5 years later presented himself as a candidate for the doctor's degree in law. The degree was refused him on account of his youth, but Leibniz quickly obtained the degree at Altdorf (Nuremberg). There he was offered a professorhip, but declined it to enter the service of the Elector of Mainz. Leibniz did much political research for the Elector, even providing him with a plan for encouraging an invasion of Egypt by France with a view to diverting French pressure from the German states. The French were interested enough to invite Leibniz to Paris, although he never obtained the interview he sought with Louis XIV.

His visit to Paris brought Leibniz in contact with many brilliant men, for Paris was the literary and scientific capital of Europe. Among others, he met Arnauld, Malebranche, and Huyghens. He devised and exhibited a mathematical computer which later won him membership in the Royal Society of London. Eventually his mathematical researches led him to the discovery of the differential and integral calculus. His project for a universal symbolic language foreshadowed many of the results of modern deductive logic.

Leaving the Elector of Mainz, Leibniz entered the employ of the house of Brunswick, remaining in the service of that family for 40 years. European travel enabled him to visit Spinoza in Amsterdam, and he took notes on the latter's *Ethics*. He carried on full correspondence with the savants of the day. In 1690 he founded the Academy of Sciences in Berlin and became its first president.

Most of Leibniz' philosophical works were composed in the last two decades of his life. His only complete philosophical book, the *Theodicy*, appeared in 1710. A sketch of his metaphysical system made in 1714 for Prince Eugene of Savoy was titled *The Monadology*. In this work Leibniz elaborates his theory of monads, points of force graded according to the clarity of their perception. Simple and self-moving, these spiritual atoms are entirely unaffected from without. Monads have no windows.

The last years of Leibniz' life were depressed by illness and saddened by the neglect of the royal and learned worlds to pay him the honors he considered due him. At his death, only his secretary followed the body to its grave.

GEORGE BERKELEY

1685–1753

With the exception of John Scotus Erigena who left Ireland in the ninth century to teach at the court of the Frankish king Charles the Bald, Berkeley is the only Irish philosopher of major importance. He was born to a family of English origin in Kilkenny, and went to boarding school there. Taking his B.A. at Trinity College, Dublin, in 1704, he remained there for 17 years as fellow and teacher. In 1710 he was ordained priest in the Irish (Anglican) Church. About this time his best known works appeared—the essay on *A New Theory of Vision* (1709), *The Principles of Human Knowledge* (1710), and *Three Dialogues between Hylas and Philonous* (1713). The young divine became famous as the philosopher of "immaterialism."

Berkeley went to London in 1713 and was befriended by many of the prominent wits of the day. He knew Pope, Addison, Steele, and Swift. Swift's friend Vanessa intended to leave her small fortune to the author of *Gulliver's Travels*, but on being informed that the satirist had married his pupil Stella, made a new will naming Berkeley and Robert Marshall as heirs. After London, Berkeley toured the continent. In Paris, an introduction with the philosopher Malebranche was arranged. On a second trip abroad, he fell in love with the island of Ischia in the bay of Naples and stayed there three months before returning to Dublin and Trinity where he received his Doctor of Divinity degree in 1721.

Berkeley remained at Trinity until 1724 when he was made Dean of Derry. In 1728, newly married, he sailed for America in an unsuccessful attempt to found a college in Bermuda. The projected College of St. Paul was to serve as a source of higher education and Christian learning for white planters and Indians alike. Berkeley got no further than Newport, Rhode Island, where he lived and preached for nearly three years. He was a friend and benefactor of "the College at Newhaven" (Yale). He visited Harvard, and gave Samuel Johnson good advice on the founding and administration of King's College (later, Columbia).

Back in London in 1732, Berkeley published his *Alciphron*, written in America. After some delay, Queen Caroline finally acknowledged his exertions by appointing him Bishop of Cloyne, a modest episcopacy near Cork. At Cloyne he wrote his *Siris* (1744) more famous for its prescription of tar water as a universal medicine than for its discussion of the Trinity. In 1752 the celebrated man, now ailing, visited Oxford to see his son settled at the University. He stayed on in the charming city and died there of apoplexy at the age of 67.

DAVID HUME

1711–1776

David Hume is more than Scotland's greatest philosopher. His writings have had deeper and more lasting effect on modern and contemporary philosophy than any other man in the notable line of British empiricists. Hume was born in Edinburgh; his father was a country gentleman who died prematurely, leaving his younger son a small income. The boy attended the University of Edinburgh between the age of 12 and 15, and left without taking a degree. In 1734, Hume made a half-hearted try at a merchant's career, but quickly abandoned it for three years' travel and study in France. At La Flèche, where Descartes went to school, he composed a considerable part of his ambitious *Treatise on Human Nature.* Taking inspiration from Newton and Hutcheson, he planned in this work "to introduce the experimental method of reasoning into moral subjects." On his return to London in 1737, the first two books of the *Treatise* were published, and fell (in Hume's words) "dead-born from the Press." In succeeding years he brought out two volumes of essays which had somewhat more success. In 1774 his friends nominated him for the professorship of Ethics and Pneumatical Philosophy (psychology) at Edinburgh, but rumor of his sceptical views on religion blocked the appointment. After an abortive experience as companion to the mad Marquis of Annandale, Hume was invited to travel with General James St. Clair as his private secretary, an appointment which brought the philosopher into contact with the diplomatic world to which he would return years later. The work we now know as *An Enquiry concerning Human Understanding*, a revision of part of the *Treatise*, appeared in 1748. In 1751 the *Enquiry concerning the Princi-*

ples of Morals was published, and this was followed by the *Political Discourses.* Ten years' retirement and research prepared Hume for the publication of his large *History of England*, a work which substantially increased his fame.

In 1763 Hume joined Lord Hertford's diplomatic mission to Paris, and served some time in that city as British *chargé d'affaires.* Hume had always admired Rousseau and in 1766 he persuaded the persecuted author of *Emile* to take refuge in England and to accept a pension from the King. Ridden by a persecution mania, Jean Jacques turned on his benefactor, accusing Hume of proffering hospitality as a cover for planned exploitation. Hume's last service as a public official was a year's duty as an undersecretary of state. In 1769 he returned to Edinburgh where he lived until his death. His controversial *Dialogues concerning Natural Religion* were published posthumously in 1779.

Hume described himself in a paper called *My Own Life* as "a man of mild Dispositions, of Command of Temper, of an open, social, and cheerful Humour, capable of Attachment, but little susceptible of Enmity, and of great moderation in all my Passions."

IMMANUEL KANT

1724–1804

For a good part of the eighteenth century, the East Prussian city of Königsberg was the center of intellectual and political life of the duchy of Prussia. Here the greatest German philosopher was born, the fourth child of a poor master saddler. His paternal grandfather came from Scotland. His mother, whom Kant describes as uneducated but of high natural intelligence and strength of character, brought him up in the tradition of Pietism, a Lutheran sect dedicated to the Bible, simple faith, and unadorned practices. Kant went to school at the Collegium Fridericianum where he received excellent training in Latin. He entered the University of Königsberg in 1740 where he studied mathematics, physics, and philosophy, reading Leibniz and Newton with close attention. Kant's early interest in natural science bore fruit in a number of scientific papers, one of which suggested the nebular origin of the solar system, a theory now known as the Kant-LaPlace hypothesis.

In 1755 Kant obtained the official but unsalaried post of *Privatdozent* in the University and for 15 years lectured and tutored in philosophy and the natural sciences. He also offered courses in such specialized subjects as pyrotechnics and the theory of fortifications. In 1770, on the nomination of King Frederick Wilhelm II, Kant was elected Professor of Logic and Metaphysics. When he was 57 years old, he published his long awaited *Critique of Pure Reason* (1781). Despite its difficulty, this master work had a great success, stimulating critical and appreciative papers on all sides and drawing crowds of students to Königsberg. Kant's only brush with the Prussian authorities occurred after the publication of his essay "Religion within the Bounds of Mere Reason" (1793). The minister of education communicated to him the king's displeasure at the philosopher's mistaken application of his powers to the truths of Holy Writ, and asked him to refrain from further writing on religion. Kant submitted and avoided such topics until the king's death.

Kant was on good terms with Herder, Hamann, and the *literati* of the German Enlightenment. He admired Rousseau, applauded the French Revolution as an attempt to organize political arrangements on the basis of reason. Physically, Kant was small and thin. Though he never travelled more than 100 miles from his birthplace, it is said that he knew the position of every stone in London Bridge. He never married, and his life had the regularity of a bachelor whose afternoon walks could be predicted a priori. His health became enfeebled in 1790 and he retired from teaching without ceasing to write.

He died in his eightieth year, full of honors and dignity. His last words were "*Es ist gut*" ("It is well").

G. W. F. HEGEL

1770–1831

Georg Wilhelm Friedrich Hegel was born in Stuttgart, Germany. His father was a revenue officer; his mother had a good classical education and taught her son Latin. Hegel studied at the Stuttgart grammar school and in 1788 entered the University of Tübingen as a student of theology. He took his Ph.D. degree at Tübingen as well as a certificate in theology, but showed little interest in a career in the church. Two influential friends of these student years were Schelling, whose philosophical renown preceded Hegel's, and Hölderlin, the brilliant and unstable poet whose love for ancient Greece inspired a similar devotion in Hegel and (a hundred years later) in Heidegger. Hegel went to Switzerland as a private tutor in the city of Bern where he attempted to work out a philosophical justification of the life and teachings of Jesus. Through Hölderlin, Hegel now secured a tutor's position in Frankfort, and in this city his philosophical ideas began to take systematic shape.

A small legacy from his father, who died in 1799, enabled Hegel to go to Jena, center of lively intellectual and literary life, and to secure a post there as *Privatdozent* at the University. Hegel began to lecture on logic and metaphysics and, after a slow start, attracted a modest following. In 1805 he was made professor *extraordinarius* (the *ordinarius* was the regular professor holding the chair) and pushed ahead with the construction of his intensely difficult philosophical system. His first great book, *The Phenomenology of the Spirit*, was composed to the sound of Napoleon's cannon at Jena in 1806. The

Phenomenology, to this day the most fascinating of Hegel's works, was published the following year. But the impoverished philosopher had to leave Jena.

In 1808 Hegel accepted the post of rector of a gymnasium at Nuremberg and remained in that office until 1816. While at Nuremberg, he married a young wife of noble birth, and the marriage seems to have been moderately happy. Two volumes of his formidable *Science of Logic* appeared, as well as two sons, and a professorship of philosophy at Heidelberg was offered to him. Hegel's stay at Heidelberg was short, for the University of Berlin pressed an earlier invitation for him to accept the chair of philosophy vacated by the death of the renowned Fichte. At Berlin, Hegel reached the height of position and fame. He saw eye to eye with the Prussian government; he was decorated, and appointed rector of the university in 1830. Despite the fact that Hegel was rarely inspiring as a lecturer, his European fame brought many brilliant students to sit at his feet. Hegel was kind to the temperamental young Arthur Schopenhauer and secured his ungrateful junior an appointment as lecturer at Berlin.

Hegel died in the cholera epidemic in Berlin at the age of 61. His death preceded Goethe's by four months. The two had met, and Goethe admired the philosopher, although he believed his system unnecessarily complex.

ARTHUR SCHOPENHAUER

1788–1860

Arthur Schopenhauer, whose name has become identified with the philosophy of pessimism, was born in Danzig. His father, a prosperous businessman, died prematurely, possibly by his own hand. Arthur grew up as a frowning young man whose presence blighted his attractive mother's parties. Joanna Schopenhauer had a gift for writing novels and loved to enter-tain artists and writers. Moving to Weimar, she welcomed Goethe to her salon. The Olympian author of *Faust* was kind to her son and encouraged him in his writing. In turn Arthur defended Goethe's anti-Newtonian theory of color to the end of his days.

Schopenhauer studied at the University of Gottingen and wrote his doctor's thesis on "The Fourfold Root of the Principle of Sufficient Reason." Then he set to work on his masterpiece. *The World as Will and Idea* is a young man's book, appearing in the philosopher's thirtieth year. He never wrote another major work, but in subsequent years added new material so that the original book grew to four volumes. Schopenhauer tried to become a professor of philosophy, and Hegel helped him to secure an appointment on his own faculty at the University of Berlin. But it was hard for the junior lecturer to compete with Hegel who was at the time at the height of his popularity. In later years the ungrateful Schopenhauer scolded Hegel, as well as Fichte and Schelling, calling them all sophists and windbags.

The young philosopher quarrelled with his mother and left her house. He spent the rest of his life travelling in Europe or sitting grumpily in German boarding houses, composing fresh essays to add to his work. Only toward the end of his life did some measure of fame come to him. Scholars and poets called at his house in Frankfort. Richard Wagner sent him a copy of his *Ring of the Nibelungens* inscribed "With Reverence." Schopenhauer was not impressed.

The philosophy of art set forth in *The World as Will and Idea* has attracted deep sympathy from artists, composers, and men of literature. Many also see in Schopenhauer's doctrine of the instinctive, irrational Will a metaphysical foundation of the theory of psychoanalysis. "Schopenhauer, as psychologist of the will," says Thomas Mann, who in his own youth fell under the philosopher's spell, "is the father of all modern psychology. From him the line runs, by way of the psychological radicalism of Nietzsche, straight to Freud."

JOHN STUART MILL

1806—1873

John Mill's father was a Scotsman in the service of the East India Company in London where he eventually rose, as did his son, to the rank of Chief Examiner. James Mill was an intimate of Jeremy Bentham and the two learned eccentrics took young John's education in hand. At the age of 3 the tot was put to the study of Greek and by 7 had mastered a number of the Platonic dialogues in the original, although he confessed he "did not yet quite understand the *Theaetetus*." This ferocious course of home study (Mill never had any formal schooling) continued throughout his childhood. In 1823 he entered India House as a clerk, reading logic, metaphysics, psychology, and political enonomy in his spare time. At 20, young Mill suffered a near breakdown which he blames on his excessively cerebral and deficiently emotional education.

With the exception of Abélard's, Mill's passion for Harriet Taylor is philosophy's most notable love affair. The beautiful Mrs. Taylor captured the scholar's heart when he was 24 and the whole course of his life and work was changed on the spot. Her kindly husband sent Harriet to the continent to restore her composure, but the amorous philosopher joined his Muse in France and accompanied her to Sorrento. Thereafter Mill lived in close, though chaste, association with Mrs. Taylor until the death of her husband enabled the lovers to marry. Harriet died of tuberculosis, probably contracted from Mill, in Avignon in 1878. Her inconsolable husband bought a house near her grave and spent much of the rest of his life there. Mill describes many of his works as "joint productions" with Harriet. Only the *System of Logic* published in 1843 seems to have been untouched by her hand.

Besides the *Logic*, Mill's only other large-scale book was his *Principles of Political Economy* which appeared in 1848. His well-known essays on liberty, utilitarianism, and the subjection of women were products of his fifties. Mill's *Autobiography* and *Three Essays on Religion* were published after his death. A great deal of Mill's writing went into his *Westminster Review* which championed Radical (liberal) causes. Mill defended the American Union, Irish Nationalism, women's suffrage, reasonableness in religion, birth control, and the rights of prostitutes. Elected to Parliament in 1865, he served as member from Westminster until his defeat for reelection three years later. Shortly before his death at the age of 67, the "Saint of Rationalism" sent a silver mug to his infant godson Bertrand Russell.

CHARLES PEIRCE

1839–1914

Inspirer of James and Dewey, and cited by many contemporary philosophers as the greatest of American pragmatists, Charles Sanders Peirce never published a book or held more than a part-time teaching job. The eccentric genius was the son of Benjamin Peirce, a prominent Harvard mathematician. He took degrees in mathematics and chemistry at Harvard, but never advanced to the Ph.D. A reading of Schiller's *Aesthetic Letters* led him to the study of Kant, and he became an enthusiastic and original philosopher. From conversations with Peirce and from papers he heard discussed at Peirce's Metaphysical Club in Cambridge, Mass., William James derived both the leading idea and the word for his pragmatism—a debt the younger philosopher repeatedly acknowledged. Peirce entered the service of the U.S. Coast and Geodetic Survey and for a time was assigned to help his father in scientific work at the Harvard Observatory. James worked hard to get Peirce appointed to the Harvard philosophy department, but Peirce's marital infelicities were notorious and President Eliot considered him an impossible person. Peirce did have five years of intermittent teaching at Johns Hopkins University, but a safer man was appointed to the regular professorship.

Peirce had an omnivorous mind and his papers are brilliant, though sometimes crochety, analyses of problems in mathematics, logic, language, theory of knowledge, scientific method, and metaphysics. He was quite at home in medieval Latin and could follow William of Ockham's arcane logical investigations with enjoyment and profit. Duns Scotus was his favorite metaphysician. Although he published a number of philosophical papers during his lifetime, much of what he wrote was not printed until the *Collected Papers of C. S. Peirce* was published in separate volumes from 1931 to 1958. The publication of these papers *in toto* elevated Peirce's reputation to that of a major twentieth century thinker.

In 1891 Peirce retired from the Coast and Geodetic Survey, and bought a house in Milford, Pennsylvania, with a small legacy. He lived there with his second wife, a French lady, until his death in 1914. "There was no money even for a decent burial," says Peirce's editor Philip Wiener. "His widow sold his manuscripts to Harvard University for five hundred dollars."

WILLIAM JAMES

1842–1910

William James's grandfather, also named William, emigrated from Ireland at the end of the eighteenth century and settled in Albany, New York, where he made a fortune in business and land. His son Henry James (Sr.) moved to New York City taking with him no settled occupation but many interests in metaphysical and religious matters including the teachings of the mystic Swedenborg. William was the oldest of five children, and his father's friend Emerson came to look at him in his cradle. Henry, the second son, grew up to become the greatest American novelist.

William did not attend school, but was tutored at home until the James family moved to Boston. There he began the study of medicine, took his M.D. at Harvard, but never practiced. European travel and study, particularly in Germany, broadened his interests. Never robust, William James was subject to fits of depression. Certain experiences of a quasi-mystical nature helped renew his confidence. In 1878 he married Alice Gibbens whose "benign influence upon her husband's happiness," says James's biographer R. B. Perry, "can scarcely be exaggerated."

James taught physiology at Harvard, then psychology. He was responsible for the introduction of the experimental method in psychology at Harvard. In 1890, at the age of 48, he published his first book, *Principles of Psychology*, a volume which some critics believe to be the most important and influential of his works.

James had always been interested in philosophy, and his friendship with Charles Peirce had stimulated him to the line of thought that was to issue in his famous "pragmatism." He became professor of philosophy at Harvard in 1885, and this appointment inaugurated the "Golden Age" of the Harvard philosophy department which was joined by Josiah Royce and George Santayana. At the turn of the century James gave the Gifford lectures in Edinburgh, later published as *The Varieties of Religious Experience*.

In 1898 James delivered a lecture at the University of California in which he inaugurated the philosophical movement known as "pragmatism." His Lowell lectures of 1906 were published under this title. *Pragmatism* confirmed James's international fame. Friendship and correspondence with Bergson and John Dewey matured. James had hoped one day to write a systematic book on philosophy, but his energies were drawn away by demands for lectures and public appearances. Weakened by a heart strain he had suffered some years earlier, he died at his beloved summer home at Chocorua, New Hampshire, at the age of 68.

As a philosopher, James was essentially a moralist. To the question raised in his *Will to Believe* ("Is Life Worth Living?"), he answered yes—life can be made worth living by giving it the quality of bold and strenuous action.

FRIEDERICH NIETZSCHE

1844–1900

"Music and tears," Nietzsche once said, "I can scarcely tell them apart. His philosophical life was spent repressing both. Friederich Nietzsche was born in Röcken, Germany, the son of a pastor who died while his boy was still small. Brought up by devoted women of his family, Nietzsche was early marked out as a pious lad and a prize scholar. From the distinguished Pforta school, he went on to Leipzig where he studied classical philology at the university and privately cultivated antireligious sentiments. On the recommendation of his teachers he was given a professorship at the University of Basel in Switzerland before he had taken his doctor's degree. He became an intimate of Richard Wagner then living in Switzerland in exile from his native Germany. It is often said that Nietzsche turned against Wagner and his music when he found that the composer was using him as an ideologue to publicize his artistic theories. But there can be little doubt that Wagner was really fond of the young professor, and missed his company even in later years when Nietzsche was writing public attacks against the composer and his successful opera theatre at Bayreuth.

The Birth of Tragedy (1872), Nietzsche's first work to

attract public attention, was written under the spell of his love affair with Wagner's music. Here he put forward one of his most famous concepts, the polarity of the Apollonian and Dionysian in Greek culture, linking the former with the rational, the latter with the instinctive and dynamic side of things. A breakdown in health forced his resignation from Basel, and the series of brilliant works which includes *Beyond Good and Evil*, *The Genealogy of Morals*, and *Thus Spake Zarathustra*, was painfully put together in a succession of boarding houses in resort areas in Switzerland and Northern Italy.

Nietzsche proclaimed himself an *immoralist*, that is, one who overturns the standards and values of his time to replace them by new values which seem to the shocked world "immoral." Nietzsche's relentless attacks on Christianity led his admirer André Gide to say, "Nietzsche is jealous of Christ." Like Kierkegaard before him, Nietzsche professed to have no use for systematic academic philosophy, although there is probably more of it in his works than his aphoristic style would suggest. Like Kierkegaard too, he suspected academic philosophy of reducing the human predicament to an abstraction. "Life," he said, "is more important than truth."

Nietzsche's last work was *Ecce Homo* (1888), a review of his philosophical writings in which brilliant insights alternate with outbursts of apparent megalomania. The next year the philosopher broke down in Turin and dragged out the remaining 10 years of his life as a physical and mental invalid. The sufferings and madness to which the philosopher fell victim were probably syphilitic in origin. Nietzsche never married, and his chief mourner at his death in 1900 was his sister Elizabeth.

HENRI BERGSON

1859–1941

The author of *Creative Evolution* was born in Paris of a cultivated assimilated Jewish family. Bergson's mother was English (some say Irish) and his brother lived in England writing stories under an assumed name. Bergson's father was the descendant of a rich Warsaw merchant, Samuel Zbitkower. Marcel Proust became Bergson's cousin-in-law when the philosopher married a niece of Proust's mother, Mlle. Neuberger, in 1891. The novelist-to-be was an usher at the wedding.

Bergson was educated at the Lycée Condorcet and the École Normale. He wavered between a career in science and in letters, finally choosing the latter to the despair of his mathematics teacher who made a scene before Bergson's parents. Bergson taught in the lycées of Angers and Clermont, at the Collège Rollin, and the Lycée Henri IV in Paris. He received his Agrégation in philosophy in 1881 and his doctor's degree in 1889 for his *Essai sur les données immédiates de la conscience.* He was appointed to the École Normale Supérieure in 1897 and a few years later became professor at the Collège de France, holding first the chair in Greek, then in philosophy.

It was in Clermont that Bergson, out for a walk one day after class, experienced a moment of luminous perception. He had been thinking about Zeno's paradoxes, and it suddenly came to him that time is not simply a measure of motion in space, but an element of our inmost being as it grows into the future. From this key concept of *duration* the whole of Bergsonian philosophy sprang. Bergson in Paris was an immense success and in the years before World War I his public lectures at the Collège de France became an attraction to visitors second only to the Eiffel Tower. Two visits to the

United States during the first war netted him an honorary degree by Columbia University and an invitation by Theodore Roosevelt to a breakfast, the early hour and stunning proportions of which puzzled the delicate Frenchman. Bergson joined the French Academy in 1914. Seven years later he won the Nobel Prize for literature.

The Immediate Data of Consciousness was followed by *Matter and Memory* (1896) and *Creative Evolution* (1907). No large scale work came from Bergson's hands after that until *The Two Sources of Morality and Religion* of 1932. The last named book deals intensively with mysticism, a religious phenomenon that exerted a compelling personal effect on Bergson, bringing him to the point of conversion to Catholicism. In World War II, Bergson, now old and sick, was excused by the Vichy authorities from registering as a Jew. But the philosopher declined the dubious privilege and, clad in his bathrobe, stood in the dreary line to register and to receive his "*étoile de David*." A passage in Bergson's will states "I would have been converted if I had not for years seen impending the formidable wave of anti-Semitism that is going to sweep the world."

JOHN DEWEY

1859—1952

John Dewey is one of few major philosophers to take a direct and practical interest in education. He actually defined philosophy as the *theory* of education. His own early education was in the public schools of Burlington, Vermont, where he was born. His father was a grocer of easy-going temperament; his mother, a Vermonter of a more prosperous family, took a sterner view of life. Young John graduated from the University of Vermont, taught high school for two years in South Oil City, Pennsylvania, and kept the village school for a shorter period in Charlotte, Vermont. His first philosophical paper, "The Metaphysical Assumptions of Materialism" appeared in W. T. Harris' journal *Speculative Philosophy* in 1882, the year Dewey began graduate study in philosophy at Johns Hopkins. On taking his doctor's degree, Dewey became instructor of philosophy at the University of Michigan where he was influenced by the Hegelianism of his senior colleague George S. Morris. But reading William James's *Principles of Psychology* made an even deeper impression on the young philosopher.

After a brief interlude at the University of Minnesota, Dewey returned to head the department of philosophy at Michigan. In 1893 he moved to the University of Chicago where the department of Philosophy and Psychology supervised the teaching of Pedagogy. With the aid of a group of parents, Dewey opened an elementary school, known as "The Laboratory School" under the auspices of his department. Dewey's early Chicago papers on education contain the key notions linking him in the public mind with "progressive education"—the school as continuous with social environment, education as growth in a democracy. Dewey's ideas on education developed in the climate of reform and progressivism of the close of the century. Jane Addams was his friend and he frequented Hull House.

A disagreement with university authorities over the administration of the Laboratory School brought about Dewey's resignation from Chicago. In 1905 he moved to the philosophy department of Columbia University, teaching two hours a week in Teachers College as an added duty. At Columbia, Dewey found himself in a completely congenial atmosphere and taught there until his retirement 25 years later. *Democracy and Education*, *Reconstruction in Philosophy*, *Human Nature and Conduct*, *Logic: the Theory of Inquiry*, and *Art as Experience* are peaks in his bibliographical mountain range. Dewey visited and lectured in Great Britain, China, Japan, Mexico, Turkey, and the U.S.S.R. In 1936 he became a member of the commission of inquiry into charges against Trotsky at his trial *in absentia* in the Soviet Union. The hearings were held at Trotsky's home in Mexico City, and the commission returned a verdict of "Not Guilty." Dewey married twice; his first wife died in 1927.

Dewey was not an elegant lecturer; his voice was harsh and his delivery that of a man trying to think through problems as he talks. The philosopher's ninetieth birthday on October 20, 1949, was the occasion for a memorable celebration in New York to which the great of the world sent greetings.

EDMUND HUSSERL

1859—1938

To philosophers on the continent, the publication of Husserl's *Ideas Pertaining to a Pure Phenomenology* (1913) was the outstanding philosophical event of the years just before World War I. Husserl was a native of Bohemia, born in the province of Moravia. He began his studies as a mathematician, but turned to philosophy under the influence of the German philosopher Friedrich Paulsen. The Cartesian ideal can be seen early in Husserl's program; it was his ambition to make philosophy into an exact and completely reliable science. The most direct influence on Husserl was the work of the philosophical psychologist Franz Brentano (1838–1916). Husserl also acknowledged indebtedness to the *Wissenschaftslehre* of Bernhard Bolzano (1781–1848).

Husserl taught philosophy at the universities of Halle and Göttingen. In 1916 he was appointed to the chair of philosophy at the University of Freiburg where he remained until his retirement in 1929. Bonn University conferred an honorary doctorate on him, and he was made a Privy Councillor. Husserl's last years were troubled by the ascendancy of the

Nazi regime. He was of Jewish ancestry, but because of his eminence (these were the early days of Hitler's rule) he was not harmed. Nevertheless, things were made unpleasant for him. Husserl's son, dean of the law faculty at Kiel University, lost his post and had to emigrate to America.

Husserl's phenomenology became the dominant twentieth century philosophical influence on the continent. He himself had the power to convert pupils into disciples, and was regarded with reverence by some of the most brilliant young men and women of Germany and France. Husserl lectured in Paris in 1929, and his last work, the *Cartesian Meditations*, was written and published in the French language.

Husserl died at Freiburg. He was succeeded in the chair of philosophy at the university by his former student Martin Heidegger.

ALFRED NORTH WHITEHEAD

1861–1947

Son of an Anglican vicar, Alfred North Whitehead was born at Ramsgate on the isle of Thanet, Kent, 16 miles from Canterbury Cathedral. He could visualize the spot where Beckett fell in 1170 and recalled how he reconstructed the incident in his own imagination. To the countryside of his youth, with its Roman and medieval archaeological remains, Whitehead credits the taste for historical comparison that pervades his writing. In that countryside Nature was alive, and the world suffused by a process analogous to feeling.

Whitehead went to school at Sherborne, then on to Trinity College, Cambridge, where he studied, then taught mathematics. Bertrand Russell was one of his first students. Both men were interested in exploring the foundations of mathematics (Whitehead's first book was the *Treatise on Universal Algebra* of 1898) and they collaborated on the monumental *Principia Mathematica*, the first volume of which appeared in 1910. In that same year Whitehead, now married, left Cambridge for London where he obtained a post at the University of London. From 1914 to 1924 he was professor of mathematics in the Imperial College of Science and Technology. During this period he published three books on the philosophy of science of which the best known is *The Concept of Nature* (1920). At the age of 63, when most professors are thinking of retirement, Whitehead accepted an appointment as professor of philosophy at Harvard. Thus his "second biography" began in the United States where his best known philosophical works appeared–*Science and the Modern World* (1925), *Process and Reality* (1929), and *Adventures of Ideas* (1933). In his lectures at Harvard, Whitehead chose his texts from the later Plato and held up to his students the ideal of a new *Timaeus*, a cosmological investigation which would unite mathematics and the Good.

Whitehead was a professional mathematician during the larger part of his life, and came late to philosophy. By his removal to America, he cut himself off from English philosophical contacts, and to this day his work lies away from the mainstream of contemporary philosophical influences. Stephen Toulmin, a younger English philosopher, writes of him, "In the history of recent British philosophy, Alfred North Whitehead stands quite alone. As a metaphysician, he had no direct ancestors, nor any effective descendants. Admired by curious amateurs, but ignored by most of his English colleagues, his great 'philosophy of organism' has already the air of a historical monument. . . . Set beside it, the most esteemed works of the present day look like prefabricated houses, or, at best, like neatly turned out young factories."

GEORGE SANTAYANA

1863–1952

Santayana was born in Madrid and spent his early childhood in the ancient town of Avila. His father had served in the Spanish foreign service in the Philippines; his mother's first husband was a Sturgis of Boston, and she lived for some time in that American city. At the age of 8 young George arrived in Boston to live with his Sturgis relatives. Successively he attended the Brimmer School, Boston Latin School, and Harvard College. At the Latin School he was a lieutenant colonel in the school cadet regiment and contributed to the literary magazine. In his early years, Santayana wrote a good deal of poetry of no great merit, and late in life produced a novel *The Last Puritan* (1936).

Santayana's principal teachers at Harvard were William James and Josiah Royce. He took his Ph.D. with a thesis on Lotze, which remains unpublished. Appointed to the Harvard faculty in 1889, he eventually became professor of philosophy. Sanatayana always protested his temperamental unfitness for the job of professor and in 1912 left Harvard and the United States for good. For the rest of his long life he remained in Europe, mostly in Italy.

His first philosophical book, *The Sense of Beauty*, appeared in 1896. Ten years later he had completed the five volumes of *The Life of Reason.* Other works include *Three Philosophical Poets* (1910), *Winds of Doctrine* (1913), *Egotism in German Philosophy* (1915), *Scepticism and Animal Faith* (1923). Publication of his four volume work, *Realms of Being*, of which the first, *The Realm of Essence* (1927), is perhaps the best known, was not completed until 1940. A series of autobiographical volumes include *Persons and Places* (1944), *The Middle Span*

(1945), and *My Host the World* (1953). His last book *Dominations and Powers*, a volume of reflections on social and political ideas, appeared the year before his death. In his final decade, Santayana lived in Rome in a nursing home under the care of the Blue Sisters.

Sanatayana belongs to no particular school and, while usually classified as an American philosopher, made his spiritual home in the Mediterranean and classical world. Although his parents were free thinkers, Santayana remained Catholic in his sympathies if not in his belief. He could not conceal his disdain for American Protestantism which seemed to him to confuse religion with earnestness and achievement. Santayana never became an American citizen, and died a Spanish national.

BERTRAND RUSSELL

1872–

When Bertrand Russell was three days old, his mother wrote of him, "He lifts his head up and looks about in a very energetic way." The philosopher retained this posture for nearly a hundred years. His father, the free-thinking Viscount Amberley, was the son of Lord John Russell, English liberal statesman and first Earl Russell. Bertrand's godfather was John Stuart Mill. The philosopher's parents died when he was still a small child, and he was brought up in a strict Puritan environment by his grandmother, Lady Russell. He had no formal schooling, but a series of tutors and wide reading prepared him for Trinity College, Cambridge, which he entered in 1890. He took honors in mathematics at Trinity, and became fellow and lecturer in Philosophy. Under the influence of McTaggart he worked at German philosophy; his first important book was a work on Leibniz. A meeting with the Italian mathematician Peano in Paris in 1900 renewed his interest in mathematical logic, and his collaboration on *Principia Mathematica* (1910) with his friend and former teacher Whitehead soon began. Correspondence with Frege on the foundations of arithmetic enriched a project which became the bible-encyclopedia of modern logic, and Russell himself maintained in later years that *Principia* was the work most likely to survive him. At Cambridge, Russell worked with G. E. Moore and later with Wittgenstein whose "logical atomism" considerably influenced him.

Apart from mathematical logic, Russell's chief contributions lay in theory of knowledge. His impact on twentieth century philosophy was felt through a sequence of important books concerned with problems of knowledge and meaning, a series extending from *Our Knowledge of the External World* of 1914 to *Human Knowledge: Its Scope and Limits* of 1948. The mingled exasperation and respect with which two generations of younger philosophers regarded him is summed up in a critic's remark, "The history of twentieth century philosophy consists in the corrections of Bertrand Russell's mistakes."

Interest in social questions was part of his family tradition, as well as native to his temperament, and Russell's writings in this area have been as voluminous as they are controversial. During World War I he went to jail for his pacificist views. He championed woman suffrage. With Dora Russell, the second of his four wives, he operated a progressive school which conservatives denounced as a scandal. In 1940 he was prevented from accepting a professorship in the College of the City of New York by a taxpayer's suit brought against the city on the ground that the philosopher was an atheist and taught immorality. Russell was a Socialist, but with little sympathy for the Soviet variety. Hitler was too much for him and he supported the Allied cause against the Nazi threat. After World War II he returned to his pacificism, denouncing what he considered the nuclear-backed power ambitions of both the U.S.S.R. and the United States.

G. E. MOORE

1873–1958

A story is told of a young American philosopher of the analytic school who was assigned by his college the task of teaching the History of Western Philosophy. When asked by his superiors whether he would begin the course with Socrates or the pre-Socratics, he replied that he considered the history of philosophy to have begun in 1903 with the publication of *Principia Ethica,* and proposed to devote his first lectures to G. E. Moore. The story is an indication of the immense personal influence Moore has had on the English-speaking philosophical world of the twentieth century.

George Edward Moore was the fifth child of a family of eight. His father was a London physician who had retired from practice and lived on his private income. His mother came from a Quaker family. Both Moore parents were Baptists. Young George went to school as a day boy at Dulwich where he acquired a formidable competence in Greek and Latin. He was fond of music, particularly of German *Lieder;* years later as a Cambridge professor his vocal rendition of Schumann's "*The Two Grenadiers*" was said to be remarkable. Moore won a scholarship to Trinity College, Cambridge, and there met Bertrand Russell who encouraged him to turn to philosophy. Like Russell, Moore fell under the spell of Hegelian idealism, and for a while believed that Bradley's arguments proving that Time was unreal were irrefutable. He was soon disillusioned, and adopted a method which applied the test of ordinary usage to terms found in philosophical disputations.

Principia Ethica established Moore's reputation both philosophical and social. The chapter on the Ideal, holding friendship and aesthetic enjoyment to be unconditional goods, made him the darling of the Bloomsbury group which included Clive

Bell, the Woolfs, John Maynard Keynes, E. M. Forster, and more. In 1911 Moore took up a lectureship at his university and, with the exception of four years in the United States during World War II, spent the rest of his life at Cambridge. Although he wrote a number of important papers, Moore's only other proper book was the *Ethics* he contributed to the Home University Library in 1912. A colleague said that the reason Moore wrote so few books was that he saw the reasons against any view so clearly that he could never make up his mind which was the more defensible. "In 1922–3, when I attended both courses of Moore's lectures," says R. B. Braithwaite, "we hunted the correct analysis of propositions about the self on Monday, Wednesday and Friday mornings, and the correct analysis of propositions of the form 'This is a pencil' on Tuesdays, Thursdays and Saturdays throughout the year. By the end of May, Moore would have got through about two and a half of the possible kinds of analysis."

Moore saw much of Wittgenstein at Cambridge, and, with Bertrand Russell constituted the examining board that recommended the award of the Ph.D. degree to the Austrian genius for his *Tractatus*. Moore was the editor of the philosophical journal *Mind* for 26 years. He was happily married to Dorothy Ely, a Newnham graduate, and had two sons. The Queen awarded him the Order of Merit after ill health forced his retirement from active life.

MARTIN HEIDEGGER

1889–

Martin Heidegger was born in Baden in southwest Germany where he lived all his life. He went to the gymnasium at Freiburg and had serious intentions toward the Catholic priesthood. He left the Church without abandoning his absorbing interest in medieval philosophy. Under his teacher Husserl's direction, he wrote his doctoral dissertation on the categories of Duns Scotus. He was appointed *Privatdozent* at Freiburg in 1915, *Ordinarius* at Marburg in 1923. Heidegger succeeded to the chair vacated by Husserl at Freiburg in 1928, and occupied it until his own retirement in 1943. His best known work *Being and Time* appeared in 1927. Although Heidegger's philosophy has had a great influence on Protestant theology, and on philosophical, philological, and literary history in Europe, his work is not well known in America.

Heidegger became a near recluse after his unfortunate acceptance of the rectorship of the University of Freiburg in 1933. Most of his hearers interpreted his somewhat obscure inaugural address as a call for wholehearted support of the newly elected National Socialists. He appeared to hold that the stated aims of the Nazis opened the way for the self-assertion of German scholarship. Of Heidegger's public exhortations during his rectorship, Karl Löwth remarked that people who listened to them were never quite sure whether to resume their study of the pre-Socratics or to don the uniform of the Storm Troopers. In any event, Heidegger became quickly disillusioned, and resigned the rectorship the following year. In 1945 the occupying powers regarded him with something less than enthusiasm, and the philosopher withdrew to his ski hut in the Black Forest, taking with him quantities of writing paper. It was not long, however, before the demand for his lectures grew to such proportions that the philosopher was prevailed upon to satisfy it by occasional public appearances at Freiburg.

A newspaper correspondent described him in 1962: "Now at 73, Martin Heidegger is everyman's conception of a German philosopher; ascetic, withdrawn, a trifle eccentric and virtually impossible to understand. A thick-set man of medium height, his face (with the help of gray hair, thin lips, and a pair of penetrating black eyes), radiate a spirit of asceticism. He has been described as a mixture of scholar and Black Forest peasant and he still favors breeches and heavy woolen stockings. From time to time he shows up at the University of Freiburg to hold crowd-attracting lectures. His last one brought a thousand savants and students into the hall. But local editors doubted that more than 20 in the audience knew precisely what the man was saying."[1]

LUDWIG WITTGENSTEIN

1889–1951

The strange and gifted man who is conceded to have been the chief influence on Anglo-American philosophy in the twentieth century was an Austrian of Jewish descent who was baptized a Roman Catholic. His father was a prominent engineer. One of his brothers, a concert pianist, lost his right arm in World War I; it was for Paul Wittgenstein that Ravel wrote his *Concerto for the Left Hand.* Ludwig studied engineering at the Technical High School in Berlin. He continued his studies in England where he became interested in Bertrand Russell's writings on the logical foundations of mathematics. Wittgenstein became Russell's student at Cambridge, and visited or corresponded with a number of philosophers and mathematicians including G. E. Moore and Frege. Encouraged by Russell, he began work on his book *Tractatus Logico-Philosophicus* and took the manuscript with him into the war, in which he served as a volunteer in the Austrian army. The *Tractatus* was published in 1922.

Wittgenstein's father died in 1912 and left his son a large fortune which Ludwig gave entirely away after his return from the war. He wandered about rural Austria for some years, doing various odd jobs, teaching school, working as a gardener's helper. It occurred to him that he might enter a monastery, but he decided against it. Not until 1929 did he return to Cambridge and to philosophy. He became a lecturer and acquired a small but devoted band of students. In 1939 he suc-

[1] *New York Times Book Review,* Nov. 11, 1962, p. 6.

ceeded Moore as professor of philosophy. His classes were usually held in his college rooms, and he philosophized, often with painful effort, before his respectful disciples.

Through these years Wittgenstein was writing his *Philosophical Investigations.* After Hitler took over Austria, the philosopher became a British subject. During World War II, he worked in hospitals, first as a porter, later as a laboratory technician. After the war, he lived for a while in a lonely hut in Galway. In 1949 he visited the United States to stay with his former pupil Norman Malcolm at Cornell University. He returned to England ill with cancer, and died in Cambridge. His last words were, "Tell them I've had a wonderful life."

JEAN-PAUL SARTRE

1905–

The French *Who's Who* describes Sartre not as a philosopher but as "*homme de lettres.*" The sheer quantity of his varied output—philosophical, political, critical, novelistic, dramatic—is more characteristic of the nineteenth century than of our own. Sartre was born in Paris, the son of Jean-Baptiste Sartre and Anne Marie Schweitzer. His grand-uncle was Albert Schweitzer, the theologian and humanitarian. Sartre has described his family in his autobiographical memoir *The Words.* Sartre attended the Lycée Henri IV in Paris and the École Normale Supérieure, where he took his *Agrégation* in philosophy. He taught in the lycées of Laon and Le Havre, the latter becoming the "Bouville" of his first novel *La Nausée.* A government fellowship enabled him to study philosophy in Berlin in 1934 where he came under the influence of the philosophies of Husserl and Heidegger. He returned to France to teach philosophy at the Lycée Pasteur at Neuilly and at the Lycée Condorcet in Paris. In 1944 Sartre abandoned teaching to devote his energies entirely to writing. His first big philosophy book *Being and Nothingness* appeared in 1943; the major philosophical work of his later period is *The Critique of Dialectical Reason* of 1960.

During World War II, Sartre was taken prisoner by the Germans and later released. In company with Albert Camus and others, he worked for the Resistance paper *Combat*, and after the war assumed the editorship of *Le Temps Moderne.* His "Existentialism" (it was Gabriel Marcel who first labelled him and his work thus) became immensely fashionable after the war; sightseers drove him and his companion Simone de Beauvoir from their table at the Cafe Flore. Later Mlle. de Beauvoir wrote a fictionalized account of those years with Sartre in her novel *Les Mandarins.* Sartre's plays (*The Flies, No Exit, Dirty Hands*, and others) were more successful than the novel sequence *Les Chemins de la Liberté* of which he completed three volumes. His preface to his edition of the plays of Jean Genet grew into an independent volume of 578 pages.

In company with some other French writers, Sartre was sent to the United States by his government in 1946, and he lectured at Harvard, Columbia, Yale, and Princeton. Although not a Communist, he sympathized with Marxist insurgencies, and later took the part of Cuba and North Vietnam against the United States. He withdrew from a commitment to lecture on Flaubert at Cornell University in 1964 because, in his words, "I do not want to find myself in New York with Hanoi being bombed."

Sartre refused the Legion of Honor in 1945, and declined the Nobel Prize for literature in 1964. Sartre's Paris apartment on the rue Bonaparte is a few doors down from Auguste Comte's old rooms; around the corner stands the house where Balzac had his printing shop.

Index

NEWARK PUBLIC LIBRARY - NEWARK, OHIO 43055
P9-CRC-873

ELEPHANTS CAN REMEMBER

NOVELS OF SUSPENSE BY AGATHA CHRISTIE

Listed in Order of Publication (*English Titles in Italics*)

The Mysterious Affair at Styles
The Secret Adversary
The Murder on the Links
The Man in the Brown Suit
The Secret of Chimneys
The Murder of Roger Ackroyd
The Big Four
The Mystery of the Blue Train
The Seven Dials Mystery
The Murder at the Vicarage
The Murder at Hazelmoor
The Sittaford Mystery
Peril at End House
Thirteen at Dinner
Lord Edgeware Dies
Murder in the Calais Coach
Murder on the Orient Express
Murder in Three Acts
Three-Act Tragedy
Death in the Air
Death in the Clouds
The Boomerang Clue
Why Didn't They Ask Evans?
The A.B.C. Murders
Murder in Mesopotamia
Cards on the Table
Poirot Loses a Client
Dumb Witness
Death on the Nile
Appointment With Death
Murder for Christmas
Hercule Poirot's Christmas
Easy to Kill
Murder Is Easy
And Then There Were None
Ten Little Niggers

Sad Cypress
The Patriotic Murders
One, Two, Buckle My Shoe
N or M?
Evil Under the Sun
The Body in the Library
Murder in Retrospect
Five Little Pigs
The Moving Finger
Towards Zero
Death Comes As the End
Remembered Death
Sparkling Cyanide
The Hollow
There Is a Tide
Taken at the Flood
Crooked House
A Murder Is Announced
They Came to Baghdad
Mrs. McGinty's Dead
Murder With Mirrors
They Do It With Mirrors
Funerals Are Fatal
After the Funeral
A Pocket Full of Rye
So Many Steps to Death
Destination Unknown
Hickory, Dickory, Death
Hickory, Dickory, Dock
Dead Man's Folly
What Mrs. McGillicuddy Saw!
The 4:50 from Paddington
Ordeal by Innocence
Cat Among the Pigeons
The Pale Horse
The Mirror Crack'd
The Mirror Crack'd from Side to Side
The Clocks
A Caribbean Mystery
At Bertram's Hotel
Third Girl
Endless Night
By the Pricking of My Thumbs
Hallowe'en Party
Passenger to Frankfurt
Nemesis

ELEPHANTS CAN REMEMBER

AGATHA CHRISTIE

DODD, MEAD & COMPANY NEW YORK

ISBN: 0-396-06742-5
Library of Congress Catalog Card Number: 72-7788
Printed in the United States of America
by Vail-Ballou Press, Inc., Binghamton, N. Y.

TO MOLLY MYERS

in return for many kindnesses

CONTENTS

Book II

LONG SHADOWS

ELEPHANTS CAN REMEMBER

1

A LITERARY LUNCHEON

Mrs. Oliver looked at herself in the glass. She gave a brief, sideways look towards the clock on the mantelpiece, which she had some idea was twenty minutes slow. Then she resumed her study of her coiffure. The trouble with Mrs. Oliver was—and she admitted it freely—that her styles of hairdressing were always being changed. She had tried almost everything in turn. A severe pompadour at one time, then a wind-swept style where you brushed back your locks to display an intellectual brow, at least she hoped the brow was intellectual. She had tried tightly arranged curls, she had tried a kind of artistic disarray. She had to admit that it did not matter very much today what her type of hairdressing was, because today she was going to do what she very seldom did—wear a hat.

On the top shelf of Mrs. Oliver's wardrobe there reposed four hats. One was definitely allotted to weddings. When you went to a wedding, a hat was a "must." But even then Mrs. Oliver kept two. One, in a round bandbox, was of feathers. It fitted closely to the head and stood up very well to sudden squalls of rain if they should overtake one unexpectedly as one passed from a car to the interior of the sacred edifice, or as so often nowadays, a registrar's office.

The other, and more elaborate, hat was definitely for attending a wedding held on a Saturday afternoon in summer. It had flowers and chiffon and a covering of yellow net attached with mimosa.

The other two hats on the shelf were of a more all-purpose character. One was what Mrs. Oliver called her country house hat, made of tan felt suitable for wearing with tweeds of almost any pattern, with a becoming brim that you could turn up or turn down.

Mrs. Oliver had a cashmere pullover for warmth and a thin pullover for hot days, either of which was suitable in color to go with this. However, though the pullovers were frequently worn, the hat was practically never worn. Because, really, why put on a hat just to go to the country and have a meal with your friends?

The fourth hat was the most expensive of the lot and it had extraordinary advantages about it. Possibly, Mrs. Oliver sometimes thought, because it was so expensive. It consisted of a kind of turban of various layers of contrasting velvets, all of rather becoming pastel shades which would go with anything.

Mrs. Oliver paused in doubt and then called for assistance.

"Maria," she said, then louder, "Maria. Come here a minute."

Maria came. She was used to being asked to give advice on what Mrs. Oliver was thinking of wearing.

"Going to wear your lovely smart hat, are you?" said Maria.

"Yes," said Mrs. Oliver. "I wanted to know whether you think it looks best this way or the other way round."

Maria stood back and took a look.

"Well, that's back to front you're wearing it now, isn't it?"

"Yes, I know," said Mrs. Oliver. "I know that quite well. But I thought somehow it looked better that way."

"Oh, why should it?" said Maria.

"Well, it's meant, I suppose. But it's got to be meant by me as well as the shop that sold it," said Mrs. Oliver.

"Why do you think it's better the wrong way round?"

"Because you get that lovely shade of blue and the dark brown, and I think that looks better than the other way, which is green with the red and the chocolate color."

At this point Mrs. Oliver removed the hat, put it on again and tried it wrong way round, right way round and sideways, which both she and Maria disapproved of.

"You can't have it the wide way. I mean, it's wrong for your face, isn't it? It'd be wrong for anyone's face."

"No. That won't do. I think I'll have it the right way round, after all."

"Well, I think it's safer always," said Maria.

Mrs. Oliver took off the hat. Maria assisted her to put on a well-cut, thin woolen dress of a delicate puce color, and helped her to adjust the hat.

"You look ever so smart," said Maria.

That was what Mrs. Oliver liked so much about Maria. If given the least excuse for saying so, she always approved and gave praise.

"Going to make a speech at the luncheon, are you?" Maria asked.

"A speech!" Mrs. Oliver sounded horrified. "No, of course not. You know I never make speeches."

"Well, I thought they always did at these here literary luncheons. That's what you're going to, isn't it? Famous writers of nineteen seventy-three—or wherever year it is we've got to now."

"I don't need to make a speech," said Mrs. Oliver. "Several other people who *like* doing it will be making speeches, and they are much better at it than I would be."

"I'm sure you'd make a lovely speech if you put your mind to it," said Maria, adjusting herself to the role of a tempter.

"No, I shouldn't," said Mrs. Oliver. "I know what I can do and I know what I can't. I can't make speeches. I get all worried and nervy and I should probably stammer or say the same thing twice. I should not only feel silly, I should probably look silly. Now it's all right with words. You can write words down or speak them into a machine or dictate them. I can do things with words so long as I know it's not a speech I'm making."

"Oh, well. I hope everything'll go all right. But I'm sure it will. Quite a grand luncheon, isn't it?"

"Yes," said Mrs. Oliver in a deeply depressed voice. "Quite a grand luncheon."

And why, she thought, but did not say, why on earth am I going to it? She searched her mind for a bit because she always really liked knowing what she was doing instead of doing it first and wondering why she had done it afterwards.

"I suppose," she said, again to herself and not to Maria, who had had to return rather hurriedly to the kitchen, summoned by a smell of overflowing jam which she happened to have on the stove, "I wanted to see what it felt like. I'm always being asked to literary lunches or something like that and I never go."

Mrs. Oliver arrived at the last course of the grand luncheon with a sigh of satisfaction as she toyed with the remains of the meringue on her plate. She was particularly fond of meringues and it was a delicious last course in a very delicious luncheon. Nevertheless, when one reached middle age, one had to be careful with meringues. One's teeth! They looked all right, they had the great advantage that they could not ache, they were white and quite agreeable-looking—just like the real thing. But it was true enough that they were *not* real teeth. And teeth that were not real teeth—or so Mrs. Oliver believed—were not really of high-class material. Dogs, she had always understood, had teeth of real ivory, but human beings had teeth merely of bone. Or, she supposed, if they were false teeth, of plastic. Anyway, the point was that you mustn't get involved in some rather shame-making appearance, which false teeth might lead you into. Lettuce was a difficulty, and salted almonds, and such things as chocolates with hard centers, clinging caramels and the delicious stickiness and adherence of meringues. With a sigh of satisfaction, she dealt with the final mouthful. It had been a good lunch, a very good lunch.

Mrs. Oliver was fond of her creature comforts. She had enjoyed the luncheon very much. She had enjoyed the company, too. The luncheon, which had been given to celebrated female writers, had fortunately not been confined to female writers only. There had been other writers, and critics, and those who read books as well as those who wrote them. Mrs. Oliver had sat between two very charming members of the male sex. Edwin Aubyn, whose poetry she always enjoyed, an extremely entertaining person who had had various entertaining experiences in his tours abroad, and various literary and personal adventures. Also he was interested in restaurants and food and they had talked very happily about food, and left the subject of literature aside.

Sir Wesley Kent, on her other side, had also been an agreeable lunch companion. He had said very nice things about her books, and had had the tact to say things that did not make her feel embarrassed, which so many people could do almost without trying. He had mentioned one or two reasons why he had liked one or other of her books, and they had been the right reasons, and therefore Mrs. Oliver had thought favorably of him for that reason. Praise from men, Mrs. Oliver thought to herself, is always acceptable. It was women who gushed. Some of the things that women wrote to her! Really! Not always women, of course. Sometimes emotional young men from very faraway countries. Only last week she had received a fan letter beginning, "Reading your book, I feel what a noble woman you must be." After reading *The Second Goldfish* he had then gone off into an intense kind of literary ecstasy which was, Mrs. Oliver felt, completely unfitting. She was not unduly modest. She thought the detective stories she wrote were quite good of their kind. Some were not so good and some were much better than others. But there was no reason, so far as she could see, to make anyone think she was a noble woman. She was a lucky woman who had established a happy knack of writing what quite a lot of people wanted to read. Wonderful luck that was, Mrs. Oliver thought to herself.

Well, all things considered, she had got through this ordeal very well. She had quite enjoyed herself, talked to some nice people. Now they were moving to where coffee was being handed round and where you could change partners and chat with other people. This was the moment of danger, as Mrs. Oliver knew well. This was now where other women would come and attack her. Attack her with fulsome praise, and where she always felt lamentably inefficient at giving the right answers because there weren't really any right answers that you could give. It went really rather like a travel book for going abroad with the right phrases.

Question: "I *must* tell you how very fond I am of reading your books and how wonderful I think they are."

Answer from flustered author: "Well, that's very kind. I am so glad."

"You must understand that I've been waiting to meet you for months. It really is wonderful."

"Oh, it's very nice of you. Very nice indeed."

It went on very much like that. Neither of you seemed to be able to talk about anything of outside interest. It had to be all about your books, or the other woman's books if you knew what her books were. You were in the literary web and you weren't good at this sort of stuff. Some people could do it, but Mrs. Oliver was bitterly aware of not having the proper capacity. A foreign friend of hers had once put her, when she was staying at an embassy abroad, through a kind of course.

"I listen to you," Albertina had said in her charming, low, foreign voice. "I have listened to what you say to that young man who came from the newspaper to interview you. You have not got—no! you have not got the pride you should have in your work. You should say 'Yes, I write well. I write better than anyone else who writes detective stories.' "

"But I don't," Mrs. Oliver had said at that moment. "I'm not bad, but—"

"Ah, do not say 'I don't' like that. You must say you *do;*

even if you do not think you do, you ought to *say* you do."

"I wish, Albertina," said Mrs. Oliver, "that you could interview these journalists who come. You would do it so well. Can't you pretend to be me one day, and I'll listen behind the door?"

"Yes, I suppose I could do it. It would be rather fun. But they would know I was not you. They know your face. But you must say, 'Yes, yes, I know that I am better than anyone else.' You must say that to everybody. They should know it. They should announce it. Oh, yes—it is terrible to hear you sitting there and say things as though you *apologize* for what you are. It must not be like that."

It had been rather, Mrs. Oliver thought, as though she had been a budding actress trying to learn a part, and the director had found her hopelessly bad at taking direction. Well, anyway, there'd be not much difficulty here. There'd be a few waiting females when they all got up from the table. In fact, she could see one or two hovering already. That wouldn't matter much. She would go and smile and be nice and say, "So kind of you. I'm so pleased. One is so glad to know people like one's books." All the stale old things.. Rather as though you put a hand into a box and took out some useful words already strung together like a necklace of beads. And then, before very long now, she could leave.

Her eyes went round the table because she might perhaps see some friends there as well as would-be admirers. Yes, she did see in the distance Maurine Grant, who was great fun. The moment came, the literary women and the attendant cavaliers who had also attended the lunch, rose. They streamed towards chairs, towards coffee tables, towards sofas, and confidential corners. The moment of peril, Mrs. Oliver often thought of it to herself, though usually at cocktails and not literary parties because she seldom went to the latter. At any moment the danger might arise, as someone whom you did not remember but who remembered you, or someone whom you definitely did not want to talk to but whom you found you could not avoid. In this case it was the first dilemma that came to her. A large woman. Ample proportions, large white champing teeth. What in French could have been called *une femme formidable,* but who definitely had not only the French variety of being formidable, but the English one of being supremely bossy. Obviously she either knew Mrs. Oliver, or was intent on making her acquaintance there and then. The last was how it happened to go.

"Oh, Mrs. Oliver," she said in a high-pitched voice. "What a pleasure to meet you today. I have wanted to for so long. I simply adore your books. So does my son. And my husband used to insist on never traveling without at least two of your books. But come, do sit down. There are so many things I want to ask you about."

Oh, well, thought Mrs. Oliver, not my favorite type of woman, this. But as well her as any other.

She allowed herself to be conducted in a firm way, rather as a police officer might have done. She was taken to a settee for two across a corner, and her new friend accepted coffee and placed coffee before her also.

"There. Now we are settled. I don't suppose you know my name. I am Mrs. Burton-Cox."

"Oh yes," said Mrs. Oliver, embarrassed, as usual. Mrs. Burton-Cox? Did she write books also? No, she couldn't really remember anything about her. But she seemed to have heard the name. A faint thought came to her. A book on politics, something like that? Not fiction, not fun, not crime. Perhaps a high-crow intellectual with political bias? That ought to be easy, Mrs. Oliver thought with relief. I can just let her talk and say, "How interesting!" from time to time.

"You'll be very surprised, really, at what I'm going to say," said Mrs. Burton-Cox. "But I have felt, from reading your books, how sympathetic you are, how much you understand of human nature. And I feel that if there is anyone who can give me an answer to the question I want to ask, you will be the one to do so."

"I don't think, really . . ." said Mrs. Oliver, trying to think of suitable words to say that she felt very uncertain of being able to rise to the heights demanded of her.

Mrs. Burton-Cox dipped a lump of sugar in her coffee and crunched it in a rather carnivorous way, as though it was a bone. Ivory teeth, perhaps, thought Mrs. Oliver vaguely. Ivory? Dogs had ivory, walruses had ivory and elephants had ivory, of course. Great big tusks of ivory. Mrs. Burton-Cox was saying:

"Now the first thing I must ask you—I'm pretty sure that I am right, though—you have a goddaughter, haven't you? A daughter who's called Celia Ravenscroft?"

"Oh," said Mrs. Oliver, rather pleasurably surprised. She felt she could deal perhaps with a goddaughter. She had a good many goddaughters—and godsons, for that matter. There were times, she had to admit as the years were growing upon her, when she couldn't remember them all. She had done her duty in due course, one's duty being to send toys to your godchildren at Christmas in their early years, to visit them and their parents, or to have them visit you during the course of their upbringing, to take the boys out from school perhaps, and the girls also. And then, when the crowning days came, either the twenty-first birthday at which a godmother must do the right thing and let it be acknowledged to be done, and do it handsomely, or else marriage, which entailed the same type of gift and a financial or other blessing. After that godchildren rather receded into the middle or far distance. They married or went abroad to foreign countries, foreign embassies, or taught in foreign schools or took up social projects. Anyway, they faded little by little out of your life. You were pleased to see them if they suddenly, as it were, floated up on the horizon again. But you had to remember to think when you had seen them last, whose daughters they were, what link had led to your being chosen as a godmother.

"Celia Ravenscroft," said Mrs. Oliver, doing her best. "Yes, yes, of course. Yes, definitely."

Not that any picture rose before her eyes of Celia Ravenscroft, not, that is, since a very early time. The christening. She'd gone to Celia's christening and had found a very nice Queen Anne silver strainer as a christening present. Very nice. Do nicely for straining milk and would also be the sort of thing a goddaughter could always sell for a nice little sum if she wanted ready money at any time. Yes, she remembered the strainer very well indeed. Queen Anne—Seventeen-eleven it had been. Britannia mark. How much easier it was to remember silver coffeepots or strainers or christening mugs than it was the actual child.

"Yes," she said, "yes, of course. I'm afraid I haven't seen Celia for a very long time now."

"Ah, yes. She is, of course, a rather impulsive girl," said Mrs. Burton-Cox. "I mean, she's changed her ideas very often. Of course, very intellectual, did very well at university, but—her political notions—I suppose all young people have political notions nowadays."

"I'm afraid I don't deal much with politics," said Mrs. Oliver, to whom politics had always been anathema.

"You see, I'm going to confide in you. I'm going to tell you exactly what it is I want to know. I'm sure you won't mind. I've heard from so many people how kind you are, how willing always."

I wonder if she's going to try and borrow money from me, thought Mrs. Oliver, who had known many interviews that began with this kind of approach.

"You see, it is a matter of the greatest moment to me. Something that I really feel I *must* find out. Celia, you see, is going to marry—or thinks she is going to marry—my son, Desmond."

"Oh, indeed!" said Mrs. Oliver.

"At least, that is their idea at present. Of course, one has to know about people, and there's something I want very much to know. It's an extraordinary thing to ask anyone and I couldn't go—well, I mean, I couldn't very well go and ask a stranger, but I don't feel you are a stranger, dear Mrs. Oliver."

Mrs. Oliver thought, I wish you did. She was getting nervous now. She wondered if Celia had had an illegitimate baby or was going to have an illegitimate baby, and whether she, Mrs. Oliver, was supposed to know about it and give details. That would be very awkward. On the other hand, thought Mrs. Oliver, I haven't seen her now for five or six years and she must be about twenty-five or -six, so it would be quite easy to say I don't know anything.

Mrs. Burton-Cox leaned forward and breathed hard. "I want you to tell me, because I'm sure you must know or perhaps have a very good idea how it all came about. Did her mother kill her father or was it the father who killed the mother?"

Whatever Mrs. Oliver had expected, it was certainly not that. She stared at Mrs. Burton-Cox unbelievingly.

"But I don't—" She stopped. "I—I can't understand. I mean—what reason—"

"Dear Mrs. Oliver, you must *know* . . . I mean, such a famous case . . . Of course, I know it's a long time ago now, well, I suppose ten—twenty years at least, but it did cause a lot of attention at the time. I'm sure you'll remember, you *must* remember."

Mrs. Oliver's brain was working desperately. Celia was her goddaughter. That was quite true. Celia's mother—yes, of course, Celia's mother had been Molly Preston Grey, who had been a friend of hers, though not a particularly intimate one, and of course she had married a man in the Army, yes—what was his name?—Sir Something Ravenscroft. Or was he an ambassador? Extraordinary, one couldn't remember these things. She couldn't even remember whether she herself had been Molly's bridesmaid. She thought she had. Rather a smart wedding at the Guards Chapel or something like that. But one *did* forget so. And after that she hadn't met them for years—they'd been out somewhere—in the Middle East? In Persia? In Iraq? One time in Egypt? India? Very occasionally, when they had been visiting England, she met them again. But they'd been like one of those photographs that one takes and looks at. One knows the people vaguely who are in it, but it's so faded that you really can't recognize them or remember who they were. And she couldn't remember now whether Sir Something Ravenscroft and Lady Ravenscroft, born Molly Preston Grey, had entered much into her life. She didn't think so. But then . . . Mrs. Burton-Cox was still looking at her. Looking at her as though disappointed in her lack of *savoir-faire,* her inability to remember what had evidently been a *cause célèbre.*

"Killed? You mean—an accident?"

"Oh, no. Not an accident. In one of those houses by the sea. Cornwall, I think. Somewhere where there were rocks. Anyway, they had a house down there. And they were both found on the cliff there and they'd been shot, you know. But there was nothing really that the police could tell whether the wife shot the husband and then shot herself, or whether the husband shot the wife and then shot himself. They went into the evidence of the—you know—of the bullets and the various things, but it was very difficult. They thought it might be a suicide pact and—I forget what the verdict was. Something—it could have been misadventure or something like that. But of course everyone knew it must have been *meant,* and there were a lot of stories that went about, of course, at the time—"

"Probably all invented ones," said Mrs. Oliver hopefully, trying to remember even one of the stories if she could.

"Well, maybe. Maybe. It's very hard to say, I know. There were tales of a quarrel either that day or before, there was some talk of another man, and then of course there was the usual talk about some other woman. And one never knows which way it was about. I think things were hushed up a good deal because General Ravenscroft's position was rather a high one, and I think it was said that he'd been in a nursing home that year, and he'd been very rundown or something, and that he really didn't know what he was doing."

"I'm really afraid," said Mrs. Oliver, speaking firmly, "that I must say that I don't know anything about it. I do remember, now you mention it, that there was such a case, and I remember the names and that I knew the people, but I never knew what happened or anything at all about it. And I really don't think I have the least idea . . ."

And really, thought Mrs. Oliver, wishing she was brave enough to say it, how on earth *you* have the impertinence to ask me such a thing, I don't know.

"It's very important that I should know," Mrs. Burton-Cox said.

Her eyes, which were rather like hard marbles, started to snap.

"It's important, you see, because of my boy, my dear boy wanting to marry Celia."

"I'm afraid I can't help you," said Mrs. Oliver. "I've never heard anything."

"But you *must* know," said Mrs. Burton-Cox. "I mean, you write these wonderful stories, you know all about crime. You know who commits crimes and why they do it, and I'm sure that all sorts of people will tell you the story behind the story, as one so much thinks of these things."

"I don't know anything," said Mrs. Oliver in a voice which no longer held very much politeness, and definitely now spoke in tones of distaste.

"But you do see that really one doesn't know who to go to to ask about it? I mean, one couldn't go to the police after all these years, and I don't suppose they'd tell you anyway, because obviously they were trying to hush it up. But I feel it's important to get the *truth*."

"I only write books," said Mrs. Oliver coldly. "They are entirely fictional. I know nothing personally about crime and have no opinions on criminology. So I'm afraid I can't help you in *any* way."

"But you could ask your goddaughter. You could ask Celia."

"Ask Celia!" Mrs. Oliver stared again. "I don't see how I

could do *that*. She was—why, I think she must have been quite a child when this tragedy happened."

"Oh, I expect she knew all about it, though," said Mrs. Burton-Cox. "Children always know everything. And she'd tell you. I'm sure she'd tell *you*."

"You'd better ask her yourself, I should think," said Mrs. Oliver.

"I don't think I could really do that," said Mrs. Burton-Cox. "I don't think, you know, that Desmond would like it. You know he's rather—well, he's rather touchy where Celia is concerned, and I really don't think that—no—I'm sure she'd tell you."

"I really shouldn't dream of asking her," said Mrs. Oliver. She made a pretence of looking at her watch. "Oh, dear," she said, "what a long time we've been over this delightful lunch. I must run now. I have a very important appointment. Good-bye, Mrs.—er—Bedley-Cox, so sorry I can't help you, but these things are rather delicate and—does it really make any difference anyway, from your point of view?"

"Oh, I think it makes *all* the difference."

At that moment, a literary figure whom Mrs. Oliver knew well drifted past. Mrs. Oliver jumped up to catch her by the arm.

"Louise, my dear, how lovely to see you. I hadn't noticed you were here."

"Oh, Ariadne, it's a long time since I've seen *you*. You've grown a lot thinner, haven't you?"

"What nice things you always say to me," said Mrs. Oliver, engaging her friend by the arm and retreating from the settee. "I'm rushing away because I've got an appointment."

"I suppose you got tied up with that awful woman, didn't you?" said her friend, looking over her shoulder at Mrs. Burton-Cox.

"She was asking me the most extraordinary questions," said Mrs. Oliver.

"Oh. Didn't you know how to answer them?"

"No. They weren't any of my business anyway. I didn't know anything about them. Anyway, I wouldn't have wanted to answer them."

"Was it about anything interesting?"

"I suppose," said Mrs. Oliver, letting a new idea come into her head, "I suppose it might be interesting, only—"

"She's getting up to chase you," said her friend. "Come along. I'll see you get out and give you a lift to anywhere you want to go if you haven't got your car here."

"I never take my car about in London, it's so awful to park."

"I know it is. Absolutely deadly."

Mrs. Oliver made the proper good-byes. Thanks, words of greatly expressed pleasure, and presently was being driven round a London square.

"Eaton Terrace, isn't it?" said the kindly friend.

"Yes," said Mrs. Oliver, "but where I've got to go now is —I think it's Whitefriars Mansions. I can't quite remember the name of it, but I know where it is."

"Oh, flats. Rather modern ones. Very square and geometrical."

"That's right," said Mrs. Oliver.

2

FIRST MENTION OF ELEPHANTS

Having failed to find her friend Hercule Poirot at home, Mrs. Oliver had to resort to a telephone inquiry.

"Are you by any chance going to be at home this evening?" asked Mrs. Oliver.

She sat by her telephone, her fingers tapping rather nervously on the table.

"Would that be—?"

"Ariadne Oliver," said Mrs. Oliver, who was always surprised to find she had to give her name because she always expected all her friends to know her voice as soon as they heard it.

"Yes, I shall be at home all this evening. Does that mean that I may have the pleasure of a visit from you?"

"It's very nice of you to put it that way," said Mrs.

Oliver. "I don't know that it will be such a pleasure."

"It is always a pleasure to see you, *chère madame.*"

"I don't know," said Mrs. Oliver. "I might be going to —well, bother you rather. Ask things. I want to know what you think about something."

"That I am always ready to tell anyone," said Poirot.

"Something's come up," said Mrs. Oliver. "Something tiresome and I don't know what to do about it."

"And so you will come and see me. I am flattered. Highly flattered."

"What time would suit you?" said Mrs. Oliver.

"Nine o'clock? We will drink coffee together, perhaps, unless you prefer a grenadine or a *Sirop de Cassis.* But no, you do not like that. I remember."

"George," said Poirot to his invaluable manservant, "we are to receive tonight the pleasure of a visit from Mrs. Oliver. Coffee, I think, and perhaps a liqueur of some kind. I am never sure what she likes."

"I have seen her drink kirsch, sir."

"And also, I think, a *crème de menthe.* But kirsch, I think, is what she prefers. Very well then," said Poirot. "So be it."

Mrs. Oliver came punctual to time. Poirot had been wondering, while eating his dinner, what it was that was driving Mrs. Oliver to visit him, and why she was so doubtful about what she was doing. Was she bringing him some difficult problem, or was she acquainting him with a crime? As Poirot knew well, it could be anything with Mrs. Oliver.

The most commonplace things or the most extraordinary things. They were, as you might say, all alike to her. She was worried, he thought. Ah, well, Hercule Poirot thought to himself, he could deal with Mrs. Oliver. He always had been able to deal with Mrs. Oliver. On occasion she maddened him. At the same time he was really very much attached to her. They had shared many experiences and experiments together. He had read something about her in the paper only that morning—or was it the evening paper? He must try and remember it before she came. He had just done so when she was announced.

She came into the room and Poirot deduced at once that his diagnosis of worry was true enough. Her hair-do, which was fairly elaborate, had been ruffled by the fact that she had been running her fingers through it in the frenzied and feverish way that she did sometimes. He received her with every sign of pleasure, established her in a chair, poured her some coffee and handed her a glass of kirsch.

"Ah!" said Mrs. Oliver with the sigh of someone who has relief. "I expect you're going to think I'm awfully silly, but still . . ."

"I see, or rather, I saw in the paper that you were attending a literary luncheon today. Famous women writers. Something of that kind. I thought you never did that kind of thing."

"I don't usually," said Mrs. Oliver, "and I shan't ever do it again."

"Ah. You suffered much?" Poirot was quite sympathetic. He knew Mrs. Oliver's embarrassing moments. Extravagant praise of her books always upset her highly because, as she had once told him, she never knew the proper answers.

"You did not enjoy it?"

"Up to a point I did," said Mrs. Oliver, "and then something very tiresome happened."

"Ah. And that is what you have come to see me about."

"Yes, but I really don't know why. I mean, it's nothing to do with you and I don't think it's the sort of thing you'd even be interested in. And I'm not really interested in it. At least, I suppose I must be or I wouldn't have wanted to come to you to know what you thought. To know what—well, what you'd do if you were me."

"That is a very difficult question, that last one," said Poirot. "I know how I, Hercule Poirot, would act in anything, but I do not know how you would act, well though I know you."

"You must have some idea by this time," said Mrs. Oliver. "You've known me long enough."

"About what—twenty years now?"

"Oh, I don't know. I can never remember what years are, what dates are. You know, I get mixed up. I know nineteen thirty-nine because that's when the war started and I know other dates because of queer things, here and there."

"Anyway, you went to your literary luncheon. And you did not enjoy it very much."

"I enjoyed the lunch but it was afterwards . . ."

"People said things to you," said Poirot, with the kindliness of a doctor demanding symptoms.

"Well, they were just getting ready to say things to me.

Suddenly one of those large, bossy women who always manage to dominate everyone and who can make you feel more uncomfortable than anyone else, descended on me. You know, like somebody who catches a butterfly or something, only she'd have needed a butterfly net. She sort of rounded me up and pushed me on to a settee and then she began to talk to me, starting about a goddaughter of mine."

"Ah, yes. A goddaughter you are fond of?"

"I haven't seen her for a good many years," said Mrs. Oliver. "I can't keep up with all of them, I mean. And then she asked me a most worrying question. She wanted me—oh, dear, how very difficult it is for me to tell this—"

"No, it isn't," said Poirot kindly. "It is quite easy. Everyone tells everything to me sooner or later. I'm only a foreigner, you see, so it does not matter. It is easy because I am a foreigner."

"Well, it is rather easy to say things to you," said Mrs. Oliver. "You see, she asked me about the girl's father and mother. She asked me whether her mother had killed her father or her father had killed her mother."

"I beg your pardon," said Poirot.

"Oh, I know it sounds mad. Well, I thought it was mad."

"Whether your goddaughter's mother had killed her father, or whether her father had killed her mother."

"That's right," said Mrs. Oliver.

"But—was that a matter of fact? Had her father killed her mother or her mother killed her father?"

"Well, they were both found shot," said Mrs. Oliver. "On the top of a cliff. I can't remember if it was in Cornwall or in Corsica. Something like that."

"It was true, then, what she said?"

"Oh, yes, that part of it was true. It happened years ago. Well, but I mean—why come to me?"

"All because you were a crime writer," said Poirot. "She no doubt said you knew all about crime. This was a real thing that happened?"

"Oh, yes. It wasn't something like what would A do—or what would be the proper procedure if your mother had killed your father or your father had killed your mother. No, it was something that really happened. I suppose really I'd better tell you all about it. I mean, I can't remember all about it, but it was quite well known at the time. It was about—oh, I should think it was about twenty years ago at least. And, as I say, I can remember the names of the people because I did know them. The wife had been at school with me and I'd known her quite well. We'd been friends. It was a well-known case—you know, it was in all the papers and things like that. Sir Alistair Ravenscroft and Lady Ravenscroft. A very happy couple and he was a colonel or a general and she'd been with him and they'd been all over the world. Then they bought this house somewhere—I think it was abroad but I can't remember. And then there were suddenly accounts of this case in the papers. Whether somebody else had killed them or whether they'd been assassinated or something, or whether they killed each other. I think it was a revolver that had been in the house for ages and—well, I'd better tell you as much as I can remember."

Pulling herself slightly together, Mrs. Oliver managed to

give Poirot a more or less clear résumé of what she had been told. Poirot from time to time checked on a point here or there.

"But why," he said finally, "why should this woman want to know this?"

"Well, that's what I want to find out," said Mrs. Oliver. "I could get hold of Celia, I think. I mean, she still lives in London. Or perhaps it's Cambridge she lives in, or Oxford. I think she's got a degree and either lectures here or teaches somewhere, or does something like that. And—very modern, you know. Goes about with long-haired people in queer clothes. I don't think she takes drugs. She's quite all right and—just very occasionally I hear from her. I mean, she sends a card at Christmas and things like that. Well, one doesn't think of one's godchildren all the time, and she's quite twenty-five or -six."

"Not married?"

"No. Apparently she is going to marry—or that is the idea—Mrs.—what's the name of that woman again?—oh, yes, Mrs. Brittle—no—Burton-Cox's son."

"And Mrs. Burton-Cox does not want her son to marry this girl because her father killed her mother or her mother killed her father?"

"Well, I suppose so," said Mrs. Oliver. "It's the only thing I can think. But what does it matter which? If one of your parents killed the other, would it really matter to the mother of the boy you were going to marry which way round it was?"

"That is a thing one might have to think about," said

Poirot. "It is—yes, you know it is quite interesting. I do not mean it is very interesting about Sir Alistair Ravenscroft or Lady Ravenscroft. I seem to remember vaguely —oh, some case like this one, or it might not have been the same one. But it is very strange about Mrs. Burton-Cox. Perhaps she is a bit touched in the head. Is she very fond of her son?"

"Probably," said Mrs. Oliver. "Probably she doesn't want him to marry this girl at all."

"Because she may have inherited a predisposition to murder the man she marries—or something of that kind?"

"How do I know?" said Mrs. Oliver. "She seems to think that I can tell her, and she's really not told *me* enough, has she? But why, do you think? What's behind it all? What does it mean?"

"It would be almost interesting to find out," said Poirot.

"Well, that's why I've come to you," said Mrs. Oliver. "You like finding out things. Things that you can't see the reason for at first. I mean, that nobody can see the reason for."

"Do you think Mrs. Burton-Cox has any preference?" said Poirot.

"You mean that she'd rather the husband killed the wife, or the wife killed the husband? I don't think so."

"Well," said Poirot, "I see your dilemma. It is very intriguing. You come home from a party. You've been asked to do something that is very difficult, almost impossible, and—you wonder what is the proper way to deal with such a thing."

"Well, what would you think is the proper way?" said Mrs. Oliver.

"It is not easy for me to say," said Poirot. "I'm not a woman. A woman whom you do not really know, whom you had met at a party, has put this problem to you, asked you to do it, giving no discernible reason."

"Right," said Mrs. Oliver. "Now what does Ariadne do? What does A do, in other words, if you were reading this as a problem in a newspaper?"

"Well, I suppose," said Poirot, "there are three things that A could do. A could write a note to Mrs. Burton-Cox and say, 'I'm very sorry, but I really feel I cannot oblige you in this matter,' or whatever words you like to put. B. You get in touch with your goddaughter and you tell her what has been asked of you by the mother of the boy, or the young man, or whatever he is, whom she is thinking of marrying. You will find out from her if she is really thinking of marrying this young man. If so, whether she has any idea or whether the young man has said anything to her about what his mother has got in her head. And there will be other interesting points, like finding out what this girl thinks of the mother of the young man she wants to marry. The third thing you could do," said Poirot, "and this really is what I firmly advise you to do, is . . ."

"I know," said Mrs. Oliver, "one word."

"Nothing," said Poirot.

"Exactly," said Mrs. Oliver. "I know that is the simple and proper thing to do. Nothing. It's darned cheek to go and tell a girl who's my goddaughter what her future mother-in-law is going about saying and asking people. But—"

"I know," said Poirot, "it is human curiosity."

"I want to know why that odious woman came and said what she did to me," said Mrs. Oliver. "Once I knew that I could relax and forget all about it. But until I know that . . ."

"Yes," said Poirot, "you won't sleep. You'll wake up in the night and, if I know you, you will have the most extraordinary and extravagant ideas which presently, probably, you will be able to make into a most attractive crime story. A whodunit—a thriller. All sorts of things."

"Well, I suppose I could if I thought of it that way," said Mrs. Oliver. Her eyes flashed slightly.

"Leave it alone," said Poirot. "It will be a very difficult plot to undertake. It seems as though there could be no good reason for this."

"But I'd like to make *sure* that there *is* no good reason."

"Human curiosity," said Poirot. "Such a very interesting thing." He sighed. "To think what we owe to it throughout history. Curiosity. I don't know who invented curiosity. It is said to be usually associated with the cat. Curiosity killed the cat. But I should say really that the Greeks were the inventors of curiosity. They wanted to *know*. Before them, as far as I can see, nobody wanted to know *much*. They just wanted to know what the rules of the country they were living in were, and how they could avoid having their heads cut off or being impaled on spikes or something disagreeable happening to them. But they either obeyed or disobeyed. They didn't want to know *why*. But since then a lot of people have wanted to know *why* and all sorts of things have happened because of that. Boats, trains, flying machines and atom bombs and penicillin and cures for various illnesses. A little boy watches his mother's kettle raising its lid because of the steam. And the next thing we know is we have railway trains, leading on in due course to railway strikes and all that. And so on and so on."

"Just tell me," said Mrs. Oliver, "do you think I'm a terrible nosey-parker?"

"No, I don't," said Poirot. "On the whole I don't think you are a woman of great curiosity. But I can quite see you getting in a het-up state at a literary party, busy defending yourself against too much kindness, too much praise. You ran yourself instead into a very awkward dilemma, and took a very strong dislike to the person who ran you into it."

"Yes. She's a very tiresome woman, a very disagreeable woman."

"This murder in the past of this husband and wife who were supposed to get on well together and no apparent sign of a quarrel was known. One never really read about any cause for it, according to you?"

"They were shot. Yes, they were shot. It could have been a suicide pact. I think the police thought it was at first. Of course, one can't find out about things all those years afterwards."

"Oh, yes," said Poirot, "I think I could find out something about it."

"You mean—through the exciting friends you've got?"

"Well, I wouldn't say the exciting friends, perhaps. Certainly there are knowledgeable friends, friends who could get certain records, look up the accounts that were given of the crime at the time, some access I could get to certain records."

"You could find out things," said Mrs. Oliver hopefully, "and then tell me."

"Yes," said Poirot, "I think I could help you to know at any rate the full facts of the case. It'll take a little time, though."

"I can see that if you do that, which is what I want you to do, *I've* got to do something myself. I'll have to see the girl. I've got to see whether she knows anything about all this, ask her if she'd like me to give her mother-in-law-to-be a raspberry or whether there is any other way in which I can help her. And I'd like to see the boy she's going to marry, too."

"Quite right," said Poirot. "Excellent."

"And I suppose," said Mrs. Oliver, "there might be people—" She broke off, frowning.

"I don't suppose people will be very much good," said Hercule Poirot. "This is an affair of the past. A *cause célèbre,* perhaps at the time. But what is a *cause célèbre* when you come to think of it? Unless it comes to an astonishing dénouement, which this one didn't. Nobody remembers it."

"No," said Mrs. Oliver, "that is quite true. There was a lot about it in the papers and mentions of it for some time, and then it just—faded out. Well, like things do now. Like that girl, the other day. You know, who left her home and they couldn't find her anywhere. Well, I mean, that was five or six years ago and then suddenly a little boy, playing about in a sand heap or a gravel pit or something, suddenly came across her dead body. Five or six years later."

"That is true," said Poirot. "And it is true that knowing from that body how long it is since death and what happened on the particular day and going back over various events of which there is a written record, one may in the end turn up a murderer. But it will be more difficult in your problem since it seems the answer must be one of two things: that the husband disliked his wife and wanted to get rid of her, or that the wife hated her husband or else had a lover. Therefore, it might have been a passionate crime or something quite different. Anyway, there would be nothing, as it were, to find out about it. If the police could not find out at the time, then the motive must have been a difficult one, not easy to see. Therefore it has remained a nine days' wonder, that is all."

"I suppose I can go to the daughter. Perhaps that is what that odious woman was getting me to do—wanted me to do. She thought the daughter knew—well, the daughter might have known," said Mrs. Oliver. "Children do, you know. They know the most extraordinary things."

"Have you any idea how old this goddaughter of yours would have been at the time?"

"Well, I have if I reckon it up, but I can't say offhand. I think she might have been nine or ten, but perhaps older, I don't know. I think that she was away at school at the time.

But that may be just my fancy, remembering back what I read."

"But you think Mrs. Burton-Cox's wish was to make you get information from the daughter? Perhaps the daughter knows something, perhaps she said something to the son, and the son said something to his mother. I expect Mrs. Burton-Cox tried to question the girl herself and got rebuffed, but thought the famous Mrs. Oliver, being both a godmother and also full of criminal knowledge, might obtain information. Though why it should matter to her, I still don't see," said Poirot. "And it does not seem to me that what you call vaguely 'people' can help after all this time." He added, "Would anybody remember?"

"Well, that's where I think they might," said Mrs. Oliver.

"You surprise me," said Poirot, looking at her with a somewhat puzzled face. "*Do* people remember?"

"Well," said Mrs. Oliver, "I was really thinking of elephants."

"Elephants?"

As he had thought often before, Poirot thought that really Mrs. Oliver was the most unaccountable woman. Why suddenly elephants?

"I was thinking of elephants at the lunch yesterday," said Mrs. Oliver.

"Why were you thinking of elephants?" said Poirot with some curiosity.

"Well, I was really thinking of teeth. You know, things one tries to eat, and if you've got some sort of false teeth —well, you can't do it very well. You know, you've got to know what you can eat and what you can't."

"Ah!" said Poirot with a deep sigh. "Yes, yes. The dentists, they can do much for you, but not everything."

"Quite so. And then I thought of—you know—our teeth being only bone and so not awfully good, and how nice it would be to be a dog, who has really ivory teeth. And then I thought of anyone else who has ivory teeth, and I thought about walruses and—oh, other things like that. And I thought about elephants. Of course when you think of ivory, you do think of elephants, don't you? Great big elephant tusks."

"That is very true," said Poirot, still not seeing the point of what Mrs. Oliver was saying.

"So I thought that what we've really got to do is to get at the people who are like elephants. Because elephants, so they say, don't forget."

"I have heard the phrase, yes," said Poirot.

"Elephants don't forget," said Mrs. Oliver. "You know, a story children get brought up on? How someone, an Indian tailor, stuck a needle or something in an elephant's tusk. No. Not a tusk, his trunk, of course, an elephant's trunk. And the next time the elephant came past he had a great mouthful of water and he splashed it out all over the tailor, though he hadn't seen him for several years. He hadn't forgotten. He remembered. That's the point, you see. Elephants remember. What I've got to do is—I've got to get in touch with some elephants."

"I do not know yet if I quite see what you mean," said Hercule Poirot. "Who are you classifying as elephants? You sound as though you were going for information to the zoo."

"Well, it's not exactly like that," said Mrs. Oliver. "Not elephants, as elephants, but the way people up to a point would resemble elephants. There are some people who *do* remember. In fact, one does remember queer things. I mean, there are a lot of things that *I* remember very well. They happened—I remember a birthday party I had when I was five, and a pink cake—a lovely pink cake. It had a sugar bird on it. And I remember the day my canary flew away and I cried. And I remember another day when I went into a field and there was a bull there and somebody said it would gore me, and I was terrified and wanted to run out of the field. Well, I remember that quite well. It was a Tuesday, too. I don't know why I should remember it was a Tuesday, but it was a Tuesday. And I remember a wonderful picnic with blackberries. I remember getting pricked terribly, but getting more blackberries than anyone else. It was wonderful! By that time I was nine, I think. But one needn't go back as far as that. I mean, I've been to hundreds of weddings in my life, but when I look back on a wedding there are only two that I remember *particularly*. One where I was a bridesmaid. It took place in the New Forest, I remember, and I can't remember who was there actually. I think it was a cousin of mine getting married. I didn't know her very well, but she wanted a good many bridesmaids and, well, I came in handy, I suppose. But I know another wedding. That was a friend of mine in the Navy. He was nearly drowned in a submarine, and then he was saved again, and then the girl he was engaged to, her people didn't want her to marry him, but then he did marry her after that and I was one of her bridesmaids at the marriage. Well, I mean, there's always things you *do* remember."

"I see your point," said Poirot. "I find it interesting. So you will go *à la recherche des éléphants?*"

"That's right. I'd have to get the date right."

"There," said Poirot, "I hope I may be able to help you."

"And then I'll think of people I knew about at that time, people that I may have known who also knew the same friends that I did, who probably knew General What-not. People who may have known them abroad, but whom I also knew although I mayn't have seen them for a good many years. You can look up people, you know, that you haven't seen for a long time. Because people are always quite pleased to see someone coming up out of the past, even if they can't remember very much about you. And then you naturally will talk about the things that were happening at that date, that you remember about."

"Very interesting," said Poirot. "I think you are very well equipped for what you propose to do. People who knew the Ravenscrofts either well or not very well; people who lived in the same part of the world where the thing happened or who might have been staying there. More difficult, but I think one could get at it. And so, somehow or other one would try different things. Start a little talk going about what happened, what they think happened, what anyone else has ever told you about what might have happened. About any love affairs the husband or wife had, about any money that somebody might have inherited. I think you could scratch up a lot of things."

"Oh, dear," said Mrs. Oliver, "I'm afraid really I'm just a nosey-parker."

"You've been given an assignment," said Poirot, "not by someone you like, not by someone you wish to oblige, but someone you entirely dislike. That does not matter. You are still on a quest—a quest of knowledge. You take your own path. It is the path of the elephants. The elephants *may* remember. *Bon voyage,"* said Poirot.

"I beg your pardon," said Mrs. Oliver.

"I'm sending you forth on your voyage of discovery," said Poirot. " *A la recherche des éléphants."*

"I expect I'm mad," said Mrs. Oliver sadly. She brushed her hands through her hair again so that she looked like the old picture books of Struwelpeter. "I was just thinking of starting a story about a golden retriever. But it wasn't going well. I couldn't get started, if you know what I mean."

"All right, abandon the golden retriever. Concern yourself only with elephants."

Book I

ELEPHANTS

3

GREAT-AUNT ALICE'S GUIDE TO KNOWLEDGE

"Can you find my address book for me, Miss Livingstone?"

"It's on your desk, Mrs. Oliver. In the left-hand corner."

"I don't mean that one," said Mrs. Oliver. "That's the one I'm using now. I mean my last one. The one I had last year, or perhaps the one before that again."

"Has it been thrown away, perhaps?" suggested Miss Livingstone.

"No, I don't throw away address books and things like that because so often you want one. I mean some address that you haven't copied into the new one. I expect it may be in one of the drawers of the tallboys."

Miss Livingstone was a fairly new arrival, replacing Miss

Sedgwick. Ariadne Oliver missed Miss Sedgwick. Sedgwick knew so many things. She knew the places where Mrs. Oliver sometimes put things, the kind of places Mrs. Oliver kept things in. She remembered the names of people Mrs. Oliver had written nice letters to, and the names of people that Mrs. Oliver, goaded beyond endurance, had written rather rude things to. She was invaluable, or rather, had been invaluable. "She was like—what was the book called?" Mrs. Oliver said, casting her mind back. "Oh, yes, I know—a big brown book. All Victorians had it. *Enquire Within upon Everything*. And you could, too! How to take iron mark stains off linen, how to deal with curdled mayonnaise, how to start a chatty letter to a bishop. Many, many things. It was all there in *Enquire Within upon Everything*." Great-aunt Alice's great stand-by.

Miss Sedgwick had been just as good as Aunt Alice's book. Miss Livingstone was not at all the same thing. Miss Livingstone stood there always, very long-faced, with a sallow skin, looking purposefully efficient. Every line of her face said, "I am very efficient." But she wasn't really, Mrs. Oliver thought. She only knew all the places where former literary employers of hers had kept things and where she clearly considered Mrs. Oliver ought to keep them.

"What I want," said Mrs. Oliver with firmness and the determination of a spoiled child, "is my nineteen seventy address book. And I think nineteen sixty-nine as well. Please look for it as quick as you can, will you?"

"Of course, of course," said Miss Livingstone.

She looked around her with the rather vacant expression of someone who is looking for something she has never heard of before but which efficiency may be able to produce by some unexpected turn of luck.

If I don't get Sedgwick back, I shall go mad, thought Mrs. Oliver to herself. I can't deal with this thing if I don't have Sedgwick.

Miss Livingstone started pulling open various drawers in the furniture in Mrs. Oliver's so-called study and writing room.

"Here is last year's," said Miss Livingstone happily. "That will be much more up-to-date, won't it? Nineteen seventy-one."

"I don't want nineteen seventy-one," said Mrs. Oliver.

Vague thoughts and memories came to her.

"Look in that tea caddy table," she said.

Miss Livingstone looked round, looking worried.

"That table," said Mrs. Oliver, pointing.

"A desk book wouldn't be likely to be in a tea caddy," said Miss Livingstone, pointing out to her employer the general facts of life.

"Yes, it could," said Mrs. Oliver. "I seem to remember."

Edging Miss Livingstone aside, she went to the tea caddy table, raised the lid, looked at the attractive inlaid work inside. "And it *is* here," said Mrs. Oliver, raising the lid of a papier-mâché round canister, devised to contain Lapsang Souchong as opposed to Indian tea, and taking out a curled-up, small brown notebook.

"Here it is," she said.

"That's only nineteen sixty-eight, Mrs. Oliver. Four years ago."

"That's about right," said Mrs. Oliver, seizing it and taking it back to the desk. "That's all for the present, Miss Livingstone, but you might see if you can find my birthday book somewhere."

"I didn't know . . ."

"I don't use it now," said Mrs. Oliver, "but I used to have one once. Quite a big one, you know. Started when I was a child. Goes on for years. I expect it'll be in the attic upstairs. You know, the one we use as a spare room sometimes when it's only boys coming for holidays, or people who don't mind. The sort of chest or bureau thing next to the bed."

"Oh. Shall I look and see?"

"That's the idea," said Mrs. Oliver.

She cheered up a little as Miss Livingstone went out of the room. Mrs. Oliver shut the door firmly behind her, went back to the desk and started looking down the addresses written in faded ink and smelling of tea.

"Ravenscroft. Celia Ravenscroft. Yes. Fourteen Fishacre Mews, S.W.Three. That's the Chelsea address. She was living there then. But there was another one after that. Somewhere like Strand-on-the-Green near Kew Bridge."

She turned a few more pages.

"Oh, yes, this seems to be a later one. Mardyke Grove. That's off Fulham Road, I think. Somewhere like that. Has she got a telephone number? It's very rubbed out, but I think—yes, I think that's right—Flaxman . . . Anyway, I'll try it."

She went across to the telephone. The door opened and Miss Livingstone looked in.

"Do you think that perhaps—"

"I found the address I want," said Mrs. Oliver. "Go on looking for that birthday book. It's important."

"Do you think you could have left it when you were in Sealy House?"

"No, I don't," said Mrs. Oliver. "Go on looking."

She murmured, as the door closed, "Be as long as you like about it."

She dialed the telephone and waited, opening the door to call up the stairs: "You might try that Spanish chest. You know, the one that's bound with brass. I've forgotten where it is now. Under the table in the hall, I think."

Mrs. Oliver's first dialing was not successful. She appeared to have connected herself to a Mrs. Smith Potter, who seemed both annoyed and unhelpful and had no idea what the present telephone number might be of anyone who had lived in that particular flat before.

Mrs. Oliver applied herself to an examination of the address book once more. She discovered two more addresses which were hastily scrawled over other numbers and did not seem wildly helpful. However, at the third attempt a somewhat illegible Ravenscroft seemed to emerge from the crossings-out and initials and addresses.

A voice admitted to knowing Celia.

"Oh, dear, yes. But she hasn't lived here for *years*. I think she was in Newcastle when I last heard from her."

"Oh, dear," said Mrs. Oliver, "I'm afraid I haven't got that address."

"No, I haven't got it either," said the kindly girl. "I think she went to be secretary to a veterinary surgeon."

It did not sound very hopeful. Mrs. Oliver tried once or twice more. The addresses in the latest of her two address books were no use, so she went back a bit further. She struck oil, as you might put it, when she came to the last one, which was for the year 1962.

"Oh, you mean Celia," said a voice. "Celia Ravenscroft, wasn't it? Or was it Finchwell?"

Mrs. Oliver just prevented herself in time from saying, "No, and it wasn't redbreast either."

"A very competent girl," said the voice. "She worked for me for over a year and a half. Oh, yes, very competent. I would have been quite happy if she had stayed longer. I think she went from here to somewhere in Harley Street, but I think I've got her address somewhere. Now let me see." There was a long pause while Mrs. X—name unknown—was seeing. "I've got one address here. It seems to be in Islington somewhere. Do you think that's possible?"

Mrs. Oliver said that anything was possible and thanked Mrs. X very much and wrote it down.

"So difficult, isn't it, trying to find people's addresses. They do send them to you usually. You know, a sort of postcard or something of that kind. Personally I always seem to lose it."

Mrs. Oliver said that she herself also suffered in this respect. She tried the Islington number. A heavy, foreign voice replied to her.

"You want, yes—you tell me what? Yes, who live here?"

"Miss Celia Ravenscroft?"

"Oh, yes, that is very true. Yes, yes, she lives here. She has a room on the second floor. She is out now and she not come home."

"Will she be in later this evening?"

"Oh, she be home very soon now, I think, because she come home to dress for party and go out."

Mrs. Oliver thanked her for the information and rang off.

"Really," said Mrs. Oliver to herself with some annoyance, "girls!"

She tried to think how long it was since she had last seen her goddaughter, Celia. One lost touch. That was the whole point. Celia, she thought, was in London now. If her boy friend was in London, or if the mother of her boy friend was in London—all of it went together. Oh, dear, thought Mrs. Oliver, this really makes my head ache. "Yes, Miss Livingstone?" She turned her head.

Miss Livingstone, looking rather unlike herself and decorated with a good many cobwebs and a general coating of dust, stood looking annoyed in the doorway holding a pile of dusty volumes.

"I don't know whether any of these things will be any use to you, Mrs. Oliver. They seem to go back for a great many years." She was disapproving.

"Bound to," said Mrs. Oliver.

"I don't know if there's anything particular you want me to search for."

"I don't think so," said Mrs. Oliver, "if you'll just put them on the corner of the sofa there I can look at them this evening."

Miss Livingstone, looking more disapproving every moment, said, "Very good, Mrs. Oliver. I think I will just dust them first."

"That will be very kind of you," said Mrs. Oliver, just stopping herself in time from saying—"and for goodness' sake, dust yourself as well. You've got six cobwebs in your left ear."

She glanced at her watch and rang the Islington number again. The voice that answered this time was purely Anglo-Saxon and had a crisp sharpness about it that Mrs. Oliver felt was rather satisfactory.

"Miss Ravenscroft?—Celia Ravenscroft?"

"Yes, this is Celia Ravenscroft."

"Well, I don't expect you'll remember me very well. I'm Mrs. Oliver. Ariadne Oliver. We haven't seen each other for a long time, but actually I'm your godmother."

"Oh, yes, of course. I know that. No, we haven't seen each other for a long time."

"I wonder very much if I could see you, if you could come and see me, or whatever you like. Would you like to come to a meal or . . ."

"Well, it's rather difficult at present, where I'm working. I could come round this evening, if you like. About half-past seven or eight. I've got a date later but . . ."

"If you do that, I shall be very, very pleased," said Mrs. Oliver.

"Well, of course I will."

"I'll give you the address." Mrs. Oliver gave it.

"Good. I'll be there. Yes, I know where that is quite well."

Mrs. Oliver made a brief note on the telephone pad and looked with some annoyance at Miss Livingstone, who had just come into the room struggling under the weight of a large album.

"I wonder if this could possibly be it, Mrs. Oliver?"

"No, it couldn't," said Mrs. Oliver. "That's got cookery recipes in it."

"Oh, dear," said Miss Livingstone, "so it has."

"Well, I might as well look at some of them anyway," said Mrs. Oliver, removing the volume firmly. "Go and have another look. You know, I've thought about the linen cupboard. Next door to the bathroom. You'd have to look on the top shelf above the bath towels. I do sometimes stick papers and books in there. Wait a minute. I'll come up and look myself."

Ten minutes later Mrs. Oliver was looking through the pages of a faded album. Miss Livingstone, having entered her final stage of martyrdom, was standing by the door. Unable to bear the sight of so much suffering, Mrs. Oliver said:

"Well, that's all right. You might just take a look in the desk in the dining room. The old desk. You know, the one that's broken a bit. See if you can find some more address books. Early ones. Anything up to about ten years old will be worth while having a look at. And after that," said Mrs. Oliver, "I don't think I shall want anything more today."

Miss Livingstone departed.

"I wonder," said Mrs. Oliver to herself, releasing a deep sigh as she sat down. She looked through the pages of the birthday book. "Who's better pleased? She to go or I to see her go? After Celia has come and gone, I shall have to have a busy evening."

Taking a new exercise book from the pile she kept on a small table by her desk, she entered various dates, possible addresses and names, looked up one or two more things in the telephone book and then proceeded to ring up Monsieur Hercule Poirot.

"Ah, is that you, Monsieur Poirot?"

"Yes, madame, it is I myself."

"Have you done anything?" said Mrs. Oliver.

"I beg your pardon—have I done what?"

"Anything," said Mrs. Oliver. "What I asked you about yesterday."

"Yes, certainly. I have put things in motion. I have arranged to make certain inquiries."

"But you haven't made them yet," said Mrs. Oliver, who had a poor view of what the male view was of doing something.

"And you, *chère madame?"*

"I have been very busy," said Mrs. Oliver.

"Ah! And what have you been doing, madame?"

"Assembling elephants," said Mrs. Oliver, "if that means anything to you."

"I think I can understand what you mean, yes."

"It's not very easy, looking into the past," said Mrs. Oliver. "It is astonishing, really, how many people one does remember when one comes to look up names. My word, the silly things they write in birthday books sometimes, too. I can't think why when I was about sixteen or seventeen or even thirty, I wanted people to write in my birthday book. There's a sort of quotation from a poet for every particular day in the year. Some of them are terribly silly."

"You are encouraged in your search?"

"Not quite encouraged," said Mrs. Oliver. "But I still think I'm on the right lines. I've rung up my goddaughter—"

"Ah. And you are going to see her?"

"Yes, she is coming to see me. Tonight between seven and eight, if she doesn't run out on me. One never knows. Young people are very unreliable."

"She appeared pleased that you had rung her up?"

"I don't know," said Mrs. Oliver, "not particularly pleased. She's got a very incisive voice and—I remember now, the last time I saw her, that must be about ten years ago, I thought then that she was rather frightening."

"Frightening? In what way?"

"What I mean is that she was more likely to bully me than I would be to bully her."

"That may be a good thing and not a bad thing."

"Oh, do you think so?"

"If people have made up their minds that they do not wish to like you, that they are quite sure they do not like you, they will get more pleasure out of making you aware of the fact and in that way will release more information to you than they would have done if they were trying to be amiable and agreeable."

"Sucking up to me, you mean? Yes, you have something there. You mean then they tell you things that they thought would please you. And the other way they'd be annoyed with you and they'd say things that they'd hope would annoy you. I wonder if Celia's like that? I really remember her much better when she was five years old than at any other age. She had a nursery governess and she used to throw her boots at her."

"The governess at the child, or the child at the governess?"

"The child at the governess, of course!" said Mrs. Oliver.

She replaced the receiver and went over to the sofa to examine the various piled-up memories of the past. She murmured names under her breath.

"Mariana Josephine Pontarlier—of course, yes, I haven't thought of her for years—I thought she was dead. Anna Braceby—yes, yes, she lived in that part of the world—I wonder now—"

Continuing all this, time passed—she was quite surprised when the bell rang. She went out herself to open the door.

4

CELIA

A tall girl was standing on the mat outside. Just for a moment Mrs. Oliver was startled, looking at her. So this was Celia. The impression of vitality and of life was really very strong. Mrs. Oliver had the feeling which one does not often get.

Here, she thought, was someone who *meant* something. Aggressive, perhaps, could be difficult, could be almost dangerous perhaps. One of those girls who had a mission in life, who was dedicated to violence, perhaps, who went in for causes. But interesting. Definitely interesting.

"Come in, Celia," she said. "It's such a long time since I saw you. The last time, as far as I remember, was at a wedding. You were a bridesmaid. You wore apricot chiffon, I remember, and large bunches of—I can't remember what it was, something that looked like goldenrod."

"Probably *was* goldenrod," said Celia Ravenscroft. "We sneezed a lot—with hay fever. It was a terrible wedding. I know. Martha Leghorn, wasn't it? Ugliest bridesmaids' dresses I've ever seen. Certainly the ugliest I've ever worn!"

"Yes. They weren't very becoming to anybody. You looked better than most, if I may say so."

"Well, it's nice of you to say that," said Celia. "I didn't feel my best."

Mrs. Oliver indicated a chair and manipulated a couple of decanters.

"Like sherry or something else?"

"No. I'd like sherry."

"There you are, then. I suppose it seems rather odd to you," said Mrs. Oliver. "My ringing you up suddenly like this."

"Oh, no, I don't know that it does particularly."

"I'm not a very conscientious godmother, I'm afraid."

"Why should you be, at my age?"

"You're right there," said Mrs. Oliver. "One's duties, one feels, end at a certain time. Not that I ever really fulfilled mine. I don't remember coming to your confirmation."

"I believe the duty of a godmother is to make you learn your catechism and a few things like that, isn't it? Renounce the devil and all his works in my name," said Celia. A faint, humorous smile came to her lips.

She was being very amiable but all the same, thought Mrs. Oliver, she's rather a dangerous girl in some ways.

"Well, I'll tell you why I've been trying to get hold of

you," said Mrs. Oliver. "The whole thing is rather peculiar. I don't often go out to literary parties, but as it happened I did go out to one the day before yesterday."

"Yes, I know," said Celia. "I saw mention of it in the paper, and you had your name in it, too, Mrs. Ariadne Oliver, and I rather wondered because I know you don't usually go to those sort of things."

"No," said Mrs. Oliver. "I rather wish I hadn't gone to that one."

"Didn't you enjoy it?"

"Yes, I did in a way because I hadn't been to one before. And so—well, the first time there's always something that amuses you. But," she added, "there's usually something that annoys you as well."

"And something happened to annoy you?"

"Yes. And it's connected in an odd sort of way with you. And I thought—well, I thought I ought to tell you about it because I didn't like what happened. I didn't like it at all."

"Sounds intriguing," said Celia, and sipped her sherry.

"There was a woman there who came and spoke to me. I didn't know her and she didn't know me."

"Still, I suppose that often happens to you," said Celia.

"Yes, invariably," said Mrs. Oliver. "It's one of the—hazards of literary life. People come up to you and say, 'I do love your books so much and I'm so pleased to be able to meet you.' That sort of thing."

"I was secretary to a writer once. I do know about that sort of thing and how difficult it is."

"Yes, well, there was some of that too, but that I was

prepared for. And then this woman came up to me and she said, 'I believe you have a goddaughter called Celia Ravenscroft.' "

"Well, that was a bit odd," said Celia. "Just coming up to you and saying that. It seems to me she ought to have led into it more gradually. You know, talking about your books first and how much she'd enjoyed the last one, or something like that. And then sliding into me. What had she got against me?"

"As far as I know she hadn't got anything against you," said Mrs. Oliver.

"Was she a friend of mine?"

"I don't know," said Mrs. Oliver.

There was a silence. Celia sipped some more sherry and looked very searchingly at Mrs. Oliver.

"You know," she said, "you're rather intriguing me. I can't see quite what you're leading into."

"Well," said Mrs. Oliver, "I hope you won't be angry with me."

"Why should I be angry with you?"

"Well, because I'm going to tell you something, or repeat something, and you might say it's no business of mine or I ought to keep quiet about it and not mention it."

"You've aroused my curiosity," said Celia.

"Her name she mentioned to me. She was a Mrs. Burton-Cox."

"Oh!" Celia's "Oh" was rather distinctive. "Oh."

"You know her?"

"Yes, I know her," said Celia.

"Well, I thought you must, because—"

"Because of what?"

"Because of something she said."

"What—about me? That she knew me?"

"She said that she thought her son might be going to marry you."

Celia's expression changed. Her eyebrows went up, came down again. She looked very hard at Mrs. Oliver.

"You want to know if that's so or not?"

"No," said Mrs. Oliver, "I don't particularly want to know. I merely mention that because it's one of the first things she said to me. She said because you were my goddaughter, I might be able to ask you to give me some information. I presume that she meant that if the information was given to me I was to pass it on to her."

"What information?"

"Well, I don't suppose you'll like what I'm going to say now," said Mrs. Oliver. "I didn't like it myself. In fact, it gives me a very nasty feeling all down my spine because I think it was—well, such awful cheek. Awful bad manners. Absolutely unpardonable. She said, 'Can you find out if her father murdered her mother or if her mother murdered her father?' "

"She said that to you? Asked you to do *that?*"

"Yes."

"And she didn't know you? I mean, apart from being an authoress and being at the party?"

"She didn't know me at all. She'd never met me, I'd never met her."

"Didn't you find that extraordinary?"

"I don't know that I'd find anything extraordinary that that woman said. She struck me," said Mrs. Oliver, "if I may say so, as a particularly odious woman."

"Oh, yes. She is a particularly odious woman."

"And are you going to marry her son?"

"Well, we've considered the question. I don't know. You knew what she was talking about?"

"Well, I know what I suppose anyone would know who was acquainted with your family."

"That my father and mother, after he had retired from India, bought a house in the country, that they went out one day for a walk together, a walk along the cliff path. That they were found there, both of them shot. There was a revolver lying there. It belonged to my father. He had had two revolvers in the house, it seems. There was nothing to say whether it was a suicide pact or whether my father killed my mother and then shot himself, or my mother shot my father and then killed herself. But perhaps you know all this already."

"I know it after a fashion," said Mrs. Oliver. "It happened I think about twelve—fifteen years ago."

"About that, yes."

"And you were about twelve or fourteen at the time."

"Yes . . ."

"I don't know much about it," said Mrs. Oliver. "I wasn't even in England myself. At the time—I was on a lecture tour in America. I simply read it in the paper. It was given a lot of space in the press because it was difficult to know the real facts—there did not seem to be any motive. Your father and mother had always been happy together and lived on good terms. I remember that being mentioned. I was interested because I had known your father and mother when we were all much younger, especially your mother. I was at school with her. After that our ways led apart. I married and went somewhere and she married and went out, as far as I remember, to India or some place like that, with her soldier husband. But she did ask me to be godmother to one of her children. You. Since your mother and father were living abroad, I saw very little of them for many years. I saw you occasionally."

"Yes. You used to take me out from school. I remember that. Gave me some specially good feeds, too. Lovely food you gave me."

"You were an unusual child. You liked caviar."

"I still do," said Celia, "though I don't get it offered to me very often."

"I was shocked to read this mention of things in the paper. Very little was said. I gathered it was a kind of open verdict. No particular motive. Nothing to show. No accounts of quarrel, there was no suggestion of there having been an attack from outside. I was shocked by it," said Mrs. Oliver, "and then I forgot it. I wondered once or twice what could have led to it, but as I was not in the country—I was doing a tour at the time, in America as I've said—the whole thing passed out of my mind. It was some years later when I next saw you and naturally I did not speak of it to you."

"No," said Celia, "I appreciate that."

"All through life," Mrs. Oliver said, "one comes across very curious things that happen to friends or to acquaintances. With friends, of course, very often you have some idea of what led to—whatever the incident might be. But if it's a long time since you've heard them discussed or talked to them, you are quite in the dark and there is nobody that you can show too much curiosity to about the occasion."

"You were always very nice to me," said Celia. "You sent me nice presents, a particularly nice present when I was twenty-one, I remember."

"That's the time when girls need some extra cash in hand," said Mrs. Oliver, "because there are so many things they want to do and have just then."

"Yes, I always thought you were an understanding person and not—well, you know what some people are like. Always questioning, and asking things and wanting to know all about you. You never asked questions. You used to take me out to shows, or give me nice meals, and talk to me as though, well, as though everything was all right and you were just a distant relation of the family. I've appreciated that. I've known so many nosey-parkers in my life."

"Yes. Everyone comes up against that sooner or later," said Mrs. Oliver. "But you see now what upset me at this particular party. It seems an extraordinary thing to be asked to do by a complete stranger like Mrs. Burton-Cox. I couldn't imagine why she should want to know. It was no business of hers, surely. Unless—"

"You thought it was, unless it was something to do with

my marrying Desmond. Desmond is her son."

"Yes, I suppose it could have been, but I couldn't see how, or what business it was of hers."

"Everything's her business. She's nosey—in fact she's what you said she was, an odious woman."

"But I gather Desmond isn't odious."

"No. No, I'm very fond of Desmond and Desmond is fond of me. I don't like his mother."

"Does he like his mother?"

"I don't really know," said Celia. "I suppose he might like her—anything's possible, isn't it? Anyway, I don't want to get married at present. I don't feel like it. And there are a lot of—oh, well, difficulties, you know there are a lot of fors and againsts. It must have made you feel rather curious," said Celia. "I mean, why Mrs. Nosey Cox should have asked you to try and worm things out of me and then run along and spill it all to her— Are you asking me that particular question, by the way?"

"You mean, am I asking you whether you think or know that your mother killed your father or your father killed your mother, or whether it was a double suicide? Is that what you mean?"

"Well, I suppose it is, in a way. But I think I have to ask you also, *if* you were wanting to ask me that, whether you were doing so with the idea of giving Mrs. Burton-Cox the information you obtained, in case you did receive any information from me."

"No," said Mrs. Oliver. "Quite decidedly no. I shouldn't dream of telling the odious woman anything of the sort. I shall tell her quite firmly that it is not any business of hers or of mine, and that I have no intention of obtaining information from you and retailing it to her."

"Well, that's what I thought," said Celia. "I thought I could trust you to that extent. I don't mind telling you what I do know. Such as it is."

"You needn't. I'm not asking you for it."

"No. I can quite see that. But I'll give you the answer all the same. The answer is—nothing."

"Nothing," said Mrs. Oliver thoughtfully.

"No. I wasn't there at the time. I mean, I wasn't in the house at the time. I can't remember now quite where I was. I think I was at school in Switzerland, or else I was staying with a school friend during the school holidays. You see, it's all rather mixed up in my mind by now."

"I suppose," said Mrs. Oliver doubtfully, "it wouldn't be likely that you would know. Considering your age at the time."

"I'd be interested," said Celia, "to know just what you feel about that. Do you think it would be likely for me to know all about it? Or not to know?"

"Well, you said you weren't in the house. If you'd been in the house at the time then, yes, I think it would be quite likely that you might know something. Children do. Teenagers do. People of that age know a lot, they see a lot, they don't talk about it very often. But they do know things that the outside world wouldn't know, and they do know things that they wouldn't be willing, shall we say, to tell to police inquirers."

"No. You're being quite sensible. I wouldn't've known. I don't think I did know. I don't think I had any idea. What did the police think? You don't mind my asking you that, I hope, because I should be interested. You see, I never read any account of the inquest or anything like that or the inquiry into it."

"I think they thought it was a double suicide, but I don't think they ever had any inkling as to the reason for it."

"Do you want to know what I think?"

"Not if you don't want me to know," said Mrs. Oliver.

"But I expect you are interested. After all, you write crime stories about people who kill themselves or kill each other, or who have reasons for things. I should think you would be interested."

"Yes, I'll admit that," said Mrs. Oliver. "But the last thing I want to do is to offend you by seeking for information which is no business of mine to know."

"Well, I wondered," said Celia. "I've often wondered from time to time why, and how, but I knew very little about things. I mean, about how things were going on at home. The holidays before that I had been away on exchange on the continent, so I hadn't seen my mother and father really very recently. I mean, they'd come out to Switzerland and taken me out from school once or twice, but that was all. They seemed much as usual, but they seemed older. My father, I think, was ailing. I mean, getting feebler. I don't know if it was heart or what it was. One doesn't really think about that. My mother, too, she was going rather nervy. Not hypochondriac, but a little inclined to fuss over her health. They were on good terms, quite friendly. There wasn't anything that I noticed. Only sometimes one would, well, sometimes one gets ideas. One doesn't think they're true or necessarily right at all, but one just wonders if—"

"I don't think we'd better talk about it any more," said Mrs. Oliver. "We don't need to know or find out. The whole thing's over and done with. The verdict was quite satisfactory. No means to show, or motive, or anything like that. But there was no question of your father having deliberately killed your mother, or of your mother having deliberately killed your father."

"If I thought which was most likely," said Celia, "I would think my father killed my mother. Because, you see, it's more natural for a man to shoot anyone, I think. To shoot a woman for whatever reason it was. I don't think a woman, or a woman like my mother, would be so likely to shoot my father. If she wanted him dead, I should think she might have chosen some other method. But I don't think either of them wanted the other one dead."

"So it could have been an outsider."

"Yes, but what does one mean by an outsider?" said Celia.

"Who else was there living in the house?"

"A housekeeper, elderly, rather blind and rather deaf, a foreign girl, an *au pair* girl, she'd been my governess once —she was awfully nice—she came back to look after my mother, who had been in hospital— And there was an aunt whom I never loved much. I don't think any of them could have been likely to have any grudge against my parents.

There was nobody who profited by their deaths, except, I suppose, myself and my brother Edward, who was four years younger than I was. We inherited what money there was, but it wasn't very much. My father had his pension, of course. My mother had a small income of her own. No. There was nothing there of any importance."

"I'm sorry," said Mrs. Oliver. "I'm sorry if I've distressed you by asking all this."

"You haven't distressed me. You've brought it up in my mind a little and it has interested me. Because, you see, I am of an age now that I wish I did know. I knew and was fond of them, as one is fond of parents. Not passionately, just normally, but I realize I don't know what they were really *like*. What their life was like. What mattered to them. I don't know anything about it all. I wish I did know. It's like a burr, something sticking into you, and you can't leave it alone. Yes. I would like to know. Because then, you see, I shouldn't have to think about it any more."

"So you do? Think about it?"

Celia looked at her for a moment. She seemed to be trying to come to a decision.

"Yes," she said, "I think about it nearly all the time. I'm getting to have a thing about it, if you know what I mean. And Desmond feels the same."

5

OLD SINS HAVE LONG SHADOWS

Hercule Poirot let the revolving door wind him round. Arresting the swing of it with one hand, he stepped forward into the small restaurant. There were not many people there. It was an unfashionable time of day, but his eyes soon saw the man he had come to meet. The square, solid bulk of Superintendent Spence rose from the table in one corner.

"Good," he said. "You have arrived here. You had no difficulty in finding it?"

"None at all. Your instructions were most adequate."

"Let me introduce you now. This is Chief Superintendent Garroway. Monsieur Hercule Poirot."

Garroway was a tall, thin man with a lean, ascetic face, gray hair which left a small round spot like a tonsure, so that he had a faint resemblance to an ecclesiastic.

"This is wonderful," said Poirot.

"I am retired now, of course," said Garroway, "but one remembers. Yes, certain things one remembers, although they are past and gone, and the general public probably remembers nothing about them. But yes."

Hercule Poirot very nearly said "Elephants do remember," but checked himself in time. That phrase was so associated in his mind now with Mrs. Ariadne Oliver that he found it difficult to restrain it from his tongue in many clearly unsuitable categories.

"I hope you have not been getting impatient," said Superintendent Spence.

He pulled forward a chair, and the three men sat down. A menu was brought. Superintendent Spence, who was clearly addicted to this particular restaurant, offered tentative words of advice. Garroway and Poirot made their choice. Then, leaning back a little in their chairs and sipping glasses of sherry, they contemplated each other for some minutes in silence before speaking.

"I must apologize to you," said Poirot, "I really must apologize to you for coming to you with my demands about an affair which is over and done with."

"What interests me," said Spence, "is what has interested you. I thought first that it was unlike you to have this wish to delve in the past. Is it connected with something that has occurred nowadays, or is it sudden curiosity about a rather inexplicable, perhaps, case? Do you agree with that?"

He looked across the table.

"Inspector Garroway," he said, "as he was at that time, was the officer in charge of the investigations into the Ravenscroft shooting. He was an old friend of mine and so I had no difficulty in getting in touch with him."

"And he was kind enough to come here today," said Poirot, "simply because I must admit to a curiosity which I am sure I have no right to feel about an affair that is past and done with."

"Well, I wouldn't say that," said Garroway. "We all have interests in certain cases that are past. Did Lizzie Borden really kill her father and mother with an ax? There are people who still do not think so. Who killed Charles Bravo and why? There are several different ideas, mostly not very well founded. But still people try to find alternative explanations."

His keen, shrewd eyes looked across at Poirot.

"And Monsieur Poirot, if I am not mistaken, has occasionally shown a leaning towards looking into cases, going back, shall we say, for murder, back into the past, twice, perhaps three times."

"Three times, certainly," said Superintendent Spence.

"Once, I think I am right, by request of a Canadian girl."

"That is so," said Poirot. "A Canadian girl, very vehement, very passionate, very forceful, who had come here to investigate a murder for which her mother had been condemned to death, although she died before sentence was carried out. Her daughter was convinced that her mother had been innocent."

"And you agreed?" said Garroway.

"I did not agree," said Poirot, "when she first told me of the matter. But she was very vehement and very sure."

"It was natural for a daughter to wish her mother to have been innocent and to try and prove against all appearances that she was innocent," said Spence.

"It was just a little more than that," said Poirot. "She convinced me of the type of woman her mother was."

"A woman incapable of murder?"

"No," said Poirot, "it would be very difficult, and I am sure both of you agree with me, to think there is anyone quite incapable of murder if one knows what kind of person they are, what led up to it. But in that particular case, the mother never protested her innocence. She appeared to be quite content to be sentenced. That was curious to begin with. Was she a defeatist? It did not seem so. When I began to inquire, it became clear that she was not a defeatist. She was, one would say, almost the opposite of it."

Garroway looked interested. He leaned across the table, twisting a bit of bread off the roll on his plate.

"And was she innocent?"

"Yes," said Poirot. "She was innocent."

"And that surprised you?"

"Not by the time I realized it," said Poirot. "There were one or two things—one thing in particular—that showed she *could not* have been guilty. One fact that nobody had appreciated at the time. Knowing that, one had only to look at what there was, shall we say, on the menu in the way of looking elsewhere." *

* *Murder in Retrospect.* [English title: *Five Little Pigs.*]

Grilled trout was put in front of them at this point.

"There was another case, too, where you looked into the past, not quite in the same way," continued Spence. "A girl who said at a party that she had once seen a murder committed." *

"There again one had to—how shall I put it?—step backward instead of forward," said Poirot. "Yes, that is very true."

"And had the girl seen the murder committed?"

"No," said Poirot, "because it was the wrong girl. This trout is delicious," he added with appreciation.

"They do all fish dishes very well here," said Superintendent Spence.

He helped himself from the sauce boat proffered to him.

"A most delicious sauce," he added.

Silent appreciation of food filled the next three minutes.

"When Spence came along to me," said Superintendent Garroway, "asking if I remembered anything about the Ravenscroft case, I was intrigued and delighted at once."

"You haven't forgotten all about it?"

"Not the Ravenscroft case. It wasn't an easy case to forget about."

"You agree," said Poirot, "that there were discrepancies about it? Lack of proof, alternative solutions?"

"No," said Garroway, "nothing of that kind. All the evidence recorded the visible facts. Deaths of which there were several former examples, yes, all plain sailing. And yet—"

"Well?" said Poirot.

* *Hallowe'en Party.*

"And yet it was all wrong," said Garroway.

"Ah," said Spence.

He looked interested.

"That's what you felt once, isn't it?" said Poirot, turning to him.

"In the case of Mrs. McGinty. Yes."

"You weren't satisfied," said Poirot, "when that extremely difficult young man was arrested. He had every reason for doing it, he looked as though he had done it, everyone thought he had done it. But you knew he hadn't done it. You were so sure of it that you came to me and told me to go along to see what I could find out."

"See if you could help—and you did help, didn't you?" said Spence.

Poirot sighed.

"Fortunately, yes. But what a tiresome young man he was. If ever a young man deserved to be hung, not because he had done a murder but because he wouldn't help anyone to prove that he hadn't. Now we have the Ravenscroft case. You say, Superintendent Garroway, something was wrong?"

"Yes, I felt quite sure of it if you understand what I mean."

"I do understand," said Poirot. "And so does Spence. One does come across these things sometimes. The proofs are there, the motive, the opportunity, the clues, the *mise en scène,* it's all there. A complete blueprint, as you might say. But all the same, those whose profession it is, *know*. They know that it's all wrong, just like a critic in the artistic world knows when a picture is all wrong. Knows when it's a fake and not the real thing."

"There wasn't anything I could do about it, either," said Superintendent Garroway. "I looked into it, around it, up above it and down below it, as you might say. I talked to the people. There was nothing there. It looked like a suicide pact, it had all the marks of the suicide pact. Alternatively, of course, it could be a husband who shot a wife and then himself, or a wife who shot her husband and then herself. All those three things happen. When one comes across them, one knows they have happened. But in most cases one has some idea of *why.*"

"There wasn't any real idea of *why* in this case, was that it?" said Poirot.

"Yes. That's it. You see, the moment you begin to inquire into a case, to inquire about people and things, you get a very good picture as a rule of what their lives have been like. This was a couple, aging, the husband with a good record, a wife affectionate, pleasant, on good terms together. That's a thing one soon finds out about. They were happy living together. They went for walks, they played picquet, and poker patience with each other in the evenings. They had children who caused them no particular anxiety. A boy in school in England and a girl in a *pensionnat* in Switzerland. There was nothing wrong with their lives as far as one could tell. From such medical evidence as one could obtain, there was nothing definitely wrong with their health. The husband had suffered from high blood pressure at one time, but was in good condition by the taking of suitable medicaments which kept him on an even keel. His wife was slightly deaf and had had a little minor heart trouble, nothing to be worried about. Of course it could be, as does happen sometimes, that one or other of them had fears for their health. There are a lot of people who are in good health but are quite convinced they have cancer, are quite sure that they won't live another year. Sometimes that leads to their taking their own life. The Ravenscrofts didn't seem that kind of people. They seemed well balanced and placid."

"So what did you really think?" said Poirot.

"The trouble is that I couldn't think. Looking back, I say to myself it was suicide. It could only have been suicide. For some reason or other they decided that life was unbearable to them. Not through financial trouble, not through health difficulties, not because of unhappiness. And there, you see, I came to a full stop. It had all the marks of suicide. I cannot see any other thing that could have happened except suicide. They went for a walk. On that walk they took a revolver with them. The revolver lay between the two bodies. There were blurred fingerprints of both of them. Both of them in fact had handled it, but there was nothing to show who had fired it last. One tends to think the husband perhaps shot his wife and then himself. That is only because it seems more likely. Well, why? A great many years have passed. When something reminds me now and again, something I read in the papers of bodies, a husband and wife's bodies somewhere, lying dead, having taken their own lives apparently, I think back and then I wonder again what happened in the Ravenscroft case. Twelve years ago or fourteen and I still remember the Ravenscroft case and wonder—well, just the one word, I think. Why—why—why? Did the husband really hate his wife, and had hated her for a long time? Did the wife really hate her husband and want to get rid of him? Did they go on hating each other until they could bear it no longer?"

Garroway broke off another piece of bread and chewed at it.

"You got some idea, Monsieur Poirot? Has somebody come to you and told you something that has awakened your interest particularly? Do you know something that might explain the 'Why'?"

"No. All the same," said Poirot, "you must have had a theory. Come now, you had a theory?"

"You're quite right, of course. One does have theories. One expects them all, or one of them at least, to work out, but they don't usually. I think that my theory was in the end that you couldn't look for the cause, because one didn't know enough. What *did* I know about them? General Ravenscroft was close on sixty; his wife was thirty-five. All I knew of them, strictly speaking, was the last five or six years of their lives. The General had retired on a pension. They had come back to England from abroad and all the evidence that came to me, all the knowledge, was of a brief period during which they had first a house at Bournemouth and then moved to where they lived in the home where the tragedy took place. They had lived there peacefully, happily, their children came home there for school holidays. It was a peaceful period, I should say, at the end of what one presumed as a peaceful life. But then I thought, but how much did I know of that peaceful life? I knew of their life after retirement in England, of their family. There was no financial motive, no motive of hatred, no motive of sexual involvement, of intrusive love affairs. No. But there *was* a period before that. What did I know about that? What I knew was a life spent mostly abroad with occasional visits home, a good record for the man, pleasant remembrances of her from friends of the wife's. There was no outstanding tragedy, dispute, nothing that one knew of. But then I mightn't have known. One doesn't know. There was a period of, say, twenty–thirty years, years from childhood to the time they married, the time they lived abroad in India and other places. Perhaps the root of the tragedy was there. There is a proverb my grandmother used to repeat: *Old sins have long shadows*. Was the cause of death some long shadow, a shadow from the past? That's not an easy thing to find out about. You find out about a man's record, what friends or acquaintances say, but you don't know any inner details. Well, I think little by little the theory grew up in my mind that that would have been the place to look, if I could have looked. Something that had happened then, in another country, perhaps. Something that had been thought to be forgotten, to have passed out of existence, but which still perhaps existed. A grudge from the past, some happening that nobody knew about, that had happened elsewhere, not in their life in England, but which may have been there. If one had known where to look for it."

"Not the sort of thing, you mean," said Poirot, "that anybody would remember. I mean, remember nowadays. Something that no friends of theirs in England, perhaps, would have known about."

"Their friends in England seem to have been mostly made since retirement, though I suppose old friends did come and visit them or see them occasionally. But one doesn't hear about things that happened in the past. People forget."

"Yes," said Poirot thoughtfully. "People forget."

"They're not like elephants," said Superintendent Garroway, giving a faint smile. "Elephants, they always say, remember everything."

"It is odd that you should say that," said Poirot.

"That I should say about long sins?"

"Not so much that. It was your mention of elephants that interested me."

Superintendent Garroway looked at Poirot with some surprise. He seemed to be waiting for more. Spence also cast a quick glance at his old friend.

"Something that happened in India, perhaps," he suggested. "I mean—well, that's where elephants come from, isn't it? Or from Africa. Anyway, who's been talking to you about elephants?" he added.

"A friend of mine happened to mention them," said Poirot. "Someone *you* know," he said to Superintendent Spence. "Mrs. Oliver."

"Oh, Mrs. Ariadne Oliver. Well!" He paused.

"Well what?" said Poirot.

"Well, does she know something, then?" he asked.

"I do not think so as yet," said Poirot, "but she might know something before very long." He added thoughtfully, "She's that kind of person. She gets around, if you know what I mean."

"Yes," said Spence. "Yes. Has she got any ideas?" he asked.

"Do you mean Mrs. Ariadne Oliver, the writer?" asked Garroway with some interest.

"That's the one," said Spence.

"Does she know a good deal about crime? I know she writes crime stories. I've never known where she got her ideas from or her facts."

"Her ideas," said Poirot, "come out of her head. Her facts—well, that's more difficult." He paused for a moment.

"What are you thinking of, Poirot? Something in particular?"

"Yes," said Poirot. "I ruined one of her stories once, or so she tells me. She had just had a very good idea about a fact, something that had to do with a long-sleeved woolen vest. I asked her something over the telephone and it put the idea for the story out of her head. She reproaches me at intervals."

"Dear, dear," said Spence. "Sounds rather like that parsley that sank into the butter on a hot day. You know. Sherlock Holmes and the dog who did nothing in the night-time."

"Did they have a dog?" asked Poirot.

"I beg your pardon?"

"I said did they have a dog? General and Mrs. Ravenscroft. Did they take a dog for that walk with them on the day they were shot? The Ravenscrofts."

"They had a dog—yes," said Garroway. "I suppose, I suppose they did take him for a walk most days."

"If it had been one of Mrs. Oliver's stories," said Spence, "you ought to have found the dog howling over the two dead bodies. But that didn't happen."

Garroway shook his head.

"I wonder where the dog is now?" said Poirot.

"Buried in somebody's garden, I expect," said Garroway. "It's fourteen years ago."

"So we can't go and ask the dog, can we?" said Poirot. He added thoughtfully, "A pity. It's astonishing, you know, what dogs can know. Who was there exactly in the house? I mean on the day when the crime happened?"

"I brought you a list," said Superintendent Garroway, "in case you like to consult it. Mrs. Whittaker, the elderly cook-housekeeper. It was her day out, so we couldn't get much from her that was helpful. A visitor was staying there who had been governess to the Ravenscroft children once, I believe. Mrs. Whittaker was rather deaf and slightly blind. She couldn't tell us anything of interest, except that recently Lady Ravenscroft had been in hospital or in a nursing home—for nerves but not illness, apparently. There was a gardener, too."

"But a stranger might have come from outside. A stranger from the past. That's your idea, Superintendent

Garroway?"

"Not so much an idea as just a theory."

Poirot was silent, he was thinking of a time when he had asked to go back into the past, had studied five people out of the past who had reminded him of the nursery rhyme "Five little pigs." Interesting it had been, and in the end rewarding, because he had found out the truth.

6

AN OLD FRIEND REMEMBERS

When Mrs. Oliver returned to the house the following morning, she found Miss Livingstone waiting for her.

"There have been two telephone calls, Mrs. Oliver."

"Yes?" said Mrs. Oliver.

"The first one was from Crichton and Smith. They wanted to know whether you had chosen the lime-green brocade or the pale blue one."

"I haven't made up my mind yet," said Mrs. Oliver. "Just remind me tomorrow morning, will you? I'd like to see it by night light."

"And the other was from a foreigner, a Mr. Hercules Poirot, I believe."

"Oh, yes," said Mrs. Oliver. "What did he want?"

"He asked if you would be able to call and see him this

afternoon."

"That will be quite impossible," said Mrs. Oliver. "Ring him up, will you? I've got to go out again at once, as a matter of fact. Did he leave a telephone number?"

"Yes, he did."

"That's all right, then. We won't have to look it up again. All right. Just ring him. Tell him I'm sorry that I can't but that I'm out on the track of an elephant."

"I beg your pardon?" said Miss Livingstone.

"Say that I'm on the track of an elephant."

"Oh, yes," said Miss Livingstone, looking shrewdly at her employer to see if she was right in the feelings that she sometimes had that Mrs. Ariadne Oliver, though a successful novelist, was at the same time not quite right in the head.

"I've never hunted elephants before," said Mrs. Oliver. "It's quite an interesting thing to do, though."

She went into the sitting room, opened the top volume of the assorted books on the sofa, most of them looking rather the worst for wear, since she had toiled through them the evening before and written out a paper with various addresses.

"Well, one has got to make a start somewhere," she said. "On the whole I think that if Julia hasn't gone completely off her rocker by now, I might start with her. She always had ideas, and after all, she knew that part of the country because she lived near there. Yes, I think we'll start with Julia."

"There are four letters for you here to sign," said Miss Livingstone.

"I can't be bothered now," said Mrs. Oliver. "I really can't spare a moment. I've got to go down to Hampton Court, and it's quite a long ride."

The Honorable Julia Carstairs, struggling with some slight difficulty out of her armchair, the difficulty that those over the age of seventy have when rising to their feet after prolonged rest, even a possible nap, stepped forward, peering a little to see who it was who had just been announced by the faithful retainer who shared the apartment which she occupied in her status of a member of "Homes for the Privileged." Being slightly deaf, the name had not come clearly to her. Mrs. Gulliver. Was that it? But she didn't remember a Mrs. Gulliver. She advanced on slightly shaky knees, still peering forward.

"I don't expect you'll remember me, it's so many years since we met."

Like many elderly people, Mrs. Carstairs could remember voices better than she did faces.

"Why," she exclaimed, "it's—dear me, it's Ariadne! My dear, how very nice to see you."

Greetings passed.

"I just happened to be in this part of the world," explained Mrs. Oliver. "I had to come down to see someone not far from here. And then I remembered that looking in my address book last night I had seen that this was quite near where you had your apartment. Delightful, isn't it?" she added, looking round.

"Not too bad," said Mrs. Carstairs. "Not quite all it's

written up to be, you know. But it has many advantages. One brings one's own furniture and things like that, and there is a central restaurant where you can have a meal, or you can have your own things, of course. Oh, yes, it's very good, really. The grounds are charming and well-kept-up. But sit down, Ariadne; do sit down. You look very well. I saw you were at a literary lunch the other day, in the paper. How odd it is that one just sees something in the paper and almost the next day one meets the person. Quite extraordinary."

"I know," said Mrs. Oliver, taking the chair that was offered her. "Things do go like that, don't they?"

"You are still living in London?"

Mrs. Oliver said yes, she was still living in London. She then entered into what she thought of in her own mind, with vague memories of going to dancing class as a child, the first figure of the Lancers. Advance, retreat, hands out, turn round twice, whirl round, and so on.

She inquired after Mrs. Carstairs's daughter and about the two grandchildren, and she asked about the other daughter, what she was doing. She appeared to be doing it in New Zealand. Mrs. Carstairs did not seem to be quite sure what it was. Some kind of social research. Mrs. Carstairs pressed an electric bell that rested on the arm of her chair, and ordered Emma to bring tea. Mrs. Oliver begged her not to bother. Julia Carstairs said:

"Of course Ariadne has got to have tea."

The two ladies leaned back. The second and third figures of the Lancers. Old friends. Other people's children. The death of friends.

"It must be years since I saw you last," said Mrs. Carstairs.

"I think it was at the Llewellyns' wedding," said Mrs. Oliver.

"Yes, that must have been about it. How terrible Moira looked as a bridesmaid. That dreadfully unbecoming shade of apricot they wore."

"I know. It didn't suit them."

"I don't think weddings are nearly as pretty as they used to be in our day. Some of them seem to wear such very peculiar clothes. The other day one of my friends went to a wedding and she said the bridegroom was dressed in some sort of quilted white satin and ruffles at his neck. Made of Valenciennes lace, I believe. *Most* peculiar. And the girl was wearing a very peculiar trouser suit. Also white, but it was stamped with green shamrocks all over.

"Well, my dear Ariadne, can you imagine it. Really, extraordinary. In church, too. If I'd been a clergyman, I'd have refused to marry them."

Tea came. Talk continued.

"I saw my goddaughter, Celia Ravenscroft, the other day," said Mrs. Oliver. "Do you remember the Ravenscrofts? Of course, it's a great many years ago."

"The Ravenscrofts? Now wait a minute. That was that very sad tragedy, wasn't it? A double suicide, didn't they think it was? Near their house at Overcliffe."

"You've got such a wonderful memory, Julia," said Mrs. Oliver.

"Always had. Though I have difficulties with names sometimes. Yes, it was very tragic, wasn't it?"

"Very tragic indeed."

"One of my cousins knew them very well in India, Roddy Foster, you know. General Ravenscroft had had a most distinguished career. Of course he was a bit deaf by the time he retired. He didn't always hear what one said very well."

"Do you remember them quite well?"

"Oh, yes. One doesn't really forget people, does one? I mean, they lived at Overcliffe for quite five or six years."

"I've forgotten her Christian name now," said Mrs. Oliver.

"Muriel, I think. But everyone called her Molly. Yes, Muriel. So many people were called Muriel, weren't they, at about that time? She used to wear a wig, do you remember?"

"Oh, yes," said Mrs. Oliver. "At least I can't quite remember, but I think I do."

"I'm not sure she didn't try to persuade me to get one. She said it was so useful when you went abroad and traveled. She had four different wigs. One for evening and one for traveling and one—very strange, you know. You could put a hat on over it and not really disarrange it."

"I didn't know them as well as you did," said Mrs. Oliver. "And of course at the time of the shooting I was in America on a lecture tour. So I never really heard any details."

"Well, of course, it was a great mystery," said Julia Carstairs. "I mean to say, one didn't know. There were so many different stories going about."

"What did they say at the inquest—I suppose they had an inquest?"

"Oh, yes, of course. The police had to investigate it. It was one of those indecisive things, you know, in that the death was due to revolver shots. They couldn't say definitely what had occurred. It seemed possible that General Ravenscroft had shot his wife and then himself, but apparently it was just as probable that Lady Ravenscroft had shot her husband and then herself. It seemed most likely, I think, that it was a suicide pact, but it couldn't be said definitely how it came about."

"There seemed to be no question of its being a crime?"

"No, no. It was said quite clearly there was no suggestion of foul play. I mean there were no footsteps or any signs of anyone coming near them. They left the house to walk after tea, as they so often did. They didn't come back again for dinner and the manservant or somebody or the gardener—whoever it was—went out to look for them, and found them both dead. The revolver was lying by the bodies."

"The revolver belonged to him, didn't it?"

"Oh, yes. He had two revolvers in the house. These ex-military people so often do, don't they? I mean, they feel safer what with everything that goes on nowadays. A second revolver was still in the drawer in the house, so that he—well, he must have gone out deliberately with the revolver, presumably. I don't think it likely that she'd have gone out for a walk carrying a revolver."

"No. No, it wouldn't have been so easy, would it?"

"But there was nothing apparently in the evidence to show that there was any unhappiness or that there'd been any quarrel between them or that there was any reason why they should commit suicide. Of course one never knows what sad things there are in people's lives."

"No, no," said Mrs. Oliver. "One never knows. How very true that is, Julia. Did you have any ideas yourself?"

"Well, one always wonders, my dear."

"Yes," said Mrs. Oliver, "one always wonders."

"It might be of course, you see, that he had some disease. I think he might have been told he was going to die of cancer, but that wasn't so, according to the medical evidence. He was quite healthy. I mean, he had—I think he had had a—what do they call those things?—coronary, is that what I mean? It sounds like a crown, doesn't it, but it's really a heart attack, isn't it? He'd had that but he'd recovered from it, and she was, well, she was very nervy. She was neurotic always."

"Yes, I seem to remember that," said Mrs. Oliver. "Of course I didn't know them well, but—" she asked suddenly —"was she wearing a wig?"

"Oh. Well, you know, I can't really remember that. She always wore her wig. One of them, I mean."

"I just wondered," said Mrs. Oliver. "Somehow I feel if you were going to shoot yourself or even shoot your husband, I don't think you'd wear your wig, do you?"

The ladies discussed this point with some interest.

"What do you really think, Julia?"

"Well, as I said, dear, one wonders, you know. There were things said, but then there always are."

"About him or her?"

"Well, they said that there was a young woman, you know. Yes, I think she did some secretarial work for him. He was writing his memoirs of his career in India—I believe commissioned by a publisher at that—and she used to take dictation from him. But some people said—well, you know what they do say sometimes, that perhaps he had got —er—tied up with this girl in some way. She wasn't very young. She was over thirty, and not very good-looking and I don't think—there were no scandals about her or anything, but still, one doesn't know. People thought he might have shot his wife because he wanted to—well, he might have wanted to marry her, yes. But I don't really think people said that sort of thing and *I* never believed it."

"What did you think?"

"Well, of course I wondered a little about *her.*"

"You mean that a man was mentioned?"

"I believe there was something out in Malaya. Some kind of story I heard about her. That she got embroiled with some young man much younger than herself. And her husband hadn't liked it much and it had caused a bit of scandal. I forget where. But anyway, that was a long time ago and I don't think anything ever came of it."

"You don't think there was any talk nearer home? No special relationship with anyone in the neighborhood? There wasn't any evidence of quarrels between them, or anything of that kind?"

"No, I don't think so. Of course I read everything about it at the time. One did discuss it, of course, because one couldn't help feeling there might be some—well, some really very tragic love story connected with it."

"But there wasn't, you think? They had children, didn't they? There was my goddaughter, of course."

"Oh, yes, and there was a son. I think he was quite young. At school somewhere. The girl was only twelve, no —older than that. She was with a family in Switzerland."

"There was no—no mental trouble, I suppose, in the family?"

"Oh, you mean the boy—yes, *might* be, of course. You do hear very strange things. There was that boy who shot his father—that was somewhere near Newcastle, I think. Some years before that. You know. He'd been very depressed and at first I think they said he tried to hang himself when he was at the university, and then he came and shot his father. But nobody quite knew why. Anyway, there wasn't anything of that sort with the Ravenscrofts. No, I don't think so, in fact, I'm pretty sure of it. I can't help thinking, in some ways—"

"Yes, Julia?"

"I can't help thinking that there might have been a man, you know."

"You mean that she—?"

"Yes, well—well, one thinks it rather likely, you know. The wigs, for one thing."

"I don't quite see how the wigs come into it."

"Well, wanting to improve her appearance."

"She was thirty-five, I think."

"More. More. Thirty-six, I think. And, well, I know she showed me the wigs one day, and one or two of them really made her look quite attractive. And she used a good deal of make-up. And that had all started just after they had come to live there, I think. She was rather a good-looking woman."

"You mean, she might have met someone—some man?"

"Well, that's what I've always thought," said Mrs. Carstairs. "You see, if a man's getting off with a girl, people notice it usually because men aren't so good at hiding their tracks. But a woman, it might be—well, I mean like someone she'd met and nobody knew much about it."

"Oh, do you really think so, Julia?"

"No, I don't really think so," said Julia, "because I mean, people always do know, don't they? I mean, you know, servants know, or gardeners or bus drivers. Or somebody in the neighborhood. And they know. And they talk. But still, there could have been something like that and either he found out about it . . ."

"You mean it was a crime of jealousy?"

"I think so, yes."

"So you think it's more likely that he shot her, then himself, than that she shot him and then herself."

"Well, I should think so, because I think if she were trying to get rid of him—well, I don't think they'd have gone for a walk together and she'd have to have taken the revolver with her in a handbag and it would have been rather a bigger handbag if so. One has to think of the practical side of things."

"I know," said Mrs. Oliver. "One does. It's very interesting."

"It must be interesting to you, dear, because you write these crime stories. So I expect really you would have better ideas. You'd know more what's likely to happen."

"I don't know what's likely to happen," said Mrs. Oliver, "because, you see, in all the crimes that I write, I've invented the crimes. I mean, what I want to happen, happens in my stories. It's not something that actually has happened or that could happen. So I'm really the worst person to talk about it. I'm interested to know what you think because you know people very well, Julia, and you knew them well. And I think she might have said something to you one day —or he might."

"Yes. Yes, now wait a minute when you say that, that seems to bring something back to me."

Mrs. Carstairs leaned back in her chair, shook her head doubtfully, half closed her eyes and went into a kind of coma. Mrs. Oliver remained silent, with a look on her face which women are apt to wear when they are waiting for the first signs of a kettle coming to the boil.

"She did say something once, I remember, and I wonder what she meant by it," said Mrs. Carstairs. "Something about starting a new life—in connection, I think, with St. Teresa. St. Teresa of Avila."

Mrs. Oliver looked slightly startled.

"But how did St. Teresa of Avila come into it?"

"Well, I don't know really. I think she must have been reading a *Life* of her. Anyway, she said that it was wonderful how women get a sort of second wind. That's not quite the term she used, but something like that. You know, when they are forty or fifty or that sort of age and they suddenly want to begin a new life. Teresa of Avila did. She hadn't done anything special up till then except being a nun, then she went out and reformed all the convents, didn't she, and flung her weight about and became a great saint."

"Yes, but that doesn't seem quite the same thing."

"No, it doesn't," said Mrs. Carstairs. "But women do talk in a very silly way, you know, when they are referring to love affairs when they get on in life. About how it's never too late."

7

BACK TO THE NURSERY

Mrs. Oliver looked rather doubtfully at the three steps and the front door of a small, rather dilapidated-looking cottage in the side street. Below the windows some bulbs were growing, mainly tulips.

Mrs. Oliver paused, opened the little address book in her hand, verified that she was in the place she thought she was, and rapped gently with the knocker after having tried to press a bell-push of possible electrical significance but which did not seem to yield any satisfactory bell ringing inside, or anything of that kind. Presently, not getting any response, she knocked again. This time there were sounds from inside. A shuffling sound of feet, some asthmatic breathing and hands apparently trying to manage the opening of the door. With this noise there came a few vague echoes in the letter box.

"Oh, drat it. Drat it. Stuck again, you brute, you."

Finally, success met these inward industries, and the door, making a creaky and rather doubtful noise, was slowly pulled open. A very old woman, with a wrinkled face, humped shoulders and a general arthritic appearance, looked at her. Visitor. Her face was unwelcoming. It held no sign of fear, merely of distaste for those who came and knocked at the home of an Englishwoman's castle. She might have been seventy or eighty, but she was still a valiant defender of her home.

"I dunno what you've come about and I—" she stopped. "Why," she said, "it's Miss Ariadne. Well, I never now! It's Miss Ariadne."

"I think you're wonderful to know me," said Mrs. Oliver. "How are you, Mrs. Matcham?"

"Miss Ariadne! Just think of that now."

It was, Mrs. Ariadne Oliver thought, a long time ago since she had been addressed as Miss Ariadne, but the intonation of the voice, cracked with age though it was, rang a familiar note.

"Come in, m'dear," said the old dame; "come in now. You're lookin' well, you are. I dunno how many years it is since I've seen you. Fifteen at least."

It was a good deal more than fifteen, but Mrs. Oliver made no corrections. She came in. Mrs. Matcham was shaking hands, her hands were rather unwilling to obey their owner's orders. She managed to shut the door and, shuffling her feet and limping, entered a small room which was obviously one that was kept for the reception of any likely or unlikely visitors whom Mrs. Matcham was prepared to admit to her home. There were large numbers of photographs—some of babies, some of adults. Some in nice leather frames which were slowly drooping but had not quite fallen to pieces yet. One in a silver frame by now rather tarnished, representing a young woman in presentation court dress with feathers rising up on her head. Two naval officers, two military gentlemen, some photographs of naked babies sprawling on rugs. There was a sofa and two chairs. As bidden, Mrs. Oliver sat in a chair. Mrs. Matcham pressed herself down on the sofa and pulled a cushion into the hollow of her back with some difficulty.

"Well, my dear, fancy seeing you. And you're still writing your pretty stories, are you?"

"Yes," said Mrs. Oliver, assenting to this though with a slight doubt as to how far detective stories and stories of crime and general criminal behavior could be called pretty stories. But that, she thought, was very much a habit of Mrs. Matcham's.

"I'm all alone now," said Mrs. Matcham. "You remember Gracie, my sister? She died last autumn, she did. Cancer it was. They operated, but it was too late."

"Oh, dear, I'm so sorry," said Mrs. Oliver.

Conversation proceeded for the next ten minutes on the subject of the demise, one by one, of Mrs. Matcham's last remaining relatives.

"And you're all right, are you? Doing all right? Got a husband now? Oh, now, I remember, he's dead years ago, isn't he? And what brings you here to Little Saltern Minor?"

"I just happened to be in the neighborhood," said Mrs. Oliver, "and as I've got your address in my little address book with me, I thought I'd just drop in and—well, see how you were and everything."

"Ah! And talk about old times, perhaps. Always nice when you can do that, isn't it?"

"Yes, indeed," said Mrs. Oliver, feeling some relief that this particular line had been indicated to her since it was more or less what she had come for. "What a lot of photographs you've got," she said.

"Ah, I have, an' that. D'you know, when I was in that home—silly name it had, Sunset House of Happiness for the Aged, something like that it was called, a year and a quarter I lived there till I couldn't stand it no more, a nasty lot they were, saying you couldn't have any of your own things with you. You know, everything had to belong to the home. I don't say as it wasn't comfortable, but you know, I like me own things around me. My photos and my furniture. And then there was ever so nice a lady, came from a Council, she did, some society or other, and she told me there was another place where they had homes of their own or something and you could take what you liked with you. And there's ever such a nice helper as comes in every day to see if you're all right. Ah, very comfortable I am here. Very comfortable indeed. I've got all my own things."

"Something from everywhere," said Mrs. Oliver, looking round.

"Yes, that table—the brass one—that's Captain Wilson,

he sent me that from Singapore or something like that. And that Benares brass, too. That's nice, isn't it? That's a funny thing on the ash tray. That's Egyptian, that is. It's a scarabee, or some name like that. You know. Sounds like some kind of scratching disease, but it isn't. No, it's a sort of beetle and it's made out of some stone. They call it a precious stone. Bright blue. A lazy—a lavis—a lazy lapin or something like that."

"Lapis lazuli," said Mrs. Oliver.

"That's right. That's what it is. Very nice, that is. That was my archeological boy what went digging. He sent me that."

"All your lovely past," said Mrs. Oliver.

"Yes, all my boys and girls. Some of them as babies, some of them I had from the month, and the older ones. Some of them when I went to India and that other time when I was in Siam. Yes. That's Miss Moya in her court dress. Ah, she was a pretty thing. Divorced two husbands, she has. Yes. Trouble with his lordship, the first one, and then she married one of those pop singers and of course that couldn't take very well. And then she married someone in California. They've got a yacht and go about places, I think. Died two or three years ago and only sixty-two. Pity dying so young, you know."

"You've been to a lot of different parts of the world yourself, haven't you?" said Mrs. Oliver. "India, Hong Kong, then Egypt, and South America, wasn't it?"

"Ah, yes, I've been about a good deal."

"I remember," said Mrs. Oliver, "when I was in India,

you were with a service family then, weren't you? A General somebody. Was it—now wait a minute, I can't remember the name—it wasn't General and Lady Ravenscroft, was it?"

"No, no, you've got the name wrong. You're thinking of when I was with the Barnabys. That's right. You came to stay with them. Remember? You were doing a tour, you were, and you came and stayed with the Barnabys. You were an old friend of hers. He was a judge."

"Ah, yes," said Mrs. Oliver. "It's difficult a bit. One gets names mixed up."

"Two nice children they had," said Mrs. Matcham. "Of course they went to school in England. The boy went to Harrow and the girl went to Roedean, I think it was, and so I moved on to another family after that. Ah, things have changed nowadays. Not so many ayahs, even, as there used to be. Mind you, the ayahs used to be a bit of a trouble now and then. I got on with our one very well when I was with the Barnabys, I mean. Who was it you spoke of? The Ravenscrofts? Well, I remember them. Yes—I forget the name of the place where they lived now. Not far from us. The families were acquainted, you know. Oh, yes, it's a long time ago, but I remember it all. I was still out there with the Barnabys, you know. I stayed on when the children went to school to look after Mrs. Barnaby. Look after her things, you know, and mend them and all that. Oh, yes, I was there when that awful thing happened. I don't mean the Barnabys. I mean to the Ravenscrofts. Yes, I shall never forget that. Hearing about it, I mean. Naturally I wasn't mixed up in it myself, but it was a terrible thing to happen, wasn't it?"

"I should think it must have been," said Mrs. Oliver.

"It was after you'd gone back to England, a good long time after that, I think. A nice couple they were. Very nice couple and it was a shock to them."

"I don't really remember now," said Mrs. Oliver.

"I know. One forgets things. I don't myself. But they said she'd always been queer, you know. Ever since the time she was a child. Some early story there was. She took a baby out of the pram and threw it in the river. Jealousy, they said. Other people said she wanted the baby to go to heaven and not wait."

"Is it—is it Lady Ravenscroft, you mean?"

"No, of course I don't. Ah, you don't remember as well as I do. It was the sister."

"Her sister?"

"I'm not sure now whether it was her sister or his sister. They said she'd been in a kind of mental place for a long time, you know. Ever since she was about eleven or twelve years old. They kept her there and then they said she was all right again and she came out. And she married someone in the Army. And then there was trouble. And the next thing they heard, I believe, was that she'd been put back again in one of them loony-bin places. They treat you very well, you know. They have a suite, nice rooms and all that. And they used to go and see her, I believe. I mean the General did or his wife. The children were brought up by someone else, I think, because they were afraid-like. However, they said she was all right in the end. So she came back to live with her husband, and then he died or something. Blood pressure I think it was, or heart. Anyway, she was very upset and she came out to stay with her brother or her sister—whichever it was—she seemed quite happy there and everything, and ever so fond of children, she was. It wasn't the little boy, I think. He was at school. It was the little girl, and another little girl who'd come to play with her that afternoon. Ah, well, I can't remember the details now. It's so long ago. There was a lot of talk about it. There was some as said, you know, as it wasn't her at all. They thought it was the ayah that had done it, but the ayah loved them and she was very, very upset. She wanted to take them away from the house. She said they weren't safe there, and all sorts of things like that. But of course the others didn't believe in it and then this came about and I gather they think it must have been whatever her name was—I can't remember it now. Anyway, there it was."

"And what happened to this sister, either of General or Lady Ravenscroft?"

"Well, I think, you know, as she was taken away by a doctor and put in some place and went back to England, I believe, in the end. I dunno if she went to the same place as before, but she was well looked after somewhere. There was plenty of money, I think, you know. Plenty of money in the husband's family. Maybe she got all right again. But, well, I haven't thought of it for years. Not till you came here asking me stories about General and Lady Ravenscroft. I wonder where they are now. They must have retired before now, long ago."

"Well, it was rather sad," said Mrs. Oliver. "Perhaps you read about it in the papers."

"Read what?"

"Well, they bought a house in England and then—"

"Ah, now, it's coming back to me. I remember reading something about that in the paper. Yes, and thinking then that I knew the name Ravenscroft, but I couldn't quite remember when and how. They fell over a cliff, didn't they? Something of that kind."

"Yes," said Mrs. Oliver, "something of that kind."

"Now look here, dearie, it's so nice to see you, it is. You must let me give you a cup of tea."

"Really," said Mrs. Oliver, "I don't need any tea. Really, I don't want it."

"Of course you want some tea. If you don't mind now, come into the kitchen, will you? I mean, I spend most of my time there now. It's easier to get about there. But I take visitors always into this room because I'm proud of my things, you know. Proud of my things and proud of all the children and the others."

"I think," said Mrs. Oliver, "that people like you must have had a wonderful life with all the children you've looked after."

"Yes. I remember when you were a little girl, you liked to listen to the stories I told you. There was one about a tiger, I remember, and one about monkeys—monkeys in a tree."

"Yes," said Mrs. Oliver, "I remember those. It was a

very long time ago."

Her mind swept back to herself, a child of six or seven, walking in button boots that were rather too tight on a road in England, and listening to a story of India and Egypt from an attendant Nanny. And this was Nanny. Mrs. Matcham was Nanny. She looked round the room as she followed her hostess out. At the pictures of girls, of schoolboys, of children and various middle-aged people, all mainly photographed in their best clothes and sent in nice frames or other things because they hadn't forgotten Nanny. Because of them, probably, Nanny was having a reasonably comfortable old age with money supplied. Mrs. Oliver felt a sudden desire to burst out crying. This was so unlike her that she was able to stop herself by an effort of will. She followed Mrs. Matcham to the kitchen. There she produced the offering she had brought.

"Well, I never! A tin of Tophole Thathams tea. Always my favorite. Fancy you remembering. I can hardly ever get it nowadays. And that's my favorite tea biscuits. Well, you are a one for never forgetting. What was it they used to call you—those two little boys who came to play—one would call you Lady Elephant and the other one called you Lady Swan. The one who called you Lady Elephant used to sit on your back and you went about the floor on all fours and pretended to have a trunk you picked things up with."

"You don't forget many things, do you, Nanny?" said Mrs. Oliver.

"Ah," said Mrs. Matcham. "Elephants don't forget. That's the old saying."

8

MRS. OLIVER AT WORK

Mrs. Oliver entered the premises of Williams & Barnet, a well-appointed chemist's shop also dealing with various cosmetics. She paused by a kind of dumbwaiter containing various types of corn remedies, hesitated by a mountain of rubber sponges, wandered vaguely toward the prescription desk and then came down past the well-displayed aids to beauty as imagined by Elizabeth Arden, Helena Rubinstein, Max Factor and other benefit providers for women's lives.

She stopped finally near a rather plump girl of thirty-five or so, and inquired for certain lipsticks, then uttered a short cry of surprise.

"Why, Marlene—it is Marlene isn't it?"

"Well, I never. It's Mrs. Oliver. I am pleased to see you. It's wonderful, isn't it? All the girls will be very excited when I tell them that you've been in to buy things here."

"No need to tell them," said Mrs. Oliver.

"Oh, now I'm sure they'll be bringing out their autograph books!"

"I'd rather they didn't," said Mrs. Oliver. "And how are you, Marlene?"

"Oh, getting along, getting along," said Marlene.

"I didn't know whether you'd be working here still."

"Well, it's as good as any other place, I think, and they treat you very well here, you know. I had a rise in salary last year and I'm more or less in charge of this cosmetic counter now."

"And your mother? Is she well?"

"Oh, yes. Mum will be pleased to hear I've met you."

"Is she still living in her same house down the—the road past the hospital?"

"Oh, yes, we're still there. Dad's not been so well. He's been in hospital for a while, but Mum keeps along very well indeed. Oh, she will be pleased to hear I've seen you. Are you staying here by any chance?"

"Not really," said Mrs. Oliver. "I'm just passing through, as a matter of fact. I've been to see an old friend and I wonder now—" she looked at her wrist watch. "Would your mother be at home now, Marlene? I could just call in and see her. Have a few words before I have to get on."

"Oh, do do that," said Marlene. "She'd be ever so pleased. I'm sorry I can't leave here and come with you, but I don't think—well, it wouldn't be viewed very well. You know, I can't get off for another hour and a half."

"Oh, well, some other time," said Mrs. Oliver. "Anyway, I can't quite remember—was it Number Seventeen or has it got a name?"

"It's called Laurel Cottage."

"Oh, yes, of course. How stupid of me. Well, nice to have seen you."

She hurried out plus one unwanted lipstick in her bag, and drove her car down the main street of Chipping Bartram and turned, after passing a garage and a hospital building, down a rather narrow road which had quite pleasant small houses built on either side of it.

She left the car outside Laurel Cottage and went in. A thin, energetic woman with gray hair, of about fifty years of age, opened the door and displayed instant signs of recognition.

"Why, so it's you, Mrs. Oliver. Ah, well, now. Not seen you for years and years, I haven't."

"Oh, it's a very long time."

"Well, come in then; come in. Can I make you a nice cup of tea?"

"I'm afraid not," said Mrs. Oliver, "because I've had tea already with a friend, and I've got to get back to London. As it happened, I went into the chemist for something I wanted and I saw Marlene there."

"Yes, she's got a very good job there. They think a lot of her in that place. They say she's got a lot of enterprise."

"Well, that's very nice. And how are you, Mrs. Buckle? You look very well. Hardly older than when I saw you last."

"Oh, I wouldn't like to say that. Gray hairs, and I've lost a lot of weight."

"This seems to be a day when I meet a lot of friends I knew formerly," said Mrs. Oliver, going into the house and being led into a small, rather overclustered sitting room. "I don't know if you remember Mrs. Carstairs—Mrs. Julia Carstairs."

"Oh, of course I do. Yes, rather. She must be getting on."

"Oh, yes, she is, really. But we talked over a few old days, you know. In fact, we went as far as talking about that tragedy that occurred. I was in America at the time so I didn't know much about it. People called Ravenscroft."

"Oh, I remember that well."

"You worked for them, didn't you, at one time, Mrs. Buckle?"

"Yes. I used to go in three mornings a week. Very nice people they were. You know, real military lady and gentleman, as you might say. The old school."

"It was a very tragic thing to happen."

"Yes, it was, indeed."

"Were you still working for them at that time?"

"No. As a matter of fact, I'd given up going there. I had my old Aunt Emma come to live with me and she was rather blind and not very well, and I couldn't really spare the time any more to go out doing things for people. But I'd been with them up to about a month or two before that."

"It seemed such a terrible thing to happen," said Mrs.

Oliver. "I understand that they thought it was a suicide pact."

"I don't believe that," said Mrs. Buckle. "I'm sure they'd never have committed suicide together. Not people that age. And living so pleasantly together as they did. Of course, they hadn't lived there very long."

"No, I suppose they hadn't," said Mrs. Oliver. "They lived somewhere near Bournemouth, didn't they, when they first came to England?"

"Yes, but they found it was a bit too far for getting to London from there, and so that's why they came to Chipping Bartram. Very nice house it was, and a nice garden."

"Were they both in good health when you were working for them last?"

"Well, they felt their age a bit as most people do. The General, he'd had some kind of heart trouble or a slight stroke. Something of that kind, you know. They'd take pills, you know, and lie up a bit from time to time."

"And Mrs. Ravenscroft?"

"Well, I think she missed the life she'd had abroad, you know. They didn't know so very many people there, although they got to know a good many families, of course, being the sort of class they were. But I suppose it wasn't like India or those places. You know, where you have a lot of servants. I suppose gay parties and that sort of thing."

"You think she missed her gay parties?"

"Well, I don't know that exactly."

"Somebody told me she'd taken to wearing a wig."

"Oh, she'd got several wigs," said Mrs. Buckle, smiling slightly. "Very smart ones and very expensive. You know, from time to time she'd send one back to the place she'd got it from in London, and they'd redress it for her again and send it. There were all kinds. You know, there was one with auburn hair, and one with little gray curls all over her head. Really, she looked very nice in that one. And two—well, not so attractive really but useful for—you know—windy days when you wanted something to put on when it might be raining. Thought a lot about her appearance, you know, and spent a lot of her money on clothes."

"What do you think was the cause of the tragedy?" said Mrs. Oliver. "You see, not being anywhere near here and not seeing any of my friends at that time because I was in America, I missed hearing anything about it and, well, one doesn't like to ask questions or write letters about things of that kind. I suppose there must have been some cause. I mean, it was General Ravenscroft's own revolver that was used, I understand."

"Oh, yes, he had two of those in the house because he said that no house was safe without. Perhaps he was right there, you know. Not that they'd had any trouble beforehand as far as I know. One afternoon a rather nasty sort of fellow came along to the door. Didn't like the look of him, I didn't. Wanted to see the General. Said he'd been in the General's regiment when he was a young fellow. The General asked him a few questions and I think thought as how he didn't—well, thought he wasn't very reliable. So he sent him off."

"You think then that it was someone outside that did it?"

"Well, I think it must have been, because I can't see any

did the gardening for them very much. He hadn't got a very good reputation and I gather he'd had a few jail sentences earlier in his life. But of course the General took up his references and he wanted to give him a chance."

"So you think the gardener might have killed them?"

"Well, I–I always thought that. But then I'm probably wrong. But it doesn't seem to me– I mean, the people who said there was some scandalous story or something about either her or him and that either he'd shot her or she'd shot him, that's all nonsense, I'd say. No, it was some outsider. One of these people that–well, it's not as bad as it is nowadays because that, you must remember, was before people began getting all this violence idea. But look at what you read in the papers every day now. Young men, practically only boys still, taking a lot of drugs and going wild and rushing about, shooting a lot of people for nothing at all, asking a girl in a pub to have a drink with them and then they see her home and next day her body's found in a ditch. Stealing children out of prams from their mothers, taking a girl to a dance and murdering her or strangling her on the way back. If anything, you feel as anyone can do anything. And anyway, there's that nice couple, the General and his wife, out for a nice walk in the evening, and there they were, both shot through the head."

"Was it through the head?"

"Well, I don't remember exactly now and of course I never saw anything myself. But anyway, just went for a walk as they often did."

"And they'd not been on bad terms with each other?"

"Well, they had words now and again, but who doesn't?"

"No boy friend or girl friend?"

"Well, if you can use that term of people of that age, oh, I mean there was a bit of talk here and there, but it was all nonsense. Nothing to it at all. People always want to say something of that kind."

"Perhaps one of them was–ill."

"Well, Lady Ravenscroft had been up to London once or twice consulting a doctor about something and I rather think she was going into hospital, or planning to go into hospital for an operation of some kind, though she never told me exactly what it was. But I think they managed to put her right–she was in this hospital for a short time. No operation, I think. And when she came back, she looked very much younger. Altogether, she'd had a lot of face treatment and you know, she looked so pretty in these wigs with curls on them. Rather as though she'd got a new lease of life."

"And General Ravenscroft?"

"He was a very nice gentleman and I never heard or knew of any scandal about him and I don't think there was any. People say things, but then they want to say something when there's been a tragedy of any kind. It seems to me perhaps as he might have had a blow on the head in India or something like that. I had an uncle or a great-uncle, you know, who fell off his horse there once. Hit it on a cannon or something and he was very queer afterwards. All right for about six months and then they had to put him into an asylum because he wanted to take his wife's life the whole

time. He said she was persecuting him and following him and that she was a spy for another nation. Ah, there's no saying what things happen or can happen in families."

"Anyway, you don't think there was any truth in some of the stories about them that I have happened to hear of, bad feeling between them so that one of them shot the other and then shot himself or herself?"

"Oh, no, I don't."

"Were her children at home at the time?"

"No. Miss—er—oh, what was her name now, Rosie? No. Penelope?"

"Celia," said Mrs. Oliver. "She's my goddaughter."

"Oh, of course she is. Yes, I know that now. I remember you coming and taking her out once. She was a high-spirited girl, rather bad-tempered in some ways, but she was very fond of her father and mother, I think. No, she was away at a school in Switzerland when it happened, I'm glad to say, because it would have been a terrible shock to her if she'd been at home and the one who saw them."

"And there was a boy, too, wasn't there?"

"Oh, yes. Master Edward. His father was a bit worried about him, I think. He looked as though he disliked his father."

"Oh, there's nothing in that. Boys go through that stage, I think. Was he very devoted to his mother?"

"Well, she fussed over him a bit too much, I think, which he found tiresome. You know, they don't like a mother fussing over them, telling them to wear thicker vests or put an extra pullover on. His father, he didn't like the way he

wore his hair. It was—well, they weren't wearing hair like the way they are nowadays, but they were beginning to, if you know what I mean."

"But the boy wasn't at home at the time of the tragedy?"

"No."

"I suppose it was a shock to him?"

"Well, it must have been. Of course, I wasn't going to the house any more at that time, so I didn't hear so much. If you ask me, I didn't like that gardener. What was his name now—Fred, I think. Fred Wizell. Some name like that. Seems to me if he'd done a bit of—well, a bit of cheating or something like that and the General had found him out and was going to sack him, I wouldn't put it past him."

"To shoot the husband and wife?"

"Well, I'd have thought it more likely he'd just have shot the General. If he shot the General and the wife came along, then he'd have had to shoot her, too. You read things like that in books."

"Yes," said Mrs. Oliver thoughtfully, "one does read all sorts of things in books."

"There was the tutor. I didn't like him much."

"What tutor?"

"Well, there was a tutor for the boy earlier. You know, he couldn't pass an exam and things at the earlier school he was at—prep school or something. So they had a tutor for him. He was there for about a year, I think. Lady Ravenscroft liked him very much. She was musical, you know, and so was this tutor. Mr. Edmunds, I think his name was. Rather a namby-pamby sort of young man, I thought my-

Rather a namby-pamby sort of young man, I thought myself, and it's my opinion that General Ravenscroft didn't care for him much."

"But Mrs. Ravenscroft did."

"Oh, they had a lot in common, I think. And I think she was the one really that chose him rather more than the General. Mind you, he had very nice manners and spoke to everyone nicely and all that—"

"And did—what's-his-name?"

"Edward? Oh, yes, he liked him all right, I think. In fact, he was quite a bit soft on him, I think. Almost a bit of hero worship. Anyway, don't you believe any stories you hear about scandals in the family or her having an affair with anyone or General Ravenscroft with that rather pi-faced girl who did filing work for him and all that sort of thing. No. Whoever that wicked murderer was, it's one who came from outside. The police never got on to anyone, no car was seen near there and there was nothing to it and they never got any further. But all the same, I think one ought to look about for somebody perhaps who'd known them in Malaya or abroad or somewhere else, or even when they were first living at Bournemouth. One never knows."

"What did your husband think about it?" said Mrs. Oliver. "He wouldn't have known as much about them as you would, of course, but still he might have heard a lot."

"Oh, he heard a lot of talk, of course. In the George and Flag, of an evening, you know. People saying all sorts of things. Said as she drank and that cases of empty bottles had been taken out of the house. Absolutely untrue, that was, I know for a fact. And there was a nephew as used to come and see them sometimes. Got into trouble with the police in some way, he did, but I don't think there was anything in that. The police didn't, either. Anyway, it wasn't at that time."

"There was no one else really living in the house, was there, except the General and Lady Ravenscroft?"

"Well, she had a sister as used to come sometimes, Lady Ravenscroft did. She was a half-sister, I think. Something like that. Looked rather like Lady Ravenscroft but not very good-looking and a year or two older, I should say. She made a bit of trouble between them, I always used to think, when she came for a visit. She was one of those who likes stirring things up, if you know what I mean. Just said things to annoy people."

"Was Lady Ravenscroft fond of her?"

"Well, if you ask me, I don't think she was really. I think the sister more or less wished herself on to them sometimes and she didn't like not to have her, but I think she found it pretty trying to have her there. The General quite liked her because she played cards well. Played chess and things with him and he enjoyed that. And she was an amusing woman in a way. Mrs. Jerryboy or something like that, her name was. She was a widow, I think. Used to borrow money from them, I think, too."

"Did you like her?"

"Well, if you don't mind my saying so, ma'am, no, I didn't like her. I disliked her very much. I thought she was one of those troublemakers, you know. But she hadn't been down for some time before the tragedy happened. I don't really remember very much what she was like. She had a son as came with her once or twice. Didn't like him very much. Shifty, I thought."

"Well," said Mrs. Oliver. "I suppose nobody will really ever know the truth. Not now. Not after all this time. I saw my goddaughter the other day."

"Did you now, ma'am. I'd be interested to hear about Miss Celia. How is she? All right?"

"Yes. She seems quite all right. I think she's thinking perhaps of getting married. At any rate she's got a—"

"Got a steady boy friend, has she?" said Mrs. Buckle. "Ah, well, we've all got that. Not that we all marry the first one we settle on. Just as well if you don't, nine times out of ten."

"You don't know a Mrs. Burton-Cox, do you?" asked Mrs. Oliver.

"Burton-Cox? I seem to know that name. No, I don't think so. Wasn't living down here or come to stay with them or anything? No, not that I remember. Yet I did hear something. Some old friend of General Ravenscroft, I think, which he'd known in India. But I don't know." She shook her head.

"Well," said Mrs. Oliver, "I mustn't stay gossiping with you any longer. It's been so nice to see you and Marlene."

9

RESULTS OF ELEPHANTINE RESEARCH

"A telephone call for you," said Hercule Poirot's manservant George. "From Mrs. Oliver."

"Ah, yes, George. And what had she to say?"

"She wondered if she could come and see you this evening, sir, after dinner."

"That would be admirable," said Poirot. "Admirable. I have had a tiring day. It will be a stimulating experience to see Mrs. Oliver. She is always entertaining as well as being highly unexpected in the things she says. Did she mention elephants, by the way?"

"Elephants, sir? No, I do not think so."

"Ah. Then it would seem perhaps that the elephants have been disappointing."

George looked at his master rather doubtfully. There were times when he did not quite understand the relevance of Poirot's remarks.

"Ring her back," said Hercule Poirot. "Tell her I shall be delighted to receive her."

George went away to carry out this order, and returned to say that Mrs. Oliver would be there about quarter to nine.

"Coffee," said Poirot. "Let coffee be prepared and some petits fours. I rather think I ordered some in lately from Fortnum and Mason."

"A liqueur of any kind, sir?"

"No, I think not. I myself will have some *Sirop de Cassis.*"

"Yes, sir."

Mrs. Oliver arrived exactly on time. Poirot greeted her with every sign of pleasure.

"And how are you, *chère madame?*"

"Exhausted," said Mrs. Oliver.

She sank down into the armchair that Poirot indicated.

"Completely exhausted."

"Ah. *Qui va à la chasse*—oh, I cannot remember the saying."

"I remember it," said Mrs. Oliver. "I learned it as a child. *'Qui va à la chasse perd sa place.'* "

"That, I am sure, is not applicable to the chase you have been conducting. I am referring to the pursuit of elephants, unless that was merely a figure of speech."

"Not at all," said Mrs. Oliver. "I have been pursuing elephants madly. Here, there and everywhere. The amount of petrol I have used, the amount of trains I have taken, the amount of letters I've written, the amount of telegrams I've sent—you wouldn't believe how exhausting it all is."

"Then repose yourself. Have some coffee."

"Nice, strong, black coffee—yes, I will. Just what I want."

"Did you, may I ask, get any results?"

"Plenty of results," said Mrs. Oliver. "The trouble is, I don't know whether any of them are any use."

"You learned facts, however?"

"No. Not really. I learned things that people told me were facts, but I strongly doubt myself whether any of them *were* facts."

"They were hearsay?"

"No. They were what I said they would be. They were memories. Lots of people who had memories. The trouble is, when you remember things, you don't always remember them right, do you?"

"No. But they are still what you might describe perhaps as results. Is not that so?"

"And what have you done?" said Mrs. Oliver.

"You are always so stern, madame," said Poirot. "You demand that I run about, that I also do things."

"Well, have you run about?"

"I have not run about, but I have had a few consultations with others of my own profession."

"It sounds far more peaceful than what I have been

doing," said Mrs. Oliver. "Oh, this coffee is nice. It's really strong. You wouldn't believe how tired I am. And how muddled."

"Come, come. Let us have good expectancy. You have got things. You have got something, I think."

"I've got a lot of different suggestions and stories. I don't know whether any of them are true."

"They could be not true, but still be of use," said Poirot.

"Well, I know what you mean," said Mrs. Oliver, "and that's what I think, too. I mean, that's what I thought when I went about it. When people remember something and tell you about it—I mean, it's often not quite actually what occurred but, it's what they themselves thought occurred."

"But they must have had something on which to base it," said Poirot.

"I've brought you a list of a kind," said Mrs. Oliver. "I don't need to go into details of where I went or what I said or why, I went out deliberately for—well, information one couldn't perhaps get from anybody in this country now. But it's all from people who knew something about the Ravenscrofts, even if they hadn't known them very well."

"News from foreign places, do you mean?"

"Quite a lot of them were from foreign places. Other people who knew them here rather slightly or from people whose aunts or cousins or friends knew them long ago."

"And each one that you've noted down had *some* story to tell—some reference to the tragedy or to people involved?"

"That's the idea," said Mrs. Oliver. "I'll tell you roughly, shall I?"

"Yes. Have a petit four."

"Thank you," said Mrs. Oliver.

She took a particularly sweet and rather bilious-looking one and champed it with energy.

"Sweet things," she said, "really give you a lot of vitality, I always think. Well, now, I've got the following suggestions. These things have usually been said to me starting by: 'Oh, yes, of course!' 'How sad it was, that whole story!' 'Of course, I think everyone knows really what happened.' That's the sort of thing."

"Yes."

"These people *thought* they knew what happened. But there weren't really any very good reasons. It was just something someone had told them, or they'd heard either from friends or servants or relations or things like that. The suggestions, of course, are all the kind that you might think they were. A. That General Ravenscroft was writing his memoirs of his Indian days and that he had a young woman who acted as his secretary and took dictation and typed things for him and was helping him, that she was a nice-looking girl and no doubt there was something there. The result being—well, there seemed to be two schools of thought. One school of thought was that he shot his wife because he hoped to marry the girl, and then when he had shot her, immediately was horror-stricken at what he'd done and shot himself . . ."

"Exactly," said Poirot. "A romantic explanation."

"The other idea was that there had been a tutor who

came to give lessons to the son who had been ill and away from his prep school for six months or so—a good-looking young man."

"Ah, yes. And the wife had fallen in love with the young man. Perhaps had an affair with him?"

"That was the idea," said Mrs. Oliver. "No kind of evidence. Just romantic suggestion again."

"And therefore?"

"Therefore I think the idea was that the General probably shot his wife and then in a fit of remorse shot himself. There was another story that the General had had an affair, and his wife found out about it, that she shot him and then herself. It's always been slightly different every time. But nobody really knew anything. I mean, it's always just a likely story every time. I mean, the General may have had an affair with a girl or lots of girls or just another married woman, or it might have been the wife who had an affair with someone. It's been a different someone in each story I've been told. There was nothing definite about it or any evidence for it. It's just the gossip that went around about twelve or thirteen years ago, which people have rather forgotten about now. But they remember enough about it to tell one a few names and get things only moderately wrong about what happened. There was an angry gardener who happened to live on the place, there was a nice elderly cook-housekeeper who was rather blind and rather deaf, but nobody seems to suspect that she had anything to do with it. And so on. I've got all the names and possibilities written down. The names of some of them wrong and some of them right. It's all very difficult. His wife had been ill, I gather, for some short time. I think it was some kind of fever that she had. A lot of her hair must have fallen out because she bought four wigs. There were at least four new wigs found among her things."

"Yes. I, too, heard that," said Poirot.

"Who did you hear it from?"

"A friend of mine in the police. He went back over the accounts of the inquest and the various things in the house. Four wigs! I would like to have your opinion on that, madame. Do you think that four wigs seems somewhat excessive?"

"Well, I do really," said Mrs. Oliver. "I had an aunt who had a wig, and she had an extra wig, but she sent one back to be redressed and wore the second one. I never heard of anyone who had four wigs."

Mrs. Oliver extracted a small notebook from her bag, ruffled the pages of it, searching for extracts.

"Mrs. Carstairs, she's seventy-seven and rather gaga. Quote from her: 'I do remember the Ravenscrofts quite well. Yes, yes, a very nice couple. It's very sad, I think. Yes. Cancer it was!' I asked them which of them had cancer," said Mrs. Oliver, "but Mrs. Carstairs had rather forgotten about that. She said she thought the wife came to London and consulted a doctor and had an operation and then came home and was very miserable, and her husband was very upset about her. So of course he shot her and himself."

"Was that her theory or did she have any exact knowledge?"

"I think it was entirely theory. As far as I can see and hear in the course of my investigations," said Mrs. Oliver, making rather a point of this last word, "when anybody has heard that any of their friends whom they don't happen to know very well have sudden illnesses or consult doctors, they always think it's cancer. And so do the people themselves, I think. Somebody else—I can't read her name here, I've forgotten, I think it began with T—she said that it was the husband who had cancer. He was very unhappy, and so was his wife. And they talked it over together and they couldn't bear the thought of it all, so they decided to commit suicide."

"Sad and romantic," said Poirot.

"Yes, and I don't think really true," said Mrs. Oliver. "It is worrying, isn't it? I mean, the people remembering so much and that they really mostly seem to have made it up themselves."

"They have made up the solution of something they knew about," said Poirot. "That is to say, they know that somebody comes to London, say, to consult a doctor, or that somebody has been in hospital for two or three months. That is a *fact* that they know."

"Yes," said Mrs. Oliver, "and then when they come to talk about it a long time afterwards, they've got the solution for it which they've made up themselves. That isn't awfully helpful, is it?"

"It is helpful," said Poirot. "You are quite right, you know, in what you said to me."

"About elephants?" said Mrs. Oliver rather doubtfully.

"About elephants," said Poirot. "It is important to know

certain facts which have lingered in people's memories although they may not know exactly what the fact was, why it happened or what led to it. But they might easily know something that we do not know and that we have no means of learning. So there have been memories leading to theories—theories of infidelity, of illness, of suicide pacts, of jealousy. All these things have been suggested to you. Further search could be made as to points if they seem in any way probable."

"People like talking about the past," said Mrs. Oliver. "They like talking about the past really much more than they like talking about what's happening now, or what happened last year. It brings things back to them. They tell you, of course, first about a lot of other people that you don't want to hear about and then you hear what the other people that they've remembered knew about somebody else that they didn't know but they heard about. You know, so that the General and Lady Ravenscroft you hear about is at one remove, as it were. It's like family relationships," she said. "You know, first cousin once removed, second cousin twice removed, all the rest of it. I don't think I've been really very helpful, though."

"You must not think that," said Poirot. "I am pretty sure that you will find that some of these things in your agreeable little purple-colored notebook will have something to do with the past tragedy. I can tell you from my own inquiries into the official accounts of these two deaths that they have remained a mystery. That is, from the police point of view. They were an affectionate couple, there was no gossip or hearsay much about them of any sex trouble, there was no illness discovered such as would have caused anyone to take their own lives. I talk now only of the time, you understand, immediately preceding the tragedy. But there was a time before that, further back."

"I know what you mean," said Mrs. Oliver, "and I've got something about that from an old Nanny. An old Nanny who is now—I don't know, she might be a hundred, but I think she's only about eighty. I remember her from my childhood days. She wasn't very young then. She used to tell me stories about people in the Services abroad—India, Egypt, Siam and Hong Kong and the rest."

"Anything that interested you?"

"Yes," said Mrs. Oliver, "there was some tragedy that she talked about. She seemed a bit uncertain about what it was. I'm not sure that it had anything to do with the Ravenscrofts, it might have been to do with some other people out there because she doesn't remember surnames and things very well. It was a mental case in one family. Someone's sister-in-law. Either General Whoever-it-was's sister or Mrs. Whoever-it-was's sister. Somebody who'd been in a mental home for years. I gathered she'd killed her own children or tried to kill her own children long ago, and then she'd been supposed to be cured or paroled or something and came out to Egypt, or India or wherever it was. She came out to stay with the people. And then it seems there was some other tragedy, connected again, I think, with children or something of that kind. Anyway, it was something that was hushed up. But I wondered. I mean, if there was something mental in the family, either Lady Ravenscroft's family or General Ravenscroft's family. I don't think it need have been as near as a sister. It could have been a cousin or something like that. But—well, it seemed to me a possible line of inquiry."

"Yes," said Poirot, "there's always possibility and something that waits for many years and then comes home to roost from somewhere in the past. That is what someone said to me. *Old sins have long shadows.*"

"It seemed to me," said Mrs. Oliver, "not that it was likely or even that old Nanny Matcham remembered it right or even really about it being the people she thought it was. But it *might* have fitted in with what that awful woman at the literary luncheon said to me."

"You mean when she wanted to know . . ."

"Yes. When she wanted me to find out from the daughter, my godchild, whether her mother had killed her father or whether her father had killed her mother."

"And she thought the girl might know?"

"Well, it's likely enough that the girl would know. I mean, not at the time—it might have been shielded from her—but she might know things about it which would make her be aware what the circumstances were in their lives and who was likely to have killed whom, though she would probably never mention it or say anything about it or talk to anyone about it."

"And you say that woman—this Mrs.—"

"Yes. I've forgotten her name now. Mrs. Burton something. A name like that. She said something about her son had this girl friend and that they were thinking of getting married. And I can quite see you might want to know, if so, whether her mother or her father had criminal relations in their family—or a loony strain. She probably thought that if it was the mother who killed the father it would be very unwise for the boy to marry her, whereas if the father had killed the mother, she probably wouldn't mind as much," said Mrs. Oliver.

"You mean that she would think that the inheritance would go in the female line?"

"Well, she wasn't a very clever type of woman. Bossy," said Mrs. Oliver. "Thinks she knows a lot, but no. I think you might think that way if you were a woman."

"An interesting point of view, but possible," said Poirot. "Yes, I realize that." He sighed. "We have a lot to do still."

"I've got another sidelight on things, too. Same thing, but second hand, if you know what I mean. You know. Someone says, 'The Ravenscrofts? Weren't they that couple who adopted a child? Then it seems, after it was all arranged, and they were absolutely stuck on it—very, very keen on it, one of their children had died in India, I think—but at any rate they had adopted this child and then its own mother wanted it back and they had a court case or something. But the court gave them the custody of the child and the mother came and tried to kidnap it back.' "

"There are simpler points," said Poirot, "arising out of your report, points that I prefer."

"Such as?"

"Wigs. Four wigs."

"Well," said Mrs. Oliver, "I thought that was interesting you, but I don't know why. It doesn't seem to *mean* anything. The Indian story was just somebody mental. There are mental people who are in homes or loony-bins because they have killed their children or some other child, for some absolutely batty reason, no sense to it at all. I don't see why that would make General and Lady Ravenscroft want to kill themselves."

"Unless one of them was implicated," said Poirot.

"You mean that General Ravenscroft may have killed someone, a boy—an illegitimate child, perhaps, of his wife's or of his own? No, I think we're getting a bit too melodramatic there. Or she might have killed her husband's child or her own."

"And yet," said Poirot, "what people seem to be, they usually are."

"You mean—?"

"They seemed an affectionate couple—a couple who lived together happily without disputes. They seem to have had no case history of illness beyond a suggestion of an operation, of someone coming to London to consult some medical authority, a possibility of cancer, of leukemia, something of that kind, some future that they could not face. And yet, somehow we do not seem to get at something beyond what is *possible*, but not yet what is *probable*. If there was anyone else in the house, anyone else at the time, the police, my friends that is to say, who have known the investigation at the time, say that nothing told was really compatible with anything else but with the facts. For some reason, those two didn't want to go on living. *Why?*"

"I knew a couple," said Mrs. Oliver, "in the war—the second war, I mean—they thought that the Germans would land in England and they had decided if that happened they would kill themselves. I said it was very stupid. They said it would be impossible to go on living. It still seems to me stupid. You've got to have enough courage to live through something. I mean, it's not as though your death was going to do any good to anybody else. I wonder—?"

"Yes, what do you wonder?"

"Well, when I said that I wondered suddenly if General and Lady Ravenscroft's deaths did any good to anyone else."

"You mean somebody inherited money from them?"

"Yes. Not quite as blatant as that. Perhaps somebody would have a better chance of doing well in life. Something there was in their life that they didn't want either of their two children ever to hear about or to know about." Poirot sighed.

"The trouble with you is," he said, "you think so often of something that well *might* have occurred, that *might* have been. You give me ideas. Possible ideas. If only they were probable ideas also. *Why?* Why were the deaths of those two necessary? Why is it—they were not in pain, they were not in illness, they were not deeply unhappy from what one can see. Then why, in the evening of a beautiful day, did they go for walk to a cliff and taking the dog with them . . ."

"What's the dog got to do with it?" said Mrs. Oliver.

"Well, I wondered for a moment. Did they take the dog,

or did the dog follow them? Where does the dog come in?"

"I suppose it comes in like the wigs," said Mrs. Oliver. "Just one more thing that you can't explain and doesn't seem to make sense. One of my elephants said the dog was devoted to Lady Ravenscroft, but another one said the dog bit her."

"One always comes back to the same thing," said Poirot. "One wants to know more." He sighed. "One wants to know more about the people, and how can you know people separated from you by a gulf of years?"

"Well, you've done it once or twice, haven't you?" said Mrs. Oliver. "You know—something about where a painter was shot or poisoned. That was near the sea on a sort of fortification or something. You found out who did that, although you didn't know any of the people."

"No. I didn't know any of the people, but I learned about them from the other people who were there." *

"Well, that's what I'm trying to do," said Mrs. Oliver. "Only I can't get near enough. I can't get to anyone who really knew anything, who was really involved. Do you think really we ought to give it up?"

"I think it would be very wise to give it up," said Poirot, "but there is a moment when one no longer wants to be wise. One wants to find out more. I have an interest now in that couple of kindly people, with two nice children. I presume they are nice children?"

"I don't know the boy," said Mrs. Oliver. "I don't think

* *Murder in Retrospect.*

I've ever met him. Do you want to see my goddaughter? I could send her to see you, if you like."

"Yes, I think I would like to see her, meet her some way. Perhaps she would not wish to come and see me, but a meeting could be brought about. It might, I think, be interesting. And there is someone else I would like to see."

"Oh! Who is that?"

"The woman at the party. The bossy woman. Your bossy friend."

"She's no friend of mine," said Mrs. Oliver. "She just came up and spoke to me, that's all."

"You could resume acquaintance with her?"

"Oh, yes, quite easily. I would think she'd probably jump at it."

"I would like to see her. I would like to know why she wants to know these things."

"Yes. I suppose that might be useful. Anyway—" Mrs. Oliver sighed—"I shall be glad to have a rest from elephants. Nanny—you know, the old Nanny I talked about—she mentioned elephants and that elephants didn't forget. That sort of silly sentence is beginning to haunt me. Ah, well, *you* must look for more elephants. It's your turn."

"And what about you?"

"Perhaps I could look for swans."

"*Mon dieu,* where do swans come in?"

"It is only what I remember, which Nanny reminded me of. That there were little boys I used to play with and one used to call me Lady Elephant and the other one used to call me Lady Swan. When I was Lady Swan, I pretended to be swimming about on the floor. When I was Lady Elephant, they rode on my back. There are no swans in this."

"That is a good thing," said Poirot. "Elephants are quite enough."

10

DESMOND

Two days later, as Hercule Poirot drank his morning chocolate, he read at the same time a letter that had been among his correspondence that morning. He was reading it now for the second time. The handwriting was a moderately good one, though it hardly bore the stamp of maturity.

Dear Monsieur Poirot,

I am afraid you will find this letter of mine somewhat peculiar, but I believe it would help if I mentioned a friend of yours. I tried to get in touch with her to ask her if she would arrange for me to come and see you, but apparently she had left home. Her secretary—I am referring to Mrs. Ariadne Oliver, the novelist—her secretary seemed to say something about her having gone on a safari in East Africa. If so, I can see she may not return for some time. But I'm sure she would help me. I would indeed like to see you so much. I am badly in need of advice of some kind.

Mrs. Oliver, I understand, is acquainted with my mother, who met her at a literary luncheon party. If you could give me an appointment to visit you one day, I should be very grateful. I can suit my time to anything you suggested. I don't know if it is helpful at all, but Mrs. Oliver's secretary did mention the word "elephants." I presume this has something to do with Mrs. Oliver's travels in East Africa. The secretary spoke as though it was some kind of password. I don't really understand this but perhaps you will. I am in a great state of worry and anxiety and I would be very grateful if you could see me.

Yours truly,
Desmond Burton-Cox.

"Nom d'un petit bonhomme!" said Hercule Poirot.

"I beg your pardon, sir?" said George.

"A mere ejaculation," said Hercule Poirot. "There are some things, once they have invaded your life, which you find very difficult to get rid of again. With me it seems to be a question of elephants."

He left the breakfast table, summoned his faithful secretary, Miss Lemon, handed her the letter from Desmond Cox and gave her directions to arrange an appointment with the writer of the letter.

"I am not too occupied at the present time," he said. "Tomorrow will be quite suitable."

Miss Lemon reminded him of two appointments which

he already had, but agreed that that left plenty of hours vacant and she would arrange something as he wished.

"Something to do with the Zoological Gardens?" she inquired.

"Hardly," said Poirot. "No, do not mention elephants in your letter. There can be too much of anything. Elephants are large animals. They occupy a great deal of the horizon. Yes. We can leave elephants. They will no doubt arise in the course of the conversation I propose to hold with Desmond Burton-Cox."

"Mr. Desmond Burton-Cox," announced George, ushering in the expected guest.

Poirot had risen to his feet and was standing beside the mantelpiece. He remained for a moment or two without speaking, then he advanced, having summed up his own impression. A somewhat nervous and energetic personality. Quite naturally so, Poirot thought. A little ill at ease but managing to mask it very successfully. He said, extending a hand,

"Mr. Hercule Poirot?"

"That is right," said Poirot. "And your name is Desmond Burton-Cox. Pray sit down and tell me what I can do for you, the reasons why you have come to see me."

"It's all going to be rather difficult to explain," said Desmond Burton-Cox.

"So many things are difficult to explain," said Hercule Poirot, "but we have plenty of time. Sit down."

Desmond looked rather doubtfully at the figure confronting him. Really, a very comic personality, he thought. The egg-shaped head, the big moustaches. Not somehow very imposing. Not quite, in fact, what he had expected to encounter.

"You—you are a detective, aren't you?" he said. "I mean you—you find out things. People come to you to find out, or to ask you to find out things for them."

"Yes," said Poirot, "that is one of my tasks in life."

"I don't suppose that you know what I've come about or that you know anything much about me."

"I know something," said Poirot.

"You mean Mrs. Oliver, your friend Mrs. Oliver. She's told you something?"

"She told me that she had had an interview with a goddaughter of hers, a Miss Celia Ravenscroft. That is right, is it not?"

"Yes. Yes, Celia told me. This Mrs. Oliver, is she—does she also know my mother—know her well, I mean?"

"No. I do not think that they know each other well. According to Mrs. Oliver, she met her at a literary luncheon recently and had a few words with her. Your mother, I understand, made a certain request to Mrs. Oliver."

"She'd no business to do so," said the boy.

His eyebrows came down over his nose. He looked angry now, angry—almost revengeful.

"Really," he said, "Mother's—I mean—"

"I understand," said Poirot. "There is much feeling these days, indeed perhaps there always has been. Mothers are continually doing things which their children would much rather they did not do. Am I right?"

"Oh you're right enough. But my mother—I mean, she interferes in things in which really she has no concern."

"You and Celia Ravenscroft, I understand, are close friends. Mrs. Oliver understood from your mother that there was some question of marriage. Perhaps in the near future?"

"Yes, but my mother really doesn't need to ask questions and worry about things which are—well, no concern of hers."

"But mothers are like that," said Poirot. He smiled faintly. He added, "You are, perhaps, very much attached to your mother?"

"I wouldn't say that," said Desmond. "No, I certainly wouldn't say that. You see—well, I'd better tell you straightaway, she's not really my mother."

"Oh, indeed. I had not understood that."

"I'm adopted," said Desmond. "She had a son. A little boy who died. And then she wanted to adopt a child, so I was adopted, and she brought me up as her son. She always speaks of me as her son, and thinks of me as her son, but I'm not really her son. We're not a bit alike. We don't look at things the same way."

"Very understandable," said Poirot.

"I don't seem to be getting on," said Desmond, "with what I want to ask you."

"You want me to do something, to find out something, to cover a certain line of interrogation?"

"I suppose that does cover it. I don't know how much

you know about—about well, what the trouble is all about."

"I know a little," said Poirot. "Not details. I do not know very much about you or about Miss Ravenscroft, whom I have not yet met. I'd like to meet her."

"Yes, well, I was thinking of bringing her to talk to you, but I thought I'd better talk to you myself first."

"Well, that seems quite sensible," said Poirot. "You are unhappy about something? Worried? You have difficulties?"

"Not really. No. No, there shouldn't be any difficulties. There aren't any. What happened is a thing that happened years ago when Celia was only a child, or a schoolgirl at least. And there was a tragedy, the sort of thing that happens—well, it happens every day, any time. Two people you know whom something has upset very much and they commit suicide. A sort of suicide pact, this was. Nobody knew very much about it or why, or anything like that. But, after all, it happens and it's no business really of people's children to worry about it. I mean, if they know the facts, that's quite enough, I should think. And it's no business of my mother's *at all.*"

"As one journeys through life," said Poirot, "one finds more and more that people are often interested in things that are none of their own business. Even more so than they are in things that *could* be considered as their own business."

"But this is all over. Nobody knew much about it or anything. But, you see, my mother keeps asking questions. Wants to know things, and she's got at Celia. She's got Celia into a state where she doesn't really know whether she wants to marry me or not."

"And you? You know if you want to marry her still?"

"Yes, of course I know. I mean to marry her. I'm quite determined to marry her. But she's got upset. She wants to know things. She wants to know why all this happened and she thinks—I'm sure she's wrong—she thinks that my mother knows something about it. That she's heard something about it."

"Well, I have much sympathy for you," said Poirot, "but it seems to me that if you are sensible young people and if you want to marry, there is no reason why you should not. I may say that I have been given some information at my request about this sad tragedy. As you say, it is a matter that happened many years ago. There was no full explanation of it. There never has been. But in life one cannot have explanations of all the sad things that happen."

"It was a suicide pact," said the boy. "It couldn't have been anything else. But—well . . ."

"You want to know the cause of it. Is that it?"

"Well, yes, that's it. That's what Celia's been worried about, and she's almost made me worried. Certainly my mother is worried, though, as I've said, it's absolutely no business of hers. I don't think any fault is attached to anyone. I mean, there wasn't a row or anything. The trouble is, of course, that we don't know. Well, I mean, I shouldn't know anyway because I wasn't there."

"You didn't know General and Lady Ravenscroft or Celia?"

"I've known Celia more or less all my life. You see, the people I went to for holidays and her people lived next door to each other when we were very young. You know —just children. And we always liked each other, and got on together and all that. And then, of course, for a long time all that passed over. I didn't meet Celia for a great many years after that. Her parents, you see, were in Malaya, and so were mine. I think they met each other again there—I mean my father and mother. My father's dead, by the way. But I think when my mother was in India she heard things and she's remembered now what she heard and she's worked herself up about them and she sort of— sort of thinks things that can't possibly be true. I'm sure they aren't true. But she's determined to worry Celia about them. I want to know what really happened. Celia wants to know what really happened. What it was all about. And why? And how? Not just people's silly stories."

"Yes," said Poirot, "it is not unnatural perhaps that you should both feel that. Celia, I should imagine, more than you. She is more disturbed by it than you are. But, if I may say so, does it really matter? What matters is the *now,* the *present*. The girl you want to marry, the girl who wants to marry you—what has the past to do with you? Does it matter whether her parents had a suicide pact or whether they died in an airplane accident or one of them was killed in an accident and the other one later committed suicide? Whether there were love affairs which came into their lives and made for unhappiness."

"Yes," said Desmond Burton-Cox, "yes, I think what

you say is sensible and quite right but—well, things have been built up in such a way that I've got to make sure that Celia is satisfied. She's—she's a person who *minds* about things although she doesn't talk about them much."

"Has it not occurred to you," said Hercule Poirot, "that it may be very difficult, if not impossible, to find out what really happened?"

"You mean which of them killed the other or why, or that one shot the other and then himself. Not unless—not unless there had been *something*."

"Yes, but that something would have been in the past, so why does it matter now?"

"It oughtn't to matter—it wouldn't matter but for my mother interfering, poking about in things. It wouldn't have mattered. I don't suppose that, well, Celia's ever thought much about it. I think probably that she was away at school in Switzerland at the time the tragedy happened and nobody told her much and, well, when you're a teen-ager or younger still you just accept things as something that happened, but that's not anything to do with you really."

"Then don't you think that perhaps you're wanting the impossible?"

"I want you to find out," said Desmond. "Perhaps it's not the kind of thing that you can find out, or that you like finding out—"

"I have no objection to finding out," said Poirot. "In fact one has even a certain—curiosity, shall I say. Tragedies, things that arise as a matter of grief, surprise, shock, illness—they are human tragedies, human things, and it is only natural that if one's attention is drawn to them one should want to know. What I say is, is it wise or necessary to rake up things?"

"Perhaps it isn't," said Desmond, "but you see . . ."

"And also," said Poirot, interrupting him, "don't you agree with me that it is rather an impossible thing to do after all this time?"

"No," said Desmond, "that's where I *don't* agree with you. I think it would be quite possible."

"Very interesting," said Poirot. "Why do you think it would be quite possible?"

"Because—"

"Of what? You have a reason."

"I think there are people who would know. I think there are people who *could* tell you if they were willing to tell you. People, perhaps, who would not wish to tell me, who would not wish to tell Celia, but *you* might find out from them."

"That is interesting," said Poirot.

"Things happened," said Desmond. "Things happened in the past. I—I've sort of heard about them in a vague way. There was some mental trouble. There was someone—I don't know who exactly, I think it might have been Lady Ravenscroft—I think she was in a mental home for years. Quite a long time. Some tragedy had happened when she was quite young. Some child who died or an accident. Something that—well, she was concerned in it in some way."

"It is not what you know of your own knowledge, I

presume?"

"No. It's something my mother said. Something she heard. She heard it in India, I think. Gossip there from other people. You know how they get together in the Services, people like that, and the women all gossip together —all the mem-sahibs. Saying things that mightn't be true at all."

"And you want to know whether they were true or were not true?"

"Yes, and I don't know how to find out myself. Not now, because it was a long time ago and I don't know who to ask. I don't know who to go to, but until we really find out what did happen and why—"

"What you mean is," said Poirot, "at least I think I am right, only this is pure surmise on my part, Celia Ravenscroft does not want to marry you unless she is quite sure that there is no mental flaw passed to her presumably by her mother. Is that it?"

"I think that is what she has got into her head somehow. And I think my mother put it there. I think it's what my mother wants to believe. I don't think she's any reason really for believing it except ill-mannered spite and gossip and all the rest of it."

"It will not be a very easy thing to investigate," said Poirot.

"No, but I've heard things about you. They say that you're very clever at finding out what did happen. Asking people questions and getting them to tell you things."

"Whom do you suggest I should question or ask? When you

say India, I presume you are not referring to people of Indian nationality. You are speaking of what you might call the mem-sahib days, the days when there were Service communities in India. You are speaking of English people and the gossip in some English station there."

"I don't really mean that that would be any good now. I think whoever it was who gossiped, who talked—I mean, it's so long ago now that they'd have forgotten all about it, that they are probably dead themselves. I think that my mother's got a lot of things wrong, that she's heard things and made up more things about them in her mind."

"And you still think that I would be capable—"

"Well, I don't mean that I want you to go out to India and ask people things. I mean, none of the people would be there now."

"So you think you could not give me names?"

"Not those sort of names," said Desmond.

"But some names?"

"Well, I'll come out with what I mean. I think there are two people who might know what happened and why. Because, you see, they'd have been *there*. They'd have *known,* really known, of their own knowledge."

"You do not want to go to them yourself?"

"Well, I could. I have in a way, but I don't think, you see, that they—I don't know. I wouldn't like to ask some of the things I want to ask. I don't think Celia would. They're very nice, and that's *why* they'd know. Not because they're nasty, not because they gossip, but because they might have helped. They might have done something to make things better, or have tried to do so, only they couldn't. Oh, I'm putting it all so badly."

"No," said Poirot, "you are doing it very well, and I am interested and I think you have something definite in your mind. Tell me, does Celia Ravenscroft agree with you?"

"I haven't said too much to her. You see, she was very fond of Maddy and of Zélie."

"Maddy and Zélie?"

"Oh, well, that's their names. Oh, I must explain. I haven't done it very well. You see, when Celia was quite a child—at the time when I first knew her, as I say, when we were living next door in the country—she had a French sort of—well, I suppose nowadays we call it an *au pair* girl, but it was called a governess then. You know, a French governess. A mademoiselle. And you see, she was very nice. She played with all of us children and Celia always called her Maddy for short—and all the family called her Maddy."

"Ah, yes. The mademoiselle."

"Yes, you see being French, I thought—I thought perhaps she would tell you things that she knew and wouldn't wish to speak about to other people."

"Ah. And the other name you mentioned?"

"Zélie. The same sort of thing, you see. A mademoiselle. Maddy was there, I think, for about two or three years and then, later, she went back to France, or Switzerland I think it was, and this other one came. Younger than Maddy was and we didn't call her Maddy. Celia called her Zélie. All the family called her Zélie. She was very young, pretty and great fun. We were all frightfully fond of her. She played games with us and we all loved her. The family did. And General Ravenscroft was very taken with her. They used to play games together, picquet, you know and lots of things."

"And Lady Ravenscroft?"

"Oh, she was devoted to Zélie too, and Zélie was devoted to her. That's why she came back again after she'd left."

"Came back?"

"Yes, when Lady Ravenscroft was ill, and had been in hospital, Zélie came back and was sort of companion to her and looked after her. I don't know, but I believe, I think, I'm almost sure that she was there when it—the tragedy—happened. And so, you see she'd know—what really happened."

"And you know her address? You know where she is now?"

"Yes. I know where she is. I've got her address. I've got both their addresses. I thought perhaps you could go and see her, or both of them. I know it's a lot to ask—" He broke off.

Poirot looked at him for some minutes. Then he said: "Yes, it is a possibility—certainly—a possibility."

BOOK II

LONG SHADOWS

11

SUPERINTENDENT GARROWAY AND POIROT COMPARE NOTES

Superintendent Garroway looked across the table at Poirot. His eyes twinkled. At his side George delivered a whisky and soda. Passing on to Poirot, he put down a glass filled with a dark purple liquid.

"What's your tipple?" said Superintendent Garroway with some interest.

"A syrup of black currant," said Poirot.

"Well, well," said Superintendent Garroway, "everyone to their own taste. What was it Spence told me? He told me you used to drink something called a tisane, wasn't it? What's that, a variant of French piano or something?"

"No," said Poirot, "it's useful for reducing fevers."

"Ah. Invalid dope of some kind." He drank from his

glass. "Well," he said, "here's to suicide!"

"It *was* suicide?" Poirot asked.

"What else can it be?" said Superintendent Garroway. "The things you wanted to know!" He shook his head. His smile grew more pronounced.

"I am sorry," said Poirot, "to have troubled you so much. I am like the animal or the child in one of your stories by Mr. Kipling. I suffer from insatiable curiosity."

"Insatiable curiosity," said Superintendent Garroway. "Nice stories he wrote, Kipling. Knew his stuff, too. They told me once that that man could go for one short tour round a destroyer and know more about it than one of the top engineers in the Royal Navy."

"Alas," said Hercule Poirot, "I do not know everything. Therefore, you see, I have to ask questions. I am afraid that I sent you rather a long list of questions."

"What intrigued me," said Superintendent Garroway, "is the way you jumped from one thing to another. Psychiatrists, doctors' reports, how money was left, who had money, who got money. Who expected money and didn't get money, particulars of ladies' hairdressing, wigs, name of the supplier of wigs, charming rose-colored cardboard boxes they came in, by the way."

"You knew all these things," said Poirot. "That has amazed me, I can assure you."

"Ah, well, it was a puzzling case and of course we made full notes on the subject. None of this was any good to us, but we kept the files and it was all there if one wanted to look for it."

He pushed a piece of paper across the table.

"Here you are. Hairdressers. Bond Street. Expensive firm. Eugene and Rosentelle was the name of it. They moved later. Same firm but went into business in Sloane Street. Here's the address, but it's a pet shop now. Two of their assistants retired some years ago now, but they were the top assistants serving people then, and Lady Ravenscroft was on their list. Rosentelle lives in Cheltenham now. Still in the same line of business. Calls herself a hair stylist—that's the up-to-date term—and you add beautician. Same man, different hat, as one used to say in my young days."

"Ah-ha!" said Poirot.

"Why ah-ha?" asked Garroway.

"I am immensely obliged to you," said Hercule Poirot. "You have presented me with an idea. How strange it is the way ideas arrive into one's head."

"You've too many ideas in your head already," said the Superintendent. "That's one of your troubles—you don't need any more. Now then, I've checked up as well as I could on the family history—nothing much there. Alistair Ravenscroft was of Scottish extraction. Father was a clergyman—two uncles in the Army—both quite distinguished. Married Margaret Preston-Grey—well-born girl—presented at Court and all the rest of it. No family scandals. You were quite right about her being one of twin sisters. Don't know where you picked that up—Dorothea and Margaret Preston-Grey—known colloquially as Dolly and Molly. Preston-Greys lived at Hatters Green in Sussex. Identical twins—usual kind of history of that kind of twin.

Cut their first tooth the same day—both got scarlet fever the same month—wore the same kind of clothes—fell in love with the same kind of man—got married about the same time—both husbands in the Army. Family doctor who attended the family when they were young died some years ago, so there's nothing of interest to be got out of him. There was an early tragedy, though, connected with one of them."

"Lady Ravenscroft?"

"No, the other one—she married a Captain Jarrow—had two children; the younger one, a boy of four, was knocked down by a wheelbarrow or some kind of a child's garden toy—or a spade or a child's hoe. Hit him on his head and he fell into an artificial pond or something and drowned. Apparently it was the older child, a girl of nine, who did it. They were playing together and quarreled, as children do. Doesn't seem much doubt, but there *was* another story. Someone said the mother did it—got angry and hit him—and someone else said it was a woman who lived next door who hit him. Don't suppose it's of any interest to you—no bearing on a suicide pact entered into by the mother's sister and her husband years after."

"No," said Poirot, "it does not seem to. But one likes to know background."

"Yes," said Garroway, "as I told you, one has to look into the past. I can't say we'd thought of looking into the past as long ago as this. I mean, as I've said, all this was twenty years before the suicide."

"Were there any proceedings at the time?"

"Yes. I managed to look up the case. Accounts of it.

Newspaper accounts. Various things. There were some doubts about it, you know. The mother was badly affected. She broke down completely and had to go into hospital. They do say she was never the same woman again afterwards."

"But they thought she had done it?"

"Well, that's what the doctor thought. There was no direct evidence, you understand. She said that she had seen this happen from a window, that she'd seen the older child, the girl, hit the boy and push him in. But her account—well, I don't think they believed it at the time. She talked so wildly."

"There was, I suppose, some psychiatric evidence?"

"Yes. She went to a nursing home or hospital of some kind, she was definitely a mental case. She was a good long time in one or two different establishments having treatment, I believe under the care of one of the specialists from St. Andrew's Hospital in London. In the end she was pronounced cured, and released after about three years, and sent home to lead a normal life with her family."

"And she was then quite normal?"

"She was always neurotic, I believe—"

"Where was she at the time of the suicide? Was she staying with the Ravenscrofts?"

"No—she had died nearly three weeks before that. She was staying with them at Overcliffe when it happened. It seemed again to be an illustration of the identical twin destiny. She walked in her sleep—had suffered from that over a period of years, it seems. She had had one or two minor accidents that way. She sometimes took too many tranquilizers and that resulted in her walking round the house and sometimes out of it during the night. She was following a path along the cliff edge, lost her footing and fell over the cliff. Killed immediately. They didn't find her until the next day. Her sister, Lady Ravenscroft, was terribly upset. They were very devoted to each other and she had to be taken to hospital suffering from shock."

"Could this tragic accident have led to the Ravenscrofts' suicide some months later?"

"There was never a suggestion of such a thing."

"Odd things happen with twins, as you say. Lady Ravenscroft might have killed herself because of the link between her and her twin sister. Then the husband may have shot himself because possibly he felt guilty in some way—"

Superintendent Garroway said: "You have too many ideas, Poirot. Alistair Ravenscroft couldn't have had an affair with his sister-in-law without everyone knowing about it. There was nothing of that kind—if that's what you've been imagining."

The telephone rang. Poirot rose and answered it. It was Mrs. Oliver.

"Monsieur Poirot, can you come to tea or sherry tomorrow? I have got Celia coming—and later on the bossy woman. That's what you wanted, isn't it?"

Poirot said it was just what he wanted.

"I've got to dash now," said Mrs. Oliver, "Going to meet an old war horse—provided by my elephant Number One, Julia Carstairs. I think she's got his name wrong—she always does—but I hope she's got his address right."

12

CELIA MEETS HERCULE POIROT

"Well, madame," said Poirot, "and how did you fare with Sir Hugo Foster?"

"To begin with, his name wasn't Foster—it was Fothergill. Trust Julia to get a name wrong. She's always doing it."

"So elephants are not always reliable in the names they remember?"

"Don't talk of elephants—I've finished with elephants."

"And your war horse?"

"Quite an old pet—but useless as a source of information. Obsessed by some people called Marchant who did have a child killed in an accident in India. But nothing to do with the Ravenscrofts. I tell you, I've finished with elephants—"

"Madame, you have been most persevering, most noble."

"Celia is coming along in about half an hour's time. You wanted to meet her, didn't you? I've told her that you are —well, helping me in this matter. Or would you rather she came to see you?"

"No," said Poirot, "I think I should like her to come in the way you have arranged."

"I don't suppose she'll stay very long. If we get rid of her in about an hour, that would be all right, just to think over things a bit, and then Mrs. Burton-Cox is coming."

"Ah, yes. That will be interesting. Yes, that will be very interesting."

Mrs. Oliver sighed. "Oh, dear, it's a pity, though, isn't it?" She said again, "We do have too much material, don't we?"

"Yes," said Poirot. "We do not know what we are looking for. All we know of still is, in all probability, the double suicide of a married couple who lived quiet and happy lives together. And what have we got to show for cause, for reason? We've gone forward and back to the right, to the left, to the west, to the east."

"Quite right," said Mrs. Oliver. "Everywhere. We haven't been to the North Pole yet," she added.

"Nor to the South Pole," said Poirot.

"So what is there, when it all comes to it?"

"Various things," said Poirot. "I have made here a list. Do you want to read it?"

Mrs. Oliver came over and sat beside him and looked over his shoulder.

"Wigs," she said, pointing to the first item. "Why wigs first?"

"Four wigs," said Poirot, "seem to be interesting. Interesting and rather difficult to solve."

"I believe the shop she got her wigs from has gone out of the trade now. People go to quite different places for wigs and they're not wearing so many as they did just then. People used to wear wigs to go abroad. You know, because it saves bother in traveling."

"Yes, yes," said Poirot, "we will do what we can with wigs. Anyway, that is one thing that interests me. And then there are other stories. Stories of mental disturbance in the family. Stories of a twin sister who was mentally disturbed and spent a good many years of her life in a mental home."

"It doesn't seem to lead anywhere," said Mrs. Oliver. "I mean to say, I suppose she could have come and shot the two of them, but I don't really see why."

"No," said Poirot, "the fingerprints on the revolver were definitely only the fingerprints of General Ravenscroft and his wife, I understand. Then there are stories of a child. A child in India was murdered or attacked, possibly by this twin sister of Lady Ravenscroft. Possibly by some quite different woman—possibly by an ayah or a servant. Point two. You know a little more about money."

"Where does money come into it?" said Mrs. Oliver in some surprise.

"It does not come into it," said Poirot. "That is what is so interesting. Money usually comes in. Money someone got as a result of that suicide. Money lost as a result of it. Money somewhere causing difficulties, causing trouble, causing covetousness and desire. It is difficult, that. Difficult to see. There does not seem to have been any large amount of money anywhere. There are various stories of love affairs, women who were attractive to the husband, men who were attractive to the wife. An affair there one side or the other could have led to suicide or to murder. It very often does. Then we come to what at the moment inclines me to the most interest. That is why I am so anxious to meet Mrs. Burton-Cox."

"Oh. That awful woman. I don't see why you think she's important. All she did was to go being a nosey-parker and wanting me to find out things."

"Yes, but why did she want you to find out things? It seems to me very odd, that. It seems to me that that is something that one has to find out about. She is the link, you see."

"The link?"

"Yes. We do not know what the link was, where it was, how it was. All we know is that she wants desperately to learn more about this suicide. Being a link, she connects both with your godchild, Celia Ravenscroft, and with the son who is not her son."

"What do you mean—not her son?"

"He is an adopted son," said Poirot. "A son she adopted because her own son died."

"How did her own child die? Why? When?"

"All these things I asked myself. She could be a link, a

link of emotion, a wish for revenge through hatred, through some love affair. At any rate I must see her. I must make up my mind about her. Yes. I cannot help but think that is very important."

There was a ring at the bell and Mrs. Oliver went out of the room to answer it.

"This, I think, could be Celia," she said. "You're sure it's all right?"

"By me, yes," said Poirot. "By her also, I hope."

Mrs. Oliver came back a few minutes later. Celia Ravenscroft was with her. She had a doubtful, suspicious look.

"I don't know," she said, "if I—" She stopped, staring at Hercule Poirot.

"I want to introduce you," said Mrs. Oliver, "to someone who is helping me, and I hope is helping you also. That is, helping you in what you want to know and to find out. This is Monsieur Hercule Poirot. He has special genius in finding out things."

"Oh," said Celia.

She looked very doubtfully at the egg-shaped head, the monstrous moustaches and the small stature.

"I think," she said rather doubtfully, "that I have heard of him."

Hercule Poirot stopped himself with a slight effort from saying firmly, "Most people have heard of me." It was not quite as true as it used to be, because many people who had heard of Hercule Poirot and known him were now reposing with suitable memorial stones over them in churchyards. He said:

"Sit down, mademoiselle. I will tell you this much about myself. That when I start an investigation I pursue it to the end. I will bring to light the truth and if it is, shall we say, truly the truth that you want, then I will deliver that knowledge to you. But it may be that you want reassuring. That is not the same thing as the truth. I can find various aspects that might reassure you. Will that be enough? If so, do not ask for more."

Celia sat down in the chair he had pushed towards her, and looked at him rather earnestly. Then she said:

"You don't think I'd care for the truth, is that it?"

"I think," said Poirot, "that the truth might be—a shock, a sorrow, and it might be that you would have said 'why did I not leave all this behind? Why did I ask for knowledge? It is painful knowledge about which I can do nothing helpful or hopeful.' It is a double suicide by a father and a mother that I—well, we'll admit it—that I loved. It is not a disadvantage to love a mother and father."

"It seems to be considered so nowadays occasionally," said Mrs. Oliver. "New article of belief, shall we say."

"That's the way I've been living," said Celia. "Beginning to wonder, you know. Catching on to odd things that people said sometimes. People who looked at me rather pityingly. But more than that. With curiosity as well. One begins to find out, you know, things about people, I mean. People you meet, people you know, people who used to know your family. I don't want this life. I want . . . you think I don't really want it, but I do—I want truth. I'm able to deal with truth. Just tell me something."

It was not a continuation of the conversation. Celia had turned on Poirot with a separate question. Something which had replaced what had been in her mind just previously.

"You saw Desmond, didn't you?" she said. "He went to see you. He told me he had."

"Yes. He came to see me. Did you not want him to do so?"

"He didn't ask me."

"If he had asked you?"

"I don't know. I don't know whether I should have forbidden him to do so, told him on no account to do such a thing, or whether I should have encouraged it."

"I would like to ask you one question, mademoiselle. I want to know if there is one clear thing in your mind that matters to you, that could matter to you more than anything else."

"Well, what is that?"

"As you say, Desmond Burton-Cox came to see me. A very attractive and likeable young man, and very much in earnest over what he came to say. Now that—that is the really important thing. The important thing is if you and he really wish to marry—because that *is* serious. That is—though young people do not always think so nowadays—that is a link together for life. Do you want to enter into that state? It matters. What difference can it make to you or to Desmond whether the death of two people was a double suicide or something quite different?"

"You think it *is* something quite different—or, it was?"

"I do not as yet know," said Poirot. "I have reason to believe that it might be. There are certain things that do not accord with a double suicide, but as far as I can go on the opinion of the police—and the police are very reliable, Mademoiselle Celia, very reliable—they put together all the evidence and they thought very definitely that it could be nothing else but a double suicide."

"But they never knew the cause of it? That's what you mean."

"Yes," said Poirot, "that's what I mean."

"And don't you know the cause of it, either? I mean, from looking into things or thinking about them, or whatever you do?"

"No, I am not sure about it," said Poirot. "I think there might be something very painful to learn and I am asking you whether you will be wise enough to say: 'The past is the past. Here is a young man whom I care for and who cares for me. This is the future we are spending together, not the past.' "

"Did he tell you he was an adopted child?" asked Celia.

"Yes, he did."

"You see, what business is it really, of hers? Why should she come worrying Mrs. Oliver here, trying to make Mrs. Oliver ask me questions, find out things. She's not his own mother."

"Does he care for her?"

"No," said Celia. "I'd say on the whole he dislikes her. I think he always has."

"She's spent money on him, schooling and on clothes and on all sorts of different things. And you think *she* cares for *him?*"

"I don't know. I don't think so. She wanted, I suppose, a child to replace her own child. She'd had a child who died in an accident, that was why she wanted to adopt someone, and her husband had died quite recently. All these dates are so difficult."

"I know, I know. I would like perhaps to know one thing."

"About her or about him?"

"Is he provided for financially?"

"I don't know quite what you mean by that. He'll be able to support me—to support a wife. I gather some money was settled on him when he was adopted. A sufficient sum, that is. I don't mean a fortune or anything like that."

"There is nothing that she could—withhold?"

"What, you mean that she'd cut off the money supplies if he married me? I don't think she's ever threatened to do that, or indeed that she could do it. I think it was all fixed up by lawyers or whoever arranges adoptions. I mean, they make a lot of fuss, these adoption societies, from all I hear."

"I would ask you something else which you might know but nobody else does. Presumably Mrs. Burton-Cox knows it. Do you know who his actual mother was?"

"You think that might have been one of the reasons for her being so nosey and all that? Something to do with, as you say, what he was really. I don't know. I suppose he might have been an illegitimate child. They're the usual ones that go for adoption, aren't they? She might have known something about his real mother or his real father, or something like that. If so, she didn't tell him. I gather she just told him the silly things they suggest you should say. That it is just as nice to be adopted, because it shows you really were wanted. There's a lot of silly slop like that."

"I think some societies suggest that that's the way you should break the news. Does he or you know of any blood relations?"

"I don't know. I don't think he knows, but I don't think it worries him at all. He's not that kind of a worrier."

"Do you know if Mrs. Burton-Cox was a friend of your family, of your mother and father? Did you ever meet her, as far as you can remember, when you were living in your own home in the early days?"

"I don't think so. I think Desmond's mother—I mean, I think Mrs. Burton-Cox went to Malaya. I think perhaps her husband died out in Malaya, and that Desmond was sent to school in England while they were out there and that he was boarded with some cousins or people who take in children for holidays. And that's how we came to be friends in those days. I always remembered him, you know. I was a great hero-worshiper. He was wonderful at climbing trees and he taught me things about birds' nests and birds' eggs. So it seemed quite natural, when I met him again I mean, met him at the university, and we both talked about where we'd lived and then he asked me my name. He said, 'Only your Christian name I know,' and then we remembered quite a lot of things together. It's what made us, you might say, get acquainted. I don't know everything about him. I don't know *anything*. I want to know. How can you arrange your life and know what you're going to do with your life if you don't know all about the things that affect you, that really happened?"

"So you tell me to carry on with my investigation?"

"Yes, if it's going to produce any results, though I don't think it will, because in a way, well, Desmond and I have tried our hand at finding out a few things. We haven't been very successful. It seems to come back to this plain fact which isn't really the story of a life. It's the story of a death, isn't it? Of two deaths, that's to say. When it's a double suicide, one thinks of it as one death. Is it in Shakespeare or where does the quotation come from—'And in death they were not divided'?" She turned to Poirot again. "Yes, go on. Go on finding out. Go on telling Mrs. Oliver or telling me direct. I'd rather you told me direct." She turned towards Mrs. Oliver. "I don't mean to be horrid to you, Godmother. You've been a very nice godmother to me always, but—but I'd like it straight from the horse's mouth. I'm afraid that's rather rude, Monsieur Poirot, but I didn't mean it that way."

"No," said Poirot, "I am content to be the horse's mouth."

"And you think you will be?"

"I always believe that I can."

"And it's always true, is it?"

"It is usually true," said Poirot. "I do not say more than that."

13

MRS. BURTON-COX

"Well," said Mrs. Oliver as she returned into the room after seeing Celia to the door. "What do you think of her?"

"She is a personality," said Poirot, "an interesting girl. Definitely, if I may put it so, she is somebody, not anybody."

"Yes, that's true enough," said Mrs. Oliver.

"I would like you to tell me something."

"About her? I don't really know her very well. One doesn't really, with godchildren. I mean, you only see them, as it were, at stated intervals rather far apart."

"I didn't mean her. Tell me about her mother."

"Oh. I see."

"You knew her mother?"

"Yes. We were in a sort of *pensionnat* in Paris together.

People used to send girls to Paris then to be finished," said Mrs. Oliver. "That sounds more like an introduction to a cemetery than an introduction into society. What do you want to know about her?"

"You remember her? You remember what she was like?"

"Yes. As I tell you, one doesn't entirely forget things or people because they're in the past."

"What impression did she make on you?"

"She was beautiful," said Mrs. Oliver. "I do remember that. Not when she was about thirteen or fourteen. She had a lot of puppy fat then. I think we all did," she added thoughtfully.

"Was she a personality?"

"It's difficult to remember because, you see, she wasn't my only friend or my greatest friend. I mean, there were several of us together—a little pack, as you might say. People with tastes more or less the same. We were keen on tennis and we were keen on being taken to the opera and we were bored to death being taken to the picture galleries. I really can only give you a general idea."

"Molly Preston-Grey. That was her name. Had few boy friends?"

"We had one or two passions, I think. Not for pop singers, of course. They hadn't happened yet. Actors usually. There was one rather famous variety actor. A girl—one of the girls—had him pinned up over her bed and Mademoiselle Girand, the French mistress, on no account allowed that actor to be pinned up there. *'Ce n'est pas convenable,'* she said. The girl didn't tell her that he was her father! We laughed," added Mrs. Oliver. "Yes, we laughed a good deal."

"Well, tell me more about Molly or Margaret Preston-Grey. Does this girl remind you of her?"

"No, I don't think she does. No. They are not alike. I think Molly was more—was more emotional than this girl."

"There was a twin sister, I understand. Was she at the same *pensionnat?*"

"No, she wasn't. She might have been since they were the same age, but no, I think she was in some entirely different place in England. I'm not sure. I have a feeling that the twin sister Dolly, whom I had met once or twice very occasionally and who of course at that time looked exactly like Molly—I mean they hadn't started trying to look different, have different hair-dos and all that, as twins do usually when they grow up. I think Molly was devoted to her sister Dolly, but she didn't talk about her very much. I have a feeling—nowadays, I mean, I didn't have it then—that there might have been something a bit wrong perhaps with the sister even then. Once or twice, I remember, there were mentions of her having been ill or gone away for a course of treatment somewhere. Something like that. I remember once wondering whether she was a cripple. She was taken once by an aunt on a sea voyage to do her health good." She shook her head. "I can't really remember, though. I just had a feeling that Molly was devoted to her and would have liked to have protected her in some way. Does that seem nonsense to you?"

"Not at all," said Hercule Poirot.

"There were other times, I think, when she didn't want to talk about her. She talked about her mother and her father. She was fond of them, I think, in the ordinary sort of way. Her mother came once to Paris and took her out, I remember. Nice woman. Not very exciting or good-looking or anything. Nice, quiet, kindly."

"I see. So you have nothing to help us there? Boy friends?"

"We didn't have so many boy friends then," said Mrs. Oliver. "It's not like nowadays when it's a matter of course. Later, when we were both back again at home we more or less drifted apart. I think Molly went abroad somewhere with her parents. I don't think it was India—I don't think so. Somewhere else, I think it was. Egypt, perhaps. I think now they were in the Diplomatic Service. They were in Sweden at one time, and after that somewhere like Bermuda or the West Indies. I think he was a governor or something there. But those sort of things one doesn't really remember. All one remembers is all the silly things that we said to each other. I had a crush on the violin master, I remember. Molly was very keen on the music master, which was very satisfying to us both and I should think much less troublesome than boy friends seem to be nowadays. I mean, you adored—longed for the day when they came again to teach you. They were, I have no doubt, quite indifferent to you. But one dreamt about them at night and I remember having a splendid kind of daydream in which I nursed my beloved Monsieur Adolphe when he had cholera and I gave him, I think, blood transfusions to save his life. How very silly one is. And think of all the other things you think of doing! There was one time when I was quite determined to be a nun and later on I thought I'd be a hospital nurse. Well, I suppose we shall have Mrs. Burton-Cox in a moment. I wonder how she will react to you?"

Poirot gazed at his watch.

"We shall be able to see that fairly soon."

"Have we anything else we ought to talk about first?"

"I think there are a few things we might compare notes on. As I say, there are one or two things that I think could do with investigation. An elephant investigation for you, shall we say? And an understudy for an elephant for me."

"What an extraordinary thing to say," said Mrs. Oliver. "I told you I was done with elephants."

"Ah," said Poirot, "but elephants perhaps have not done with you."

The front doorbell sounded once again. Poirot and Mrs. Oliver looked at each other.

"Well," said Mrs. Oliver, "here we go."

She left the room once more. Poirot heard sounds of greeting going on outside and in a moment or two Mrs. Oliver returned, ushering the somewhat massive figure of Mrs. Burton-Cox.

"What a delightful flat you have," said Mrs. Burton-Cox. "So charming of you to have spared time—your very valuable time, I'm sure—and asked me to come and see you." Her eyes shot sideways to Hercule Poirot. A faint expression of surprise passed over her face. For a moment her eyes went from him to the baby grand piano that stood in one window. It occurred to Mrs. Oliver that Mrs. Burton-Cox was thinking that Hercule Poirot was a piano tuner. She hastened to dispel this illusion.

"I want to introduce you," she said, "to Mr. Hercule Poirot."

Poirot came forward and bent over her hand.

"I think he is the only person who might be able to help you in some way. You know. What you were asking me about the other day concerning my godchild, Celia Ravenscroft."

"Oh, yes, how kind of you to remember. I do so hope you can give me a little more knowledge of what really happened."

"I'm afraid I haven't been very successful," said Mrs. Oliver, "and that is really why I asked Mr. Poirot to meet you. He is a wonderful person, you know, for information on things generally. Really on top of his profession. I cannot tell you how many friends of mine he has assisted and how many, well, I can really call them mysteries, he has elucidated. And this was such a tragic thing to have happened."

"Yes, indeed," said Mrs. Burton-Cox. Her eyes were still somewhat doubtful. Mrs. Oliver indicated chairs and remarked:

"Now what will you have? A glass of sherry? It's too late for tea, of course. Or would you prefer a cocktail of some kind?"

"Oh, a glass of sherry. You are very kind."

"Monsieur Poirot?"

"I, too," said Poirot.

Mrs. Oliver could not help being thankful that he had not asked for *Sirop de Cassis* or one of his favorite fruit drinks. She got out glasses and a decanter.

"I have already indicated to Monsieur Poirot the outlines of the inquiry you want to make."

"Oh, yes," said Mrs. Burton-Cox.

She seemed rather doubtful and not so sure of herself as it would seem she was in the natural habit of being.

"These young people," she said to Poirot, "so difficult nowadays. These young people. My son, such a dear boy, we have great hopes of his doing well in the future. And then there is this girl, a very charming girl, who, as probably Mrs. Oliver told you, is her goddaughter, and—well, of course one never knows. I mean these friendships spring up and very often they don't last. They are what we used to call calf love, you know, years ago, and it is very important to know a little at least about the—antecedents of people. You know, what their families are like. Oh, of course I know Celia's a very well-born girl and all that, but there *was* this tragedy. Mutual suicide, I believe, but nobody has been really able to enlighten me at all on what led to it or what led up to it, shall we say. I have no actual friends who were friends in common with the Ravenscrofts and so it is very difficult for me to have ideas. I know Celia is a charming girl and all that, but one would like to know, to know more."

"I understand from my friend, Mrs. Oliver, that you wanted to know something specifically. You wanted to know, in fact—"

"What you said you wanted to know," said Mrs. Oliver, chipping in with some firmness, "was whether Celia's father shot her mother and then himself or whether Celia's mother shot her father and then herself."

"I feel it makes a difference," said Mrs. Burton-Cox. "Yes, definitely I feel it makes a difference."

"A very interesting point of view," said Poirot.

His tone was not very encouraging.

"Oh, the emotional background, shall I say, the emotional events that led up to all this. In a marriage, you must admit, one had to think of the children. The children, I mean, that are to come. I mean heredity. I think now we realize that heredity does more than environment. It leads to certain formation of character and certain very grave risks that one might not want to take."

"True," said Poirot. "The people who undertake the risks are the ones that have to make the decision. Your son and this young lady, it will be their choice."

"Oh, I know, I know. Not mine. Parents are never allowed to choose, are they, or even to give any advice. But I would like to know something about it. Yes, I would like to know very much. If you feel that you could undertake any—investigation I suppose is the word you would use. But perhaps—perhaps I am being a very foolish mother. You know. Overanxious about my dear son. Mothers are like that."

She gave a little whinny of laughter, putting her head slightly on one side.

"Perhaps," she said, as she tipped up the sherry glass,

"perhaps you will think about it and I also will let you know. Perhaps the exact points and things that I am worried about."

She looked at her watch.

"Oh, dear. Oh, dear, I'm late for another appointment. I shall have to go. I am so sorry, dear Mrs. Oliver, to have to run away so soon, but you know what it is. I had great difficulties finding a taxi this afternoon. One after another just turned his head aside and drove straight past me. Ah, very, very difficult, isn't it? I think Mrs. Oliver has your address, has she not?"

"I will give you my address," said Poirot. He removed a card from his pocket and handed it to her.

"Oh, yes, yes. I see. Monsieur Hercule Poirot. You are French, is that right?"

"I am Belgian," said Poirot.

"Oh, yes, yes. Belgique. Yes, yes. I quite understand. I am so pleased to have met you and I feel so hopeful. Oh, dear, I must go very, very fast."

Shaking Mrs. Oliver warmly by the hand, then extending the same hand to Poirot, she left the room and the door sounded in the hall.

"Well, what do you think of that?" said Mrs. Oliver.

"What do you?" said Poirot.

"She ran away," said Mrs. Oliver. "She ran away. You frightened her in some way."

"Yes," said Poirot, "I think you've judged quite right."

"She wanted me to get things out of Celia, she wanted me to get some knowledge out of Celia, some expression some sort of secret she suspected was there, but she doesn't want a real proper investigation, does she?"

"I think not," said Poirot. "That is interesting. Very interesting. She is well-to-do, you think?"

"I should say so. Her clothes are expensive, she lives at an expensive address, she is—it's difficult to make out. She's a pushing woman and a bossy woman. She sits on a lot of committees. There's nothing, I mean, suspicious about her. I've asked a few people. Nobody likes her very much. But she's a sort of public-spirited woman who takes part in politics, all those sorts of things."

"Then what is wrong with her?" said Poirot.

"You think there is something wrong with her. Or do you just not like her, like I do?"

"I think there is something there that she does not want to come to light," said Poirot.

"Oh. And are you going to find out what it is?"

"Naturally, if I can," said Poirot. "It may not be easy. She is in retreat. She was in retreat when she left us here. She was afraid of what questions I was going to ask her. Yes. It is interesting." He sighed. "One will have to go back, you know, even farther than one thought."

"What, back into the past again?"

"Yes. Somewhere in the past, in more cases than one, there is something that one will have to know before we can come back again to what happened—what is it now? —fifteen years ago, twenty years ago, at a house called Overcliffe. Yes. One will have to go back again."

"Well, that's that," said Mrs. Oliver. "And now, what is

there to do? What is this list of yours?"

"I have heard a certain amount of information through police records on what was found in the house. You will remember that among the things there were four wigs."

"Yes," said Mrs. Oliver, "you said that four wigs were too many."

"It seemed to be a little excessive," said Poirot. "I have also got certain useful addresses. The address of a doctor that might be helpful."

"The doctor? You mean, the family doctor?"

"No, not the family doctor. The doctor who gave evidence at an inquest on a child who met with an accident. Either pushed by an older child or possibly by someone else."

"You mean by the mother?"

"Possibly the mother, possibly by someone else who was in the house at the time. I know the part of England where that happened, and Superintendent Garroway has been able, through sources known to him and also through journalistic friends of mine, who were interested in this particular case, to get some information about the doctor."

"And you're going to see him. He must be a very old man by now."

"It is not him I shall go to see. It is his son. His son is also qualified as a specialist in various forms of mental disorders. I have an introduction to him and he might be able to tell me something interesting. There have also been inquiries into a case of money."

"What do you mean by money?"

"Well, there are certain things we have to find out. That is one of the things in anything which might be a crime. Money. Who has money to lose by some happening, who has money to gain by something happening. That, one has to find out."

"Well, they must have found out in the case of the Ravenscrofts."

"Yes, that was all quite natural, it seems. They had both made normal wills leaving, in each case, the money to the other partner. The wife left her money to the husband and the husband left his money to his wife. Neither of them benefited by what happened because they both died. So that the people who did profit were the daughter, Celia, and a younger child, Edward, who I gather is now at a university abroad."

"Well, that won't help. Neither of the children were there or could have had anything to do with it."

"Oh, no, that is quite true. One must go further—further back, further forward, further sideways, to find out if there is some financial motive somewhere that is—well, shall we say, significant."

"Well, don't ask me to do that sort of thing," said Mrs. Oliver. "I've no real qualifications for that. I mean, that's come up, I suppose, fairly reasonably in the—well, in the elephants that I've talked to."

"No. I think the best thing for you to do would be to, shall we say, take on the subject of the wigs."

"Wigs?"

"There had been a note made in the careful police report

at the time of the suppliers of the wigs, who were a very expensive firm of hairdressers and wigmakers in London, in Bond Street. Later, that particular shop closed and the business was transferred somewhere else. Two of the original partners continued to run it and I understand it has now been given up, but I have here an address of one of the principal fitters and hairdressers, and I thought perhaps that it would come more easily if inquiries were made by a woman."

"Ah," said Mrs. Oliver, "me?"

"Yes, you."

"All right. What do you want me to do?"

"Pay a visit to Cheltenham to an address I shall give you and there you will find a Madame Rosentelle. A woman no longer young but who was a very fashionable maker of ladies' hair adornments of all kinds, and who was married, I understand, to another in the same profession, a hairdresser who specialized in surmounting the problems of gentlemen's baldness. Toupees and other things."

"Oh, dear," said Mrs. Oliver, "the jobs you do give me to do. Do you think they'll remember anything about it?"

"Elephants remember," said Hercule Poirot.

"Oh, and who are you going to ask questions of? This doctor you talked about?"

"For one, yes."

"And what do you think he'll remember?"

"Not very much," said Poirot, "but it seems to me possible that he might have heard about a certain accident. It must have been an interesting case, you know. There must be records of the case history."

"You mean of the twin sister?"

"Yes. There were two accidents as far as I can hear connected with her. One when she was a young mother living in the country, at Hatters Green I think the address was, and again later when she was in India. Each time an accident which resulted in the death of a child. I might learn something about—"

"You mean that as they were twin sisters, that Molly—my Molly, I mean—might also have had mental disability of some kind? I don't believe it for a minute. She wasn't like that. She was affectionate, loving, very good-looking, emotional and—oh, she was a terribly nice person."

"Yes. Yes, so it would seem. And a happy person on the whole, would you say?"

"Yes. She was a happy person. A *very* happy person. Oh, I know I never saw anything of her later in life, of course; she was living abroad. But it always seemed to me on the very rare occasions when I got a letter or went to see her that she was a happy person."

"And the twin sister you did not really know?"

"No. Well, I think she was . . . well, quite frankly she was in an institution of some kind, I think, on the rare occasions that I saw Molly. She wasn't at Molly's wedding, not as a bridesmaid even."

"That is odd in itself."

"I still don't see what you're going to find out from that."

"Just information," said Poirot.

14

DR. WILLOUGHBY

Hercule Poirot got out of the taxi, paid the fare and a tip, verified the fact that the address he had come to was the address corresponding to that written down in his little notebook, took carefully a letter from his pocket addressed to Dr. Willoughby, mounted the steps to the house and pressed the bell. The door was opened by a manservant. On reception of Poirot's name he was told that Dr. Willoughby was expecting him.

He was shown into a small, comfortable room with bookshelves up the side of it. There were two armchairs drawn to the fire and a tray with glasses on it and two decanters. Dr. Willoughby rose to greet him. He was a man between fifty and sixty with a lean, thin body, a high forehead, dark-haired and with very piercing gray eyes. He shook hands and motioned him to a seat. Poirot produced the letter from his pocket.

"Ah, yes."

The doctor took it from him, opened it, read it and then, placing it beside him, looked at Poirot with some interest.

"I had already heard," he said, "from Superintendent Garroway and also, I may say, from a friend of mine in the Home Office, who also begged me to do what I can for you in the matter that interests you."

"It is a rather serious favor to ask, I know," said Poirot, "but there are reasons which make it important for me."

"Important for you after this number of years?"

"Yes. Of course I shall quite understand if those particular events have passed out of your mind altogether."

"I can't say they've done that. I am interested, as you may have heard, in special branches of my profession, and have been for many years."

"Your father, I know, was a very celebrated authority on them."

"Yes, he was. It was a great interest in his life. He had a lot of theories, some of them triumphantly proved right and some of them which proved disappointing. It is, I gather, a mental case you are interested in?"

"A woman. Her name was Dorothea Preston-Grey."

"Yes. I was quite a young man at the time. I was already interested in my father's line of thought although my theories and his did not always agree. The work he did was interesting and the work I did in collaboration interested me very much. I don't know what your particular interest was in Dorothea Preston-Grey, as she was at the time, Mrs. Jarrow later."

"She was one of twins, I gather," said Poirot.

"Yes. That was at that moment, I may say, my father's particular field of study. There was a project on hand at that time to follow up the general lives of selected pairs of identical twins. Those who were brought up in the same environment, those who through various chances of life were brought up in entirely different environments. To see how alike they remained, how similar the things were that happened to them. Two sisters, perhaps, or two brothers who had hardly spent any of their life together and yet in an extraordinary way the same things seemed to happen to them at the same time. It was all—indeed it has been all—extremely interesting. However, that is not your interest in the matter, I gather."

"No," said Poirot, "it is a case, I think—the part of it that is to say that I'm interested in—of an accident to a child."

"That is so. It was in Surrey, I think. Yes, a very pleasant area, that, in which people lived. Not very far from Camberley, I think. Mrs. Jarrow was a young widow at that time and she had two small children. Her husband had recently died in an accident. She was, as a result—"

"Mentally disturbed?" asked Poirot.

"No, she was not thought to be so. She was deeply shocked by her husband's death and had a great sense of loss, but she was not recovering very satisfactorily in the impression of her own doctor. He did not quite like the way her convalescence was tending, and she did not seem to be getting over her bereavement in the way that he would have liked. It seemed to be causing her rather peculiar reactions. Anyway, he wanted a consultation and my father was asked by him to come and see what he could make of it. He found her condition interesting, and at the same time he thought it held very decided dangers, and he seemed to think that it would be as well if she was put under observation in some nursing home where particular care could be taken. Things like that. Even more so after the case when this accident to the child happened. There were two children, and according to Mrs. Jarrow's account of what happened, it was the older child, a girl, who attacked the little boy who was four or five years younger than she was, hitting him with a garden spade or hoe, so that he fell into an ornamental pond they had in the garden and was drowned. Well, these things, as you know, happen quite often among children. Children are pushed in a perambulator into a pond sometimes because an older child, being jealous, thinks that 'Mummy will have so much less trouble if only Edward or Donald, or whatever his name is, wasn't here,' or, 'It would be much nicer for her.' It all results from jealousy. There did not seem to be any particular case or evidence of jealousy in this case, though. The child had not resented the birth of her brother. On the other hand, Mrs. Jarrow had not wanted this second child. Although her husband had been pleased to have this second child coming, Mrs. Jarrow did not want it. She had tried two doctors with the idea of having an abortion, but did not succeed in finding one who would perform what was then an illegal operation. It was said by one of the servants, and also by a boy who was bringing a telegram, I believe, to the house, that it was a woman who attacked the boy, not the other child. And one of the servants said very definitely she had been looking out of the window and that it was her mistress. She said, 'I don't think the poor thing knows what she is doing nowadays. You know, just since the master died she's been in, oh, such a state as never was.' Well, as I say, I don't know exactly what you want to know about the case. A verdict was brought in of accident. It was considered to be an accident, and the children had been said to be playing together, pushing each other, et cetera, and that therefore it was undoubtedly a very unfortunate accident. It was left at that, but my father, when consulted, and after a conversation with Mrs. Jarrow and certain tests, questionnaires, sympathetic remarks to her and questions, he was quite sure she had been responsible for what happened. According to his advice it would be advisable for her to have mental treatment."

"But your father was quite sure that she had been responsible?"

"Yes. There was a school of treatment at the time which was very popular and which my father believed in. That school's belief was that after sufficient treatment, lasting sometimes quite a long time, a year or longer, people could resume a normal everyday life, and it was to their advantage to do so. They could be returned to live at home and with a suitable amount of attention, both medical and from those, usually near relatives, who were with them and could observe them living a normal life, everything would go well. This, I may say, did meet with success at first in many cases, but later there was a difference. Several cases had most unfortunate results. Patients who appeared to be cured came home to their natural surroundings, to a family, a husband, their mothers and fathers, and slowly relapsed, so that very often tragedies or near-tragedies occurred. One case my father was bitterly disappointed in—also a very important case in his knowledge—was a woman who came back to live with the same friend she lived with before. All seemed to be going happily, but after about five or six months she sent urgently for a doctor and when he came said, 'I must take you upstairs because you will be angry at what I have done, and you will have to send for the police, I am afraid. I know that must happen. But you see, I was commanded to do this. I saw the Devil looking out of Hilda's eyes. I saw the Devil there so I knew what I had to do. I knew I had to kill her.' The woman was lying dead in a chair, strangled, and after her death her eyes had been attacked. The killer died in a mental home with never any feeling about her crime except that it had been a necessary command laid upon her because it was her duty to destroy the Devil."

Poirot shook his head sadly.

The doctor went on: "Yes. Well, I consider that in a mild way Dorothea Preston-Grey suffered from a form of mental disorder that was dangerous and that she could only be considered safe if she lived under supervision. This was not generally accepted, I may say, at the time, and my father did consider it most inadvisable. After she had been committed once more to a very pleasant nursing home a very good treatment was given. And again, after a period of years she appeared to be completely sane, left the establishment, lived an ordinary life with a very pleasant nurse more or less in charge of her, though considered in the household as a lady's maid. She went about, made friends and sooner or later went abroad."

"To India," said Poirot.

"Yes. I see you've been correctly informed. She went to India to stay with her twin sister."

"And there another tragedy happened?"

"Yes. A child of a neighbor was attacked. It was thought at first by an ayah, and afterwards I believe one of the native servants, a bearer, was suspected. But there again there seemed no doubt that Mrs. Jarrow had, for one of those mental reasons known only to her, been guilty of the attack. There was no definite evidence, I understand, which could be brought against her. I think General—I forget his name now—"

"Ravenscroft?" said Poirot.

"Yes, yes, General Ravenscroft agreed to arrange for her to go back to England and again undergo medical treatment. Is that what you wanted to know?"

"Yes," said Poirot, "that is what I have partly heard already, but mainly, I may say, by hearsay, which is not dependable. What I want to ask you was, this was a case concerned with identical twins. What about the other twin?

Margaret Preston-Grey. Afterwards the wife of General Ravenscroft. Was she likely to be affected by the same malady?"

"There was never any medical case about her. She was perfectly sane. My father was interested, visited her once or twice and talked to her because he had so often seen cases of almost identical illnesses or mental disturbances happen between identical twins who had started life very devoted to each other."

"Only started life, you said?"

"Yes. On certain occasions a state of animosity can arise between identical twins. It follows on a first keen protective love one for the other, but it can degenerate into something which is nearer hatred, if there is some emotional strain that could trigger it off or could arouse it, or any emotional crisis to account for animosity arising between two sisters.

"I think there might have been that here. General Ravenscroft as a young subaltern or captain or whatever he was, fell deeply in love, I think, with Dorothea Preston-Grey, who was a very beautiful girl. Actually the more beautiful of the two. She also fell in love with him. They were not officially engaged, but Captain Ravenscroft transferred his affections fairly soon to the other sister, Margaret—or Molly, as she was called. He fell in love with her, and asked her to marry him. She returned his affection and they were married as soon as it became feasible in his career. My father had no doubt that the other twin, Dolly, was bitterly jealous of her sister's marriage and that she continued to be in love with Alistair Ravenscroft and to resent his marriage.

However, she got over it all, married another man in due course—a thoroughly happy marriage, it seemed, and later she used frequently to go to visit the Ravenscrofts, not only on that one occasion in Malaya, but later when they were in another station abroad and after they returned home. She was by that time apparently cured again, was no longer in any kind of mental dejection and lived with a very reliable nurse-companion and staff of servants. I believe, or so my father had always told me, that Lady Ravenscroft, Molly, remained very devoted to her sister. She felt very protective towards her and loved her dearly. She wanted often, I think, to see more of her than she did, but General Ravenscroft was not so keen on her doing so. I think it possible that the slightly unbalanced Dolly—Mrs. Jarrow—continued to feel a very strong attachment to General Ravenscroft, which I think may have been embarrassing and difficult for him, though I believe that his wife was quite convinced that her sister had got over any feelings of jealousy or anger."

"I understand Mrs. Jarrow was staying with the Ravenscrofts about three weeks or so before the tragedy of their suicide happened."

"Yes, that was quite true. Her own tragic death happened then. She was quite frequently a sleepwalker. She went out one night walking in her sleep and had an accident, falling down a portion of the cliff to which a pathway which had been discarded appeared to lead. She was found the next day and I believe died in hospital without recovering consciousness. Her sister Molly was extremely upset and bitterly unhappy about this, but I would like to say, which you probably want to know, I do not think that this can in any way be held responsible for the subsequent suicide of the married couple who were living so happily together. Grief for a sister's or a sister-in-law's death would hardly lead you to commit suicide. Certainly not to a double suicide."

"Unless, perhaps," said Hercule Poirot, "Margaret Ravenscroft had been responsible for her sister's death."

"Good heavens!" said Dr. Willoughby, "surely you are not suggesting—"

"That it was Margaret who followed her sleepwalking sister, and that it was Margaret's hand that was stretched out to push Dorothea over the cliff edge?"

"I refuse absolutely," said Dr. Willoughby, "to accept any such idea."

"With people," said Hercule Poirot, "one never knows."

15

EUGENE AND ROSENTELLE, HAIR STYLISTS BEAUTICIANS

Mrs. Oliver looked at Cheltenham with approval. As it happened, she had never been to Cheltenham before. How nice, said Mrs. Oliver to herself, to see some houses that are really like houses, proper houses.

Casting her mind back to youthful days, she remembered that she had known people, or at least her relations, her aunts, had known people who lived at Cheltenham. Retired people usually. Army or Navy. It was the sort of place, she thought, where one would like to come and live if one had spent a good deal of time abroad. It had a feeling of English security, good taste and pleasant chat and conversation.

After looking in one or two agreeable antique shops, she

found her way to where she wanted—or rather Hercule Poirot wanted her—to go. It was called The Rose Green Hairdressing Saloons. She walked inside it and looked round. Four or five people were in process of having things done to their hair. A plump young lady left her client and came forward with an inquiring air.

"Mrs. Rosentelle?" said Mrs. Oliver, glancing down at a card. "I understand she said she could see me if I came here this morning. I don't mean," she added, "having anything done to my hair, but I wanted to consult her about something and I believe a telephone call was made and she said if I came at half-past eleven she could spare me a short time."

"Oh, yes," said the girl. "I think Madam is expecting someone."

She led the way through a passage down a short flight of steps and pushed a swing door at the bottom of it. From the hairdressing saloon they had passed into what was obviously Mrs. Rosentelle's house. The plump girl knocked at the door and said, "The lady to see you," as she put her nose in, and then asked rather nervously, "What name did you say?"

"Mrs. Oliver," said Mrs. Oliver.

She walked in. It had a faint effect of what might have been yet another showroom. There were curtains of rose gauze and roses on the wallpaper and Mrs. Rosentelle, a woman Mrs. Oliver thought of as roughly her own age or possibly a good many years older, was just finishing what was obviously a cup of morning coffee.

"Mrs. Rosentelle?" said Mrs. Oliver.

"Yes?"

"You did expect me?"

"Oh, yes. I didn't quite understand what it was all about. The lines are so bad on the telephone. That is quite all right. I have about half an hour to spare. Would you like some coffee?"

"No, thank you," said Mrs. Oliver. "I won't keep you any longer than I need. It is just something that I want to ask you about, that you may happen to remember. You have had quite a long career, I understand, in the hairdressing business."

"Oh, yes. I'm quite thankful to give over to the girls now. I don't do anything myself these days."

"Perhaps you still advise people?"

"Yes, I do do that." Mrs. Rosentelle smiled.

She had a nice, intelligent face with well-arranged brown hair with somewhat interesting gray streaks in it here and there.

"I'm not sure what it's all about."

"Well, really, I wanted to ask you a question about, well, I suppose in a way about wigs generally."

"We don't do as much in wigs now as we used to do."

"You had a business in London, didn't you?"

"Yes. First in Bond Street and then we moved to Sloane Street, but it's very nice to live in the country after all that, you know. Oh, yes, my husband and I are very satisfied here. We run a small business, but we don't do much in the wig line nowadays," she said, "though my husband does advise and get wigs designed for men who are bald. It really makes a big difference, you know, to many people in their business if they don't look too old and it often helps in getting a job."

"I can quite imagine that," said Mrs. Oliver.

From sheer nervousness she said a few more things in the way of ordinary chat and wondered how she would start on her subject. She was startled when Mrs. Rosentelle leaned forward and said suddenly, "You are Ariadne Oliver, aren't you? The novel writer?"

"Yes," said Mrs. Oliver, "as a matter of fact—" she had her usual somewhat shamefaced expression when she said this, that was habitual to her—"yes, I do write novels."

"I'm so fond of your books. I've read a lot of them. Oh, this is very nice indeed. Now tell me in what way can I help you?"

"Well, I wanted to talk about wigs and about something that happened a great many years ago and probably you mayn't remember anything about it."

"Well, I rather wonder—do you mean fashions of years ago?"

"Not exactly. It's a woman, a friend of mine—actually I was at school with her—and then she married and went out to India and came back to England, and there was a tragedy later and one of the things I think that people found surprising after it was that she had so many wigs. I think they had been all supplied by you, by your firm, I mean."

"Oh, a tragedy. What was her name?"

"Well, her name when I knew her was Preston-Grey, but afterwards her name was Ravenscroft."

"Oh. Oh, yes, that one. Yes, I do remember Lady Ravenscroft. I remember her quite well. She was so nice and really very, very good-looking still. Yes, her husband was a colonel or a general or something and they'd retired and they lived in—I forget the county now—"

"And there was what was supposed to be a double suicide," said Mrs. Oliver.

"Yes. Yes, I remember reading about it and saying, 'Why, that's our Lady Ravenscroft,' and then there was a picture of them both in the paper, and I saw that it was so. Of course, I'd never seen him, but it was her all right. It seemed so sad, so much grief. I heard that they discovered that she had cancer and they couldn't do anything about it so this happened. But I never heard any details or anything."

"No," said Mrs. Oliver.

"But what is it you think I can tell you?"

"You supplied her with wigs and I understand the people investigating, I suppose the police, thought four wigs was quite a lot to have, but perhaps people did have four wigs at a time?"

"Well, I think that most people had two wigs at least," said Mrs. Rosentelle. "You know, one to send back to be serviced, as you might say, and the other one that they wore while it was away."

"Do you remember Lady Ravenscroft ordering an extra two wigs?"

"She didn't come herself. I think she'd been or was ill in hospital, or something, and it was a French young lady who came. I think a French lady who was companion to her or something like that. Very nice. Spoke perfect English. And she explained all about the extra wigs she wanted, sizes and colors and styles and ordered them. Yes. Fancy my remembering it. I suppose I wouldn't have except that about—oh, it must have been a month later—a month, perhaps, more, six weeks—I read about the suicide, you know. I'm afraid they gave her bad news at the hospital or wherever she was, and so she just couldn't face living any more, and her husband felt he couldn't face life without her—"

Mrs. Oliver shook her head sadly and continued her inquiries.

"They were different kinds of wigs, I suppose."

"Yes, one had a very pretty gray streak in it, and then there was a party one and one for evening wear, and one close-cropped with curls. Very nice, that you could wear under a hat and it didn't get messed up. I was sorry not to have seen Lady Ravenscroft again. Even apart from her illness, she had been very unhappy about a sister who had recently died. A twin sister."

"Yes, twins are very devoted, aren't they?" said Mrs. Oliver.

"She'd always seemed such a happy woman before," said Mrs. Rosentelle.

Both women sighed. Mrs. Oliver changed the subject.

"Do you think that I'd find a wig useful?" she asked.

The expert stretched out a hand and laid it speculatively on Mrs. Oliver's head.

"I wouldn't advise it—you've got a splendid crop of hair—very thick still. I imagine"—a faint smile came to her lips—"you enjoy doing things with it?"

"How clever of you to know that. It's quite true—I enjoy experimenting. It's such fun."

"You enjoy life altogether, don't you?"

"Yes, I do. I suppose it's the feeling that one never knows what might be going to happen next."

"Yet that feeling," said Mrs. Rosentelle, "is just what makes so many people never stop worrying!"

16

MR. GOBY REPORTS

Mr. Goby came into the room and sat, as indicated by Poirot, in his usual chair. He glanced around him before choosing what particular piece of furniture or part of the room he was about to address. He settled, as often before, for the electric fire, not turned on at this time of year. Mr. Goby had never been known to address the human being he was working for directly. He selected always the cornice, a radiator, a television set, a clock, sometimes a carpet or a mat. Out of a briefcase he took a few papers.

"Well," said Hercule Poirot, "you have something for me?"

"I have collected various details," said Mr. Goby.

Mr. Goby was celebrated all over London, indeed possibly all over England and even further, as a great purveyor of information. How he performed these miracles, nobody ever really quite knew. He employed a not excessive staff. Sometimes he complained that his legs, as he sometimes called them, were not as good as they used to be. But his results were still able to astonish people who had commissioned them.

"Mrs. Burton-Cox," he said, announcing the name much as though he had been the local churchwarden having his turn at reading the lessons. He might equally have been saying, "Third verse, fourth chapter, the book of Isaiah."

"Mrs. Burton-Cox," he said again. "Married Mr. Cecil Aldbury, manufacturer of buttons on a large scale. Rich man. Entered politics, was MP for Little Stansmere. Mr. Cecil Aldbury was killed in a car accident four years after their marriage. The only child of the marriage died in an accident shortly afterwards. Mr. Aldbury's estate was inherited by his wife, but was not as much as had been expected, since the firm had not been doing well of late years. Mr. Aldbury also left quite a considerable sum of money to a Miss Kathleen Fenn, with whom it seemed he had been having intimate relations quite unknown to his wife. Mrs. Burton-Cox continued her political career. Some three years after that she adopted a child which had been born to Miss Kathleen Fenn. Miss Kathleen Fenn insisted that the child was the son of the late Mr. Aldbury. This, from what I have been able to learn in my inquiries, is somewhat difficult to accept," continued Mr. Goby. "Miss Fenn had had many relationships, usually with gentlemen of ample means and generous dispositions, but after all, so many people have their price, have they not? I'm afraid this is quite a serious bill I may have to send you in."

"Continue," said Hercule Poirot.

"Mrs. Aldbury, as she then was, agreed to adopt the child. A short while later she married Major Burton-Cox. Miss Kathleen Fenn became, I may say, a most successful actress and pop singer and made a very large amount of money. She then wrote to Mrs. Burton-Cox, saying she would be willing to take back the adopted child. Mrs. Burton-Cox refused. Mrs. Burton-Cox has been living quite comfortably since, I understand. Major Burton-Cox was killed in Malaya. He left her moderately well off. A further piece of information I have obtained is that Miss Kathleen Fenn, who died a very short while ago—eighteen months, I think—left a will by which her entire fortune, which amounted by then to a considerable sum of money, was left to her natural son Desmond, at present known under the name of Desmond Burton-Cox."

"Very generous," said Poirot. "Of what did Miss Fenn die?"

"My informant tells me that she contacted leukemia."

"And the boy has inherited his mother's money?"

"It was left in trust for him to acquire at the age of twenty-five."

"So he will be independent, will have a substantial fortune? And Mrs. Burton-Cox?"

"Has not been happy in her investments, it is understood. She has sufficient to live on but not much more."

"Has the boy Desmond made a will?" asked Poirot.

"That," said Mr. Goby, "I fear I do not know as yet. But I have certain means of finding out. If I do, I will acquaint you with the fact without loss of time."

Mr. Goby took his leave, absent-mindedly bowing a farewell to the electric fire.

About an hour and a half later the telephone rang.

Hercule Poirot, with a sheet of paper in front of him, was making notes. Now and then he frowned, twirled his moustaches, crossed something out and rewrote it and then proceeded onward. When the telephone rang, he picked up the receiver and listened.

"Thank you," he said; "that was quick work. Yes . . . yes, I'm grateful. I really do not know sometimes how you manage these things . . . Yes, that sets out the position clearly. It makes sense of something that did not make sense before . . . Yes . . . I gather . . . yes, I'm listening . . . you are pretty sure that that *is* the case. He knows he is adopted . . . but he never has been told who his real mother was . . . yes. Yes, I see . . . Very well. You will clear up the other point, too? Thank you."

He replaced the receiver and started once more writing down words. In half an hour the telephone rang once more. Once again he picked up the phone.

"I'm back from Cheltenham," said a voice which Poirot had no difficulty in recognizing.

"Ah, *chère madame,* you have returned? You have seen Mrs. Rosentelle?"

"Yes. She is nice. Very nice. And you were quite right, you know. She *is* another elephant."

"Meaning, *chère madame?*"

"I mean that she remembered Molly Ravenscroft."

"And she remembered her wigs?"

"Yes."

Briefly she outlined what the retired hairdresser had told her about the wigs.

"Yes," said Poirot, "that agrees. That is exactly what Superintendent Garroway mentioned to me. The four wigs that the police found. Curls, an evening type of headdress, and two other plainer ones. Four."

"So I really only told you what you knew already?"

"No, you told me something more than that. She said—that is what you told me just now, is it not?—that Lady Ravenscroft wanted two extra wigs to add to the two that she already had and that this was about three weeks to six weeks before the suicide tragedy occurred. Yes, that is interesting, is it not?"

"It's very natural," said Mrs. Oliver. "I mean, you know that people, women, I mean, may do awful damage to things. To false hair and things of that kind. If it can't be redressed and cleaned, if it's got burnt or got stuff spilt on it you can't get out, or it's been dyed and dyed all wrong—something like that—well then, of course you have to get two new wigs or switches or whatever they are. I don't see what makes you excited about that."

"Not exactly excited," said Poirot, "no. It is a point, but the more interesting point is what you have just added. It was a French lady, was it not, who brought the wigs to be copied or matched?"

"Yes. I gathered some kind of companion or something. Lady Ravenscroft had been or was in hospital or in a nursing home somewhere and she was not in good health and she could not come herself to make a choice or anything of that kind."

"I see."

"And so her French companion came."

"Do you know the name of that companion, by any chance?"

"No. I don't think Mrs. Rosentelle mentioned it. In fact I don't think she knew. The appointment was made by Lady Ravenscroft and the French girl or woman just brought the wigs along for size and matching and all the rest of it, I suppose."

"Well," said Poirot, "that helps me towards the further step that I am about to take."

"What have *you* learned?" said Mrs. Oliver. "Have you done anything?"

"You are always so skeptical," said Poirot. "You always consider that I do nothing, that I sit in a chair and repose myself."

"Well, I think you sit in a chair and think," admitted Mrs. Oliver, "but I quite agree that you don't often go out and do things."

"In the near future I think I may possibly go out and do things," said Hercule Poirot, "and that will please you. I may even cross the Channel, though certainly not in a boat. A plane, I think, is indicated."

"Oh," said Mrs. Oliver. "Do you want me to come, too?"

"No," said Poirot, "I think it would be better if I went alone on this occasion."

"You really will go?"

"Oh, yes, oh, yes. I will run about with all activity and so you should be pleased with me, madame."

When he had rung off, he dialed another number which he looked up from a note he had made in his pocketbook. Presently he was connected to the person whom he wished to speak to.

"My dear Superintendent Garroway, it is Hercule Poirot who addresses you. I do not derange you too much? You are not very busy at this moment?"

"No, I am not busy," said Superintendent Garroway. "I am pruning my roses, that's all."

"There is something that I want to ask you. Quite a small thing."

"About our problem of the double suicide?"

"Yes, about our problem. You said there was a dog in the house. You said that the dog went for walks with the family, or so you understood."

"Yes, there was some mention made of a dog. I think it may have been either the housekeeper or someone who said that they went for a walk with the dog as usual that day."

"In examination of the body, was there any sign that Lady Ravenscroft had been bitten by a dog? Not necessarily very recently or on that particular day?"

"Well, it's odd you should say that. I can't say I'd have remembered about it if you hadn't mentioned such a thing. But, yes, there were a couple of scars. Not bad ones. But again the housekeeper mentioned that the dog had attacked its mistress more than once and bitten her, though not very severely. Look here, Poirot, there was no rabies about, if that's what you are thinking. There couldn't have been anything of that kind. After all, she was shot—they were both shot. There was no question of any septic poisoning or danger of tetanus."

"I do not blame the dog," said Poirot; "it was only something I wanted to know."

"One dog bite was fairly recent, about a week before, I think, or two weeks, somebody said. There was no case of necessary injections or anything of that kind. It had healed quite well. What's that quotation?" went on Superintendent Garroway. " '*The dog it was that died.*' I can't remember where it comes from, but—"

"Anyway, it wasn't the dog that died," said Poirot. "That wasn't the point of my question. I would like to have known that dog. He was perhaps a very intelligent dog."

After he had replaced the receiver with thanks to the Superintendent, Poirot murmured: "An intelligent dog. More intelligent perhaps than the police were."

17

POIROT ANNOUNCES DEPARTURE

Miss Livingstone showed in a guest. "Mr. Hercules Porrett."

As soon as Miss Livingstone had left the room, Poirot shut the door after her and sat down by his friend, Mrs. Ariadne Oliver.

He said, lowering his voice slightly, "I depart."

"You do what?" said Mrs. Oliver, who was always slightly startled by Poirot's methods of passing on information.

"I depart. I make the departure. I take a plane to Geneva."

"You sound as though you were UNO or UNESCO or something."

"No. It is just a private visit that I make."

"Have you got an elephant in Geneva?"

"Well, I suppose you might look at it that way. Perhaps two of them."

"I haven't found out anything more," said Mrs. Oliver. "In fact, I don't know who I can go to to find out any more."

"I believe you mentioned, or somebody did, that your goddaughter, Celia Ravenscroft, had a young brother."

"Yes. He's called Edward, I think. I've hardly ever seen him. I took him out once or twice from school, I remember. But that was years ago."

"Where is he now?"

"He's at university, in Canada, I think. Or he's taking some engineering course there. Do you want to go and ask him things?"

"No, not at the moment. I should just like to know where he is now. But I gather he was not in the house when this suicide happened?"

"You're not thinking—you're not thinking for a moment that *he* did it, are you? I mean, shot his father and his mother, both of them. I know boys do sometimes. Very queer they are sometimes when they're at a funny age."

"He was not in the house," said Poirot. "That I know already from my police reports."

"Have you found out anything else interesting? You look quite excited."

"I am excited, in a way. I have found out certain things that may throw light upon what we already know."

"Well, what throws light on what?"

"It seems to me possible now that I can understand why Mrs. Burton-Cox approached you as she did and tried to get you to obtain information for her about the facts of the suicide of the Ravenscrofts."

"You mean she wasn't just being a nosey-parker?"

"No. I think there was some motive behind it. This is where, perhaps, money comes in."

"Money? What's money got to do with that? She's quite well off, isn't she?"

"She has enough to live upon, yes. But it seems that her adopted son, whom she regards apparently as her true son —he knows that he was adopted although he knows nothing about the family from which he really came. It seems that when he came of age he made a will, possibly urged by his adopted mother to do so. Perhaps it was merely hinted to him by some friends of hers or possibly by some lawyer that she had consulted. Anyway, on coming of age he may have felt that he might as well leave everything to her, to his adopted mother. Presumably at that time he had nobody else to leave it to."

"I don't see how that leads to wanting news about a suicide."

"Don't you? She wanted to discourage the marriage. If young Desmond had a girl friend, if he proposed to marry her in the near future, which is what a lot of young people do nowadays—they can't wait or think it over. In that case, Mrs. Burton-Cox would not inherit the money he left, since the marriage would invalidate any earlier will, and presumably if he did marry his girl, he would make a new will leaving everything to her and not to his adopted mother."

"And you mean Mrs. Burton-Cox didn't want that?"

"She wanted to find something that would discourage him from marrying the girl. I think she hoped, and probably really believed as far as that goes, that Celia's mother killed her husband, afterwards shooting herself. That is the sort of thing that might discourage a boy. Even if her father killed her mother, it is still a discouraging thought. It might quite easily prejudice and influence a boy at that age."

"You mean he'd think if her father or mother was a murderer, the girl might have murderous tendencies?"

"Not quite as crude as that, but that might be the main idea, I should think."

"But he wasn't rich, was he? An adopted child."

"He didn't know his real mother's name or who she was, but it seems that his mother, who was an actress and a singer and who managed to make a great deal of money before she became ill and died, wanted at one time to get her child returned to her, and when Mrs. Burton-Cox would not agree to that, I should imagine she thought about this boy a great deal and decided that she would leave her money to him. He will inherit this money at the age of twenty-five, but it is held in trust for him until then. So of course Mrs. Burton-Cox doesn't want him to marry, or only to marry someone that she really approves of or over whom she might have influence."

"Yes, that seems to me fairly reasonable. She's not a nice woman, though, is she?"

"No," said Poirot, "I did not think her a very nice

woman."

"And that's why she didn't want you coming to see her and messing about with things and finding out what she was up to."

"Possibly," said Poirot.

"Anything else you have learned?"

"Yes, I have learned—that is, only a few hours ago really—when Superintendent Garroway happened to ring me up about some other small matters, but I did ask him and he told me that the housekeeper, who was elderly, had very bad eyesight."

"Does that come into it anywhere?"

"It might," said Poirot. He looked at his watch. "I think," he said, "it is time that I left."

"You are on your way to catch your plane at the airport?"

"No. My plane does not leave until tomorrow morning. But there is a place I have to visit today—a place that I wish to see with my own eyes. I have a car waiting outside now to take me there—"

"What is it you want to see?" Mrs. Oliver asked with some curiosity.

"Not so much to *see*—to *feel*. Yes, that is the right word—to feel and to recognize what it will be that I feel . . ."

18

INTERLUDE

Hercule Poirot passed through the gate of the churchyard. He walked up one of the paths, and presently, against a moss-grown wall, he stopped, looking down on a grave. He stood there for some minutes looking first at the grave, then at the view of the Downs and sea beyond. Then his eyes came back again. Flowers had been put recently on the grave. A small bunch of assorted wild flowers, the kind of bunch that might have been left by a child, but Poirot did not think that it was a child who had left them. He read the lettering on the grave.

TO THE MEMORY OF
DOROTHEA JARROW Died Sept. 15th, 1952
ALSO OF
MARGARET RAVENSCROFT Died Oct. 3rd, 1952
SISTER OF ABOVE

ALSO OF
ALISTAIR RAVENSCROFT Died Oct. 3rd, 1952
HER HUSBAND
In their Death they were not divided

Forgive us our trespasses
As we forgive those that trespass against us.
Lord, have mercy upon us.
Christ, have mercy upon us.
Lord, have mercy upon us.

Poirot stood there a moment or two. He nodded his head once or twice. Then he left the churchyard and walked by a footpath that led out on to the cliff and along it. Presently he stood still again, looking out to the sea. He spoke to himself.

"I am sure now that I know what happened and why. I understand the pity of it and the tragedy. One has to go back such a long way. *In my end is my beginning,* or should one put it differently? 'In my beginning was my tragic end'? The Swiss girl must have known—but will she tell me? The boy believes she will. For their sakes—the girl and the boy. They cannot accept life unless they know."

19

MADDY AND ZÉLIE

"Mademoiselle Rouselle?" said Hercule Poirot. He bowed.

Mademoiselle Rouselle extended her hand. About fifty, Poirot thought. A fairly imperious woman. Would have her way. Intelligent, intellectual, satisfied, he thought, with life as she had lived it, enjoying the pleasures and suffering the sorrows life brings.

"I have heard your name," she said. "You have friends, you know, both in this country and in France. I do not know exactly what I can do for you. Oh, I know that you explained, in the letter that you sent me. It is an affair of the past, is it not? Things that happened. Not exactly things that happened, but the clue to things that happened many, many years ago. But sit down. Yes. Yes, that chair is quite comfortable, I hope. There are some petits fours and the decanter is on the table."

She was quietly hospitable without any urgency. She was unworried but amiable.

"You were at one time a governess in a certain family," said Poirot. "The Ravenscrofts. Perhaps now you hardly remember them."

"Oh, yes, one does not forget, you know, things that happen when you were young. There was a girl, and a boy about four or five years younger in the family I went to. They were nice children. Their father was a general in the Army."

"There was also another sister."

"Ah, yes, I remember. She was not there when I first came. I think she was delicate. Her health was not good. She was having treatment somewhere."

"You remember their mother's Christian name?"

"Margaret, I think was one. The other one I am not sure of by now."

"Dorothea."

"Ah, yes. A name I have not often come across. But they called each other by shorter names. Molly and Dolly. They were identical twins, you know, remarkably alike. They were both very handsome young women."

"And they were fond of each other?"

"Yes, they were devoted. But we are, are we not, becoming slightly confused? Preston-Grey is not the name of the children I went to teach. Dorothea Preston-Grey married a major—ah, I cannot remember the name now. Arrow? No, Jarrow."

"Ravenscroft," said Poirot.

"Ah, that. Yes. Curious how one cannot remember names. The Preston-Greys are a generation older. Margaret Preston-Grey had been in a *pensionnat* in this part of the world, and when she wrote after her marriage asking Madame Benoît, who ran that *pensionnat,* if she knew of someone who would come to her as nursery-governess to her two children, I was recommended. That is how I came to go there. I spoke only of the other sister because she happened to be staying there during part of my time of service with the children. The children were a girl, I think then of six or seven. She had a name out of Shakespeare, I remember. Rosalind or Celia."

"Celia," said Poirot.

"And the boy was only about three or four. His name was Edward. A mischievous but lovable child. I was happy with them."

"And they were happy, I hear, with you. They enjoyed playing with you and you were very kind in your playing with them."

"Moi, j'aime les enfants," said Mademoiselle Rouselle.

"They called you Maddy, I believe."

She laughed.

"Ah, I like hearing that word. It brings back past memories."

"Did you know a boy called Desmond? Desmond Burton-Cox?"

"Ah, yes. He lived, I think, in a house next door or nearly next door. We had several neighbors and the children very often came to play together. His name was Desmond. Yes, I remember."

"You were there long, mademoiselle?"

"No. I was only there for three or four years at most. Then I was recalled to this country. My mother was very ill. It was a question of coming back and nursing her, although I knew it would not be perhaps for very long. That was true. She died a year and a half or two years at the most after I returned here. After that I started a small *pensionnat* out here, taking in rather older girls who wanted to study languages and other things. I did not visit England again, although for a year or two I kept up communication with the country. The two children used to send me a card at Christmastime."

"Did General Ravenscroft and his wife strike you as a happy couple?"

"Very happy. They were fond of their children."

"They were very well suited to each other?"

"Yes, they seemed to me to have all the necessary qualities to make their marriage a success."

"You said Mrs. Ravenscroft was devoted to her twin sister. Was the twin sister also devoted to her?"

"Well, I had not very much occasion of judging. Frankly, I thought that the sister—Dolly, as they called her—was very definitely a mental case. Once or twice she acted in a very peculiar manner. She was a jealous woman, I think, and I understood that she had at one time thought she was engaged, or was going to be engaged, to Major Ravenscroft. As far as I could see, he'd fallen in love with her first, then later, however, his affections turned towards her sister, which was fortunate, I thought, because Molly Ravenscroft was a well-balanced and very sweet woman. As for Dolly—sometimes I thought she adored her sister, sometimes that she hated her. She was a very jealous woman and she decided too much affection was being shown to the children. There is one who could tell you about all this better than I. Mademoiselle Meauhourat. She lives in Lausanne and she went to the Ravenscrofts about a year and a half to two years after I had to leave. She was with them for some years. Later I believe she went back as companion to Mrs. Ravenscroft when Celia was abroad at school."

"I am going to see her. I have her address," said Poirot.

"She knows a great deal that I do not, and she is a charming and reliable person. It was a terrible tragedy that happened later. She knows if anyone does what led to it. She is very discreet. She has never told me anything. Whether she will tell you, I do not know. She may do, she may not."

Poirot stood for a moment or two looking at Mademoiselle Meauhourat. He had been impressed by Mademoiselle Rouselle. He was impressed also by the woman who stood waiting to receive him now. She was not so formidable, she was much younger, at least ten years younger, he thought, and she had a different kind of impressiveness. She was alive, still attractive, eyes that watched you and made their own judgment on you, willing to welcome you, looking with kindliness on those who came her way, but without undue softness. Here is someone, thought Hercule Poirot, very remarkable.

"I am Hercule Poirot, mademoiselle."

"I know. I was expecting you either today or tomorrow."

"Ah. You received a letter from me?"

"No. It is no doubt still in the post. Our posts are a little uncertain. No. I had a letter from someone else."

"From Celia Ravenscroft?"

"No. It was a letter written by someone in close touch with Celia. A boy or a young man, whichever we like to regard him as, called Desmond Burton-Cox. He prepared me for your arrival."

"Ah. I see. He is intelligent and he wastes no time, I think. He was very urgent that I should come and see you."

"So I gathered. There's trouble, I understand. Trouble that he wants to resolve, and so does Celia. They think you can help them?"

"Yes, and they think that *you* can help *me*."

"They are in love with each other and wish to marry."

"Yes, but there are difficulties being put in their way."

"Ah, by Desmond's mother, I presume. So he lets me understand."

"There are circumstances, or have been circumstances, in Celia's life that have prejudiced his mother against his early marriage to this particular girl."

"Ah. Because of the tragedy, for it was a tragedy."

"Yes, because of the tragedy. Celia has a godmother who was asked by Desmond's mother to try and find out from Celia the exact circumstances under which that suicide occurred."

"There's no sense in that," said Mademoiselle Meauhourat. She motioned with her hand. "Sit down. Please sit down. I expect we shall have to talk for some little time. Yes, Celia could not tell her godmother—Mrs. Ariadne Oliver, the novelist, is it not? Yes, I remember. Celia could not give her the information because she has not got the information herself."

"She was not there when the tragedy occurred, and no one told her anything about it. Is that right?"

"Yes, that is right. It was thought inadvisable."

"Ah. And do you approve of that decision or disapprove of it?"

"It is difficult to be sure. Very difficult. I've not been sure of it in the years that have passed since then, and there are quite a lot. Celia, as far as I know, has never been worried. Worried, I mean, as to the why and wherefore. She's accepted it as she would have accepted an airplane accident or a car accident. Something that resulted in the death of her parents. She spent many years in a *pensionnat* abroad."

"Actually I think the *pensionnat* was run by you, Mademoiselle Meauhourat."

"That is quite true. I have retired recently. A colleague of mine is now taking it on. But Celia was sent out to me and I was asked to find for her a good place for her to continue her education, as many girls do come to Switzerland for that purpose. I could have recommended several places. At the moment I took her into my own."

"And Celia asked you nothing, did not demand information?"

"No. It was, you see, before the tragedy happened."

"Oh. I did not quite understand that."

"Celia came out here some weeks before the tragic occurrence. I was at that time not here myself. I was still with General and Lady Ravenscroft. I looked after Lady Ravenscroft, acting as a companion to her rather than as a governess to Celia, who was still at that moment in boarding-school. But it was suddenly arranged that Celia should come to Switzerland and finish her education there."

"Lady Ravenscroft had been in poor health, had she not?"

"Yes. Nothing very serious. Nothing as serious as she had herself feared at one time. But she had suffered a lot of nervous strain and shock and general worry."

"You remained with her?"

"A sister whom I had living in Lausanne received Celia on her arrival and settled her into the institution which was only for about fifteen or sixteen girls, but there she would start her studies and await my return. I returned some three or four weeks later."

"But you were at Overcliffe at the time it happened."

"I was at Overcliffe. General and Lady Ravenscroft went for a walk, as was their habit. They went out and did not return. They were found dead, shot. The weapon was found lying by them. It was one that belonged to General Ravenscroft and had been always kept in a drawer in his study. The fingermarks of both of them were found on that weapon. There was no definite indication of who had held it last. Impressions of both people, slightly smeared, were on it. The obvious solution was a double suicide."

"You found no reason to doubt that?"

"The police found no reason, so I believe."

"Ah," said Poirot.

"I beg your pardon?" said Mademoiselle Meauhourat.

"Nothing. Nothing. Just something upon which I reflect."

Poirot looked at her. Brown hair as yet hardly touched with gray, lips closed firmly together, gray eyes, a face which showed no emotion. She was in control of herself completely.

"So you cannot tell me anything more?"

"I fear not. It was a long time ago."

"You remember that time well enough."

"Yes. One cannot entirely forget such a sad thing."

"And you agreed that Celia should not be told anything more of what had led up to this?"

"Have I not just told you that I had no extra information?"

"You were there, living at Overcliffe, for a period of time before the tragedy, were you not? Four or five weeks—six weeks, perhaps."

"Longer than that, really. Although I had been governess to Celia early, I came back this time, after she went to school, in order to help Lady Ravenscroft."

"Lady Ravenscroft's sister was living with her also about that time, was she not?"

"Yes. She had been in hospital having special treatment for some time. She had shown much improvement and the authorities had felt—the medical authorities I speak of—that she would do better to lead a normal life with her own relations and the atmosphere of a home. As Celia had gone to school, it seemed a good time for Lady Ravenscroft to invite her sister to be with her."

"Were they fond of each other, those two sisters?"

"It was difficult to know," said Mademoiselle Meauhourat. Her brows drew together. It was as though what Poirot had just said aroused her interest. "I have wondered, you know. I have wondered so much since, and at the time, really. They were identical twins, you know. They had a bond between them, a bond of mutual dependence and love and in many ways they were very alike. But there were ways also in which they were not alike."

"You mean? I should be glad to know just what you mean by that."

"Oh, this has nothing to do with the tragedy. Nothing of that kind. But there was a definite, as I shall put it, a definite physical or mental flaw—whichever way you like to put it. Some people nowadays hold the theory that there is some physical cause for any kind of mental disorder. I believe that it is fairly well recognized by the medical profession that identical twins are born either with a great bond between them, a great likeness in their characters which means that although they may be divided in their environment, where they are brought up, the same things will happen to them at the same time of life. They will take the same trend. Some of the cases quoted as medical examples seem quite extraordinary. Two sisters, one living in Europe, one, say, in France, the other in England, they have a dog of the same kind which they choose at about the same date. They marry men singularly alike. They give birth perhaps to a child almost within a month of each other. It is as though they have to follow the pattern wherever they are and without knowing what the other one is doing. Then there is the opposite to that. A kind of revulsion, a hatred almost, that makes one sister draw apart, or one brother reject the other as though they seek to get away from the sameness, the likeness, the knowledge, the things they have in common. And that can lead to very strange results."

"I know," said Poirot. "I have heard of it. I have seen it once or twice. Love can turn to hate very easily. It is easier to hate where you have loved than it is to be indifferent where you have loved."

"Ah, you know that," said Mademoiselle Meauhourat.

"Yes, I have seen it not once but several times. Lady Ravenscroft's sister was very like her?"

"I think she was still very like her in appearance, though, if I may say so, the expression on her face was very different. She was in a condition of strain as Lady Ravenscroft was not. She had a great aversion to children. I don't know why. Perhaps she had had a miscarriage in early life. Perhaps she had longed for a child and never had one, but she had a kind of resentment against children. A dislike of them."

"That had led to one or two rather serious happenings, had it not?" said Poirot.

"Someone has told you that?"

"I have heard things from people who knew both sisters when they were in India. Lady Ravenscroft was there with her husband and her sister, Dolly, came out to stay with them there. There was an accident to a child there, and it was thought that Dolly might have been partially responsible for it. Nothing was proved definitely, but I gather that Molly's husband took his sister-in-law home to England and she had once more to go into a mental home."

"Yes, I believe that is a very good account of what happened. I do not of course know it of my own knowledge."

"No, but there are things you do know, I think, from your own knowledge."

"If so, I see no reason for bringing them back to mind now. Is it not better to leave things when at least they have been accepted?"

"There are other things that could have happened that day at Overcliffe. It may have been a double suicide, it could have been a murder, it could have been several other things. You were told what had happened, but I think, from one little sentence you just said, that you know what happened of your own knowledge. You know what happened that day and I think you know what happened perhaps—or began to happen, shall we say?—sometime before that. The time when Celia had gone to Switzerland and you were still at Overcliffe. I will ask you one question. I would like to know what your answer would be to it. It is not a thing of direct information. It is a question of what you believe. What were the feelings of General Ravenscroft towards those two sisters, the twin sisters?"

"I know what you mean."

For the first time her manner changed slightly. She was no longer on her guard. She leaned forward now and spoke to Poirot almost as though she definitely found a relief in doing so.

"They were both beautiful," she said, "as girls. I heard that from many people. General Ravenscroft fell in love with Dolly, the mentally afflicted sister. Although she had a disturbed personality, she was exceedingly attractive—sexually attractive. He loved her very dearly, and then I don't know whether he discovered in her some characteristic, something perhaps that alarmed him or in which he found a repulsion of some kind. He saw perhaps the beginnings of insanity in her, the dangers connected with her. His affections went to her sister. He fell in love with the sister and married her."

"He loved them both, you mean. Not at the same time, but in each case there was genuine fact of love."

"Oh, yes, he was devoted to Molly, relied on her and she on him. He was a very lovable man."

"Forgive me," said Poirot. "You, too, were in love with him, I think."

"You—you dare say that to me?"

"Yes. I dare say it to you. I am not suggesting that you and he had a love affair. Nothing of that kind. I'm only saying that you loved him."

"Yes," said Zélie Meauhourat. "I loved him. In a sense, I still love him. There's nothing to be ashamed of. He trusted me and relied on me, but he was never in love with me.

You can love and serve and still be happy. I wanted no more than I had. Trust, sympathy, belief in me—"

"And you did," said Poirot, "what you could to help him in a terrible crisis in his life. There are things you do not wish to tell me. There are things that I will say to you, things that I have gathered from various information that has come to me, that I know something about. Before I have come to see you, I have heard from others, from people who have known not only Lady Ravenscroft, not only Molly, but who have known Dolly. And I know something of Dolly, the tragedy of her life, the sorrow, the unhappiness and also the hatred, the streak perhaps of evil, the love of destruction that can be handed down in families. If she loved the man she was engaged to, she must have, when he married her sister, felt hatred perhaps towards that sister. Perhaps she never quite forgave her. But what of Molly Ravenscroft? Did she dislike her sister? Did she hate her?"

"Oh, no," said Zélie Meauhourat, "she loved her sister. She loved her with a very deep and protective love. That I do know. It was she who always asked that her sister should come and make her home with her. She wanted to save her sister from unhappiness, from danger too, because her sister would often relapse into fits of rather dangerous rages. She was frightened sometimes. Well, you know enough. You have already said that there was a strange dislike of children from which Dolly suffered."

"You mean that she disliked Celia?"

"No, no, not Celia. The other one. Edward. The younger one. Twice Edward had dangers of an accident. Once some kind of tinkering with a car and once some outburst of violent annoyance. I know Molly was glad when Edward went back to school. He was very young, remember—much younger than Celia. He was only eight or nine at preparatory school. He was vulnerable. Molly was frightened about him."

"Yes," said Poirot, "I can understand that. Now, if I may, I will talk of wigs. Wigs, the wearing of wigs. Four wigs. That is a lot for one woman to possess at one time. I know what they were like, what they looked like. I know that when more were needed, a French lady went to the shop in London and spoke about them and ordered them. There was a dog, too. A dog who went for a walk on the day of the tragedy with General Ravenscroft and his wife. Earlier that dog, some little time earlier, had bitten his mistress, Molly Ravenscroft."

"Dogs are like that," said Zélie Meauhourat. "They are never quite to be trusted. Yes, I know that."

"And I will tell you what I think happened on that day, and what happened before that. Some little time before that."

"And if I will not listen to you?"

"You will listen to me. You may say that what I have imagined is false. Yes, you might even do that, but I do not think you will. I am telling you and I believe it with all my heart, that what is needed here is the truth. It is not just imagining, it is not just wondering. There is a girl and a boy who care for each other and who are frightened of the future because of what may have happened and what there might be handed down from the father or the mother to the child. I am thinking of the girl, Celia. A rebellious girl, spirited, difficult perhaps to manage but with brains, a good mind, capable of happiness, capable of courage, but needing—there are people who need—truth. Because they can face truth without dismay. They can face it with that brave acceptance that you have to have in life if life is to be any good to you. And the boy that she loves, he wants that for her, too. Will you listen to me?"

"Yes," said Zélie Meauhourat, "I am listening. You understand a great deal, I think, and I think you know more than I could have imagined you would know. Speak and I will listen."

20

COURT OF INQUIRY

Once more Hercule Poirot stood on the cliff overlooking the rocks below and the sea breaking against them. Here where he stood the bodies of a husband and wife had been found. Here, three weeks before that a woman had walked in her sleep and fallen to her death.

"Why had these things happened?" That had been Superintendent Garroway's question.

Why? What had led to it?

An accident first—and three weeks later a double suicide. Old sins that had left long shadows. A beginning that had led years later to a tragic end.

Today there would be people meeting here. A boy and a girl who sought the truth. Two people who knew the truth.

Hercule Poirot turned away from the sea and back along

the narrow path that led to a house once called Overcliffe.

It was not very far. He saw cars parked against a wall. He saw the outline of a house against the sky. A house that was clearly empty, that needed repainting. A house agent's board hung there, announcing that "this desirable property" was for sale. On the gate the word Overcliffe had a line drawn over it and the name Down House replaced it. He went to meet two people who were walking towards him. One was Desmond Burton-Cox and the other was Celia Ravenscroft.

"I got an order from the house agent," said Desmond, "saying we wanted to view it or however they put it. I've got the key in case we want to go inside. It's changed hands twice in the last five years. But there wouldn't be anything to see there now, would there?"

"I shouldn't think so," said Celia. "After all, it's belonged to lots of people already. Some people called Archer who first bought it, and then somebody called Fallowfield, I think. They said it was too lonely. And now these last people are selling it, too. Perhaps they were haunted."

"Do you really believe in haunted houses?" said Desmond.

"Well now, of course I don't think so really," said Celia, "but this might be, mightn't it? I mean, the sort of things that happened, the sort of place it is and everything . . ."

"I do not think so," said Poirot. "There was sorrow here and death, but there was also love."

A taxi came along the road.

"I expect that's Mrs. Oliver," said Celia. "She said she'd

come by train and take a taxi from the station."

Two women got out of the taxi. One was Mrs. Oliver and with her was a tall, elegantly dressed woman. Since Poirot knew she was coming, he was not taken by surprise. He watched Celia to see if she had any reactions.

"Oh!" Celia sprang forward.

She went towards the woman and her face had lit up.

"Zélie!" she said. "It *is* Zélie? It is really Zélie! Oh, I am so pleased. I didn't know you were coming."

"Monsieur Hercule Poirot asked me to come."

"I see," said Celia. "Yes, yes, I suppose I see. But I—I didn't—" she stopped. She turned her head and looked at the handsome boy standing beside her. "Desmond, was it —was it you?"

"Yes. I wrote to Mademoiselle Meauhourat—to Zélie, if I may still call her that."

"You can always call me that, both of you," said Zélie. "I was not sure I wanted to come. I did not know if I was wise to come. That I still do not know, but I hope so."

"I want to *know,*" said Celia. "We both want to know. Desmond thought you could tell us something."

"Monsieur Poirot came to see me," said Zélie. "He persuaded me to come today."

Celia linked her arm in Mrs. Oliver's.

"I wanted you to come, too, because you put this in hand, didn't you? You got Monsieur Poirot and you found out some things yourself, didn't you?"

"People told me things," said Mrs. Oliver; "people whom I thought might remember things. Some of them did remember things. Some of them remembered them right and some of them remembered them wrong. That was confusing. Monsieur Poirot says that that does not really matter."

"No," said Poirot, "it is just as important to know what is hearsay and what is certain knowledge. Because from one you can learn facts even if they are not quite the right facts or had not got the explanation that you think they had. With the knowledge that you got for me, madame, from the people whom you designated elephants—" He smiled a little.

"Elephants?" said Mademoiselle Zélie.

"It is what she called them," said Poirot.

"Elephants can remember," explained Mrs. Oliver. "That was the idea I started on. And people can remember things that happened a long time ago just like elephants can. Not all people, of course, but they can usually remember *something*. There were a lot of people who did. I turned a lot of the things I heard over to Monsieur Poirot and he—he has made a sort of—oh, if he was a doctor I should call it a sort of diagnosis, I suppose."

"I made a list," said Poirot. "A list of things that seemed to be pointers to the truth of what happened all those years ago. I shall read the various items to you to see perhaps if you who were concerned in all this feel that they have any significance. You may not see their significance or you may see it plainly."

"One wants to know," said Celia. "Was it suicide, or was it murder? Did somebody—some outside person—kill both my father and my mother, shoot them for some reason we don't know about, some motive. I shall always think there was something of that kind or something else. It's difficult, but—"

"We will stay here, I think," said Poirot. "We will not go into the house as yet. Other people have lived in it and it has a different atmosphere. We will perhaps go in if we wish when we have finished our court of inquiry here."

"It's a court of inquiry, is it?" said Desmond.

"Yes. A court of inquiry into what happened."

He moved towards some iron seats which stood near the shelter of a large magnolia near the house. Poirot took from the case he carried a sheet of paper with writing on it. He said to Celia:

"To you, it has got to be that way? A definite choice. Suicide or murder."

"One of them must be true," said Celia.

"I shall say to you that both are true, and more than those two. According to my ideas, we have here not only a murder and also a suicide, but we have as well what I shall call an execution, and we have a tragedy also. A tragedy of two people who loved each other and who died for love. A tragedy of love may not always belong to Romeo and Juliet. It is not necessarily only the young who suffer the pains of love and are ready to die for love. No. There is more to it than that."

"I don't understand," said Celia.

"Not yet."

"Shall I understand?" said Celia.

"I think so," said Poirot. "I will tell you what I think

happened and I will tell you how I came to think so. The first things that struck me was the things that were not explained by the evidence that the police examined. Some things were very commonplace, were not evidence at all, you'd think. Among the possessions of the dead Margaret Ravenscroft, were four wigs." He repeated with emphasis, "*Four* wigs." He looked at Zélie.

"She did not use a wig all the time," said Zélie. "Only occasionally. If she traveled or if she'd been out and got very disheveled and wanted to tidy herself in a hurry, or sometimes she'd use one that was suitable for evening wear."

"Yes," said Poirot, "it was quite the fashion at that particular date. People certainly when they traveled abroad usually had a wig or two wigs. But in her possession were *four* wigs. Four wigs seemed to me rather a lot. I wondered *why* she needed four. According to the police whom I asked, it was not that she had any tendency to baldness. She had the ordinary hair a woman of her age would have and in good condition. All the same, I wondered about those. One of the wigs had a gray streak in it, I learned later. It was her hairdresser who told me that. And one of the wigs had little curls. It was the latter wig she was wearing the day she died."

"Is that significant in any way?" asked Celia. "She might have been wearing any of them."

"She might. I also learned the housekeeper told the police that she had been wearing that particular wig almost all the time for the last few weeks before she died. It appeared to be her favorite one."

"I can't see—"

"There was also a saying that Superintendent Garroway quoted to me, 'Same man—different hat.' It gave me furiously to think."

Celia repeated, "I don't see—"

Poirot said, "There was also the evidence of the dog—"

"The dog—what did the dog do?"

"The dog bit her. The dog was said to be devoted to its mistress, but in the last few weeks of her life, the dog turned on her more than once and bit her quite severely."

"Do you mean it knew she was going to commit suicide?" Desmond stared.

"No, something much simpler than that—"

"I don't—"

Poirot went on—"No, it knew what no one else seemed to know. It knew she was not its mistress. She looked like its mistress. The housekeeper who was slightly blind and also deaf saw a woman who wore Molly Ravenscroft's clothes and the most recognizable of Molly Ravenscroft's wigs—the one with little curls all over the head. The housekeeper said only that her mistress had been rather different in her manner the last few weeks of her life. 'Same man—different hat,' had been Garroway's phrase. And the thought—the conviction—came to me then. Same *wig*—different *woman*. The dog knew—he knew by what his nose told him. A different woman, not the woman he loved—a woman whom he disliked and feared. And I thought, suppose that woman was not Molly Ravenscroft—but who could she be? Could she be Dolly—the twin sister?"

"But that's impossible," said Celia.

"No, it was not impossible. After all, remember, they were twins. I must come now to the things that were brought to my notice by Mrs. Oliver. The things people told her or suggested to her. The knowledge that Lady Ravenscroft had recently been in hospital or in a nursing home and that she perhaps had known that she suffered from cancer, or thought that she did. Medical evidence was against that, however. She still might have thought she did, but it was not the case. Then I learned little by little the early history of her and her twin sister, who loved each other very devotedly as twins do, did everything alike, wore clothes alike, the same things seemed to happen to them, they had illnesses at the same time, they married about the same time or not very far removed in time. And eventually, as many twins do, instead of wanting to do everything in the same fashion and the same way, they wanted to do the opposite. To be as unlike each other as they could. And even between them grew a certain amount of dislike. More than that. There was a reason in the past for that. Alistair Ravenscroft as a young man fell in love with Dorothea Preston-Grey, the elder twin of the two. But his affection shifted to the other sister, Margaret, whom he married. There was jealousy then, no doubt, which led to an estrangement between the sisters. Margaret continued to be deeply attached to her twin, but Dorothea no longer was devoted in any way to Margaret. That seemed to me to be the explanation of a great many things. Dorothea was a tragic figure. By no fault of her own but by some accident of genes, of birth, of hereditary characteristics, she was always mentally unstable. At quite an early age she had, for some reason which has never been made clear, a dislike of children. There is every reason to believe that a child came to its death through her action. The evidence was not definite, but it was definite enough for a doctor to advise that she should have mental treatment, and she was for some years treated in a mental home. When reported cured by doctors, she resumed normal life, came often to stay with her sister and went out to India, at a time when they were stationed out there, to join them there. And there, again, an accident happened. A child of a neighbor. And again, although perhaps there was no very definite proof, it seems again Dorothea might have been responsible for it. General Ravenscroft took her home to England and she was placed once more in medical care. Once again she appeared to be cured, and after psychiatric care it was again said that she could go once more and resume a normal life. Margaret believed this time that all would be well, and thought that she ought to live with them so that they could watch closely for any signs of any further mental disability. I don't think that General Ravenscroft approved. I think he had a very strong belief that just as someone can be born deformed, spastic or crippled in some way, she had a deformity of the brain which would recur from time to time and that she would have to be constantly watched and saved from herself in case some other tragedy happened."

"Are you saying," asked Desmond, "that it was she who

shot both the Ravenscrofts?"

"No," said Poirot, "that is not my solution. I think what happened was that Dorothea killed her sister, Margaret. They walked together on the cliff one day and Dorothea pushed Margaret over. The dormant obsession of hatred and resentment of the sister who, though so like herself, was sane and healthy, was too much for her. Hate, jealousy, the desire to kill all rose to the surface and dominated her. I think that there was one outsider who knew, who was here at the time that this happened. I think *you* knew, Mademoiselle Zélie."

"Yes," said Zélie Meauhourat, "I knew. I was here at the time. The Ravenscrofts had been worried about her. That is when they saw her attempt to injure their small son, Edward. Edward was sent back to school and I and Celia went to my *pensionnat*. I came back here—after seeing Celia settled in. Once the house was empty except for myself, General Ravenscroft and Dorothea and Margaret, nobody had any anxiety. And then one day *it happened*. The two sisters went out together. Dolly returned alone. She seemed in a very queer and nervous state. She came in and sat down at the tea table. It was then General Ravenscroft noticed that her right hand was covered with blood. He asked her if she had had a fall. She said, 'Oh, no, it was nothing. Nothing at all. I got scratched by a rosebush.' But there were no rosebushes on the Downs. It was a purely foolish remark and we were worried. If she had said a gorse bush, we might have accepted the remark. General Ravenscroft went out and I went after him. He kept saying as he walked, 'Something has happened to Margaret. I'm sure something has happened to Molly.' We found her on a ledge a little way down the cliff. She had been battered with a rock and stones. She was not dead, but she had bled heavily. For a moment we hardly knew what we could do. We dared not move her. We must get a doctor, we felt, at once, but before we could do that, she clung to her husband. She said, gasping for breath, 'Yes, it was Dolly. She didn't know what she was doing. She didn't *know,* Alistair. You mustn't let her suffer for it. She's never known the things she does or why. She can't help it. She's never been able to help it. You must promise me, Alistair. I think I'm dying now. No—no, we won't have time to get a doctor and a doctor couldn't do anything. I've been lying here bleeding to death—and I'm very close to death. I know that, but promise me. *Promise* me you'll save her. Promise me you won't let the police arrest her. Promise me that she'll not be tried for killing me, not shut up for life as a criminal. Hide me somewhere so that my body won't be found. Please, please, it's the last thing I ask you. You whom I love more than anything in the world. If I could live for you I would, but I'm not going to live. I can feel that. I crawled a little way, but that was all I could do. Promise me. And you, Zélie, you love me, too. I know. You've loved me and been good to me and looked after me always. And you loved the children, so you must save Dolly. You must save poor Dolly. Please, please. For all the love we have for each other, Dolly must be saved.' "

"And then," said Poirot, "what did you do? It seems to

me that you must in some way between you—"

"Yes. She died, you know. She died within about ten minutes of those last words, and I helped him. I helped him to hide her body. It was a place a little further along the cliff. We carried her there and there were rocks and boulders and stones, and we covered her body as best we could. There was no path to it, really, or no way. You had to scramble. We put her there. All Alistair said again and again was—'I promised her. I must keep my word. I don't know how to do it, I don't know how anyone can save her. I don't know. But—' Well, we did do it. Dolly was in the house. She was frightened, desperate with fright, but at the same time she showed a horrible kind of satisfaction. She said, 'I always knew. I've known for years that Molly was really evil. She took you away from me, Alistair. You belonged to me—but she took you away from me and made you marry her and I always knew one day I should get even with her. I always knew. Now I'm frightened. What'll they do to me—what'll they say? I can't be shut up again. I can't, I can't. I shall go mad. You won't let me be shut up. They'll take me away and they'll say I'm guilty of murder. It wasn't murder. I just had to do it. Sometimes I do have to do things. I wanted to see the blood, you know. I couldn't wait to see Molly die, though. I ran away. But I knew she would die. I just hoped you wouldn't find her. She just fell over the cliff. People would say it was an accident.' "

"It's a horrible story," said Desmond.

"Yes," said Celia, "it's a horrible story, but it's better to know. It's better to know, isn't it? I can't even feel sorry for her. I mean for my mother. I know she was sweet. I know there was never any trace of evil in her—she was good all through—and I know, I can understand, why my father didn't want to marry Dolly. He wanted to marry my mother because he loved her and he had found out by then that there was something wrong with Dolly. Something bad and twisted. But how—how did you do it all?"

"We told a good many lies," said Zélie. "We hoped the body would not be found so that later perhaps it might be removed in the night or something like that to somewhere where it could look as though she'd fallen down into the sea. But then we thought of the sleepwalking story. What we had to do was really quite simple. Alistair said, 'It's frightening, you know. But I promised—I swore to Molly when she was dying. I swore I'd do as she asked. There's a way, a possible way to save Dolly, if only Dolly can do her part. I don't know if she's capable of it.' I said, 'Do what?' And Alistair said, 'Pretend she's Molly and that it's Dorothea who walked in her sleep and fell to her death.'

"We managed it. Took Dolly to an empty cottage we knew of and I stayed with her there for some days. Alistair said Molly had been taken to hospital suffering from shock after the discovery that her sister had fallen over the cliff while walking in her sleep at night. Then we brought Dolly back—brought her back as Molly—wearing Molly's clothes and Molly's wig. I got extra wigs—the kind with curls, which really did disguise her. The dear old housekeeper, Janet, couldn't see very well. Dolly and Molly were really very much alike, you know, and their voices were alike. Everyone accepted quite easily that it was Molly, behaving rather peculiarly now and then because of still suffering from shock. It all seemed quite natural. That was the horrible part of it—"

"But how could she keep it up?" asked Celia. "It must have been dreadfully difficult."

"No—she did not find it difficult. She had got, you see, what she wanted—what she had always wanted. She had got Alistair—"

"But Alistair—how could *he* bear it?"

"He told me why and how—on the day he had arranged for me to go back to Switzerland. He told me what I had to do and then he told me what he was going to do."

"He said: 'There is only one thing for me to do. I promised Margaret that I wouldn't hand Dolly over to the police, that it should never be known that she was a murderess, that the children were never to know that they had a murderess for an aunt. No one need ever know that Dolly committed murder. She walked in her sleep and fell over the cliff—a sad accident and she will be buried here in the church, and under her own name.'

" 'How can you let that be done?' I asked. I couldn't bear it.

"He said: 'Because of what I am going to do—you have got to know about it.'

" 'You see,' he said, 'Dolly has to be stopped from living. If she's near children, she'll take more lives—poor soul; she's not fit to live. But you must understand, Zélie, that because of what I am going to do, I must pay with my own life, too. I shall live here quietly for a few weeks with Dolly playing the part of my wife—and then there will be another tragedy—'

"I didn't understand what he meant. I said, 'Another accident? Sleepwalking again?' And he said, 'No—what will be known to the world is that I and Molly have both committed suicide. I don't suppose the reason will ever be known. They may think it's because she was convinced she had cancer—or that I thought so—all sorts of things may be suggested. But you see—you must help me, Zélie. You are the only person who really loves me and loves Molly and loves the children. If Dolly has got to die, I am the only person who must do it. She won't be unhappy or frightened. I shall shoot her and then myself. Her fingerprints will show on the revolver because she handled it not long ago, and mine will be there too. Justice has to be done and I have to be the executioner. The thing I want you to know is that I did—that I still do—love them both. Molly more than my life. Dolly because I pity her so much for what she was born to be.' He said, 'Always remember that—' "

Zélie rose and came towards Celia. "Now you know the truth," she said. "I promised your father that you should never know. I have broken my word. I never meant to reveal it to you or to anyone else. Monsieur Poirot made me feel differently. But—it's such a horrible story—"

"I understand how you felt," said Celia. "Perhaps you

were right from your point of view, but I—I am glad to know, because now a great burden seems to have been lifted off me—"

"Because now," said Desmond, "we both know. And it's something we'll never mind about knowing. It was a tragedy. As Monsieur Poirot here has said, it was a real tragedy of two people who loved each other. But they didn't kill each other, because they loved each other. One was murdered and the other executed a murderer for the sake of humanity so that more children shouldn't suffer. One can forgive him if he was wrong, but I don't think it was wrong, really."

"She was a frightening woman always," said Celia. "Even when I was a child I was frightened of her, but I didn't know why. But I do know why now. I think my father was a brave man to do what he did. He did what my mother asked him to do, begged him to do with her dying breath. He saved her twin sister, whom I think she'd always loved very dearly. I like to think—oh, it seems a silly thing for me to say—" she looked doubtfully at Hercule Poirot. "Perhaps you won't think so. I expect you're a Catholic, but it's what's written on their tombstone. 'In death they were not divided.' It doesn't mean that they died together, but I think they are together. I think they came together afterwards. Two people who loved each other very much, and my poor aunt whom I'll try to feel more kindly about than I ever did—my poor aunt didn't have to suffer for what she couldn't perhaps help herself doing. Mind you," said Celia, suddenly breaking into her ordinary everyday voice, "she wasn't a nice person. You can't help not liking people if they're not nice people. Perhaps she *could* have been different if she tried, but perhaps she couldn't. And if so, one has to think of her as someone who was very ill—like somebody, for instance, who had plague in a village and they wouldn't let her go out or feed her and she couldn't go among other people because the whole village would have died. Something like that. But I'll try and be sorry for her. And my mother and father—I don't worry about them any more. They loved each other so much, and loved poor, unhappy, hating Dolly."

"I think, Celia," said Desmond, "we'd better get married now as soon as possible. I can tell you one thing. My mother is never going to hear anything about this. She's not my own mother and she's not a person I can trust with this sort of secret."

"Your adopted mother, Desmond," said Poirot, "I have good reason to believe was anxious to come between you and Celia and tried to influence you in the idea that from her mother and father she might have inherited some terrible characteristic. But you know, or you may not know and I see no reason why I should not tell you, you will inherit from the woman who was your real mother and who died not very long ago leaving all her money to you. You will inherit a very large sum when you reach the age of twenty-five."

"If I marry Celia, of course we shall need the money to live on," said Desmond. "I quite understand. I know my present adopted mother is very keen on money and I often lend her money even now. She suggested my seeing a lawyer the other day because she said it was very dangerous now that I was over twenty-one, not leaving a will behind me. I suppose she thought she'd get the money. I had thought of probably leaving nearly all the money to her. But of course now Celia and I are getting married I shall leave it to Celia—and I didn't like the way my mother tried to put me against Celia."

"I think your suspicions are entirely correct," said Poirot. "I dare say she could tell herself that she meant it all for the best, that Celia's origin is something that you ought to know if there is a risk for you to take, but—"

"All right," said Desmond, "but—I know I'm being unkind. After all, she adopted me and brought me up and all the rest of it, and I dare say if there's enough money I can settle some of it on her. Celia and I will have the rest and we're going to be happy together. After all, there are things that'll make us feel sad from time to time, but we shan't worry any more, shall we, Celia?"

"No," said Celia, "we'll never worry again. I think they were rather splendid people, my mother and father. Mother tried to look after her sister all her life, but I suppose it was a bit too hopeless. You can't stop people from being like they are."

"Ah, dear children," said Zélie. "Forgive me for calling you children, because you are not. You are a grown man and woman. I know that. I am so pleased to have seen you again and to know I have not done any harm in what I did."

"You haven't done any harm at all and it's lovely seeing you, dear Zélie." Celia went to her and hugged her. "I've always been terribly fond of you," she said.

"And I was very fond of you, too, when I knew you," said Desmond. "When I lived next door. You had lovely games you played with us."

The two young people turned.

"Thank you, Mrs. Oliver," said Desmond. "You've been very kind and you've put in a lot of work. I can see that. Thank you, Monsieur Poirot."

"Yes, thank you," said Celia. "I'm very grateful."

They walked away and the others looked after them.

"Well," said Zélie, "I must leave now." She said to Poirot, "What about you? Will you have to tell anyone about this?"

"There is one person I might tell in confidence. A retired police force officer. He is no longer actively in the Service now. He is completely retired. I think he would not feel it is his duty to interfere with what time has now wiped out. If he was still in active service, it might be different."

"It's a terrible story," said Mrs. Oliver, "terrible. And all those people I talked to—yes, I can see now, they all remembered something. Something that was useful in showing us what the truth was, although it was difficult to put together. Except for Monsieur Poirot, who can always put things together out of the most extraordinary things. Like wigs and twins."

Poirot walked across to where Zélie was standing looking out over the view.

"You do not blame me," he said, "for coming to you,

persuading you to do what you have done?"

"No. I am glad. You have been right. They are very charming, those two, and they are well suited, I think. They will be happy. We are standing here where two lovers once lived. Where two lovers died, and I don't blame him for what he did. It may have been wrong, I suppose it was wrong, but I can't blame him. I think it was a brave act even if it was a wrong one."

"You loved him too, did you not?" said Hercule Poirot.

"Yes. Always. As soon as I came to the house. I loved him dearly. I don't think he knew it. There was never anything, what you call, between us. He trusted me and was fond of me. I loved them both. Both he and Margaret."

"There is something I would like to ask you. He loved Dolly as well as Molly, didn't he?"

"Right up to the end. He loved them both. And that's why he was willing to save Dolly. Why Molly wanted him to. Which did he love the best of those sisters? I wonder. That is a thing I shall perhaps never know," said Zélie. "I never did—perhaps I never shall."

Poirot looked at her for a moment, then turned away. He rejoined Mrs. Oliver.

"We will drive back to London. We must return to everyday life, forget tragedies and love affairs."

"Elephants can remember," said Mrs. Oliver, "but we are human beings, and mercifully human beings can forget."